# APPLIED INDUSTRIAL/ORGANIZATIONAL PSYCHOLOGY

**SECOND EDITION**

# APPLIED INDUSTRIAL/ORGANIZATIONAL PSYCHOLOGY

**SECOND EDITION**

**MICHAEL G. AAMODT**
**Radford University**

**Brooks/Cole Publishing Company**

I(T)P™ An International Thomson Publishing Company

Pacific Grove • Albany • Bonn • Boston • Cincinnati • Detroit • London • Madrid • Melbourne
Mexico City • New York • Paris • San Francisco • Singapore • Tokyo • Toronto • Washington

Sponsoring Editor: Marianne Taflinger
Marketing Team: Carolyn Crockett and
        Romy Fineroff
Editorial Assistant: Laura Donahue
Production Coordinator: Penelope Sky
Manuscript Editor: Joan Harlan
Permissions Editor: Catherine Gingras
Interior Design: ColorType, San Diego
Interior Illustration: Martha Roach

Cover Design: Roy R. Neuhaus
Cover Photo: PhotoDisc, Inc.
Photo Editor: Kathleen Olson
Production Service: ColorType, San Diego
Indexer: Joyce Teague
Typesetting: ColorType, San Diego
Cover Printing: Color Dot Graphics, Inc.
Printing and Binding: Quebecor/Fairfield

*For more information, contact:*

BROOKS/COLE PUBLISHING COMPANY
511 Forest Lodge Road
Pacific Grove, CA  93950
USA

International Thomson Publishing Europe
Berkshire House 168-173
High Holborn
London WC1V 7AA
England

Thomas Nelson Australia
102 Dodds Street
South Melbourne, 3205
Victoria, Australia

Nelson Canada
1120 Birchmount Road
Scarborough, Ontario
Canada M1K 5G4

International Thomson Editores
Campos Eliseos 385, Piso 7
Col. Polanco
11560 México D. F. México

International Thomson Publishing GmbH
Königswinterer Strasse 418
53227 Bonn
Germany

International Thomson Publishing Asia
221 Henderson Road
#05-10 Henderson Building
Singapore 0315

International Thomson Publishing Japan
Hirakawacho Kyowa Building, 3F
2-2-1 Hirakawacho
Chiyoda-ku, Tokyo 102
Japan

Printed in the United States of America

10  9  8  7  6  5  4  3  2  1

**Library of Congress Cataloging-in-Publication Data**
Aamodt, Michael G.
    Applied industrial/organizational psychology/Michael G. Aamodt.
    —2nd ed.
        p.   cm.
    Includes bibliographical references and index.
    ISBN 0-534-33880-1
    1. Psychology, Industrial.    I. Title.
HF5548.8.A17    1995
158.7—dc20                                                    95-17007
                                                                  CIP

This edition is dedicated to Dr. Wilson W. Kimbrough,
my advisor, mentor, and friend,

and to the late Dr. Daniel L. Johnson,
whose wisdom and guidance I greatly miss.

# CONTENTS

# PREFACE

Industrial/organizational psychologists usually love their field. You can be a scientist, a detective, a lawyer, an advisor, a statistician, an inventor, a writer, a teacher, a mentor, a trainer, a high stakes gambler, a motivator, and an engineer — all at the same time. In no other field can you experience such challenging opportunities along with the satisfaction of bettering the lives of others.

I wrote this book because there was a strong need for a text that would appeal directly to undergraduates without sacrificing scholarship. It contains many real-world examples that illustrate important points; employment profiles that demonstrate the wide variety of I/O career paths; and charts and tables that integrate and simplify complicated issues, including employment law, job satisfaction, and work motivation. The applied approach is apparent both in such topics as how to survive an interview or to write a résumé or rejection letter and in the large number of meta-analyses.

## NEW TO THIS EDITION

The second edition of *Applied Industrial/Organizational Psychology* differs from the first in the following significant ways:

- It contains an entire chapter on employment law.
- The chapters on job analysis, performance appraisal, and communication have been completely reorganized.
- The chapter on research methods has been expanded.
- Meta-analysis is explained in greater detail.

- Such new topics as e-mail, workplace violence, and repetitive motion injuries are discussed.
- The references have been updated.
- Humor is used generously throughout.

## SUPPLEMENT

The accompanying workbook, *I/O Psychology in Action,* allows the student to conduct the critical incident technique, determine the utility of a test, take a personality test, write a job description and a résumé, and develop a theory of leadership. The workbook also contains practice tests the student can use to prepare for exams.

## ACKNOWLEDGMENTS

I am grateful to the excellent staff at Brooks/Cole; including Marianne Taflinger, Laura Donahue, Penelope Sky, Kathleen Olson, and Lynne Bush. The quality of the text was improved by the thoughtful responses of reviewers, including Jay Brand, Loma Linda University; Donald Fisher, Southwest Missouri State; Steven Hurwitz, Tiffin University; Jean Kirnan, Trenton State College; Juan Sanchez, Florida International University; Eugene Sheehan, University of Northern Colorado; and William Siegfried, University of North Carolina at Charlotte.

I would also like to thank my students for accommodating my time spent writing and for their ideas and support. I appreciate my colleagues Nora Reilly, Michael Surrette, and Ge Ge Beall, who patiently allowed me to bounce what must have seemed like a million ideas off them. Thanks also to my IPMA, SIOP, and SHRM colleagues for their insight and stories.

Finally, I thank Bobbie Raynes for her editorial help ("Are you sure this is what you wanted to say?"), her reality checks ("So, just what student do you think would be interested in this topic?"), her humor policing ("I know you think this is funny, but I'm not sure anyone without a pocket protector would"), and most of all for her love and support.

Michael G. Aamodt

# 1

# INTRODUCTION TO INDUSTRIAL/ORGANIZATIONAL PSYCHOLOGY

Wouldn't it be wonderful if all employees loved their jobs so much that they couldn't wait to get to work and were so well suited and trained that their performances were outstanding? Well, such a situation would be great, and ultimately it is the goal of industrial psychology. Unfortunately, not every employee will enjoy his or her job, and not every employee will do well. The purpose of this book, however, is to provide the reader with techniques developed by industrial/organizational (I/O) psychologists that will at least show the way toward reaching the goal of creating a happy and productive work force.

Before we can talk about these techniques, several areas must be discussed so that you will have the basics to help you better understand the rest of the book. In this chapter, you will find two distinct sections. The first provides a brief overview of the field of I/O psychology, and the second discusses the research methods that will be mentioned throughout the text.

## DIFFERENCES BETWEEN I/O PSYCHOLOGY AND BUSINESS PROGRAMS

**Industrial/organizational psychology** applies the principles of psychology to the workplace. For example, principles of learning are used to develop training programs and incentive plans, principles of social psychology are used to form work groups and understand employee conflict, and principles of motivation and emotion are used to motivate and satisfy employees. The application of psychological principles is what best distinguishes I/O psychology from related fields typically taught in business colleges. Although many of the topics covered in this text are similar to those found in a personnel management or organizational behavior text, the techniques and the reasons behind them are quite different. For example, many personnel texts advocate the interview as an excellent means of selecting the best employees. I/O psychologists consider the interview to be of less value than alternatives such as psychological tests, weighted application blanks, and assessment centers (Thayer, 1988).

A second difference between I/O psychology and other business fields is that I/O psychology examines factors that affect the *people* in an organization rather than such broader aspects of running an organization as marketing channels, transportation networks, and cost accounting (Feldman, 1986). As you can see from the typical graduate courses listed in Table 1.1, business programs examine areas such as accounting, marketing, and transportation, whereas I/O programs focus almost exclusively on human resource issues (Peggans, Chandra, & McAlarnis, 1986).

I/O psychology differs also from clinical and counseling psychology. I/O psychology relies extensively on research, quantitative methods, and testing techniques. I/O psychologists are trained to use empirical data and statistics rather than clinical judgment in making decisions. I/O psychologists are not clinical psychologists who happen to be in industry, and they do not conduct therapy for workers. There are psychologists who work for

**Table 1.1**   Comparison of MBA and I/O master's degree coursework

| Typical I/O Coursework | Typical MBA Coursework |
| --- | --- |
| Statistics | Statistics |
| Experimental Methodology | Business Research |
| Psychometric Theory | Organizational Behavior |
| Employee Selection and Placement | Administrative Policy |
| Organizational Psychology | Managerial Economics |
| Employee Training and Development | Financial Management |
| Performance Appraisal | Marketing Management |
| Job Analysis | Managerial Accounting |

organizations and help employees with such problems as drug and alcohol abuse, but these psychologists are serving as counselors rather than as I/O psychologists.

One reason that I/O psychology continually increases in popularity is that professionals in this field can have a positive impact on the lives of other people. Let us look at a typical day in the life of a typical person:

| Activity | Time Spent |
|---|---|
| Work | 8 hours |
| Commuting to work | 1 hour |
| Watching T.V. | 3 hours |
| Sleeping | 8 hours |
| Eating | 2 hours |
| Other | 2 hours |

People spend more time at their jobs than at any other activity in life, with the possible exception of sleeping. Thus, it makes sense that people who are happy and productive in their jobs will lead more fulfilling lives than people who are unhappy at work. The residual effect of unhappiness at work affects the quality of family and leisure life.

From a societal perspective, I/O psychologists also increase employee effectiveness, which in turn improves product quality and reduces the cost of goods, which in turn reduces repair and replacement costs by improving organizational efficiency, which can result in decreases in such activities as waiting in line.

Thus, I/O psychology can improve the quality of life at levels equal to, and often exceeding, counseling psychology and medicine. Although I/O psychologists make good salaries, the real benefits of their work are their positive effects on the lives of others.

## MAJOR FIELDS OF I/O PSYCHOLOGY

### Personnel Psychology

I/O psychologists and human resource management (HRM) professionals involved in **personnel psychology** practice and do research in such areas as employee-selection techniques, job analysis, employment tests, evaluation of employee performance, absenteeism, and job evaluation. Professionals working in these areas choose existing tests or create new tests to select and promote employees. These tests are then constantly evaluated to ensure both their fairness and validity.

Personnel psychologists also analyze jobs to obtain a complete picture of what each employee does, often assigning monetary values to each position. After obtaining job descriptions, personnel psychologists construct performance-appraisal instruments to evaluate employees.

To do all of these things, personnel psychologists rely heavily on research and statistical analysis. A survey conducted by Rassenfoss and Kraut (1988) indicated that the most common activities of personnel researchers are:

1. Developing, administering, and analyzing employee attitude surveys
2. Constructing performance-appraisal instruments
3. Validating tests
4. Developing employee-selection tests
5. Conducting job analyses

### Organizational Psychology

Psychologists involved in **organizational psychology** practice and do research in leadership, job satisfaction, employee motivation, organizational communication, conflict management, and group processes. Organizational psychologists often conduct surveys of employee attitudes to determine employees' beliefs about an organization's strengths and weaknesses. An organizational psychologist, usually serving as a consultant, will then make recommendations on ways problem areas can be improved. For example, the level of job satisfaction might be increased by allowing employees to participate in making certain company decisions, and poor communication might be improved by implementing an employee suggestion system.

### Training and Development

Psychologists interested in training and development examine various methods to develop the talents of both new and current employees. People within this subfield usually work in a training department of an organization and are involved in such activities as identifying the training needs of an organization, developing training systems, and evaluating their success. Practitioners also operate as consultants and provide workshops on many topics.

### Human Factors: Ergonomics

Psychologists involved in **human factors** concentrate on workplace design, human-machine interaction, ergonomics, and physical fatigue and stress. Sample activities in this subfield include designing the optimal way to draw a map, designing the most comfortable chair, and investigating the optimal work schedule.

## BRIEF HISTORY OF I/O PSYCHOLOGY

I/O psychology has a relatively recent history. Although various experts disagree about the exact origin of I/O psychology (see Table 1.2), it is generally thought to have begun either in 1903 when Walter Dill Scott wrote *The Theory of Advertising*, in which psychology was first applied to business, or in

**Table 1.2**  Important events in I/O psychology

| Year | Event |
|------|-------|
| 1903 | Walter Dill Scott publishes *The Theory of Advertising* |
| 1913 | Hugo Munsterberg publishes *Psychology and Industrial Efficiency* |
| 1918 | World War I provides I/O psychologists with first opportunity for large-scale employee testing and selection |
| 1921 | First Ph.D. in I/O Psychology awarded to Bruce Moore at Pennsylvania State University |
| 1939 | Hawthorne studies published |
| 1945 | Society for Industrial Psychology established |
| 1963 | Equal Pay Act passed |
| 1964 | Civil Rights Act passed |
| 1973 | Division 14 of the American Psychological Association changes name from Society for Industrial Psychology to Society for Industrial and Organizational Psychology (SIOP) |
| 1986 | SIOP holds first annual national conference separate from APA meeting |
| 1989 | U.S. Supreme Court sets conservative trend and becomes more "employer friendly" |
| 1990 | Americans with Disabilities Act passed |
| 1991 | Civil Rights Act of 1991 passed to overcome 1989 conservative Supreme Court decisions |

1913 when Hugo Munsterberg wrote *Psychology and Industrial Efficiency*. Regardless of the official starting date, I/O psychology was born in the early 1900s.

I/O psychology had its first big impact during World War I. Because of the large number of soldiers who had to be assigned to various units within the armed forces, I/O psychologists were employed to test recruits and then place them into appropriate positions. The testing was mainly accomplished through the **Army Alpha** and **Army Beta** tests of mental ability. The more intelligent recruits were assigned to officer training and the less intelligent to the infantry.

In the 1930s, I/O psychology greatly expanded its scope. Until then, it had been primarily involved in personnel issues such as the selection and placement of employees. However, in the 1930s, with the findings from the famous **Hawthorne studies,** psychologists became more involved in the quality of the working environment as well as in the attitudes of employees.

The 1960s were characterized by the passage of several major pieces of civil rights legislation, which will be discussed in the next chapter. These laws focused the attention of human resource professionals on developing fair-selection techniques. As a result, the need for I/O psychologists greatly increased.

In the 1970s, research focused on such issues as employee satisfaction and motivation, and many theories about employee behavior in organizations were developed.

The 1980s and 1990s brought three major changes to I/O psychology. The first involved an increased use of fairly sophisticated statistical techniques and methods of analysis. This change is evident if one compares journal articles published in the 1960s with those written since 1980. More recent articles use such complicated statistics as path analysis, multivariate analysis of variance (MANOVA), and causal modeling, whereas articles from the 1960s used simpler statistics such as t-tests and analysis of variance. This reliance on statistics explains why typical I/O psychology doctoral students take at least five statistics courses.

A second change concerned a new interest in the application of cognitive psychology to industry. For example, researchers in the 1970s primarily described and tested new methods for evaluating employee performance. In the 1980s and early 1990s, however, researchers approached the same issue by examining the thought process used by managers when they conduct performance appraisals.

The final major change, in the 1980s and 1990s, was that I/O psychologists were more aggressive in developing methods to select employees. In the 1960s and 1970s, the courts were still interpreting the major civil rights acts of the early 1960s, which resulted in I/O psychologists taking cautious approaches in selecting employees. By the mid-1980s, however, the courts became less strict, and a wider variety of selection instruments was developed and used, including cognitive ability tests, personality tests, and situational interviews. Other changes during the 1980s and 1990s that have had significant effects on I/O psychology include massive organizational downsizing, greater concern for diversity and gender issues, an aging workforce, and increased concern about the effects of stress.

With the passage of the Civil Rights Act in 1991 and the election of Bill Clinton in 1992, the legal atmosphere is again more restrictive for human resource professionals. As of 1995, I/O psychologists still are taking aggressive approaches to selecting employees but increasingly are worried about such issues as adverse impact and invasion of privacy, which will be discussed in Chapter 2.

## EMPLOYMENT OF I/O PSYCHOLOGISTS

Throughout this text, you will find several "Employment Profiles" that look at the jobs held by people with degrees in I/O psychology. As indicated in Table 1.3, the greatest number of I/O psychologists holding Ph.D.s work at universities, followed by consulting firms and private industry (Balzer & Howard, 1994). Also, as shown in Table 1.3, I/O psychologists holding master's degrees have a different employment profile, with most of them working in industry (Ekeberg, Switzer, & Siegfried, 1991; Erffmeyer & Mendel, 1990; Frizzell, 1989). They more often are employed as personnel generalists, data analysts, trainers, and compensation analysts and less often as academicians (Schippman, Schmitt, & Hawthorne, 1992).

I/O professionals who work in industrial settings perform a wide range of activities such as training, research, performance appraisal, productivity

**Table 1.3** Employment settings for I/O psychologists

| Employment Setting | Highest Degree Obtained | |
| --- | --- | --- |
| | M.A. | Ph.D. |
| Education | 1.4% | 35.0% |
| Industry | 55.6 | 19.0 |
| Government | 24.3 | n/a |
| Consulting | 15.9 | 34.0 |
| Other | 2.8 | 11.0 |

Note: n/a = information not available

enhancement, test construction, test validation, job analysis, employee motivation, recruitment, and personnel selection (Cederbloom, Pence, & Johnson, 1984; Schippman, Schmitt, & Hawthorne, 1992). Those employed by state and local governments usually perform job analysis and test construction and other human resource-related functions.

At least a Master's degree is usually required to become an I/O psychologist. As of 1989, starting salaries for these Master's level positions were approximately $27,000, with average salaries reaching $42,000 after several years of experience (Frizzell, 1989). Starting salaries for Ph.D.s in nonacademic environments are $5,000 to $10,000 higher.

A variety of jobs await I/O psychology graduates.

## EDUCATIONAL REQUIREMENTS
## AND TYPES OF PROGRAMS

To obtain reasonable employment in I/O psychology, a Master's degree is required for most jobs and a Ph.D. for some. Obtaining a Master's takes one to two years. Admissions requirements vary greatly from school to school, but an undergraduate grade-point average (G.P.A.) of at least 3.0 and a score of 1,000 on the **Graduate Record Exam (G.R.E.)** — the graduate school version of the Scholastic Aptitude Test, or SAT, that you took after high school — are not uncommon (Koppes, 1991). Advice for getting into graduate school can be found in Box 1.1.

### Types of Graduate Programs

Master's degree programs come in two varieties: terminal Master's degree programs and those that are part of a Ph.D. program. Schools with **terminal Master's degree programs** do not have Ph.D. programs. Thus, a Master's degree is the highest that can be earned at such a school. Schools with doctoral programs have both the Master's degree and the Ph.D. Terminal programs are best suited for students wanting an applied human resource position in an organization. These programs usually have less-stringent entrance requirements and provide more financial aid and individual attention to Master's students than do Ph.D. programs. Doctoral programs, on the other hand, usually have more well-known faculty members as well as better facilities and research funding. Doctoral programs are best suited for students who eventually want to teach, research, or consult.

Most Master's programs require about 40 hours of graduate coursework (Koppes, 1991). Although 15 to 18 hours is considered to be a full undergraduate semester load, 12 hours is considered a full graduate load. In addition to coursework, many programs require a student to complete a thesis, which is usually an original research work created and conducted by the student. The thesis is completed in the second year of graduate school.

Most programs also allow the student to complete an **internship** or **practicum** with a local organization (Lowe, 1993). These internship requirements vary by program. For example, at Radford University in Virginia, students work 10 hours per week at an organization during their last semester of graduate school. At East Carolina University, the student takes a semester off to work full time with a company.

Finally, most programs require a student to pass a comprehensive oral or written exam or both before graduation (Lowe, 1993). These exams usually are taken during the final semester and cover material from all courses taken during the graduate program. As you can see, completing a Master's degree program in I/O psychology is tough, but it will lead to excellent employment and professional benefits.

Obtaining a Ph.D. is more difficult than obtaining a Master's, with the typical doctoral program taking five years to complete. Common entrance requirements are a 3.5 G.P.A. and G.R.E. score of 1,200 (Lowe, 1993).

This section may seem out of place in an I/O textbook, but the information contained here is often not learned by students until it is too late. This information also can be applied to fields other than I/O psychology.

Although different graduate programs often emphasize different entrance requirements, most place some weight on G.R.E. scores, G.P.A., letters of recommendation, and previous research or professional experience. With this in mind, following the advice below should increase your chances of being selected for a graduate program.

1. Take extra mathematics and English courses. The G.R.E. consists of four parts: quantitative, verbal, analytic, and psychology. The quantitative portion requires knowledge of algebra, geometry, and some trigonometry. Thus, often the only way to do well on this section is to take extra courses in these subjects. Taking English courses in reading comprehension and vocabulary will help your score on the verbal section.

It is important to understand that the G.R.E. is a test of knowledge, not intelligence. Thus, with extra course work, you can improve your scores. Remember, it will have been a long time since you took these courses in high school.

2. Take at least one psychology course in each of the areas of statistics, experimental methods, abnormal psychology, personality, social psychology, physiological psychology, learning, perception, and cognitive psychology; each area is covered in the G.R.E.'s psychology portion. Although courses in sex and group dynamics are interesting and will help you in the future, they will not help you to score well on the G.R.E.

3. Make sure that you have at least three people who can write good letters of recommendation for you. Getting an A in a professor's class is not enough to expect a good letter that will carry weight with the admissions committee. Let the professors get to know you as both student and person. Talk with different professors and become involved with their research; this will not only allow you to have research of your own to show prospective graduate programs, but also it will result in better and more complete letters of recommendation.

4. Get involved! Conduct independent research projects, join professional clubs, get a summer job. Anything to demonstrate your desire to be a professional.

5. Study for your G.R.E. and get a good night's sleep before you take the test. You may not be able to learn much new material by studying, but you can at least refresh your memory about material that you have already learned but may have forgotten. Remember that the G.R.E. will determine your future and is probably the most important test that you will ever take. Treat it as such and prepare.

The first two years of a doctoral program involve taking a wide variety of courses in psychology. In most programs, the student does not concentrate on I/O courses until the third and fourth years. In addition to a thesis, a student working toward a Ph.D. must complete a **dissertation.** No formal definition distinguishes a thesis from a dissertation, but the major differences are that the dissertation involves answering a series of questions, is evaluated more critically, and requires more original and independent effort than does the thesis. Doctoral programs also involve a series of comprehensive exams that are similar to, but more extensive than, the exams taken in a Master's program.

For a complete list of I/O psychology graduate programs, see Appendixes A and B. Though no formal ranking exists for I/O psychology graduate programs, Appendix C contains rankings on a number of dimensions.

## RESEARCH IN I/O PSYCHOLOGY

One of the essential foundations of the upcoming chapters is research. This section will not provide you with an in-depth discussion of research, but it will provide enough information so that when a study is mentioned in the text, you will understand the method that was used.

### WHY CONDUCT RESEARCH?

Though most of you will probably not go on to careers as researchers, understanding research and statistics is important for several reasons.

#### *Answering Questions and Making Decisions*

One of the characteristics of I/O psychology is its extensive use of research and statistics. Although there are many reasons for this reliance on research, the most important is that research ultimately saves an organization money. To many of you, this last statement may seem a bit insensitive. Keep in mind, however, that for most organizations, the most important thing is the bottom line. If an I/O psychologist is not able to save the company considerably more money than it pays for her salary and expenses, she will be without a job.

These monetary savings can result from many factors, including increased employee satisfaction, increased productivity, and fewer accidents. Perhaps an excellent example of how research can save a company money involves the employment interview. For years, many organizations relied on the employment interview as the main method for selecting employees (most still do). But research has shown that the employment interview is not the best predictor of future behavior on the job (Hunter & Hunter, 1984). Thus, without research, an organization might still be spending money on a method that actually lowers its profits rather than raises them.

#### *Research and Everyday Life*

Research confronts us on an almost daily basis, both at home and on the job. As a student, you will encounter research throughout this and other courses. As a professional, you will receive advertisements and sales pitches containing references to research supporting a particular project. At home, you read the results of political polls in the newspaper and are bombarded with TV commercials trumpeting the results of the *Pepsi Challenge* or that "Nine out of ten dentists . . ." recommend a product. Understanding research helps you to critically listen and analyze results of these studies to make more intelligent decisions. After all, you would hate to buy a soft drink based on the results of poorly conducted research!

When I was an undergraduate at Pepperdine University in Malibu, California (yes, the surf was always up), the students attempted to hold the first dance ever at the university. Until this point, dancing was prohibited and the students wanted the prohibition removed. The dance proposal came under heavy attack by the church sponsoring the university as well as by several administrators. In support of its position, the church cited research showing that "in a study of Catholic confessionals, nine out of ten fallen women had their downfall on the dance floor."

When confronted with this devastating piece of research, we pulled out our trusty experimental psychology books and, using our finely honed research skills, challenged the validity of the study on such grounds as the poorly defined dependent variable (what is a fallen woman?), the sample size (how many women fell?), and the question of whether the study actually existed; there is no way the Catholic church would allow a study of confessionals. After our impressive critique, the administration gave in, and we were allowed to hold our dance off-campus but to advertise it on-campus. If you consider allowing 200 students with no rhythm to dance as a victory, then our superior knowledge of research made us victors.

A crazy story? Sure. But the fact that intelligent people actually used such research to support their point underscores the importance of understanding research.

### Common Sense Is Often Wrong

Often, there is a temptation not to conduct research because the answer to a question is "common sense." Unfortunately, common sense is not so common and is often wrong. Until the end of the fifteenth century, common sense said that the world was square and a person sailing toward the horizon would fall off the earth. Until late in this century, common sense said that women could not perform as well as men. In other words, many of our commonsense policies have been, and continue to be, wrong.

As a more recent example, imagine taking a multiple-choice test. After finishing the test, you go back and read question 32 but can't decide if you should stick with your original response of "b" or change it to "c." What would you do? Most students respond with what they have always been told: *stick with your first answer.* If you stuck with this piece of common advice, you probably would miss the question. Contrary to common sense, five studies investigating this question all concluded that 70% of the time an answer will be changed from wrong to right. Another victory for research over common sense!

## CONSIDERATIONS IN CONDUCTING RESEARCH

### Ideas, Hypotheses, and Theories

The first step in conducting research is to decide *what to research.* It is true that some psychologists have "great theoretical and research minds," but it is probably more true that most research ideas stem from a person starting a sentence with "I wonder." For example, a manager might say "I wonder why some of my employees can't get to work on time," an employee might say "I wonder if I could assemble more parts if my chair were higher," or a supervisor might ask "I wonder which of my employees is the best to promote." All three seem to be ordinary questions, but each is just as valid and important in research as those asked by a professor in a university. Thus, everyone is a researcher at heart, and conducting some form of research to answer a question will undoubtedly lead to a better answer than could be obtained by guesswork alone.

Once a question has been asked, the next step is to form a **hypothesis**— an educated prediction about the answer to a question. This prediction is usually based on a **theory,** previous research, or logic (Smith, 1993). For example, as shown in Table 1.4, a researcher is curious about the effect of noise on employee performance (the question) and believes that high levels of noise will result in decreased performance (the hypothesis). The prediction is based on the theory that distracting events reduce the ability to concentrate. To see if the hypothesis is correct, the researcher would need to conduct a study.

If the results support the hypothesis, it becomes important to test the theory. In psychology, competing theories often predict the same outcome, but for different reasons. Take the situation depicted in Table 1.5 as an example. An industrial psychologist wants to know which method of recruiting employees is best. She predicts that employee referrals will result in longer employee tenure (employees staying with the company) than will other recruitment methods. Though she is sure about her hypothesis, she is not sure about the reason as there are three possible theories or explanations for her hypothesis:

1. Applicants referred by a current employee will stay with the company longer because they were given an accurate picture of the job and the company by the person telling them about the job (realistic job preview theory).

2. The personalities of applicants using employee referrals are different than the personalities of applicants using other methods to find jobs (differential recruitment source theory).

3. Friends have similar personalities; thus, if one person has the type of personality that makes her want to stay with her current job, her friend should also like the job in question (personality similarity theory).

**Table 1.4**  Hypothesis example 1

| Does all this noise affect my employees' performance? | High levels of noise will increase the number of errors made in assembling electronic components | Noise causes a distraction making it difficult to concentrate |
| --- | --- | --- |
| *Idea or Question* | *Hypothesis or prediction* | *Theory or explanation* |
| | **What will happen** | **Why it will happen** |

**Table 1.5**  Hypothesis example 2

| What employee recruitment source is best? | Employee referrals will result in employees who stay with the company longer than will the other recruitment methods | 1. Realistic job preview theory<br>2. Differential source theory<br>3. Personality similarity theory |
| --- | --- | --- |
| *Idea or Question* | *Hypothesis or prediction* | *Theory or explanation* |
| | **What will happen** | **Why it will happen** |

Thus, even though a study might support a hypothesis, it is still important to determine the *reason* why the hypothesis is true. In this example, it would be necessary to conduct further studies to determine which of the three theories, if any, best explains the results. This is important because our ability to understand and use the best theory allows us to develop new methods to improve productivity in the workplace. If the first theory were true, we would give every applicant a realistic job preview. If the third theory were true, we would encourage successful employees to recruit their friends.

At times, forming a hypothesis can be difficult. In some cases, this difficulty is because no previous research has been conducted or theory proposed that would suggest a clear hypothesis about the answer to a question. For example, a student of mine wanted to see if personality was related to handwriting neatness. She couldn't find any research on handwriting neatness, much less on the relationship between personality and handwriting. There were also no theories or logical reason to predict what types of personalities would write a particular way. So, she conducted an *exploratory study* without a hypothesis; a practice that is not uncommon but is generally frowned upon by scientists.

In other cases, it is difficult to form a hypothesis because a prediction could go either way. For example, another of my students was curious about whether a recommendation letter written by an important person (such as a senator) would be more influential than one written by a professor (Hey, I thought professors were important!). She had trouble forming a hypothesis because there were just as many reasons that a reference by an important person would be more influential as there were that such a reference would be less influential.

At times, a hypothesis may not be supported by a study even though the logic and theory behind it are correct. Often, a poor research design is the culprit. Other times, it is because the topic is more complicated than originally thought. When studying a topic, psychologists wish for simple answers. Unfortunately, most situations in life are not simple. For example, psychologists have been trying for years to understand aggression and violence. They have postulated many theories for why people are violent: genetics, brain abnormalities, learning, and frustration to name a few. Some studies support these reasons while others don't. Why the lack of consistency? Because none of the theories by itself is the answer. Each of the theories explains violence in certain people under certain circumstances. Furthermore, violent behavior may be the result of a cumulation of several factors, each of which by itself will not result in violence.

Confused? I hope not. But the purpose of the preceding paragraphs was to show you the complexity of research. At times, many theories can explain a particular behavior. At other times, behavior can be predicted, but the reason for the behavior may not be known. At still other times, we have questions but can't predict what the answer will be. This complexity of life is what makes research fun.

### Literature Reviews

Once a research idea has been created, the next step is to search the literature for similar research. This search is important because if the question you are interested in answering has already been researched in 20 studies, it is probably not necessary for you to conduct a new study. As a graduate student, it took me a while to realize that most of my research ideas that were "so brilliant, no one else could have thought of them" had already been conducted several times over. I guess the moral of this last story is that when you finish school, don't forget about your university library. I would venture to say that most questions that you will have can be answered by a quick trip to the library: it is not necessary, nor smart, to constantly reinvent the wheel.

Even if your specific question has not been researched before, the probability is high that similar research has been conducted. This research is useful because even though it does not directly answer your question, it can provide some good ideas on how to conduct your study.

When reviewing literature, you are likely to encounter three types of periodicals: journals and journal/magazines which are listed in Table 1.6, and magazines. **Journals** consist of articles written by researchers directly reporting the results of a study. Journals may be difficult (and boring) to read but are the best source of unbiased and accurate information about a topic. The leading journal in I/O psychology is the *Journal of Applied Psychology*.

**Journal/Magazines** contain articles usually written by professional writers who have expertise in a given field. This type of publication is usu-

**Table 1.6**   List of I/O psychology periodicals

| Journals | Journal/Magazines |
|---|---|
| *Academy of Management Journal* | *HRMagazine* |
| *Academy of Management Review* | *Personnel* |
| *Applied H.R.M. Research* | *Personnel Journal* |
| *Erognomics* | *Training* |
| *Human Factors* | *Training and Development Journal* |
| *Human Performance* | |
| *Journal of Applied Psychology* | |
| *Journal of Business and Psychology* | |
| *Journal of Occupational Psychology* | |
| *Journal of Vocational Behavior* | |
| *Organizational Behavior and Human Decision Processes* | |
| *Personnel Psychology* | |
| *Public Personnel Management* | |

ally read by practitioners in the field. Journal/magazines summarize the research on a topic in an easy to understand format; however, the articles in these publications do not cover all the research on a topic and can be somewhat biased. *HRMagazine* and *Personnel Journal* are examples of I/O-related journal/magazines.

You are already familiar with **magazines** such as *People, Time,* and *Soldier of Fortune.* These periodicals are designed to entertain as well as inform. Magazines are good sources of ideas but inadequate to support a scientific hypothesis. Magazine articles are written by professional writers with no particular expertise in a topic. As a result, the "scientific" information in magazines is often wrong (Aamodt, 1986).

### The Location Where the Study Will Be Conducted

Once a research idea has been created and a hypothesis formed, you must decide whether to conduct the study in the laboratory or the field.

**Laboratory Research**   Often when one hears the word *research*, the first thing that comes to mind is an experimenter in a white coat testing subjects in a basement laboratory. Few experimenters actually wear white coats, but much I/O psychology research *is* conducted in laboratories. Usually, this is done at a university, but it also can be conducted by researchers in such organizations as AT&T and IBM.

One disadvantage of laboratory research is **external validity.** That is, will the results of laboratory research *generalize* to organizations in the real world? An example of this issue involves research about employee-selection methods. It is not uncommon in such research for subjects to view a résumé or a videotape of an interview and make a judgment about a hypothetical applicant. The problem: Is the situation similar enough to actual employment decisions made in the real world or is the laboratory environment so controlled and hypothetical that the results will not generalize? Although the answers to these questions still have not been resolved, research often is conducted in laboratories because they allow a researcher to control many variables that are not of interest to the researchers.

**Field Research** Another location for research is away from the laboratory and out in the "field," which could be the assembly line of an automotive plant, the secretarial pool of a large insurance company, or the interviewing room at a personnel agency. **Field research** has a problem opposite to that of laboratory research. What field research obviously gains in external validity it loses in control of extraneous variables that are not of interest to the researcher (internal validity).

Does the location of a study make a difference? It can. A meta-analysis by Sadri and Robertson (1993) found that self-efficacy predicts performance in laboratory studies more than in field studies, and Miller and Monge (1986) found a stronger relationship between participation and job satisfaction in field studies than in laboratory studies.

Field research also provides researchers with an ethical dilemma. Psychologists require that subjects participate in studies of their own free will — a concept called **informed consent.** In laboratory studies, informed consent is seldom an issue as potential subjects are told the nature of a study, asked to sign-up for the study, and then asked to sign an informed consent form indicating they understand their rights as a subject and have chosen to voluntarily participate (an example of an informed consent form can be found

Conducting research in field settings can be difficult.

in Figure 1.1). In field studies, however, obtaining informed consent can not only be difficult, but can change the way in which people behave.

For example, suppose we think that making a supervisor's office more pleasant looking will increase the number of employees who visit the supervisor's office. After decorating five supervisors' offices with plants and paintings and making five other supervisors' offices look messy and cold, we use a video camera to record the number of office visitors. Would the results of our study be affected if we told our employees that they were going to be part of a study? Probably so.

How then do we solve the ethical dilemma of informed consent and yet still protect the integrity of our research project? Our ethical guidelines allow us to balance the harm or inconvenience imposed on a subject with the importance of the study. In this example, our study is not of great importance, but informed consent would not be necessary because no negative consequences — pain, inconvenience, embarrassment — were associated with being a subject in our study.

When studies involve negative consequences for a subject, as would be the case if we subjected employees to intense heat so that we could study the effects of temperature, informed consent can only be waived if the importance of the study outweighs the negative consequences. Universities have **Institutional Review Boards** to monitor research to ensure ethical treatment of subjects. One area to which these review boards pay close attention is *confidentiality.* Because the data collected in research can be of a sensitive nature (for example, performance ratings or test scores), researchers ensure confidentiality by using subject ID numbers rather than names and avoiding discussion of individual subjects.

### The Research Method to Be Used

After deciding the location for the research, the researcher must determine which type of research method to use. The choices include experimental and nonexperimental methods, archival research, surveys, and meta-analyses.

**Experimental Method**   As you might recall from your general psychology course, the experimental method is the most powerful of all research methods because it is the only method that can determine **cause-and-effect** relationships. Thus, if it is important to know whether one variable produces or causes another variable to change, then the **experiment** is the only method that should be used. What makes a research study an experiment? For a research study to be an experiment, the researcher must actually **manipulate** a variable, which is called the **independent variable.** It is important to understand that the word *experiment* refers only to a study in which the independent variable has been manipulated by a researcher. Any study not involving such a manipulation cannot technically be called an experiment; instead, it is called a study, a survey, or an investigation.

For example, suppose we were interested in finding out whether wearing a three-piece suit to an interview is better than wearing a coat and

ADULT INFORMED CONSENT FORM

Title of Investigation:

Investigator(s): (List Faculty and Graduate Students)

This is to certify that I, _____, hereby agree to participate as a volunteer in a scientific investigation (experiment, program, study) as an authorized part of the education and research program of Radford University under the supervision of _____.

The investigation and my part in the investigation have been defined and fully explained to me by _____, and I understand his/her explanation. A copy of the procedures of this investigation and a description of any risks and discomforts has been provided to me and has been discussed in detail with me.

I have been given an opportunity to ask whatever questions I may have had and all such questions and inquiries have been answered to my satisfaction.

I understand that I am free to deny any answers to specific items or questions in interviews or questionnaires.

I understand that any data or answers to questions will remain confidential with regard to my identity.

I understand that, in the event of physical injury resulting from this investigation, neither financial compensation nor free medical treatment will be provided by Radford University for the injury. Further, I agree that I will not hold Radford University responsible for any liability for personal injury I may incur in the course of or as a result of the study.

I certify that to the best of my knowledge and belief, I have no physical or mental illness or weakness that would increase the risk to me of participation of this investigation. (Use this statement if it applies to your investigation.)

I understand that my participation is voluntary and that my decision whether or not to participate will not affect any present or future relationship with Radford University.

I FURTHER UNDERSTAND THAT I AM FREE TO WITHDRAW MY CONSENT AND TERMINATE MY PARTICIPATION AT ANY TIME

_____          _____
            Date                                          Signature of subject

I, the undersigned, have defined and fully explained the investigation to the above subject.


_____          _____
            Date                                          Investigator's signature

        I was present when the study was explained to the subject(s) in detail and to my best knowledge and belief it was understood. (Use this statement if it applies to your investigation.)

_____          _____
            Date                                                    Witness

NOTE:  WHEN A SIGNED CONSENT DOCUMENT IS USED, A COPY MUST BE GIVEN TO THE SUBJECT
            SO EACH WILL HAVE A RECORD OF THEIR AGREEMENT TO PARTICIPATE.

**Figure 1.1** Sample informed consent form

slacks. We could study this issue by observing job applicants at a specific company and comparing the interview scores of people with three-piece suits with those of people wearing coats and slacks. We might find that the better dressed applicants received higher scores, but we could not conclude that the wearing of a three-piece suit *caused* the higher scores; something other than the suit may be at work. Perhaps applicants who own three-piece suits are more assertive than other applicants; it then might have been assertiveness and not dress style that led to the higher interview scores.

If we wanted to be more sure that dress style affects interview scores, we would have to manipulate the variable of interest and hold all other variables as constant as possible. How could we turn this into an experiment? Let us take 100 people and give 50 of them three-piece suits to wear and the other 50 sports coats and slacks. Each subject would then go through an interview with a personnel director. Afterward, we would compare the interview scores of our two groups. The variable that we expect to change as a result of our manipulating the independent variable is called the **dependent variable.** In this case, the dependent variable would be the interview score.

Although this particular research design has some problems (see if you can spot them), the fact that we manipulated the applicant's dress style gives us greater confidence that dress style would cause higher interview scores. Even though the results of experiments provide more confidence regarding cause-and-effect relationships, ethical and practical considerations do not always make experimental designs possible.

Suppose we wish to study the effect of loud noise on worker performance. To make this an experimental design, we could have 50 subjects work on an assembly line while being subjected to very loud noise and 50 subjects work on an assembly line with no noise. Two months later we compare the productivity of the two groups. But what is wrong with this study? In addition to having lower productivity, the high-noise group now has poorer hearing—not a very ethical sounding experiment (yes, the pun *was* intended).

**Nonexperimental Methods**   Even though researchers would always like to use the experimental method, it is not always possible. Nonexperimental designs are then used. As an example, let us go back to our noise study.

Because we cannot manipulate the level of noise, we will instead test the noise level of 100 manufacturing plants and compare the average productivity of plants with lower noise levels with that of plants with higher noise levels. As you can easily see, this is not as good a research design as the unethical experiment that we created earlier. Too many variables other than noise could account for any differences found in productivity; however, given the circumstances, it still provides us with more information than we had before the study.

**Nonexperimental methods** are often used to evaluate the results of a new program implemented by an organization. For example, an organization that had instituted a child-care center wanted to see whether the center affected employee absenteeism. To find the answer, the organization compared absenteeism levels from the year before the center was introduced with the

**Table 1.7** Why nonexperimental studies are difficult to interpret: the child-care center

| Date | Absenteeism | External Factor | Internal Factor |
|---|---|---|---|
| 1/85 | 2.8% | | |
| 2/85 | 3.1 | | |
| 3/85 | 4.7 | Local unemployment rate at 4.1% | |
| 4/85 | 4.7 | | |
| 5/85 | 4.8 | | |
| 6/85 | 6.7 | Main highway closed | |
| 7/85 | 6.5 | | |
| 8/85 | 4.9 | Highway reopens | |
| 9/85 | 4.5 | | |
| 10/85 | 4.4 | | |
| 11/85 | 8.7 | Terrible snow storm | |
| 12/85 | 5.3 | | |
| 1/86 | 5.3 | | Child-care center started |
| 2/86 | 5.4 | | |
| 3/86 | 5.1 | | Flextime program started |
| 4/86 | 2.1 | Local unemployment rate hits 9.3% | |
| 5/86 | 2.1 | | |
| 7/86 | 1.8 | | Wellness program started |
| 8/86 | 1.8 | | |
| 9/86 | 2.0 | | New attendance policy |
| 10/86 | 2.3 | | |
| 11/86 | 4.0 | Mild weather | |
| 12/86 | 4.2 | Mild weather | |

Note: Absenteeism rate in 1985 prior to child-care center = 5.09%; rate in 1986 after child-care center = 3.01%

absenteeism levels for the year following the implementation; the organization found that both absenteeism and turnover had decreased.

Although it would be tempting to conclude that the child-care center was a success, such a conclusion would not be prudent. Many other variables might have caused the reduction. As shown in Table 1.7, the organization implemented several other progressive programs during the same period. Thus, the decrease in absenteeism and turnover could have resulted from other programs or some combination of programs. Furthermore, the economy changed, and jobs became more difficult to obtain. Workers may have reduced their absentee rates out of fear of being fired, and turnover may have been reduced because employees realized that there were few jobs available. In addition, the weather improved in the second year, which meant workers were rarely unable to get to work.

Taken by itself, we would certainly not want to bet the mortgage on the results of our nonexperimental study. But, if 10 other researchers use different nonexperimental designs to study the same question and find similar results, we might feel confident enough to make changes or reach conclusions based on the available research evidence.

**Archival Research**   Another research method commonly used in I/O psychology is **archival research,** which involves using previously collected data or records to answer a research question. For example, if we wanted to know what distinguishes good workers from poor workers, we could look in the personnel files to see whether the backgrounds of good workers have common characteristics that are not shared by poor workers. The advantages of archival research are its unobtrusiveness and relatively low cost, but it also has severe drawbacks. Records in files are not always accurate, and they are not always kept up to date. Furthermore, the type of data needed by a researcher may not be in the archives because the data were never recorded in the first place.

As an undergraduate, (this was before the big dance), I was involved with an archival study designed to determine why some students in a Master of business administration (M.B.A.) program dropped out while others completed their coursework. What was supposed to be an easy job of getting records from a few files turned into a nightmare. The records of more than 300 students were scattered in storage rooms in three locations in southern California and were not filed in any order. Furthermore, almost every student had at least one important item missing from his or her file. Needless to say, these problems kept the results of the study from being as accurate as desired. As we approach the twenty-first century, the computerization of information greatly increases the potential for and ease of archival research.

**Surveys**   Another method of conducting research is to *ask* people about their opinion on some topic. Surveys might ask employees about their attitudes toward the company, human resource directors about their opinions regarding the best résumé format, or managers about success of their child-care centers.

*Survey Method*   Surveys can be conducted by mail, personal interviews, phone, fax, e-mail, and magazines. The method chosen depends on such factors as sample size, budget, amount of time available to conduct the study, and need for a representative sample. For example, mail surveys are less expensive and time consuming than personal interviews but result in lower response rates and, at times, lower quality answers. E-mail surveys are inexpensive but are limited to people who have access to e-mail (not a representative sample) and are more subject to size and format restrictions than are mail surveys. Surveys contained in magazines and professional publications are common *(for example, HRNews and Training and Development Journal),* but, as with e-mail, they may not result in a representative sample.

A high response rate is essential for trust to be placed in survey results. Appropriate response rates are 60% for mail surveys and 80% for interviews (Babbie, 1992). Response rates can be increased by providing either monetary or nonmonetary incentives with a survey mailing; making the incentive contingent on returning the survey does not greatly improve response rates (Church, 1993). Response rates can also be increased by making several contacts with respondents, providing a stamped return envelope, and personalizing the survey request letter (Yammarino, Skinner, & Childers, 1991).

***Survey Questions*** Well-designed survey questions are easy to understand, use simple language, do not ask about hypothetical situations, and are relatively short in length (Converse & Presser, 1986). Extreme care must be taken in choosing the words used in each question. For example, in a survey about abortion attitudes, would the questions "Are you pro-choice?" or "Are you anti-life" get the same response? How about "Are you pro-life?" or "Are you anti-choice?" As this example clearly points out, biased wording can easily alter the results of a survey.

***Accuracy of Responses*** A final issue involving surveys is the extent to which responses to the survey questions are accurate. This issue is especially important when asking about sensitive or controversial issues. That is, if I ask if you "believe that males and females are equally qualified to be managers," would you tell the truth if you thought men were better qualified? Would people honestly respond to questions about their former drug use, poor performance at work, or unethical behavior? Probably not.

Inaccurately responding to survey questions is not always an intentional attempt to be dishonest. Instead, inaccurate responses can be the result of a person not actually knowing the correct answer to a question. For example, an employee might respond to a question about attendance by stating she has missed three days of work in the past year when in fact she missed five. Was she lying or just mistaken about her attendance record?

**Meta-Analysis** Perhaps the newest research method, **meta-analysis** is a statistical method of reaching conclusions based on previous research. Prior to meta-analysis, a researcher interested in reviewing the literature on a topic would read all of the available research and then make a rather subjective conclusion based on the articles. With meta-analysis, the researcher goes through each article, determines the **effect size** for each article, and then finds a statistical average of effect sizes across all articles. Thus, meta-analysis will result in one number, called the **mean effect size** ($d$), that indicates the effectiveness of some variable.

To make this process clearer, let's go through a hypothetical meta-analysis. For example, if we were interested in determining whether child-care centers effectively reduce absenteeism, we would start our meta-analysis by searching for articles on child care. After a thorough search, we find 60 such articles. Only 10 of the articles, however, represent actual empirical research; thus, our meta-analysis would concentrate on only those 10.

The next step in meta-analysis would be to compute an *effect size* for each article. This can be done in two ways. One way is to take the results of the statistical test used in the study (for example, $F, t, x^2$) and convert them into an effect size using one of the formulas shown in Figure 1.2 (don't worry, the formulas are for demonstration purposes only; it would be too

A meta-analysis is a statistical summary of related research studies.

dangerous to use these at home without the direct supervision of a trained psychologist). The other way is to directly compute the effect size by using **means** and **standard deviations.** The formula for doing this is:

$$\text{effect size} = \frac{\bar{x}_e - \bar{x}_c}{sd}$$

where $x_e$ is the mean of the experimental group, $x_c$ is the mean of the control group, and $sd$ is the overall standard deviation. In the first article, suppose we find that during the year before the child-care center's establishment the average employee missed six days, and in the following year the average employee missed three days; the standard deviation is three. Our effect size for this study would be:

$$\frac{6 - 3}{3} = 1$$

We would then compute effect sizes for each study until we had an effect size for all 10. The next step is to multiply each effect size by the number of people in each study, add these products, and then divide by the total number of subjects in all 10 studies. The resulting number is our mean effect size. The purpose of this last step is to provide more weight for studies with large sample sizes: it makes sense that the results of a study with 1,000 subjects should carry more weight than a study with 25 subjects. An example of this process is shown in Table 1.8.

**Figure 1.2**
List of meta-analysis conversion formulas

| Statistic to Be Converted | | Formula for Transformation to $r$ |
|:---:|:---:|:---:|
| $t$ | $r=$ | $\sqrt{\dfrac{t^2}{t^2 + df}}$ |
| $F$ | $r=$ | $\sqrt{\dfrac{F}{F + df\,(error)}}$ |
| $\chi^2$ | $r=$ | $\sqrt{\dfrac{\chi^2}{n}}$ |
| $d$ | $r=$ | $\dfrac{d}{\sqrt{d^2 + 4}}$ |
| | $r=$ | $\sqrt{\dfrac{Z^2}{N}}$ |

| Statistic to Be Converted | | Formula for Transformation to $d$ |
|:---:|:---:|:---:|
| $t$ | $d=$ | $\dfrac{2t}{\sqrt{df}}$ |
| $F$ | $d=$ | $\dfrac{2\sqrt{F}}{\sqrt{df\,(error)}}$ |
| $r$ | $d=$ | $\dfrac{2r}{\sqrt{1 - r^2}}$ |

Rather than using $d$ scores, meta-analyses can be conducted using correlation coefficients ($r$) as the effect size. Correlation coefficients are used as the effect size when researchers are interested in the *relationship* between two variables and the majority of studies use correlation as their statistical test. Examples would be studies looking at the relationship between honesty test scores and employee theft or the relationship between job satisfaction and performance. An example of a meta-analysis using correlation coefficients is shown in Table 1.9.

A $d$ is used as the effect size when researchers are looking at the *difference* between two groups; the majority of studies use $F$, $t$, or $x^2$ as their statistical test. Examples would be studies looking at the effectiveness of a training method, the effect of goal setting, or the effects of shift work. The results of meta-analyses using $r$ and $d$ as the effect size will be used throughout this text.

After computing a mean effect size, several other steps would then be taken—computing the observed variance, the variance expected by sampling

**Table 1.8** Example of a simple meta-analysis using *d* scores

| Study | Performance Rating | | sd | d | n | d × n |
| --- | --- | --- | --- | --- | --- | --- |
| | Training | No Training | | | | |
| Cruise (1993) | 6.3 | 4.1 | 2.2 | 1.00 | 52 | 52.00 |
| Baldwin (1994) | 5.1 | 4.8 | 1.4 | .21 | 44 | 9.24 |
| Gibson (1993) | 8.2 | 6.3 | 3.5 | .54 | 100 | 54.00 |
| Ford (1995) | 7.3 | 7.1 | 1.5 | .13 | 200 | 26.00 |
| Reeves (1994) | 6.9 | 7.4 | 2.9 | −.17 | 30 | −5.17 |
| Total | | | | | 426 | 136.07 |
| Mean effect size (*d*) | | | | .32 | | |

**Table 1.9** Example of a simple meta-analysis using correlation coefficients

| Study | Correlation (*r*) | n | r × n |
| --- | --- | --- | --- |
| Stone (1995) | .10 | 43 | 4.30 |
| Peiffer (1994) | .33 | 206 | 67.98 |
| Ryan (1993) | .42 | 320 | 134.40 |
| Bassinger (1993) | .63 | 24 | 15.12 |
| Griffith (1994) | .35 | 189 | 66.15 |
| Total | | 782 | 287.95 |
| Mean effect size (*r*) | .37 | | |

error alone, and a confidence interval (we I/O folks love our statistics as much as a good meal!) — but a complete discussion of meta-analysis is beyond the scope of this book and probably beyond the reader's interest as well. It is important, however, that you be able to interpret the outcomes of meta-analyses because they will not only be used in this text, but also they appear to be the emerging trend in reviewing previous research.

The question remains regarding how effect sizes should be interpreted. If you have not yet had a statistics course under your belt (and we all know how painful that can be), understanding effect size can be difficult. However, effect sizes can be interpreted in two ways: by comparing them to norms or directly applying them to a particular situation. When using norms, effect sizes (*d*) less than .40 are considered to be small, those between .40 and .80 are moderate, and those higher than .80 are considered large (Cohen, 1977). Of course, these numbers are "rules of thumb" and the actual **practical significance** of an effect size depends on many factors — formulas are available to achieve more precision. The average effect size for an organizational intervention is .44 (Guzzo, Jette, & Katzell, 1985).

When directly applying an effect size to a particular situation, one needs to know the standard deviation of the variable in question. This standard deviation is then multiplied by the effect size from the meta-analysis to yield a meaningful score.

For example, suppose employees at an AT&T manufacturing plant miss an average of 9.5 days of work per year with a standard deviation of 3.6 days. AT&T is considering a new incentive system to improve attendance that a meta-analysis indicates has an effect size of .32 in reducing absenteeism. What can AT&T expect to gain from this incentive system? By multiplying their absenteeism standard deviation (3.6 days) by the effect size from the meta-analysis (.32), AT&T can expect the incentive system to reduce absenteeism by an average of 1.15 days per employee (3.6 × .32 = 1.15). If the attendance data for IBM were an average of 10.4 days per year missed with a standard deviation of 5.6, it could expect an annual reduction in absenteeism of 1.79 days per employee (5.6 × .32 = 1.79). AT&T and IBM would each have to decide if the predicted reduction in savings would be worth the cost of the incentive system.

### Sample

Decisions also must be made regarding the size, composition, and method of selecting the subjects who will serve as the sample in a study. Although it is nice to have a large sample for any research study, it is not necessary if the experimenter can choose a random sample and control for many of the extraneous variables. But unless the study will be conducted in a laboratory using the experimental method, it is doubtful that a small sample size will be sufficient.

The method of selecting the sample depends on the nature of the organization. A small organization will probably be forced to use all of its employees, which means that the sample will be small but highly representative of the intended population. For economical and practical reasons, a large organization will select only certain employees to participate in a study rather than use the entire work force. The problem then becomes one of which employees will participate.

If the study involves a questionnaire, it would be no problem to randomly select a desired number of employees and have them complete the survey. If, however, the study is more elaborate, such as investigating the effects of lighting on performance, it would be difficult to randomly select employees. That is, it would not be practical to have one employee work under high levels of light while the person next to her was uninvolved with the experiment. If we decide to have one plant work with high levels of light and another with lower levels, what we gain in practicality we lose in randomness and control. So we try to strike a balance between practicality and experimental rigor.

To increase experimental rigor and decrease the costs of conducting research, many studies are conducted at universities using students rather than employees as subjects. In fact, college students serve as subjects in 87%

of all published I/O research (Gordon, Slade, & Schmitt, 1986). This use of students has led to considerable debate regarding the **generalizability** of university research; that is, do students behave in the same fashion as employees? Some authors (for example, Sears, 1986) point out that, compared to adults in the working world, college students are younger, more educated, and more egocentric; possess a less formulated sense of self; and have a stronger need for peer approval. Because of these differences, it makes sense that in research, students would behave differently than adults in the working world.

Research on this issue, however, is mixed. Some researchers have found differences between student subjects and professional subjects, while others have not. For example, Landy and Bates (1973) found that students are more subject to contrast effects than are managers, but Hakel, Ohnesorge, and Dunnette (1970) did not find sample differences in an earlier study. In general, however, the preponderance of research indicates that college student samples behave differently than do real world or nonacademic samples (Barr & Hitt, 1986; Burnett & Dunne, 1986; Gordon, Slade, & Schmitt, 1986). Furthermore, some research suggests that results will differ based on the *major* of the college sample. For example, both Staw and Ross (1985) and Forst (1987) found that business students rated managers differently than did psychology students. These findings suggest that in certain cases, research using students for subjects will not generalize to the real world.

A final important issue concerns the method used to recruit subjects. To obtain the best research results, it is essential to use a **random sample** so that the sample will be as representative as possible. This means that if a survey is randomly sent to 100 employees, the research will be most accurate only if all employees return the survey. However, if study participation is voluntary, a 100% return rate is unlikely. The ethics of the American Psychological Association (APA) require voluntary participation, whereas accurate research often requires compulsory participation. How do researchers solve this dilemma? In some organizations, employees are required to sign a statement when they are hired agreeing to participate in any organizational research studies. To underscore this agreement, each employee's job description lists research participation.

Proponents of this method argue that participation in research is still voluntary because the individual had the choice of either not taking the job or taking it with the advance knowledge of research requirements. Opponents argue that taking a job or not taking a job in order to make a living does not constitute a proper and completely free choice. Similarly, in some universities students have the option of participating in a few research studies or writing a term paper. Even though the students are given an alternative to research participation, some psychologists argue that the choice between writing a term paper that will take several days and participating in two or three experiments that will take a few hours is not a legitimate choice (Sieber & Saks, 1989).

Because obtaining random samples is difficult, especially in industry, many studies use a **convenience sample** and then randomly assign subjects to the various experimental conditions. A convenience sample is one, such as students in a psychology class, that is easily available to a researcher. With **random assignment,** each subject in a nonrandom sample is randomly *assigned* to a particular experimental condition. For example, in a study designed to test the effectiveness of a training method, 60 subjects agree to participate in the study — 30 of the subjects are randomly assigned to the group receiving training, and another 30 are randomly assigned to the control group that does not receive training.

### Running the Study

Once all of the above decisions have been made, it is finally time to run the study and collect data. To ensure that data collection proceeds in an unbiased fashion, it is important that all instructions to the subjects be stated in a standardized fashion and at a level that is understandable. Once the subjects finish their participation, they should be **debriefed,** or told the purpose of the experiment and given a chance to ask questions about their participation.

### Statistical Analysis

After all data have been collected, the results are statistically analyzed. A discussion of statistics is beyond the scope of this book, but it is important to understand why statistics are used. Statistical analysis helps us to determine how confident we are that our results are real and did not occur by chance alone. For example, if we conducted a study in your classroom in which we compared the average social security number of students on the left side of the room with that of students on the right side of the room, we would no doubt get a difference. That is, the average social security number of the students on the right would not be exactly the same as that for students on the left. If we did not conduct a statistical analysis of our data, we could conclude that people on the right side have higher social security numbers than people on the left side. Perhaps we could even develop a theory about our results!

Does this sound ridiculous? Of course it does. But it points out the idea that any set of numbers we collect will in all probability be different. The question is, are they *significantly* different? Statistical analysis provides the answer by determining the probability that our data were the result of chance. In psychology, we use the .05 level of significance, which means that if our analysis indicates that the probability that our data resulted from chance is 5% or less, we would consider our results to be statistically significant. This means that if someone were to replicate our research, we would be confident that other researchers would get results similar to ours 95% of the time. Although the .05 level of significance is the most commonly used, some researchers have suggested that we should be more flexible and use either more conservative or more liberal levels, depending on the situation (Serlin & Lapsley, 1985).

At this point, a caution must be made about the interpretation of significance levels. Significance levels only indicate the level of confidence that we can place on a result being the product of chance. They say nothing about the strength of the results. Thus, a study finding results significant at the .01 level does not necessarily show a stronger effect than a study with results significant at the .05 level.

To determine the strength of a finding, we use the effect size discussed earlier in the section on meta-analysis. Significance levels tell us the *statistical significance* of a study, and effect sizes (combined with logic) tell us the *practical significance* of a study.

For example, suppose that we conduct a study comparing the SAT scores of male and female high school students. Based on a sample of five million students, we find that males average 490 and females 489. With such a huge sample size, we will probably find that the two means are statistically different. However, with only a one-point difference between the two groups on a test with a maximum score of 800, we would probably not place much practical significance in the difference.

**Correlation**　A detailed discussion of statistics is beyond our scope. But it is necessary to discuss one particular statistic—correlation—because it is so widely used in I/O psychology and throughout this book.

**Correlation** is a statistical procedure that allows a researcher to determine the *relationship* between two variables—For example, the relationships found between an employment test and future employee performance, or job satisfaction and job attendance, or performance ratings made by workers and supervisors. A correlational analysis does not necessarily say anything about causality.

The result of correlational analysis is a number called a **correlation coefficient.** The values of this coefficient range from 0 to + 1 and from 0 to − 1. The further the coefficient is from 0, the greater the relationship between two variables. That is, a correlation of .40 shows a stronger relationship between two variables than a correlation of .20. Likewise, a correlation of −.39 shows a stronger relationship than a correlation of +.30. The + and − signs indicate the *direction* of the correlation. A positive (+) correlation means that as the values of one variable increase, so do the values of a second variable. For example, we might find a positive correlation between intelligence and scores on a classroom exam. This would mean that the more intelligent the student, the higher his score on the exam.

A negative (−) correlation means that as the values of one variable increase, the values of a second variable decrease. For example, we would probably find a negative correlation between the number of beers that you drink the night before a test and your score on that test. In I/O psychology, we find negative correlations between job satisfaction and absenteeism, age and reaction time, and nervousness and interview success.

Why does a correlation coefficient not indicate a cause and effect relationship? Because a third variable, an **intervening variable,** often accounts for the relationship between two variables (Mitchell, 1985). Take the example often used by psychologist David Schroeder. Suppose there is a correlation of +.80 between the number of ice cream cones sold in New York during

August and the number of babies that die during August in India. Does eating ice cream kill babies in another nation? No, that would not make sense. Instead, we look for the third variable that would explain our high correlation. In this case, the answer is clearly the summer heat.

Another interesting example was provided by Mullins (1986) in a presentation about the incorrect interpretation of correlation coefficients. Mullins pointed out that data show a strong negative correlation between the number of cows per square mile and the crime rate. With his tongue firmly planted in his cheek, Mullins suggested that New York City could rid itself of crime by importing millions of head of cattle. Of course, the real interpretation for the negative correlation is that crime is greater in urban areas than in rural areas.

As demonstrated above, a good researcher should always be cautious about variables that seem related. A few years ago, *People* magazine reported on a minister who conducted a "study" of 500 pregnant teenaged girls and found that rock music was being played when 450 of them became pregnant. The minister concluded that because the two are related (that is, they occurred at the same time), rock music must cause pregnancy. His solution? Outlaw rock music and teenage pregnancy would disappear. In my own "study," however, I found that in all 500 cases of teenage pregnancy, a pillow also was present. To use the same logic as that used by the minister, the real solution would be to outlaw pillows, not rock music. Although both "solutions" are certainly strange, the point should be clear: just because two events occur at the same time or seem to be related does not mean that one event or variable causes another (Brigham, 1989).

## CHAPTER SUMMARY

In this chapter, we discussed the field of I/O psychology and research methods used by I/O psychologists.

In the first section, you learned that I/O psychology is relatively young and consists of four major subfields: personnel psychology, training, organizational psychology, and human factors. Industrial psychologists work in a variety of settings including industry, government, education, and consulting firms. At least a Master's degree is required to find employment in the field, and starting salaries are around $27,000 at the Master's level and $37,000 at the Ph.D. level. The work performed by Master's level graduates is different from that performed by doctoral level graduates.

In the second section, research was described as an important part of the I/O psychologist's job. Research decisions that must be made include what to research, the location of the research (laboratory or field), the research method that will be used (experimental method, nonexperimental method, survey, archival research, meta-analysis), the sample that will be used, and the statistics that will be used to analyze the research data.

**Archival research**   Research that involves the use of previously collected data.

**Army alpha**   An intelligence test developed during World War I and used by the army for soldiers who can read.

**Army beta**   An intelligence test developed during World War I and used by the army for soldiers who cannot read.

**Cause-effect relationship**   The result of a well-controlled experiment about which the researcher can confidently state that the independent variable caused the change in the dependent variable.

**Convenience sample**   A non-random research sample that is used because it is easily available.

**Correlation**   A statistical procedure used to measure the relationship between two variables.

**Correlation coefficient**   A statistic, resulting from performing a correlation, that indicates the magnitude and direction of a relationship.

**Debriefing**   Informing the subject in an experiment about the purpose of the study in which he or she was a participant and providing any other relevant information.

**Dependent variable**   The measure of behavior that is expected to change as a result of changes in the independent variable.

**Dissertation**   A formal research paper required of most doctoral students in order to graduate.

**Effect size**   Used in meta-analysis, a statistic that indicates the amount of change caused by an experimental manipulation.

**Experiment**   A type of research study in which the independent variable is manipulated by the experimenter.

**External validity**   The extent to which research results can be expected to hold true outside the specific setting in which they were obtained.

**Field research**   Research conducted in a natural setting as opposed to in a laboratory.

**Generalizability**   Like external validity, the extent to which research results hold true outside the specific setting in which they were obtained.

**Graduate Record Exam (G.R.E.)**   A standardized admission test required by most psychology graduate schools.

**Hawthorne studies**   A series of studies conducted at the Western Electric Plant in Hawthorne, Illinois, that have come to represent any change in behavior that occurs when people react to a change in the environment.

**Human factors**   A field of study concentrating on the interaction between humans and machines.

**Hypothesis**   An educated prediction about the answer to a research question.

**Independent variable**   The manipulated variable in an experiment.

**Industrial/organizational psychology**   A branch of psychology that applies the principles of psychology to the workplace.

**Informed consent**   The formal process by which subjects give permission to be included in a study.

**Institutional Review Board**   A committee designated to ensure the ethical treatment of research subjects.

**Internship**   A situation in which a student works for an organization, either for pay or as a volunteer, in order to receive practical work experience.

**Intervening variable**   A third variable that can often explain the relationship between two other variables.

**Journal**   A collection of articles describing the methods and results of new research.

**Journal/magazine**   A collection of articles about related professional topics that seldom directly report the methods and results of new research.

**Magazine**   An unscientific collection of articles about a wide range of topics.

**Manipulation**   The alteration of a variable by an experimenter in expectation that alteration will result in a change in the dependent variable.

**Mean**   The arithmetic average of a series of scores.

**Mean effect size**   Used in meta-analysis, a statistic that is the average of the effect sizes for all studies included in the analysis.

**Meta-analysis**   A statistical method for cumulating research results.

**Nonexperimental methods**   Research methods in which the experimenter does not manipulate the independent variable.

**Organizational psychology**   The field of study that investigates the behavior of employees within the context of an organization.

**Personnel psychology**   The field of study that concentrates on the selection and evaluation of employees.

**Practical significance**   The extent to which the results of a study have actual impact on human behavior.

**Practicum**   A paid or unpaid position with an organization that gives the student practical work experience.

**Random assignment**   The random, nonbiased assignment of subjects in a research sample to the various experimental and control conditions.

**Random sample**   A sample in which every member of the relevant population has an equal chance of being chosen to participate in the study.

**Standard deviation**   A statistic that indicates the variation of scores in a distribution.

**Terminal Master's degree programs**   Graduate programs that offer a Master's degree but not a Doctoral degree.

**Theory**   A systematic set of assumptions regarding the cause and nature of an event.

## Appendix A: I/O Terminal Master's Degree Programs

| University | State | Average G.R.E. | Average G.P.A. | Jr./Sr. G.P.A. | Number Applied | Number Admitted | Number Enrolled |
|---|---|---|---|---|---|---|---|
| California State University, Long Beach | CA | 1080 | | | 107 | 57 | 46 |
| California State University, Northridge | CA | | | | | | |
| California State University, Sacramento | CA | 1100 | 3.40 | | 60 | 24 | 20 |
| California State University, San Bernardino | CA | | 3.50 | 3.50 | 30 | 15 | 10 |
| St. Mary's College | CA | | | | | | |
| San Diego State University | CA | 1134 | | | 120 | 14 | 11 |
| San Francisco State University | CA | 1200 | 3.40 | 3.60 | 100 | 25 | 20 |
| San Jose State University | CA | | | | | | |
| University of Colorado, Denver | CO | 1160 | 3.50 | | 48 | 10 | 6 |
| University of Hartford | CT | 1013 | 3.13 | | 30 | 14 | 7 |
| University of New Haven | CT | | 3.20 | 3.40 | 120 | 75 | 35 |
| Florida Institute of Technology | FL | 1070 | 3.40 | 3.40 | 40 | 14 | 10 |
| University of Central Florida | FL | 1160 | 3.40 | 3.50 | 80 | 14 | 14 |
| University of West Florida | FL | 1028 | | 3.60 | 54 | 24 | 11 |
| Valdosta State College | GA | 1000 | 3.00 | | 24 | 13 | 12 |
| Illinois State University | IL | 1149 | 3.30 | 3.46 | 81 | 17 | 10 |
| Southern Illinois University, Edwardsville | IL | 1011 | 3.09 | | 47 | 31 | 18 |
| Indiana University-Purdue University at Indianapolis | IN | 1267 | 3.44 | | 51 | 6 | 4 |
| Emporia State University | KS | | | | | | |
| Western Kentucky University | KY | 1000 | 3.10 | 3.25 | 34 | 13 | 7 |
| University of Baltimore | MD | | 3.30 | | 43 | 35 | 18 |
| Springfield College | MA | | 3.00 | 3.00 | 90 | 44 | 40 |
| Western Michigan University | MI | | | | | | |
| Mankato State University | MN | 1002 | 3.02 | 3.35 | 25 | 6 | 4 |
| Farleigh Dickinson University | NJ | 1100 | 3.25 | | 60 | 30 | 25 |
| Montclair State College | NJ | 990 | 3.30 | | 35 | 18 | 7 |
| City University of New York | NY | | 3.20 | | 150 | 30 | 20 |
| Polytechnic University | NY | | 3.30 | | | | |
| Rensselaer Polytechnic University | NY | 1128 | 3.32 | | 90 | 38 | 22 |
| Appalachian State University | NC | 975 | 3.25 | | 48 | 31 | 11 |
| East Carolina University | NC | 975 | 3.02 | 3.30 | 16 | 8 | 6 |
| University of North Carolina-Charlotte | NC | 1105 | 3.40 | 3.50 | 65 | 22 | 13 |
| Xavier University | OH | | 3.40 | | 18 | 11 | 5 |
| West Chester University | PA | | 3.23 | | 30 | 15 | 10 |
| Clemson University | SC | 1188 | 3.61 | | 80 | 23 | 21 |
| Middle Tennessee State University | TN | 1000 | 3.25 | | 25 | 20 | 15 |
| University of Tennessee-Chattanooga | TN | | | | | | |
| Lamar University | TX | 1060 | 3.35 | | 32 | 9 | 8 |
| Stephen F. Austin University | TX | | | | | | |
| Radford University | VA | 1024 | 3.21 | 3.43 | 98 | 42 | 21 |
| University of Central Washington | WA | | | | | | |
| University of Wisconsin-Oshkosh | WI | 1067 | 3.38 | 3.43 | 40 | 10 | 8 |

Source: Society for Industrial and Organizational Psychology, Inc., 1992, *Graduate Training Programs in Industrial/Organizational Psychology and Related Fields*, Arlington Heights, IL: Society for Industrial and Organizational Psychology, Inc.

## Appendix B:  I/O Ph.D. Programs

| University | State | Average G.R.E. | Average G.P.A. | Jr./Sr. G.P.A. | Number Applied | Number Admitted | Number Enrolled |
|---|---|---|---|---|---|---|---|
| Auburn University | AL | 1127 | 3.65 | | 25 | 6 | 4 |
| University of Alabama | AL | 1080 | 3.40 | 3.50 | 25 | 9 | 5 |
| University of California, Berkeley | CA | | | 3.80 | 13 | 2 | 1 |
| Claremont Graduate School | CA | | 3.20 | | 42 | 12 | 7 |
| California School of Professional Psychology | CA | | 3.20 | | 30 | 15 | 12 |
| Queen's University | Canada | 1300 | | | 30 | 4 | 2 |
| University of Waterloo | Canada | 1375 | 3.70 | 3.70 | 8 | 3 | 3 |
| University of British Columbia | Canada | 1200 | 3.00 | 3.50 | 8 | 1 | 1 |
| University of Calgary | Canada | | 3.19 | | 2 | 0 | 0 |
| University of Guelph | Canada | | | | | | |
| University of Western Ontario | Canada | | | | 35 | 2 | 1 |
| Colorado State University | CO | 1221 | | 3.50 | 100 | 15 | 5 |
| University of Connecticut | CN | 1310 | 3.70 | | 108 | 10 | 4 |
| George Washington University | D.C. | 1223 | 3.64 | | 83 | 5 | 3 |
| Florida International University | FL | 1100 | 3.30 | | 22 | 5 | 5 |
| University of South Florida | FL | 1216 | | 3.67 | 120 | 14 | 7 |
| Georgia Institute of Technology | GA | 1240 | 3.50 | | 98 | 15 | 10 |
| University of Georgia | GA | 1120 | 3.40 | 3.50 | 120 | 16 | 8 |
| DePaul University | IL | 1195 | 3.56 | 3.88 | 90 | 10 | 5 |
| Illinois Institute of Technology | IL | 1165 | 3.40 | | 53 | 25 | 11 |
| Northern Illinois University | IL | 1262 | 3.51 | | 29 | 5 | 5 |
| University of Illinois at Chicago | IL | | | | | | |
| University of Illinois at Urbana-Champaign | IL | 1350 | | 3.80 | 80 | 10 | 4 |
| Purdue University | IN | | 3.80 | 4.00 | 130 | 2 | 2 |
| Iowa State University | IO | 1100 | 3.19 | | 53 | 8 | 4 |
| Kansas State University | KS | 1144 | 3.79 | | 47 | 13 | 4 |
| Louisiana State University | LA | 1200 | 3.40 | | 33 | 3 | 3 |
| Tulane University | LA | 1265 | 3.70 | 3.70 | 62 | 8 | 4 |
| University of Maryland | MD | 1300 | 3.70 | | 125 | 4 | 3 |
| Central Michigan University | MI | 1122 | 3.31 | | 29 | 15 | 6 |
| Michigan State University | MI | 1320 | 3.70 | 3.80 | 110 | 10 | 4 |
| University of Michigan | MI | | 3.70 | | 120 | 8 | 7 |
| Wayne State University | MI | 1212 | 3.60 | 3.80 | 60 | 10 | 6 |
| University of Minnesota | MN | | | | | | |
| University of Southern Mississippi | MS | 1200 | | 3.50 | 30 | 5 | 4 |
| St. Louis University | MO | | | | | | |
| University of Missouri-St. Louis | MO | 1190 | 3.73 | | 60 | 9 | 5 |
| University of Nebraska-Omaha | NB | | | 3.74 | 12 | 5 | 3 |
| Stevens Institute of Technology | NJ | 1130 | 3.40 | | 25 | 10 | 6 |
| City University of New York | NY | 1250 | 3.40 | | 85 | 10 | 6 |
| Columbia University | NY | 1220 | 3.50 | 3.70 | 70 | 10 | 7 |
| Fordham University | NY | 1150 | 3.25 | 3.40 | 5 | 3 | 2 |

**Appendix B** *(continued)*

| University | State | Average G.R.E. | Average G.P.A. | Jr./Sr. G.P.A. | Number Applied | Number Admitted | Number Enrolled |
|---|---|---|---|---|---|---|---|
| New York University | NY | 1322 | 3.48 | 3.64 | 94 | 9 | 4 |
| SUNY-Albany | NY | 1180 | 3.60 | | 50 | 19 | 7 |
| SUNY-Buffalo | NY | | | | | | |
| North Carolina State University | NC | 1271 | | | 64 | 14 | 4 |
| Bowling Green State University | OH | 1230 | 3.56 | | 100 | 10 | 6 |
| Ohio University | OH | 1320 | 3.70 | | 40 | 8 | 4 |
| The Ohio State University | OH | 1410 | 3.70 | 3.80 | 145 | 10 | 3 |
| University of Akron | OH | 1240 | 3.20 | | 155 | 25 | 17 |
| Wright State University | OH | | | | | | |
| University of Tulsa | OK | 1190 | 3.20 | 3.20 | 46 | 10 | 5 |
| Portland State University | OR | 1075 | 3.23 | | 21 | 12 | 9 |
| Carnegie Mellon University | PA | | | | 50 | 6 | 3 |
| Penn State University | PA | 1258 | 3.65 | 3.80 | 145 | 15 | 10 |
| Caribbean Center for Advanced Studies | PR | | | | | | |
| University of Puerto Rico | PR | | | | | | |
| University of Tennessee | TN | 1250 | 3.41 | 3.51 | 137 | 13 | 6 |
| Rice University | TX | 1238 | 3.75 | | 94 | 7 | 5 |
| Texas A&M University | TX | 1317 | | 3.69 | 68 | 9 | 5 |
| Texas Tech | TX | | | | | | |
| University of Houston | TX | 1300 | | 3.50 | 124 | 12 | 6 |
| University of North Texas | TX | 1250 | | 3.80 | 1 | 1 | 1 |
| George Mason University | VA | 1201 | | 3.50 | 119 | 31 | 21 |
| Old Dominion University | VA | 1243 | 3.65 | | 65 | 8 | 4 |
| Virginia Tech | VA | 1263 | | 3.65 | 91 | 12 | 5 |

Source: Society for Industrial and Organized Psychology, Inc., 1992, *Graduate Training Programs in Industrial/Organizational Psychology and Related Fields,* Arlington Heights, IL: Society for Industrial and Organizational Psychology, Inc.

**Appendix C:** Program Ranking Based on Presentations at the Annual Graduate Conference in I/O Psychology and Organizational Behavior (1992–1994)

| University | Program Type | Year 1992 | Year 1993 | Year 1994 | Total | Rank |
|---|---|---|---|---|---|---|
| Radford University | M.A. | 7 | 11 | 7 | 25 | 1 |
| Bowling Green State University | Ph.D. | 6 | 10 | 8 | 24 | 2 |
| DePaul University | Ph.D. | 9 | 3 | 7 | 19 | 3 |
| University of Wisconsin - Oshkosh | M.A. | 6 | 4 | 0 | 10 | 4 |
| Penn State | Ph.D | 0 | 6 | 3 | 9 | 5 |
| Ohio State University | Ph.D. | 2 | 4 | 2 | 8 | 6 |
| University of Guelph | Ph.D. | 2 | 0 | 5 | 7 | 7 |
| Illinois Institute of Technology | Ph.D. | 0 | 0 | 7 | 7 | 7 |
| University of Michigan | Ph.D. | 1 | 5 | 0 | 6 | 9 |
| University of Nebraska - Omaha | Ph.D. | 1 | 1 | 3 | 5 | 10 |
| University of Illinois | Ph.D. | 0 | 3 | 2 | 5 | 10 |
| University of Hartford | Ph.D. | 0 | 5 | 0 | 5 | 10 |
| University of Tennessee | Ph.D. | 0 | 5 | 0 | 5 | 10 |
| Purdue University | Ph.D. | 0 | 0 | 4 | 4 | 14 |
| Wayne State University | Ph.D. | 2 | 2 | 0 | 4 | 14 |
| University of Waterloo | Ph.D. | 0 | 3 | 0 | 3 | 16 |
| Michigan State University | Ph.D. | 0 | 3 | 0 | 3 | 16 |
| Georgia Tech | Ph.D. | 0 | 0 | 3 | 3 | 16 |
| Tulane University | Ph.D. | 0 | 0 | 2 | 2 | 19 |
| Kent State University | Ph.D. | 0 | 0 | 2 | 2 | 19 |
| North Carolina State | Ph.D. | 0 | 1 | 1 | 2 | 19 |
| Clemson University | M.A. | 2 | 0 | 0 | 2 | 19 |
| University of Illinois - Chicago | Ph.D. | 0 | 0 | 1 | 1 | 22 |
| Brigham Young University | Ph.D. | 0 | 0 | 1 | 1 | 22 |
| Virginia Tech | Ph.D. | 1 | 0 | 0 | 1 | 22 |
| University of Missouri - St. Louis | Ph.D. | 0 | 1 | 0 | 1 | 22 |
| University of Toronto | Ph.D. | 0 | 0 | 1 | 1 | 22 |
| University of Montreal | Ph.D. | 0 | 1 | 0 | 1 | 22 |
| New York University | Ph.D. | 0 | 0 | 1 | 1 | 22 |
| Central Michigan | Ph.D. | 0 | 1 | 0 | 1 | 22 |
| St. Louis University | Ph.D. | 0 | 1 | 0 | 1 | 22 |
| University of Central Florida | M.A. | 1 | 0 | 0 | 1 | 22 |
| SUNY - Buffalo | Ph.D. | 0 | 1 | 0 | 1 | 22 |
| Auburn University | Ph.D. | 1 | 0 | 0 | 1 | 22 |
| University of Georgia | Ph.D. | 1 | 0 | 0 | 1 | 22 |
| Texas A&M | Ph.D. | 1 | 0 | 0 | 1 | 22 |
| George Washington | Ph.D. | 0 | 0 | 1 | 1 | 22 |

**Appendix D:** Program Ranking Based on Publications in the Journal of Applied Psychology (1992–1994)

| University | Year | | | Total | Rank |
|---|---|---|---|---|---|
| | 1992 | 1993 | 1994 | | |
| Michigan State University | 5.5 | 4.5 | 5.5 | 15.5 | 1 |
| University of Minnesota | 5.0 | 6.5 | 2.0 | 13.5 | 2 |
| University of Iowa | 3.0 | 3.5 | 2.5 | 9.0 | 3 |
| Penn State University | 3.0 | 1.5 | 3.0 | 7.5 | 4 |
| Cornell University | 2.0 | 2.5 | 2.5 | 7.0 | 5 |
| University of Missouri-St. Louis | 0.5 | 2.5 | 3.0 | 6.0 | 6 |
| Bowling Green State University | 2.5 | 1.0 | 2.0 | 5.5 | 7 |
| University of Illinois | 0.5 | 3.0 | 2.0 | 5.5 | 7 |
| Purdue University | 1.5 | 0.5 | 3.0 | 5.0 | 9 |
| Iowa State | 1.0 | 2.5 | 1.0 | 4.5 | 10 |
| Louisiana State University | 2.0 | 0.5 | 2.0 | 4.5 | 10 |
| New York University | 1.5 | 1.5 | 1.5 | 4.5 | 10 |
| University of Western Ontario | 1.0 | 1.5 | 2.0 | 4.5 | 10 |
| Colorado State | 2.0 | 2.0 | 0.0 | 4.0 | 14 |
| Ohio State University | 2.0 | 0.0 | 2.0 | 4.0 | 14 |
| Texas A&M | 0.0 | 2.5 | 1.5 | 4.0 | 14 |
| University of Maryland | 2.0 | 1.0 | 1.0 | 4.0 | 14 |
| Florida International | 1.0 | 2.5 | 0.0 | 3.5 | 18 |
| Carnegie Mellon | 1.0 | 0.5 | 1.5 | 3.0 | 19 |
| SUNY-Albany | 1.0 | 0.0 | 2.0 | 3.0 | 19 |
| University of Houston | 0.5 | 1.0 | 1.5 | 3.0 | 19 |
| University of Nebraska-Lincoln | 0.5 | 1.5 | 1.0 | 3.0 | 19 |
| University of Washington | 0.5 | 1.5 | 1.0 | 3.0 | 19 |
| Georgia State | 1.0 | 1.0 | 0.5 | 2.5 | 24 |
| Georgia Tech | 0.5 | 1.5 | 0.5 | 2.5 | 24 |
| Indiana University | 1.0 | 0.5 | 1.0 | 2.5 | 24 |
| Notre Dame | 2.0 | 0.5 | 0.0 | 2.5 | 24 |
| Queens College | 0.0 | 0.5 | 2.0 | 2.5 | 24 |
| SUNY-Buffalo | 1.5 | 0.5 | 0.5 | 2.5 | 24 |
| Stanford | 1.5 | 1.0 | 0.0 | 2.5 | 24 |
| Texas Christian University | 1.5 | 1.0 | 0.0 | 2.5 | 24 |
| Tulane University | 0.5 | 1.0 | 1.0 | 2.5 | 24 |
| University of Arkansas | 2.0 | 0.5 | 0.0 | 2.5 | 24 |
| University of Georgia | 0.5 | 0.5 | 1.5 | 2.5 | 24 |
| University of Southern California | 0.5 | 1.5 | 0.5 | 2.5 | 24 |
| University of Tennessee | 1.0 | 1.0 | 0.5 | 2.5 | 24 |
| Virginia Tech | 1.5 | 1.0 | 0.0 | 2.5 | 24 |

# 2

# LEGAL ISSUES
# IN EMPLOYEE SELECTION

In the human resource field, it is not a question of *will* you get sued by an applicant or former employee but *when* and *how often*? In 1993 alone, 87,942 discrimination complaints were filed with the Equal Employment Opportunity Commission (EEOC) resulting in over $161 million in awards and settlements. This is an increase over the 72,000 complaints filed in 1992 and 67,000 filed in 1991. These statistics should convince anyone entering the human resource field that knowledge of employment law is essential.

To know whether a given employment practice is legal, it is important to understand the legal process as it relates to employment law. The first step in the legal process is for some legislative body, such as the U.S. Congress or a state legislature, to pass a law. If a law is passed at the federal level, states may pass laws that *expand* the rights granted in the federal law; states may not, however, pass laws that *diminish* the rights granted in federal legislation. For example, if Congress passed a law that gave women six months of maternity leave, a state or local government could pass a law extending the leave to eight months, but they could not reduce the amount of maternity leave to less than the mandated six months. Thus, to be on firm legal ground, it is important to be aware of state and local laws as well as federal legislation.

Once a law has been passed, situations will always arise in which the intent of the law is not clear. For example, a law might be passed to protect disabled employees. Two years later, an employee is denied promotion because he has high blood pressure. The employee may file a charge against the employer claiming discrimination based on a disability. He may claim that high blood pressure is a disability but that he can still work in spite of the disability and consequently deserves the promotion. The organization, on the other hand, might claim that high blood pressure is not a disability and that even if it were, an employee with high blood pressure could not perform the job.

As shown in Figure 2.1, a charge of discrimination is usually filed with a government agency. A state agency is used if the alleged violation involves a

Lawyers and human resource professionals work closely to avoid law suits.

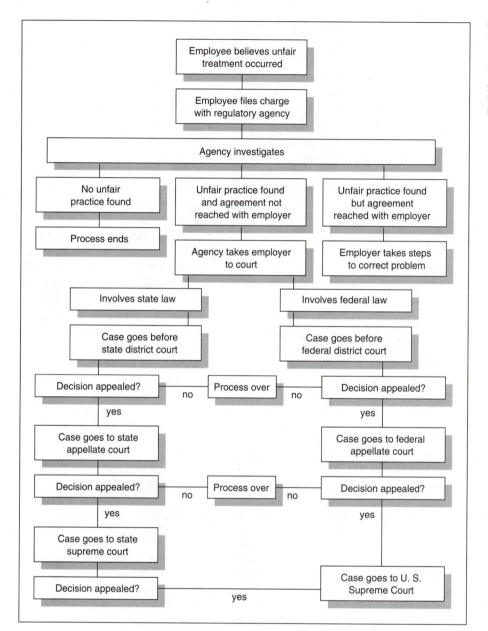

**Figure 2.1**
Legal process in employment law

Source: *Federal Register* (1988, April11) *53*(69), p. 11970.

Employee believes unfair treatment occurred

Employee files charge with regulatory agency

Agency investigates

No unfair practice found

Process ends

Unfair practice found and agreement not reached with employer

Unfair practice found but agreement reached with employer

Agency takes employer to court

Employer takes steps to correct problem

Involves state law

Involves federal law

Case goes before state district court

Case goes before federal district court

Decision appealed?

Process over

Decision appealed?

no          no

yes          yes

Case goes to state appellate court

Case goes to federal appellate court

Decision appealed?

Process over

Decision appealed?

no          no

yes          yes

Case goes to state supreme court

Decision appealed?

Case goes to U. S. Supreme Court

yes

state law and a federal agency; usually the EEOC handles alleged violations of federal law. The complaint must be filed within 180 days of the discriminatory act. The governmental agency will notify the employer within 10 days about the complaint, obtain further information from both parties if necessary, and then review the charge to determine whether it has merit; if it does, the agency will try to work out a settlement between the claimant and employer without taking the case to court.

These settlements might include an employer offering a job or promotion to the person filing the complaint, the payment of back wages, or the payment of compensatory or punitive damages. These settlements can range in size from a few dollars to over $100 million. One of the largest recent settlements was the $105 million that Shoney's agreed to pay in 1993, mostly to approximately 10,000 Blacks who either worked for or were denied employment with Shoney's over a seven-year period. The size of the settlement was based not only on the high number of victims, but also on the severity of the discrimination. For example, the number of Black employees in each restaurant was limited to the percentage of Black customers. When Blacks were hired, they were placed in "low-paying, low-visibility kitchen jobs" (Smothers, 1993). In addition to the $105 million, Shoney's agreed to institute an affirmative-action program over the next 10 years.

If a settlement cannot be reached, however, the case will go to either a state or a federal district court with the EEOC representing (physically and financially) the person filing the complaint. When the court makes a decision, the decision becomes **case law.** Case law is a judicial interpretation of a law and is important because it establishes a precedent for future cases. If one side does not like the decision rendered in a lower court, it may appeal to higher courts, perhaps eventually going to a state's supreme court or even to the U.S. Supreme Court. Obviously, a ruling by the U.S. Supreme Court carries more weight than rulings of district courts or state supreme courts.

If, after reviewing a complaint, the governmental agency does not find merit, one of two things can happen based on whether the person filing the complaint accepts the decision. If the person filing the complaint accepts the decision, the process ends. If the person filing the complaint does not accept the decision, he is issued a *right to sue* letter, which entitles him to hire a private attorney and file the case himself.

## DETERMINING WHETHER AN EMPLOYMENT DECISION IS LEGAL

At first glance, the legal aspects of making employment decisions seem complicated. After all, many laws and court cases apply to employment decisions. The basic legal aspects, however, are not that complicated and use of the flow chart in Figure 2.2 will help make that process easier to understand. Following is a discussion of each stage shown in Figure 2.2.

### DOES THE EMPLOYMENT PRACTICE DIRECTLY REFER TO A MEMBER OF A FEDERALLY PROTECTED CLASS?

The first step in determining the legality of an employment practice is to decide whether the employment practice directly refers to a member of a protected class. A **protected class** is any group of people for which protective legislation has been passed. A federally protected class is any group of indi-

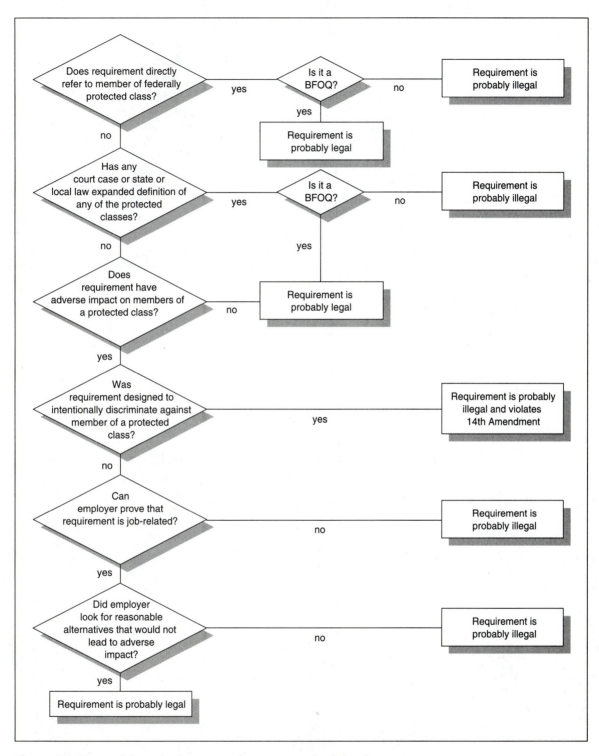

**Figure 2.2** Determining whether an employment practice is legal

**Table 2.1**  Federally protected classes

| Protected Class | Federal Law |
| --- | --- |
| Age (over 40) | Age Discrimination in Employment Act |
| Disability | Americans with Disabilities Act<br>Vocational Rehabilitation Act of 1973 |
| National origin | Civil Rights Acts of 1964, 1991 |
| Pregnancy | Pregnancy Discrimination Act of 1978 |
| Race | Fourteenth Amendment (intentional)<br>Civil Rights Acts of 1964, 1991 (unintentional) |
| Religion | Civil Rights Acts of 1964, 1991 |
| Gender | Civil Rights Acts of 1964, 1991<br>Equal Pay Act of 1963 |
| Vietnam veterans | Vietnam-Era Veterans Readjustment Act of 1974 |

viduals specifically protected by *federal* law. A list of federally protected classes is shown in Table 2.1.

### Race

Based on the Civil Rights Acts of 1866, 1964, and 1991, as well as the Fourteenth Amendment to the U.S. Constitution, it is illegal to discriminate against a person based on race. According to Congress, but not many anthropologists (Rushton, 1995), the four races are African American (Black), European American (White), Asian American, and Native American Indian.

The *equal protection* clause of the **Fourteenth Amendment** mandates that no state may deny a person equal protection under the law. Basically, this implies that a government may not *intentionally* discriminate or allow intentional discrimination to take place. Because any suit filed under the Fourteenth Amendment must demonstrate intent, it is not often used.

The Civil Rights Acts of 1964 (known as Title VII) and 1991 extended the scope of the Fourteenth Amendment. Title VII makes it illegal for employers with more than 15 employees, labor unions, employment agencies, state and local governmental agencies, and educational institutions to

1. Fail, refuse to hire, discharge any individual, or otherwise discriminate against any individual with respect to his compensation, terms, conditions, or privileges of employment because of the individual's race, color, religion, sex, or national origin; or

2. Limit, segregate, or classify employees or applicants for employment in any way that would deprive, or tend to deprive, any individual of employment opportunities or otherwise adversely affect his stature as an employee because of an individual's race, color, religion, sex, or national origin.

Unlike the Fourteenth Amendment, for an employment practice to be potentially illegal under Title VII, the discrimination does not have to be intentional (Arvey, 1979). Instead, proof of discrimination is determined through statistical analysis of selection rates and by the presence or absence of adverse impact, which will be discussed in detail later in this chapter.

In addition to employment decisions such as selection and promotion, Title VII also has been interpreted by the courts to cover the "atmosphere" of the organization, which includes such behavior as sexual harassment (*Broderick* v. *Ruder*, 1988; *Brundy* v. *Jackson*, 1971), age harassment (*Louis* v. *Federal Prison Industries*, 1986), and race harassment (*Hunter* v. *Allis-Chalmers*, 1986).

## Color

Also protected by the Civil Rights Acts of 1964 and 1991 is color. Though commonly used as a synonym for race, the reference to color protects individuals within one race against discrimination based on variations in skin color. For example, in the 1989 case of *Walker* v. *Secretary of the Treasury*, a district court found that a darker skinned Black supervisor at the IRS illegally fired a lighter skinned Black employee.

## Gender

The Civil Rights Acts of 1964 and 1991 as well as the Equal Pay Act (1963) prohibit discrimination based on gender. The courts have ruled that intentional discrimination against either females or males is illegal (*Diaz* v. *Pan American Airways*, 1991) but discrimination against transsexuals is not (*Sommers* v. *Budget Marketing*, 1991).

## National Origin

National origin is protected under the Civil Rights Acts of 1964 and 1991. Note that Hispanics are protected under national origin, not race. Claims of discrimination based on national origin have increased greatly over the past few years due primarily to high unemployment and "unprecedented" immigration (Barton, 1993). One of the most common complaints is "English only" or "understandable English" speaking requirements. The courts have generally ruled that language requirements are legal if they are job related (Quinn & Petrick, 1993) and limited to communication during "company time" rather than on breaks.

## Religion

Also protected under the Civil Rights Acts of 1964 and 1991 is religion. It is illegal to use an individual's religion in an employment decision unless the nature of the job is religious. For example, the Catholic church can require its priests to be Catholic but not its clerical staff. Courts have extended this reasoning to allow wearing of religious garments to work, to forbid an employer from requiring its employees to say "Merry Christmas" to customers, and to require a trucking company to allow some employees Sunday off from work.

### Age

The **Age Discrimination in Employment Act (ADEA)** and its later amendments forbid an employer or union from discriminating against an individual over the age of 40. In part, this act was designed to protect older workers from employment practices aimed at reducing costs by firing older workers with higher salaries and replacing them with lower-paid younger workers. To file suit under this act, an individual must demonstrate that he is in the specified age bracket and has been intentionally or unintentionally discriminated against due to his age (Faley, Kleiman, & Lengnick-Hall, 1984). Though mandatory retirement ages are allowed in certain circumstances (for example, in colleges), they are usually illegal because, as research indicates, in general, work performance does not decline with age.

### Disability

Discrimination against people with disabilities by the federal government is forbidden by the **Vocational Rehabilitation Act** (1973), and discrimination against people with disabilities by any other employer with 15 or more employees is forbidden by the **Americans with Disabilities Act (ADA)** (1990).

The Americans with Disabilities Act, signed into law by former President Bush in 1990, is the most important piece of employment legislation since the 1964 Civil Rights Act. The ADA requires organizations with 15 or more employees to make "reasonable accommodation" for people with physical and mental disabilities unless to do so "would impose an undue hardship." Though Congress did not provide a list of disabilities, it did define disability as:

1. A physical or mental impairment that substantially limits one or more of the major life activities of an individual,
2. A record of such impairment, or
3. Being regarded as having such an impairment.

For the first part of the definition, major life activities include such things as walking, hearing, and speaking. Examples of conditions considered disabilities by case law or the Department of Labor are blindness, paralysis, asthma, muscular dystrophy, and various learning disabilities such as dyslexia. Conditions not considered disabilities include fear of heights and sprained ankles.

The second part of the definition was designed to protect people who were once disabled but no longer are. Examples include recovering alcoholics, cancer patients in remission, people who spent time in a mental health facility, and drug addicts who have successfully completed treatment.

The final part of the definition protects individuals who don't have a disability but are treated as if they do. Examples of people protected under this clause are those with facial scarring or severe burns.

The ADA does not require an organization to hire or give preference to the disabled; only that the disabled be given an equal chance and that reasonable attempts be made to accommodate their disability. Although there are no guidelines regarding what is "reasonable," accommodations can include providing readers or interpreters, modifying work schedules, modifying equipment, and making facilities more accessible. Most accommodations cost less than $50.

If a disability keeps a person from performing the "essential functions" of a job, the person does not have to be hired or retained. For example, in *Caston v. Trigon Engineering* (1993), a district court ruled that a woman with 44 personalities was unable to perform her job as an environmental engineer. In another case (*DiPompo v. West Point*, 1991), a district court ruled that a dyslexic applicant, though considered disabled, was not able to perform essential job functions such as inspecting vehicles and buildings for the presence of dangerous materials and recording information such as work schedules and emergency calls.

### Pregnancy

The **Pregnancy Discrimination Act** states that "women affected by pregnancy, childbirth, or related medical conditions shall be treated the same for all employment-related purposes, including receipt of benefit programs, as other persons not so affected but similar in their ability or inability to work." Simply put, this act requires pregnancy to be treated as any other disability. For example, in *Adams v. North Little Rock Police Department* (1992), the U.S. Court of Appeals ruled that a police department discriminated against a pregnant police officer when the department denied her "light duty" yet granted light duty to male officers with temporary disabilities such as strained backs.

In the case of *California Federal Savings and Loan Association v. Guerra* (1987), the U.S. Supreme Court expanded the scope of the law. Pregnant women may receive better treatment than other persons with disabilities but cannot receive worse treatment.

### Vietnam Veteran Status

Due to the large scale of discrimination in the 1960s and 1970s against soldiers returning from duty in Vietnam, in 1974 Congress passed the **Vietnam-Era Veterans Readjustment Act.** This act mandates any contractor or subcontractor with more than $10,000 in federal government contracts to take affirmative action to employ and promote Vietnam-era veterans. This law is one reason that veterans applying for civil service jobs receive credit for their military service as well as for their qualifications.

### BFOQs: An Exception to Intentional Discrimination

Employment decisions based on membership in a protected class (for example, "We will not hire females because they are not strong enough to do the

*Victor O. Cardwell,
Attorney
Labor and Employment
Law
Woods, Rogers &
Hazlegrove, P.L.C.*

I am 1 of 8 attorneys and 1 paralegal specializing in labor and employment law in a law firm of 70 attorneys in Southwestern Virginia. Due to the nature of labor and employment law, my practice encompasses a wide range of legal issues that are addressed in a variety of ways to best serve the needs of my clients. One day I may be advising a client on steps to help them remain "union-free," and the next day I may find myself training supervisors in avoiding sexual harassment lawsuits.

The majority of our clients consist of medium-size to large businesses, and, therefore, I typically work on the management side of legal issues. In this context I, as a labor- and employment-law attorney, am able to work directly with representatives from human resource departments to offer advice in a number of areas, which may include: establishing company policy, determining appropriate employee discipline, and developing employee training. I really enjoy this involvement in my clients' day-to-day operations.

As a labor- and employment-law attorney, I perform many of the tasks that people usually think of when they think of lawyers. For example, upon receipt of a new case file involving a sexual harassment lawsuit, I first interview the company's human resource director to get an overall idea of what has happened to instigate the suit. Next, I conduct witness interviews in an effort to comprehend all of the facts of the situation. It is imperative that I understand all of the facts involved in the case. I follow this same procedure in most Title VII or discrimination cases.

After I thoroughly understand what has taken place, it then becomes my job to present the circumstances of the case in the best possible light for my client. Taking facts that on face value may appear detrimental to my client and presenting them to a judge in the best possible light sometimes can be extremely difficult. Admittedly, there are times when clients are at fault and have to be advised to settle claims. Settlement requires negotiation on the part of the clients and attorneys involved. Fortunately, these situations are uncommon, especially when I have been working with the company's human resource director on an ongoing basis to minimize these types of issues.

When handling cases dealing with overtime and exempt-status regulations that are brought under the Fair Labor Standards Act, I must first investigate why an employer made the decision he or she did. Again, this requires interviewing witnesses. Once I have a firm understanding of the facts, I then explain to the Department of Labor why the employer's decision complied with the law. In some instances, employers do not realize they have violated a law such as the Fair Labor Standards Act, and, at this point, I must explain the client's mistake to the Department of Labor investigator. I work with other governmental agencies, such as the National Labor Relations Board, which deals with issues affecting unionized employees, in much the same manner.

Another aspect of my profession that I particularly enjoy is training my clients' employees. Being in front of a group requires good communication skills and the ability to understand the audience in order to give the trainees what they need. My particular training style works best when I have a lot of feedback and audience participation. The clients request training in all areas of employment, such as performance evaluations. Once again, I assess with my client exactly what he or she is seeking from the training. Next, I meticulously research a myriad of labor and employment laws that could conceivably apply to the training. Finally, I develop written materials so that the trainees, who may include front-line supervisors, will job") are illegal unless the employer can demonstrate that the requirement is a **bona fide occupational qualification (BFOQ).**

If a job can only be performed by a person in a particular class, the requirement is considered a BFOQ. Actually some jobs can only be performed by a person of a particular gender; for instance, only a female could be a wet nurse and only a male could be a sperm donor. However, very few jobs in our society can only be performed by a particular race, gender, or national origin. Take, for example, a job that involves lifting 150-pound crates. Although it is true that, on average, males are stronger than females, a company could not set a male-only requirement. The real BFOQ in this example is strength, not gender. Thus, restricting employment to males would be illegal.

Prison guards provide an interesting example of how strictly the courts interpret BFOQ cases (Surrette, 1993; 1995). Out of a concern for privacy, it is common for prisons and jails to have males guard male inmates and females guard female inmates. The courts, however, have ruled this practice illegal (*Canedy* v. *Bordman,* 1992) because the essential function of the job is to guard prisoners, and either sex can perform this duty regardless of the inmate's gender.

The courts have clearly stated that a BFOQ must involve the ability to perform the job, not satisfy a customer's or client's preferences. For example, in *Diaz* v. *Pan American Airways* (1991), the court ruled that even though airline passengers prefer female flight attendants, the nature of the business is to transport passengers safely, and males can perform the essential job functions as well as females. In another interesting case, in 1989 Caesar's Casino in Atlantic City was fined $250,000 for removing Black and female card dealers from a table to appease a high-stakes gambler who preferred white male dealers.

## HAS ANY COURT CASE, STATE LAW, OR LOCAL LAW EXPANDED THE DEFINITION OF ANY OF THE PROTECTED CLASSES?

An employment decision may not violate a federal law, but it may violate one of the many state and local laws that have been passed to protect additional groups of people. For example, at the state level, Maryland outlaws discrimination against obese people, Wisconsin prohibits discrimination based on sexual orientation, and Virginia forbids discrimination based on marital status. At the local level, Santa Cruz, California, has outlawed discrimination based on height and physical appearance, and Cincinnati, Ohio, prohibits discrimination against people of Appalachian heritage.

In addition to state and local laws, the definitions of protected classes can be expanded or narrowed by court decisions. For example, in a variety of cases, the courts have ruled that the definition of disability should be expanded to include obesity but not former drug use and that transsexuals are not protected as a gender.

## DOES THE REQUIREMENT HAVE ADVERSE IMPACT AGAINST A MEMBER OF A PROTECTED CLASS?

If the employment practice does not refer directly to a member of a protected class, the next step is to determine whether the requirement adversely affects members of a protected class. **Adverse impact** means a particular employment decision results in negative consequences more often for members of one protected group than for members of the non-protected group. For example, an employee-selection requirement of a college degree would lead to a lower percentage of Black applicants being hired when compared to White applicants. Thus, even though such a requirement does not mention Blacks (a protected class), it does adversely impact them because 22% of Whites have bachelor's degrees compared to 11% of Blacks.

Adverse impact is legally determined through the "four-fifths rule." That is, the percentage of Blacks hired must be at least 80% of the percentage of Whites who are hired. It is important to keep in mind that adverse impact refers to *percentages* rather than raw numbers. For example, as shown in Table 2.2, if we hire 25 of 50 white applicants, the hiring percentage would be 50%. If we had 10 black applicants, at least 4 would need to be hired to avoid adverse impact. Why 4? Because the hiring percentage for Blacks must be at least 80% of the White hiring percentage. Because our White hiring percentage was 50%, our hiring percentage for Blacks must be at least four-fifths (80%) of 50%. Thus, $.50 \times .80 = .40$, indicating that we would need

**Table 2.2**  Adverse impact example

| | Race | |
| --- | :---: | :---: |
| | *White* | *Black* |
| Applicants | 50 | 10 |
| Hires | 25 | 4 |
| Selection ratio | .50 | .40 |

to hire at least 40% of all Black applicants to avoid adverse impact and a potential charge of unfair discrimination. With 10 applicants, this results in hiring at least 4 of the 10 applicants.

Though it is illegal to intentionally discriminate against White males, employment practices that result in adverse impact against White males are not illegal. For example, it was mentioned previously that requiring a college degree adversely impacts Blacks because 22% of Whites have bachelor's degrees compared to 11% of Blacks. Though 33% of Asian Americans have college degrees, a White applicant could not file a discrimination charge based on adverse impact.

## WAS THE REQUIREMENT DESIGNED TO INTENTIONALLY DISCRIMINATE AGAINST A PROTECTED CLASS?

If an employment practice does not refer directly to a member of a protected class but adversely affects a protected class, the courts will look closely at whether the practice was initiated to intentionally reduce the pool of qualified minority applicants. For example, suppose that a city requires all of its employees to live within the city limits. The city believes this is a justifiable requirement because salaries are paid by tax dollars, the city employees should contribute to that tax base. Though such a requirement is not illegal, the court might look deeper to see if the tax base was in fact the reason for the residency requirement. That is, if the city population was 99% White and the population of the area surrounding the city was 90% Black, the court might argue that the residency requirement was a subtle way of discriminating against Blacks.

Though such subtle requirements are probably no longer common in the employment sector, they have been used throughout history. For example, prior to the 1970s, some states required voters to pass a "literacy test" to be eligible to vote. Though the stated purpose of the test was to ensure that voters would make intelligent and educated decisions, the real purpose was to reduce the number of minority voters.

The scoring method for tennis provides another example. Why is tennis scored 15, 30, 40, and then deuce? Why not 1, 2, 3, and 4? Rather than banning poor people from public tennis courts, the complicated scoring system confused less-educated people — often poor and black — and thus discouraged them from learning tennis, which stopped them from taking the limited number of available public tennis courts.

## CAN THE EMPLOYER PROVE THAT THE REQUIREMENT IS JOB RELATED?

As shown in the flowchart in Figure 2.2, if our employment practice does not result in adverse impact, it is probably legal. If adverse impact does result, then the burden of proof shifts to the employer to demonstrate that the employment practice is either **job related** or exempt from adverse impact. Before discussing these two strategies, two points need to be made. First, adverse impact is a fact of life in personnel selection. Almost any test is going to have adverse impact against some protected class, though some tests may have less adverse impact than others (Bradburn & Villar, 1992).

Second, the burden of proof in employment law is different than in criminal law. In criminal law, a defendant is innocent until proven guilty. In employment law, both the Civil Rights Act of 1991 and the court's ruling in *Griggs* v. *Duke Power* (1972) shift the burden of proof: once adverse impact is established, an employer (the defendant) is considered guilty unless it can prove its innocence by establishing the job relatedness of the test. That employers are treated more harshly than criminals by Congress and the courts is a constant source of frustration among human resource professionals.

### Valid Testing Procedures

An employment practice resulting in adverse impact may still be legal as long as the test is professionally developed, job related (valid), and reasonable attempts have been made to find other tests that might be just as valid but have less adverse impact. For example, if an employer uses an intelligence test to select employees, there is a strong possibility that adverse impact will occur. If the employer can demonstrate, however, that the intelligence test predicts performance on the job and that no other available test will equally predict performance, the use of the test is probably justified. A more in-depth discussion of validity strategies is found in Chapter 4.

### Exceptions

**Bona Fide Seniority System** An organization that has had a long-standing policy of promoting employees with the greatest seniority or laying off employees with the least seniority can continue to do so even though adverse impact occurs. But if discrimination occurred earlier in the organization and was the reason that members of a protected class were lower on the seniority list, a court probably will discredit the seniority system, declaring that it is not bona fide (Twomey, 1986).

**National Security** In certain circumstances, it is legal for an employer to discriminate against a member of a particular national origin or other protected class when it is in the best interest of the nation's security to do so. For example, for years Russian citizens living in the United States were prohibited from working for any defense-related industry.

**Veteran's Preference Rights** Most civil-service jobs provide extra points on tests for veterans of the armed forces. Because most people in the military are male, awarding these extra points for military service results in adverse impact against females. However, according to the Civil Rights Act of 1964, such practices are exempt from legal action.

## DID EMPLOYER LOOK FOR REASONABLE ALTERNATIVES THAT WOULD NOT LEAD TO ADVERSE IMPACT?

As shown in Figure 2.2, if an employer proves a test is job related, the final factor looked at by the courts is the extent to which the employer looked for other valid selection tests that would have less adverse impact. For example, if an organization wanted to use a particular cognitive-ability test, did it explore such alternatives as education level or other cognitive-ability tests that would be just as valid but have less adverse impact?

# AFFIRMATIVE ACTION

**Affirmative action** is one of the most misunderstood legal concepts concerning employment. Though most people associate affirmative action with hiring goals or quotas, affirmative action can actually involve several strategies (Robinson, Allen, & Abraham, 1992).

## AFFIRMATIVE-ACTION STRATEGIES

### Intentional Recruitment of Minority Applicants

A common affirmative-action strategy is to target underrepresented groups for more extensive recruitment. Such efforts might include advertising in magazines and newspapers with a minority readership, recruiting at predominantly minority or female universities, visiting minority communities, or paying current employees a bonus for recruiting a member of a protected class.

A related technique is to set up training programs designed to teach minorities the skills needed to obtain employment with the organization. For example, Hogan and Quigley (1994) found that providing a six-week exercise program would result in fewer female applicants failing physical agility tests for positions such as firefighter.

### Identification and Removal
### of Employment Practices Working against
### Minority Applicants and Employees

A second affirmative-action strategy involves identifying and removing practices that might discourage minority applicants from applying to an organization or minority employees from being promoted within an organization. Such practices might involve company policy, supervisor attitudes, or the way in which an organization is decorated. For example, a Black employee in a southern city filed a lawsuit alleging race as the reason he wasn't promoted. As evidence, he cited the embroidered Confederate flag hanging in his supervisor's office. The city's affirmative-action officer suggested the flag be removed because, even though the supervisor was a Civil War enthusiast rather than a racist, a Confederate flag in a supervisor's office might give the perception of institutional acceptance of racism.

As another example, it is a common practice for police applicants to receive information and obtain employment applications directly from the police department. However, many minorities are uncomfortable going to a police station and asking White police officers for information and application materials. As a result, an easy affirmative-action strategy would be to have employment applications available only at the city's personnel office.

When I presented this example to a meeting of police chiefs, the overwhelming response was "How can someone be a cop if they don't feel comfortable going to a police station?" I responded that it is uncomfortable for anyone to go into any new environment, much less one with the stigma associated with a police station. I then told the group a story of how scared I was when, back in high school, I had to go to a police station to register a car rally that our school group was having. I still recall the icy stare and gruff voice of the desk sergeant, which quickly turned my legs to jelly. When a few others in the crowd joined in with similar stories, it drove home the point that many seemingly trivial things deter others from applying for jobs.

### Preferential Hiring and Promotion of Minorities

This is certainly the most controversial and misunderstood of the affirmative-action strategies. Under this strategy, minority applicants will be given preference over an equally qualified nonminority applicant. It is important to note that in no way does affirmative action require an employer to hire an unqualified minority over a qualified White male. Instead, affirmative action requires employers to monitor their employment records to determine whether minority groups are underrepresented. If they are, affirmative action requires that an organization do the best it can to remedy the situation. One such remedy might be preferential hiring and promotion.

### REASONS FOR AFFIRMATIVE-ACTION PLANS

Organizations have affirmative-action plans for one of four reasons, two of which are involuntary and two voluntary (Robinson et al., 1992).

## Involuntary: Government Regulation

Most affirmative-action requirements are the result of Presidential Executive Order 11246. This order, as well as sections of several laws, requires federal contractors and subcontractors with more than 100 employees and federal contracts in excess of $100,000 to have formal affirmative-action plans. Most state and local governments also have such requirements, though the number of employees and dollar amounts of contracts will differ. These required affirmative-action plans typically involve analyses of all major job categories that indicate which categories have underrepresentations of the protected classes as well as goals and plans for overcoming such underrepresentations.

## Involuntary: Court Order

When a court finds a public agency such as a police or fire department guilty of not hiring or promoting enough members of a protected class, it can order the agency to begin an affirmative-action program. As previously discussed, this program might involve increased recruitment efforts or may entail specific hiring or promotion goals.

## Voluntary: Consent Decree

If a discrimination complaint has been filed with a court, a public agency can "voluntarily" agree to an affirmative-action plan rather than have a plan forced upon it by the court. With a consent decree, the agency agrees that it has not hired or promoted enough members of a protected class and is willing to make changes. The specific nature of these changes is agreed upon by the group filing the complaint and the agency that is the subject of the complaint. This agreement is then approved and monitored by the court.

## Voluntary: Desire to Be a Good Citizen

Rather than wait for a discrimination complaint, some organizations develop affirmative-action programs out of a desire to be good citizens. That is, they want to voluntarily ensure that their employment practices are fair to all groups of people.

## LEGALITY OF AFFIRMATIVE-ACTION PLANS

As shown in Figure 2.3, the courts will use five criteria to determine the legality of an affirmative-action plan involving preferential hiring. It is always legal to actively recruit minorities and remove barriers.

## History of Discrimination

The first criterion examined is whether there has been a history of discrimination by a particular organization. If no discrimination has previously occurred, then an affirmative-action plan is neither necessary nor legal.

**Figure 2.3**
Determining the legality of an affirmative action plan

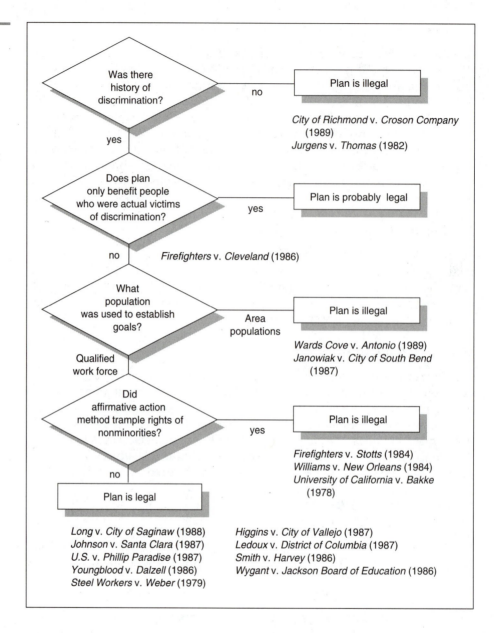

*Was there history of discrimination?* — no → Plan is illegal

*City of Richmond* v. *Croson Company* (1989)
*Jurgens* v. *Thomas* (1982)

yes

*Does plan only benefit people who were actual victims of discrimination?* — yes → Plan is probably legal

no — *Firefighters* v. *Cleveland* (1986)

*What population was used to establish goals?* — Area populations → Plan is illegal

*Wards Cove* v. *Antonio* (1989)
*Janowiak* v. *City of South Bend* (1987)

Qualified work force

*Did affirmative action method trample rights of nonminorities?* — yes → Plan is illegal

*Firefighters* v. *Stotts* (1984)
*Williams* v. *New Orleans* (1984)
*University of California* v. *Bakke* (1978)

no

Plan is legal

*Long* v. *City of Saginaw* (1988)        *Higgins* v. *City of Vallejo* (1987)
*Johnson* v. *Santa Clara* (1987)        *Ledoux* v. *District of Columbia* (1987)
*U.S.* v. *Phillip Paradise* (1987)        *Smith* v. *Harvey* (1986)
*Youngblood* v. *Dalzell* (1986)        *Wygant* v. *Jackson Board of Education* (1986)
*Steel Workers* v. *Weber* (1979)

### *Beneficiaries of the Plan*

The second criterion concerns the extent to which the plan benefits people who were not actual victims of discrimination. If the plan only benefits actual victims, it will probably be considered legal, but if it benefits people not directly discriminated against by the organization, other criteria will be considered.

For example, imagine an organization consisting of 100 male but no female managers. Twenty female assistant managers, after being denied promotions for several years, file suit charging discrimination. The organization agrees to hire 10 of the females to fill the next 10 openings. Because the beneficiaries of this plan were themselves the actual victims of the organization's previous discrimination, the plan would be legal. If the plan, however, involved promoting females who had not previously applied for the management positions, the courts, before determining the legality of the plan, would consider three factors: the population used to set the goals, the impact on nonminorities, and the ending point for the plan.

### Population Used to Set Goals

The third criterion concerns which of two types of populations was used to statistically determine discrimination and to set affirmative-action goals. With area populations, an organization compares the number of minorities in the general area with the number of minorities in each position in the organization. If a discrepancy occurs, the organization sets hiring goals to remedy the discrepancy. For example, if 80% of the area surrounding an organization is Hispanic but only 20% of the salaried workers in the organization are Hispanic, the organization might set hiring goals for Hispanics at 90% until the work force becomes 80% Hispanic.

Although the use of area population figures has been traditional, recent U.S. Supreme Court decisions have declared them inappropriate. Instead, the population that must be used in goal setting is that of the **qualified work force** in the area rather than the area population.

For example, several southern states are under court supervision to increase the number of minority faculty in their public universities. Rather than a goal consistent with the percentage of Blacks in the United States (roughly 12%), the goal of 2% is based on the qualified work force: Blacks with Ph.D.s. This example is important because it illustrates that the courts are not unreasonable when it comes to setting affirmative-action goals. They realize that a university cannot hire minorities in numbers equal to the national population because a lower percentage of minorities than nonminorities have doctorates.

Another example is the case of *City of Richmond* v. *Croson* (1989). Because 50% of the Richmond population is minority, the city required that contractors receiving city funds subcontract at least 30% of their work to minority-owned businesses. The J. A. Croson company received a contract with the city but was unable to subcontract the required 30% because there were not enough minority-owned businesses in the city. The U.S. Supreme Court found Richmond's plan illegal because the goal of 30% was based on the area population rather than the percentage of relevant qualified minority-owned businesses (less than 5%).

### Impact on Nonminorities

The fourth criterion used by courts to determine the legality of an affirmative-action program is whether the remedy designed to help minorities "unnecessarily tramples" the rights of nonminorities. That is, a plan that helps females cannot deny the rights of males. Preference can be given to a qualified minority over a qualified nonminority, but an unqualified minority can never be hired over a qualified nonminority.

Affirmative action becomes controversial when an organization realizes it has discriminated against a particular protected group. For example, police and fire departments have long been staffed by White males. In some cases, this composition has been accidental, in others it has been intentional. To remedy such situations, police and fire departments often set goals for minority hiring. These goals are objectives and are not to be confused with quotas, which *require* a certain percentage of minorities to be hired.

To help with affirmative-action hiring, an organization usually keeps separate lists of qualified Whites and qualified minorities. If the goal is to hire females for half of its work force, then the top male is hired from the male list and the top female is hired from the female list. This process continues until all openings have been filled. Although this process often results in minorities with lower test scores being hired over White males with higher test scores, the important point is that everyone who is hired has been determined to be qualified based on their test scores.

Should only a small number of minority applicants test highly enough to be considered qualified, the organization is under no obligation to hire unqualified applicants. In fact, if an organization hires unqualified minorities over qualified minorities, or if it sets unreasonable goals, it can be found guilty of reverse discrimination (Levin-Epstein, 1987). For example, in *Bishop* v. *District of Columbia* (1986), the U.S. Court of Appeals ruled that reverse discrimination occurred when a Black battalion chief was promoted ahead of five higher-ranking White deputy chiefs. The court ruled the promotion to be illegal because it was the result of political pressure rather than qualifications and previous job performance. A similar decision was reached in *Black Firefighters Association* v. *City of Dallas* (1994) when the U.S. Court of Appeals ruled that "skip promotions" were not legal.

In *Higgins* v. *City of Vallejo* (1987), however, the U.S. Court of Appeals ruled that promotion of a minority applicant with the third highest score over a nonminority applicant with the highest score was legal. The court's decision was based on the idea that even though the two applicants had different scores, they were close enough to be considered "equally qualified." When two candidates are equally qualified, affirmative-action needs can be taken into consideration to decide which of the candidates will be chosen. As one can imagine, the question of how close different qualifications need to be before two candidates are no longer considered equal is difficult to answer. In Chapter 4, methods to answer this question, such as banding and passing scores, will be discussed.

### Ending Point for the Plan

The fifth and final criterion concerns the presence of an ending point for the plan. That is, an affirmative-action plan cannot continue indefinitely: it must end when certain goals have been obtained. For example, in *Detroit Police Officers Association* v. *Coleman Young* (1993), the U.S. Court of Appeals ruled that an affirmative-action plan that had been utilized for 19 years had reached its intended goal: 50% of the Detroit police department was minority. Continuing the plan would be illegal, reasoned the court, because the plan would result in a substantial hardship on nonminority applicants.

## CONSEQUENCES OF AFFIRMATIVE-ACTION PLANS

Though affirmative-action programs are an important tool in ensuring equal opportunity, they can result in some negative consequences for people hired or promoted as the result of affirmative action. Research indicates that employees hired due to affirmative-action programs are perceived by co-workers as less competent (Heilman, Block, & Lucas, 1992), have a tendency to devalue their own performance (Heilman, Lucas, & Kaplow, 1990), and behave negatively toward others who are hired based on affirmative-action programs (Heilman, Kaplow, Amato, & Stathatos, 1993). These effects can be reduced when applicants are given positive information about their abilities (Heilman et al., 1993). Not surprisingly, women and ethnic minorities hold more positive views toward affirmative action than do males and nonminorities (Kravitz & Platania, 1993).

The previously mentioned studies suggest that affirmative-action programs can have negative consequences for their recipients. Affirmative-action programs may also have negative consequences for an organization. Silva and Jacobs (1993) found that hiring minorities above their level of representation in the applicant pool (affirmative action) resulted in decreased organizational performance. With these studies in mind, it is essential that an organization weigh the many benefits of affirmative-action programs against the programs' unintended side effects.

# PRIVACY ISSUES

As discussed previously in the chapter, an employment practice is illegal if it results in adverse impact and is not job related. An employment practice can also be illegal if it unnecessarily violates an individual's right to privacy.

The **Fourth Amendment** to the U.S. Constitution protects citizens against unreasonable search or seizure. Its importance to I/O psychology is in the areas of drug testing, locker searches, and psychological testing. Several courts have ruled that drug testing must be considered a "search," and, therefore, to be legal, drug testing programs must be reasonable and show cause. It is important to understand that the Fourth Amendment is limited to public agencies such as state and local governments. Private industry is not restricted from drug testing by the Fourth Amendment unless government regulations require drug testing (for example, with trucking companies and railroads), but drug testing and searches by a private organization must be conducted in "good faith and with fair dealing."

Generally, employers are free, even encouraged by the government, to test job applicants for current drug use. Drug testing, however, can be illegal when current employees, rather than applicants, are the ones being tested.

## DRUG TESTING

Drug testing conducted by a public agency must be based on "reasonable suspicion" and with "just cause." Based on prior cases, reasonable suspicion means that there is reason to suspect that employees are using drugs at work. Such suspicion can be produced from a variety of sources including "tips" that employees are using drugs (*Copeland* v. *Philadelphia Police Department,* 1989; *Feliciano* v. *Cleveland,* 1987), accidents or discipline problems (*Allen* v. *City of Marietta,* 1985; *Burnley* v. *Railway,* 1988), or actual observation of drug usage (*Everett* v. *Napper,* 1987). For jobs involving the safety of the public, random testing rather than testing based on reasonable suspicion will probably be legal (Asquith & Feld, 1993).

Traditionally, the courts view as just cause the degree to which an employee's behavior affects the safety and trust of the public. For example, an air traffic controller has been deemed to be responsible for the safety of the public (*Government Employees* v. *Dole,* 1987), but a school bus attendant has not (*Jones* v. *McKenzie,* 1987).

Other factors taken into consideration by the courts include the accuracy of the drug tests and the care and privacy taken during the testing (*Triblo* v. *Quality Clinical Laboratories,* 1982; *Hester* v. *City of Milledgeville,* 1986). The issue of privacy is an especially interesting one because employees who use drugs often try to "cheat" on their drug tests. Attempts at cheating include bringing in "clean" urine that has been taken or purchased from a friend or diluting the urine sample with soap, toilet water, or other chemicals. To stop such attempts, some organizations have required employees to strip so that the employee cannot bring anything into the test area; they also may require that the employee be observed while he provides the urine specimen. Testing conditions such as these would be allowed only under the most serious situations involving national security. The federal guidelines for collecting urine specimens are shown in Box 2.1.

Two other important issues are the appeal process (*Harvey* v. *Chicago Transit Authority,* 1984) and the confidentiality of test results (*Ivy* v. *Damon Clinical Laboratory,* 1984). Employees must be given the opportunity to have their specimens retested and to explain why their tests were positive even though they may not have taken illegal drugs. Thus, for a drug testing program to be legal, the organization must have reason to suspect drug usage, the job must involve the safety or trust of the public, the testing process must be accurate and reasonably private, the results should be handled in a confidential manner, and employees who test positive must be

Box 2.1
Federal Guidelines for Workplace Drug Testing

To ensure that drug testing of federal government employees is conducted properly, the National Institute on Drug Abuse developed the following guidelines. Although these guidelines were developed for use by the federal government, they provide an excellent model for other employers as well.

### Integrity and Identity of Specimen

Agencies shall take precautions to ensure that a urine specimen not be adulterated or diluted during the collection procedure and that information on the urine bottle and in the record book can identify the individual from whom the specimen was collected. The following minimum precautions shall be taken to ensure that unadulterated specimens are obtained and correctly identified.

1. To deter the dilution of specimens at the collection site, toilet bluing agents shall be placed in toilet tanks wherever possible, so the reservoir of water in the toilet bowl always remains blue. There shall be no other source of water (no shower or sink) in the enclosure where urination occurs.

2. When an individual arrives at the collection site, the collection site person shall request the individual to present photo identification. If the individual does not have proper photo identification, the collection site person shall contact the supervisor of the individual, the coordinator of the drug testing program, or any other agency official who can positively identify the individual. If the individual's identity cannot be established, the collection site person shall not proceed with the collection.

3. If the individual fails to arrive at the assigned time, the collection site person shall contact the appropriate authority to obtain guidance on the action to be taken.

4. The collection site person shall ask the individual to remove any unnecessary outer garments such as coat or jacket that might conceal items or substances that could be used to tamper with or adulterate the individual's urine specimen. The collection site person shall ensure that all personal belongings such as a purse or briefcase remain with the outer garments. The individual may retain his or her wallet.

5. The individual shall be instructed to wash and dry his or her hands prior to urination.

6. After washing hands, the individual shall remain in the presence of the collection site person and shall not have access to any water fountain, faucet, soap dispenser, cleaning agent or any other materials which could be used to adulterate the specimen.

7. The individual may provide his or her specimen in the privacy of a stall or otherwise partitioned area that allows for individual privacy.

8. The collection site person shall note any unusual behavior or appearance in the permanent record book.

9. In the exceptional event that an agency-designated collection site is not accessible and there is an immediate requirement for specimen collection (for example, an accident investigation), a public rest room may be used according to the following procedures: A collection site person of the same gender as the individual shall accompany the individual into the public rest room, which shall be made secure during the collection procedure. If possible, a toilet bluing agent shall be placed in the bowl and any accessible toilet tank. The collection site person shall remain in the rest room, but outside the stall until the specimen is collected. If no bluing agent is available to deter specimen dilution, the collection site person shall instruct the individual not to flush the toilet until the specimen is delivered to the collection site person. After the collection site person has possession of the specimen, the individual will be instructed to flush the toilet and to participate with the collection site

*(continued)*

**Box 2.1** (continued)

person in completing the chain of custody procedures.

10. Upon receiving the specimen from the individual, the collection site person shall determine that it contains at least 60 milliliters of urine. If there is less than 60 milliliters of urine in the container, additional urine shall be collected in a separate container to reach a total of 60 milliliters. (The temperature of the partial specimen in each separate container shall be measured in accordance with paragraph (f)(12) of this section, and the partial specimens shall be combined in one container.) The individual may be given a reasonable amount of liquid to drink for this purpose (for example, a glass of water). If the individual fails for any reason to provide 60 milliliters of urine, the collection site person shall contact the appropriate authority to obtain guidance on the action to be taken.

11. After the specimen has been provided and submitted to the collection site person, the individual shall be allowed to wash his or her hands.

12. Immediately after the specimen is collected, the collection site person shall measure the temperature of the specimen. The temperature measuring device used must accurately reflect the temperature of the specimen and not contaminate the specimen. The time from urination to temperature measurement is critical and in no case shall exceed 4 minutes.

13. If the temperature of a specimen is outside the range of 32.5°–37.7°C/90.5°–99.8°F, that is a reason to believe that the individual may have altered or substituted the specimen, and another specimen shall be collected under direct observation of a same gender collection site person and both specimens shall be forwarded to the laboratory for testing. An individual may volunteer to have his or her oral temperature taken to provide evidence to counter the reason to believe the individual may have altered or substituted the specimen caused by the specimen's temperature falling outside the prescribed range.

14. Immediately after the specimen is collected, the collection site person shall also inspect the specimen to determine its color and look for any signs of contaminants. Any unusual findings shall be noted in the permanent record book.

15. All specimens suspected of being adulterated shall be forwarded to the laboratory for testing.

16. Whenever there is reason to believe that a particular individual may alter or substitute the specimen to be provided, a second specimen shall be obtained as soon as possible under the direct observation of a same gender collection site person.

17. Both the individual being tested and the collection site person shall keep the specimen in view at all times prior to its being sealed and labeled. If the specimen is transferred to a second bottle, the collection site person shall request the individual to observe the transfer of the specimen and the placement of the tamperproof seal over the bottle cap and down the sides of the bottle.

18. The collection site person and the individual shall be present at the same time during procedures outlined in paragraphs (f)(19)–(f)(22) of this section.

19. The collection site person shall place securely on the bottle an identification label which contains the date, the individual's specimen number, and any other identifying information provided or required by the agency.

20. The individual shall initial the identification label on the specimen bottle for the purpose of certifying that it is the specimen collected from him or her.

21. The collection site person shall enter in the permanent record book all information identifying the specimen. The collection site person shall sign the permanent record book next to the identifying information.

22. The individual shall be asked to read and sign a statement in the permanent record book certifying that the specimen

**Box 2.1**

identified as having been collected from him or her is in fact that specimen he or she provided.

23. A higher level supervisor shall review and concur in advance with any decision by a collection site person to obtain a specimen under the direct observation of a same gender collection site person based on a reason to believe that the individual may alter or substitute the specimen to be provided.

24. The collection site person shall complete the chain of custody form.

25. The urine specimen and chain of custody form are now ready for shipment. If the specimen is not immediately prepared for shipment, it shall be appropriately safeguarded during temporary storage.

26. While any part of the above chain of custody procedures is being performed, it is essential that the urine specimen and custody documents be under the control of the involved collection site person. If the involved collection site person leaves his or her work station momentarily, the specimen and custody form shall be taken with him or her or shall be secured. After the collection site person returns to the work station, the custody process will continue. If the collection site person is leaving for an extended period of time, the specimen shall be packaged for mailing before he or she leaves the site.

**Collection Control**

To the maximum extent possible, collection site personnel shall keep the individual's specimen bottle within sight both before and after the individual has urinated. After the specimen is collected, it shall be properly sealed and labeled. An approved chain of custody form shall be used for maintaining control and accountability of each specimen from the point of collection to final disposition of the specimen. The date and purpose shall be documented on an approved chain of custody form each time a specimen is handled or transferred and every individual in the chain shall be identified. Every effort shall be made to minimize the number of persons handling specimens.

**Transportation to Laboratory**

Collection site personnel shall arrange to ship the collected specimens to the drug testing laboratory. The specimens shall be placed in containers designed to minimize the possibility of damage during shipment, for example, specimen boxes or padded mailers; and those containers shall be securely sealed to eliminate the possibility of undetected tampering. On the tape sealing the container, the collection site supervisor shall sign and enter the date specimens were sealed in the containers for shipment. The collection site personnel shall ensure that the chain of custody documentation is attached to each container sealed for shipment to the drug testing laboratory.

Source: *Federal Register* (1988, April 11) *53*(69), p. 1970.

given opportunities to appeal and undergo rehabilitation. A detailed discussion of the use and validity of drug testing for employee selection can be found in Chapter 6.

## OFFICE AND LOCKER SEARCHES

Office and locker searches are allowed under the law as long as they are reasonable and with cause (*O'Conner* v. *Ortega,* 1987). Allowing employees to place their own locks on lockers, however, removes the right of the organization to search the locker.

**Table 2.3** Do these true-false test questions violate an applicant's right to privacy?

| |
|---|
| I go to church almost every week. |
| I am very religious. |
| I believe there is a God. |
| My sex life is satisfactory. |
| I like to talk about sex. |
| I have never indulged in any unusual sex practices. |

## PSYCHOLOGICAL TESTS

An employment test may be illegal if its questions unnecessarily invade the privacy of an applicant (O'Meara, 1994). At most risk are psychological tests originally developed to measure psychopathology. These tests often include questions about such topics as religion and sexual preference that some applicants feel uncomfortable answering. In *Soroka* v. *Dayton Hudson* (1991), three applicants for store security guard positions with Target Stores filed a class action suit after taking a 704-item psychological test (Psychscreen). The applicants believed that some of the questions, a few of which are shown in Table 2.3, violated their right to privacy guaranteed by the California Constitution.

Though the two sides in this case reached a settlement prior to the case being decided by the U.S. Supreme Court, the case focused attention on the questions used in psychological testing. Of particular concern to I/O psychologists in this case was that the tests were scored by a consulting firm and Target Stores never saw the individual answers to the questions. Instead, it only received overall scores indicating the applicant's level of emotional stability, interpersonal style, addiction potential, dependability, and socialization. The finding by courts that use of the test was an invasion of privacy was troubling to psychologists who routinely make decisions based on overall test scores rather than the answers to any one particular question (Brown, 1993).

# HARASSMENT

An issue of growing concern in the workplace is sexual harassment: research indicates that as many as 40% of women and 15% of men have been sexually harassed (Moulton, 1994). These percentages increase when employees are the sole representative of their gender (called gender pioneers) or consist of a small minority of the employees in a particular work setting (Niebuhr & Oswald, 1992). Though the following discussion focuses on *sexual* harassment, the courts have ruled that racial, religious, disability, and age harassment are also illegal (Platt, 1994).

Sexual harassment complaints are increasing each year.

Legally, sexual harassment can take one of two forms: *quid pro quo* or hostile environment. With *quid pro quo,* the granting of sexual favors is tied to employment decisions such as promotions or salary increases. An example of a *quid pro quo* case of harassment is a supervisor who tells his secretary that she must sleep with him in order to keep her job. In *quid pro quo* cases, a *single* sexual advance may be enough to constitute sexual harassment.

In a hostile atmosphere case, sexual harassment occurs when a *pattern* of conduct related to sex or gender unreasonably interferes with an individual's work performance. Such conduct can include comments, unwanted sexual or romantic advances, or the display of demeaning posters, signs, or cartoons (*Jenson* v. *Eveleth Taconite Co.*, 1993). Members of a police department consistently referring to female officers as "babes" or "honey" would be an example of sexual harassment because the comments are based on gender and are demeaning to the female officers. A male officer calling a female officer "stupid" would be an example of rude behavior, but not sexual harassment because the nature of the comment was neither sexual nor based on gender.

The idea is that any pattern of behavior, based on gender, that causes an employee discomfort might constitute sexual harassment (Egler, 1995). In *Harris* v. *Forklift Systems* (1993), the court found that a male supervisor's comments such as "Let's go to the Holiday Inn and negotiate your raise" and "You're just a dumb-ass woman" constituted harassment even though the female employee did not suffer any great psychological damage or have a nervous breakdown.

For conduct to be considered sexual harassment based on a hostile atmosphere claim, it generally must be a pattern of behavior rather than an isolated incident. It would not be harassment to ask a co-worker for a date, even if the co-worker does not agree to the date. It becomes harassment if the employee *continually* makes unwanted romantic or sexual overtures.

To be illegal, the conduct must also be unwanted and considered negative to the "reasonable person." For example, about once a week, a male employee tells a female co-worker that she "looks nice today" or that the color of her dress is "a good color" for her. Would this behavior constitute sexual harassment? The answer would depend on the court's opinion about the extent to which the "reasonable woman" would consider the behavior degrading. In this case, the court would probably rule that the behavior is not harassment. However, because the behavior upsets a particular employee, the organization probably should direct the male employee to stop complimenting his female co-worker.

If an employee complains of sexual harassment, the organization should investigate the complaint quickly and then promptly take any necessary action to rectify the situation and punish the offender. To reduce an organization's liability for sexual harassment, Robinson, Allen, Franklin, and Duhon (1993) and Bloch (1995) advise the following:

1. All complaints, no matter how trivial or farfetched they appear, must be investigated.

2. The organization's policy must encourage victims to come forward and allow them multiple channels or sources with which to file their complaint.

3. Complaints must be kept confidential to protect both the accused and the accuser.

4. Action must be taken to protect the accuser during the time the complaint is being investigated. Actions might include physically separating the two parties or limiting the amount of contact between them.

5. Both the accused and the accuser must be given due process and care must be taken to avoid an initial assumption of guilt.

6. The results of the investigation must be communicated in writing to both parties.

7. The severity of the punishment (if any) must match the severity of the violation.

The proper handling of a sexual-harassment complaint can protect an employer from legal liability. In *Saxton* v. *AT&T* (1993), the Court of Appeals ruled that AT&T was not liable for sexual harassment because it investigated a sexual-harassment complaint in a timely manner and then took prompt corrective action against the harasser. In contrast, in *Intlekofer* v. *Turnage* (1992), the Court of Appeals found the Veteran's Administration liable for the harassment of one of its employees because it ignored nearly two dozen complaints by a female employee and refused to take corrective action against the harasser.

Rather than simply reacting to sexual-harassment complaints, it is in the best interests of an organization to take proactive steps to prevent harassment. These include having a strong organizational policy against harassment (Moulton, 1994) and training employees about behavior that constitutes harassment (Moynahan, 1993).

In addition to the obvious legal costs, sexual harassment has other financial ramifications for an organization. It results in higher levels of turnover, greater absenteeism, and lower levels of productivity (Petrocelli & Repa, 1992).

## FAMILY LEAVE ACT (1993)

In 1993, Congress passed the **Family Medical Leave Act (FMLA),** which entitles eligible employees (both male and female) to a minimum of 12 weeks of unpaid leave to deal with the following matters: birth, adoption, or the serious illness of a child, parent, or the employee. All public agencies and private organizations with 50 or more employees physically employed within a 70-mile radius of one another are covered by the act (Fitzpatrick & Topuzian, 1995).

Employees are eligible if they

1. Work for a covered employer,
2. Have worked for the organization for at least one year, and
3. Have worked at least 1,250 hours over the previous 12 months.

If employees take advantage of family or medical leave, the organization must continue their health-care coverage and guarantee employees that when they return, they will either have the same or an equivalent position. In return, employees must provide a doctor's certification and give 30-days' notice if the leave is foreseeable (for example, birth or adoption).

To protect employers from potential problems in complying with the FMLA, Congress allowed employers to exempt their key employees from using the FMLA. Key employees are the highest paid 10% in the organization or those whose leave would cause economic problems for the organization. Other than record-keeping headaches, however, the FMLA has not resulted in many hardships for most organizations (Martinez, 1994).

The Family Medical Leave Act was designed to help working parents.

## CHAPTER SUMMARY

In this chapter, the legal process was discussed. Here you learned that important laws include the Fourth Amendment, which has been extended to cover drug testing and employee locker searches; the Fourteenth Amendment, which covers intentional discrimination; the 1964 Civil Rights Act, which covers unintentional discrimination; the Equal Pay Act of 1963, which requires equal pay for equal work; the Age Discrimination in Employment Act, which prohibits discrimination against people over age 40; the Americans with Disabilities Act and the Vocational Rehabilitation Act, which forbid discrimination against the disabled; the Vietnam-Era Veterans Readjustment Act, which protects and helps Vietnam veterans; and the Pregnancy Discrimination Act and Family Medical Leave Act, which protect the rights of employees to have and care for families.

Also discussed were affirmative-action programs designed to encourage the employment of females and minorities. Affirmative-action strategies include increased efforts to recruit minorities, removal of employment practices working against minorities, and the controversial preferential hiring and promotion of minorities. Organizations enter into affirmative-action programs because of government regulations, court orders, consent decrees, and a desire to be a good citizen. Legal affirmative-action programs were developed because organizations had a history of discrimination, have hiring goals based on the percentage of minorities in the qualified work force rather than the general population, do not deny nonminorities of their rights, and have ending points.

Organizations using drug testing, office searches, and psychological tests are potentially liable for violating an individual's privacy. Organizations can also be held liable for the sexual harassment conduct of their employees. This harassment can take the form of *quid pro quo* or hostile environment.

# GLOSSARY

**Adverse impact**   An employment practice that results in members of a protected class being negatively affected at a higher rate than members of the majority class.

**Affirmative action**   The process of ensuring proportional representation of employees based on variables such as race and sex.

**Age Discrimination in Employment Act (ADEA)**   A federal law that, with its amendments, forbids discrimination against an individual who is over the age of 40.

**Americans with Disabilities Act (ADA)**   A federal law, passed in 1990, that forbids discrimination against people who are physically and mentally disabled.

**Bona fide occupational qualification (BFOQ)**   A selection requirement that is necessary for the performance of job-related duties and for which there is no substitute.

**Case law**   The interpretation of a law by a court through a verdict in a trial that sets precedent for subsequent court decisions.

**Family Medical Leave Act**   Passed in 1993, this federal law provides 12 weeks of unpaid leave for birth, adoption, or serious illness of a child, parent, spouse, or the employee.

**Fourteenth Amendment**   The amendment to the U.S. Constitution that mandates that no state may deny a person equal protection under the law.

**Fourth Amendment**   The amendment to the U.S. Constitution that protects against unreasonable search or seizure; it has been ruled to cover drug testing.

**Job-related**   The case in which requirements needed to score well on a selection test are the same as those needed to perform well on the job.

**Pregnancy Discrimination Act**   A 1978 federal law protecting the rights of pregnant women.

**Protected class**   Any group of people for which protective legislation has been passed.

**Qualified work force**   The percentage of people in a given geographic area that have the qualifications (skills, education, and so on) to perform a certain job.

**Uniform guidelines**   Federal guidelines that are used to guide an employer in establishing fair selection methods.

**Vietnam-Era Veterans Readjustment Act**   A 1974 federal law that mandates that federal government contractors and subcontractors take affirmative action to employ and promote Vietnam-era veterans.

**Vocational Rehabilitation Act**   Federal act passed in 1973 that prohibits federal government contractors or subcontractors from discriminating against the physically or mentally handicapped.

# 3
# JOB ANALYSIS AND EVALUATION

In 1585, fifteen English settlers landed at and established a colony on Roanoke Island near what is now the Outer Banks of the North Carolina coast. When John White arrived at Roanoke Island in 1590, he found no trace of the colony and only the word "Croatan" carved on a tree. To this day, it is not known what happened to the settlers of the Lost Colony of Roanoke.

Many theories have been put forth to explain the fate of the lost colony — killed by Indians, moved to another location, and so on. One theory, however, is that the members of the colony were not prepared to survive in the new continent; that is, the group consisted of politicians, soldiers, and sailors. Although worthy individuals were sent to the New World, few had the necessary training and skills to survive. In fact, the colony might have survived if settlers with more appropriate skills, such as farmers, had been sent instead.

Thus, a better match between job requirements and personnel might have saved the colony.

Does this sound farfetched? Perhaps so, but the story does underscore the importance of a process called **job analysis**—the breaking down of a job into its component activities and requirements (Levine, 1983).

# JOB ANALYSIS

## LEGAL IMPORTANCE

From Chapter 2, recall that any employment decision must be based on job-related information. One legally acceptable way to directly determine job relatedness is by *job analysis*. No law specifically requires a job analysis, but several important guidelines and court cases mandate job analysis for all practical purposes.

First, in the Uniform Guidelines discussed in Chapter 2, there are several direct references to the necessity of job analysis. Even though the Uniform Guidelines are not law, courts have granted them "great deference" (Levine, 1983).

Second, several court cases have discussed the concept of job relatedness. For example, in *Griggs* v. *Duke Power* (1971), employment decisions were based in part upon applicants' possession of high school diplomas. Because a higher percentage of Blacks than Whites did not meet this requirement, a smaller percentage of Black applicants was hired. Thus, a suit was filed against the Duke Power Company charging that a high school diploma was not necessary to carry out the demands of the job. The court agreed with Griggs, the plaintiff, stating that the company had indeed not established the job relatedness of the high school diploma requirement.

Although not specifically mentioning the term *job analysis,* the decision in *Griggs* was the first one that addressed the issue of job relatedness. Subsequent cases such as *Albermarle* v. *Moody* (1975) and *Chance* v. *Board of Examiners* (1971) further established the necessity of job relatedness and the link between it and job analysis.

## PRACTICAL IMPORTANCE

Even if job analysis were not legally required, it has so many uses that it should still be an integral part of an organization's human resource system. Potential uses for job analysis include job descriptions, employee selection, training, personpower planning, performance appraisal, job classification, job evaluation, job design, and organizational analysis (Ash & Levine, 1980).

### Job Descriptions

Often confused with job analysis, **job descriptions** are brief, two- to five-page summaries of the tasks and job requirements found in the job analysis.

In other words, the job analysis is the *process* of determining the work activities and requirements, and the job description is the written *result* of the job analysis.

A complete discussion on how to write job descriptions is presented later in this chapter. It is more essential now, however, to realize just how important job descriptions really are. They provide guidelines that can be followed by employees, which can lead to greater employee performance by clearly defining the employer's expectations of the employee in a particular job (Campbell, 1983).

### Employee Selection

It is difficult to imagine how an employee can be selected unless there is a clear understanding of the job's requirements. By identifying such requirements, it is possible to select tests or interview questions that will determine whether a particular applicant possesses the necessary knowledge, skills, and abilities to carry out the requirements of the job. Although this seems like common sense, the discussion of the employment interview in Chapter 5 demonstrates that many non–job-related variables are often used to select employees. Examples are height requirements for police officers, firm handshakes for most jobs, and physical attractiveness for flight attendants.

### Training

Again, it is difficult to see how employees can be trained unless the requirements of the job are known. Job analyses yield lists of job activities that can be systematically used to create training programs.

### Personpower Planning

One important but seldom utilized use of job analysis is to determine *worker mobility* within an organization. That is, if an individual is hired for a particular job, to what other jobs can she expect to eventually be promoted and become successful? Many organizations have a policy of promoting the person who performs the best in the job immediately below the one in question. Although this approach has its advantages, it can result in the so-called **Peter Principle**: promoting a person until she eventually reaches her highest level of incompetence (Peter & Hull, 1969). For example, consider an employee who is the best sales person in the company. Even though this person is known to be excellent in sales, it is not known what type of supervisor she will be. Promotion solely on the basis of sales performance does not guarantee that the individual will do well as a supervisor. Suppose, however, that job analysis results are used to compare all jobs in the company to the supervisor's job. Instead of promoting the person in the job immediately below the supervisor, we promote the best employee from the most similar job, that is, a job that already involves much of the same knowledge, skills, and abilities as the supervisor's job. With this approach, there is a better match between the person being promoted and the requirements of the job.

### Performance Appraisal

Another important use of job analysis is the construction of a performance appraisal instrument. As in employee selection, the evaluation of employee performance must be job related. Employees are often evaluated with forms that use vague categories such as "dependability," "knowledge," and "initiative." The use of specific, job-related categories leads to more accurate performance appraisals that are not only better accepted by employees, but also accepted more readily by the courts (Field & Holley, 1982). In addition, when properly administered and utilized, job-related performance appraisals can serve as an excellent source of employee training and counseling.

### Job Classification

Job analysis allows a human resource professional to classify jobs into groups based on similarities in requirements and duties. Job classification is useful for determining pay levels, transfers, and promotions.

### Job Evaluation

Job analysis information also can be used to determine the *worth* of a job. Job evaluation will be discussed in greater detail later in this chapter.

### Job Design

Job analysis information can be used to determine the optimal way in which a job should be performed. By analyzing a job, wasted motions can be eliminated, work stations moved closer together, or two jobs can be combined into one.

### Organizational Analysis

During a job analysis, the job analyst often becomes aware of certain problems within an organization. For example, during a job-analysis interview, an employee may indicate that she does not know how she is evaluated or to whom she is supposed to report. The discovery of such lapses in organizational communication can then be used to correct problems and help an organization function better. For example, while conducting job-analysis interviews of credit union positions, job analyst Deborah Peggans discovered that none of the workers knew how their job performances were evaluated, which indicated that the organization had not done an adequate job of communicating performance standards to its employees.

## WRITING A GOOD JOB DESCRIPTION

As mentioned earlier, one of the most useful results of a job analysis is the **job description.** A job description is a relatively short summary of a job and should be about two to five pages in length. This suggested length is not typical of most job descriptions used in industry; they tend to be only one page. But for a job description to be of any value, it must describe a job in enough detail that decisions about activities such as selection and training can be made. Such decisions probably cannot be made if the description is just one page.

Though I/O psychologists believe that job descriptions should be detailed and lengthy, many professionals in organizations resist such efforts. These professionals worry that listing each activity will limit their ability to direct employees to perform tasks not listed on the job description. The concern is that an employee, referring to the job description as support, might respond "it's not my job." This fear, however, can be countered with two arguments. The first is that duties can always be added to a job description and job descriptions can, and should, be updated on a regular basis. The second is to include the statement "and performs other job-related duties as assigned" to the job description. In fact, Virginia Tech has a policy stating that the university can require employees to perform any duties not on the employees' job descriptions for a period not to exceed three months. After three months, the duty must be either eliminated or permanently added to the employee's job description, at which time a review also will be made to determine if the addition is significant enough to merit a salary increase.

Job descriptions can be written in many ways, but the following format has been used successfully for many jobs and is a combination of methods used by many companies and suggested by several researchers. A job description should contain the following seven sections: job title, brief summary, work activities, tools and equipment used, work context, performance standards, and personal requirements.

### Job Title and DOT Code

A job title is important for several reasons. An accurate title describes the nature of the job. When industrial psychologist David Faloona started a new job at Washington National Insurance in Chicago, his title was Psychometric Technician. Unfortunately, none of the other workers knew what he did. To correct that problem, his title was changed to Personnel Assistant, and supervisors then began consulting with him on human resource-related problems. A job analysis conducted by your author provides another example. After analyzing the position of "secretary" for one credit union, we found that her duties were actually those of a position that other credit unions title "loan officer." This change in title resulted in the employee receiving a higher salary as well as vindication that she was indeed "more than a secretary."

An accurate title also aids in employee selection and recruitment. If the job title indicates the true nature of the job, potential applicants for a position will be better able to determine if their skills and experience match those required for the job—the "secretary story" is a good example because secretarial applicants would not possess the lending and decision-making skills needed by a "loan officer."

When conducting a job analysis, it is not unusual for an analyst to discover that some workers do not have job titles. But, job titles provide workers with some form of identity. Instead of just saying that she is a "worker at the foundry," a woman can say that she is a "welder" or a "machinist." At Radford University, hundreds of students receiving financial aid are called "work-study students" rather than titles such as clerk, computer operator, or mail sorter. This inaccurate title causes many students to think they are supposed to study as they work rather than sort mail or operate a computer.

Job titles can also affect perceptions of the status and worth of a job. For example, job descriptions containing such gender-neutral titles as administrative assistant are evaluated as being worth more money than ones containing titles with a female sex linkage such as executive secretary (Naughton, 1988). As another example, Smith, Hornsby, Benson, and Wesolowski (1989) had subjects read identical job descriptions that differed only in the status of the title. Jobs with higher status titles were evaluated as being worth more money than jobs with lower status titles. Some authors, however, have questioned the gender effects associated with titles (Mount & Ellis, 1989; Rynes, Weber, & Milkovich, 1989).

In addition to a title, the Uniform Guidelines suggest that a job description contain a code from the **Dictionary of Occupational Titles (DOT).** The DOT is produced by the federal government and contains descriptions of thousands of jobs, each of which is accompanied by an identifying code, commonly referred to as the **DOT Code.** Use of this code makes it easier to compare jobs and summarize industry-related information such as affirmative action, safety, and career guidance reports. DOT Codes contain nine numbers divided into three groups of three numbers. For example, the DOT Code for a physical therapist is 076.121-014.

The first three numbers identify a specific occupational group. As shown in Figure 3.1, the first number refers to one of nine broad categories such as professional, clerical, agricultural, and machine trades. The *0* in our

**Figure 3.1**
D.O.T. code example

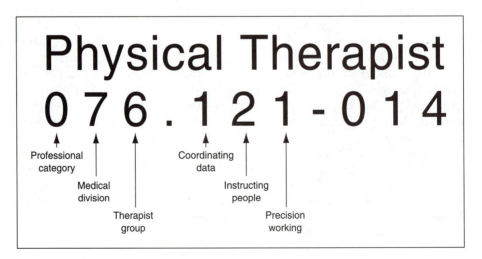

**Table 3.1** Data, people, things levels

| Date | People | Things |
|---|---|---|
| 0 Synthesizing | 0 Mentoring | 0 Setting up |
| 1 Coordinating | 1 Negotiating | 1 Precision Working |
| 2 Analyzing | 2 Instructing | 2 Operating–Controlling |
| 3 Compiling | 3 Supervising | 3 Driving–Operating |
| 4 Computing | 4 Diverting | 4 Manipulating |
| 5 Copying | 5 Persuading | 5 Tending |
| 6 Comparing | 6 Speaking–Signaling | 6 Feeding–Offbearing |
| | 7 Serving | 7 Handling |
| | 8 Taking instructions | |
| | 9 Helping | |

example indicates that the job falls under the professional category, whereas a *2* would indicate a clerical or sales category. The second number refers to a division within the occupational group. In our example, the *7* indicates that our job is in medicine and health, whereas a *9* would indicate a professional job in education. The third number refers to a specific occupation within the division. In our example, the *6* indicates a therapist, whereas a *5* would indicate a registered nurse.

As shown in Figure 3.1 and Table 3.1, the middle three numbers identify the level of work performed by incumbents in the occupation. The fourth number indicates the level at which the incumbent deals with data, the fifth number indicates the level at which the incumbent deals with people, and the sixth number indicates the level at which the incumbent deals with things. In our example, the middle three numbers are *121* indicating that the job involves coordinating data, instructing people, and precisely working with things.

The last three digits identify a specific job. For example, the first three numbers indicate that the job is professional, in the medical field, and is a therapist position. However, we still do not know which type of therapist (for example, physical, vocational, respiratory); thus, the last three numbers allow us to assign a unique code to specifically identify the position as a physical therapist.

### Brief Summary

The summary need only be a paragraph in length but should briefly describe the nature and purpose of the job. This summary can be used in help wanted advertisements, internal job postings, and company brochures.

### Work Activities

The work activities section lists the tasks and activities in which the worker is involved. These tasks and activities should be organized into meaningful categories to make the job description easier to read and understand. The category labels are also convenient to use in the brief summary. As the reader can see in the sample job description in Box 3.1, the 72 work activities performed by the bookkeeper are divided into seven main areas: accounting, clerical, teller, share draft, collections, payroll, and financial operations.

Much has been written about the proper way to write a task statement (McCormick, 1979), but a job analyst should not get too bogged down worrying about format. Instead, the task statements in this section should be short and written at a level that can be read and understood by a person with the same reading ability as the typical job incumbent. The statement should make sense by itself. That is, "makes photocopies" does not provide as much detail as "makes photocopies of transactions for credit union members," which indicates what types of materials are photocopied and for whom they are copied. It also has been suggested that for those activities that involve decision making, the level of authority should be indicated. This level lets the incumbent know which decisions she is allowed to make on her own and which ones she needs approval from a higher level (Campbell, 1983).

### Tools and Equipment Used

A section should be included that lists all the tools and equipment used to perform the work activities in the previous section. Even though tools and equipment may have been mentioned in the activities section, placing them in a separate section makes their identification simpler. Information in this section is primarily used for employee selection and training. That is, an applicant can be asked if she can operate an adding machine, a computer, and a credit history machine.

### Work Context

This section should describe the environment in which the employee works and should mention stress level, work schedule, physical demands, level of responsibility, temperature, number of co-workers, degree of danger, and any other relevant information. This information is especially important in providing applicants with disabilities with information they can use to determine their ability to perform a job under a particular set of circumstances.

### Performance Standards

The job description should outline standards of performance. This section contains a relatively brief description of how an employee's performance is evaluated and what work standards are expected of the employee.

### Personal Requirements

The personal requirements section contains what are commonly called **job specifications.** These are the knowledge, skills, abilities, and other **(KSAOs)** characteristics (such as interest, personality, training) that are necessary to be successful on the job. This section should be divided into two subsections. The first subsection contains KSAOs that an employee must have at

Box 3.1
Example of a Job Description

**Bookkeeper**
**Radford Pipe Shop Employee's**
**Federal Credit Union**

**Job Summary** Under the general supervision of the office manager, the Bookkeeper is responsible for all of the accounting duties of the office. Specifically, the Bookkeeper is responsible for: keeping all financial records accurate and up-to-date; processing loans; and preparing and posting statements, reports, and bonds.

**Work Activities** The work activities of the Bookkeeper are divided into seven main functional areas:

### Accounting Activities

- Prepares quarterly income statement
- Maintains and posts all transactions in general ledger book
- Pays credit union bills
- Prepares statistical reports
- Updates undivided earnings account
- Prepares and files tax returns and statements
- Completes IRA forms and reports in co-operation with CUNA
- Annually computes Cumis Bond
- Balances journal and cash records

### Clerical Activities

- Looks up members' account information when requested
- Answers phone
- Makes copies of transactions for members
- Drafts statements of account to members
- Types Certificates of Deposit
- Makes copies of letters that are sent to members
- Picks up, sorts, and disperses credit union mail
- Folds monthly and quarterly statements and places into an envelope to be mailed to members

- Processes and mails savings and share draft statements
- Sorts checks or copies of checks in numerical order
- Orders supplies
- Types reports and minutes from board meetings
- Maintains and updates files for members
- Prepares, types, and files correspondence
- Enters change-of-address information into the computer

### Teller Activities

- Enrolls new members and opens and closes accounts
- Reconciles accounts
- Issues money orders and traveler's checks
- Conducts history of accounts
- Processes and issues receipts for transactions
- Asks for identification if person making transaction is not known
- Daily enters transaction totals onto a list sent to the bank
- Orders new or replacement checks for members
- Prints and issues checks
- Makes proper referrals

### Share Draft Activities

- Deducts fee from member's account when a share is returned
- Processes statements for share draft accounts
- Issues stop payments and sends copy of form to member
- Deducts fee in form of an overdraft when more than three transfers have occurred for any one member in a month
- Checks and records share drafts or additions from previous day
- Receives share draft totals for each member from CUNA data

*(continued)*

**Box 3.1** *(continued)*

• Decides on an individual basis whether overdrafts will be covered by credit union

• Determines if overdrafts on account have been paid

• Checks to see if share drafts have cleared

• Telephones Chase-Manhattan Bank when a member does not have enough money to cover a share draft

### Collections Activities

• Holds money from member's check in order to meet loan payments

• Decides if a member who has a delinquent loan will be able to take money out of account

• Locates and communicates with members having delinquent loans

• Completes garnishee form to send to courts on delinquent loans

• Resubmits garnishee form once every three months until delinquent loan has been paid in full by member

• Makes collection on delinquent loans

• Checks on previous member's address and current job to see if loan payments can be made

• Determines number and length of time of delinquent loans

• Sends judgment form to court, which sends it to delinquent member

• If a member is delinquent, finds out if they are sick or on vacation

### Payroll and Data-Processing Activities

• Checks and verifies payroll run for all necessary deductions

• Reads and interprets computer printouts

• Computes and subtracts deductions from payroll

• Sets up and changes deduction amounts for payroll savings plan

• Runs payroll on computer

• Annually sends out backup disk to outside vendor who transfers information to a magnetic tape that is sent to IRS

• Computes payroll

• Runs daily trial balances and transaction registers

• Loads paper into printer

• Makes backup copies of all daily computer transactions

• Runs quarterly and/or monthly statements on computer

### Financial Operations Activities

• Scans business/financial environment to identify potential threats and opportunities

• Makes recommendations to the board regarding investments

• Invests all excess money into accounts that will earn interest

• Computes profits and amounts to be used for investments

• Prepares statements of financial condition and federal operating fee report

• Obtains enough funds for day-to-day operation of branch

• Notifies and makes available investment funds to the NCUA

**Machines Used**   The Bookkeeper uses the following machines and equipment:

• Adding machine

• Typewriter

• Computer printer

• CRT

• Mainframe computer

• Credit history machine

• Motor vehicle

• Photocopy machine

• Folding machine

• Microfiche reader

• Safe

• Telephone

• Security check writer

*(continued)*

**Box 3.1**

**Job Context**  The Bookkeeper spends the majority of time making entries in and balancing journals and ledgers. The work day is spent in a climate-controlled office with four co-workers. Physical demands are minimal and sitting is required for most of the day. Stress is moderate.

**Work Performance**  To receive an excellent performance appraisal, the Bookkeeper should:

- Maintain neat and accurate records
- Meet all deadlines
- Maintain an orderly office
- Make sure all ledgers and journals balance
- Perform duties of other jobs when the need arises

**Job Qualifications**  Upon hire, the Bookkeeper must:

- Have a basic knowledge of math and English
- Understand financial documents
- Be able to make limited financial decisions
- Have completed advanced coursework in accounting and finance
- Have had training in data processing

After hire, the Bookkeeper must:

- Learn general office procedures
- Learn credit union style accounting procedures and regulations
- Learn how to complete the various forms

the time of hiring. The second contains the KSAOs that are an important part of the job but which can be obtained after being hired. The first set of KSAOs are used for employee selection and the second for training purposes (Wooten, 1993).

## CONDUCTING THE JOB ANALYSIS

### Who Will Conduct the Analysis?

Typically a job analysis is conducted by a trained individual in the personnel department, but it can also be conducted by job incumbents, supervisors, and outside consultants. If job incumbents or supervisors are used, it is essential that they be thoroughly trained in job analysis procedures. The Uniform Guidelines state that a job analysis must be "professionally conducted," and a job analyst certainly cannot be called a professional unless she has been trained. In addition, research indicates that analysts who have been trained produce slightly different results from those produced by untrained analysts (Cellar, Curtis, Kohlepp, Poczapski, & Mohiuddin, 1989; Surrette, Aamodt, & Johnson, 1990).

Time is always an issue when using supervisors or incumbents. Telling a supervisor to "write job descriptions in your spare time" is not likely to go over well. Thus, supervisors and employees will need to be released from other duties—a situation that is seldom possible.

The state of Virginia developed a system in which all employees were asked to follow set guidelines and write their own job descriptions. The system itself was well conceived, but employees were not given enough job-analysis training, which resulted in substantial confusion and, in some cases, inaccurate job descriptions.

Some jobs
involve high
levels of danger.

Consultants are a good choice for conducting job analyses because, in general, they are well trained and have extensive experience. The main drawback, though, is their expense. Consultants typically charge between $50 to $250 per hour based on their education, experience, and reputation. Given that 10 hours is probably the least amount of time that will be spent analyzing the simplest job, and the most complex jobs can take months of analysis, an organization must carefully weigh the benefits of consultants against their cost.

An alternative to hiring a consultant is to use college interns. Graduate students from I/O psychology programs tend to have job-analysis training and experience and can be employed for a relatively small cost (often, at no cost). In fact, Radford University operates the *Community Human Resource Center* in which graduate students obtain job-analysis experience by conducting job analyses free of charge for such local nonprofit institutions as schools, towns, and hospitals. In this way, graduate students obtain experience, and the institutions receive professional quality job analyses and job descriptions at no cost.

### Which Employees Should Participate?

For organizations with relatively few people in each job, it is advisable to have all employees participate in the job analysis. But, in organizations in which many people perform the same job (for example, teachers at a university or assemblers in a factory), every person need not participate. Rouleau and Krain (1975) have designed a system for estimating the number of employees who should participate in a job analysis, and Green and Stutzman (1986) have indicated that the number should be greater than three. Unfortunately, no research is available to verify these estimates.

After the number of participants has been determined, a decision needs to be made about *which particular employees* will participate. If every employee will not participate, the same sampling rules used in research should be used in job analysis. That is, participants should be selected in as random a way as practical yet still be representative. The reason for this, according to research, is that employee differences in gender, race, job performance level, experience, job enjoyment, and personality can, at times, result in slightly different job analysis outcomes (Aamodt, Kimbrough, Keller, & Crawford, 1982; Landy & Vasey, 1991; Love, Bishop, & Scionti, 1991; Machungwa & Schmitt, 1983; Mullins & Kimbrough, 1988; Schmitt & Cohen, 1989; Veres, Green, & Boyles, 1991).

The consideration of which employees are chosen to participate is an important issue because a job often can be performed in several ways. If males and females perform equally well on a job, yet perform the job in different ways, then the job analyses must contain information about both styles. For example, suppose that research indicates that male supervisors lead by setting goals and being directive and female supervisors use more of a participative approach. Consequently, a job analysis conducted only on male supervisors would result in a different set of KSAOs than a job analysis using both male and female supervisors. Because job analysis is the basis for every personnel decision, it can be seen that equal opportunity efforts begin as early as the job analysis.

The issue of using the best employees or the typical employees is also important. During a job analysis at a large printing factory, it was discovered that one employee performed his job differently than the employees on the other two shifts. Further investigation revealed that the one employee was also rated much higher in job performance than the other two. Thus, it appeared the logical thing to do was write the job analysis results based on the way the best employee performed the job and then retrain the other two.

### What Types of Information Should Be Obtained?

An important decision concerns the *level of specificity*. That is, should the job analysis break down a job into very minute, specific behaviors (for example, "tilts arm at a 90 degree angle" or "moves foot forward three inches") or should the job be analyzed at a more general level ("makes financial decisions," "speaks to clients")? Although most jobs are analyzed at levels somewhere between these two extremes, at times the level of analysis will be closer to one end of the spectrum than to the other.

For some jobs that involve intricate work, extensive and expensive efforts have been undertaken to identify the optimal way in which they should be performed. For example, in a window manufacturing plant, job analysis determined that many more windows could be mounted in frames by lifting the glass just six inches and then sliding it into place rather than lifting the glass higher and placing it in the frame. In such a situation, the work obviously must be performed in a specific manner for the greatest financial savings; thus, the job analysis is more effective at a more detailed level.

A related decision addresses the issue of *formal versus informal requirements*. Formal requirements for a secretary might include typing letters or filing memos. Informal requirements might involve making coffee or picking up the boss's children from school. Including informal requirements has the advantages of identifying and eliminating duties that may be illegal or unnecessary.

For example, suppose a job analysis reveals that a secretary in one department picks up the boss's children from school and takes them to a child care center. This is an important finding because the company may not want this to occur. However, because the manager makes $130,000 per year, the company may prefer the lower-paid secretary taking an hour a day to pick up the children rather than the higher-paid executive. If this task was in the job description, an applicant would know about this duty in advance and could decide at the time of hire if it were acceptable.

In addition, informal requirements, such as picking up the mail, may need to be made more formal to reduce potential confusion regarding who is responsible for the task. At one credit union, a continued source of bickering involved whose job or whose turn it was to pick up the mail, especially when the weather was bad and post office parking was limited. This problem could have been eliminated if the task were assigned to one individual.

### How Should Information Be Obtained?

Consideration should be given to what methods will be used to obtain the information to include in a job description. Though most job analyses will be conducted through interviews and observations, many other job analysis methods are available, each of which provides information suitable for one or more parts of the job description. A discussion of these methods follows:

**Interview**  The most common method of conducting a job analysis is the **job-analysis interview** (Jones & DeCotiis, 1969). Job-analysis interviews differ greatly from employment interviews; the purpose of the job-analysis interview is to obtain information about the job itself rather than about the person doing the job. Job-analysis interviews come in two main forms: individual and group. In the individual interview, the **job analyst** interviews only one employee at a time. In the group interview, a larger number of employees are interviewed together. Individual interviews are, of course, more costly and time-consuming than group interviews. The greater cost often can be justified, however, by the increased openness during an individual

*Deborah L. Gebhardt,*
*Ph.D.*
*President of Human Per-*
*formance Systems, Inc.*
*Hyattsville, Maryland*

My company conducts research to develop and validate physical performance and cognitive tests and medical guidelines. To provide our clients with valid, defensible selection, evaluation, and promotion instruments we conduct detailed job analyses to determine job requirements. Job analysis provides the foundation for establishing the validity of selection and promotion procedures. To develop valid, defensible procedures that reflect the essential job functions, the job tasks, knowledges, skills, and abilities must be defined. Conducting the job analysis can be one of the most rewarding aspects of a project because the job analyst is exposed to new environments and new people.

To become an effective job analyst one must be able to learn the details involved in another person's job. This is a highlight of the process because it affords us the opportunity to visit job sites and interview incumbents. These site visits have provided us with some exciting and interesting experiences. For example, our work in the natural gas industry involved observing work performed on a drilling platform 100 miles out in the Gulf of Mexico to learn how to repair engines with five-foot long pistons. Similarly, interviewing workers in a manhole while they repair telephone cable provides a true understanding of why there may be occasional static on your home phone line.

Each project provides new challenges to the job analyst in capturing the purpose and details associated with the job tasks. In many instances this information is best obtained by accompanying the worker on a shift and participating in the work. To understand the work of public safety personnel, we rode with paramedics in New York City, followed firefighters into a burning building, and answered domestic dispute calls with police officers.

When developing physical performance assessment procedures and medical guidelines, it is important to gather information about the ergonomic parameters that affect the work place and the worker. Ergonomics applies knowledge of human capabilities and requirements to the design of work devices, systems, and the physical work setting. Ergonomic evaluations can involve specific analysis of working postures and their effect on muscle fatigue or general gathering of data such as heights, weights, and forces involved in task performance. This again involves on-site measurements and observations. For instance, we obtained measurements of the forces required to open the hatches and doors on Navy destroyers and in nuclear power plants. In another study learning to climb telephone poles was necessary to obtain the ergonomic data needed to determine whether men and women used different climbing techniques.

Conducting a job analysis provides an appreciation and understanding for the ingenuity of the American workforce. We observed first hand the advances in mechanized and electronic control systems and administrative procedures that have increased productivity, made work environments more pleasant, and decreased work related injuries.

The key to performing an accurate job analysis is to get involved in the process by learning as much as possible about the job. All jobs are not exciting, but as a job analyst it is important to be interested in the job and allow the incumbent to provide relevant information. This requires asking many questions about the work to obtain detailed information. To do this effectively, the job analyst must be fully and genuinely engaged in the process.

interview because employees are more confident that what they say will remain confidential. This may result in more accurate information.

Regardless of whether individual or group interviews are used, certain guidelines should be followed that will make the interview go more smoothly (McCormick, 1979).

1. *Prepare* for the interview by announcing the job analysis to the employees well in advance of the interviews and by selecting a quiet and private interview location.

2. *Open* the interview by establishing rapport, putting the worker at ease, and explaining the purpose of the interview.

3. *Conduct* the interview by asking open-ended questions, using easy-to-understand vocabulary, and allowing sufficient time for the employee to talk and answer questions—avoid being condescending.

Most workers are proud of their jobs and willing to talk about them in great detail. Once the initial apprehensions and jitters are over, most job-analysis interviews go well. A good way to start the actual interview is by asking the employee to describe what she does from the moment she first enters the parking lot at work to the moment she arrives back at her house. A question such as this provides some structure for the employee in recalling the various aspects of her job and also provides the interviewer with many follow-up questions and areas that will provide additional information.

A slightly more formal method for conducting group interviews is the technique described by Kosidiak (1987). With this technique, a committee of experts meet to brainstorm the major duties involved in a job. Once this has been done, the committee identifies the tasks (work-related activities) that must be completed for each of the duties. The results are then summarized in job descriptions or a job-analysis report. The employment profile of Deborah Gebhardt shows a particular use for interview results.

An excellent job-analysis interview technique for use with small organizations was developed by Ammerman (1965) and reported by Robinson (1981). The basic steps for the **Ammerman Technique** are:

1. Convene a panel of experts that includes representatives from all levels of the organization.

2. Have the panel identify the objectives and standards that are to be met by the ideal incumbent.

3. Have the panel list the specific behaviors necessary for each objective or standard to be attained.

4. Have the panel identify which of the behaviors from Step 3 are "critical" to reaching the objective.

5. Have the panel rank order the objectives on the basis of importance.

**Table 3.2** Example of Ammerman Technique objectives and tasks for a bank teller

Cross-sell bank products.
- Study daily rate charts.
- Explain new products to customers.

Balance drawer within 30 minutes at end of day.
- Accurately count money.
- Trail balance drawer during down times.

Comply with federal and state regulations.
- Notify federal government of cash transactions in excess of $10,000.
- Treat customers equally regardless of age, race, gender, or national origin.

Accurately complete paperwork.
- Obtain all necessary information from customers.
- Obtain all necessary signatures.

Make each customer feel a "part of the family".
- Know each customer's name.
- Refer to customers by their first names.
- Smile and greet each customer.

The results of these procedures will yield a set of important objectives and the behaviors necessary to meet these objectives. These behaviors can be used to create employee-selection tests, develop training programs, or evaluate the performance of current employees. An example of Ammerman-style objectives and behaviors is shown in Table 3.2.

**Observation**   **Observations** are useful job-analysis methods, especially when used in conjunction with other methods such as interviews. During a job-analysis observation, the job analyst observes incumbents performing their jobs in the work setting. The advantage to this method is that it lets the job analyst actually see the worker do her job and thus obtain information that the worker may have forgotten to mention during the interview. This is especially important because many employees have difficulty describing exactly what they do; to them, performing their job is second nature and takes little thought. A good demonstration of this point is to name the locations of keys on a typewriter or the locations of gears when you drive. We all type and shift gears without thinking (well, most of us do), but quickly describing to another person the location of the *v* key on our typewriter or *reverse* in our manual transmission is difficult.

The method's disadvantage is that it is very obtrusive: observing someone without their knowing is difficult. The best way to underscore this point is for you to think of the jobs at which you have worked. Seldom can an analyst observe a job being performed without being seen by employees. This is a problem because once employees know they are being watched, their behavior changes, which keeps an analyst from obtaining an accurate picture of the way jobs are done. When I was in college and working third shift at a bookbinding factory, the company hired an efficiency expert to analyze our performance. The expert arrived in a three-piece suit, armed with a stop watch and clipboard. He stuck out like a sore thumb! You can bet that for the two weeks the efficiency expert observed us, we were ideal employees (I can even remember calling my supervisor "sir") because we knew he was watching. Once he left, we went back to being our normal, time-wasting, soda-drinking, wise-cracking selves.

**Task Analysis**     Another commonly used job-analysis technique is **task analysis.** Task analysis involves compiling a list of tasks required to perform a job and then having job incumbents rate the task on several scales, such as frequency of occurrence, relative time spent, difficulty in performing, and importance. The trick to this technique is in compiling an accurate list of tasks. Such a list typically is developed by reading old job descriptions, observing workers, and interviewing incumbents and supervisors (Gael, 1983).

Once the task list has been created (which may include 200 tasks), incumbents rate each task. Tasks that receive ratings of importance, high frequency, or both are considered when writing job descriptions, developing training programs, and so on. Most **task inventories** are created with at least two scales. For example, consider the task "accurately shooting a gun." For a police officer, this task occurs infrequently, but when it does, its importance is paramount. If a frequency scale alone were used, shooting a gun might not be covered in training. Research suggests that many of the scales tap similar types of information (Sanchez & Fraser, 1992; Sanchez & Levine, 1989) and thus using the two scales of frequency of occurrence and importance should be sufficient. In fact, some researchers advise that rather than asking for ratings of frequency of occurrence or relative time spent on a task, the task inventory should simply ask "Do you perform this task?" (Wilson & Harvey, 1990).

It also has been suggested that a few tasks not part of a job be placed into the task inventory, and incumbents who rate these irrelevant tasks as part of their job can be removed from the job analysis due to their carelessness (Green & Stutzman, 1986). An example of a task inventory created for university-housing resident assistants is shown in Figure 3.2.

**Job Participation**     A job can be analyzed by actually performing it. This technique, called **job participation,** is especially useful because it is easier to understand every aspect of a job once you've done it yourself. The technique is easily used when the analyst has previously performed the job. An excellent candidate to use this technique would be a supervisor who has worked her way up through the ranks. However, as mentioned earlier, the problem with using a supervisor or an incumbent is that neither has been trained in job-analysis techniques.

A professional job analyst also can perform an unfamiliar job for a short period of time, although this, of course, is limited to certain occupations that involve quick training and minimal consequences from an error. The job of a brain surgeon probably would not be a good one to analyze using this method.

Figure 3.2
Example of a task
inventory

**Instructions**

Listed below are tasks that may be involved in your job. If you do not perform the task at all, circle 0. If you perform the task on occasion, circle 1. If you perform the task on at least a weekly basis, circle 2. If you perform the task at least daily, circle 3.

| Task | Rating | | | |
|------|--------|---|---|---|
| 1. Patrol floors to ensure that building is secure and safe. | 0 | 1 | 2 | 3 |
| 2. Write up residents who break rules. | 0 | 1 | 2 | 3 |
| 3. Advise residents having problems with roommates. | 0 | 1 | 2 | 3 |
| 4. Attend meetings of House Council. | 0 | 1 | 2 | 3 |
| 5. Design bulletin boards and posters. | 0 | 1 | 2 | 3 |
| 6. Issue keys to new residents. | 0 | 1 | 2 | 3 |
| 7. Change hallway light bulbs that have burned out. | 0 | 1 | 2 | 3 |

The analyst should spend enough time on the job to properly sample work behavior in addition to job difficulty. Yet spending long periods of time can be very expensive and still not guarantee that all aspects of behavior will be covered. Psychologist Wayman Mullins used job-participation techniques to analyze the job of a firefighter. Mullins spent two weeks living at the fire station and performing all the duties of a firefighter. The only problem during this two-week period? No fires. Thus, if Mullins had not already had a good idea of what a firefighter did, he would have concluded that the most important duties were sleeping, cleaning, cooking, and playing cards!

### Obtaining General Information about Tasks and Activities

The methods discussed in the previous section yield *specific* information about the tasks and activities performed by an incumbent in a *particular* job. Though such detailed information is ideal, obtaining it can be both time consuming and expensive. As an alternative, several questionnaires have been developed to analyze jobs at a more general level, which not only saves time and money, but allows jobs to be more easily compared with one another than is the case if interviews, observations, job participation, or task analysis are used.

**Position Analysis Questionnaire (PAQ)** The **Position Analysis Questionnaire (PAQ)** is a structured questionnaire that was developed at Purdue University by McCormick, Jeanneret, and Mecham (1972). The PAQ contains 194 items that are organized into six main dimensions: information input, mental processes, work output, relationships with other persons, job context, and other job-related variables such as work schedule, pay, and responsibility. Notice that in the sample PAQ page shown in Figure 3.3, the level of analysis is fairly general. That is, the PAQ tells us if a job involves interviewing but does not indicate the type of interviewing that is performed

**RELATIONSHIPS WITH OTHER PERSONS**

| Code Importance to This Job (I) |
|---|
| N Does not apply |
| 1 Very minor |
| 2 Low |
| 3 Average |
| 4 High |
| 5 Extreme |

**4  Relationships with Other Persons**
This section deals with different aspects of interaction between people involved in various kinds of work.

**4.1  Communications**
Rate the following in terms of how important the activity is to the completion of the job. Some jobs may involve several or all of the items in this section.

**4.1.1  Oral (communicating by speaking)**

99  I  Advising (dealing with individuals in order to counsel and/or guide them with regard to problems that may be resolved by legal, financial, scientific, technical, clinical, spiritual, and/or other professional principles)

100  I  Negotiating (dealing with others in order to reach an agreement or solution, for example, labor bargaining, diplomatic relations, etc.)

101  I  Persuading (dealing with others in order to influence them toward some action or point of view, for example, selling, political campaigning, etc.)

102  I  Instructing (the teaching of knowledge or skills, in either an informal or a formal manner, to others, for example, a public school teacher, a machinist teaching an apprentice, etc.)

103  I  Interviewing (conducting interviews directed toward some specific objective, for example, interviewing job applicants, census taking, etc.)

104  I  Routine information exchange: job related (the giving and/or receiving of job-related information of a routine nature, for example, ticket agent, taxicab dispatcher, receptionist, etc.)

105  I  Nonroutine information exchange (the giving and/or receiving of job-related information of a nonroutine or unusual nature, for example, professional committee meetings, engineers discussing new product design, etc.)

106  I  Public speaking (making speeches or formal presentations before relatively large audiences, for example, political addresses, radio/TV broadcasting, delivering a sermon, etc.)

**4.1.2  Written (communicating by written/printed material)**

107  I  Writing (for example, writing or dictating letters, reports, etc., writing copy for ads, writing newspaper articles, etc,: do not include transcribing activities described in item 43, but only activities in which the incumbent creates the written material)

**4.1.3  Other Communications**

108  I  Signaling (communicating by some type of signal, for example, hand signals, semaphore, whistles, horns, bells, lights, etc.)

109  I  Code communications (telegraph, cryptography, etc.)

**Figure 3.3** Example of PAQ questions

Source: E. J. McCormick, P. R. Jeannert, & R. C. Mecham, *Position Analysis Questionnaire,* copyright 1969 by Purdue Research Foundation, West Lafayette, Indiana 47907. Reprinted with permission of the publisher.

(interviewing job applicants versus interviewing a witness to a crime) nor how the interview is conducted. Thus, the results would be difficult to use for functions such as training or performance appraisal.

The PAQ offers many advantages. It is inexpensive and takes relatively little time to use (Levine, Ash, & Bennett, 1980). It is one of the most standardized job-analysis methods, and its results for a particular position can be compared through computer analysis with thousands of other positions. Furthermore, it is both reliable (Taylor, 1978) and robust (Jones, Main, Butler, & Johnson, 1982). In one survey, the PAQ was rated by experienced job analysts as being the most useful of the standardized techniques for job evaluation (Levine, Ash, Hall, & Sistrunk, 1983).

Although the PAQ has considerable support, research indicates its strengths are also the source of its weaknesses.

The PAQ's instructions suggest that incumbents using the questionnaire have education levels between grades 10 and 12. Research has found, however, that the PAQ questions and directions are written at the college-graduate level (Ash & Edgell, 1975); thus, many workers may not be able to understand the PAQ.

In addition, the PAQ was designed to cover all jobs, but, limited to 194 questions and six dimensions, the PAQ has not proven very sensitive. For example, a homemaker and a police officer have similar PAQ profiles (Arvey & Begalla, 1975). Similar profiles also are obtained regardless of whether an analyst actually observes the job or just looks at a job title (Smith & Hakel, 1979) or a job description (Friedman & Harvey, 1986; Jones, Main, Butler, & Johnson, 1982).

Finally, having a large amount of information about a job yields the same results as having little information (Arvey, Davis, McGowen, & Dipboye, 1982; Surrette, Aamodt, & Johnson, 1990). Although these studies speak favorably about the reliability of the PAQ, they also provide cause to worry because the PAQ appears to yield the same results regardless of how familiar the analyst is with a job. DeNisi, Cornelius, and Blencoe (1987), however, have suggested that even though job experts and nonexperts agree on whether or not a job involves a certain task, they disagree about the degree of the task's involvement.

**Job Structure Profile (JSP)**   A revised version of the PAQ was developed by Patrick and Moore (1985). The major changes in the revision, which is called the **Job Structure Profile (JSP),** include item content and style, new items to increase the discriminatory power of the intellectual and decision-making dimensions, and an emphasis on having a job analyst, rather than the incumbent, use the JSP. Research by JSP's developers has indicated that the instrument is reliable, but further research is needed before it is known whether the JSP is a legitimate improvement over the PAQ.

**Job Elements Inventory (JEI)**   Another method designed as an alternative to the PAQ is the **Job Element Inventory (JEI)** developed by Cornelius and Hakel (1978). The JEI contains 153 items and has a readability level

**Figure 3.4**
Sample elements
from the job ele-
ment inventory

Use visual displays

Answer questions from others

Contact high officials

Judge distances

Treat the sick or injured

Work in a cramped space

appropriate for an employee with only a 10th-grade education (Cornelius, Hakel, & Sackett, 1979). Research comparing the JEI with the PAQ indicates that the scores from each method are very similar (Harvey, Friedman, Hakel, & Cornelius, 1988); thus, the JEI may be a better replacement for the difficult-to-read PAQ. But as mentioned with the JSP, much more research is needed before conclusions can be confidently drawn. A list of sample elements from the JEI is shown in Figure 3.4.

**Functional Job Analysis (FJA)** **Functional Job Analysis (FJA)** was designed by Fine (1955) as a quick method that could be used by the federal government to analyze and compare thousands of jobs. All of the jobs listed in the DOT were analyzed using FJA. Although rarely used in industry, FJA is important to understand for two reasons. First, it serves as the base for the DOT, and, as discussed earlier in the chapter, DOT codes must be used on many occasions when dealing with the federal government. Second, FJA is the job-analysis foundation upon which many government validity generalization programs using the **General Aptitude Test Battery (GATB)** are based.

Jobs analyzed by FJA are broken down into the percentage of time the incumbent spends on three functions: data (information and ideas), people (clients, customers, and co-workers), and things (machines, tools, and equipment). An analyst is given 100 points to allot to the three functions. The points are usually assigned in multiples of 5, with each function receiving a minimum of 5 points. Once the points have been assigned, the highest level at which the job incumbent functions is then chosen from the chart shown back in Table 3.1 (Fine & Wiley, 1971).

### Obtaining Information about Tools and Equipment

**Job Components Inventory (JCI)** To take advantage of the PAQ's strengths while avoiding some of its problems, Banks, Jackson, Stafford, and Warr (1983) developed the **Job Components Inventory (JCI)** for use in England. The JCI consists of more than 400 questions covering five major categories: tools and equipment, perceptual and physical requirements, mathematical requirements, communication requirements, and decision making and responsibility. It is the only job-analysis method containing a detailed section on tools and equipment. An example of one JCI question is shown in Figure 3.5.

Because the JCI is fairly new, the published research on its use is not abundant. But it does appear to be a promising technique, with research indicating that it is reliable (Banks & Miller, 1984), can differentiate between jobs (Banks, Jackson, Stafford, & Warr, 1983), can cluster jobs based on their similarity to one another (Stafford, Jackson, & Banks, 1984), and, contrary to the PAQ, is affected by the amount of information available to the analyst (Surrette, Aamodt, & Johnson, 1990).

## DO YOU OPERATE PRINTING EQUIPMENT?

FOR EXAMPLE:

01   DUPLICATORS

02   SPIRIT DUPLICATORS

03   PHOTOCOPYING MACHINES

04   ADDRESSOGRAPH MACHINES

05   SCREEN PRINTING

06   PRINTING STENCILS

07   COLLATING MACHINES

08   FOLDING MACHINES

ANY OTHERS?

WHAT FOR?

A22.

**Figure 3.5**
JCI questions

Source: Banks, M. H., Jackson, P. R., Stafford, E. M., & Warr, P. B. (1983). The Job Components Inventory and the analysis of jobs requiring limited skill. *Personnel Psychology, 36,* 57–66. Reprinted with permission of the authors.

Some jobs require great physical stamina.

### *Obtaining Information about the Work Environment*

The techniques discussed so far provide information about the activities that are performed and the equipment used to perform them. The job analyst still needs information about the conditions under which the activities are performed. For example, two employees might perform the task "delivers mail," yet one might do it by carrying 50-pound mail bags in very hot weather while the other delivers mail by driving a golf cart through an air conditioned warehouse. To obtain information about the work environment, a job analyst might use the **AET,** an acronym for *Arbeitswissenschaftliches Erhebungsverfahren zur Tatigkeitsanalyse,* which means "ergonomic job-analysis procedure." By *ergonomic,* we mean that it is primarily concerned with the relationship between the worker and work objects. Developed in Germany by Rohmert and Landau (1983), the AET is a 216-item standardized questionnaire that analyzes a job along the dimensions shown in Figure 3.6. Sample items from the AET can be found in Figure 3.7. Although the AET appears to be a promising method for obtaining certain types of job-analysis information, there has not been enough published research to draw any real conclusions.

**Part A   Work System Analysis**
1  Work objects
   1.1  material work objects (physical condition, special properties of the material, quality of surfaces, manipulation delicacy, form, size, weight, dangerousness)
   1.2  energy as work object
   1.3  information as work object
   1.4  man, animals, plants as work objects
2  Equipment
   2.1  working equipment
      2.1.1  equipment, tools, machinery to change the properties of work objects
      2.1.2  means of transport
      2.1.3  controls
   2.2  other equipment
      2.2.1  displays, measuring instruments
      2.2.2  technical aids to support human sense organs
      2.2.3  work chair, table, room
3  Work environment
   3.1  Physical environment
      3.1.1  environmental influences
      3.1.2  dangerousness of work and risk of occupational diseases
   3.2  Organizational and social environment
      3.2.1  temporal organization of work
      3.2.2  position in the organization of work sequence
      3.2.3  hierarchical position in the organization
      3.2.4  position in the communication system
   3.3  Principles and methods of remuneration
      3.3.1  principles of remuneration
      3.3.2  methods of remuneration

**Part B   Task Analysis**
1  Tasks relating to material work objects
2  Tasks relating to abstract work objects
3  Man-related tasks
4  Number and repetitiveness of tasks

**Part C   Job Demand Analysis**
1  Demands on perception
   1.1  mode of perception
      1.1.1  visual
      1.1.2  auditory
      1.1.3  tactile
      1.1.4  olfactory
      1.1.5  proprioceptive
   1.2  absolute/relative evaluation of perceived information
   1.3  accuracy of perception
2  Demands for decision
   2.1  complexity of decision
   2.2  pressure of time
   2.3  required knowledge
3  Demands for response/activity
   3.1  body postures
   3.2  static work
   3.3  heavy muscular work
   3.4  light muscular work
   3.5  strenuousness and frequency of movements

**Figure 3.6**  AET dimensions

Source: Rohmert, W., & Landau, K. (1983). *A new technique for job analysis.* New York: Taylor & Francis. Reprinted with permission of the publisher.

**Figure 3.7**
Sample AET items

Source: Rohmert, W., & Landau, K. (1983). *A new technique for job analysis.* New York: Taylor & Francis. Reprinted with permission of the publisher.

CNO    CC
1.1.7    Weight

Answer questions 22–24 indicating the individual proportions of *time* during which the incumbent performs tasks involving work materials of *different weights.*

22    D    *Low* weight
objects weighing up to 1 kg can normally be manipulated with fingers or hands

23    D    *Medium* weight
1–10 kg can normally be manipulated with hands

24    *Heavy* weight
more than 10 kg can partly be manipulated by one person without using additional auxiliaries, partly including the use of handling equipment and hoisting machines

1.1.8    Danger

Answer questions 25–30 indicating the individual proportions of *time* during which the incumbent performs tasks involving *dangerous work materials.*

25    D    Work materials that are *explosive*
e.g., explosives and igniting mixtures, ammunition, fireworks

26    D    Work materials that are *conducive to fire or inflammable*
e.g., petrol, technical oils, lacquers, and varnishes

27    D    Work materials that are *poisonous or caustic*
e.g., basic chemicals, chemical-technical materials, plant protectives, cleaning materials

28    D    Work materials that are *radioactive*
e.g., uranium concentrate, nuclear materials

29    D    Work materials *irritating skin or mucous membrane*
e.g., quartz, asbestos, Thomas meal, flax, raw cotton

30    D    Work materials *causing other health hazards*
If characteristic 1 is rated D = 5, continue with characteristic 34.

## Obtaining Information about KSAOs

The techniques in this section provide information about the KSAOs needed to perform the tasks and use the equipment identified by the job-analysis techniques discussed previously.

**Critical Incident Technique**    The **Critical Incident Technique (CIT)** was first developed and used by John Flanagan and his students at the University of Pittsburgh in the late 1940s and early 1950s. The CIT is used to discover actual incidents of job behavior that make the difference between a job's successful and unsuccessful performance (Flanagan, 1954). This technique can be conducted in many ways, but the basic procedure is as follows:

1. Job incumbents each generate between one and five incidents of both excellent and poor performance they have seen on the job. These incidents can be obtained in many ways — log books, questionnaires, interviews, and so on; research has shown that the method used makes little difference (Campion, Greener, & Wernli, 1973), although questionnaires are usually used because they are easiest. A convenient way to word requests for critical incidents is by asking incumbents to think of times they saw workers perform in an especially outstanding way and then to write down exactly what occurred. Incumbents are then asked to do the same for times they saw workers perform poorly. This process is repeated as needed. Two examples of critical incidents are shown in Figure 3.8.

2. Job experts examine each incident and decide whether it is an example of excellent or poor behavior. This step is necessary because approximately 5% of incidents initially cited as poor examples by employees are actually excellent examples and vice versa (Aamodt, Reardon, & Kimbrough, 1986). For example, in a recent job analysis of the position of university instructor, a few students described their worst teachers as those who lectured from material not included in their textbooks. A committee of faculty members and students who reviewed the incidents determined that lecturing from nontext material actually was excellent. Thus, the incidents were counted as examples of excellent rather than poor performance.

3. The incidents generated in the first stage are then given to three or four incumbents to sort into an unspecified number of categories. The incidents in each category are then read by the job analyst, who combines, names, and defines the categories.

4. To verify the judgments made by the job analyst in Step 3, three other incumbents are given the incidents and category names and asked to sort the incidents into the newly created categories. If two of the three incumbents sort an incident into the same category, the incident is considered part of that category. Any incident that is not agreed upon by two sorters is either thrown out or placed into a new category.

5. The numbers of both types of incidents sorted into each category are then tallied and used to create a table similar to Table 3.3. The categories provide the important dimensions of a job, and the numbers provide the relative importance of these dimensions.

The CIT is an excellent addition to a job analysis because the actual critical incidents can be used for future activities such as performance appraisal (Smith & Kendall, 1963) and training (Glickman & Vallance, 1958). The CIT's greatest drawback is that its stress on the difference between excellent and poor performance ignores routine duties. Thus, the CIT cannot be used as the sole method of job analysis.

**Figure 3.8**
Critical incident examples

About a year ago, I was driving home from school and had a flat tire. I was having trouble changing the tire, when the police officer stopped and helped me. He then followed me to the nearest gas station to make sure that I didn't have any more trouble. Most cops probably wouldn't have done a darn thing to help.

I got pulled over for doing 45 in a 25 MPH zone. Instead of just writing me up, the cop told me what a jerk I was for speeding and that if he ever saw me speed again, I would get more than a ticket. He was the one who was the jerk!

**Table 3.3**  CIT categories and frequencies for excellent and poor resident assistants

| Category | Excellent | Poor | Total |
|---|---|---|---|
| Interest in residents | 31 | 19 | 50 |
| Availability | 14 | 27 | 41 |
| Responsibility | 12 | 20 | 32 |
| Fairness | 18 | 10 | 28 |
| Self-adherence to the rules | 0 | 28 | 28 |
| Social skills | 19 | 7 | 26 |
| Programming | 13 | 7 | 20 |
| Self-confidence | 12 | 8 | 20 |
| Rule enforcement | 4 | 14 | 18 |
| Authoritarianism | 1 | 16 | 17 |
| Counseling skills | 12 | 4 | 16 |
| Self-control | 5 | 2 | 7 |
| Confidentiality | 1 | 2 | 3 |

**Table 3.4**   Example of threshold traits analysis

| Problem Solving | | | |
|---|---|---|---|
| **Job functions include** | | **Incumbent must** | |
| *Processing information* to reach specific conclusions, answering problems, adapting and assessing ideas of others, and revising into workable form. | | Analyze information and, by inductive reasoning, arrive at a specific conclusion or solution (trait also known as *convergent thinking, reasoning*). | |
| Level | Job activities that require solving | Level | Incumbent must solve |
| 0 | Very minor problems with fairly simple solutions (running out of supplies or giving directions). | 0 | Very minor problems with fairly simple solutions. |
| 1 | Problems with known and limited variables (diagnosing mechanical disorders or customer complaints). | 1 | Problems with known and limited variables. |
| 2 | More complex problems with many known variables (programming or investment analysis). | 2 | Problems with many known and complex variables. |
| 3 | Very complex and abstract problems with many unknown variables (advanced systems design or research). | 3 | Very complex and abstract problems with many unknown variables. |

Source: Adapted from Lopez, F. M., Kesselman, G. A., & Lopez, F. E. (1981). An empirical test of a trait-oriented job analysis technique. *Personnel Psychology, 34,* 479–502. Reprinted with permission of authors.

**Job Components Inventory (JCI)**   Discussed earlier, in addition to information about tools and equipment used on the job, the JCI also provides information about the perceptual, physical, mathematical, communication, decision-making, and responsibility skills needed to perform the job.

**Threshold Traits Analysis (TTA)**   An approach similar to the JCI is **Threshold Traits Analysis (TTA),** which was developed by Lopez, Kesselman, and Lopez (1981). Its unique style makes it worthy of mentioning. The TTA questionnaire's 33 items identify the traits that are necessary for the successful performance of a job. The 33 items cover five trait categories: physical, mental, learned, motivational, and social. Examples of the items and their trait categories can be found in Tables 3.4 and 3.5. The TTA's greatest advantages are that it is short, reliable, and can correctly identify important traits (Lopez, Kesselman, & Lopez, 1981). TTA's greatest disadvantage is that it is not available commercially. Because the TTA also focuses on traits, its main uses would be in the development of an employee-selection system or a career plan (Lopez, Rockmore, & Kesselman, 1980).

**Fleishman Job Analysis Survey (F-JAS)**   Based on over 30 years of research (Fleishman & Reilly, 1992), the **Fleishman Job Analysis Survey (F-JAS)** requires incumbents or job analysts to view a series of abilities,

**Table 3.5** Threshold traits analysis categories

| Area | Job Functions | Trait | Description: Can |
|---|---|---|---|
| Physical | Physical exertion | 1 Strength | Lift, pull, or push objects |
| | | 2 Stamina | Expend physical energy for long periods |
| | Bodily activity | 3 Agility | React quickly; has good coordination |
| | Sensory inputs | 4 Vision | See details and color of objects |
| | | 5 Hearing | Recognize sound, tone, and pitch |
| Mental | Vigilance and attention | 6 Perception | Observe and differentiate details |
| | | 7 Concentration | Attend to details and distractions |
| | | 8 Memory | Retain and recall ideas |
| | Information processing | 9 Comprehension | Understand spoken and written ideas |
| | | 10 Problem solving | Reason and analyze abstract information |
| | | 11 Creativity | Produce new ideas and products |
| Learned | Quantitative computation | 12 Numerical computation | Solve arithmetic and mathematical problems |
| | Communications | 13 Oral expression | Speak clearly and effectively |
| | | 14 Written expression | Write clearly and effectively |
| | Action selection and projection | 15 Planning | Project a course of action |
| | | 16 Decision making | Choose a course of action |
| | Application of information | 17 Craft knowledge | Apply specialized information |
| | | 18 Craft skill | Perform a complex set of activities |

Source: Adapted from Lopez, F. M., Kesselman, G. A., & Lopez, F. E. (1981). An empirical test of a trait-oriented job analysis technique. *Personnel Psychology, 34,* 479–502. Reprinted with permission of authors.

such as the one shown in Figure 3.9, and rate the level of ability needed to perform the job. These ratings are performed for each of the 72 abilities and knowledge shown in Table 3.6. The F-JAS is easy to use, supported by years of research, and can be used by either incumbents or trained analysts. Its advantages over TTA are that it is more detailed and is commercially available. Its advantage over the CIT is that it is highly structured and thus more reliable and easier to use. It does not, however, have as many uses as the CIT.

**Job-element Approach** The **job-element approach** was developed by Ernest Primoff (1975) as a job-analysis system for use in the federal government. This

**Table 3.5**

| Area | Job Functions | Trait | Description: Can |
|---|---|---|---|
| Motivational | Working conditions | | |
| | Unprogrammed | 19 Adaptability — change | Adjust to interruptions and changes |
| | Cycled | 20 Adaptability — repetition | Adjust to repetitive activities |
| | Stressful | 21 Adaptability — pressure | Adjust to critical and demanding work |
| | Secluded | 22 Adaptability — isolation | Work alone or with little personal contact |
| | Unpleasant | 23 Adaptability — discomfort | Work in hot, cold, or noisy workplaces |
| | Dangerous | 24 Adaptability — hazards | Work in dangerous situations |
| | Absence of direct supervision | 25 Control — dependability | Work with minimum of supervision |
| | Presence of difficulties | 26 Control — perseverance | Stick to a task until completed |
| | Unstructured conditions | 27 Control — initiative | Act on own, take charge when needed |
| | Access to valuables | 28 Control — integrity | Observe regular ethical and moral codes |
| | Limited mobility | 29 Control — aspirations | Limit desire for promotion |
| Social | Interpersonal contact | 30 Personal appearance | Meet appropriate standards of dress |
| | | 31 Tolerance | Deal with people in tense situations |
| | | 32 Influence | Get people to cooperate |
| | | 33 Cooperation | Work as member of a team |

technique basically involves a group interview in which six incumbents generate job elements, which are properties such as KSAOs that are important in a job's performance. The resulting job elements are then rated on four variables:

1. The extent to which barely acceptable workers have the element
2. The importance of the element in picking out superior workers
3. How much trouble is likely to occur if the element is not considered
4. The practicality of requiring applicants to possess the element

For each element, the ratings of these four variables are combined in a rather complicated fashion to provide a number that indicates each element's

**Figure 3.9**
F-JAS example

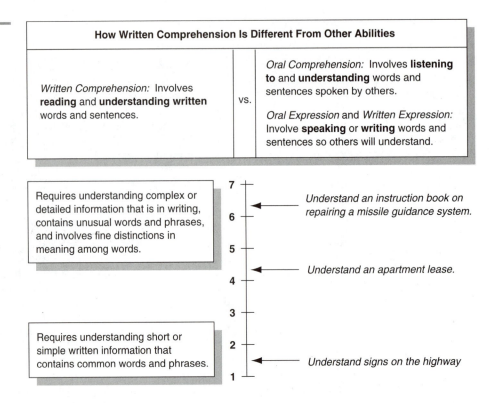

importance. These numerically weighted elements can be used to design an employee-selection system. The job-element approach is seldom used today but is mentioned in this text because of its unique rating scales and historic value (historic to job-analysis lovers, but probably not to anyone with a real life).

## EVALUATION OF METHODS

In the previous pages, many job-analysis methods were presented. But the question left unanswered is, which of the methods is best? Unfortunately, there is no clear answer to this question. The best method to use in analyzing a particular job depends on the end-use of the job-analysis information. That is, different methods are best for different uses—*worker-oriented methods,* such as CIT and TTA, are best for such uses as employee selection and performance appraisal; *Job-oriented methods,* such as task analysis, are best for such uses as work design and writing job descriptions. To get the most out of a job analysis, several techniques should be utilized (Rouleau & Krain, 1975). At least one of these methods should be worker oriented and one job-oriented (Prien, 1977).

From a legal perspective, courts have ruled that job analysis is necessary (Ledvinka & Schoenfeldt, 1978) and that acceptable job analyses should use several up-to-date sources, be conducted by experts, use a large number of job incumbents, and cover the entire range of worker activities and qualifi-

**Table 3.6**  F-JAS dimensions

| Cognitive Abilities | Physical Abilities | Interactive/Social Scales |
|---|---|---|
| Oral comprehension | Static strength | Persuasion |
| Written comprehension | Explosive strength | Social sensitivity |
| Oral expression | Dynamic strength | Oral fact finding |
| Written expression | Trunk strength | Oral defense |
| Fluency of ideas | Extent flexibility | Resistance to premature |
| Originality | Dynamic flexibility | judgment |
| Memorization | Gross body coordination | Persistence |
| Problem sensitivity | Gross body equilibrium | Resilience |
| Mathematical reasoning | Stamina | Behavior flexibility |
| Number facility | | Sales interest |
| Deductive reasoning | | |
| Inductive reasoning | Sensory Abilities | Knowledge/Skills Scales |
| Information ordering | | |
| Category flexibility | Near vision | Electrical/electronic |
| Speed of closure | Far vision | knowledge |
| Flexibility of closure | Visual color discrimination | Mechanical knowledge |
| Spatial orientation | Night vision | Knowledge of tools and uses |
| Visualization | Peripheral vision | Map reading |
| Perceptual speed | Depth perception | Drafting |
| Selective attention | Glare sensitivity | Reading plans |
| Time sharing | Hearing sensitivity | Driving |
| | Auditory attention | Typing |
| | Sound localization | Shorthand |
| Psychomotor Abilities | Speech recognition | Spelling |
| | Speech clarity | Grammar |
| Control precision | | |
| Multilimb coordination | | |
| Response orientation | | |
| Rate control | | |
| Reaction time | | |
| Arm-hand steadiness | | |
| Manual dexterity | | |
| Finger dexterity | | |
| Wrist-finger speed | | |
| Speed of limb movement | | |

cations (Thompson & Thompson, 1982). Interviews and the CIT seem to hold up well in court, while the job-elements approach does not (Kleiman & Faley, 1978; Thompson & Thompson, 1982).

Unfortunately, research directly comparing job-analysis methods is not abundant. This is primarily because direct comparison of methods is virtually impossible: each method yields results that differ in both the number and type of dimensions (Cornelius, Carron, & Collins, 1979). Thus, the comparative research that has been conducted has focused on opinions of job analysts.

Survey research by Levine, Ash, and their colleagues (Levine, Ash, & Bennett, 1980; Levine, Ash, Hall, & Sistrunk, 1983) has found the following:

1. PAQ is seen as the most standardized technique and CIT the least standardized.

2. CIT takes the least amount of job-analyst training, and task analysis takes the most.

3. PAQ is the least costly method, CIT the most.

4. PAQ takes the least amount of time to complete, task analysis the most.

5. Task analysis has the highest quality results, TTA the lowest.

6. Task-analysis reports are longest, job elements shortest.

7. CIT was rated at being the most useful, PAQ the least.

8. Task analysis gave the best overall job picture, PAQ the worst.

Keep in mind, however, that the above findings were based on users' opinions rather than actual empirical comparison.

# JOB EVALUATION

**Job evaluation** is the process of determining a job's *worth*. Such evaluation is important because most workers want to be paid fairly; that is, they want to be paid an amount equal to the actual worth of their particular job and also in amounts consistent with those paid to other workers in the same company (internal equity) as well as to workers in other organizations (external equity). Arriving at "fair and accurate" pay levels is difficult because most job-evaluation procedures determine the worth of a job based on the skill needed as well as on the demands that the job makes on the worker. But the results of job evaluations are often controversial because job-evaluation techniques do not take into account important factors that are not directly related to the job itself. These other factors include the status level of the job (physician versus hair stylist), intrinsic satisfaction of a job (teaching versus assembly-line work), local cost of living (California versus Arkansas), prevailing wage rates, and union agreements. With these limitations in mind, compensable job factors and the method of job evaluation—by ranking or by point—must be considered if the job evaluation is to be reasonable.

### DETERMINING INTERNAL PAY EQUITY

Internal pay equity involves comparing jobs within a company to ensure that people with jobs worth the most money are paid accordingly. The difficulty in this process, of course, is determining the worth of each job. Though a complete discussion of all job evaluation methods is beyond the scope of this text, two common methods, *ranking* and *point*, will be discussed.

On average, females still make less than males.

### Compensable Job Factors

The first step in evaluating a job is to decide what factors differentiate the relative worth of jobs. Possible **compensable job factors** include:

- Level of responsibility
- Physical demands
- Mental demands
- Educational requirements
- Training and experience requirements
- Working conditions
- Availability of workers in the workforce

The philosophical perspectives of the job evaluator can affect these factors. Some evaluators argue that the most important compensable factors are responsibility and education and the least important are physical demands; thus, the choice of compensable factors is often more philosophical than empirical.

### Choice of Methods

The second step in determining job worth is choosing which evaluation method to use. Just as there are many job-analysis techniques, there are many methods of job evaluation. The method used is determined by such factors as the number of jobs to be evaluated, the expertise of the person conducting the job evaluation, and the philosophical leaning of the person conducting the job evaluation.

**Ranking Method** The **ranking method** is the easiest to use and often is used in smaller organizations (Mann, 1965). Basically, jobs within an organization are rank ordered either on the basis of their perceived overall worth or compensable factors selected from the list in the previous section. If the latter method is used, the rankings for each factor are then summed to form an overall ranking. Overall rankings are then compared to the actual salaries that are paid to workers in each position. In Table 3.7, for example, the receptionist job has been ranked higher than the gardener job. In such a case, the salary for the receptionist would be raised above the gardener's. Although this method is excellent for assigning **relative amounts** of compensation, it does not yield enough information to determine **absolute amounts** of compensation. Furthermore, it is difficult to find individuals to do the ranking who are familiar enough with all of the jobs in an organization.

A more complicated version of the ranking method is the assignment of differential weights to each factor by a job-evaluation committee (Yoder & Heneman, 1979). The average ranks for each factor are then multiplied by the weight assigned to the factors. The products of these calculations are then summed to provide an overall rank order. Most of these calculations are done by computer programs purchased from consultants specializing in job evaluation. Typically, these programs already contain standard compensable factors and weights for each factor. Thus, the main job of the job-evaluation committee is to rank the jobs on each of the factors.

**Table 3.7** Example of ranking method of job evaluation

| Job | Rank | Previous Salary |
| --- | --- | --- |
| Manager | 1 | $30,000 |
| Assistant Manager | 2 | 22,000 |
| Salesperson | 3 | 18,000 |
| Secretary | 4 | 15,000 |
| Receptionist | 5 | 10,000 |
| Gardener | 6 | 12,000 |
| Janitor | 7 | 9,000 |

One version of this method, the **classification method,** is used by many governmental agencies including those of the federal government. In this version, jobs that are ranked near one another are grouped together to form several **grades.** Jobs within each grade level are considered to be of equal value and are paid at the same rate.

**Point Method**   The **point method** is the most commonly used method of job evaluation (Hills, 1987). To use this method, a five-step process is followed:

1. A job-evaluation committee determines the total number of points that will be distributed among the factors. Usually, the number is a multiple of 100 (for example, 100, 500, 1000) and is based on the number of compensable factors. The greater the number of factors, the greater the number of points.

2. Each factor is weighted by assigning different numbers of points to the factors. The more important the factor, the greater the number that will be assigned.

3. Each factor is divided into degrees. For example, if one of the factors is education, the degrees might be

   - High school education or less
   - Two years of college
   - Bachelor's degree
   - Master's degree
   - Ph.D.

   The number of points assigned to a factor is then divided into each of the degrees. If 100 points were assigned to the factor of education, then 20 points (100 points/5 degrees) would be assigned to each degree. An example of this procedure is shown in Table 3.8.

4. The job-evaluation committee takes the job descriptions for each job and assigns points based on the factors and degrees created in the previous steps.

5. The total number of points for a job is compared with the salary currently being paid for the job. This comparison is typically graphed in a fashion similar to the **wage trend line** shown in Figure 3.10. Wage trend lines are drawn based on the results of a regression formula in which salary is predicted by the number of job analysis points. Jobs whose point values fall below the line (as with job D's in Figure 3.10) are considered underpaid and are immediately assigned higher salary levels. Jobs with point values above the line (as with job H) are considered overpaid and the salary level is decreased once current jobholders leave.

**Other Methods**   A few other methods can be used to evaluate jobs. The **factor-comparison method** (Benge, Burk, & Hay, 1941), the job-components method, and **time span of discretion** (Jaques, 1961) are examples, but

**Table 3.8** Example of the point method of job evaluation

| Factors | Points |
|---|---|
| Education (200 points possible) | |
| High school education or less | 0 |
| Two years of college | 50 |
| Bachelor's degree | 100 |
| Master's degree | 150 |
| Ph.D. | 200 |
| Responsibility (300 points possible) | |
| Makes no decisions | 0 |
| Makes decisions for self | 100 |
| Makes decisions for 1–5 employees | 200 |
| Makes decisions for more than 5 employees | 300 |
| Physical demands (100 points possible) | |
| Lifts no heavy objects | 0 |
| Lifts objects between 25 and 100 pounds | 50 |
| Lifts objects more than 100 pounds | 100 |

because they are both complex and not commonly used, they will not be discussed here.

## DETERMINING EXTERNAL EQUITY

### Salary Surveys

The techniques described above are used to establish the **internal equity** of an organization's compensation plan. To recruit and retain employees, however, it is essential that an organization's compensation plan reflect **external equity.** In other words, it must be competitive with the compensation plans of other organizations. That is, a fast-food restaurant that pays cooks $6.00 per hour will probably have trouble hiring and keeping high-caliber employees if other fast-food restaurants in the area pay $7.00 per hour.

To determine external equity, organizations use **salary surveys.** Sent to other organizations, these surveys ask how much their organization pays their employees in various positions. An organization can either construct and send out its own survey or use the results of surveys conducted by trade groups, an option that many companies choose. A page from an actual salary survey is shown in Figure 3.11. Notice that in this survey, information about the gender and race of the incumbents has been requested. Such information is seldom requested in salary surveys but was included in this particular example because the trade group conducting the survey wanted industry-specific information about potential pay inequity.

Based on the results of these surveys, an organization can decide where it wants to be, called *market position,* when compared with the compensation policies of other organizations. That is, an organization might choose to offer compensation at higher levels to attract the best applicants as well as

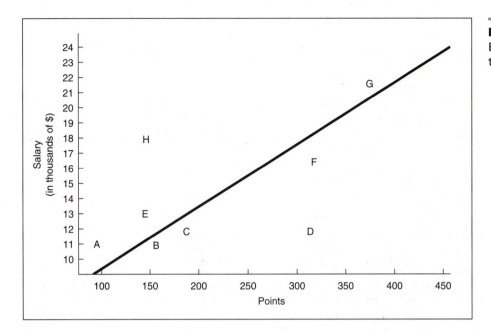

**Figure 3.10**
Example of a wage trend line

keep current employees from going to other organizations. Other organizations might choose to pay at the "going rate" so that they have a reasonable chance of competing for applicants, even though they will often lose the best applicants to higher-paying organizations. Market position is most important in a good economy where jobs are plentiful and applicants have several job options. It may seem surprising that competing organizations would supply salary information to each other, but because every organization needs salary data from other organizations, compensation analysts tend to cooperate well with one another.

Roanoke County, Virginia, provides an excellent example of the importance of market position. The county was concerned about the high turnover rate of its police dispatchers and undertook a study to determine the reason for the problem. Possible reasons were thought to be working conditions, location, reputation, and pay. The study revealed that most of the turnover was due to a neighboring city paying its dispatchers $2,500 more per year. This resulted in Roanoke County dispatchers resigning after a year of experience to take a higher-paying job only five miles away. Adjusting the salary greatly reduced the turnover rate.

Keep in mind that job evaluation concerns the worth of the *job itself*, not the worth of a *person* in the job. For example, suppose that a salary survey reveals that the going rate for a job falls within the range of $20,000 to $30,000, and an organization, deciding to be at the upper end of the market, sets its range for the position at $27,000 to $32,000. Decisions must then be made regarding where in the $5,000 range each particular employee will be paid. This decision is based on such factors as years of experience, years with the company, special skills, education, local cost of living, and performance level.

**Figure 3.11**
Example of a salary
survey

Job title: `Loan Interviewer`    Total number of employees in this position: _____

Job description

The loan interviewer is responsible for servicing credit
union members in reference to prospective loans by
accepting loan applications, interviewing loan applicants,
running credit reports, processing loan applications, and
communicating decision results to members.  The factor
that most differentiates a loan interviewer from a loan
clerk is the amount of contact with the public.

Annual salary range for position

   Minimum $__ __ , __ __ __          Maximum $__ __ , __ __ __

Compensation data for each employee in this position

| Incumbent number | Current actual annual salary | Sex of employee | Race of employee | Years in position | Education level |
|---|---|---|---|---|---|
| 01 | $__ __ , __ __ __ | _____ | _____ | _____ | _____ |
| 02 | $__ __ , __ __ __ | _____ | _____ | _____ | _____ |
| 03 | $__ __ , __ __ __ | _____ | _____ | _____ | _____ |
| 04 | $__ __ , __ __ __ | _____ | _____ | _____ | _____ |
| 05 | $__ __ , __ __ __ | _____ | _____ | _____ | _____ |
| 06 | $__ __ , __ __ __ | _____ | _____ | _____ | _____ |
| 07 | $__ __ , __ __ __ | _____ | _____ | _____ | _____ |
| 08 | $__ __ , __ __ __ | _____ | _____ | _____ | _____ |
| 09 | $__ __ , __ __ __ | _____ | _____ | _____ | _____ |
| 10 | $__ __ , __ __ __ | _____ | _____ | _____ | _____ |
| 11 | $__ __ , __ __ __ | _____ | _____ | _____ | _____ |
| 12 | $__ __ , __ __ __ | _____ | _____ | _____ | _____ |

In the previous few pages, we discussed the amount of money that a job is worth: this amount is called **direct compensation.** Employees are also compensated in other ways, such as pay for time not worked (for example, holidays, vacation, sick days), deferred income (for example, social security and pension plans), health protection, such as medical and dental insurance, and perquisites (perks), such as a company car (Henderson, 1994). Consequently, a job with a direct compensation of $30,000 might actually be worth more than one at $35,000 because of the *indirect compensation* package. In fact, any time I complain to my neighbors about low faculty salaries,

**Table 3.9** Salary levels of women as percentage of men's salaries, and women's share of total employment in selected occupations, 1981

| Occupation | Female–Male Pay Ratio[a] | Female Share of Total Employment |
|---|---|---|
| **Professional** | | |
| Accountant | 83 | 23% |
| Auditor | 86 | 22 |
| Attorney | 78 | 15 |
| Chemist | 75 | 14 |
| **Administrative** | | |
| Director of personnel | 87 | 13 |
| Job analyst | 79 | 62 |
| Buyer | 80 | 20 |
| **Technical** | | |
| Engineering technician | 85 | 8 |
| Drafter | 82 | 13 |
| Computer operator | 92 | 34 |
| Photographer | 80 | 7 |
| **Clerical** | | |
| Accounting clerk | 82 | 92 |
| Messenger | 101 | 46 |
| Purchasing assistant | 74 | 85 |

Source: Sieling, M. S. (1984). Staffing patterns prominent in female–male earnings gap. *Monthly Labor Review, 107*(6), 29.

[a]Includes data only for workers identified by sex.

they shed few tears as they mention such benefits as three-week Christmas vacations and three-month summer holidays.

## PAY EQUITY FOR PROTECTED CLASSES

In addition to internal and external equity, pay audits should also be conducted to ensure that employees are not paid differently based on gender or race. Two types of audits should be conducted: one that looks at pay rates of employees within positions with identical or similar duties (equal pay for equal work) and a second that looks at pay rates of employees in jobs of similar worth as determined by the job evaluation process (comparable worth).

**Comparable worth** is an issue very much related to the discussion of job evaluation. Recently, comparable worth has been in the news because some groups claim that female workers are paid less than male workers. This perception of pay inequity stems from the statistic that, on average, female workers in 1993 were paid only 72% of what male workers were paid (U.S. Department of Labor, 1993). But as Table 3.9 shows, this statistic is misleading.

**Table 3.10** Salary level by sex and occupational level

| Occupational Work Level | Average Monthly Salary[a] | Female–Male Pay Relationship[b] | Female Share of Total Employment |
|---|---|---|---|
| Professional | | | |
| Accountant I | $1,372 | 99 | 46% |
| Accountant II | 1,679 | 98 | 34 |
| Accountant III | 1,962 | 96 | 19 |
| Accountant IV | 2,402 | 95 | 11 |
| Accountant V | 2,928 | 90 | 5 |
| Auditor I | 1,364 | 98 | 36 |
| Auditor II | 1,651 | 97 | 27 |
| Auditor III | 2,033 | 92 | 21 |
| Auditor IV | 2,456 | 90 | 8 |
| Attorney I | 1,873 | 103 | 28 |
| Attorney II | 2,338 | 99 | 24 |
| Attorney III | 3,031 | 95 | 13 |
| Attorney IV | 3,738 | 94 | 9 |
| Chemist I | 1,508 | 96 | 38 |
| Chemist II | 1,757 | 94 | 29 |
| Chemist III | 2,120 | 93 | 15 |
| Chemist IV | 2,567 | 92 | 10 |
| Administrative | | | |
| Buyer I | 1,350 | 96 | 52 |
| Buyer II | 1,089 | 95 | 23 |
| Buyer III | 2,100 | 92 | 9 |
| Director of personnel I | 2,321 | 101 | 21 |
| Director of personnel II | 2,933 | 94 | 10 |
| Director of personnel III | 3,574 | 90 | 7 |
| Job analyst I | 1,412 | 87 | 75 |
| Job analyst II | 1,525 | 92 | 85 |
| Job analyst III | 1,900 | 90 | 66 |
| Job analyst IV | 2,393 | 94 | 29 |

Source: Sieling, M.S. (1984). Staffing patterns prominent in female–male earnings gap. *Monthly Labor Review, 107*(6), 29.
[a]Includes data for workers not identified by sex.
[b]Includes data only for workers identified by sex.

When males and females in the same jobs are compared, this percentage increases to around 80%. Often not taken into account in these statistics are that males have been in the workforce longer, have a higher percentage of full-time jobs, and have a higher percentage of college degrees (Mellor, 1984). As shown in Table 3.10, when males and females are compared in *identical* jobs with identical requirements, the percentage is approximately

**Table 3.10**

| Occupational Work Level | Average Monthly Salary[a] | Female–Male Pay Relationship[b] | Female Share of Total Employment |
|---|---|---|---|
| Technical | | | |
| Engineering technician I | $1,137 | 97 | 24% |
| Engineering technician II | 1,307 | 98 | 17 |
| Engineering technician III | 1,527 | 97 | 9 |
| Drafter I | 923 | 103 | 34 |
| Drafter II | 1,075 | 101 | 26 |
| Drafter III | 1,301 | 96 | 18 |
| Drafter IV | 1,611 | 94 | 8 |
| Computer operator I | 906 | 99 | 37 |
| Computer operator II | 1,049 | 102 | 49 |
| Computer operator III | 1,220 | 97 | 35 |
| Computer operator IV | 1,475 | 97 | 24 |
| Computer operator V | 1,733 | 92 | 17 |
| Photographer II | 1,425 | 96 | 6 |
| Photographer III | 1,704 | 106 | 5 |
| Clerical | | | |
| Accounting clerk I | 798 | 94 | 95 |
| Accounting clerk II | 953 | 89 | 94 |
| Accounting clerk III | 1,121 | 89 | 91 |
| Accounting clerk IV | 1,407 | 84 | 82 |
| Purchasing assistant I | 1,002 | 93 | 95 |
| Purchasing assistant II | 1,278 | 87 | 84 |
| Messenger | 783 | 101 | 46 |

95%. Thus, the issue of comparable worth is often less an issue of pay discrimination than one of vocational choice and educational opportunity discrimination. To alleviate gender differences in pay, it is essential that young females be encouraged to enter historically male-dominated fields (assembly lines, management, police) and that young males be encouraged to enter historically female-dominated fields (nursing, clerical, elementary education).

# CHAPTER SUMMARY

The first section of this chapter discussed the job-analysis process. Even if job analysis were not legally required, it would still be useful in such areas as performance appraisal, employee selection, training, and job design. Before a job analysis is begun, decisions must be made about the type of information that will be obtained, who will conduct the job analysis, and who will participate in it. These are important decisions: Research indicates that different types of people and different types of information collected will result in different job-analysis outcomes.

The chapter also discussed 14 different methods of job analysis. Although no method is always better than another, each is better for certain purposes. For example, the PAQ is an excellent method for compensation uses, and the CIT is an excellent method for performance appraisal.

When a job analysis is completed, job descriptions can be written. A good job-description format includes a job title, a brief summary of the job, and information about work activities, tools and equipment, the work context, performance standards, and the personal requirements that are needed to perform the job.

The second section of the chapter discussed job evaluation—the process of assigning a monetary value to a job. This process can be accomplished by first choosing compensable factors and then using a job evaluation method such as the point or ranking method to determine the relative worth of the job. Salary surveys are used to determine how competitive an organization's compensation plan is relative to other organizations.

# GLOSSARY

**Absolute amounts**   The actual salary paid for a particular job.

**AET**   An ergonomic job-analysis method developed in Germany.

**Ammerman Technique**   A job-analysis method in which a group of job experts identifies the objectives and standards that are to be met by the ideal incumbent.

**Classification method**   A job-evaluation system in which jobs of similar worth are placed into the same category and are paid at the same level.

**Comparable worth**   The idea that jobs requiring the same level of skill and responsibility should be paid the same regardless of supply and demand.

**Compensable job factors**   Factors, such as responsibility and educational requirements, that differentiate the relative worth of jobs.

**Critical Incident Technique (CIT)**   A job-analysis method developed by John Flanagan that utilizes written reports of excellent and poor employee behavior.

**Dictionary of Occupational Titles (DOT)**   A directory published by the federal government that supplies information for almost 30,000 jobs.

**Direct compensation**  The amount of money paid to an employee (does not count benefits, time-off, and so on).

**Dot Code**  The number assigned to each job listed in the Dictionary of Occupational Titles.

**External equity**  The extent to which employees within an organization are paid fairly compared to employees in other organizations.

**Factor-comparison method**  A job-evaluation technique in which dollar amounts rather than point values are assigned to jobs.

**Fleishman Job Analysis Survey (F-JAS)**  A job-analysis method in which jobs are rated based on the abilities needed to perform them.

**Functional Job Analysis (FJA)**  A job-analysis method developed by Fine that rates the extent to which a job incumbent is involved with functions in the categories of data, people, and things.

**General Aptitude Test Battery (GATB)**  The most commonly used ability test to select employees.

**Grade**  A cluster of jobs of similar worth.

**Internal equity**  The extent to which employees within an organization are paid fairly compared to other employees within the same organization.

**Job analysis**  The process of identifying how a job is performed as well as the requirements that it takes to perform the job.

**Job-analysis interview**  Obtaining information about a job by talking to the person performing the job.

**Job analyst**  The person conducting the job analysis.

**Job Components Inventory (JCI)**  A structured job-analysis technique developed by Banks that concentrates on worker requirements for performing a job rather than on specific tasks.

**Job description**  A written summary of the tasks performed in a job, the conditions under which the job is performed, and the requirements needed to perform the job.

**Job-element approach**  A job-analysis method developed by Primoff that involves the identification and rating of job elements.

**Job Element Inventory (JEI)**  A structured job-analysis technique developed by Cornelius and Hakel that is similar to the PAQ but easier to read.

**Job elements**  Used in the job-element approach, job elements are factors such as knowledge, skills, and abilities that are important to the performance of a job.

**Job evaluation**  The process of determining the monetary worth of a job.

**Job participation**  A job-analysis method in which the job analyst actually performs the job being analyzed.

**Job specifications**  The knowledge, skills, and abilities needed to successfully perform a job.

**Job Structure Profile (JSP)**  A revised version of the PAQ designed to be used more by the job analyst than the job incumbent.

**KSAOs**  Acronym for knowledge, skills, abilities, and other characteristics required to perform a job.

**Observation**  A job-analysis method in which the job analyst watches job incumbents perform their jobs.

**Peter Principle**   The idea that organizations tend to promote good employees until they reach the level at which they are not competent; in other words, their highest level of incompetence.

**Point method**   A job-evaluation system in which jobs are assigned points across several compensable factors to determine the worth of the job.

**Position Analysis Questionnaire (PAQ)**   A structured job-analysis method developed by McCormick.

**Ranking method**   Job-evaluation technique in which jobs in an organization are rank ordered based on their perceived worth.

**Relative amounts**   The relationship of one salary to another (for example, a secretary being paid more than a clerk).

**Salary survey**   A questionnaire sent to other organizations to see how much they are paying their employees in positions similar to those in the organization sending the survey.

**Task analysis**   A job-analysis method in which the job analyst identifies the tasks that are performed on the job.

**Task inventory**   A questionnaire containing a list of tasks for which the job incumbent rates each task on a series of scales such as importance and time spent.

**Threshold Traits Analysis (TTA)**   A 33-item questionnaire developed by Lopez that is designed to identify traits necessary to successfully perform a job.

**Time span of discretion**   A job-evaluation technique in which the worth of a job is determined by the length of time an employee goes without receiving direction from a supervisor.

**Wage trend line**   A line that represents the ideal relationship between the number of points that a job has been assigned (using the point method of evaluation) and the salary range for that job.

# 4

# EVALUATING SELECTION TECHNIQUES AND DECISIONS

In Chapter 2, you learned that many laws and regulations affect employee selection methods. In Chapters 5 and 6, recruiting and selecting employees will be discussed. Before we can discuss the available methods of selection, you need to know what determines the fairness and usefulness of a selection technique or decision. This chapter discusses *how to evaluate* the effectiveness, fairness, and usefulness of employee-selection techniques. Throughout this chapter you will encounter the word *test*. Though this word often conjures up an image of a paper-and-pencil test, in I/O psychology we use *test* to mean any technique used to evaluate someone. Thus, employment tests include such methods as references, interviews, and assessment centers.

# CHARACTERISTICS OF EFFECTIVE SELECTION TECHNIQUES

## RELIABILITY

**Reliability** is the extent to which a score from a test is stable and free from error. If a test score is not stable or error free, it is not useful. For example, suppose that we are using a ruler to measure the lengths of boards that will be used to build a doghouse. We want each board to be 4 feet long, but each time we measure a board, we get a different number. If the ruler does not yield the same number each time the same board is measured, the ruler cannot be considered reliable and, thus, is of no use. The same is true of employment tests. If test-takers score differently each time they take a test, we are unsure of their actual scores. Consequently, the scores from the tests are of little value. Therefore, reliability is an essential characteristic of an effective test.

### Characteristics Related to Test Reliability

**Test Length**   In general, the longer the test, the higher its **internal reliability,** that is, the agreement among responses to the various test items (Cureton, 1965). To illustrate this point, let us look at the final exam for this course. If the final were based on three chapters, would you want a test consisting of only three multiple-choice items? Probably not. If you make a careless mistake in marking your answer or fell asleep during part of the lecture from which a question was taken, your score will be low. But if the test has 100 items, one careless mistake or one missed part of a lecture will not severely affect the total score.

**Homogeneity of Test Items**   Another factor that can affect the internal reliability of a test is **item homogeneity.** That is, do all of the items measure the same thing or do they measure different constructs? The more homogeneous the items, the higher the internal reliability. To illustrate this concept, let us again look at your final exam based on three chapters.

If we computed the reliability of the entire exam, it would probably be relatively low. Why? Because the test items are not homogeneous. They are measuring knowledge from three topic areas (three chapters), two sources (lecture and text), and two knowledge types (factual and conceptual). If we broke the test down by chapter, source, and item type, the reliability of the separate test components would be higher because we are looking at groups of homogeneous items.

**Scorer Reliability**   A final factor that can affect a test's reliability is **scorer reliability.** A test can have homogeneous items and yield heterogeneous scores and still not be reliable if the person scoring the test makes mistakes. Scorer reliability is an issue especially in projective or subjective tests in which there is no one correct answer, but even tests scored with the use of keys suffer from scorer mistakes.

When human judgment of performance is involved, scorer reliability is discussed in terms of *interrater reliability*. That is, will two interviewers give an applicant similar ratings or will two supervisors give an employee similar performance ratings?

### Determining the Reliability of a Test

Test reliability is determined in three ways: test-retest reliability, alternate-forms reliability, and internal reliability. Each of these techniques will be discussed in the sections that follow.

**Test-Retest Reliability**   With the **test-retest reliability** method, several people take the same test twice. The scores from the first administration of the test are correlated with scores from the second to determine whether they are similar. If they are, the test is said to have **temporal stability**: The test scores are stable across time and not highly susceptible to random daily conditions such as illness, fatigue, stress, or uncomfortable testing conditions (Anastasi, 1988). There is no standard amount of time that should elapse between the two administrations of the test. The time interval should be long enough, however, so that the specific test answers have not been memorized but short enough so that the person has not changed significantly.

For example, if three years have elapsed between administrations of a personality test, there may be a very low correlation between the two sets of scores; but the low correlation may not be the result of low test reliability. Instead, it could be caused by personality changes of the people in the sample over time. This is a problem especially when the sample used in the reliability study is composed of young people (Pinneau, 1961). Likewise, if only 10 minutes separate the two administrations, a very high correlation between the two sets of scores might occur. This high correlation may only represent what the people remembered from the first testing rather than what they actually believe. Typical time intervals between test administrations range from three days to three months. Usually, the longer the time interval, the lower the reliability coefficient (Anastasi, 1988).

Test-retest reliability is not appropriate for all kinds of tests. For example, it would not make sense to measure the test-retest reliability of a test designed to measure short-term moods or feelings. For example, the *State–Trait Anxiety Inventory* measures two types of anxiety. *Trait anxiety* refers to the amount of anxiety that an individual normally has all the time, while *state anxiety* is the amount of anxiety an individual has at any given moment. For the test to be useful, it would be important for the measure of trait anxiety to have temporal stability, whereas the measure of state anxiety need not.

**Alternate-Forms Reliability**   With the **alternate-forms reliability** method, two forms of the same test are constructed. As shown in Table 4.1, a sample of 100 people are administered both forms of the test; one-half of the sample first receives form A and the other half form B. This **counterbalancing** of

**Table 4.1**  Design for typical alternate forms reliability study

| Subjects | Administration Order | |
| | First | Second |
| --- | --- | --- |
| 1–50 | Form A | Form B |
| 51–100 | Form B | Form A |

test-taking order is designed to eliminate any effects that first taking one form of the test may have on scores on the second form.

The scores on the two forms are then correlated to determine whether they are similar. If they are, the test is said to have **form stability.** Why would anyone use this method? If there is a high probability that people will take a test more than once, two forms of the test are needed to reduce the potential advantage to individuals who take the test a second time. This situation might occur in police department examinations. To be promoted, most police officers must pass a promotion exam. If the officer fails the exam one year, the officer can retake the exam the next year. If only one form of the test were available, the officer retaking the test for the seventh time could remember many of the questions and possibly score higher than an officer taking the test for the first time.

Multiple forms also might be used in large groups of test-takers where there may be the possibility of cheating. Perhaps one of your professors has used more than one form of the same test to discourage cheating. The last time you took your written driver's test, multiple forms probably were used, just as they were when you took the SAT or ACT to be admitted to college. As you can see, multiple forms of a test are common.

Recall that with test-retest reliability, the time interval between administrations usually ranges from three days to three months. With alternate-forms reliability, however, the time interval should be as short as possible. If the two forms are administered three weeks apart and a low correlation results, the cause of the low reliability is difficult to determine. That is, it could be that the test lacks form stability or temporal stability. Thus, to determine the cause of the unreliability, the interval needs to be short.

In addition, a *t*-test used to determine differences between two means should be conducted on the mean scores for each form to ensure equivalency. The test in Table 4.2, for example, shows a perfect correlation between the two forms. People who scored well on form A also scored well on form B. But the average score on form B is two points higher than on form A. Thus, even though the perfect correlation shows that the scores on the two forms are parallel, the difference in mean scores indicates that the two forms are not equivalent. In such a case, either the forms must be revised or different standards (norms) must be used to interpret the results of the test.

Any change in a test potentially changes its reliability, validity, difficulty, or all three. Such changes might include the order of the items, examples

**Table 4.2** Example of two parallel but nonequivalent forms

| Subjects | Test Scores | |
| | Form A | Form B |
| --- | --- | --- |
| 1 | 12 | 14 |
| 2 | 18 | 20 |
| 3 | 11 | 13 |
| 4 | 6 | 8 |
| 5 | 24 | 26 |
| 6 | 19 | 21 |
| 7 | 17 | 19 |
| 8 | 12 | 14 |
| 9 | 21 | 23 |
| 10 | 9 | 11 |
| Average score | 14.9 | 16.9 |

used in the questions, method of administration, time limits, and, conceivably, such characteristics as paper color. Research on the actual effects of these variables is mixed. For example, studies indicate that administering a test on a computer rather than on paper can (but does not always) affect test scores (Lee, Moreno, & Sympson, 1986) but a meta-analysis indicates that changing the order of items does not seem to greatly affect test scores (Aamodt & McShane, 1992).

**Internal Reliability**   One problem with the alternate-forms and test-retest methods is that, in both cases, reliability can be determined only by giving two administrations of a test. This is often neither possible nor practical. For example, if your instructor wanted to determine the reliability of the final exam, how could it be done? In the test-retest method, each student would take the exam at the end of the semester and then again during the next semester. Not only would few students want to retake a final exam, but much of the course knowledge would be lost.

In the alternate-forms method, each student would have to take two final exams, which would not be popular. However, with internal reliability, the test need be administered only once and would measure **item stability.**

Internal reliability can be determined in many ways, but perhaps the easiest is to use the **split-half method.** With this method, the items on a test are split into two groups. Usually, all of the odd-numbered items comprise one group and the even-numbered items the second group. The scores on each group are then correlated. Because the number of items in the test has been reduced, the **Spearman-Brown prophecy formula** is used to adjust the correlation; This formula is easy to use and takes the following form:

$$\text{Corrected reliability} = \frac{2 \times \text{Split-half correlation}}{1 + \text{Split-half correlation}}$$

Thus, if the correlation between the two test halves is .60, the corrected reliability using the Spearman-Brown prophecy formula would be:

$$\frac{2 \times .60}{1 + .60} = \frac{1.20}{1.60} = .75$$

Cronbach's **coefficient alpha** (Cronbach, 1951) and the **Kuder-Richardson formula 20 (K-R 20)** (Kuder & Richardson, 1937) are more popular and accurate methods of determining internal reliability, although they are more complicated to use and thus are calculated by computer rather than by hand. Essentially, both the coefficient alpha and the K-R 20 represent the reliability coefficient that would be obtained from all possible combinations of split halves. The difference between the two is that the K-R 20 is used for tests containing dichotomous items (for example, yes/no, true/false), while the coefficient alpha is used for tests containing interval and ratio items, such as five-point rating scales.

## VALIDITY

**Validity** is the degree to which inferences from scores on tests or assessments are justified by the evidence. As with reliability, a test must be valid to be useful. For example, suppose that we want to use height requirements to hire typists. Our measure of height (a ruler) would certainly be reliable; most adults will get no taller, and two people measuring an applicant's height will probably get very similar measurements. It is doubtful, however, that height is related to typing performance. Thus, height would be a reliable but not valid measure of typing performance.

Even though reliability and validity are not the same, they are related. The potential validity of a test is limited by its reliability. Thus, if a test has poor reliability, it cannot have high validity. But as we saw in the preceding example, a test's reliability does not imply validity. Instead, we think of reliability as having a *necessary but not sufficient relationship* with validity.

### Methods for Determining Validity

**Content Validity**   One way to determine a test's validity is to look at its degree of **content validity** — the extent to which tests or test items sample the content that they are supposed to measure. For example, your instructor tells you that the final exam will measure your knowledge of Chapters 8, 9, and 10. Each chapter is the same length, and your instructor spent three class periods on each chapter. The test will have 60 questions. For the test to be content-valid, the items must constitute a representative sample of the material contained in the three chapters; therefore, the test should have 20 questions from each chapter. If there are 30 questions each from Chapters 8 and 9, the test will not be content-valid because it left out Chapter 10. Likewise, if there are questions from Chapter 4, the test will not be content-valid because it requires knowledge that is outside of the appropriate domain.

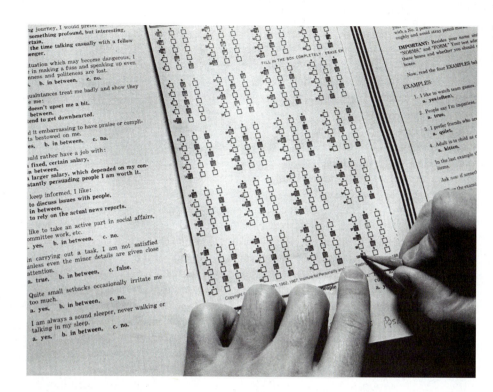

In industry, the appropriate content for a test or test battery is determined by the job analysis. All of the important dimensions identified in the job analysis should be covered somewhere in the selection process. Anything that was not identified in the job analysis should be left out.

The readability of a test is a good example of how tricky content validity can be. Suppose we determine that independence is an important aspect of a job. We find a test that measures independence, and we are confident that our test is content-valid because it measures a dimension identified in the job analysis. But the "independence test" is very difficult to read and most of our applicants are only high school graduates. Is our test content-valid? No, because it requires a high level of reading ability, and reading ability was not identified as an important dimension for our job.

**Criterion Validity**   Another measure of validity is **criterion validity,** which refers to the extent to which a test score is related to some measure of job performance called a **criterion** (criteria will be discussed more thoroughly in Chapter 7). Criterion validity takes content validity a step further. Just because a test is reliable and has content validity does not necessarily mean that it will be related to job performance.

Criterion validity is established using one of two research designs: concurrent or predictive. With **concurrent-validity** design, a test is given to a group of employees who are already on the job. The scores on the test are then correlated with a measure of the employees' current performance.

With **predictive-validity** design, the test is administered to a group of job applicants who are going to be hired. The test scores are then compared to a future measure of job performance. In the ideal predictive-validity situation, every applicant is hired (or a random sample of applicants), and the test scores are hidden from the people who will later make performance evaluations. By hiring every applicant, a wide range of both test scores and employee performance is likely to be found. Remember that the wider the range of scores, the higher the validity coefficient. But because it is rarely practical to hire every applicant, the ideal predictive design is not often used. Instead, most criterion-validity studies use a concurrent design. Why is a concurrent design weaker than a predictive design? The answer lies in the homogeneity of performance scores. In a given employment situation, very few employees are at the extremes of a performance scale. Employees who would be at the bottom of the performance scale were either never hired or have since been terminated. Employees at the upper end of the performance scale often get promoted. Thus the **restricted range** of performance scores makes obtaining a significant validity coefficient more difficult.

A major issue concerning the criterion validity of tests is **validity generalization (VG),** which is the extent to which a test found valid for a job in one location is valid for the same job in a different location. In the past, the job of typist in one company was not the same as that in another company, the job of police officer in one small town was not the same as that in another small town, and that of retail store supervisor was not the same as supervisor in a fast-food restaurant.

Recently, however, the work of Hunter and Hunter (1984); Schmidt, Hunter, Pearlman, and Hirsh (1985); and Schmidt, Gast-Rosenberg, and Hunter (1980) has indicated that a test valid for a job in one organization also is valid for the same job in another organization. Schmidt, Hunter, and their associates have tested hundreds of thousands of employees to arrive at their conclusions. They suggest that previous thinking resulted from studies with small sample sizes, and test validity in one location but not another was the product primarily of sampling error. With large sample sizes, a test found valid in one location probably will be valid in another—providing that the jobs actually are similar and not merely sharing the same job title.

The two building blocks for validity generalization are meta-analysis, discussed in Chapter 1, and job analysis, discussed in Chapter 3. Meta-analysis can be used to determine the average validity of specific types of tests for a variety of jobs. For example, several studies have shown that cognitive ability is an excellent predictor of police performance. If we were to conduct a meta-analysis of all the studies looking at this relationship, we would be able to determine the average validity of cognitive ability in predicting police performance. If this validity coefficient is significant, then police departments similar to those used in the meta-analysis could adopt the test without conducting criterion-validity studies of their own. This would be especially useful for small departments that have neither the number of officers necessary to properly conduct criterion-validity studies nor the financial resources necessary to hire professionals to conduct such studies. Validity generalization should only be used if a job analysis has been conducted and the results of the job analysis show that the job in question is similar to those used in the meta-analysis.

**Construct Validity**   **Construct validity** is the most theoretical of the methods for determining validity. Basically, it is the extent to which a test actually measures the construct that it purports to measure. Construct validity is concerned with inferences about test scores; in contrast, content validity is concerned with inferences about test construction (Cascio, 1987).

Perhaps a good example of the importance of construct validity is a situation I encountered during graduate school. We had just completed a job analysis of the entry-level police officer position for a small town. One of the important constructs that emerged was honesty. Almost every officer insisted that a good police officer is honest, so we searched for tests that measure honesty; we quickly discovered that there are many types of honesty tests. Some measure theft, some cheating, while others measure moral judgment. None measured the honesty construct as it was defined by these police officers: not taking bribes and not letting friends get away with crimes. No test measured that particular construct even though all of the tests measured "honesty."

Construct validity usually is determined by correlating scores on a test with scores from other tests. Some of the tests measure the same construct, while others do not. For example, suppose we have a test that measures knowledge of psychology. One hundred people are administered our "knowledge-of-psychology test" as well as another psychology knowledge test, a test of reading ability, and a test of general intelligence. If our test really measures the construct we say it measures—knowledge of psychology—it should correlate highly with the other test of psychology knowledge but not very highly with the other two tests. If our test correlates highest with the reading-ability test, our test may be content-valid (it contained psychology items), but not construct-valid because scores on our test are based more on reading ability than on knowledge of psychology.

**Face Validity**   Although face validity is not one of the three major methods of determining test validity cited in the Uniform Guidelines, it is still important (Anastasi, 1988). **Face validity** refers to the extent to which a test appears to be valid. This is important because if a test or its items do not appear valid, the test takers and administrators will not have confidence in the results. Likewise, if employees involved in a training session on interpersonal skills take a personality test and are given results that to them seem inaccurate, they will not be motivated to change or to use the results of the test. The face validity and acceptance of test results can be increased by telling applicants how a test relates to job performance (Lounsbury, Bobrow, & Jensen, 1989).

But just because a test has face validity does not mean it is valid (Jackson, O'Dell, & Olson, 1982). For example, have you ever read a personality description based on your astrological sign and found the description to be quite accurate? Does this mean that astrological forecasts are accurate? Not at all. If you also have read the description of a different astrological sign, you probably found it to be as accurate as the one based on your own sign. Why is this? Because of something called **Barnum statements** (Dickson & Kelly, 1985); which are statements that are so general they can be true of almost everyone. For example, if I were to describe you as "sometimes sad, sometimes successful, and at times unable to get along with your best friend," I would probably be very accurate. However, these statements describe almost anyone. So face validity by itself is not enough.

A technique created by Aamodt and Kimbrough (1982), however, allows a researcher to determine the face validity of a test while controlling for the effect of Barnum statements. In this technique, a test is administered to a group of individuals. Half of the individuals are given test results that correspond to their test scores, whereas the other half are given test results that correspond to another person's test scores. Each subject then is asked to rate the extent to which the test results describe their behavior. If the ratings from the group receiving its own results are significantly higher than the ratings from the group receiving others' results, some support is established for the test's face validity. If the average ratings from the two groups are equal, the test results can be said to suffer from Barnum statements.

Though face validity is often not related to the content, construct, or criterion validity of a test, it is related to several important applicant behaviors (Gilliland, 1993; Roberts & Lozada-Larsen, 1994). Face-valid tests that are accepted by applicants decrease the chance of law suits (Rynes & Connerley, 1993), reduce the number of applicants dropping-out of the employment process (Thornton, 1993), and increase the chance that an applicant will accept a job offer (Hoff Macan, Avedon, & Paese, 1994).

**Known-Group Validity**   Another method of measuring validity is **known-group validity** (Hattie & Cooksey, 1984). This method is not a common one and should be used only when other methods are not practical. With known-group validity, a test is given to two groups of people who are "known" to be different on the trait in question.

For example, suppose we want to determine the validity of our new honesty test. The best approach might be a criterion-validity study in which we correlate our employees' test scores with their dishonest behavior, such as stealing or lying. The problem is, how do we know who stole or who lied? We could ask them, but would dishonest people tell the truth? Probably not. Instead, we decide to validate our test by administering it to a group known as honest (priests) and to another group known as dishonest (criminals).

After administering the test to both groups we find that, sure enough, the priests score higher on honesty than do the convicts. Does this mean our test is valid? Not necessarily. It means that the test has known-group validity but not necessarily other types of validity. We do not know whether the test will predict employee theft (criterion validity), nor do we know if the test is even measuring honesty (construct validity). It is possible that the test is actually measuring another construct on which the two groups differ (for example, intelligence). Because of these problems, the best approach to take with known-group validity is that if the known groups do not differ on test scores, consider the test invalid. If scores do differ, one still cannot be sure of its validity.

Even though known-group validity usually should not be used to establish test validity, it is important to understand because some test companies use known-group validity studies to sell their tests, claiming that the tests are valid. Personnel analyst Jeff Rodgers once was asked to evaluate a test that his company was considering for selecting bank tellers. The test literature sounded impressive, mentioning that the test was "backed by over 100 validity studies." Rodgers was suspicious and requested copies of the studies. After several months of "phone calls and teeth pulling," he obtained reports of the validity studies. Most of the studies used known-group methodology and compared the scores of groups such as monks and priests. Not one study involved a test of criterion validity to demonstrate that the test could actually predict bank-teller performance. Thus, upon hearing that a test is valid, it is important to obtain copies of the research reports.

With at least five ways of measuring validity, one might logically ask which of the methods is the "best" to use. As with most questions in psychology, the answer is "it depends." In this case, the answer depends on the situation as well as on what the person conducting the validity study is trying to accomplish. If the question is whether the test will be a useful predictor of employee performance, then content validity would usually be used, and a criterion-validity study also would be conducted if there were enough employees and a good measure of job performance was available.

If the person conducting the validity study is trying to create a test that can be used by a variety of organizations, then all five methods of establishing validity should be used. If only one of the five were to be used in this situation, most I/O psychologists would probably agree that construct validity would be the most desirable.

Finally, a test itself can never be valid. When we speak of validity, we are speaking about the validity of the *test scores* as they relate to a particular job. A test may be a valid predictor of tenure for counselors but not of performance for shoe salespeople. Thus, when we say that a test is valid, we mean that it is valid for a particular job and a particular criterion. No test will ever be valid for all jobs and all criteria.

## FINDING RELIABILITY AND VALIDITY INFORMATION

Over the previous pages, we have discussed different ways to measure reliability and validity. But even though most of you will eventually be involved with some form of employee testing, few of you will actually conduct a study on a test's reliability and validity. Consequently, where do you get information about a test's reliability and validity? Many excellent sources containing reliability and validity information are available in the reference section of most university libraries.

**Wonderlic Personnel Test**

**Purpose:** "For testing adults in business and industrial situations. It is useful as a selection instrument in hiring and placing applicants and also as an indicator of future promotion and reassignment possibilities."
**Population:** Adults.
**Publication Dates:** 1939–89.
**Acronym:** WPT.
**Scores:** Total score only.
**Administration:** Group.
**Forms:** Available in 16 comparable and similar forms; forms for business, industry, and government: A, B, I, II, IV, V; forms available on restricted basis to business, industry, and government: T-11, T-21, T-31, T-14; forms for those involved in job counseling other than ultimate employers: EM, APT, BPT, CPT; forms restricted to use of educational institutions evaluating the academic potential of students: Scholastic Level Exam (SLE), created in 1982 by reformatting of Forms T-51 and T-71 (4 equivalent forms of SLE now available: IV, V, T-51,T-71); WPT Interpretive Software available for use on IBM-PC/XT/ST/PS-2 and compatibles.
**Price Data, 1990:** $45 per 25 tests (any form), scoring key, and manual ('83, 28 pages); $65 per 25 large-print version tests, scoring key, and manual; $225 per Interpretive Software (specify 5 1/4-inch or 3 1/2-inch disk).
**Foreign Language and Special Editions:** French, Spanish, Cuban, Mexican, Puerto Rican, and large-print editions available.
**Time:** 12(20) minutes.

**Author:** E. F. Wonderlic.
**Publisher:** E. F. Wonderlic Personnel Test, Inc.
**Cross References:** For reviews by Frank L. Schmidt and Lyle F. Schoenfeldt, see 9:1385 (8 references); see also T3: 2638 (24 references) and T2:482 (10 references); for reviews by Robert C. Droege and John P. Foley, Jr., see 7:401 (28 references); for reviews by N. M. Downie and Marvin D. Dunnette, see 6:513 (17 references); see also 5:400 (59 references); for reviews by H. E. Brogden, Charles D. Flory, and Irving Lorge, see 3:269 (7 references); see also 2:1415 (2 references).

TEST REFERENCES

1. Davou, D., & McKelvie, S. J. (1984). Relationship between study habits and performance on an intelligence test with limited and unlimited time. *Psychological Reports, 54,* 367-371.
2. Hines, M., & Shipley, C. (1984). Prenatal exposure to diethylstilbestrol (DES) and the development of sexually dimorphic cognitive abilities and cerebral lateralization. *Developmental Psychology, 20,* 81-94.
3. Deffenbacher, J. L., & Hazaleus, S. L. (1985). Cognitive, emotional, and physiological components of test anxiety. *Cognitive Therapy and Research, 9,* 169-180.
4. Edinger, J. D., Shipley, R. H., Watkins, C. E., Jr., & Hammet, E. B. (1985). Validity of the Wonderlic Personnel Test as a brief IQ measure in psychiatric patients. *Journal of Consulting and Clinical Psychology, 53,* 937-939.
5. Adams, N. A., & Holcomb, W. R. (1986). Analysis of the relationship between anxiety about mathematics and performance. *Psychological Reports, 59,* 943-948.
6. Arnkoff, D. B. (1986). A comparison of the coping and restructuring components of cognitive restructuring. *Cognitive Therapy and Research, 10,* 147-158.
7. Crowley, C., Crowley, D., & Clodfelter, C. (1986). Effects of a self-coping cognitive treatment for test anxiety. *Journal of Counseling Psychology, 33,* 84-86.
8. Hakstian, A. R., Wooley, L. K., & Schroeder, M. L. (1987). Validity of a large-scale assessment battery in an industrial setting. *Educational and Psychological Measurement, 47* (1), 165-178.
9. Raphall, D. (1988). High school conceptual level as an indicator of young adult adjustment. *Journal of Personality Assessment, 52,* 679-690.
10. Frisch, M. B., & Jessop, N. S. (1989). Improving WAIS-R estimates with the Shipley-Harford and Wonderlic Personnel Tests: Need to control for reading ability. *Psychological Reports, 65,* 923-928.

**Figure 4.1** Example of entry in *The Eleventh Mental Measurements Yearbook*
Source: *The Eleventh Mental Measurements Yearbook,* by J. J. Kramer and J. C. Conoley, 1992, Lincoln, NE: University of Nebraska Press.

**Figure 4.2**
Example of entry in
*Tests*

Source: *Tests*, R. C. Sweetland and D. J. Keyser,
1983, Kansas City, MO:
Test Corporation of Amer-
ica. Reprinted by permis-
sion of the publisher.

---

### I. P. I. Job Test Field Series: Dental Technician
*Industrial Psychology, Inc.*

---

Adult                                                          ☞ ✍

---

**Purpose:** Assesses skills of applicants for a position as a dental
technician. Used in screening laboratory worker in four classification
levels: cast metal, denture, crown and bridge, porcelain and acrylic.

---

**Decription:** Multiple item paper-pencil battery of two achievement
tests and two personality tests. Tests are: Dexterity, Dimension,
Neurotic Personality Factor, and Contact Personality Factor. For
individual test descriptions, see I. P. I. Aptitude-Intelligence Test
Series. Examiner required. Suitable for group use. Available in
French and Spanish.

**Timed:** 25 minutes

**Range:** Adult

**Scoring:** Hand key

**Cost:** Instruction kits $10.00; test packages $6.00.

**Publisher:** Industrial Psychology, Inc.

---

Perhaps the most common source of test information is **The Eleventh
Mental Measurements Yearbook (MMY)** (Kramer & Conoley, 1992). This
book contains information about thousands of different psychological tests
as well as reviews by test experts. One *MMY* test description is shown in
Figure 4.1.

Another excellent source of information is a compendium titled *Tests*
(Sweetland & Keyser, 1983), which contains information similar to the
*MMY* without the test reviews. Figure 4.2 shows a test description from
*Tests*. Box 4.1 lists other test compendia.

Bonjean, C. M., Hill, R. J., & McLemore, S. D. (1967). *Sociological Measurement: An inventory of scales and indices.*

Buros, O. K. (1975a). *Personality tests and reviews II.*

Buros, O. K. (1975b). *Vocational tests and reviews.*

Goldman, B. A., & Busch, J. C. (1978). *Directory of unpublished experimental measures—Volume II.*

Goldman, B. A., & Busch, J. C. (1982). *Directory of unpublished experimental measures—Volume III.*

Goldman, B. A., & Osborne, W. L. (1985). *Directory of unpublished experimental measures—Volume IV.*

Goldman, B. A., & Saunders, J. L. (1974). *Directory of unpublished experimental measures—Volume I.*

Kramer, J. J., & Conoley, J. C., (1992). *The eleventh mental measurements yearbook.*

Mitchell, J. V. (1983). *Tests in print III.*

Robinson, J. P., Anthanasious, R., & Head, K. B. (1969). *Measurements of occupational attitudes and occupational characteristics.*

Sweetland, R. C., & Keyser, D. J. (1983). *Tests.*

One problem with most test compendia is that to find information about a potential selection test, we must know the name of the test. Unfortunately, sometimes we do not know which test we want. Instead, we conduct a job analysis, identify important constructs, and then attempt to identify tests that measure the desired constructs. If only the test compendia are used, every page in each compendia must be examined to find which tests measure the appropriate construct.

## ESTABLISHING THE USEFULNESS OF A SELECTION DEVICE

Even though a test is both reliable and valid, it is not necessarily useful. At first, this may not make much sense, but consider a test that has been shown to be valid for selecting employees for a fast-food restaurant chain. Suppose there are 100 job openings and 100 job seekers apply for those openings. Even though the test is valid, it would have no impact because the restaurant chain must hire every applicant.

As another example, imagine an organization that already has a test that does a good job of predicting performance. Even though a new test being considered may be valid, the old test may have worked so well that the current employees are all successful. Thus, a new test (even though it is valid) might not provide any improvement.

To determine how useful a test would be in any given situation, several formulas and tables have been designed. Each formula and table provides slightly different information to an employer. The *Taylor-Russell tables* provide an estimate of the percentage of total new hires who will be successful employees if a test is adopted (organizational success), both *expectancy charts* and the *Lawshe tables* provide a probability of success for a particular applicant based on test scores (individual success), and the *utility formula* provides an estimate of the amount of money that an organization will save if it adopts a new testing procedure.

## TAYLOR-RUSSELL TABLES

The **Taylor-Russell tables** (Taylor & Russell, 1939) are designed to estimate the percentage of future employees who will be successful on the job if an organization uses a particular test. To use the Taylor-Russell tables, three pieces of information must be obtained.

The first information needed is the test's *criterion-validity coefficient*. There are two ways to obtain this. The best would be to actually conduct a criterion-validity study with test scores correlated with some measure of job performance. Often, however, an organization wants to know whether testing is useful before investing time and money in a criterion-validity study. This is where validity generalization comes into play. Based on findings by researchers such as Hunter and Hunter (1984) and Ghiselli (1973), we have a good idea of the typical validity coefficients that will result from various methods of selection. To estimate the validity coefficient that an organization might obtain, one of the coefficients from Table 4.3 is used. The higher the validity coefficient, the greater the possibility the test will be useful.

The second information that must be obtained is the **selection ratio,** which is simply the percentage of people that an organization must hire. The ratio is determined by the formula:

$$\text{Selection ratio} = \frac{\text{Number of openings}}{\text{Number of applicants}}$$

The lower the selection ratio, the greater the potential usefulness of the test.

The final information needed is the **base rate** of current performance—the percentage of employees currently on the job who are considered successful. This figure usually is obtained in one of two ways. The first method is the most simple but the least accurate. Employees are split into two equal groups based on their scores on some criterion such as tenure or performance. The base rate using this method is always .50, because one-half of the employees are considered satisfactory.

The second and more meaningful method is to choose a criterion measure score above which all employees are considered successful. For example, a real estate agent who sells more than $150,000 in real estate makes a profit for the agency after training and operating expenses have been deducted. In this case, agents selling more than $150,000 in property would be considered successful because they made money for the company. Agents selling less than $150,000 in property would be considered failures because they cost the company more money than was brought in.

In this example, there is a clear point at which an employee can be considered a success. Most of the time, however, there are no such clear points.

**Table 4.3** Typical validity coefficients for selection

| Selection Technique | Validity |
| --- | --- |
| Cognitive and psychomotor ability tests | .53 |
| Job knowledge tests | .50 |
| Biographical information blanks | .35 |
| Structured interviews | .34 |
| Assessment centers | .25 |
| Personality tests | .24 |
| Experience | .18 |
| Interviews | .17 |
| Reference checks | .13 |
| College grades | .13 |
| Vocational interests tests | .10 |
| Amount of education | .10 |
| Handwriting analysis | .00 |
| Projective personality tests | .00 |
| Age | .00 |

Note: These coefficients result from combinations of various meta-analyses.

In these cases, a manager will choose a point on the criterion that she feels separates successful from unsuccessful employees.

After the validity, selection ratio, and base rate figures have been obtained, the Taylor-Russell tables are consulted (see Table 4.4). To understand how they are used, let us take the following example. Suppose we have a test validity of .40, a selection ratio of .30, and a base rate of .40. Locating the table corresponding to the .40 base rate, we look along the top of the chart until we find the .30 selection ratio. Next we locate the validity of .40 on the left side of the table. We then trace across the table until we locate the intersection of the selection ratio column and the validity row; we have found .59.

This number indicates that if the organization uses that particular selection test, 59% of future employees are likely to be considered successful. This figure is compared with the previous base rate of .40, indicating a 19% increase in successful employees.

## EXPECTANCY CHARTS

**Expectancy charts** are easier to use but less accurate than the Taylor-Russell tables. The only information that is needed for an expectancy chart are employee test scores and the criterion. The two scores from each employee are graphed on a chart similar to that in Figure 4.3 on page 136. Lines are drawn from the point on the *y*-axis (criterion score) that represents a successful applicant and from the point on the *x*-axis that represents the lowest test score of a hired applicant. As you can see in Figure 4.3, these lines divide the scores into four quadrants. The points located in quadrant I represent employees who scored poorly on the test but performed well on

**Table 4.4**  Taylor–Russell tables

| Employees Considered Satisfactory | r | Selection Ratio | | | | | | | | | | |
|---|---|---|---|---|---|---|---|---|---|---|---|---|
| | | .05 | .10 | .20 | .30 | .40 | .50 | .60 | .70 | .80 | .90 | .95 |
| 10% | .00 | .10 | .10 | .10 | .10 | .10 | .10 | .10 | .10 | .10 | .10 | .10 |
| | .10 | .14 | .13 | .13 | .12 | .12 | .11 | .11 | .11 | .11 | .10 | .10 |
| | .20 | .19 | .17 | .15 | .14 | .14 | .13 | .12 | .12 | .11 | .11 | .10 |
| | .30 | .25 | .22 | .19 | .17 | .15 | .14 | .13 | .12 | .12 | .11 | .10 |
| | .40 | .31 | .27 | .22 | .19 | .17 | .16 | .14 | .13 | .12 | .11 | .10 |
| | .50 | .39 | .32 | .26 | .22 | .19 | .17 | .15 | .13 | .12 | .11 | .11 |
| | .60 | .48 | .39 | .30 | .25 | .21 | .18 | .16 | .14 | .12 | .11 | .11 |
| | .70 | .58 | .47 | .35 | .27 | .22 | .19 | .16 | .14 | .12 | .11 | .11 |
| | .80 | .71 | .56 | .40 | .30 | .24 | .20 | .17 | .14 | .12 | .11 | .11 |
| | .90 | .86 | .69 | .46 | .33 | .25 | .20 | .17 | .14 | .12 | .11 | .11 |
| 20% | .00 | .20 | .20 | .20 | .20 | .20 | .20 | .20 | .20 | .20 | .20 | .20 |
| | .10 | .26 | .25 | .24 | .23 | .23 | .22 | .22 | .21 | .21 | .21 | .20 |
| | .20 | .33 | .31 | .28 | .27 | .26 | .25 | .24 | .23 | .22 | .21 | .21 |
| | .30 | .41 | .37 | .33 | .30 | .28 | .27 | .25 | .24 | .23 | .21 | .21 |
| | .40 | .49 | .44 | .38 | .34 | .31 | .29 | .27 | .25 | .23 | .22 | .21 |
| | .50 | .59 | .52 | .44 | .38 | .35 | .31 | .29 | .26 | .24 | .22 | .21 |
| | .60 | .68 | .60 | .50 | .43 | .38 | .34 | .30 | .27 | .24 | .22 | .21 |
| | .70 | .79 | .69 | .56 | .48 | .41 | .36 | .31 | .28 | .25 | .22 | .21 |
| | .80 | .89 | .79 | .64 | .53 | .45 | .38 | .33 | .28 | .25 | .22 | .21 |
| | .90 | .98 | .91 | .75 | .60 | .48 | .40 | .33 | .29 | .25 | .22 | .21 |
| 30% | .00 | .30 | .30 | .30 | .30 | .30 | .30 | .30 | .30 | .30 | .30 | .30 |
| | .10 | .38 | .36 | .35 | .34 | .33 | .33 | .32 | .32 | .31 | .31 | .30 |
| | .20 | .46 | .43 | .40 | .38 | .37 | .36 | .34 | .33 | .32 | .31 | .31 |
| | .30 | .54 | .50 | .46 | .43 | .40 | .38 | .37 | .35 | .33 | .32 | .31 |
| | .40 | .63 | .58 | .51 | .47 | .44 | .41 | .39 | .37 | .34 | .32 | .31 |
| | .50 | .72 | .65 | .58 | .52 | .48 | .44 | .41 | .38 | .35 | .33 | .31 |
| | .60 | .81 | .74 | .64 | .58 | .52 | .47 | .43 | .40 | .36 | .33 | .31 |
| | .70 | .89 | .62 | .72 | .63 | .57 | .51 | .46 | .41 | .37 | .33 | .32 |
| | .80 | .96 | .90 | .80 | .70 | .62 | .54 | .48 | .42 | .37 | .33 | .32 |
| | .90 | 1.00 | .98 | .90 | .79 | .68 | .58 | .49 | .43 | .37 | .33 | .32 |
| 40% | .00 | .40 | .40 | .40 | .40 | .40 | .40 | .40 | .40 | .40 | .40 | .40 |
| | .10 | .48 | .47 | .46 | .45 | .44 | .43 | .42 | .42 | .41 | .41 | .40 |
| | .20 | .57 | .54 | .51 | .49 | .48 | .46 | .45 | .44 | .43 | .41 | .41 |
| | .30 | .65 | .61 | .57 | .54 | .51 | .49 | .47 | .46 | .44 | .42 | .41 |
| | .40 | .73 | .69 | .63 | .59 | .56 | .53 | .50 | .48 | .45 | .43 | .41 |
| | .50 | .81 | .76 | .69 | .64 | .60 | .56 | .53 | .49 | .46 | .43 | .42 |
| | .60 | .89 | .83 | .75 | .69 | .64 | .60 | .55 | .51 | .48 | .44 | .42 |
| | .70 | .95 | .90 | .82 | .76 | .69 | .64 | .58 | .53 | .49 | .44 | .42 |
| | .80 | .99 | .96 | .89 | .82 | .75 | .68 | .61 | .55 | .49 | .44 | .42 |
| | .90 | 1.00 | 1.00 | .97 | .91 | .82 | .74 | .65 | .57 | .50 | .44 | .42 |

*(continued)*

**Table 4.4** *(continued)*

| Employees Considered Satisfactory | r | Selection Ratio | | | | | | | | | | |
|---|---|---|---|---|---|---|---|---|---|---|---|---|
| | | .05 | .10 | .20 | .30 | .40 | .50 | .60 | .70 | .80 | .90 | .95 |
| 50% | .00 | .50 | .50 | .50 | .50 | .50 | .50 | .50 | .50 | .50 | .50 | .50 |
| | .10 | .58 | .57 | .56 | .55 | .54 | .53 | .53 | .52 | .51 | .51 | .50 |
| | .20 | .67 | .64 | .61 | .59 | .58 | .56 | .55 | .54 | .53 | .52 | .51 |
| | .30 | .74 | .71 | .67 | .64 | .62 | .60 | .58 | .56 | .54 | .52 | .51 |
| | .40 | .82 | .78 | .73 | .69 | .66 | .63 | .61 | .58 | .56 | .53 | .52 |
| | .50 | .88 | .84 | .76 | .74 | .70 | .67 | .63 | .60 | .57 | .54 | .52 |
| | .60 | .94 | .90 | .84 | .79 | .75 | .70 | .66 | .62 | .59 | .54 | .52 |
| | .70 | .98 | .95 | .90 | .85 | .80 | .75 | .70 | .65 | .60 | .55 | .53 |
| | .80 | 1.00 | .99 | .95 | .90 | .85 | .80 | .73 | .67 | .61 | .55 | .53 |
| | .90 | 1.00 | 1.00 | .99 | .97 | .92 | .86 | .78 | .70 | .62 | .56 | .53 |
| 60% | .00 | .60 | .60 | .60 | .60 | .60 | .60 | .60 | .60 | .60 | .60 | .60 |
| | .10 | .68 | .67 | .65 | .64 | .64 | .63 | .63 | .62 | .61 | .61 | .60 |
| | .20 | .75 | .73 | .71 | .69 | .67 | .66 | .65 | .64 | .63 | .62 | .61 |
| | .30 | .82 | .79 | .76 | .73 | .71 | .69 | .68 | .66 | .64 | .62 | .61 |
| | .40 | .88 | .85 | .81 | .78 | .75 | .73 | .70 | .68 | .66 | .63 | .62 |
| | .50 | .93 | .90 | .86 | .82 | .79 | .76 | .73 | .70 | .67 | .64 | .62 |
| | .60 | .96 | .94 | .90 | .87 | .83 | .80 | .76 | .73 | .69 | .65 | .63 |
| | .70 | .99 | .97 | .94 | .91 | .87 | .84 | .80 | .75 | .71 | .66 | .63 |
| | .80 | 1.00 | .99 | .98 | .95 | .92 | .88 | .83 | .78 | .72 | .66 | .63 |
| | .90 | 1.00 | 1.00 | 1.00 | .99 | .97 | .94 | .88 | .82 | .74 | .67 | .63 |
| 70% | .00 | .70 | .70 | .70 | .70 | .70 | .70 | .70 | .70 | .70 | .70 | .70 |
| | .10 | .77 | .76 | .75 | .74 | .73 | .73 | .72 | .72 | .71 | .71 | .70 |
| | .20 | .83 | .81 | .79 | .78 | .77 | .76 | .75 | .74 | .73 | .71 | .71 |
| | .30 | .88 | .86 | .84 | .82 | .80 | .78 | .77 | .75 | .74 | .72 | .71 |
| | .40 | .93 | .91 | .88 | .85 | .83 | .81 | .79 | .77 | .75 | .73 | .72 |
| | .50 | .96 | .94 | .91 | .89 | .87 | .84 | .82 | .80 | .77 | .74 | .72 |
| | .60 | .98 | .97 | .95 | .92 | .90 | .87 | .85 | .82 | .79 | .75 | .73 |
| | .70 | 1.00 | .99 | .97 | .96 | .93 | .91 | .88 | .84 | .80 | .76 | .73 |
| | .80 | 1.00 | 1.00 | .99 | .98 | .97 | .94 | .91 | .87 | .82 | .77 | .73 |
| | .90 | 1.00 | 1.00 | 1.00 | 1.00 | .99 | .98 | .95 | .91 | .85 | .78 | .74 |
| 80% | .00 | .80 | .80 | .80 | .80 | .80 | .80 | .80 | .80 | .80 | .80 | .80 |
| | .10 | .85 | .85 | .84 | .83 | .83 | .82 | .82 | .81 | .81 | .81 | .80 |
| | .20 | .90 | .89 | .87 | .86 | .85 | .84 | .84 | .83 | .82 | .81 | .81 |
| | .30 | .94 | .92 | .90 | .89 | .88 | .87 | .86 | .84 | .83 | .82 | .81 |
| | .40 | .96 | .95 | .93 | .92 | .90 | .89 | .88 | .86 | .85 | .83 | .82 |
| | .50 | .98 | .97 | .96 | .94 | .93 | .91 | .90 | .88 | .86 | .84 | .82 |
| | .60 | .99 | .99 | .98 | .96 | .95 | .94 | .92 | .90 | .87 | .84 | .83 |
| | .70 | 1.00 | 1.00 | .99 | .98 | .97 | .96 | .94 | .92 | .89 | .85 | .83 |
| | .80 | 1.00 | 1.00 | 1.00 | 1.00 | .99 | .98 | .96 | .94 | .91 | .87 | .84 |
| | .90 | 1.00 | 1.00 | 1.00 | 1.00 | 1.00 | 1.00 | .99 | .97 | .94 | .88 | .84 |

**Table 4.4**

| Employees Considered Satisfactory | r | Selection Ratio | | | | | | | | | | |
|---|---|---|---|---|---|---|---|---|---|---|---|---|
| | | .05 | .10 | .20 | .30 | .40 | .50 | .60 | .70 | .80 | .90 | .95 |
| 90% | .00 | .90 | .90 | .90 | .90 | .90 | .90 | .90 | .90 | .90 | .90 | .90 |
| | .10 | .93 | .93 | .92 | .92 | .92 | .91 | .91 | .91 | .91 | .90 | .90 |
| | .20 | .96 | .95 | .94 | .94 | .93 | .93 | .92 | .92 | .91 | .91 | .90 |
| | .30 | .98 | .97 | .96 | .95 | .95 | .94 | .94 | .93 | .92 | .91 | .91 |
| | .40 | .99 | .98 | .98 | .97 | .96 | .95 | .95 | .94 | .93 | .92 | .91 |
| | .50 | 1.00 | .99 | .99 | .98 | .97 | .97 | .96 | .95 | .94 | .92 | .92 |
| | .60 | 1.00 | 1.00 | .99 | .99 | .99 | .98 | .97 | .96 | .95 | .93 | .92 |
| | .70 | 1.00 | 1.00 | 1.00 | 1.00 | .99 | .99 | .98 | .97 | .96 | .94 | .93 |
| | .80 | 1.00 | 1.00 | 1.00 | 1.00 | 1.00 | 1.00 | .99 | .99 | .97 | .95 | .93 |
| | .90 | 1.00 | 1.00 | 1.00 | 1.00 | 1.00 | 1.00 | 1.00 | 1.00 | .99 | .97 | .94 |

Source: "The relationship of validity coefficients to the practical effectiveness of tests in selection: Discussion and tables," by H. C. Taylor and J. T. Russell, 1939, *Journal of Applied Psychology, 23,* 565–578.

the job. Points located in quadrant II represent employees who scored well on the test and were successful on the job. Points in quadrant III represent employees who scored high on the test yet did poorly on the job, and points in quadrant IV represent employees who scored low on the test and did poorly on the job.

If a test is a good predictor of performance, there should be more points in quadrants II and IV because the points in the other two quadrants represent "predictive failures." That is, in quadrants I and III, no correspondence is seen between test scores and criterion scores.

To estimate the test's effectiveness, the number of points in each quadrant is totaled, and the following formula is used:

Points in quadrants II and IV / Total points in all quadrants

The resulting number represents the percentage of time that we expect to be accurate in making a selection decision in the future. To determine whether this is an improvement, we use the following formula:

Points in quadrants I and II / Total points in all quadrants

If the percentage from the first formula is higher than that from the second, our proposed test should increase selection accuracy. If not, it is probably better to stick with the selection method currently used.

As an example, look again at Figure 4.3. There are 5 data points in quadrant I, 10 in quadrant II, 4 in quadrant III, and 11 in quadrant IV. The percentage of time that we expect to be accurate in the future would be:

$$\frac{\text{II} + \text{IV}}{\text{I} + \text{II} + \text{III} + \text{IV}} = \frac{10 + 11}{5 + 10 + 4 + 11} = \frac{21}{30} = .70$$

**Figure 4.3**
Example of an expectancy chart

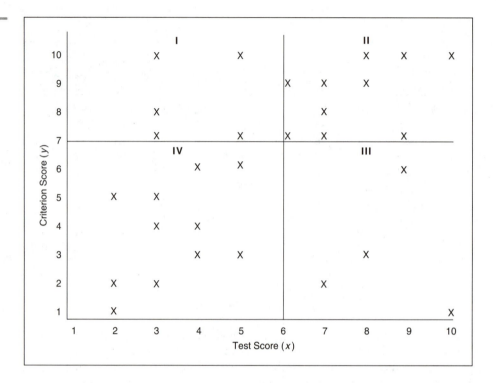

To compare this figure to the test we were previously using to select employees, we compute the satisfactory performance baseline:

$$\frac{\text{I} + \text{II}}{\text{I} + \text{II} + \text{III} + \text{IV}} = \frac{5 + 10}{5 + 10 + 4 + 11} = \frac{15}{30} = .50$$

Using the new test would result in a 20% increase in selection accuracy (.70 − .50) over the selection method previously used.

### LAWSHE TABLES

The Taylor-Russell tables were designed to determine the overall impact of a testing procedure. But we often need to know the probability that a *particular applicant* will be successful. The **Lawshe tables** (Lawshe, Bolda, Brune, & Auclair, 1958) were created to do just that. To use these tables, three pieces of information are needed. The validity coefficient and the base rate are found in the same way as for the Taylor-Russell tables. The third piece of information is the applicant's test score. More specifically, did the person score in the top 20%, the next 20%, the middle 20%, the next lowest 20%, or the bottom 20%?

Once we have all three pieces of information, the Lawshe tables, as shown in Table 4.5, are examined. For our example, we have a base rate of .50, a validity of .40, and an applicant who scored third highest out of 10. First, we locate the table with the base rate of .50. Then we locate the appropriate category at the top of the chart. Our applicant scored third highest out of 10 applicants, so she would be in the second category, the next highest one-fifth or 20%. Using the validity of .40, we locate the intersection of the validity row and the test score column and find 59. This means that the applicant has a 59% chance of being a successful employee.

**Table 4.5**  Lawshe individual prediction tables

| Percentage of Current Employees Considered Satisfactory | r | Applicant Scores on Selection Test | | | | |
|---|---|---|---|---|---|---|
| | | Top 20% | Next 20% | Middle 20% | Next 20% | Bottom 20% |
| 30% | .20 | 40 | 34 | 29 | 26 | 21 |
| | .30 | 46 | 35 | 29 | 24 | 16 |
| | .40 | 51 | 37 | 28 | 21 | 12 |
| | .50 | 58 | 38 | 27 | 18 | 09 |
| | .60 | 64 | 40 | 26 | 15 | 05 |
| 40% | .20 | 51 | 45 | 40 | 35 | 30 |
| | .30 | 57 | 46 | 40 | 33 | 24 |
| | .40 | 63 | 48 | 39 | 31 | 19 |
| | .50 | 69 | 50 | 39 | 28 | 14 |
| | .60 | 75 | 53 | 38 | 24 | 10 |
| 50% | .20 | 61 | 55 | 50 | 45 | 39 |
| | .30 | 67 | 57 | 50 | 43 | 33 |
| | .40 | 73 | 59 | 50 | 41 | 28 |
| | .50 | 78 | 62 | 50 | 38 | 22 |
| | .60 | 84 | 65 | 50 | 35 | 16 |
| 60% | .20 | 71 | 63 | 60 | 56 | 48 |
| | .30 | 76 | 66 | 61 | 54 | 44 |
| | .40 | 81 | 69 | 61 | 52 | 37 |
| | .50 | 86 | 72 | 62 | 47 | 25 |
| | .60 | 90 | 76 | 62 | 47 | 25 |
| 70% | .20 | 79 | 75 | 70 | 67 | 59 |
| | .30 | 84 | 76 | 71 | 65 | 54 |
| | .40 | 88 | 79 | 72 | 63 | 49 |
| | .50 | 91 | 82 | 73 | 62 | 42 |
| | .60 | 95 | 85 | 74 | 60 | 36 |

Source: "Expectancy charts II: Their theoretical development," C. H. Lawshe and R. A. Brune, 1958, *Personnel Psychology, 11,* 545–599.

Note: Percentages indicate probability that applicant with a particular score will be a successful employee.

## BROGDEN-CRONBACH-GLESER UTILITY FORMULA

Another way to determine the value of a test in a given situation is by computing the amount of money that an organization would save if it used the test to select employees. Fortunately, Hunter and Schmidt (1983) have devised a fairly simple **utility formula** to estimate the monetary savings to an organization. To use this formula, five things must be known:

1. *Number of employees hired per year (n)*. This number is easy to determine: It is simply the number of employees who are hired for a given position in a year.

2. *Average tenure (t)*. This is the average amount of time that employees in the position tend to stay with the company. The num-

Utility formulas allow organizations to estimate the financial impact of using a particular employment test.

ber is computed by using information from company records to identify the time that each employee in that position stayed with the company. The number of years of **tenure** for each employee is then summed and divided by the total number of employees.

3. *Test validity (r).* This figure is the criterion-validity coefficient that was obtained through either a validity study or validity generalization (Cascio, 1987).

4. *Standard deviation of performance in dollars (SD$).* For many years, this number was difficult to compute. Research has shown, however, that for jobs in which performance is normally distributed, a good estimate of the difference in performance between an average and a good worker (one standard deviation away in performance) is 40% of the employee's annual salary (Hunter & Schmidt, 1982). To obtain this, the total salaries of current employees in the position in question should be averaged.

5. *Mean standardized predictor score of selected applicants (m).* This number is obtained in one of two ways. The first method is to obtain the average score on the selection test for both the applicants who are hired and those who are not. The average test score of the nonhired applicants is subtracted from the average test score of the hired applicants. This difference is divided by the standard deviation of all the test scores.

For example, we administer a test of mental ability to a group of 100 applicants and hire the 10 with the highest scores. The average score of the 10 hired applicants was 34.6, the average test score of the other 90 applicants was 28.4, and the standard deviation of all test scores was 8.3. The desired figure would be:

$$\frac{34.6 - 28.4}{8.3} = \frac{6.2}{8.3} = .747$$

The second way to find $m$ is to compute the proportion of applicants who are hired and then use a conversion table such as that in Table 4.6 to convert the proportion into a standard score. This second method is used when an organization plans to use a test, knows the probable selection ratio based on previous hirings, but does not know the average test scores because the organization has never used the test. Using the above example, the proportion of applicants hired would be:

$$\frac{\text{Number of applicants hired}}{\text{Total number of applicants}} = \frac{10}{100} = .10$$

From Table 4.6, we see that the standard score associated with a selection ratio of .10 is 1.76. To determine the savings to the company, we use the following formula:

$$\text{Savings} = (n)\ (t)\ (r)\ (SD\$)\ (m) - \text{Cost of testing}$$

**Table 4.6**  Selection-ratio conversion table for utility formula

| Selection Ratio | $m$ |
|:---:|:---:|
| 100 | 0.00 |
| 90 | 0.20 |
| 80 | 0.35 |
| 70 | 0.50 |
| 60 | 0.64 |
| 50 | 0.80 |
| 40 | 0.97 |
| 30 | 1.17 |
| 20 | 1.40 |
| 10 | 1.76 |
| 5 | 2.08 |

As an example, suppose we will hire 10 auditors per year, the average person in this position stays two years, the validity coefficient is .40, average annual salary for the position is $30,000, and we have 50 applicants for 10 openings. Thus,

$n = 10$

$t = 2$

$r = .40$

$SD\$ = \$30,000 \times .40 = 12,000$

$m = 10/50 = .20 = 1.40$ (.20 is converted to 1.40 by using Table 4.6)

Cost of testing = $10 per person

Using the above formula, we would have

$$(10)\,(2)\,(.40)\,(12,000)\,(1.40) - \$500 = \$133,900$$

This means that, after accounting for the cost of testing, using this particular test instead of selecting employees by chance will save a company $133,900 over the two years that auditors typically stay with the organization. Because a company seldom selects employees by chance, the same formula should be used with the validity of the test (interview, psychological test, references, and so on) that the company currently uses. The result of this computation should then be subtracted from the first.

This final figure, of course, is just an estimate based on the assumption that the highest-scoring applicants will accept the job offer. To be most accurate, it must be adjusted by such factors as variable costs, discounting, corporate tax rates, and changes in strategic goals (Boudreau, 1983; Cascio, 1987; Russell, Colella, & Bobko, 1993). Though utility estimates should provide data supporting the usefulness of testing, there is some question about the extent to which managers trust the validity of the estimated financial savings (Latham & Whyte, 1994), especially considering that these estimates are often in the millions of dollars. When one considers the costs of constant poor performance, however, the size of these estimates should not be surprising. The high estimated savings are even more believable when one considers the cost of one employee's mistake. For example:

- An employee of Oxford Organics Inc. mislabeled an artificial vanilla flavoring sent to General Mills resulting in $150,000 in damaged cake frosting.
- A Navy mechanic left a 5-inch wrench inside the wheel compartment of a jet causing the $33 million plane to crash.
- A typo made in a letter by a car dealer told customers to call a 900-number instead of an 800-number. The 900-number turned out to be a sex line and the dealership had to send out an additional 1,000 letters to apologize and correct the mistake.

Thus, the cost of daily poor performance combined with the cost of occasional mistakes provide support for the validity of high utility estimates.

## DETERMINING THE FAIRNESS OF A TEST

Once a test has been determined to be reliable, valid, and have utility for an organization, the next step is to ensure its fairness. Fairness means that the test does not adversely impact any of the groups protected by law (see Chapter 2).

### ADVERSE IMPACT

The first step in determining a test's fairness is finding out whether it will result in **adverse impact.** There are two basic ways to determine this. The most common method is to find the percentage of people in each Equal Employment Opportunity (EEO) group who are hired after taking the test. This procedure was discussed in Chapter 2.

If the selection rate for any of the protected groups is less than 80% of the selection rate for either White applicants or males, the test is considered to have adverse impact. Remember that a legal defense for adverse impact is job relatedness, and a valid test is a job-related test. Thus, even if the test has adverse impact, it *probably* will be considered a fair test.

But even though the test might be considered legally fair, an organization still might not want to use it. If a test results in adverse impact, the organization probably will have to go to court to defend itself. Even though a valid test most likely will allow the organization to win the case, going to court is expensive. Thus, if the utility of the test is low, potential court costs will outweigh the minimal savings to the organization. Furthermore, a test with adverse impact will lead to poor public relations with minority communities, which could hurt recruitment or marketing efforts by the organization.

Using the 80% rule to determine a test's fairness means that an organization must wait until it has used the test to select employees, at which time damage already has been done. Another method of determining adverse impact compares the average scores of minority applicants with those of White and male applicants. This is most easily done by looking in the test manual to determine whether Blacks and Whites or males and females have significantly different test scores. If so, the test probably will have adverse impact and an alternative test can be sought.

A more sophisticated method of estimating potential adverse impact was suggested by Aamodt, Johnson, and Freeman (1992). These researchers developed a table based on the normal curve, which uses selection ratios and effect sizes (*d scores*) obtained from test-manual information to determine the minority–majority selection ratio. The table, shown in Table 4.7, is used by finding the point in the table where the selection ratio and the effect size intersect. This point represents the percentages of minorities that will be selected as a percentage of the nonminority selection ratio. Any number less than .80 or four-fifths indicates that the selection technique will probably result in adverse impact.

Using this table requires two pieces of information. The first is the effect size *(d)* representing the standard difference between the scores of two groups on a test (the effect size can be obtained using the means and standard deviations provided in test manuals). For example, suppose an organization is considering using a mechanical knowledge test to hire maintenance employees. For this type of position, the organization usually has about ten people applying for each opening (a selection ratio of .10). According to the information in the testing manual supplied by the company marketing the test, the average score for females is 72.1 and the average for males is 80.2. The standard deviation for the test is 33.69. The following formula is used to compute the effect size *(d)*:

(Minority test mean – Majority test mean)/Overall standard deviation

For the above data, the effect size *(d)* would be $(72.1 - 80.2)/33.69 = -.24$.

To predict whether this test will result in adverse impact, the intersection of the row containing the effect size of $-.24$ (use the absolute value of .24) and the column containing the selection ratio of .10 is located in Table 4.7. The number .34, found at this intersection, indicates that the selection ratio for females will be 34% of the selection ratio for males, substantially below the 80% figure indicating adverse impact.

Viewing the results from this table shows how difficult it is to avoid adverse impact using a strictly linear selection procedure. For example, with a selection ratio of .10, a test in which groups differ by only .06 of a standard deviation would result in adverse impact if applicants were hired in a top-down order based on their raw test scores, and the top scoring applicants accepted the job offer.

**Table 4.7** Minority selection ratio as a proportion of the nonminority selection ratio

| | Selection Ratio | | | | | | | | |
|---|---|---|---|---|---|---|---|---|---|
| Effect Size | .10 | .20 | .30 | .40 | .50 | .60 | .70 | .80 | .90 |
| .01 | .96 | .98 | .99 | .99 | .99 | .99 | .99 | .99 | .99 |
| .02 | .92 | .96 | .97 | .98 | .98 | .98 | .99 | .99 | .99 |
| .03 | .89 | .94 | .96 | .97 | .98 | .98 | .98 | .99 | .99 |
| .04 | .85 | .92 | .95 | .96 | .97 | .97 | .98 | .98 | .98 |
| .05 | .82 | .91 | .94 | .95 | .96 | .97 | .97 | .98 | .98 |
| .06 | .79 | .89 | .92 | .94 | .95 | .96 | .97 | .97 | .97 |
| .07 | .76 | .87 | .91 | .93 | .95 | .95 | .96 | .97 | .97 |
| .08 | .72 | .85 | .90 | .92 | .94 | .95 | .96 | .96 | .97 |
| .09 | .70 | .83 | .89 | .91 | .93 | .94 | .95 | .96 | .96 |
| .10 | .67 | .82 | .88 | .91 | .92 | .94 | .94 | .95 | .96 |
| .15 | .54 | .74 | .82 | .86 | .89 | .91 | .92 | .93 | .94 |
| .20 | .43 | .67 | .77 | .82 | .85 | .88 | .89 | .91 | .92 |
| .25 | .34 | .60 | .72 | .78 | .82 | .85 | .87 | .88 | .90 |
| .30 | .26 | .54 | .67 | .74 | .79 | .82 | .84 | .86 | .88 |
| .35 | .19 | .49 | .63 | .71 | .76 | .80 | .82 | .84 | .86 |
| .40 | .13 | .44 | .59 | .67 | .73 | .77 | .80 | .82 | .84 |
| .45 | .07 | .39 | .55 | .64 | .70 | .75 | .78 | .80 | .82 |
| .50 | .02 | .35 | .52 | .61 | .68 | .72 | .76 | .79 | .81 |
| .55 | .00 | .31 | .48 | .59 | .65 | .70 | .74 | .77 | .79 |
| .60 | .00 | .28 | .45 | .56 | .63 | .68 | .72 | .75 | .78 |
| .65 | .00 | .24 | .42 | .54 | .61 | .66 | .71 | .74 | .76 |
| .70 | .00 | .22 | .40 | .51 | .59 | .64 | .69 | .72 | .75 |
| .75 | .00 | .19 | .37 | .49 | .57 | .63 | .67 | .71 | .74 |
| .80 | .00 | .16 | .35 | .47 | .55 | .61 | .66 | .69 | .72 |
| .85 | .00 | .14 | .33 | .45 | .54 | .60 | .64 | .68 | .71 |
| .90 | .00 | .12 | .31 | .43 | .52 | .58 | .63 | .67 | .70 |
| .95 | .00 | .10 | .29 | .42 | .50 | .57 | .62 | .66 | .69 |
| 1.00 | .00 | .08 | .27 | .40 | .49 | .56 | .61 | .65 | .68 |
| 1.10 | .00 | .05 | .24 | .37 | .47 | .53 | .59 | .63 | .66 |
| 1.20 | .00 | .02 | .22 | .35 | .44 | .51 | .57 | .61 | .65 |
| 1.30 | .00 | .00 | .20 | .33 | .43 | .50 | .55 | .60 | .63 |
| 1.40 | .00 | .00 | .18 | .31 | .41 | .48 | .54 | .58 | .62 |
| 1.50 | .00 | .00 | .16 | .30 | .40 | .47 | .53 | .57 | .61 |
| 1.60 | .00 | .00 | .15 | .28 | .38 | .46 | .52 | .56 | .60 |
| 1.70 | .00 | .00 | .14 | .27 | .37 | .45 | .51 | .56 | .60 |
| 1.80 | .00 | .00 | .13 | .27 | .37 | .44 | .50 | .55 | .59 |
| 1.90 | .00 | .00 | .12 | .25 | .36 | .44 | .50 | .54 | .58 |

## SINGLE-GROUP VALIDITY

In addition to adverse impact, an organization must also determine whether
a test has **single-group validity,** which means that the test will significantly

predict performance for one group and no others. For example, a test of reading ability might predict performance of White clerks but not for Blacks.

To test for single-group validity, separate correlations are computed between the test and the criterion for each group. If both correlations are significant, the test does not exhibit single-group validity and it passes this fairness hurdle. If, however, only one of the correlations is significant, the test is considered fair for only the one group.

Single-group validity is very rare (O'Connor, Wexley, & Alexander, 1975) and is usually the result of small sample sizes and other methodological problems (Schmidt, 1988; Schmidt & Hunter, 1978). Where it occurs, an organization has three choices: to disregard single-group validity because research indicates that it probably occurred by chance, to stop using the test, or to use it for only the one group and find another test to use for other groups.

Disregarding single-group validity probably is the most appropriate choice given that most I/O psychologists believe that it occurs only by chance. As evidence of this, think of a logical reason why a test would predict differently for Blacks than for Whites or differently for males than for females. That is, why would a test of intelligence predict performance for males but not for females? Or, why would a personality test predict performance for Blacks but not for Whites? There may be many cultural reasons why two groups *score* differently on a test (e.g., educational opportunities, socioeconomic status), but finding a logical reason why the test would *predict* differently for two groups is difficult.

If we do not believe that single-group validity is the result of chance, we must adopt one of the other two options. As you can see, even though the third option (to use different tests for different groups) is legally and statistically correct, many public-relations problems may result. For example, if an applicant asks, "Why did I get one test and my friend another?" we could respond that "Blacks get one test and Whites get another." Such a response, however, is provocative and ultimately may be counterproductive for an organization.

## DIFFERENTIAL VALIDITY

The last test of fairness that must be conducted involves differential validity. With **differential validity** a test is valid for two groups, but more valid for one than for the other. Single-group validity and differential validity are easily confused, but there is a big difference between the two. Remember, with single-group validity, the test is valid only for one group. With differential validity, the test is valid for both groups, but it is more valid for one than for the other.

Like single-group validity, differential validity is rare (Schmidt & Hunter, 1981; Katzell & Dyer, 1977). When it does occur, it usually is in single-sex dominated occupations and tests are most valid for the dominant sex (Rothstein & McDaniel, 1992). If differential group validity occurs, the organization has two choices. The first is not to use the test. Usually, this is not a good option—finding a test that is valid and has utility is difficult; throwing away a good test would be a shame.

The second option is to use the test with separate regression equations for each group. Because applicants do not realize the test is scored differently, there are not the public-relations problems that exist with using separate tests. Unfortunately, the 1991 Civil Rights Act prohibits score adjustments based on race or gender. As a result, using separate equations may be statistically acceptable but may not be legally defensible.

If a test does not lead to adverse impact, does not have single-group validity, and does not have differential validity, it is considered to be fair. If the test fails to pass one of these three fairness hurdles, it may or may not be fair, depending on which model of fairness is followed (Arvey, 1979). But to be used with complete confidence, a test must be valid, have utility, and be fair.

## MAKING THE HIRING DECISION

After valid and fair selection tests have been administered to a group of applicants, a final decision must be made as to which applicant or applicants to hire. At first, this may seem to be an easy decision—hire the applicants with the highest test scores. But the decision becomes more complicated as both the number and variety of tests increase.

### LINEAR APPROACHES

Linear approaches assume that the relationship between the test score and the criterion is **linear.** That is, the higher applicants score on the test, the better they will do on the job. Usually, tests that are criterion-valid have linear relationships with criteria. Thus, if a criterion-valid test is used, selection decisions usually are based on the highest test scores.

If more than one criterion-valid test is used, the scores on the tests must be combined. This is done by a statistical procedure known as **multiple regression,** with each test score weighted according to how well it predicts the criterion. Research has shown, however, that converting test scores into standard scores, adding the standardized test scores, and then selecting applicants with the highest composite score is comparable to multiple regression (Aamodt & Kimbrough, 1985; Schmidt, 1971; & Wainer, 1976).

Linear approaches to hiring usually take one of three forms: unadjusted top-down selection, passing scores, or banding.

#### Unadjusted Top-Down Selection

With **top-down selection,** applicants are rank ordered based on their test scores. Selection is then made by starting with the highest score and moving

*T. R. Lin, Ph.D.*
*Senior Personnel Examiner*
*Los Angeles Unified School*
*District*

The Los Angeles Unified School District, the second largest district in the nation, has approximately 30,000 nonteaching employees performing more than 900 different jobs. I am one of the two examining supervisors who oversee a team of ten personnel analysts in all their recruitment and selection projects relating to these positions.

Some of our major responsibilities are as follows:

• Identifying, developing, and utilizing recruitment sources and strategies to attract qualified job applicants from diverse segments of the population.

• Conducting job analyses to identify current critical job competencies required for successful job performance.

• Constructing, validating, analyzing, and administering job-related employment and promotional assessment procedures that are in compliance with state and federal laws, regulations, guidelines, and professional standards.

• Researching, developing, validating, and administering proficiency tests to assess fluency in a wide variety of foreign languages and high school equivalency for use by the district and clients.

The majority of routine validation studies on selection procedures that I have performed are content oriented. Criterion-oriented validation strategies are being used in special projects such as the construction of the high school equivalency test. Nevertheless, the construction of alternate and parallel test forms for more than a dozen school-based examination series are needed.

In the real world, a successful test validation and administration project requires full support from the administrative department. One of my most recent and successful large-scale test construction and validation efforts was accomplished with the support of a competent and efficient project team. The team, led by a personnel analyst, involved an administrative staff intern, two line managers, and several incumbents.

One of my other duties is the coordination of our graduate internship program. I believe in the internship experience. During the last ten years, we have successfully "mentored" more than 30 interns, mostly I/O psychology graduate students, in a variety of projects. Many of these interns now work full-time in personnel-related fields.

I also believe in professional development. As a testing practitioner, I frequently attend and present at I/O psychology–related conferences such as APA, SIOP, and Academy of Management. I also am very much in touch with the real-world testing community and highly involved in organizations such as Personnel Testing Council of Southern California, International Personnel Management Association Assessment Council, and Western Region Intergovernmental Personnel Assessment Council. I have found that this is one of the best ways to exchange ideas and learn from other testing professionals about real-world test-validation strategies.

down until all openings have been filled. For example, using the data in Table 4.8, if we had four openings, we would hire the top four scorers who, in this case, would be Shawcross, Harris, Witherspoon, and Phillips. Notice that all four are males. If, for affirmative-action purposes, we wanted to hire two females, top-down selection would not allow us to do so.

The advantage to top-down selection is that by hiring the top scorers on a valid test, an organization will gain the most utility (Schmidt, 1991). The disadvantages are that this approach can result in high levels of adverse impact and reduces an organization's flexibility to use nontest factors such as references or "organizational fit."

### Passing Scores

**Passing scores** are a means for reducing adverse impact and increasing flexibility. With this system, an organization determines the lowest score on a test that is associated with acceptable performance on the job. For example, we know that a student scoring 1300 on the SAT will probably have better grades in college than a student scoring 800. However, what is the lowest SAT score that we can accept and still be confident that the student will be able to pass classes and eventually graduate?

Notice the distinct difference between top-down selection and passing scores. With top-down selection, the question is "Who will perform the *best* the future?" With passing scores, the question becomes "Who will be able to perform at an *acceptable level* in the future?"

As you can imagine, passing scores provide an organization with much flexibility. Again, using Table 4.8 as an example, suppose we determine that any applicant scoring 70 or above will be able to adequately perform the duties of the job in question. If we set 70 as the passing score, we can fill our four openings with any of the eight applicants scoring 70 or better. Because, for affirmative-action reasons, we would like two of the four openings to be filled by females, we are free to hire Starkweather and Wilson. Use of pass-

**Table 4.8** Hypothetical testing information

| Applicant | Gender | Test Score |
|---|---|---|
| Shawcross | M | 99 |
| Harris | M | 98 |
| Witherspoon | M | 91 |
| Phillips | M | 90 |
| Starkweather | F | 88 |
| Gallego | M | 87 |
| Gacy | M | 72 |
| Wilson | F | 70 |
| | | (passing score) |
| Speck | F | 68 |
| Manson | M | 62 |
| King | M | 60 |
| Whitman | F | 57 |
| Buono | F | 54 |
| Bundy | M | 49 |
| Dahmer | M | 31 |

ing scores allows us to reach our affirmative-action goals, which would not have been met with top-down selection. By hiring applicants with lower scores, however, the quality of our future employees may be lower than if we used top-down selection (Schmidt, 1991).

Though use of passing scores appears to be a reasonable step toward reaching affirmative-action goals, determining the actual passing score can be a complicated process full of legal pitfalls (Biddle, 1993). The most common methods for determining passing scores (e.g., the Angoff and Nedelsky methods) involve having experts read each item on a test and provide an estimation about the percentage of minimally qualified employees who could answer the item correctly. The passing score then becomes the average of the estimations for each question. Legal problems occur when unsuccessful applicants challenge the validity of the passing score (Cascio, Alexander, & Barrett, 1988).

### Banding

As mentioned previously, a problem with top-down hiring is that the process results in the highest levels of adverse impact. On the other hand, use of passing scores decreases adverse impact but reduces utility. As a compromise, **banding** attempts to hire the top test scorers while still allowing some flexibility for affirmative action.

Banding takes into consideration the degree of error associated with any test score. Thus, even though one applicant might score two points higher than another, the two-point difference might be the result of chance (error) rather than actual differences in ability. The question then becomes, "How many points apart do two applicants have to be before we say their test scores are significantly different?"

We can answer this question using a statistic called the **standard error (SE).** To compute this statistic, we obtain the reliability and standard deviation *(SD)* of a particular test from the test catalog (or we can compute it ourselves if we have nothing better to do on a weekend!). This information is then plugged into the following formula:

$$SE = SD \sqrt{1 - \text{Reliability}}$$

For example, suppose we have a test with a reliability of .90 and a *SD* of 13.60. The calculation of the *SE* would be:

$$
\begin{aligned}
SE &= 13.60 \sqrt{1 - .90} \\
&= 13.60 \sqrt{.10} \\
&= 13.60 \times .316 \\
&= 4.30
\end{aligned}
$$

Bands are typically, but do not have to be, determined by multiplying the *SE* by 1.96 (the standard score associated with a 95% level of confidence). Because the *SE* of our test is 4.30, test scores within 8.4 points (4.3 × 1.96) of one another would be considered statistically the same. If we take this concept a bit further, we can establish a hiring band. For example, look at the applicants depicted in Table 4.8. Suppose that we have four openings and would like to hire at least two females if possible. Because the highest scoring female in our example is Starkweather at 88, a top-down approach would not result in any females being hired. With banding, however, we start with the highest score (Shawcross at 99) and subtract from it the band width. In this case, $99 - 8.4 = 90.6$, meaning that all applicants scoring between 91 and 99 are considered statistically to have the same score. Because no female falls within this band, we hire Shawcross and then consider the next score of Harris at 98. Our next band of 98 through 90 ($98 - 8.4$) still does not contain a female so we hire Harris and then consider the next score of Witherspoon at 91. Our new band of 91 to 83 contains four applicants, one of whom is a female. Because we are free to hire anyone within a band, we would probably hire Starkweather to meet our affirmative-action goals. We would then hire Witherspoon as our fourth person. With banding, one more female was hired than would have occurred under a top-down system. Note, however, that our goal to hire two females was not reached as it would have been had we used passing scores.

Banding has been approved in several court cases (*Officers for Justice v. City and County of San Francisco*, 1992; *Bridgeport Police v. Bridgeport Guardians*, 1989) and seems to be a good compromise between top-down hiring and passing scores (Cascio, Outtz, Zedeck, & Goldstein, 1991). Banding, however, is not without its critics. Research indicates that banding will result in lower utility than will top-down hiring (Schmidt, 1991), and its usefulness in achieving affirmative-action goals is affected by such factors as the selection ratio and the percentage of minority applicants (Sackett & Roth, 1991).

## NONLINEAR APPROACHES

Often employee-selection tests do not show a linear relationship between test scores and job performance. For example, suppose that the distance between the floor and the ceiling of an airplane cabin is 6 feet. Because the job of airline attendant would require that he stand while serving meals and assisting passengers, a content-valid requirement would be that the applicant be shorter than 6 feet. Thus, as part of the selection-testing process, we measure each applicant. Any applicant taller than 6 feet would be unable to perform the job regardless of other test scores. If we use a linear approach, however, a person 5 feet 3 inches tall would get more points than a person 5 feet 8 inches tall. This would not make sense. Both applicants are able to satisfy the requirement of moving through the aisles of the airplane while standing. Being shorter would not give one person an advantage over another.

In such a situation, we would use a **cutoff approach** in which all nonlinear tests are scored on a pass/fail basis. Applicants are administered the complete battery of tests and must pass every nonlinear one. The regression, or standardized composite, method discussed earlier then is used to select applicants based on their scores on the linearly related tests.

For example, suppose our job analysis finds that a good police officer is intelligent, confident, in good health, can lift 100 pounds, is psychologically sound, and does not have a criminal record. Our validity study indicates that the relationship between both intelligence and confidence and job performance are linear—the smarter and more confident the officer, the better he or she performs.

The other tests have a nonlinear relationship with performance. To underscore this point, let us examine good health. Would an applicant who has had one cold in the last two years be a better officer than an applicant who has had two in the past two years? Probably not, but with a physically active job, we could be confident that an applicant with a bad back would not be able to handle the routine requirements of the job. Thus, physical health would be determined on a pass/fail basis—the applicant is either healthy enough to do the job or not.

Because we have more than one nonlinearly related test, we would adapt our procedure and use a *multiple-cutoff approach* combined with a linear approach as opposed to either a single-cutoff approach or a strictly linear approach. One disadvantage of a multiple-cutoff approach is the cost. If an applicant passes only three out of four tests, he will not be hired, but the organization has paid for the applicant to take all four tests.

To reduce the costs associated with applicants failing one or more tests, **multiple-hurdle approaches** are often used. With a multiple-hurdle approach, applicants are administered one test at a time, usually beginning with the least expensive. Applicants who fail a test are eliminated from further consideration and take no more tests. Applicants who pass all of the tests are then administered the linearly related tests; the applicants with the top scores on these tests are hired.

To clarify the difference between a multiple-cutoff and multiple-hurdle approach, look at the following example. Suppose that we will use four pass/fail tests to select employees. The tests have the following costs and failure rates:

| Test | Cost of Test | Failure Rate |
| --- | --- | --- |
| Background check | $ 25 | 10% |
| Psychological screening | 50 | 10 |
| Medical checkup | 100 | 10 |
| Strength | 5 | 10 |
| Total per applicant | $180 | |

If the tests cost $180 per applicant and 100 applicants apply for a position, a multiple-cutoff approach would cost our organization $18,000 (100 applicants × $180) to administer the tests to all applicants. But with a multiple-hurdle approach, we can administer the cheapest test (the strength test) to all 100 applicants. Because 10% of the applicants will fail this test, we then can administer the next cheapest test to the remaining 90. This process continues until all tests have been administered. A savings of $3,900 will result based on the following calculations:

| Test | Test Cost | Applicants | Total Cost |
|---|---|---|---|
| Strength | $ 5 | 100 | $ 500 |
| Background check | 25 | 90 | 2,250 |
| Psychological screening | 50 | 81 | 4,050 |
| Medical checkup | 100 | 73 | 7,300 |
| Total cost | | | $14,100 |

If a multiple-hurdle approach usually saves a company money, why is it not *always* used instead of a multiple-cutoff approach? First, many tests take time to conduct or score. For example, it might take a few weeks to run a background check or a few days to interpret a psychological screening. Therefore, the tests usually must be administered on several occasions, and an applicant would have to miss several days of work to apply for a particular job. Because people often cannot or will not take more than one day off from one job to apply for another, many potentially excellent applicants are lost before testing begins.

Second, research has shown that in general the longer the time between submission of a job application and the hiring decision, the smaller the number of Black applicants who will remain in the applicant pool (Arvey, Gordon, Massengill, & Mussio, 1975). Black populations have higher unemployment rates than Whites, and people who are unemployed are more hurried to obtain employment than people with jobs. Thus, because the multiple-hurdle approach takes longer than multiple-cutoff, it may bring an unintended adverse impact, and affirmative-action goals may not be met.

## CHAPTER SUMMARY

In this chapter, we have learned that an organization should choose only selection techniques that are reliable, valid, fair, and useful. *Reliability* refers to the stability of scores and can be measured using (1) the test-retest method, which measures temporal stability; (2) the alternate-forms method, which measures forms stability; and (3) the internal-consistency method (split-half, K-R 20, and coefficient alpha), which measures item homogeneity. *Validity* refers to the degree to which inferences from scores on tests or assessments are justified by the evidence. Validity can be assessed in one of three major ways: (1) content validity, which examines the extent to which the test items sample the appropriate domain; (2) criterion validity, or the extent to which a test score is related to some measure of job performance; and (3) construct validity, or the extent to which the test measures the construct that it purports to measure.

Once a test has been found both reliable and valid, its usefulness must be established. Taylor-Russell tables, Lawshe tables, expectancy charts, and utility formulas are used to establish the usefulness of a test.

The last step in evaluating a test's usefulness in selection is examining its fairness by testing for adverse impact, single-group validity, and differential validity. If the test is valid, fair, and useful, we can feel confident in its use.

Once a test has been selected and administered to a group of applicants, decisions have to be made about how to use the scores. If the relationship between test score and performance score is linear, hiring those applicants with the highest scores is acceptable. If there is no linear relationship, then the multiple-hurdle or multiple-cutoff approaches can be used.

# GLOSSARY

**Adverse impact**   When the selection ratio for minority applicants is less than 80% of the selection ratio for nonminorities.

**Alternate-forms reliability**   The extent to which two forms of the same test are similar.

**Banding**   A statistical technique based on the standard error of measurement that allows similar test scores to be grouped.

**Barnum statements**   Statements, such as those used in astrological forecasts, that are so general they can be true of almost anyone.

**Base rate**   Percentage of current employees who are considered successful.

**Coefficient alpha**   A statistic used to determine internal reliability of tests that utilize interval or ratio scales.

**Concurrent validity**   A form of criterion validity that compares test scores and measures of job performance for employees currently working for an organization.

**Construct validity**   The extent to which a test actually measures the construct that it purports to measure.

**Content validity**   The extent to which tests or test items sample the content they are supposed to measure.

**Counter-balancing**   A method of controlling for order effects by giving half of a sample test A first, followed by test B, and giving the other half of the sample test B first, followed by test A.

**Criterion**   A measure of job performance, such as attendance, productivity, or a supervisor rating.

**Criterion validity**   The extent to which a test score is related to some measure of job performance.

**Cut-off approach**   A method of hiring in which an applicant must score higher than a particular score in order to be considered for employment.

**Differential validity**   The characteristic of a test that significantly predicts a criterion for two groups, such as both minorities and nonminorities, but predicts significantly better for one of the two groups.

**Expectancy charts**   Charts that indicate the probability of future success for an applicant with a particular test score.

**Face validity**   The extent to which a test looks like it is valid.

**Form stability**   The extent to which the scores on two forms of a test are similar.

**Internal reliability**   The extent to which responses to test items measuring the same construct are consistent.

**Item homogeneity**   The extent to which test items measure the same construct.

**Item stability**   The extent to which responses to the same test items are consistent.

**Known-group validity**   A form of validity in which test scores from two contrasting groups "known" to differ on a construct are compared.

**Kuder-Richardson Formula 20 (K-R 20)**   A statistic used to determine internal reliability of tests which utilize items with dichotomous answers (yes/no, true/false)

**Lawshe tables**   Tables that use the base rate, test validity, and applicant percentile on a test to determine the probability of future success for that applicant.

**Linear**   A straight-line relationship between the test score and the criterion of measurement.

**Mental Measurements Yearbook (MMY)**   A book that contains information about the reliability and validity of various psychological tests.

**Multiple-hurdle approach**   When applicants are administered one test at a time and must pass that test before being allowed to take the next test.

**Multiple regression**   A statistical procedure in which the scores from more than one criterion-valid test are weighted according to how well each test score predicts the criterion.

**Passing score**   The minimum test score an applicant must achieve to be considered for employment.

**Predictive validity**   A form of criterion validity in which test scores of applicants are compared at a later date with a measure of job performance.

**Reliability**   The extent to which a score from a test is stable and free from error.

**Restricted range**   A narrow range of performance scores that makes it difficult to obtain a significant validity coefficient.

**Scorer reliability**   The extent to which two people scoring a test agree on the test score, or the extent to which a test is scored correctly.

**Selection ratio**   The percentage of applicants that an organization hires.

**Single-group validity**   The characteristic of a test that significantly predicts a criterion for one class of people but not for another.

**Spearman-Brown prophecy formula**   A formula that is used to correct reliability coefficients resulting from the split-half method.

**Split-half method**   A form of internal reliability in which the consistency of item responses is determined by comparing scores on half of the items with scores on the other half of the items.

**Standard error** *(SE)*   The number of points that a test score could be off due to test unreliability.

**Taylor-Russell tables**   A series of tables based on selection ratio, base rate, and test validity that yield information about the percentage of future employees who will be successful if a particular test is used.

**Temporal stability**   The consistency of test scores over time.

**Tenure**   The length of time that an employee has been employed by an organization.

**Test-retest reliability**   The extent to which repeated administration of the same test will achieve similar results.

***Tests***   A book containing information about psychological tests.

**Top-down selection**   Selecting applicants in straight rank order of their test scores.

**Utility formula**   The extent to which an organization will benefit from the use of a particular selection system.

**Validity**   The degree to which inferences from scores on tests or assessments are justified by the evidence.

**Validity generalization (VG)**   The extent to which inferences from test scores from one organization can be applied to another organization.

# 5

# EMPLOYEE SELECTION: RECRUITING AND INTERVIEWING

In the motion picture *Sudden Impact,* actor Clint Eastwood played police detective Harry Callahan, who, upon learning that he had been transferred from homicide to personnel, replied "Personnel . . . only idiots work in personnel!" Although this statement is a bit strong, it represents the attitude that many people once held about the field of personnel. That is, if you couldn't do anything else, you could always work in personnel.

The image of the personnel field, however, has been greatly enhanced by its recent application of modern, scientific principles to employee selection and by industry's realization that properly designed employee-selection procedures can save companies a lot of money.

In this chapter, we will first explore employee recruitment and job-hunting methods and then interviewing techniques. Then we will offer some tips that you can use to help find and obtain a desired job.

**Figure 5.1**
Steps in selecting
employees

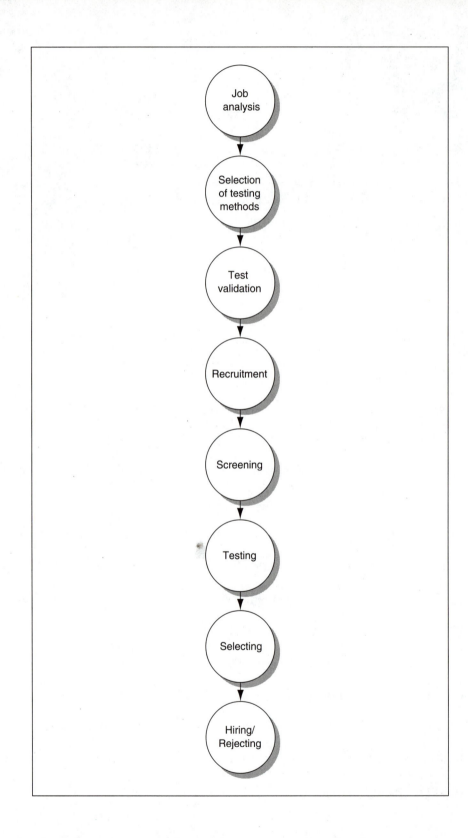

As shown in Figure 5.1, certain steps can be taken to successfully choose employees. Some of the steps are designed to attract excellent applicants to the company, others to select the best applicants, and still others to give applicants a good image of not only the company but the job-search process in general. Keep in mind that for most job openings, many more people will apply than will be hired. If you consider the number of people who are not hired and multiply that number by the number of job openings each year, it is clear that a lot of people will be in contact with a particular company. Those people not hired are potential customers with friends who are also potential customers. Leaving applicants with a positive image of the company should be a priority.

## JOB ANALYSIS

As discussed in Chapter 3, job analysis is the cornerstone of personnel selection. Remember, unless a complete and accurate picture of a job is obtained, it is virtually impossible to select excellent employees. The job analysis process involves identifying the important tasks and duties of a job and the knowledge, skills, and abilities needed to perform the job.

Therefore, the methods used to select employees should relate directly to the results of the job analysis. In other words, every essential knowledge, skill, and ability identified in the job analysis should be tested, and every test must somehow relate back to the job analysis. For example, if a job analysis reveals that an office manager types correspondence and proofreads reports to ensure the reports are grammatically correct, then the battery of selection tests should include a typing and a grammar test.

## RECRUITMENT

An important step in selecting employees is **recruitment:** attracting people with the right qualifications (as determined in the job analysis) to apply for the job. The first step is to decide whether to promote someone from within the organization (**internal recruitment**) or to hire someone from outside the organization (**external recruitment**). Organizations such as AT&T and Norfolk and Southern Railroad first advertise employment openings for two weeks to current employees. If no qualified applicants are found, these organizations then advertise outside.

To enhance employee morale and motivation, current employees should be given an advantage when applying for new internal positions (Brumback, 1986). However, if an organization always promotes employees from within, it runs the risk of having a stale workforce that is devoid of the many ideas that new employees bring from their previous employment settings. Heavy reliance on internal hiring is thought to perpetuate the racial, gender, and age composition of the workforce. Thus, a balance between promoting current employees and hiring outside applicants is needed.

# RECRUITMENT AND JOB-HUNTING METHODS

## MEDIA ADVERTISEMENTS

### Newspaper Ads

Running ads in periodicals such as local newspapers or professional journals is a common method of recruiting employees. In a survey of 188 organizations, personnel executives claimed newspaper advertising to be one of the most effective avenues of applicant recruitment (Mason & Belt, 1986).

As shown in Figure 5.2, newspaper ads typically ask the applicant to respond in one of four ways: by calling, applying in person, sending a résumé directly to the organization, or sending a résumé to a blind box.

Applicants are asked to **respond by calling** when an organization wants either to quickly screen applicants or hear an applicant's phone voice (e.g., for telemarketing or receptionist positions). Applicants responding to these ads should:

- Practice their first few sentences such as, "I saw your help-wanted ad in the local newspaper and would like to obtain more information." Don't count on being able to ad lib, or you might sound as inarticulate as the typical person leaving a message on an answering machine.

- Be prepared for a short interview by making sure you have time to talk, having your résumé handy to answer questions, and having paper and pencil close by. Ge Ge Beall, a human resource consultant, once received a phone call just as she was stepping out of the shower and before she had time to get dressed. The caller turned out to be an employer who interviewed Beall for the next hour. The employer told Beall that she liked phone interviews because the applicant "didn't have to worry about putting on her interview suit." In this case, she didn't realize just how accurate her statement was!

Organizations use **apply-in-person** ads when they don't want their phones tied up by applicants calling (e.g., a travel agency or pizza delivery restaurant), want the applicants to fill out a specific job application, or want to see the applicant. Good advice for applicants responding in person include:

- Be prepared to interview on the spot. It may be that the organization will simply take your résumé and call at a later date to schedule an interview; however, it is not unusual for an organization to interview applicants as they drop off their résumés.

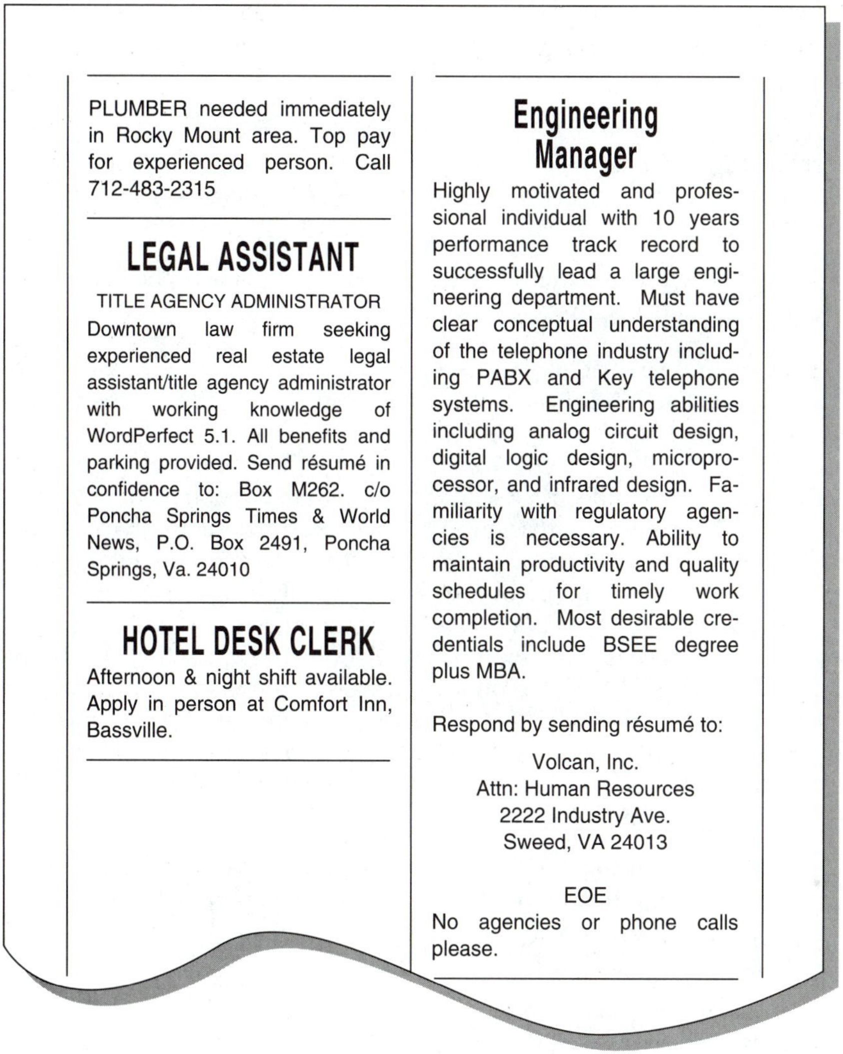

PLUMBER needed immediately in Rocky Mount area. Top pay for experienced person. Call 712-483-2315

**LEGAL ASSISTANT**

TITLE AGENCY ADMINISTRATOR

Downtown law firm seeking experienced real estate legal assistant/title agency administrator with working knowledge of WordPerfect 5.1. All benefits and parking provided. Send résumé in confidence to: Box M262. c/o Poncha Springs Times & World News, P.O. Box 2491, Poncha Springs, Va. 24010

**HOTEL DESK CLERK**

Afternoon & night shift available. Apply in person at Comfort Inn, Bassville.

**Engineering Manager**

Highly motivated and professional individual with 10 years performance track record to successfully lead a large engineering department. Must have clear conceptual understanding of the telephone industry including PABX and Key telephone systems. Engineering abilities including analog circuit design, digital logic design, microprocessor, and infrared design. Familiarity with regulatory agencies is necessary. Ability to maintain productivity and quality schedules for timely work completion. Most desirable credentials include BSEE degree plus MBA.

Respond by sending résumé to:

Volcan, Inc.
Attn: Human Resources
2222 Industry Ave.
Sweed, VA 24013

EOE

No agencies or phone calls please.

**Figure 5.2**
Examples of help-wanted ads

- Dress as if you were going to an interview. It might be convenient to drop off your résumé on your way to the beach, but dressing poorly will leave a bad impression whether you receive an immediate interview or not.
- Bring copies of your résumé and leave one even if you are asked to complete a job application.
- Bring a pen. Many organizations automatically eliminate applicants who do not do this.
- Be nice to the receptionist or any other person with whom you come in contact. The organization's first look at you is probably

the most important, and you can be sure that word of a rude or poorly dressed applicant will quickly get back to the person making the actual hiring decision.

Applicants are asked to **send a résumé directly to the company** when the organization expects a large response and does not have the resources to speak with the thousands of applicants. Responders to this type of ad should:

- Always include a cover letter (to be discussed later in the chapter).
- Type the envelope if possible.

The fourth type of ad directs applicants to send a résumé to a **blind box.** Organizations use blind boxes for three main reasons. First, the company doesn't want its name in public. This might be the case when a well-known company such as AT&T or IBM has a very specific job opening and is concerned that rumors will spread that there are many openings for a variety of positions. This could result in an avalanche of résumés—many from unqualified applicants. Second, the company might fear that people wouldn't apply if they knew the name of the company. For example, an ad for sales positions would probably not draw a large response if applicants were asked to send their résumés to a funeral home (even though selling burial plots can be a lucrative job). Third, on rare occasions a company plans to terminate an employee but first wants to find a replacement. As you can imagine, running an ad containing the name of the company would not be smart if the current employee was not aware that he or she was about to be fired.

When considering blind ads:

- Don't be afraid to respond to these types of ads; most of the time they will result in good jobs with respectable organizations.
- Respond promptly; boxes are assigned to advertisers only for the period in which the ad runs.

### Writing Recruitment Ads

Although little research is available, there is plenty of expert advice on the best way for an employer to write recruitment advertisements (see Table 5.1). Kaplan, Aamodt, and Wilk (1991) tested some of this expert advice by first determining the characteristics of help-wanted ads and then comparing the design of actual help-wanted ads in 10 newspapers with the quantity and quality of applicants who responded. After examining thousands of ads, Kaplan and her colleagues identified the 23 advertising characteristics found in Table 5.2. After comparing the presence or absence of the 23 characteristics with the quantity and quality of applicants who responded to the ad, the researchers found that ads displaying the company emblem and using creative illustrations attracted the greatest *number* of applicants, while ads that included the salary range and a company phone number attracted the highest *quality* applicants.

**Table 5.1** Expert advice on writing help-wanted ads

| Author | Advice |
|---|---|
| Bucalo (1983) | Ads should be creative, written in language that is familiar to the applicant, and should emphasize the benefits of the position. |
| Fyock (1988) | Recruitment ads should be placed in other sections of the newspaper to attract more applicants. |
| | Recruitment advertisers should team with the company's marketing or advertising departments to create unique and distinctive ads. |
| Ilaw (1985) | Ads that use "attention-getting" words may be confusing and misleading to the applicant. |
| Mason and Belt (1986) | Ads that specify job qualifications screen out unqualified applicants. |
| Rawlinson (1988) | Recruitment ads should represent the image that the company wants. |

In recent years, a new trend in help-wanted advertising is to use such creative ads as those shown in Figure 5.3. By using innovative advertising, On-Line Software tripled the number of applicants who responded to its help-wanted ad for secretarial positions. Hyundai's innovative ad cost only $5,000 and had almost 2,000 responses to advertised positions (Rawlinson, 1988). Thus, using the same techniques and imagination used in product advertisements may increase the recruitment yield from help-wanted ads. That is one reason why major advertising firms such as Bernard Hodes and Austin-Knight are increasingly involved in the development of recruitment ads and campaigns.

### Electronic Media

Recruitment advertisements are fairly common in newspapers, but aside from commercials run by the armed forces, they are not as common in the other two mass media areas—namely, television and radio. Perhaps the greatest use of television recruitment in the private sector has been by McDonald's, whose television commercials show McDonald's to be the ideal place for retirees to work part-time. In addition to generating applicants, the commercials are an excellent public-relations vehicle.

An interesting twist in television recruiting was developed by Videosearch—a California-based employment agency. Videosearch's 30-minute television program titled "Meet Your Next Employer" is paid for by organizations that advertise their job opportunities. The cost for this service is about $1,500 per minute for national exposure. A similar program called "CareerLine" is broadcast weekly on the Financial News Network. Although

**Table 5.2**  Important characteristics of help-wanted ads

| Characteristic | Percentage of Ads with Characteristic |
|---|---|
| Ad design | |
| Company emblem included | 21% |
| Creative illustrations used | 26 |
| Creative wording | 8 |
| Size of ad | a |
| White space around ad | 5 |
| Job title enlarged or in boldface | 74 |
| Legal information | |
| Affirmative-action statement | 38 |
| EEO statement | 41 |
| Information about the job | |
| Benefit package listed | 38 |
| Job title mentioned | 96 |
| Salary description | 36 |
| Multiple jobs listed in same ad | 75 |
| Information about the company | |
| Company address listed | 83 |
| Company description included | 63 |
| Company name mentioned | 59 |
| Phone number listed | 40 |
| Applicant qualifications | |
| Education requirements | 19 |
| Personality traits desired | 30 |
| Previous experience requirements | 64 |
| Skills needed by applicants | 50 |
| Salary history requested | 21 |

Source: Kaplan, A., & Wilk, D. (1989). Relationship between characteristics of recruitment advertisements and applicant pool quantity and quality. *Proceedings of the 10th annual graduate conference in I/O psychology and organizational behavior,* New Orleans, LA.
[a]Information not available.

television advertising sounds promising, it is an area that needs much more empirical investigation to determine its actual effectiveness.

### Situation-Wanted Ads

Situation-wanted ads are placed by the applicant rather than by organizations. As shown in Figure 5.4, these ads take a variety of forms: some list extensive qualifications, some give applicants' names, and some generally are more creative than others. As shown in Table 5.3, two studies (Williams & Garris, 1991; Willis, Miller, & Huff, 1991) investigated the effectiveness of

CLERICAL

**Figure 5.3**
Creative help-wanted ads

Source: Reprinted with permission of Ad Masters, Inc.

these ads by contacting applicants who had placed situation-wanted ads in a variety of daily and professional publications. The results of the two studies are encouraging: 69.4% of those applicants placing ads were contacted. However, not all contacts were from employers. Instead, some were from employment agencies, résumé writing services, and even an encyclopedia salesman (how could the applicant afford an encyclopedia when she doesn't even have a job?). Of the applicants who placed the ads, 21.5% did receive actual job offers. So, situation-wanted ads appear to be a useful way of looking for a job, and given that they don't cost an organization any money, may be a beneficial method of recruitment.

**Figure 5.4**
Examples of situation-wanted ads

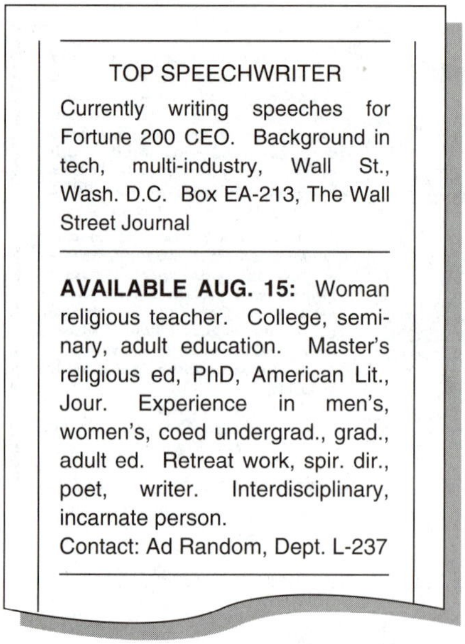

> **TOP SPEECHWRITER**
> Currently writing speeches for Fortune 200 CEO. Background in tech, multi-industry, Wall St., Wash. D.C. Box EA-213, The Wall Street Journal
>
> **AVAILABLE AUG. 15:** Woman religious teacher. College, seminary, adult education. Master's religious ed, PhD, American Lit., Jour. Experience in men's, women's, coed undergrad., grad., adult ed. Retreat work, spir. dir., poet, writer. Interdisciplinary, incarnate person.
> Contact: Ad Random, Dept. L-237

## POINT-OF-PURCHASE METHODS

This method of recruitment is based on point-of-purchase advertising principles used to market products to consumers. For example, consider shopping at a local grocery store. As you push your cart through one aisle of the store, you see a special display for potato chips; on the next aisle a display for cookies. When you get to the checkout stand, products such as the *National Enquirer,* candy, and batteries are conveniently placed so that you can examine them while you wait in line. The idea is to encourage you to buy more items once you are already in the store.

In employee recruitment, job-vacancy notices are posted in places where customers who are already familiar with the company or its products or current employees are likely to see them: store windows, bulletin boards, restaurant placemats, and the sides of trucks. The advantages to this method are that it is inexpensive and is targeted toward people who frequent the business. The disadvantage is that only a limited number of people are exposed to the sign.

Many fast-food restaurants are using innovative point-of-purchase techniques. McDonald's, Arby's, Burger King, and Carl's Jr. have all printed help-wanted ads with application blanks on their paper placemats. To apply for a job, customers simply wipe the spilled ketchup off the placemat, fill in their name and address, and give the placemat to the manager. Examples of these are shown in Figure 5.5.

**Table 5.3** Effectiveness of situation-wanted ads: percentage of people receiving inquiries and job offers

| Number of Responses | Type of Response | |
| --- | --- | --- |
| | *Inquiries* | *Job Offers* |
| None | 30.6% | 78.5% |
| 1 | 13.9 | 6.7 |
| 2 | 18.1 | 7.4 |
| 3 | 12.5 | 1.3 |
| 4 | 5.6 | 1.3 |
| 5 | 6.3 | 2.0 |
| 6 | 4.2 | 0.7 |
| 7 | 2.8 | 0.7 |
| 10 | 2.8 | 0.0 |
| 12 | 1.4 | 0.0 |
| 15 | 0.0 | 0.7 |
| 20 or more | 2.1 | 0.7 |

Note: These figures represent the combined data from Willis (1991) and Williams (1991).

Wendy's printed the words "Now hiring smiling faces" on their cash register receipts, Domino's Pizza placed help-wanted ads on its pizza boxes, and Kentucky Fried Chicken placed signs on vans that stopped at student gathering places to distribute free sodas and application materials.

Lauriat's Books took the unique approach of placing a help-wanted advertisement on the side of milk cartons. It placed a job posting and mini-résumé on the bookmark shown in Figure 5.5. The cost of the recruitment campaign was minimal because the company had already borne the expense of creating and printing the milk cartons on which the bookmark appeared.

## CAMPUS RECRUITERS

Many organizations send recruiters to college campuses to answer questions and to interview students for available positions. Though campus recruiters are not necessarily effective at selecting the best applicants (Aamodt & Carr, 1988), their behavior can greatly influence applicants' decisions to accept jobs that are offered (Glueck, 1973; Powell, 1991; Rynes, Bretz, & Gerhart, 1991).

## OUTSIDE RECRUITERS

Organizations often use outside recruiting sources such as private employment agencies, public employment agencies, and executive search firms. Private employment agencies and executive search firms are designed to

**Figure 5.5**
Points-of-purchase
recruitment
examples

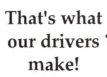

# $6 - $10 Per Hour

### That's what our drivers make!

- Earn TIPS and mileage
- Must have own car
- Must be 18 years or older
- Excellent working environment
  (*We have fun!*)
- Health Insurance Plan available
- *Must* be a safe driver

*Come by the location nearest you to talk
with us about Domino's Pizza!
No phone calls please.*

```
* * * *            WENDY'S            * * * *
  * *   THE BEST BURGERS IN THE BUSINESS   * *




CHILI                                     1.05
1/4 LB SINGLE CHZ                         1.65
   EVERYTHING                              .00
FRIES                                      .79
FRIES                                      .79
   REGULAR COLA                            .69
   REGULAR COLA                            .69
TAX     .34            INSIDE TOTAL       6.00

 ***     NOW HIRING SMILING FACES !!!     ***

01809651     00035414    19:33:10   07/24/88
```

make a profit from their recruitment activities, whereas public employment agencies are strictly nonprofit.

### Employment Agencies

Employment agencies operate in one of two ways. They either charge the company or the applicant when the applicant takes the job. The amount usually ranges from 10% to 30% of the applicant's first-year salary.

From an organization's perspective, few risks are involved in using an employment agency that charges the applicant for its services. That is, if the employment agency cannot find an appropriate candidate, the organization has not wasted money. But, if the employment agency is successful, the organization gets a qualified employee at no cost.

Employment agencies are especially useful if a personnel department is overloaded with work or an organization does not have an individual with the skills and experience needed to properly select employees. The disadvantage of employment agencies is that a company loses some control over its recruitment process and may end up with undesirable applicants. Remember, most "counselors" at employment agencies are hired because of their skill in sales, not because of their solid background in the area of personnel selection. In fact, one employment agency turned down one of its own job applicants because the applicant had earned a degree in personnel management. During the interview the head of the agency told the applicant, "We are not really looking for a personnel professional. What we want is the type of person who could sell aluminum siding to the owner of a brick home."

The applicant can seldom go wrong using an employment agency. If the fee is charged to the company, the applicant gets a job at no cost. However, even if the fee is charged to the applicant, the applicant may still benefit. For example, suppose you are having difficulty finding a job, and an employment agency finds you a good job paying $26,000 per year. Spending $2,600 to obtain a good job might be worthwhile because every month of unemployment is costing you $2,167 in lost income. So, the fee is essentially one month's salary that you would not have earned anyway without the job.

### Executive Search Firms

Executive search firms, better known as *head hunters* differ from employment agencies in several ways. First, the jobs they represent tend to be higher paying, non–entry-level positions such as executives, engineers, and computer programmers. Second, reputable executive search firms always charge their fees to organizations rather than to applicants. Third, fees charged by executive search firms tend to be about 30% of the applicant's first-year salary.

A word of caution about both employment agencies and executive search firms: Because these firms make their money on the number of applicants they place, they tend to exert tremendous pressure on applicants to take jobs that are offered. But, applicants are not obligated to take jobs and so should not be intimidated about turning down a position that appears to be a poor match.

### *Public Employment Agencies*

The third type of outside recruitment organization are state and local employment agencies. These public agencies primarily are designed to help the unemployed find work, but they often offer services such as career advisement and résumé preparation. From the organization's perspective, public employment agencies can be of great value in filling blue collar and clerical positions. Not only is there no cost involved in hiring the applicants, but often there are government programs available that will help pay training costs. In addition, with the advent of standardized testing programs (which will be discussed in Chapter 6), the quality of employees hired through public agencies is now much higher than in the past.

## EMPLOYEE REFERRALS

Another way to recruit is by **employee referral,** where current employees recommend family members and friends for specific job openings. Some organizations are so convinced of the attractiveness of this method that they provide financial incentives to employees who recommend applicants who are hired. For example, Washington National Insurance in Chicago gave employees $500 for each applicant the employee recommended who was hired and stayed with the company for at least six months; Providence Hospital awarded employees $1,500 for a successful recommendation; and White Memorial Medical Center provided recommenders of successful employees free maid service for a full year. The average amount of such bonuses is $462. The typical time period that a new employee must stay with the company before the referring employee is eligible for a bonus is three months (Stewart, Ellenburg, Hicks, Kremen, & Daniel, 1990).

Surprisingly, Stewart and his colleagues (1990) found neither a significant relationship between the size of the bonus and the number of referrals nor that organizations offering referral bonuses received more referrals than organizations not offering bonuses. Thus, further research is needed to determine if the popularity of employee-referral programs is justified. Surveys investigating this popularity indicate that about 40% of private organizations with over 100 employees have formal referral programs (Stewart et al., 1990; Bernard Hodes Advertising, 1985) and 89% use employee referrals in some way (Smith, Smits, & Hoy, 1992). Only 5% of public organizations such as state and city governments have such programs, and the few that do have them to encourage minority recruitment of police officers and firefighters (Stewart et al., 1990).

Although the idea of employee referrals sounds good, not all referrals are the same. Aamodt and Carr (1988) and Rupert (1989) compared the success of employees who had been referred by currently successful and unsuccessful employees and found that employees referred by successful employees had longer tenure than did employees who had been referred by unsuccessful employees. Thus, only those referrals made by successful employees should be considered. This finding, explained by social psychology research, indicates that our friends tend to be similar to us in characteristics such as personality, values, and interests. If a particular employee is a good employee, then the same characteristics that made her a good employee are probably shared by her friends and family. The same would be true of an unsuccessful employee.

Even though referrals by successful employees are a good recruitment avenue, the similarity of friends can also pose some problems. The biggest problem is that our friends also tend to be the same gender, race, national origin, and religion as us. Thus, if an organization uses employee referrals and the organization consists predominantly of white, male, Protestants, it will never hire blacks or females. Thus, even though the organization didn't intend to discriminate, the consequences of the recruitment policy may have that effect.

### DIRECT MAIL

Because direct mail has been successful in product advertising, several organizations have used this method to recruit applicants. An employer typically obtains a mailing list and sends help-wanted letters or brochures to people through the mail. Mailing lists can be purchased for about $100 per 1,000 names, and response rates run about 1 or 2% (Bargerstock, 1989).

One California branch of Allstate Insurance had been using newspaper advertisements and getting limited response. However, from a single mailing of 64,000 letters that explained the career opportunities available at Allstate to current policy holders, the company received more than 500 calls and hired 20 new employees (Halcrow, 1989). Union Special, an Illinois manufacturer of sewing machines, had difficulty filling 10 engineering positions. So, they direct mailed 3,300 cards to Chicago-area engineers at a cost of about $5,000. Consequently, the company received 100 responses and conducted 30 interviews. A third company that successfully used direct-mail recruitment is the Bank of America. To save money, Bank of America did something different than Allstate and Union Special. Instead of sending a special recruitment mailing, Bank of America included recruitment literature in the regular monthly mailing of bank statements to its customers. An example of direct mail recruiting is shown in Figure 5.6.

### COMPUTER DATABASES

Computer databases are a relatively recent recruitment technique and operate in a manner similar to employment agencies. In some systems, applicants pay a fee to have their résumés listed in an on-line database, whereas in other systems the organization pays the fee to use the database, and the

## If You're Looking For:

- An OUTSIDE sales position with earnings between 40-50K and more for high performances, and a company car
- A TELEPHONE sales position with earnings between 30-40K and more for high performances
- A reputable, well accepted and needed product to sell
- Provided leads/Protected accounts
- An exceptional benefits package including health, dental, & 401K plan
- Five weeks paid comprehensive training
- Excellent opportunity for advancement
- A top notch work environment & management team
- A position that offers minimal travel

## We're Looking For:

- Seasoned sales professionals with two years proven experience in commissioned outside or telephone sales to sell yellow page advertising space
- Individuals with strong professional selling skills

- Competitive, articulate and dedicated business men and women with integrity
- Team players

## Consider CDSC.

CDSC, Chesapeake Directory Sales Company, is a new partnership between Bell Atlantic Corporation and GTE Directories Corporation and will be the official sales company for C&P Telephone Yellow Pages.

## Opportunities Exist In The Following Areas:

- Washington, D.C. metro area
- Baltimore, MD metro area
- Richmond, VA
- Norfolk, VA
- Roanoke, VA
- Charleston, WV

If interested and for immediate consideration, please fill out and return the self-addressed Mini-Resume coupon by **JUNE 24**. We're hiring **NOW**.

CDSC is an equal opportunity employer.

---

**MINI-RESUME**

Name _____

Address _____

City _____

State/Zip _____

Phone (h)_____ (w)_____

Degree/College _____

_____

Current Employer _____

Current Position _____

Responsibilities _____

_____

_____

Other Related Experience _____

_____

_____

Position/City Interested In _____

_____

applicants list their résumés for free. Though this method appears promising, not many companies are using it (DeLong & St. Clair, 1990), and its effectiveness has been investigated in only one study. McDaniel and Johnson (1992) tracked 64 applicants listing their résumés in three separate databases and found that only one of the 64 was contacted by an employer (the person did not get the job).

## JOB FAIRS

Job fairs are designed to provide information in a personal fashion to as many applicants as possible. Job fairs typically are conducted in one of three ways. In the first, many types of organizations have booths at the same location. Your college probably has one or two of these job fairs each year in which dozens of organizations send representatives to discuss employment opportunities with students and to collect résumés. In addition, company representatives usually hand out literature and souvenirs such as t-shirts, yardsticks, and cups.

The second type of job fair is to have many similar organizations in one location. For example, a nursing job fair in New York City in 1988 had over 100 medical organizations represented and attracted over 1,500 potential nurses (Harper, 1988). The advantage to this type of job fair is that each visitor is a potential applicant for every organization. The drawback, of course, is that each organization must compete directly with the others at the fair.

The third approach is for an organization to hold its own job fair. Although this approach is certainly more expensive, it has the advantage of focusing the attention of the applicants on only one company. Such an approach was taken by Compaq Computer Corporation. Because of a shortage of applicants with technical skills, Compaq created a traveling job fair called "Compaq, Texas." The job fair traveled from city to city and was set-up in hotel ballrooms. Before the job fair arrived in each city, Compaq conducted a media blitz to inform prospective applicants about the fair. Upon arrival at the hotel, each prospective applicant was assigned a personal recruiter who would lead the applicant through "Compaq, Texas" with its product displays, videos, literature, and company representatives. The cost to Compaq for each job fair was about $100,000. This amount seems high, but each job fair draws 1,000 or more applicants; if the company hires just 5 or more applicants, it spends less than it would if it used outside recruiters (Chauran, 1989).

## EVALUATING THE EFFECTIVENESS
## OF RECRUITMENT SOURCES

Considering the number of potential recruitment sources, it is important to determine which source is the best to use. Such an evaluation can be conducted in several ways. As shown in Table 5.4, one method is to examine the *number of applicants* that each recruitment source yields. That is, if a newspaper ad results in 100 applicants and an in-store sign results in 20 applicants, newspaper ads could be considered the better method.

But looking at only the number of applicants who apply does not take into account the cost of the recruitment campaign. Thus, a second method for evaluating the success of a recruitment campaign would be to consider the *cost per applicant*, which is determined by dividing the number of applicants by the amount spent for each source. Continuing with the example

**Table 5.4** Evaluating the effectiveness of recruitment strategies

| | Recruitment Sources | | |
| Criterion | Advertisements | Referrals | Walk-ins |
| --- | --- | --- | --- |
| Number of applicants | 40 | 30 | 20 |
| Number qualified | 10 | 15 | 5 |
| Number hired | 2 | 7 | 1 |
| Number successful | 0 | 4 | 1 |

above, suppose our newspaper ad cost $200 and yielded 100 applicants and our in-store sign cost $5 and yielded 20 applicants. The cost per applicant for the newspaper ad would be $2, while the cost per applicant for the in-store sign would be just 25 cents. Using this method of evaluation, the in-store sign would be best as long as it generated the number of applicants needed by the organization. That is, a method such as an in-store sign will probably not cost an organization much money. But if the organization needs to hire 10 new employees and only five applicants apply for jobs, this recruitment source by itself is not effective.

Although the cost-per-applicant evaluation method is an improvement on the applicant-yield method, it too has a serious drawback. Even though an organization might receive a large number of applicants at a relatively low cost per applicant, as shown in the humorous example in Figure 5.7, none may be qualified for the job. Therefore, the third and fourth methods of evaluation would be to look at either the *number of qualified applicants* or the *cost per qualified applicant*.

A final method, and perhaps the best one, for evaluating the effectiveness of various recruitment sources looks at the number of successful employees generated by each recruitment source. This is an effective method because, as shown in Table 5.4, not only will every applicant not be qualified, but also, not every qualified applicant will become a successful employee.

Research investigating the relationship between recruitment source and the success of future employees has been mixed. Some research (Decker & Cornelius, 1979) has indicated that informal sources such as employee referrals lead to lower turnover than do formal sources such as advertisements. However, other research (Swaroff, Bass, & Barclay, 1985) has found no differences in tenure or performance between applicants recruited through formal or informal sources. Other research has suggested that informal recruiting sources will lead to longer tenure for Whites, whereas formal recruiting sources will lead to longer tenure for Blacks (Caldwell & Spivey, 1983).

A meta-analysis conducted by Aamodt and Carr (1988) found that employee referrals were the best method for finding employees who would stay with the organization, but no method of employee referral resulted in better employee performance than another. Even though employee referrals are superior when tenure alone is used as the criterion, several theories have been postulated about why referrals result in better employees. The first the-

**Figure 5.7**
The wording of an ad can result in unintended consequences

Source: Corporate Organizing and Research Services, Inc. © CORS Inc. 1989. Used with permission.

ory suggests that applicants who are referred by other employees receive more accurate information about the job than do employees recruited by other methods (Wanous, 1980). This theory has been supported in research by Breaugh and Mann (1984) and by Quaglieri (1982) who found that applicants referred by current employees received not only more information but

**Table 5.5** Summary of relationship of personal variables to various recruitment sources

| | Research Finding | |
| Recruitment Source | Related | Unrelated |
| --- | --- | --- |
| Employment agencies<br>Advertisements | Low self-esteem<br>Low self-esteem<br>Age (older)<br>Sex (males) | Age<br>Race<br>Education<br>Sex<br>Employment status<br>Experience<br>Ability<br>Personality<br>G.P.A.<br>Financial standing |
| Employee referral | Age (young) | Self-esteem<br>Race<br>Sex<br>Education<br>Employment status<br>Experience<br>Ability<br>G.P.A.<br>Personality<br>Financial standing |
| Direct application | Age (young)<br>Sex (female) | Self-esteem<br>Sex<br>Education<br>Employment status<br>Experience<br>Ability<br>Race<br>G.P.A.<br>Personality<br>Financial standing |

also more accurate information about the job than did applicants who had been recruited through other channels.

The second theory postulates that differences in recruitment-source effectiveness are the result of different recruitment sources reaching and being used by different types of applicants (Schwab, 1982). Although some research has supported this theory (Breaugh & Mann, 1984; Ellis & Taylor, 1983; Swaroff, Barclay, & Bass, 1985; Taylor & Schmidt, 1983), other research has not (Aamodt & Carr, 1988; Breaugh, 1981). In fact, as shown in Table 5.5, more variables have been found *not* to relate to the differential use of recruitment strategies. Furthermore, as shown in Table 5.6, the typical

**Table 5.6** How applicant Joe Smith was recruited for various jobs

| Position | Recruitment Source |
|---|---|
| Cook, Burger King | Newspaper ad |
| Clerk, Kmart | Friend |
| Waiter, Big Sizzle | Sign in window |
| Camp counselor | State employment agency |

person looking for a job uses a wide variety of job-search strategies. To underscore this point, think of the part-time jobs that you have held. How did you find out about each one? Was it the same method each time? As you can see, it is unlikely that a certain type of person responds only to newspaper ads, while another type goes only to employment agencies.

A third theory might better explain the finding that employee referrals result in greater tenure than other recruitment strategies. This theory, cited earlier in the discussion on employee referral programs, has its roots in the interpersonal attraction literature, which indicates that people tend to be friends with those who are similar to themselves (Byrne, 1971). If true, and research strongly suggests that it is, then an employee recommending a friend for a job will more than likely recommend one similar to herself. Thus, it would make sense that a person who is happy with her job would recommend a person who, because of her similarity to the incumbent, should also be happy with the job. Likewise, an unhappy employee would recommend similar friends who would also be unhappy and would probably have short tenure with the organization.

This theory has not been heavily researched but it has been supported by two studies. As discussed earlier, both Aamodt and Carr (1988) and Rupert (1989) found that long-tenured employees referred applicants who, after being hired, stayed in their jobs longer than applicants who were referred by short-tenured employees. No significant differences were found when job performance was examined instead of tenure.

Regardless of the actual reason for the success of employee referrals, given that the effect size for employee tenure was small and that the effect size for employee performance was not significant, recruitment methods probably make a difference primarily in the number of applicants who are attracted per recruitment dollar spent rather than in actual performance of future employees.

## REALISTIC JOB PREVIEWS

Because recruitment sources have only a slight effect on tenure of future employees, using other methods during the recruitment process may be helpful in recruiting applicants who will be successful. One such method is the **realistic job preview (RJP).** RJPs involve giving an applicant an honest assessment of a job. Instead of telling the applicant how much fun she will have working on the assembly line, the recruiter tells the applicant about both the positive and negative aspects of the job.

The logic behind RJPs is that even though telling the truth may scare away many applicants, the ones who stay will not be surprised about the job. Because they know what to expect, informed applicants will tend to stay on the job longer than applicants who did not understand the nature of the job.

In a meta-analysis of 21 RJP studies, Premack and Wanous (1985) found that RJPs have only a small effect on future employee tenure—the average effect size for tenure was only .12. (If you don't remember what an effect size is, you may want to review the meta-analysis section in Chapter 1.) The relationship between RJPs and performance was more complicated. RJPs that are administered in writing or orally had almost no effect at all—the mean effect size was −.04. But if the RJP was conducted using multimedia methods, the mean effect size was a respectable .32.

In a more recent meta-analysis, Shetzer and Stackman (1991) found that RJPs discussing opportunities for career advancement ($d = .19$) were more effective than ones without a career component ($d = .05$). These two meta-analyses indicate that RJPs, especially if they are conducted using multimedia methods and containing a career component, may be useful in the recruitment process.

## THE EMPLOYMENT INTERVIEW

If the recruitment process was successful, an organization will have several applicants from which to choose. Many selection techniques can be used to pick the best person from this pool of applicants.

Undoubtedly, the most commonly used method to select employees is the **employment interview.** In fact, if you think back to all of the part-time and summer jobs for which you have applied, most of those jobs were obtained after you went through an interview process. You might even remember the sweaty palms that went along with the interview. Because the interview is the most commonly used method to select employees, it might logically follow that it must be the most effective. Unfortunately, most evidence suggests otherwise. The typical unstructured interview is a poor predictor of future employee performance (Hunter & Hunter, 1984; McDaniel, Whetzel, Schmidt, & Maurer, 1994).

Perhaps the most critical look at the interview process was conducted by Meehl (1965), who examined the relative effectiveness of *clinical* versus *statistical prediction.* **Clinical prediction** in the employment setting looks at information about an applicant, combining that information in some subjective way (such as using intuition, hunches, experience, and so on), and then making a judgment about that person. **Statistical prediction** uses numerical formulas that take the information gathered about an individual and mathematically determines a probability regarding that person's future behavior. If the interview is a good method to use for selecting employees, then clinical prediction should be better than statistical prediction. Such is not the case, however. In examining the results of 51 studies that investigated clinical versus statistical prediction, Meehl (1965) found that only one study concluded that clinical prediction was more accurate than statistical prediction. These results have been confirmed by others who more directly investigated the accuracy of the employment interview; they found a lack of both reliability and validity for the interview (Arvey & Campion, 1982; Mayfield, 1964; Ulrich & Trumbo, 1965).

## REASONS FOR LACK OF INTERVIEW VALIDITY

Why does the interview seem *not* to predict future employee performance? Researchers have investigated this question for years and have identified eight factors that contribute to the poor reliability and validity of the interview process: poor intuitive ability, lack of job relatedness, primacy effects, contract effects, negative-information bias, interviewer-interviewee similarity, interviewee appearance, and nonverbal cues.

### Poor Intuitive Ability

Interviewers often base their hiring decisions on "gut reactions," or intuition (Goodale, 1992). However, as suggested by Meehl (1965), people are not good at using intuition to predict behavior. Divorce rates provide an excellent example of this poor predictive ability. Couples involved in romantic relationships spend on average of two years together before getting married. In spite of this time together, 50% of all marriages fail—an important reason for which is lack of compatibility. So, if after two years of "interviewing" a prospective spouse, we make the wrong choice 50% of the time, is it logical to assume that after spending only 15 minutes interviewing an applicant we can predict how well she will get along with the varied members of an organization?

### Lack of Job Relatedness

Research by Bolles (1995) and Biegeleisen (1994) has identified the most common questions asked by interviewers. As you can see in Box 5.1, these questions are not related to any particular job (Overman, 1995). Furthermore, the proper answers to these questions have not been empirically determined. Research has shown which answers personnel managers prefer (Bolles, 1995), but preference for an answer does not imply that it will actually predict future performance on the job. As discussed earlier in this and preceding chapters, information that is used to select employees *must* be job related if it is to have any chance of predicting future employee performance.

---

### Box 5.1
### Commonly Asked Employment Interview Questions

1. Why should I hire you?
2. What do you see yourself doing five years from now?
3. What do you consider your greatest strengths and weaknesses?
4. How would you describe yourself?
5. What college subjects did you like best? least?
6. What do you know about our company?
7. Why did you decide to seek a position with the company?
8. Why did you leave your last job?
9. What do you want to earn five years from now?
10. What do you really want to do in life?

---

### Primacy Effects

Research indicates that information presented early in the interview (primacy) carries more weight than does information presented later in the interview (Farr, 1973). Furthermore, research suggests that interviewers decide about a candidate within 5 minutes after the start of a 15-minute interview (Dessler, 1984). In fact, of a group of personnel professionals, 74% said they can make a decision within the first 5 minutes of an interview (Buckley & Eder, 1989). Thus, the **primacy effect** may help explain why research has shown no relationship between interview length and outcome (Aamodt, 1986; Huegli & Tschirgia, 1975). To reduce the primacy effect, interviewers are advised to make repeated judgments throughout the interview rather than one overall judgment at the end of the interview (Farr & York, 1975). That is, the interviewer might rate the applicant's response after each question or series of questions rather than waiting until the end of the interview to make a single rating or judgment.

### Contrast Effects

With the **contrast effect,** the interview performance of one applicant may affect the interview score given to the next applicant. Early research on this topic seemed to indicate that contrast effects do indeed occur (Carlson, 1970; Wexley, Sanders, & Yukl, 1973). If a terrible applicant precedes an average applicant, the interview score for the average applicant would be higher than if no applicant or a very qualified applicant had preceded her. In other words, an applicant's performance is judged in relation to the performance(s) of previous interviewees. Thus, it may be advantageous to be interviewed immediately after someone who has done poorly.

Research by Wexley, Yukl, Kovacs, and Sanders (1972) found that interviewers who were trained to be aware of the occurrence of contrast effects were able to reduce them significantly. Other researchers (Aamodt, 1986; Landy & Bates, 1973), however, have questioned whether the contrast effect actually plays a significant role in the interview process.

### Negative-Information Bias

Negative information apparently weighs more heavily than positive information (Rowe, 1989; Springbett, 1958), and positive information is under-weighed (Hollmann, 1972). **Negative-information bias** seems to occur only when interviewers aren't aware of job requirements (Langdale & Weitz, 1973). It seems to support the observation that most job applicants are afraid of being honest in interviews for fear that one negative response will cost them their job opportunities. Perhaps that is why interviewees are often not honest earlier, such as during the application process itself (Goldstein, 1971).

This lack of honesty may be especially evident in the interview, where the face-to-face nature of the process increases the odds that an applicant would respond in such a way as to look better to the interviewer. In a study conducted to increase the honesty of applicants during the interview process, Martin and Nagao (1989) had applicants interview for a job in one of four conditions. In the first, applicants read written interview questions and then wrote their responses to the questions. In the second condition, applicants were interviewed by a computer. In the third condition, applicants were interviewed face-to-face by an interviewer who behaved warmly; and in the fourth condition, applicants were interviewed by an interviewer who seemed cold. As expected, Martin and Nagao found that applicants were more honest in reporting their G.P.A.s and their SAT scores under the nonsocial conditions that involved paper and pencil and computer interviewing. Thus, one might increase the accuracy of information obtained in the interview by reducing social pressure and using written or computerized interviews.

### Interviewer-Interviewee Similarity

If an interviewee's personality (Foster, 1990) and perhaps attitudes (Frank & Hackman, 1975) are similar to those of the interviewer, the interviewee will receive a higher score. Available research, however, indicates that neither racial (Rand & Wexley, 1975) nor gender similarity (Rose & Andiappan, 1978) greatly affects interview ratings.

Interviewer-interviewee similarity affects interviews other than those for employment. Golightly, Huffman, and Byrne (1972) found that loan officers gave more money to loan applicants with attitudes similar to their own than they did to loan applicants whose attitudes were dissimilar.

### Interviewee Appearance

The majority of evidence indicates that, in general, physically attractive applicants have an advantage over less attractive applicants (Dipboye, Fromkin, & Wilback, 1975; Gilmore, Beehr, & Love, 1986; Raza & Carpenter, 1987). Interestingly enough, for females this relationship is moderated by the type of position for which they apply. Attractive females tend to get higher ratings for nonmanagerial jobs than unattractive females, but less attractive females get higher ratings than attractive females for managerial positions (Heilmann & Saruwatari, 1979). Interviewee appearance, it seems, is a potent hiring factor.

Along these same lines, Cash, Gillen, and Burns (1977) found that attractive males received the highest ratings for jobs traditionally held by men and attractive females received the highest ratings for jobs traditionally held by women. When the job was gender-neutral, attractive applicants in general received higher ratings than unattractive applicants.

Interviewers, however, are not as attuned to fashion or dress style as the popular press would suggest (see, for example, Molloy, 1978 and 1975). Still, research indicates that a job applicant should dress well and conservatively. That is, applicants should wear business attire. For males, three-piece suits appear not to offer any more advantage than two-piece suits (Aamodt, 1986). For females, wearing a business suit may lead to higher interview scores (Forsythe, Drake, & Cox, 1985).

Strangely enough, Baron (1983) found that even something as trivial as the wearing of cologne or perfume can affect interview scores. Male interviewers gave lower scores to applicants who wore a pleasant scent, whereas female interviewers gave higher scores to applicants who wore perfume or cologne.

### Nonverbal Cues

Perhaps the one interview variable that accounts most for high or low interview scores is **nonverbal communication.** Amalfitano and Kalt (1977) found that making eye contact led to higher interview scores. Aamodt (1986) found that making eye contact was the single best predictor of an applicant's interview score and that a firm handshake also led to a higher interview score. Young and Beier (1977) reported results that indicate that 80% of the interview score variance can be accounted for by the presence or absence of eye contact, smiling, and head nodding.

Although many more studies and variables could be listed, the preceding discussion illustrates that the interview contains many sources of bias that are not job-related. Remember that one of the major purposes of the employment interview is to determine which applicant will be the most successful in performing a job. To determine this, decisions must be based on ability to do the job and not on such variables as physical attractiveness and eye contact.

Does this mean that the interview is useless as a predictor of employee performance? Not at all. It just means that care must be taken to ensure that interview questions and decisions are job related. Even if the interview does not predict future employee success, it can still serve useful recruitment and orientation purposes by allowing the interviewer to answer any questions an applicant might have and to "sell" the organization to the applicant (Goodale, 1992). Furthermore, most people do not feel comfortable hiring someone they have not seen. Fortunately, research has discovered techniques that will make the interview more job-related and valid.

# IMPROVING INTERVIEW RELIABILITY AND VALIDITY

## Interviewer Training

As discussed earlier, Wexley and his associates (1972) have found that interviewers can be trained to avoid some of the more common types of interview bias. For example, simply being cautioned about the contrast effect led to a 20% reduction in its effect on interviewers. Participating in a week-long workshop decreased the influence of the contrast effect by more than 90%. Success in training interviewers also has been found by Dougherty, Ebert, and Callender (1986), Mayfield, Brown, and Hamstra (1980), and by Howard and Dailey (1979). Keenan (1978) found that training improved some aspects of interviewer behavior but not others. Perhaps exposure to the interview biases discussed in this text will help minimize the errors that interviewers make.

## Structured Interviews

Conducting a **structured interview** is perhaps the best way to ensure that interviewers base their decisions on relevant, job-related information. To create a structured interview, information about the job is obtained (job analysis), and questions are designed to find out the extent to which applicants' skills and experiences match those needed to successfully perform the job. These questions are incorporated into an interview form used by all interviewers for all applicants. Examples of good and poor answers are located next to the questions to help an interviewer score applicants' responses. Research has shown that structured interviews are not only fairly reliable (Schwab & Heneman, 1969) but also are much more valid than the traditional unstructured interview (Campion, Pursell, & Brown, 1988; Pursell, Campion, & Gaylord, 1980; Reynolds, 1979; Wiesner & Cronshaw, 1988; Wright, Lichtenfels, & Pursell, 1989). Interviews in which both the questions and the scoring procedures are structured are more valid than both unstructured interviews and interviews in which only the questions or the scoring procedures are structured (Huffcut & Arthur, 1994).

**Situational Interviews**   The **situational interview,** a type of structured interview, was introduced by Latham, Saari, Pursell, and Campion (1980). As shown in Box 5.2, the first step in creating a situational interview is to conduct a critical-incident job analysis, a technique that you learned in Chapter 3. This analysis is then given to job experts, such as supervisors, who are asked to choose one or two incidents that typify each of the important job dimensions determined by the job analysis.

The incidents are then rewritten into questions that will be used during the interview. Each job expert is asked to create three levels of answers for each question—excellent, mediocre, and terrible. These three answers will serve as benchmarks for points 5, 3, and 1 on a 5-point scale. Research by

Box 5.2
Steps in Developing a Situational Interview

1. Collect critical incidents.
2. Rewrite incidents into situations.
3. Translate incidents into situational questions.
4. Brainstorm several answers for each question.
5. On a 5-point scale, rate the level of performance represented by each answer.
6. Choose the answers that most closely represent the 5 points on the scale.
7. Conduct a validation study.

Buchner (1990) and Lin and Adrian (1993) indicates that increasing the number of **benchmark answers** will greatly increase the scoring reliability. Because the number of possible answers to any question is finite, it might be a good idea at this stage to brainstorm all possible answers to a question and then benchmark each of the answers. This approach would result in 10 or so benchmarked answers per question rather than the traditional 3. This process is demonstrated in Box 5.3.

The job-related questions are then asked during the employment interview. The answers given by the applicant are compared to the benchmark answers, and each answer is given a score ranging from 1 to 5. At the end of the interview, the scores from the questions are summed and the resulting figure is the applicant's interview score, which has been arrived at without being affected by such variables as eye contact and the interviewee's attractiveness.

Following this procedure, Latham et al. (1980) were able to create interviews that were not only reliable but also correlated .30 for supervisors and .46 for hourly workers. In other research:

1. Latham and Saari (1984) were able to obtain significant correlations between situational interview scores and performance by clerical workers ($r = .39$) and utility workers ($r = .14$).
2. Weekley and Gier (1987) also were successful in using a situational interview to predict success of sales clerks.
3. Maurer and Fay (1988) found that situational interviews were evaluated more reliably than traditional interviews.
4. Lin, Petersen, and Manligas (1987) found that Black, White, and Hispanic applicants scored equally on a situational interview for custodians.
5. Gousie (1992) and Lin et al. (1987) found that racial bias can still occur with situational interviews.
6. Aamodt, VanMarter, Pearson, and Martin (1993) found that scores on a situational interview designed for tellers correlated

**The Incident**

A customer entered a bank and began yelling about how the bank had messed up his account. He became so angry that he began to swear, saying that he would not leave the bank until the problem was solved. Unfortunately, the information needed by the teller was not at this branch, so there was nothing she could do.

**The Question**

You are working as a teller and have a long line of waiting customers. One customer runs to the front of the line and yells that he bounced a check and was charged $20, which caused other checks to bounce. He then swears at you and tells you that he will not leave until

the problem is solved. You are unable to check on his account because the information is at another branch. What would you do?

**The Benchmark Answers**

**Worst**

> 1—I would tell him to get at the end of the line and wait his turn.
>
> 3—I would explain to him that I cannot help him, try to calm him down, and ask him to come back tomorrow.
>
> 5—Because I do not have the information and the line is long. I would call my supervisor and have her talk to the customer in her office away from everyone else.

**Best**

---

highly with scores on a situational interview for resident assistants ($r = .67$).

7. McShane (1993) found that nonverbal cues do not affect situational interview scores.

Overall, according to published research, situational interviews have an average validity of .38 and an average interrater reliability of .80.

Though the first situational interviews were designed to be conducted face-to-face with an applicant, recently several variations of this process have been used. In the public sector, critical incidents are commonly acted out, videotaped, and then shown to large groups of applicants for such positions as police officer and prison guard. The applicants then write down what they would do in each situation, and the answers are later scored by a panel of experts. Videotaped incidents appear more realistic and are more efficient than face-to-face interviews, and they result in scores similar to those used in oral or written situational interviews (Martin & Andrews, 1992).

An interesting variation using situational exercises was developed for the New York State Civil Service Commission by Kaiser and Brull (1987). Instead of presenting the situations face-to-face or through videotape, Kaiser and Brull placed the situations in booklets with a series of possible answers. The applicant read each situation and then used a special latent ink pen to darken her response. The special pen reveals a message telling the applicant, based on her answer, the page to turn to for the next situation. As innovative as the process may be, its validity is low ($r = .13$), and it needs further refinement if it is to be useful. Furthermore, research indicates that providing potential answers from which to choose significantly raises interview scores (Aamodt et al., 1993; Martin, 1993) and lowers validity (Martin, 1993) but reduces adverse impact (Aamodt et al., 1993).

### Patterned Behavior Description Interviews (PBDI)

Patterned Behavior Description Interviews (PBDI) differ from situational interviews by focusing on *previous* behavior rather than projected behavior. That is, as shown in Figure 5.8, applicants are asked to provide specific examples of how they demonstrated job-related skills in previous jobs (Janz, Hellervik, & Gilmore, 1986). The small amount of research investigating PBDIs indicates that they have an average validity of .55 (Janz, 1982; Orpen, 1985), an average reliability of only .46 (Janz, 1982; Maas, 1965; Orpen, 1985), and are perceived by applicants as more difficult than unstructured interviews (Gilmore, 1989). Based on these results, we can conclude that PBDIs are a promising approach but are in need of much more research. An attempt to improve this technique by increasing the degree of structure resulted in higher reliability ($r = .64$) but lower validity ($r = .22$); (Motowidlo, Carter, Dunnette, Tippins, Werner, Burnett, & Vaughan, 1992).

## SURVIVING THE INTERVIEW PROCESS

Even though the employment interview has many problems, the odds are high that a person being considered for a job will be interviewed. Research and experience both indicate that an applicant can take several steps to increase an interview score.

### Scheduling the Interview

Contrary to advice given in popular magazines, neither day of week nor time of day affect interview scores (Aamodt, 1986; Willihnganz & Myers, 1993). What will affect the score, however, is when the applicant *arrives* for the interview. If she arrives late, the score will be drastically lower. In fact, in a study I conducted (Aamodt, 1986), no applicant who arrived late was hired. No differences, however, were found in interview scores based on whether an applicant arrived on time or 5 or 10 minutes early. Therefore, the interview can be scheduled for anytime of the day or week, but the applicant must not be late!

### Before the Interview

Learn about the company. Recall from Box 5.1 that one of the most commonly asked interview questions ("What do you know about our company?") is used to determine the applicant's knowledge of the organization.

## Bank Teller

**Behavior Dimensions**

- Is pleasant, courteous, helpful to all customers *versus* is curt, rude, or insulting to difficult customers.
- Works steadily, is timely *versus* wastes time, is tardy.
- Checks for errors, omissions *versus* makes mistakes.
- Contributes to pleasant, cooperative relations with peers *versus* argues, bickers, causes resentment and dissension.
- Reports problems or difficulties to the supervisor promptly *versus* hides problems or blames others.

**Interview Questions**

1.1  Let's begin by having you fill me in on your duties and responsibilities at your most recent job that are related to our opening for a teller position.

1.2  I'm sure you realize how important it is to serve customers cheerfully and pleasantly. Tell me about the nicest compliment you received when serving a customer.

- What did the customer want?
- Do you remember what you said at the time?
- What did the customer say when he or she complimented you?
- Did the customer tell anyone else?
- How often did this type of event come up last year?
- Tell me about another one. [repeat probes]

1.3  Not all customers are that nice. Sometimes customers are irritating or rude. Tell me about the most irritating customer you have had to deal with.

- When did this happen?
- What did the person do that was irritating?
- What did you say in response?
- How did you overcome the person's rudeness?
- Was the person satisfied when he or she left?

- Did the person say anything to your boss? What?
- How often did this kind of customer show up?
- Tell me about another one. [repeat probes]

1.4  Everyone has said something to a customer, especially the difficult ones, that they wish they hadn't said. What is the thing you most regretted saying to a customer?

- What led up to this particular event?
- What happened after that?
- Did you take any steps to make sure it didn't happen again?
- What were they? Was it effective?

2.1  Let's move on from your customer relations. Now I'd like to find out a bit about your success in catching errors. What do you do that helps you pick out mistakes?

2.2  Can you think of the mistake you picked out on your last job that saved the company the most money?

- When did that happen?
- What was the mistake? Who was responsible?
- Was the mistake avoidable? How?
- What did you do to correct the mistake?
- What did you do to avoid it in the future?
- When was the next time this kind of mistake came up?

2.3  We can all think of the one that got away—the mistake we would most like the chance to do over. Tell me about the mistake you would most like to do over.

- What was your responsibility in this instance?
- What actually happened? For how long?
- What did your boss say about this mistake?
- What did you do to avoid this in future?
- Did this kind of mistake ever happen again?

**Figure 5.8** Example of a patterned behavior description interview (PBDI)

Source: From *Behavior Description Interviewing,* (p. 122–123), T. Janz, L. Hellervik, & D. C. Gilmore, 1986, Boston: Allyn and Bacon.

Information about companies can be found in your college library or Career Services Center.

Not only does this advice make sense, but research has found an applicant's knowledge significantly correlated (.32) with their interview rating (Aamodt, 1986). Organizations are especially impressed if an applicant knows its products and services, future needs, major problems faced, and philosophy or mission. Knowing statistics such as market share and sales volume are not as valuable (Gardner, 1994).

A former student of mine tells the story about an interview she had for a managerial position with Allstate Insurance Company. The night before the interview she read all the available information on Allstate at her local library. During the interview, she was asked why she wanted to work for Allstate. She replied that she was active in the community and was attracted to Allstate because of its "Helping Hands" community program—which she had read about the night before. The interviewer was greatly impressed and spent the next 10 minutes describing the program and its importance. The interview was a success because the applicant had done her homework.

On the day of the interview, dress neatly and professionally, and adjust your style as necessary to fit the situation. Avoid wearing accessories such as flashy large earrings and brightly colored ties. Hair should be worn conservatively—avoid "big hair" and colors such as purple and green (we've all seen it!).

### During the Interview

Most suggestions about how best to behave in an interview take advantage of interviewer biases that we have discussed in this chapter. Nonverbal behaviors should include a firm handshake, eye contact, smiling, and head

Conservative clothing is best for interviewing.

nodding. Desired verbal behaviors include asking questions, subtly pointing out how you are similar to the interviewer, not asking about the salary, not speaking slowly, and not hesitating before answering questions. Keep in mind that first impressions are the most important. If you want to appear similar to the interviewer, look around the office. Kopitzke and Miller (1984) found that the contents of an interviewer's office are often related to her personality and interests.

### After the Interview

Immediately following the interview, write a brief letter thanking the interviewer for her time. Although research evidence supports all of the suggestions offered in this section, no research has been done on the effects of thank you letters. Still, this nice touch certainly cannot hurt.

# COVER LETTERS

**Cover letters** tell an employer that you are enclosing your résumé and would like to apply for a job. Cover letters should never be longer than one page. As shown in the sample letters in Figures 5.9 and 5.10, cover letters contain a salutation, four basic paragraphs, and a closing signature.

### Salutation

If possible, get the name of the person to whom you want to direct the letter. If you aren't sure of the person's name, call the company and simply ask for the name of the person (have it spelled) to whom you should send your résumé. If the first name leaves doubt about the person's gender, (for example, Kim, Robin, Paige), ask if the person is male or female so that you can properly address the letter to Mr. or Ms. Smith. Do not refer to the person by first name (e.g., Dear Sarah). If you can't get the person's name, a safe salutation is "Dear Human Resource Director." Avoid phrases such as "Dear Sir or Madam" or "To Whom it May Concern."

### PARAGRAPHS

The opening paragraph should be one or two sentences long and communicate three pieces of information: the fact that your résumé is enclosed, the name of the job you are applying for, and how you know about the job opening (such as a newspaper ad or from a friend). The second paragraph states that you are qualified for the job and provides three reasons why. This paragraph should be only four or five sentences in length and should not rehash the contents of your résumé. The third paragraph explains why you are interested in the particular company to which you are applying. The final paragraph closes your letter and provides information on the best days and times to reach you.

### SIGNATURE

Above your signature, use words such as "cordially" or "sincerely." "Yours truly" is not advised, and words such as "Love," "Peace," or "Hugs and snuggles" are strongly discouraged. Personally sign each cover letter, and type your name, address, and phone number below your signature.

Employment consultant Ge Ge Beall provides job applicants with the following tips about cover letters:

- Avoid sounding desperate, and don't beg (I really need a job badly! Please, please, please hire me!).
- Avoid grammar, spelling, and typing errors. Employers view cover letters and résumés as examples of the best work applicants can produce. If a cover letter contains errors, an employer will be concerned about the quality of your regular work.

**Figure 5.9**
Example of a cover
letter

November 8, 1985

Mr. John Smith
Alco, Inc.
217 West Street
Johnson, VA 24132

Dear Mr. Smith:

Enclosed find a copy of my résumé. Please consider me
for the position of welder that was advertised in the
*Roanoke Times and World News.*

For several reasons, I believe that I am qualified for
your position. First, I have six years of welding
experience in an industrial setting. Second, I am a
very dependable worker as shown by the fact that I have
missed only two days of work in the last five years.
Finally, I am available to work any shift at any of your
three plants.

I look forward to hearing from you. I can best be
reached after 3:00 p.m. on weekdays and any time on
weekends.


Cordially,


Andrew S. Jones

- Avoid officious words or phrases. Don't use a large word when a small word will do. Not only will employers be unimpressed by large words, but applicants often misuse them. As an example, one applicant tried to describe his work productivity by saying that his writings were "voluptuous" rather than "voluminous," as we think he meant to say.
- Don't discuss personal circumstances such as, "I find myself looking for a job because I am recently divorced." Employers are only interested in your qualifications.

July 15, 1995

Ms. Maria Duffie, Director
Human Resource Department
Walters Cosmetics, Inc.
69 Beall Avenue
Amityville, NY 00312

Dear Ms. Duffie:

Enclosed find a copy of my résumé. Please consider me for the position of sales representative that was advertised this past Sunday in the *Washington Post*. As you can see below, I am confident that my qualifications are a good match for the requirements stated in your advertisement.

| Your Requirements | My Qualifications |
|---|---|
| Bachelor's degree | B.A. in marketing from Radford University |
| Two years sales experience | Five years of sales experience |
| History of success in sales | Received three sales awards at AT&T |
| Strong clerical skills | A.A.S. in secretarial science<br>Three years clerical experience<br>55 words per minute typing speed |

I am especially interested in working for your company because I have used your products for over ten years and thus am familiar with both your product line and the high quality of your cosmetics.

I am looking forward to hearing from you. Please feel free to call me at home after 6:00 p.m. or at work from 8:00 a.m. until 5:00 p.m. Because AT&T is downsizing, my employer will not mind your calling me at work.

Cordially,


Mable Leane

2345 Revlon Blvd.
Avon, Virginia 24132
Home: (703) 435-1122
Work: (703) 435-4343

**Figure 5.10**  Example of a customized cover letter

- If possible, tailor your letter to each company. Standard cover letters are efficient but not as effective as those written specifically for each job you are applying for.

## RÉSUMÉS

A **résumé** is a summary of an applicant's professional and educational background. Although résumés are commonly requested by employers, little is known about their value in predicting employee performance. Harrison (1986) used résumé data to construct a weighted application blank (a concept that will be discussed in Chapter 6). Other studies have found that when an interviewer reads a résumé before interviewing an applicant, the validity of the employment interview may actually be *reduced* (Dipboye, Stramler, & Fontenelle, 1984; Phillips & Dipboye, 1989). Beyond these studies, however, it is unclear how much predictive value, if any, résumés have.

Résumés may not predict performance partly because they are intended to be advertisements for an applicant. Companies that specialize in résumé design openly brag about their ability to "make your strengths more obvious and your weaknesses hard to find." In fact, Janice Rulnick of Credential Check and Personnel Services in Michigan estimates that 30% of the résumés her company investigates contain exaggerations; this is close to the 25% exaggeration figure estimated by LoPresto, Mitcham, and Ripley (1985) and by Broussard and Brannen (1986). Such attempts to enhance an applicant's chances of getting a job are compounded by résumé fraud.

**Résumé fraud** is the intentional placement of untrue information on a résumé. Thomas Norton, president of Fidelifacts, a company specializing in the investigation of applicant information, believes that there are six very common types of résumé fraud, which are listed in Box 5.4.

Résumé fraud may not initially seem like a great problem, but consider the following examples: Paul Crafton used 33 aliases to receive university teaching jobs; Abraham Asante, posing as a doctor, improperly administered anesthesia resulting in a patient suffering brain damage; and a man on probation for a felony conviction posed as an electrical engineer and received a $95,000-a-year job by falsely claiming he spoke 13 languages. These stories are tragic and may not be typical of résumé fraud cases, but more than 80% of companies believe that it is enough of a problem to merit reference checks (Muchinsky, 1979).

### WRITING RÉSUMÉS

There is no one best way to write a résumé. Because people have such different backgrounds, a format that works for one individual may not work for another. Therefore, this section will provide only general advice about résumé writing; the rest is up to you.

Box 5.4
Forms of Résumé Fraud

Résumé fraud takes many forms. Six of the most prominent are:

**1. Misleading educational credits** In the typical educational fraud, the person usually did attend the school, but only for two years instead of the four years claimed. In many other educational fraud cases, one usually finds the job applicant took courses towards a degree, but did not complete them. You have to read the résumé carefully and question the applicant closely.

**Caution:** Many applicants will say that they majored in Business at Harvard (or other schools) for an MBA degree, but nowhere on the résumé do they actually claim to have been awarded a degree. Check carefully on Ph.D. degrees. Some applicants who claim them may be working toward a doctorate, but still have a long way to go—a thesis or orals.

**2. Omitting a period of employment and/or stretching dates of employment** An applicant may show the years he or she worked for another company, but not the number of months. Thus, if the applicant left ABC Co. in January 1980 and was hired by DEF Co. in November 1981, the applicant was really unemployed for almost two years. This gap is covered up if the applicant shows one job ending in 1980 and the next beginning in 1981—and the continuity of the years suggests continuous employment, which it was not.

**3. Exaggerated or misleading claims of expertise and experience** Terms of achievement such as *supervised* (a department) . . . *managed* (an office) . . . *increased* (sales or profits) . . . *created* (a program or a campaign) frequently appear on applicants' résumés. They may be true, but can be misleading unless they are related to, and supported by, specific measures of accomplishment (the size of the department or budget;

the number of employees, the percentage of sales and profits, the scope of the program) which are brought to light through a probing interview and thorough background check.

**4. The self-employment smoke-screen** Always be alert to claims of self-employment. Many résumé fakers make this claim to cover periods of unemployment or a job that they don't want uncovered for a variety of reasons. It is very difficult for an employer to confirm self-employment without actually going to the business address or examining court/county clerk records or interviewing people with whom the applicant did business when he or she was self-employed. As a result, many employers (to their future regret) tend to skip checking out self-employment claims.

**5. The consultant "con"** Another favorite ploy is for an applicant to claim to have been a consultant out of a home address for five to six months. When you see such a claim, be sure to ask for the names of a few customers and a bank reference—and then check them.

**6. The out-of-business blind** It is not unusual for a résumé faker to claim employment with a company that is out of business, believing there is no way for you to check his or her record there. But many times, just by checking how long the firm was in business, one can prove that a résumé faker did not work during the period claimed. This investigative approach is one that is virtually impossible to work out by a mail check. One has to go to the address to check, or have the proper research tools with which to determine if, where, and for how long the alleged former employer was in business. In such a case, an investigative agency has the advantage in having the research material needed to determine if the company existed or, in many cases, to locate the former owners.

Source: Reprinted from Norton, T. W., *Personnel Marketplace,* P.O. Box 301, Huntington, NY 11743, (516) 427-3680. Reprinted with permission of the author.

### Views of Résumés

Résumés can be viewed in one of two ways: a history of your life or an advertisement of your skills. Résumés written as a history of one's life may tend to be long and contain every job ever worked as well as personal information such as hobbies, marital status, and personal health. Résumés written as an advertisement of skills tend to be shorter and contain only information that is both positive and relevant to a job seeker's desired career. This latter view of résumés is the most commonly held today.

### Characteristics of Effective Résumés

One of the most frustrating aspects of writing a résumé is that if you ask 100 people for advice, you will get 100 different opinions. However, though there are many *preferences*, only three *rules* must be followed to write an effective résumé.

**The Résumé Must Be Attractive and Easy to Read.**   To do this, try to leave at least a one-inch margin on all sides, allow plenty of white space, and limit the length to one page (Pibal, 1985); that is, do not "pack" information into the résumé. An undergraduate student of mine came to me with the "great idea" of typing his résumé onto a legal-sized sheet and then using a photocopy machine to reduce the size to regular paper with a one-inch margin. While this technique may fit the size requirement, it probably will be difficult to read because information is still packed into a small space. Also, personnel directors do not want to spend much time reading résumés. A résumé can have great content but if the "package" is not attractive, few employers will want to read it.

This rule is hardly surprising as physical attractiveness provides a first impression for many activities such as interviewing, dating, and purchasing products. White is probably the best paper color, and it is not necessary to use a special grade of paper or have the résumé typeset (Faloona, Henson, Jahn, & Snyder, 1985).

**The Résumé Cannot Contain Typing, Spelling, Grammatical, or Factual Mistakes.**   When Walter Pierce, Jr. was a personnel officer for Norfolk-Southern Corporation, his boss received a résumé from an excellent applicant for a job as a computer programmer. However, even though the applicant had outstanding credentials, the personnel director would not even offer him an interview because the applicant had misspelled two words on his résumé. A similar story is told by Dick Williams, the general manager for N & W Credit Union. He once received two cover letters stapled together—both referring to the résumé that wasn't there. To make matters worse, four words were misspelled. I could tell you more horror stories, but the point should be clear—do not make careless mistakes!

**Résumé Should Make the Applicant Look as Qualified as Possible— Without Lying.**   This is an important rule in determining what information should be included. If including hobbies, summer jobs, and a list of courses will make you look more qualified for *this particular job*, then, by all means, include them.

If a résumé follows these three rules—that is, it looks nice, doesn't contain mistakes, and makes the applicant look as good as possible—then it is an effective résumé. Opinions to the contrary (such as "use boldface type instead of underlining" or "outline your duties instead of putting them in a paragraph," and so on) probably represent individual preferences rather than any major problem with the résumé.

### Types of Résumés

There are three main types of résumés: chronological, functional, and psychological. As shown in Figure 5.11, the **chronological résumé** lists previous jobs in order from the most to the least recent. This type of résumé is useful for applicants whose previous jobs are related to their future plans and whose work histories do not contain gaps.

The **functional résumé,** as shown in Figure 5.12, organizes jobs based on the skills required to perform them rather than the order in which they were worked. Functional résumés are especially useful for applicants who are either changing careers or have gaps in their work histories. The problem with this type of résumé is that it may be more difficult to read and comprehend than other résumé types—this problem makes functional résumés the least popular with employees (Toth, 1991).

The **psychological résumé** is the style I prefer because it contains the strengths of both the chronological and functional styles and is based on sound psychological theory and research. As shown in Figure 5.13, the résumé should begin with a short summary of your strengths. This section takes advantage of the impression-formation principles of *priming* (preparing the reader for what is to come), *primacy* (early impressions are most important), and *short-term memory limits* (the list should not be longer than seven items).

The next section of the résumé should contain information about either your education or your experience—whichever is strongest for you. The design of the education section is intended to provide an organizational framework that will make it easier for the reader to remember the contents.

In deciding which information to put into these two sections, three impression-management rules should be used: relevance, unusualness, and positivity. If information is *relevant* to your desired career, it probably should be included. For example, you might mention that you have two children if you are applying for daycare or elementary school teaching positions but not if you are applying for a job involving a lot of travel. How far back should one go in listing jobs? Using the principle of relevance, the answer would be back far enough to include all relevant jobs.

*Unusual information* should be included when possible as people pay more attention to it than to typical information. A problem for college seniors is that their résumés look identical to those of their classmates. That

**CHRISTOPHER R. MILLER**

812 Main Street, Gainsville, FL  32789                                    (904) 645-1001

| | |
|---|---|
| Objective | Entry-level management position in financial services. |
| Education | B.S., University of Florida, May 1991 |

Major:      Business Administration
GPA:         3.43/4.0
Minor:       Information Systems
Business-Related Courses:  Accounting, Money & Banking, Principles of Marketing,  Economics, Statistics

Professional Experience

July 1995–Present
Assistant Manager, TCBY Yogurt, Gainsville, FL
    Responsible for posting daily receipts and making bank deposits. Further responsible for supervising and scheduling counter personnel, writing progress reports, and handling employee disputes.

August 1994–July 1995
Cashier/Customer Service, TCBY Yogurt, Gainsville, FL
    Responsible for assisting customers promptly and courteously, maintaining a balanced cash drawer, and cleaning work station.

May 1993–August 1994
Bank Teller, Barnett Bank, Gainsville, FL
    Responsible for assisting and advising customers with financial transactions.  Cash drawer balanced 99% of the time.  Received excellent performance ratings.

August 1992–May 1993
Waiter, Shakers Restaurant, Gainsville, FL
    Responsible for taking food and drink orders from customers and serving them courteously and efficiently.  Worked in a high-volume, fast-paced environment.

Activities

Member of Phi Kappa Phi Honor Society
Member of Phi Beta Lambda Business Organization
Vice President, Kappa Alpha Pi Social Fraternity
Member of Circle K Service Organization
Participated in Intramural Football

**Figure 5.11** Chronological résumé

**MATTHEW F. JOHNSON**

816 Broadway Road, Lexington, KY 63189
(606) 814-7282

Career Objective      Management-level position in banking services.

Banking & Management Experience

*Posted receipts* and made bank deposits daily for Dunkin' Donuts coffee shop in Lexington, Kentucky.  July 1994–present.

*Supervised and scheduled* cashier personnel for Dunkin' Donuts coffee shop in Lexington, Kentucky.  July 1994–present.

*Bank teller* for Citizen's Fidelity Bank in Lexington, Kentucky.  Maintained balanced cash drawer 99% of the time.  Trained in various financial transactions of the banking field.  May 1994–August 1995.

Customer Service Experience

*Customer service/cashier* for Dunkin' Donuts coffee shop in Lexington, Kentucky. Assisted customers with placing orders and responsible for maintaining a balanced cash drawer.

*Assisted customers* promptly and courteously with financial transactions at Citizen's Fidelity Bank in Lexington, Kentucky.  Received excellent performance ratings.  May 1995–August 1995.

*Waited on customers* at El Torito Mexican Restaurant in Lexington, Kentucky.  After taking customers' orders, served customers promptly and courteously.  August 1993–May 1994.

Leadership Experience

*Vice President* of Sigma Epsilon Phi Social Fraternity.  Was responsible for assisting pledges with the transition into the fraternity and for raising money for the fraternity philanthropy through various fundraisers.

*Coordinated* and participated in the softball intramural team for the fraternity.

Community Service and Campus Activities

*Member of Key Club* Service Organization on campus.

*Member of Management Association.*

*Member of Phi Kappa Phi* Honor Society.

Education          B.A., Management, University of Kentucky, May 1995
GPA: 3.44/4.0      Minor: Information Systems
Courses:  Accounting, Economics, Marketing, Money & Banking, Principles of Management

**Figure 5.12** Functional résumé

**ALEXANDER G. BELL**

1421 Watson Drive                    Ringem, Virginia 24147                    (730) 555-1756

**PROFESSIONAL STRENGTHS**
- Associate's Degree in Business
- Twelve Years Sales and Customer Relations Experience
- Ten Years Data Entry Experience
- Excellent Oral and Written Communication Skills
- Excellent Work Performance and Attendance History
- Extensive Knowledge in Woodworking and Electronics
- Computer Literate (WordPerfect, dBase, Lotus, UNIX)

**PROFESSIONAL EXPERIENCE**

**Sales Representative** (May 1985–present)
AT&T—Vienna, Virginia

Responsible for helping customers within the federal government choose the phone system that best suits their organizational needs and for solving problems that occur after an agency has placed an order. Specific duties include talking with customers to determine their needs, suggesting systems that would satisfy those needs, entering relevant data into the computer, setting up a schedule to install or repair systems, determining how the phone network should be routed through the system, and preparing the necessary billing information.

High level of performance demonstrated by receiving three raises, maintaining an excellent attendance record, and receiving a cash award for an employee suggestion. Leaving AT&T due to workforce reduction.

**Sales Clerk** (April 1983–May 1985)
Sears – Woodbridge, Virginia

Responsible for helping customers purchase hand and power tools. Specific duties included providing customers with product information, answering questions, and ringing-up merchandise.

Demonstrated a high level of performance by consistently earning sales bonuses, balancing cash drawer, and seldom receiving complaints from customers. Left Sears to take higher-paying job at AT&T.

**EDUCATION**

A.A.S., Business Administration (1993)
Northern Virginia Community College, Annandale, Virginia

Certificate of Completion (1988)
Dale Carnegie Interpersonal Skills Program

Diploma (1985)
Beall High School, Duffie, West Virginia

Additional Training and Courses:
- Personal Financial Planning
- Computer Applications (dBase, Lotus)
- AT&T Sales Course

**Figure 5.13** Psychological résumé

**Rhonda Duffie, M.S., PHR**
*Human Resources
Administrator
Warner-Lambert, Sales &
Marketing Support
Center*

I am the human resources administrator for a small distribution center in Southwestern Virginia. We distribute promotional materials for Warner-Lambert, a large pharmaceutical, consumer health products, and confectionery manufacturer. I am responsible for employee relations, employee training and development, compensation and benefits administration, employee recruitment, administration of selection tests, interviewing, and employee orientation. A large part of my time is spent recruiting and interviewing applicants for open positions. Recruiting and hiring highly qualified applicants is very important for center operations, as well as for the reputation of the human resources department.

Whether a position is a new or existing one, the first step is ensuring that a thorough job description exists for the position. Information from this job description is then used for recruitment. In advertising the position, it is important to target the appropriate market, which depends, in large part, on the type of position to be filled and the availability of qualified local applicants.

For entry-level and mid-level positions, an advertisement in a local newspaper is placed, and an internal open-position notice is posted. The local state employment office is contacted and provided with a copy of the employment advertisement. In addition, several local college placement offices are notified concerning the open position. Recruiting for upper-level positions has a broader focus for internal and external recruiting efforts. We also use internal open-position notices, but for upper-level positions, these are distributed to company locations throughout the nation. Newspaper advertisements would be placed regionally or nationally, depending on the position to be filled. Because our center is located in a rural area, we have difficulty attracting qualified applicants. Therefore, it is essential to use a variety of recruitment methods to reach more potential applicants.

As with most organizations, an important part of the selection process is the employment interview. In order to increase the usefulness of the interview, our center uses a structured interview for all open positions. For each position, a set of important competencies is identified. Questions for each competency are established and may be either technical or situational in nature. Applicants are interviewed by me, then by the position's supervisor, and lastly, by another supervisor. Using a structured interview and having several independent interviewers increases the amount of pertinent information received and reduces the bias involved in typical interviews. Depending on the position, applicants also may be required to pass such tests as typing or data-entry. At Warner-Lambert, the final component of the selection process is a post-offer, pre-employment physical and substance abuse screening for all new hires.

is, most business majors take the same classes, belong to the same clubs, and have had similar part-time jobs. To stand out from other graduates, an applicant needs something unusual such as an internship, an interesting and relevant hobby, or an unusual life experience (for example, spent a year in Europe, rode a bike across the country).

Though it is advisable to have unusual information, the information must also be *positive*. It probably would not be a good idea to list unusual information such as, "I've been arrested more times than anyone in my class," or "I enjoy bungee jumping without cords." The unacceptability of these two examples is obvious, and few applicants would make the mistake of actually including such information on their résumés; however, more subtle items can have the same effect. For example, suppose you enjoy hunting and are a member of the Young Democrats on campus. Including these items might make a negative impression on Republicans and those who oppose hunting. Only include information that most people will find positive (such as Red Cross volunteer, worked to help finance education, and so on), and avoid information that may be viewed negatively such as political affiliation, religion, and dangerous hobbies (Bonner, 1993).

Of the many positive activities and accomplishments that you could list, list only your best. Do not list everything that you have done; research by Spock and Stevens (1985) found that it is better to list a few great things rather than many good things. This finding is based on Anderson's (1965) *averaging-versus-adding model* of impression formation, which implies that activity quality is more important than quantity (for example, it is not necessary nor desirable to list all of your coursework [Pibal, 1985]).

## CHAPTER SUMMARY

The beginning of the chapter discussed the first steps in the employee selection process, starting with a job analysis. After the job analysis, the human resource professional recruits employees and then, based on the results of the job analysis, uses some formal means to determine whether the applicant will make a good employee.

Several methods for recruiting employees then were discussed. These methods included help-wanted and situation-wanted ads, employee referrals, employment agencies, point-of-purchase methods, direct mail, and job fairs. Research indicates that for longer employee tenure, employee referrals are the best method, especially when the referrals are made by a current employee who has a long tenure. In terms of future employee performance, recruitment methods appear to be equal.

The chapter also discussed the interview process. In this discussion, factors such as contrast effects, negative information bias, use of nonverbal cues, interviewer-interviewee similarity, and primacy effects were cited as reasons for the poor reliability and minimal validity of the unstructured interview. Traditional employment interviews apparently are not good at predicting employee performance, but new developments such as situational interviews and patterned behavior description interviews (PBDI) show promise as valid predictors of future employee success.

The chapter concluded with a discussion of résumés and cover letters. Tips for writing cover letters and résumés were provided.

# GLOSSARY

**Apply-in-person ads**   Recruitment ads that instruct applicants to apply in person rather than call or send résumés.

**Averaging-versus-adding model**   A model proposed by Anderson that postulates that our impressions are based more on the average value of each impression rather than the sum of the values for each impression.

**Benchmark answers**   Standard answers to interview questions, the quality of which have been agreed on by job experts.

**Blind box ads**   Recruitment ads that instruct applicants to send their résumé to a box at the newspaper; neither the name nor the address of the company is provided.

**Chronological résumé**   A résumé in which jobs are listed in order from most to least recent.

**Clinical prediction**   When an individual looks at information about an applicant, combines that information in some subjective way, and then makes a judgment about that person.

**Contrast effect**   When the performance of one applicant affects the perception of the performance of the next applicant.

**Cost per applicant**   The amount of money spent on a recruitment campaign divided by the number of people who apply for jobs as a result of the recruitment campaign.

**Cost per qualified applicant**   The amount of money spent on a recruitment campaign divided by the number of qualified people who apply for jobs as a result of the recruitment campaign.

**Cover letter**   A letter that accompanies a résumé or job application.

**Direct mail**   A method of recruitment in which an organization sends out mass-mailings of information about job openings to potential applicants.

**Employee referral**   A method of recruitment in which a current employee refers a friend or family member for a job.

**Employment agency**   An organization that specializes in finding jobs for applicants and finding applicants for organizations looking for employees.

**Employment interview**   A method of selecting employees in which an interviewer asks questions of an applicant and then makes an employment decision based on the answers and the way in which they were answered.

**Executive search firms**   Employment agencies, also called *headhunters*, that specialize in placing applicants in high-paying jobs.

**External recruitment**   Recruiting employees from outside the organization.

**Functional résumé**   A résumé format in which jobs are grouped by function rather than listed in order by date.

**Internal recruitment**   Recruiting employees already employed by the organization.

**Job fairs**   A recruitment method in which several employers are available at one location so that many applicants can obtain information at one time.

**Media advertisements**   A recruitment method using newspapers, radio, and television.

**Negative-information bias**   Negative information may receive more weight in an employment decision than does positive information.

**Nonverbal cues**   Factors such as eye contact and posture that are not associated with actual words spoken.

**Number of qualified applicants**   A method of evaluating the effectiveness of a recruitment program by looking at the number of qualified applicants who apply.

**Patterned behavior description interview (PBDI)**   A structured interview in which the questions focus on behavior in previous jobs.

**Primacy effect**   Information that is presented early in an interview may carry more weight than information presented later.

**Psychological résumé**   A résumé style that takes advantage of psychological principles pertaining to memory organization and impression formation.

**Realistic job preview (RJP)**   A method of recruitment in which job applicants are told both the positive and negative aspects of a job.

**Recruitment**   The process of attracting employees to an organization.

**Respond-by-calling ads**   Recruitment ads in which applicants are instructed to call rather than apply in person or send résumés.

**Résumé**   A formal summary of an applicant's professional and educational background.

**Résumé fraud**   The intentional placement of untrue information on a résumé.

**Send-résumé ads**   Recruitment ads in which applicants are instructed to send their résumés to the company rather than call or apply in person.

**Signs**   A method of recruitment based on point-of-purchase advertising principles in which help-wanted signs are placed so that they can be viewed by people who visit the organization.

**Situational interview**   A structured interview technique in which applicants are presented with a series of situations and asked how they would handle each one.

**Situation-wanted ads**   Newspaper ads run by applicants looking for jobs rather than by organizations looking for applicants.

**State employment agency**   An employment service, operated by a state government, designed to match applicants with job openings.

**Statistical prediction**   The use of numerical formulas that take the information gathered about an applicant and mathematically determine a probability regarding that applicant's future behavior.

**Structured interviews**   Interviews in which every applicant is asked the same questions, and identical answers are given identical scores.

# 6

# EMPLOYEE SELECTION: REFERENCES AND TESTING

In the last chapter, interviews and résumés were described as the most commonly used methods to screen and select employees. But even though these methods are the most commonly used, they are certainly not the best. In this chapter, we discuss several other techniques that are preferred by industrial psychologists to select employees.

In psychology, a common belief is that the best predictor of future performance is past performance. Thus, if an organization wants to hire a salesperson, the best applicant might be the one who has been a successful salesperson in jobs that were similar to the one for which he now applies.

Verifying previous employment is not difficult, but it can be difficult to verify the *quality* of past performance. I recently watched the National Football League's draft of college players on television and was envious of the fact that professional football teams can assess a player's previous performance by watching game films. That is, the scouts do not have to rely on the opinions of other coaches. Instead, the scouts can watch literally every minute a player has spent on the field while in college.

Unfortunately, few applicants bring "game films" of their previous employment performances. Instead, an employer must obtain information about the quality of previous performance by relying on an applicant's references: either by calling those references directly or asking for **letters of recommendation** from previous employers; a practice used by over 90% of all organizations (Muchinsky, 1979).

## REASONS FOR USING REFERENCES AND RECOMMENDATIONS

### Confirming Details on a Résumé

As mentioned in Chapter 5, it is not uncommon for applicants to engage in **résumé fraud**—lying on their résumés about what experience or education they actually have. Thus, one reason to check references or ask for letters of recommendation is simply to confirm the truthfulness of information provided by the applicant (Beason & Belt, 1976). An excellent example of résumé fraud is the bizarre 1994 assault against figure skater Nancy Kerrigan arranged by Shawn Eckardt, the bodyguard of Kerrigan's skating rival Tonya Harding. Harding hired Eckardt as her bodyguard because his résumé indicated he was an expert in counterintelligence and international terrorism, graduated from an elite executive protection school, and had spent four years "tracking terrorist cells" and "conducting a successful hostage retrieval operation" (Meehan, 1994). After the attack against Kerrigan, however, a private investigator discovered that Eckardt never graduated from a security school and would have been 16 during the time he claimed he was in Europe saving the world from terrorists. The president of a school he did attend stated that he "wouldn't hire Eckardt as a bodyguard in a lifetime"—an opinion that would have been discovered had Harding checked Eckardt's references.

### Checking for Discipline Problems

A second reason to check references or obtain letters of recommendation is to determine if the applicant has a history of discipline problems such as poor attendance, sexual harassment, or violence. Such a history is important for an organization to discover to avoid future problems as well as to protect itself from a potential charge of **negligent hiring.** If an organization hires an applicant without checking his references and background, and he later commits a crime while in the employ of the organization, the organization may be found guilty of negligent hiring.

Negligent hiring cases are typically filed in court as common law cases, or torts. These cases are based on the premise that an employer has the duty to protect its employees and customers from harm caused by its employees or products. In determining negligent hiring, courts look at the nature of the job. Organizations involved with the safety of the public, such as police departments and daycare centers, must conduct more thorough background and reference checks than organizations such as retail stores.

For example, a child-care center in California hired an employee without checking his references. A few months later, the employee molested a child at the center. The employee had a criminal record of child abuse that would have been discovered with a simple call to his previous employer. As one would expect, the court found the employer guilty of negligent hiring because the employer had not taken "reasonable care" in ensuring the well-being of its customers.

In Virginia in 1989, an employee of a grocery store copied the address of a female customer from a check she had written to the store. The employee later went to the customer's home and raped her. In this example, a case for negligent hiring could not be made because the company had contacted the employee's previous employment references and had found no reason not to hire him. Because there was nothing to discover and because the store took reasonable care to check its employees, it was not guilty of negligent hiring.

### Discovering New Information about the Applicant

Employers use a variety of methods to understand the personality and skills of job applicants: references and letters of recommendation certainly can be two of these methods. Former employers and professors can provide information about an applicant's work habits, character, personality, and skills. Care must be taken, however, when using these methods because the opinion provided by any particular reference may be inaccurate or purposefully untrue. For example, a reference might describe a former employee as "difficult to work with," implying that everyone has trouble working with the applicant. It may be, however, that only the person providing the reference had trouble working with the applicant. This is an important point because each of us has people we don't get along with even though, all things considered, we are basically good people. Thus, reference

**Figure 6.1**
Predicting future
performance from
past performance

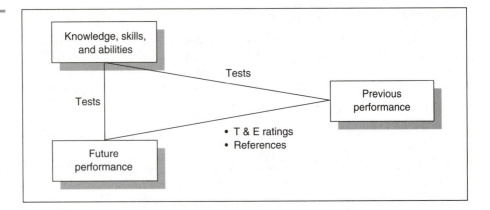

checkers should always obtain specific behavioral examples and try to get
consensus from several references.

### Predicting Future Performance

I/O Psychologists use tests to predict future employee performance. As mentioned earlier, however, psychologists believe that the best predictor of future
performance is past performance. Thus, as shown in Figure 6.1, it makes
theoretical sense that performance on previous jobs should be a better
predictor of performance on future jobs if the two jobs are similar. It is on
this use of references that our discussion will focus.

## PROBLEMS WITH USING REFERENCES
## TO PREDICT FUTURE PERFORMANCE

Even though references are commonly used to screen and select employees,
they have not been successful in predicting future employee success
(Muchinsky, 1979). In fact, the average validity coefficient for references and
performance is only .13 (Browning, 1968; Mosel & Goheen, 1958). This low
validity is due largely to four main problems with references and letters of
recommendation: leniency, knowledge of the applicant, low reliability, and
extraneous factors involved in writing and reading such letters.

### Leniency

Research is clear that most letters of recommendation are positive (Carroll
& Nash, 1972; Miller & Van Rybroek, 1988; Myers & Errett, 1959; Whitcomb
& Bryan, 1988; Yoder, 1962); especially those written by personal acquaintances (Mosel & Goheen, 1959). Because we have all worked with terrible
employees at some point in our lives, it would at first seem surprising that
references typically are so positive. But keep in mind that *applicants choose
their own references!* Even Nazi leader Adolph Hitler, serial killer Ted Bundy,
or terrorist Timothy McVeigh would have been able to find three people who
could provide them with favorable references.

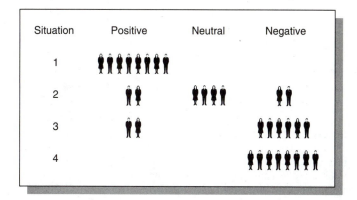

**Figure 6.2**
Co-workers' attitudes toward employee

Figure 6.2 shows how co-workers' attitudes toward an employee affect the references they give that person. In the first situation, all of the applicant's eight co-workers have positive feelings about the applicant. Thus, if we ask for references from two co-workers, both would be positive *and* representative of the other six co-workers. In situation 2, most co-workers have neutral regard for the applicant, with two having positive feelings and two having negative feelings. In this situation, however, both references chosen by the applicant would be positive—and *more favorable* than most co-workers' attitudes. In situation 3, only two of eight people like the applicant—yet the two reference letters will be the same as in the first and second situations even though most co-workers have negative feelings about our applicant. In situation 4, no one likes our applicant. In this case, our request for references either would keep the person from applying for our job or force the applicant to find references from somewhere else. But if we *require* work-related references, they probably, but not necessarily, would be negative because research has shown that co-workers *are* willing to say negative things about unsatisfactory employees (Nash & Carroll, 1970).

A second factor that influences the degree of leniency is the *confidentiality of the reference*. By law, people have the right to see their reference letters. By signing a waiver such as that shown in Figure 6.3, however, applicants can give up that right. This may be more beneficial for a potential employer; research by Ceci and Peters (1984) and Shaffer and Tomarelli (1981) indicates that people providing references tend to be less lenient when an applicant waives her right to see a reference letter. That is, when a person writing a reference letter knows that the applicant is allowed to see the letter, the writer is more inclined to provide a favorable evaluation.

A third cause of leniency stems from the *fear of legal ramifications*. A person providing references can be charged with defamation of character (slander if the reference was oral, libel if it was written) if the content of the reference is both untrue and made with malicious intent. It is this fear that keeps many organizations from providing references at all (Kleiman & White, 1991). However, people providing references are granted what is called a "conditional privilege" which means that they have the right to express their opinion provided they believe what they say is true and have reasonable

**Figure 6.3**
A typical reference
waiver

**Statement of Release**

_____     _____
Name of person asked to write                Date
this recommendation

I request that you complete this recommendation form, which I
understand will become a part of my file in the Radford
University Graduate College.  I further understand:

(1) that this recommendation statement from you will be a
candid evaluation of my scholarship, work habits, and
potential;

(2) that the completed statement will be sent to the Radford
University Graduate College; and

(3) that it will be held in confidence from me and the public
by the Radford University Graduate Office.

_____     _____
Applicant's name (print)            Applicant's signature

grounds for this belief (Ryan & Lasek, 1991). A good way to reduce the possibility of a lawsuit is to have the applicant sign waivers such as those shown in Figures 6.4 to 6.6 (Morse, 1988). The waiver in Figure 6.4 is used by a reference writer and the other two by the organization checking references: one waives claims against people providing references to the organization and the other waives future claims against the organization so that the organization can provide references about the employee should he leave the organization.

Because an employer can be guilty of negligent hiring for not contacting references, a former employer also can be guilty of **negligent reference** if it does not provide relevant information to an organization that requests it. For example, if Dinero Bank fires John Smith for theft and fails to divulge that fact to a bank that is thinking of hiring Smith, Dinero Bank may be found liable if Smith steals money at his new bank.

A number of years ago, based on several letters of recommendation, our department hired a part-time instructor. Two weeks after he started the job,

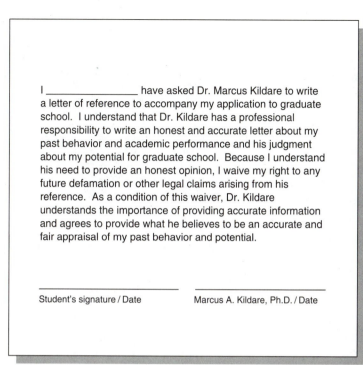

**Figure 6.4**
Sample waiver used
by a reference
writer

I _____ have asked Dr. Marcus Kildare to write a letter of reference to accompany my application to graduate school. I understand that Dr. Kildare has a professional responsibility to write an honest and accurate letter about my past behavior and academic performance and his judgment about my potential for graduate school. Because I understand his need to provide an honest opinion, I waive my right to any future defamation or other legal claims arising from his reference. As a condition of this waiver, Dr. Kildare understands the importance of providing accurate information and agrees to provide what he believes to be an accurate and fair appraisal of my past behavior and potential.

_____        _____
Student's signature / Date         Marcus A. Kildare, Ph.D. / Date

we discovered that he had to return to his home in another state to face charges of stealing drugs from his former employer, a psychology department at another university. We were upset because neither of the references from his former job mentioned the charges. After a rather heated conversation with one of the references, we learned that the applicant was the son of the department chairman and the faculty were afraid to say anything that would anger their boss.

These last examples show why providing references and letters of recommendations can be so difficult. On the one hand, a former employer can be charged with slander or libel if it says something bad about an applicant that cannot be proven. On the other hand, an employer can be held liable if it does not provide information about a potentially dangerous applicant. Because of these competing responsibilities, as mentioned previously, many organizations will only confirm employment dates and salary information unless a former employee has been convicted of a criminal offense that resulted in termination of the employee.

Three other factors that affect the leniency of references are the *gender of the letter writer, gender of the applicant,* and *race of the letter reader.* Carroll and Nash (1972) found that female reference letter writers are more lenient when referring female applicants. Kryger and Shikiar (1978) found that letters written about female applicants were rated higher than identical letters written about male applicants, and Bryan (1992) found that Black professionals are more lenient than White professionals in evaluating letter con-

**Figure 6.5**
Employee's consent to obtain information

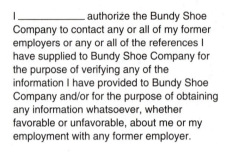

I _____ authorize the Bundy Shoe Company to contact any or all of my former employers or any or all of the references I have supplied to Bundy Shoe Company for the purpose of verifying any of the information I have provided to Bundy Shoe Company and/or for the purpose of obtaining any information whatsoever, whether favorable or unfavorable, about me or my employment with any former employer.

**Figure 6.6**
Employee's consent to release information

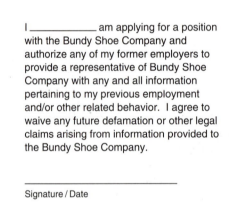

I _____ am applying for a position with the Bundy Shoe Company and authorize any of my former employers to provide a representative of Bundy Shoe Company with any and all information pertaining to my previous employment and/or other related behavior.  I agree to waive any future defamation or other legal claims arising from information provided to the Bundy Shoe Company.

_____
Signature / Date

tent. Thus, as shown in Figure 6.7, when an applicant chooses his own references, retains his right to see reference letters, is referred by a female co-worker, and is evaluated by a Black professional, his references are far more positive than if based solely on his actual performance.

### Knowledge of the Applicant

A second problem with letters of recommendation is that the person writing the letter often does not know the applicant well, has not observed all aspects of an applicant's behavior, or both. Professors are often asked to provide recommendations for students whom they know from only one or two classes. Such recommendations are not likely to be as accurate and com-

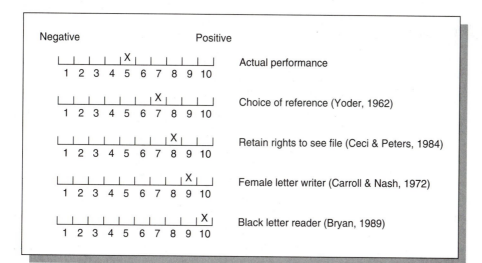

Figure 6.7
Effects of various factors in evaluation of reference letters

plete as those provided by professors who have had students in several classes and perhaps worked with them outside the classroom setting.

Even in a work setting in which a supervisor provides the recommendation, he often does not see all aspects of an employee's behavior (see Figure 6.8). Employees often act very differently around their supervisors than they would around co-workers and customers. Furthermore, as Figure 6.8 shows and as will be discussed in greater detail in a later chapter, those behaviors that a reference writer actually recalls are only a fraction of the behaviors actually occurring in the presence of the person writing the recommendation.

### Reliability

The third problem with references and letters of recommendation involves the *lack of agreement* between two people who provide references for the same person. Research reveals that reference **reliability** is less than .40 (Aamodt, Dwight, & Michals, 1994; Baxter, Brock, Hill, & Rozelle, 1981; Mosel & Goheen, 1959; Mosel & Goheen, 1952). The reliability problem is so severe that Baxter and his colleagues (1981) found more agreement between recommendations written *by the same person* for two different applicants than between two people writing recommendations *for the same person*. Thus, letters of recommendation may say more about the person writing the letter than about the person for whom it is being written.

This low level of reliability probably results from the point cited earlier that a reference writer has not seen all aspects of an applicant's behavior. Thus, a reference provided by a professor who has observed an applicant in a classroom may not agree with a reference provided by a supervisor who has observed the same applicant in a work setting. But even though there may be good reasons for the low levels of reliability in reference letters, limiting their validity, research has yet to answer the question: If references do not agree, which one should be taken the most seriously?

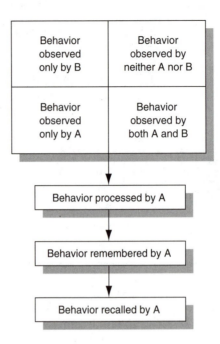

**Figure 6.8**
A reference writer often lacks complete knowledge of an employee's behavior

| Behavior observed only by B | Behavior observed by neither A nor B |
| Behavior observed only by A | Behavior observed by both A and B |

Behavior processed by A

Behavior remembered by A

Behavior recalled by A

### *Extraneous Factors*

The fourth problem with letters of recommendation concerns extraneous factors that affect their writing and evaluation. Research has indicated that the method used by the letter writer is often more important than the actual content. For example:

1. Knouse (1983) found that letters that contained specific examples were rated higher than letters that contained generalities.
2. Cowan and Kasen (1984) found that male and female writers use different titles when referring to applicants in their letters. Female writers refer to applicants as "Mr." or "Mrs.," while male writers refer to applicants by their first names.
3. Mehrabian (1965) and Weins, Jackson, Manaugh, and Matarazzo (1969) found that even though most letters of recommendation are positive, letters written by references who like applicants are longer than those written by references who do not.

### IMPROVING THE VALIDITY OF REFERENCES

To improve the validity of references, Peres and Garcia (1962) developed, and Aamodt and his colleagues (Aamodt, Bryan, & Whitcomb, 1993; Aamodt, Dwight, & Michals, 1994) refined, the *Trait Approach*, which is a unique way to make reference letters more useful by focusing on their relevant content rather than on their positiveness. As an example, see the two letters of recommendation in Figure 6.9. Although both describe the

**Figure 6.9**
Two letters of
recommendation

Dear Personnel Director:

Mr. John Anderson asked that I write this
letter in support of his application as an
assistant manager, and I am pleased to do
so.  I have known John for six years as he
was my assistant in the accounting
department.

John always had his work completed
accurately and promptly.  In his six years
here, he never missed a deadline.  He is
very detail oriented, alert in finding
errors, and methodical in his problem-
solving approach.  Interpersonally, John is
a very friendly and helpful person.

I have great confidence in John's ability.
If you desire more information, please let
me know.

Dear Personnel Director:

Mr. John Anderson asked that I write this
letter in support of his application as an
assistant manager, and I am pleased to do
so.  I have known John for six years as he
was my assistant in the accounting
department.

John was one of the most popular employees
in our agency as he is a friendly,
outgoing, sociable individual.  He has a
great sense of humor, is poised, and is
very helpful.  In completing his work, he
is independent, energetic, and industrious.

I have great confidence in John's ability.
If you desire more information, please let
me know.

**Table 6.1**  Complete list of words used in the trait approach to scoring letters of recommendation

### Urbanity

| | | | |
|---|---|---|---|
| active in class discussions | delight (to work with) | lively | sense of humor |
| affable | delightful | member of group (pres., secretary) | sociable |
| animated | engaging personality | | sophisticated |
| articulate | enjoyable | motivator | sparkling |
| assured | expressive | oral | speaks well |
| chatty | friendly | out going | talkative |
| cheerful | gregarious | particpates in discussion | teaching assistant |
| commanding | interacts (interacted) | personable | very-involved |
| confident | interpersonal (skilled) | pleasant | well-bred |
| contributor | jokes | poised | well-liked |
| conversational | leader (a) | polished | well-rounded |
| cultured | leadership (shown) | refined | (be aware of context) |
| | likable | relates well to others | |

### Cooperation-Consideration

| | | | |
|---|---|---|---|
| accommodating | easy-going | incorruptible | restrained |
| altruistic | emotionally stable (mature) | integrity (shows) | sacrificing |
| attentive | | kindly | sensitive |
| big-hearted | empathetic | levelheaded | serious |
| calm | encouraging (peers) | liberal | sincere |
| caring | ethical | loyal | sober |
| clean-cut | even keel emotionally | mature | staid |
| congeneial | faithful | modest | strong character |
| considerate | fine person | moral | takes suggestions well |
| compassionate | generous | nonjudgmental | team player |
| composed | gentle | obliging | team work (promotes) |
| conscientious (toward a person) | genuine | open | thoughtful |
| | good listener | open minded | trustworthy |
| cooperative | good-natured | patient | upstanding |
| counselor (good) | gracious | placid | volunteer |
| courteous | group-centered | professional (in interactions) | (be aware of context) |
| decent | helpful | | warm |
| desire (to help others) | honest | quiet | well mannered |
| down to earth | human relations (outstanding) | respectable | willing |
| earnest | | respectful | works well (with others) |

### Dependability-Reliability

| | | | |
|---|---|---|---|
| ability to follow through | critical | follows through | prompt |
| accurate | decisive | independent (works) | proofreads |
| attended (class) | dedicated | methodical | reliable |
| business-like | definite | neat | responsible |
| careful | dependable | never have to remind | self-reliant |
| certain | detail-minded | on time | sure |
| committed | diligent | orderly | thorough |
| completed (projects) | disciplined | organized | well prepared |
| conscientious (toward work) | efficient | practical | work completed on time |
| | fastidious | precise | |
| committed | focused (be aware of context) | prepared | |
| | | pride (toward work) | |

**Table 6.1**

| Mental Agility | | | |
|---|---|---|---|
| able to apply (information, knowledge) | common sense (shows) | inquisitive | research skills (excellent) |
| able to use common sense | competent | insightful | retains knowledge |
| able to use good judgment | creative | intellectual | resourceful |
| able to retain information | curious (intellectually) | intelligent | sagacious |
| above average | did very well | imaginative | sensible |
| academic ability (high) | discerning | judicious | skilled |
| adaptable | effective | knowledgeable | skillful (handles material) |
| adventurous | esthetic | learns quickly | sound judgment |
| alert | excellent student | logical | technically competent |
| analytical | excels (scholastically) | on-target | thinks clearly |
| aptitude | farsighted | on the ball | thinker |
| artistic | fine _____ skills | original | thoughtful |
| artistic talent | fluent (in a language) | perceptive | top 10%, etc. |
| astute | good common sense | performed well | understanding (good) |
| bright | good student | potential (demonstrated, has) | wise |
| capable | good writing skills | practical (uses common sense) | |
| | held in high regard | proficient | |
| | honor roll | quick to comprehend | |
| | informed | | |
| | ingenious | | |

| Vigor | | | |
|---|---|---|---|
| achiever | defends (ideas, positions) | hard-worker | pursues opportunities |
| active | devoted (extra time) | high energy | quick |
| aggressive | eager | hustling | resolute |
| ambitious | ebullient | independent | self-assured |
| assertive | energetic | industrious | self-confident |
| autonomous | enterprising | initiative (shows) | self-directed |
| challenges (an assertion) | enthusiastic | interest (high level of) | self-driving |
| compulsion (to achieve) | fast | involved (highly) | self-improvement |
| courageous | forthrightness | pace-setting | self-reliant |
| demanding | forward | persevere | self-starting |
| desire (to succeed) | frank | persistent | sought opportunities (info.) |
| determined | goal-directed | probes beyond . . . | speedy |
| | | productive | |

applicant in favorable terms, they differ greatly in the content words used to describe the applicant.

After examining thousands of letters of recommendation, Peres and Garcia (1962) found that the adjectives contained in such letters fall into one of five categories: **dependability-reliability, consideration-cooperation, mental agility, urbanity,** and **vigor.** A complete list of the trait words in each category is shown in Table 6.1.

Thus, to use letters of recommendation to accurately predict performance, an employer would use the following five-step process:

1. Determine the importance of each of these five categories to the performance of a particular job.

**Figure 6.10**
Identified traits
in letters of
recommendation

Dear Personnel Director:

Mr. John Anderson asked that I write this letter in support of his application as an assistant manager, and I am pleased to do so. I have known John for six years as he was my assistant in the accounting department.

John was one of the most popular employees in our agency as he is a <u>friendly</u>, <u>outgoing</u>, <u>sociable</u> individual. He has a great <u>sense of humor</u>, is <u>poised</u>, and is very <u>helpful</u>. In completing his work, he is <u>independent</u>, <u>energetic</u>, and <u>industrious</u>.

I have great confidence in John's ability. If you desire more information, please let me know.

U _4_ cc _2_ DR _0_ MA _0_ V _3_

Dear Personnel Director:

Mr. John Anderson asked that I write this letter in support of his application as an assistant manager, and I am pleased to do so. I have known John for six years as he was my assistant in the accounting department.

John always had his work completed <u>accurately</u> and <u>promptly</u>. In his six years here, he <u>never missed a deadline</u>. He is very <u>detail oriented</u>, <u>alert</u> in finding errors, and <u>methodical</u> in his problem-solving approach. Interpersonally, John is a very <u>friendly</u> and <u>helpful</u> person.

I have great confidence in John's ability. If you desire more information, please let me know.

U _0_ cc _2_ DR _6_ MA _0_ V _0_

**Figure 6.11**
Forced choice reference form

**Instructions:** In each set of traits, choose the one that most describes the applicant.

1.  friendly

    responsible

    creative

2.  detailed

    outgoing

    inventive

2.  Read each letter of recommendation and underline the traits in each letter used to describe the applicant.

3.  Use the list of words composed by Peres and Garcia (1962) and expanded by Aamodt et al. (1994) to place each trait into one of the five categories.

4.  Total the number of words for each of the five categories.

5.  Divide each category total by the total number of traits.

To demonstrate this process, Figure 6.10 shows the traits in the two letters first shown in Figure 6.9. The traits have been underlined and summed to provide a score for each of the five categories.

Two studies investigating the validity of the Trait Approach (Aamodt, Bryan, and Whitcomb, 1993; Aamodt et al., 1994) found that the number of "mental agility" adjectives mentioned in a letter of recommendation significantly correlated with graduate grade point averages, and the number of traits in the "urbanity" category significantly correlated with teaching ratings received by general psychology instructors. Thus, the Trait Approach may indeed be a useful way to determine the validity of letters of recommendation.

Carroll and Nash (1972) developed another potentially useful method to improve the validity of references. These researchers created a rating form, similar to that shown in Figure 6.11, containing 24 sets of behavioral statements. Although the words in each pair had the same level of social desirability, only one of the two predicted success on the job. A reference writer was asked to complete the form, and the applicant's score was the number of "predictive" words that were chosen. This method was found to correlate with the performance ratings of a second clerical group.

Daniel (1990) developed a reference checklist similar to that used by Carroll and Nash (1972) but based on the Peres and Garcia trait categories. Daniel compared the trait checklist results with supervisors' ratings of their desire to rehire college work-study students and found significant correlations of .38 with cooperation-consideration and .45 with mental agility.

As this discussion illustrates, references and letters of recommendation often are unable to predict performance. But with further refinement and research, techniques such as those developed by Peres and Garcia (1962) and Carroll and Nash (1972) may increase the predictive abilities of such references.

### Ethical Issues

Because providing references and letters of recommendation is a subjective process, ethical problems may arise involving their use. The following are three ethical guidelines that referees should follow:

1. *Explicitly state your relationship* with the person you are recommending. That is: Are you the applicant's professor, boss, co-worker, friend, relative, or some combination of the five? This is important because people often have dual roles: a person may be a supervisor as well as a good friend. Without understanding the exact nature of the referee-referent relationship, making judgments about the content of a reference can be difficulty. For example, I was told of a situation in which an applicant received a glowing letter of recommendation from a co-worker, and the applicant was hired in part due to the strength of that letter. Within a few months, the new employee was engaged in discipline problems, and it was only then that the organization discovered that the person who wrote the glowing letter was the applicant's daughter. Because the mother and daughter's last names were different, and the exact relationship between the two was not stated in the letter, the organization never suspected they were related.

2. *Be honest* in providing details. A referee has both an ethical and a legal obligation to provide relevant information about an applicant (Range, Menyhert, Walsh, Hardin, Craddick, & Ellis, 1991). A good rule is to ask "If I were in the reference seeker's shoes, what would I need to know?" Of course, deciding what information to provide can often be a difficult process. I was recently contacted by a Secret Service agent conducting a reference check on an applicant for a position in the human resource department. My reservations about the student concerned his excessive use of alcohol in social situations and his negative attitude toward women. After some soul searching (as much as can be done with a federal agent staring at you), I decided to provide information about the student's attitude toward women as I thought it was relevant to a human resource job but not mention the social drinking problem. Had the student been an applicant for a position as an agent, I would have mentioned the drinking. I'm not sure that my decision was correct, but the example demonstrates the dilemma of balancing the duty to provide information to the reference seeker with a duty to treat an applicant fairly.

3. Let the *applicant see your reference* before sending it, and give him the chance to decline to use it. Such a procedure is fair to the applicant and reduces the referee's liability for any defamation charge. Though this last piece of advice seems wise, it can result in some uncomfortable discussions about the content of references that are not positive. After one such discussion, a student told me that "I will get you for this"; even though the reference was never sent because the student declined to use the letter. Fortunately, after two months of harassment by the student and several calls to campus police to remove the student from the building, the episode finally ended. Thus, being fair and open with former employers or students can have its price.

# PSYCHOLOGICAL TESTING

One of the most criticized and abused methods of employee selection is **psychological testing.** For several years, psychological tests were used by many organizations, mostly because it was in vogue. But in the 1960s and 1970s, the use of psychological testing declined sharply for several reasons. First, with the passage of the 1964 Civil Rights Act, many employers felt that psychological testing could lead to discrimination against minorities and women. Second, many personnel professionals questioned the usefulness of tests in the selection process.

In recent years, however, psychological testing has again become popular, primarily because abundant and recent research has indicated that properly used psychological tests are excellent in predicting future employee performance (Hunter & Hunter, 1984). Furthermore, psychologists have realized that tests do not discriminate as much as once believed. As discussed in Chapter 4, though Blacks and Whites do score differently on many tests, these differences can be either overcome by using separate norms or justified by actual differences in work behavior (Donnoe, 1986).

## FACTORS TO CONSIDER WHEN CHOOSING TESTS

### Reliability and Validity

As discussed in Chapter 4, tests should only be used if they are both reliable and valid. Thus, in considering tests, it is essential to obtain reliability and validity information and choose the test or tests with the highest available validity. Tests for which there is no reliability or validity information available should almost always be ignored.

### Cost and Ease of Use

If two or more tests have similar validities, then cost should be considered. For example, in selecting police officers it is common to use a test of cognitive

The use of computerized testing is rapidly increasing.

ability such as the Wonderlic Personnel Test or the Wechler Adult Intelligence Scale (WAIS). Both tests have similar reliabilities and validities, yet the Wonderlic costs only a few dollars per applicant and can be administered to groups of people in only 12 minutes. The WAIS must be administered individually at a time cost of at least an hour per applicant and a financial cost of over $100 per applicant. In situations that are not so clear, the utility formula discussed in Chapter 4 can be used to determine the best test.

Tests can be administered either to individual applicants or groups of applicants. Certainly, group testing is usually less expensive and more efficient than individual testing, although important information may be lost in group testing. For example, one reason for administering an individual intelligence test is to observe the *way* in which a person solves a problem or answers a question. With group tests, only the answer can be scored.

A recent innovation in the administration of psychological tests involves the use of computers. An applicant takes a test at a computer terminal, the computer scores the test, and the test's results and interpretation are immediately available. Computer-assisted testing can lower testing costs, decrease feedback time, and yield results in which the test takers can have great confidence (Johnson & King, 1988). As with group testing, however, the testing process usually cannot be observed.

### Potential for Legal Problems

A third factor to consider in choosing a test is its potential for legal problems—either in the form of adverse impact or invasion of privacy, two terms discussed in detail in Chapter 2. In employee selection, most psychological tests will result in adverse impact because minorities and women often score differently than white males; however, some have less impact than others. Thus, given a choice of two tests with similar validities and costs, it might be smarter to choose the test with the least potential for adverse impact.

Use of psychological tests can also result in invasion-of-privacy charges. To reduce the possibility of such charges, tests that have good face validity should be given preference; that is, when applicants see the relationship between the test items and the requirements of the job, law suits are less likely.

### Scoring Methods

Tests can be scored primarily in two ways: objectively and subjectively. Tests that are **objectively scored** typically involve the use of a scoring key so that an applicant's score will be the same, regardless of who does the scoring. Multiple-choice tests such as those you have taken in school are examples of objective tests. Conversely, **subjective scoring** relies on the experience and knowledge of the scorer to interpret the meaning of the applicant's answers. The essay exams you have taken in school are examples.

The **Rorschach Inkblot Test** is a good example of a subjectively (or projectively) scored test. In the Rorschach Test, an applicant is asked what pictures he sees in a series of inkblots. The answers are scored and then interpreted by a trained psychologist to reveal characteristics of the individual's personality.

Objectively scored tests are more common in employee selection, more accurate, and less expensive than subjectively scored tests.

### Type of Test: Speed versus Power

The major differences between speed and power tests is the amount of time an applicant is given to complete the test. With **speed tests,** applicants are given a large number of items with little time to complete them. High scorers correctly complete many items in the allowed period of time. Speed tests are primarily used to test applicants for jobs that require the rapid completion of relatively simple tasks such as typing, filing, and checking addresses. With **power tests,** applicants are given as much time as necessary to answer the questions. Power tests typically are used where quality is more important than quantity. Examples include tests for supervisors and law enforcement officers.

## TYPES OF PSYCHOLOGICAL TESTS

### Personality Tests

Personality tests fall into one of two categories based on their intended purpose: measurement of types of normal personality and measurement of psychopathology (abnormal personality). *Tests of normal personality* measure the traits exhibited by normal individuals in everyday life. Examples of such traits include extroversion, shyness, assertiveness, and friendliness. Tests of normal personality have been criticized in the personnel field, primarily because few personnel professionals have the knowledge to use the tests properly.

Another problem with personality tests is that the thousands of available tests measure thousands of different types of personalities. The problem is not so much in the tests themselves as with the methods used to construct the personality dimensions measured by the tests. The number and type of personality dimensions measured by a test are usually determined in one of three ways: theory-based, statistically based, and empirically based. The number of dimensions in a *theory-based test* is identical to the number postulated by a well-known theorist. For example, the Myers-Briggs test has four scales and is based on the personality theory of Carl Jung, whereas the Edwards Personal Preference Schedule, with 15 dimensions, is based on a theory by Murray. The number of dimensions in a *statistically based test* is determined through a statistical process called factor analysis. The most well-known test of this type, the 16-PF, was created by Raymond Cattell and, as its name implies, contains 16 dimensions. The number and location of dimensions under which items fall in an *empirically keyed test* is determined by grouping answers given by people known to possess a certain characteristic. For example, in developing the Minnesota Multiphasic Personality Inventory (MMPI), hundreds of items were administered to groups of psychologically healthy people and to people known to have certain psychological problems such as paranoia. Items that were endorsed more often by paranoid patients than healthy individuals were keyed under the paranoia dimension of the MMPI.

Though there is some disagreement, psychologists today generally agree that people exhibit five main personality dimensions. Popularly known as the *Big Five*, these dimensions are openness to experience, conscientiousness, extroversion, agreeableness, and neuroticism. Most modern personality tests will contain scales topping the Big Five dimensions.

Examples of common tests of normal personality used in employee selection include the California Psychological Inventory, the Hogan Personality Inventory, the 16-PF, and the Edwards Personal Preference Schedule.

*Tests of psychopathology* (abnormal behavior) determine if individuals have serious psychological problems such as depression, bipolar disorder, and schizophrenia. Though used extensively by clinical psychologists, these tests are seldom used by I/O psychologists except in the selection of law enforcement officers.

As mentioned earlier, tests of abnormal personality are generally scored in one of two ways: objectively or projectively. **Projective tests** provide the respondent with unstructured tasks such as describing inkblots and drawing pictures. Because projective tests are of questionable reliability and validity and are time-consuming and expensive, they are rarely used in employee selection. One notable exception is the New York City Police Department's use of the House-Tree-Person test in which applicants are asked to draw pictures of a house, a tree, and a person. These drawings are then ana-

```
True / False:

I enjoy meeting new people        True        False

I am assertive                    True        False


Forced Choice

Choose the adjective most like you and the adjective least like you.

                                  Most        Least

Assertive                         _____     _____

Energetic                         _____     _____

Playful                           _____     _____
```

lyzed by trained clinical psychologists and are thought to reveal the psychological stability of potential police officers. Common tests in this category also include the Rorschach Ink Blot Test and the **Thematic Apperception Test (TAT).**

   **Objective tests** are structured so that the respondent is limited to a few answers that will be scored by standardized keys. Samples of different question formats are shown in Figure 6.12. By far the most popular and heavily studied test of this type is the revised **Minnesota Multiphasic Personality Inventory (MMPI-2).** Another test in this category is the Millon Clinical Multiaxial Inventory (MCMI-III).

   A meta-analysis by Tett, Jackson, and Rothstein (1991) indicates that objective personality tests are useful in predicting performance, particularly when a job analysis is conducted prior to choosing the tests and scales. The Big Five personality dimensions of agreeableness and openness to experience are most positively related to performance while neuroticism is most negatively related to performance.

### Interest Inventories

These tests are designed to tap vocational interests. The most commonly used **interest inventory** is the **Strong Inventory Interest (SII),** which asks individuals to indicate whether they like or dislike 325 items such as bargaining, repairing electrical wiring, or taking responsibility. The answers to these questions provide a profile that shows how similar a person is to people already employed in 89 occupations that have been classified into 23 basic interest scales and six general occupational themes. The theory behind these tests is that an individual with interests similar to those of people in a particular field will more likely be satisfied in the field than in a field composed of people whose interests are dissimilar. Other popular interest inventories include the Minnesota Vocational Interest Inventory, the Kuder Occupational Interest Inventory, and the California Occupational Preference System.

Even though interest inventories have shown limited success in helping to select employees, they are useful in **vocational counseling** (helping people find the careers for which they are best suited). Conducted properly, vocational counseling uses a battery of tests which, at a minimum, should include an interest inventory and a series of ability tests. The interest inventory scores suggest careers for which the individual's interests are compatible; the ability tests will tell him if he has the necessary abilities to enter into those careers. If interest scores are high in a particular occupational area but ability scores are low, the individual is advised about the type of training that would best prepare him for a career in that particular area.

### Ability Tests

**Ability tests** are designed to measure an applicant's abilities and talents and can be divided into one of two types: general and specific. A **specific aptitude test** measures an individual's ability in only one aptitude. More than 400 specific aptitude tests measure such abilities as mechanical aptitude, spatial aptitude, musical aptitude, and verbal aptitude (Donnoe, 1986). Although these tests are excellent in predicting future employee performance, the sheer number of specific aptitude tests leads to administrative problems because most jobs involve more than one type of aptitude. Therefore, several specific aptitude tests must be included in the test battery administered to applicants, which makes the battery both lengthy and costly.

Recall from the discussion of legal issues in Chapter 2 that any test used in industry must be job-related. One way in which the courts determine job relatedness is by asking whether test scores have been shown to correlate with some relevant aspect of job performance. With more than 400 specific aptitude tests available, a tremendous amount of research time and money would have to be invested to validate the test scores for a particular type of job. Thus, specific aptitude tests are considered useful but not always practical tools for employee selection.

To overcome some of the problems with specific aptitude tests, **general aptitude tests** were created. Popular tests of this type include the General Aptitude Test Battery (GATB), Career Ability Placement Survey (CAPS), and Differential Aptitude Tests (DAT). As shown in Figure 6.13, most general ability test batteries place the many specific aptitudes into one of three main dimensions: cognitive, perceptual, and psychomotor.

The **cognitive ability** dimension includes verbal (grammar, vocabulary, spelling), numerical, logic (verbal reasoning, mechanical reasoning), and general learning aptitudes. Aptitudes from this dimension are important for professional, clerical, and supervisory jobs, including occupations such as supervisor, accountant, and secretary. Tests of cognitive ability are designed to measure the amount of knowledge an individual possesses. Note that the vast majority of cognitive ability tests used by industrial psychologists (as

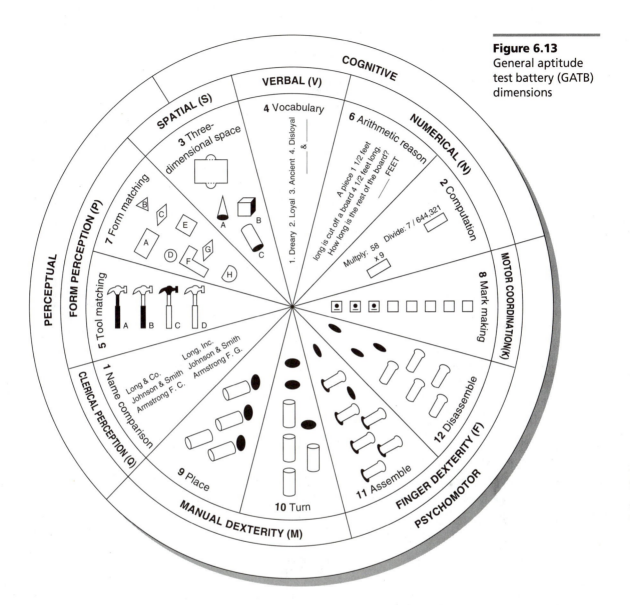

**Figure 6.13**
General aptitude test battery (GATB) dimensions

opposed to clinical psychologists) measure how much an individual *already* knows rather than how much he is *capable* of knowing. The SAT or ACT tests that you probably took to get into college are good examples. One of the most widely used cognitive ability tests in industry is the **Wonderlic Personnel Test.** The short amount of time (12 minutes) necessary to take the test as well as the fact that it can be administered in a group setting make the test popular. Sample items from the Wonderlic are shown in Figure 6.14. Other popular mental ability tests are the Miller Analogies Test, Quick Test, and Raven Progressive Matrices (Anastasi, 1988). Cognitive ability tests are excellent predictors of employee performance (Hunter &

# PERSONNEL TEST

## FORM II

_____    _____

NAME                                    (Please Print)                          Date

READ THIS PAGE CAREFULLY.  DO EXACTLY AS YOU ARE TOLD.
DO NOT TURN OVER THIS PAGE UNTIL YOU ARE
INSTRUCTED TO DO SO.

PROBLEMS MUST BE WORKED WITHOUT THE AID OF A CALCULATOR
OR OTHER PROBLEM-SOLVING DEVICE.

This is a test of problem-solving ability.  It contains various types of questions.  Below is a sample question correctly filled in.

PLACE
ANSWERS
HERE

REAP is the opposite of
   1  obtain.   2  cheer.   3  continue.   4  exist.   5  <u>sow.</u>

[ <u>5</u> ]

The correct answer is "sow."  (It is helpful to underline the correct word.)  The correct word is numbered 5.  Then write the figure 5 in the brackets <u>at the end of the line.</u>

Answer the next sample question yourself.

Paper sells for 23 cents per pad.  What will 4 pads cost?

[ ___ ]

The correct answer is 92¢.  There is nothing to underline so just place "92¢" in the brackets.

Here is another example:

MINER   MINOR  —  Do these words
   1  have similar meanings?   2  have contradictory meanings?   3  mean neither the same nor opposite?

[ ___ ]

The correct answer is "mean neither the same nor opposite" which is number 3 so all you have to do is place a figure "3" in the brackets <u>at the end of the line.</u>

When the answer to a question is a letter or a number, put the letter or number in the brackets.
All letters should be printed.

This test contains 50 questions.  It is unlikely that you will finish all of them, but do your best.  After the examiner tells you to begin, you will be given exactly 12 minutes to work as many as you can.  Do not go so fast that you make mistakes since you must try to get as many right as possible.  The questions become increasingly difficult, so do not skip about.  Do not spend too much time on any one problem.  The examiner will not answer any questions after the test begins.

Now, lay down your pencil and wait for the examiner to tell you to begin!

> *Do not turn the page until you are told to do so.*

**Figure 6.14** Instructions and example from the Wonderlic Personnel Test

Source: E. F. Wonderlic Personnel Test, Inc., Northfield, IL. Reprinted by permission.

Hunter, 1984), but because they almost always result in adverse impact, they should be used with caution.

The **perceptual ability** dimension consists of spatial relations, form perception, and clerical perception aptitudes. Abilities from this dimension are useful for jobs involving setting-up machines and occupations such as machinist, cabinet maker, die setter, and tool and die maker. An example of a perceptual ability test is shown in Figure 6.15.

The **psychomotor ability** dimension contains motor coordination, finger dexterity, and manual dexterity aptitudes. Abilities from this dimension are useful for jobs involving feeding and offbearing and occupations such as folding-machine operator, sewing-machine operator, post office clerk, and truck driver. An example of a psychomotor test is shown in Figure 6.16.

### Integrity Tests

**Integrity tests** (also called *honesty tests*) are designed to tell an employer the probability that an applicant would steal money or merchandise. Honesty tests are used mostly in the retail industry, and more than 3 million are sold each year. Such extensive use is due to the fact that 42% of retail employees, 62% of fast-food employees, and 32% of hospital employees have admitted stealing from their employers (Jones & Terris, 1989).

Until recently, employers used both electronic and paper-and-pencil honesty tests to screen applicants. In 1988, however, the U.S. Congress passed the Employee Polygraph Protection Act making general use of electronic honesty tests, such as the **polygraph** and the **voice stress analyzer,** illegal except in a few situations involving national security. The law did, however, allow the use of paper-and-pencil honesty tests.

Paper-and-pencil integrity tests fall into one of two categories: overt and personality-based (Sackett, Burris, & Callahan, 1989). **Overt integrity tests** are based on the premise that a person's attitudes about theft as well as his previous theft behavior will accurately predict his future honesty. Honesty tests measure attitudes by asking the test taker to estimate the frequency of theft in society, how harsh penalties against thieves should be, how easy it is to steal, how often he has personally been tempted to steal, how often his friends have stolen, and how often he personally has stolen. **Personality-based integrity tests** are more general in that they tap a variety of personality traits thought to be related to a wide range of counterproductive behavior such as theft, absenteeism, and violence. Overt tests are more reliable and valid in predicting theft and other counterproductive behaviors than are personality-based tests (Ones, Viswesvaran, & Schmidt, 1993; Snyman et al., 1991). In addition to predicting counterproductive behavior, both overt and personality-based integrity tests have been shown to predict job performance (Ones et al., 1993).

Table 6.2 shows some of the many honesty tests on the market, several of which do a decent job of predicting either polygraph results or admissions of theft (Ones et al., 1993; Snyman et al., 1991). Unfortunately, few studies have attempted to correlate test scores with actual theft. Of course,

2. SPATIAL RELATIONS (SR)

This is a test of Spatial Relations. Following are patterns which can be folded into figures. You are to choose which figure can be correctly made by folding the pattern and then darken the answer space above it. Only one of the four figures is correct for each pattern shown. Practice on these examples.

Example 1:

Example 2:

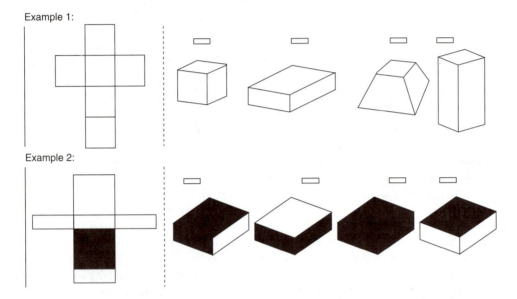

In Example 1. the first figure, the cube, is correct. You should have darkened the answer space above the first figure. In Example 2, all of the figures are correct in shape, but only one of them is shaded correctly. The last figure is correct.

Remember the surfaces you are shown in the pattern must always be the outside of the folded figure.

When the signal is given turn the page over and begin. Work as quickly and as carefully as you can.

NOTE: If you change an answer, mark a heavy "X" on the answer you wish to change then darken the correct answer.

You will have 5 minutes to complete this section.

## DO NOT TURN THIS PAGE UNTIL YOU ARE TOLD TO DO SO.

**Figure 6.15** Example of a perceptual ability test measuring spatial relations

### 8. MANUAL SPEED AND DEXTERITY (MSD)

This is a test of Manual Speed and Dexterity. Following is a series of arrows arranged in columns. You are to draw straight vertical lines connecting the tips of the adjacent arrows.

Start each line at the tip of the top arrow and draw to the tip of the bottom arrow. Make sure that you touch both arrow tips without crossing the tips into the shaded area. Start at the top of each column and work down making sure the lines you draw are straight, heavy and dark. Practice on the following examples:

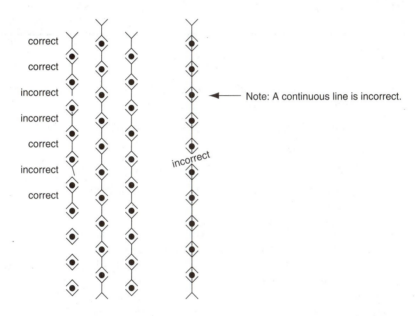

When the signal is given turn the page over and begin. Work as quickly and as accurately as you can. Your score will depend on both speed and accuracy. You will have 5 minutes to complete this section.

## DO NOT TURN THIS PAGE UNTIL YOU ARE TOLD TO DO SO.

**Figure 6.16** Example of a psychomotor test measuring manual speed and dexterity

**Table 6.2**  Validity of several honesty tests

| Test | Reliability | Overall Validity | Specific Criterion | | |
|------|-------------|------------------|--------------------|-----------|-------------------|
| | | | Polygraph | Predictive | Theft Admission |
| Phase II | .91 | .56 | .89 | .14 | .64 |
| P.O.S. | .76 | .72 | .72 | — | — |
| P.S.I. | .67 | .39 | .47 | .27 | .55 |
| Reid Report | .92 | .42 | .48 | — | .29 |
| Stanton | .91 | .61 | .79 | — | .42 |
| Milby Profile | — | .74 | — | .74 | — |
| T.A.S. | .95 | .65 | .65 | — | — |
| Wilkerson | — | .69 | .75 | — | .63 |
| P.E.A.Q. | — | .49 | — | — | .49 |
| Compu-Scan | .84 | .45 | .45 | — | — |
| Total | .90 | .58 | .65 | .38 | .50 |

Source: Snyman et al., 1991.

these would be difficult to conduct. Instead, the validity of honesty tests has been determined by comparing test scores with:

- polygraph test results
- self-admissions of theft
- shrinkage (the amount of goods lost by a store)
- known groups (for example, priests versus convicts)
- future theft

Unfortunately, all of these measures have problems. If polygraph results are used, the researcher is essentially comparing honesty test scores with the scores of a test—the polygraph—that has been made illegal partly because of questions about its accuracy. If self-admissions are used, the researcher is relying on dishonest people to be honest about their crime history. If **shrinkage** is used, the researcher does not know which of the employees is responsible for the theft or, for that matter, what percentage of the shrinkage can be attributed to employee theft as opposed to customer theft or incidental breakage. Even if actual employee theft is used, the test may only predict employees who *get caught* stealing as opposed to those who steal and do not get caught. The problems with known-group comparisons were discussed in great detail in Chapter 4.

As indicated by this discussion and the data in Table 6.2, integrity tests do a good job of predicting theft, especially when one considers that not all theft is caused by a *personal tendency* to steal (Murphy, 1993). Normally honest people might steal from an employer due to *economic pressure* caused by factors such as high debts or financial emergencies or by an organizational culture in which it is considered *normal to steal* (for example, "It's ok because everyone takes food home with them"). Employee theft can also be the result of a *reaction to organizational policy* such as layoffs or a change in rules that employees perceive as unfair. To reduce theft caused by situational factors, nontesting methods such as increased security, explicit policy, and availability of appeal and suggestion systems are needed.

Although paper-and-pencil honesty tests are inexpensive and may be useful in predicting theft, they also have serious drawbacks. The most important disadvantage might be that males have higher failure rates than do females and younger people have higher failure rates than do older people. Adverse impacts on these two groups pose little legal threat, but telling the parents of a 17-year-old boy that their son has just failed an honesty test is not the best way to foster good public relations. Failing an honesty test has a much greater psychological impact than failing a spatial relations test. For these reasons, some legal experts advise against letting applicants know they were not hired because they failed an honesty test (Douglas, Feld, & Asquith, 1989).

### Job-Knowledge Tests

Used primarily in the public sector, **job-knowledge tests** are designed to measure how much a person knows about a job. These tests are similar to the exams given several times a semester in a college class. They are typically given in multiple-choice fashion for ease of scoring, but they also can be written in essay format.

Job-knowledge tests have some of the same advantages as work samples. They have excellent content and criterion validity, and because of their high face validity, they are positively accepted by applicants (Robertson & Kandola, 1982). The major disadvantage to job-knowledge tests is that even though they do a good job of predicting performance (Ward, 1989), they often result in adverse impact (Schmidt et al., 1977).

## PHYSICAL AGILITY TESTS

**Physical-agility tests** are often used for jobs that require physical strength and stamina such as police officer, firefighter, and lifeguard. Physical agility is measured in one of two ways: job simulations and physical agility tests. With a job simulation, applicants actually demonstrate job-related physical behaviors. For example, firefighter applicants might climb a ladder and drag a 48-pound hose 75 feet across a street, police applicants might fire a gun and chase down a suspect, and lifeguard applicants might swim 100 yards and drag a drowning victim back to shore. Though job simulations are highly content valid, from a financial or safety perspective, they are often impractical (Hoover, 1992).

Testing the physical agility of police applicants is an excellent example of this impracticality. Job analyses consistently indicate that the physical requirements of police officers can be divided into two categories: athletic and

Physical agility tests are useful for jobs with high physical demands.

defensive. *Athletic requirements* are easy to simulate because they involve such behaviors as running, crawling, and pulling. *Defensive requirements,* however, are difficult to safely and accurately simulate because they involve such behaviors as applying restraining holds, kicking, and fending-off attackers. One can imagine the liability and safety problems of physically attacking applicants to see if they can defend themselves.

Because of the difficulty in using simulations to measure these last types of behaviors, physical agility tests are used. Instead of simulating the defensive behaviors listed in the above example, tests are developed that measure the basic abilities needed to perform the defensive behaviors. Tests commonly used to measure the abilities needed to perform defensive behaviors including pushups, situps, and grip strength. Research has shown that there are seven basic physical abilities (Daniel, 1987; Fleishman, 1979):

- dynamic strength (strength requiring repetitions)
- trunk strength (stooping or bending over)

- explosive strength (jumping or throwing objects)
- static strength (strength not requiring repetitions)
- dynamic flexibility (muscle flexibility)
- gross body equilibrium (balance)

Because physical agility tests have tremendous adverse impact against females (Arvey, Nutting, & Landon, 1992; Hoover, 1992; Mijares, 1993), they have been criticized on three major points: job relatedness, passing scores, and the time at which they should be required.

## JOB RELATEDNESS

Though few people would disagree that it is *better* for a police officer to be strong and fit than weak and out-of-shape, many argue whether it is *necessary* to be physically fit. Critics of physical-agility testing cite two reasons for questioning the necessity of physical agility: currently out-of-shape cops and technological alternatives. Currently, there are many police officers who are overweight, slow, and out-of-shape, yet they perform safely and at high levels. Furthermore, research suggests that physical size is not related to police safety (Griffiths & McDaniel, 1993). Thus, critics argue that physical agility is not an essential part of the job. This is especially true due to technological advances in policing. As an example, Sollie and Sollie (1993) presented data showing that the use of "pepper spray" in Meridian, Mississippi, almost completely reduced the need for officers to physically restrain drunk or physically aggressive suspects.

## PASSING SCORES

A second problem with physical-agility tests is determining passing scores; that is, how fast must an applicant run or how much weight must be lifted to pass a physical agility test. Passing scores for physical agility tests are set based on one of two types of standards: relative or absolute. Relative standards indicate how well an individual scores compared to others in a group such as females, police applicants, or current police officers. The advantage to using relative standards is that adverse impact is eliminated because males are compared with males and females with other females. The problem with relative scales, however, is that a female applicant might be strong compared to other females, yet not strong enough to perform the job. In contrast, absolute passing scores are set at the minimum level needed to perform a job. For example, if a police officer needs to drag 170-pound people from a burning car, the 170 pounds becomes the passing score. As one can imagine, the problem comes in determining the minimum amounts. That is, how fast does an officer *need* to run in order to adequately perform the job? Because people come in all sizes, how many pounds does an officer *need* to be able to drag?

## WHEN THE ABILITY MUST BE PRESENT

A third problem with physical agility requirements is with the point at which the ability must be present. Most police departments require applicants to pass physical agility tests the same day that other tests are being completed. However, the applicant doesn't need the strength or speed until he is actually in the academy or on the job. Showing awareness of this problem, cities such as San Francisco and Philadelphia provide applicants with a list of physical abilities that will be required of them once they arrive at the academy. Applicants are then given suggestions on how they can get themselves into the proper condition. Some cities even hold conditioning programs for applicants! Such policies greatly reduce adverse impact by increasing the physical agility of female applicants.

An interesting example of the importance of monitoring physical-ability testing was provided in a study by Padgett (1989) who was hired to determine vision requirements for a municipal fire department. Prior to Padgett's study, national vision standards for firefighters had been set without any empirical research. The standards stipulated that firefighters needed a minimum uncorrected vision of 20/40 and could not wear contact lenses because they might be "blown out of their eyes."

After conducting his study of actual job-related duties, however, Padgett discovered that the minimum vision needed to perform firefighting tasks was 20/100 if the person wore glasses and that there was no minimum if the person wore contacts. The difference in requirements for contacts and glasses was because certain duties might result in a loss of glasses, but it was very unlikely a firefighter would lose contacts while performing a task requiring acute vision. As a result of this study, many qualified applicants who had been turned away because of the archaic vision requirements were now allowed the chance to become firefighters.

# WEIGHTED APPLICATION BLANKS (BIODATA)

Because interviews and references have generally been found to be poor linear predictors of future employee success, industrial psychologists have developed many better prediction techniques. In the past few decades, of these many methods, one has clearly stood out as the single best predictor of future employee tenure: the weighted application blank based on biographical information (Ghiselli, 1966; Beall, 1991).

**Weighted application blanks (WAB)** use statistical weighting techniques (mentioned in Chapter 5), which are superior to the clinical techniques used in the interview and résumé evaluation processes. In a nutshell, the WAB is an application blank containing questions that research has shown measure the difference between successful and unsuccessful performers on a job. Each question receives a weight that indicates how well it differentiates poor from good performers. The better the differentiation, the higher the weight. The WAB has several advantages.

1. Research has shown that WABs can predict work behavior in many jobs, including sales, management, clerical work, mental health counseling, hourly work in processing plants, grocery clerking, fast-food work, and supervising.

2. WABs have been able to predict criteria as varied as supervisor ratings, absenteeism, accidents, employee theft, loan defaults, sales, and tenure.

3. Unlike other methods, use of WABs results in higher organizational profit and growth (Terpstra & Rozell, 1993).

4. WABs are easy to use, quickly administered, inexpensive, and not as subject to individual bias as interviews, references, and résumé evaluation.

The major disadvantage to using a WAB is that it can only be created properly when data from a large number of employees (at least 150) are available.

## DEVELOPMENT

With these considerations in mind, we can now develop a typical weighted application blank. In the first step, we obtain information about employees. Information can be gathered in one of two ways.

First, we can use personnel files because they contain a lot of employee information for such areas as previous employment, education, interests, and family. As mentioned in the discussion of archival research in Chapter 1, the major disadvantage of the **file approach** is that information is often missing or incomplete.

Second, we can create a biographical questionnaire that is administered to all employees and applicants. An example is shown in Figure 6.17. The major drawback to the **questionnaire approach** is that information cannot be obtained from employees who have quit or been fired.

After the necessary information has been obtained, an appropriate criterion is chosen. As will be discussed in detail in Chapter 7, a **criterion** is a measure of work behavior such as quantity, absenteeism, or tenure. It is essential that a chosen criterion be relevant, reliable, and fairly objective. As an example of developing a WAB with a poor criterion, I was once asked to create a WAB to help reduce absenteeism in an organization by selecting applicants who had a high probability of superior future attendance. When initial data were gathered, it was realized that absenteeism was not an actual problem for this company. Less than one-half of the work force had missed more than one day in six months; but the company perceived a problem because a few key workers had missed many days of work. Thus, using a WAB (or any other selection device) to predict a nonrelevant criterion would not have been an accurate method.

**Figure 6.17**
Biodata
questionnaire

1. Member of high school student government?
   ☐ No   ☐ Yes

2. Number of jobs in past 5 years?
   ☐ 1   ☐ 2   ☐ 3–5   ☐ More than 5

3. Length of time at present address?
   ☐ Less than 1 year   ☐ 1–3 years
   ☐ 4–5 years   ☐ More than 5 years

4. Transportation to work:
   ☐ Walk   ☐ Bike   ☐ Own car
   ☐ Bus   ☐ Ride with a friend   ☐ Other

5. Education:
   ☐ Some high school
   ☐ High school diploma or G. E. D.
   ☐ Some college
   ☐ Associate's degree
   ☐ Bachelor's degree
   ☐ Master's degree
   ☐ Doctoral degree

Once a criterion has been chosen, employees are split into two **criterion groups** based on their criterion scores. For example, if tenure is selected as the criterion measure, employees who have worked for the company for at least one year might be placed into the "long-tenure" group, while workers who quit or were fired in less than one year would be placed into the "short-tenure" group.

After the employee data have been obtained and the criterion and criterion groups chosen, each piece of employee information is then compared with criterion-group membership. The purpose of this stage is to determine which pieces of information will distinguish the members of the high-criterion group from those in the low-criterion group. Traditionally, the **vertical percentage method** (England, 1971) has been used to do this. Percentages are calculated for each group on each item. The percentage of a particular response for the low group is subtracted from the percentage of the same response in the high group to obtain a weight for that item. An example of this weighting process is shown in Table 6.3.

Once weights have been assigned to the items, the information is weighted and then summed to form a **composite score** for each employee. Composite scores are then correlated with the criterion to determine whether the newly created WAB will significantly predict the criterion. Although this procedure sounds complicated, it actually is fairly easy although time-consuming.

Two items also must be mentioned about the construction of the WAB. First, the method has been used quite successfully for more than 20 years

**Table 6.3** WAB weighting process

| Variable | Long Tenure | Short Tenure | Difference in Percentages | Weight |
|---|---|---|---|---|
| Education | | | | |
| High School | 40% | 80% | 40 | −10 |
| Bachelor's | 59 | 15 | 44 | +11 |
| Masters | 1 | 5 | 4 | −1 |

(England, 1971). Telenson, Alexander, and Barrett (1983) proposed that a new method, **rare-response scoring,** be used instead of the vertical percentage method. Basically, the rare-response method assigns weights on the basis of how typical employees respond to a specific item. That is, if a particular response to an item is given by few people, that response will receive the highest weight.

Such weighting is done because research from the fields of clinical psychology and social psychology tell us that the most revealing information about a person comes from unusual behavior. For example, if we find out that Bob enjoys eating pizza, we cannot make much of a judgment about Bob because almost everyone likes pizza (especially this author). However, if we are told that Bob runs around town naked, we would probably give that information more weight because it tells us that Bob is different from most people.

But even though the rare-response method sounds interesting, subsequent research (Aamodt & Pierce, 1987) has indicated that it has many problems: in its present state of development, it is not as good as the vertical percentage method. Future improvements, however, could lead to the rare-response method being used more frequently.

The second item for discussion concerns problems with **sample size.** To accurately create a WAB, it is desirable to have data from hundreds of employees. For most organizations, however, such large sample sizes are difficult if not impossible to obtain. In creating a WAB with a small sample, the risk of using items that do not really predict the criterion increases. This issue is important because most industrial psychologists advise that when a WAB is created, the employees should be split into two samples: One sample, the **derivation sample,** is used to form the weights; the other sample, the **hold-out sample,** is used to double-check the selected items and weights. Although this sample splitting sounds like a great idea, it is not practical when one is dealing with a small or moderate (less than 300) sample size.

Research by Schmitt, Coyle, and Rauschenberger (1977) suggests that there is less chance of error when a sample is not split. Discussion on whether to split samples is bound to continue in the years ahead, but because many human resource professionals will be dealing with relatively small numbers of employees, it might be best to create and validate a WAB without splitting employees into derivation and hold-out samples.

A final issue to consider is the sample used to create WABs. Responses of current employees can be used to select the items and create the weights that will be applied to applicants. Stokes and her colleagues (Stokes, Hogan, & Snell, 1993) found that incumbents and applicants respond in very different ways, indicating that the use of incumbents to create and scale items may reduce validity.

## CRITICISMS

Even though WABs do a good job of predicting future employee behavior, they have been criticized on two major points. The first holds that the validity of WABs may not be stable—that is, their ability to predict employee behavior decreases with time. For example, Wernimont (1962) found that only three questions retained their predictive validity over the five-year period of 1954 to 1959. Similar results were reported by Hughes, Dunn, and Baxter (1956).

More recent research (Brown, 1978), however, suggests that declines in validity found in earlier studies may have resulted from small samples in the initial development of the WAB. Brown (1978) used data from more than 10,000 life insurance agents to develop his WAB, but data from only 85 agents were used to develop the WAB samples that were earlier criticized by Wernimont (1962). Brown compared the validity of his original sample (1933) with those from samples taken six years later (1939) and 38 years later (1971). The results indicated that the same items that significantly predicted the criterion in 1933 predicted at similar levels in 1971. Thus, WABs may be more stable across time than was earlier thought (Rothstein, Schmidt, Erwin, Owens, & Sparks, 1990).

The second criticism is that some WABs may not meet the legal requirements stated in the Uniform Guidelines (Pace & Schoenfeldt, 1977), the federal guidelines that establish fair hiring methods. Of greatest concern is that certain biodata items might lead to racial or sexual discrimination. For example, consider the selection item "distance from work." Applicants who live close to work might get more points than applicants who live farther away. The item may lead to racial discrimination if the organization is located in a predominantly White area. Removal of such discriminatory items, however, should eliminate most legal problems while still allowing for significant predictive validity (Reilly & Chao, 1982). Though WABs are valid and no more prone to adverse impact than other selection methods, the fact that applicants view them and personality tests as being the least job-related selection methods (Smither, Reilly, Millsap, Pearlman, & Stoffey, 1993) may increase the chance of a lawsuit *being filed,* but not the chance of *losing* a lawsuit.

To make WAB use less disagreeable to critics, Gandy and Dye (1989) developed one containing items that had to meet four standards:

1. The item must deal with events under a person's control.
2. The item must be job-related.
3. The answer to the item must be verifiable.
4. The item must not invade an applicant's privacy.

Even though these four standards eliminated many potential items, Gandy and Dye (1989) still obtained a validity coefficient of .33. Just as impressive as the high validity coefficient was that the WAB showed good prediction for Whites, Blacks, and Hispanics.

The third criticism is that WABs can be faked, a charge that has been made against every selection method except work samples and ability tests. Research indicates that applicants do in fact respond to items in socially desirable ways (Stokes, Hogan, & Snell, 1993). However, warning applicants of the presence of a lie scale (Kluger & Colella, 1993) and using objective, verifiable items (Becker & Colquitt, 1992; Shaffer, Saunders, & Owens, 1986) will reduce this tendency to lie. Furthermore, it is uncertain if applicants who lie will actually score higher on a WAB (Crosby, 1990).

# ASSESSMENT CENTERS

An assessment center is a selection technique characterized by the use of multiple assessment methods that allow multiple assessors to actually *observe* applicants perform job-related tasks. Its major advantages are that assessment methods are all job-related and multiple trained assessors help to guard against many (but not all) types of selection bias. For a selection technique to be considered an assessment center, it must meet the following seven requirements (Ross, 1979):

1. Multiple assessment techniques, at least one of which must be a simulation, are used.
2. Multiple trained assessors are used.
3. The overall judgment regarding an applicant must be based on a combination of information from the multiple assessors and multiple techniques.
4. The overall evaluation of an applicant cannot be made until all assessment center tasks have been completed.
5. Simulation exercises that are reliable, objective, and job-related must be used.
6. All behaviors that are measured must be job-related.
7. All exercises must be designed to tap the job behaviors mentioned in requirement 6.

## DEVELOPMENT AND COMPONENTS

Although many different techniques may be used in assessment centers, the basic development and types of exercises are fairly standard. The first step in creating an assessment center is, of course, to do a job analysis. From this analysis, exercises are developed that measure different aspects of the job (Yager, 1980). Common exercises include the in-basket technique, simulations, work samples, leaderless group discussions, and business games. Each of these techniques can be used by itself. It is only when they are used in combination that they become part of an assessment center.

### The In-Basket Technique

The **in-basket technique** is designed to simulate the types of daily information that appear on a manager's or employee's desk. The technique takes its name from the wire baskets typically seen on office desks. Usually these baskets have two levels: the "in" level, which holds paperwork that must be handled, and the "out" level, which contains completed paperwork.

During the assessment center, examples of job-related paperwork are placed into a basket and the job applicant is asked to go through the basket and respond to the paperwork as if he were actually on the job. Examples of such paperwork might include a phone message from an employee who cannot get his car started and does not know how to get to work or a memo from the accounting department stating that an expense voucher is missing.

The applicant is observed by a group of assessors who score the applicant on several dimensions that can include the quality of the decision, the manner in which the decision was carried out, and the order in which the applicant handled the paperwork—that is, did he start at the top of the pile or did he start with the most important papers? Research on the reliability and validity of the in-basket technique provides only modest support for its usefulness (Schippmann, Prien, & Katz, 1990).

### Simulations

Simulation exercises are the real backbone of the assessment center because they allow assessors to see an applicant "in action." **Simulations,** which can include such diverse activities as role plays and work samples, place an applicant in a situation that is as similar as possible to that which will be encountered on the job (Kaman & Bentson, 1988). To be effective, simulations must be based on job-related behaviors and should be reasonably realistic.

A good example of a role-playing simulation is an assessment center used by a large city to select emergency telephone operators. The applicant sits before a switchboard to handle a distressed caller who is describing an emergency situation. The applicant must properly answer the call, calm the caller, and obtain the necessary information in as little time as possible. Other examples include a police applicant writing a traffic citation for an angry citizen and an applicant for a resident assistant position breaking up an argument between two roommates.

To reduce the high costs associated with actual simulations, many public organizations such as the New York Civil Service Commission and the City of Fairfax, Virginia, have developed situational exercises shown on videotape. Organizations using video simulations administer them to a group of applicants who view the situations in the tape and then write down what they would do in each situation. The written responses are scored by personnel analysts in a fashion similar to that used with situational interviews.

Because the development of simulation exercises can be expensive, prepackaged exercises can be purchased at a much lower price (Cohen, 1980) or less complicated simulations can be used (McDaniel, 1995).

### Work Samples

Usually, when a simulation does not involve a situational exercise, it is called a **work sample.** With a work sample, the applicant performs actual job-related tasks. For example, an applicant for a job as automotive mechanic might be asked to fix a torn fan belt, a secretarial applicant might be asked to type a letter, and an applicant for a position as a truck driver might be asked to back up a truck to a loading dock.

Work samples are excellent selection tools for several reasons. First, because they are directly related to job tasks, they have excellent content validity. Second, scores from work samples tend to predict actual work performance and thus have excellent criterion validity (Asher & Sciarrino, 1974). Third, because job applicants are able to see the connection between the job sample and the work performed on the job, the samples have excellent face validity and thus are challenged less often in civil service appeals or in court cases (Whelchel, 1985). Finally, minorities tend to score better on work samples than on written exams (Cascio & Phillips, 1979; Schmidt, Greenthal, Hunter, Berner, & Seaton, 1977). The main reason for not using work samples is that they can be expensive both to construct and administer. For this reason, work samples are best used for well-paying jobs for which many employees will be hired.

### Leaderless Group Discussions

In this exercise, applicants meet in small groups and are given a job-related problem to solve or a job-related issue to discuss. For example, supervisory applicants might be asked to discuss ways to motivate employees or resident assistant applicants might be asked to discuss ways to reduce noise in residence halls. No leader is appointed, hence the term **leaderless group discussion.** As the applicants discuss the problem or issue, they are individually rated on such dimensions as cooperativeness, leadership, and analytical skills.

### Business Games

**Business games** are exercises that allow the applicant to demonstrate such attributes as creativity, decision making, and ability to work with others. A business game in one assessment center used a series of Tinker Toy models. Four individuals joined a group and were told that they were part of a company that manufactured goods. The goods ranged from Tinker Toy tables to Tinker Toy scuba divers, and the group's task was to buy the parts, manufacture the products, and then sell the products at the highest profit in an environment in which prices constantly changed.

## EVALUATION OF ASSESSMENT CENTERS

The typical assessment center has 6 assessors, each of whom has been trained for an average of 3 to 5 days; has 4 to 7 exercises, which take an average of 2 to 5 days to complete; and evaluates 6 to 12 applicants at one time (Bender, 1973).

Research indicates that the assessment center has been successful in predicting a wide range of employee behavior (Gaugler, Rosenthal, Thornton, & Benston, 1987; Mento, 1980). Klimoski and Strickland (1977), however, have questioned the relative value of the assessment center by pointing out that many of the validation criteria (for example, salary and management level achieved) are measures of survival and adaptation rather than actual performance. Furthermore, other methods can predict the same criteria better and less expensively than assessment centers (Hunter & Hunter, 1984). Thus, even though an assessment center may be excellent in predicting certain aspects of employee behavior, other, less-expensive methods may be as good if not better. Furthermore, there is some question regarding the ability of an assessment center developed at one location to predict performance in similar jobs at other locations (Schmitt, Schneider, & Cohen, 1990).

# DRUG TESTING

**Drug testing** certainly is one of the most controversial testing methods used by personnel professionals. The reasons for its high usage are that human resource professionals believe that not only is drug use dangerous, but also that many employees are under the influence of drugs at work. Their beliefs are supported by research that indicates drug users are 16 times more likely to miss work, are 3 times as likely to be late, and have 4 times as many accidents on the job than non-drug users (Pendleton, 1986).

Because of such statistics, organizations are increasing their drug testing before applicants are hired. In fact, as of 1988, nearly half of the Fortune 500 companies were testing for drugs (Douglas, Feld, & Asquith, 1989).

Drug testing usually is done in two stages. In the first, an employee or applicant provides a urine or hair sample that is subjected to an initial screening test. The most common initial drug screens for urine are the **Enzyme Multiplied Immunoassay Technique (EMIT)** and **radioimmunoassay (RIA).** EMIT uses enzymes as reagents, while RIA uses radioactive tagging. Both cost approximately $10 per sample.

If the initial test for drugs is positive, then second-stage testing is done. The urine sample undergoes a more expensive confirmation test such as **thin-layer chromatography** or **gas chromatography/mass spectometry**

**analysis.** These tests can range anywhere from $30 to more than $100 per sample.

When both stages are used, testing is very accurate in detecting the presence of drugs. But drug tests are not able to determine whether an individual is impaired by drug use (Rosen, 1987). An employee smoking marijuana on Saturday night will test positive for the drug on Monday, even though the effects of the drug have long since gone away. Most drugs can be detected two to three days after they have been used. The exceptions are the benzodiazepines, which can be detected for two weeks after use, and marijuana, which can be detected up to 5 days for the casual user and up to 30 days for the frequent user (Douglas, Feld, & Asquith, 1989).

Because positive drug tests have a certain degree of uncertainty, if an applicant fails a preemployment drug test, he can usually reapply six months later. With such a policy, there are few legal pitfalls.

In the public sector or in the union environment, however, drug testing becomes complicated when it occurs after applicants are hired. Testing of employees usually takes one of three forms:

1. All employees or randomly selected employees are tested at predetermined times.
2. All employees or randomly selected employees are tested at random times.
3. Employees who have been involved in an accident or disciplinary action are tested following the incident.

The second form of testing is probably the most effective in terms of punishing or preventing drug usage, but the third form of testing is legally the most defensible (Veglahn, 1989).

Another important issue in the use of drug testing is the consequence facing an employee who fails a test. Most organizations allow employees to keep their jobs as long as they undergo treatment for drug abuse and do not test positive again in the future. With such a policy, the organization is usually on better legal ground than if it fires any employee who tests positive.

## HANDWRITING ANALYSIS

An interesting method used to select employees by more than 3,000 American organizations and by 85% of all European organizations is **handwriting analysis,** or **graphology.** The idea behind handwriting analysis is that the way people write reveals their personality, which in turn should indicate work performance.

To analyze a person's writing, a graphologist looks at the size, slant, width, regularity, and pressure of a writing sample (Patterson, 1976). From these writing characteristics, information about temperament, mental traits, social traits, work traits, and moral traits is obtained (Currer-Briggs, 1971).

**Table 6.4** Handwriting analysis research

| Study | Year | Country | Sample | Criterion | Validity |
|---|---|---|---|---|---|
| Sonnemann & Kernan | 1962 | Germany | Executives | Supervisor ratings | .74 |
| Keinan & Barak | 1984 | Israel | Military officers | Training success | .26 |
| Ben-Shakhar et al. | 1986 | Israel | Bank tellers | Supervisor ratings | .25 |
| Rafaeli & Klimoski | 1983 | U.S.A. | Salesmen | Sales performance | .04 |
| Rafaeli & Klimoski | 1983 | U.S.A. | Salesmen | Supervisor ratings | .00 |
| Zdep & Weaver | 1967 | U.S.A. | Salesmen | Sales commissions | −.05 |
| Total | | | | | .21 |

Research on graphology has revealed interesting findings. First, graphologists are consistent in their judgments about script features (Lockowandt, 1976) but not in their interpretation about what these features mean (Keinan & Barak, 1984; Rafaeli & Klimoski, 1983). Second, trained graphologists are no more accurate or reliable at interpreting handwriting samples than untrained undergraduates (Rafaeli & Klimoski, 1983) or psychologists (Ben-Shakhar, Bar-Hillel, Bilu, Ben-Abba, & Flug, 1986; Jansen, 1973). Finally, as shown in Table 6.4, handwriting analysis seems to predict performance in other countries but not in the United States. This mysterious finding might explain why graphology is used more in Europe than in the United States.

## COMPARISON OF TECHNIQUES

After reading this chapter, you are probably asking the same question that industrial psychologists have been asking for years: Which method of selecting employees is best? It is clear that the unstructured interview, education, and previous experience are not good predictors of future employee performance (Hunter & Hunter, 1984). It is also clear that ability (as measured by aptitude tests), work samples, biodata, structured interviews, and assessment centers do a fairly good job of predicting future employee performance (Hunter & Hunter, 1984; Schmitt, Gooding, Noe, & Kirsch, 1984). Personality tests predict some criteria fairly well (wages, performance ratings, sales) and others not so well (turnover, status change) (Ghiselli, 1973). Furthermore, personality tests may predict an employee's performance after accounting for ability (Day & Silverman, 1989) or after he has been with the company a few years better than they predict performance immediately after hire (Helmreich, Sawin, & Carsrud, 1986).

As shown in Table 6.5, the issue of which method is best depends on the criteria being measured and the type of job involved. For example, Ghiselli

**Table 6.5** Typical validity coefficients for recruitment and selection

| | | | Criterion | | | |
|---|---|---|---|---|---|---|
| Technique | Satisfaction | Tenure | Training | Promotion | Performance | Theft |
| **Recruitment** | | | | | | |
| Realistic job previews[a] | .06 | .06 | — | — | .03 | |
|   Written | — | — | — | — | −.02 | |
|   Audiovisual | — | — | — | — | .15 | |
| Recruitment methods[b] | | | | | | |
|   Employee referral | — | .13 | — | — | −.02 | |
|   Media | — | −.20 | — | — | .02 | |
|   Employment agencies | — | −.18 | — | — | .10 | |
| **Selection** | | | | | | |
| Ability tests | — | — | — | — | .53 | |
| Assessment centers[c] | — | — | — | — | .25 | |
| Educational requirements | — | .27 | — | — | .15 | |
| Experience | — | — | — | — | .37 | |
| Grade point average[d] | — | — | — | — | .18 | |
| Handwriting analysis | — | — | — | — | .21 | |
|   United States | — | — | — | — | .00 | |
|   Israel and Germany | — | — | — | — | .42 | |
| Integrity (honesty) tests[e] | | | | | .21 | .33 |
| Interviews[f] | | | | | | |
|   Unstructured | — | .08 | .19 | .17 | .17 | |
|   Situational | — | .25 | .27 | .32 | .39 | |
|   Patterned behavior | — | — | — | — | .55 | |
| Job knowledge | — | — | — | — | .51 | |
| References | | | | | | |
|   Traditional | — | — | — | — | .13 | |
|   Peres and Garcia method | — | — | — | — | .35 | |
| Personality tests | | | | | | |
|   Objective | — | — | — | — | .24 | |
|   Projective | — | — | — | — | .00 | |
| Vocational interest | — | — | — | — | .10 | |
| Weighted application blanks[g] | — | .28 | — | — | .36 | .38 |
| Work samples | — | — | — | — | .21 | |

[a]Premack and Wanous (1985)
[b]Aamodt and Carr (1988)
[c]Gaugler, Rosenthal, Thornton, and Bentson (1987)
[d]Bretz (1989)
[e]Ones, Viswesvaran, Schmidt (1993)
[f]Wiesner and Cronshaw (1988)
[g]Beall (1991)

(1973) found that personality tests best predicted sales success, mental ability tests best predicted service occupation success, and mechanical aptitude tests best predicted success for machine operators. Schmitt et al. (1984) found biodata to be the best predictor of performance ratings and mental ability to be the best predictor of achievement. Thus, different methods are best for different occupations and different criteria.

But even though some selection techniques are better than others, *all* are potentially useful methods for selecting employees. In fact, a properly constructed selection battery usually contains a variety of tests that tap different dimensions of a job. Take, for example, the job of police officer. We might use a physical ability test to make sure the applicant has the strength and speed necessary to chase suspects and defend herself, a situational interview to tap his decision-making ability, a personality test to ensure that he has the traits needed for the job, and a background check to determine whether he has a history of antisocial behavior.

The late industrial psychologist Dan Johnson likened the selection process to a fishing trip. During our trip, we can try to catch one huge fish to make our meal or we can catch several small fish that, when cooked and placed on a plate, make the same size meal as one large fish. With selection tests, we try for one or two tests that will predict performance at a high level. But by combining several tests with smaller validities, we can predict performance just as well as with one test with a very high validity.

## REJECTION LETTERS

Once a decision has been made regarding which applicants will be hired, those who will not be hired must be notified. As mentioned earlier in the chapter, applicants who are rejected should still be treated well because they are potential customers and potential applicants for other positions that might become available in the company. With this in mind, what is the best way to reject an applicant? Even though specific rules of courtesy will be discussed, only one study has indicated what effect, if any, different kinds of **rejection letters** have on an applicant's attitude or behavior.

The best type of letter to use is not known, but it is believed that a few rules should be followed when rejecting an applicant. First, always respond to an application as quickly as possible. If you think back on your job-hunting experiences, nothing can be more irritating than never to hear from a company or to wait a long period of time before being notified of the status of your application. Once it is known that certain applicants will not be hired, they should be notified so that they can continue their job hunting. Excuses about not having the funds to notify applicants are probably not justified when one considers the ill feelings that may result from not contacting applicants.

Second, be as personable and as specific as possible in the letter. With the use of word processors, it is fairly easy to individually address each letter, express the company's appreciation for applying, and perhaps explain who was hired and what their qualifications were.

**Mark Foster, Ph.D.**
*Consultant*
*Carl Vinson Institute of*
*Government*
*University of Georgia*

The Vinson Institute of Government is one of several service units of the University of Georgia. The human services division provides technical assistance to municipal, county, and state government agencies. Within this division, assistance is provided primarily in human resource management.

My position is primarily as a consultant. Our clients are mainly public safety agencies such as police and fire departments. The types of agencies we serve range from small municipalities that need assistance in selecting a new police chief to state law-enforcement agencies that need assistance in developing and administering their promotional testing program.

We develop and administer written job-knowledge tests and assessment centers. Much of my time is spent ensuring that these testing instruments are valid predictors of future job performance. The primary strategy we use is content validity. The basis of this approach is ensuring that the questions on the job-knowledge tests and the dimensions and exercises in the assessment center measure actual duties and responsibilities that are required by the individual who performs the job.

The content-validation approach relies heavily on conducting a thorough job analysis. This is a lengthy process in which I will spend time with job incumbents while they perform their jobs. For example, if we are developing test materials for police sergeants, I will ride with a representative sample of police sergeants and observe while they perform their jobs. During this time I ask questions and take extensive notes on exactly what they are doing and why. From this information a task list and a

knowledges and skills list are developed. Job incumbents then are asked to complete a two-phase questionnaire. In the first phase they rate each task for frequency and importance of performance. In the second phase they link these tasks to the knowledges and skills required to perform them. Based on this information, we know which knowledges to test for on the written examination and which skills to test for during the assessment center. This job-analysis information is the first line of defense should the testing process ever be challenged in court.

Examples of knowledges might include basic laws, departmental policy and procedures, proper collection and handling of evidence, and so on. Examples of skills might include recognizing and handling performance problems of a subordinate, making decisions, oral and written communication, and organization and planning. The testing process is usually two-fold: first, a written exam is given to measure if a candidate knows what he or she should do in certain circumstances; and second, an assessment center is used to measure if the candidate can do what needs to be done in a given set of circumstances.

The development of written examinations is relatively straightforward; the development of assessment centers is much more involved. The assessment center is a series of job simulations that require the candidate to perform skills that are required by the job. These job simulations or exercises can take many different forms. We typically use three or four different exercises. These exercises might include a role play, an oral presentation, and a written problem exercise.

To prepare for the role-play exercise, the candidate is given a packet of information to study for a 30- to 45-minute period. During this time they review the material and plan to meet with the role player. The information concerns recent events that involve the role player, such as a brief work history of the role player, recent disciplinary action taken against the role player, letters of commendation, complaints, and so on. Based on this information, the candidate then goes and meets with the role

*(continued)*

player to gather more information. Based on a consolidation of this information, the candidate must then take appropriate action. This action might include recommending counseling or providing discipline.

An oral presentation typically takes the form of a roll-call briefing. The candidate will prepare for the presentation by reviewing a packet of information. During the presentation the candidate should make appropriate announcements, assign personnel to duty posts, and alert personnel to potential problems.

During the written problem exercise, the candidate is asked to review a packet of information. Based on this information the candidate prepares a written memorandum to his or her superior, which details his or her findings and recommendations.

I have detailed only three basic exercises that could comprise an assessment center. While all

assessment centers may not contain these three exercises, there are some consistencies in the process. Exercises are used that simulate actual requirements of the job, and trained assessors evaluate the candidates' performance. These evaluations are then consolidated into a final evaluation of the candidate's ability to perform the tasks that are required for the job.

The development of the assessment center is from a content-validation approach. We typically evaluate the ability of the assessment center to predict future job performance from a statistical approach as well. Our research has demonstrated that the assessment-center method is a very good predictor of who will be successful in these positions. Our findings are consistent with other researchers who have found this methodology to be very helpful in making selection decisions.

---

Aamodt and Peggans (1988) found that rejection letters differ to the extent that they do or do not contain the following types of responses:

- a personally addressed and signed letter
- the company's appreciation to the applicant for applying for a position with the company
- a compliment about the applicant's qualifications
- a comment about the high qualifications possessed by the other applicants
- information about the individual who was actually hired
- a wish of good luck in future endeavors
- a promise to keep the applicant's résumé on file

Furthermore, it was found that a statement about the individual who received the job actually increased applicant satisfaction with both the selection process and the organization.

Examples of good and bad rejection letters are shown in Figures 6.18 and 6.19 respectively. Notice that in the example of a bad letter, only two types of response—an appreciation for applying and a promise to keep the résumé on file—were included, while in the example of a good letter at least four types of response were included.

Perhaps the most important thing to consider when writing a letter of rejection is to be honest. Do not tell an applicant that his résumé will be kept

**Figure 6.18**
Example of a well-designed rejection letter

Dear Mr. Jones:

I am writing concerning your recent application for our position in sales. This has been a long and arduous process as we received more than 100 applications. We have finally chosen a new Sales Representative who seemed to best fit our needs as she possesses a bachelor's degree in marketing as well as five years of sales experience.

We certainly appreciate your interest in our position, and thank you for your application. Your qualifications were outstanding, but as you can see from both the number of applications we received and the high quality of the person we selected, the competition was tough.

We wish you the best of luck in your efforts to obtain employment. We will keep your application on file for six months and should a position arise corresponding with your qualifications, we will keep you in mind.

**Figure 6.19**
Example of a poorly designed rejection letter

Dear Applicant:

The sales position for which you applied has been filled, and we appreciate your interest in the position. We will keep your application on file for six months should another opening arise.

on file if the files for each job opening will not be used. Adair and Pollen (1985) think that rejection letters treat job applicants like unwanted lovers; they either beat around the bush ("There were many qualified applicants") or stall for time ("We'll keep your résumé on file").

## CHAPTER SUMMARY

In this chapter, several employee-selection methods were discussed. References are not good linear predictors of performance, although they still are necessary because of negligent hiring concerns. Weighted application blanks, psychological tests, work samples, job-knowledge tests, and assessment centers are excellent potential predictors of employee performance. Physical ability tests are good measures for some jobs, and paper-and-pencil honesty tests were found to be reasonably good predictors of employee theft. The chapter also pointed out that applicants should be treated professionally, and that both recruitment techniques and rejection letters can help turn unsuccessful applicants into friends of the organization.

## GLOSSARY

**Aptitude test**   A test designed to measure an applicant's abilities and talents.

**Assessment center**   A method of selecting employees in which applicants participate in several job-related activities, at least one of which must be a simulation, and are rated by several trained evaluators.

**Business game**   An exercise, usually found in assessment centers, that is designed to simulate the business and marketing activities that take place in an organization.

**Cognitive Ability**   Abilities involving the knowledge and use of information such as math and grammar.

**Composite score**   A single score that is the sum of the scores of several items or dimensions.

**Cooperation/Consideration**   One of five categories from the trait approach to scoring letters of recommendation.

**Criterion**   A measure of work behavior such as quantity, quality, absenteeism, or tenure.

**Criterion group**   Division of employees into groups based on high and low scores on a particular criterion.

**Dependability/reliability**   One of five categories from the trait approach to scoring letters of recommendation.

**Derivation sample**   A group of employees that was used in creating the initial weights for a weighted application blank.

**Drug testing**   Tests that indicate if an applicant has recently used a drug.

**Enzyme Multiplied Immunoassay Technique (EMIT)**   A method of drug testing that utilizes enzymes to detect the presence of drugs in a urine sample.

**File approach**   The gathering of WAB data from employee files rather than by questionnaire.

**Gas chromatography/Mass spectometry analysis**   A means of analyzing urine samples for the presence of drugs in which the urine sample is vaporized and then bombarded with electrons.

**General aptitude test**   A test battery that measures several different aptitudes.

**General Aptitude Test Battery (GATB)**   The most widely used general aptitude test.

**Graphology**   See *Handwriting analysis.*

**Handwriting analysis**   A method of measuring personality by looking at the way in which a person writes.

**Hold-out sample**   A group of employees that are not used in creating the initial weights for a weighted application blank but instead are used to double-check the accuracy of the initial weights.

**Honesty test**   A psychological test designed to predict an applicant's tendency to steal.

**In-basket technique**   An assessment-center exercise designed to simulate the types of information that daily come across a manager's or employee's desk in order to observe the applicant's responses to such information.

**Interest inventory**   A psychological test designed to identify vocational areas in which an individual might be interested.

**Job-knowledge test**   A test that measures the amount of job-related knowledge that an applicant possesses.

**Leaderless group discussion**   A selection technique, usually found in assessment centers, in which applicants meet in small groups and are given a problem to solve or an issue to discuss.

**Leniency**   An evaluation error in which an evaluator has a tendency to rate a person higher than that person should be rated.

**Letter of recommendation**   A letter written to a prospective employer in support of an applicant's qualifications for a job.

**Mental ability tests**   Tests designed to measure the level of intelligence or the amount of knowledge possessed by an individual.

**Mental agility**   A category referring to intelligence, among the categories developed by Peres and Garcia for analyzing the adjectives used in letters of recommendation.

**Minnesota Multiphasic Personality Inventory (MMPI)**   The most widely used objective test of psychopathology.

**Negligent hiring**   The idea that an organization has the legal duty to protect its employees and customers from potential harm caused by its employees.

**Negligent reference**   The idea that an organization has the legal duty to supply relevant information to a prospective employer about a former employee's potential for legal trouble.

**Objective scoring**   A method of scoring psychological tests in which people scoring the test use keys or guides and have high scoring agreement.

**Objective tests**   A type of personality test that is structured to limit the respondent to a few answers that will be scored by standardized keys.

**Overt integrity test**   A type of honesty test that asks questions about applicants' attitudes toward theft and their previous theft history.

**Perceptual ability** Abilities such as spatial relations and form perception.

**Personality-based integrity test** A type of honesty test that measures personality traits thought to be related to antisocial behavior.

**Personality test** A psychological test designed to measure various aspects of an applicant's personality.

**Physical tests** Tests that measure an applicant's level of physical ability required for a job.

**Polygraph** An electronic test that is intended to determine honesty by measuring an individual's physiological changes that occur after being asked questions.

**Power tests** Tests in which an applicant is asked to correctly complete as many items as possible and is given an unlimited amount of time to complete the test.

**Projective tests** A subjective test in which a subject is asked to perform relatively unstructured tasks, such as drawing pictures, and a psychologist analyzes his or her responses.

**Psychological testing** A selection technique involving the use of paper-and-pencil tests, such as filling out a questionnaire, to determine an applicant's suitability for the job.

**Psychomotor ability** Abilities such as finger dexterity and motor coordination.

**Questionnaire approach** The method of obtaining WAB data from questionnaires rather than from employee files.

**Radioimmunoassay (RIA)** A method of drug testing that uses radioactive tagging to determine the presence of drugs in a urine sample.

**Rare-response scoring** A method of weighting WAB items in which unusual answers to an item get the most weight.

**Rejection letter** A letter from an organization to an applicant informing the applicant that he or she will not receive a job offer.

**Reliability** The extent to which a score from a test or from an evaluation is consistent and free from error.

**Résumé fraud** The intentional placement of untrue information on a résumé.

**Rorschach Inkblot Test** A projective personality test.

**Sample size** The number of people that participate in a study.

**Shrinkage** The amount of goods lost by an organization as a result of theft, breakage, or other loss.

**Simulation** An exercise, usually found in assessment centers, that is designed to place an applicant in a situation that is similar to the one that will be encountered on the job.

**Specific aptitude test** An aptitude test that measures an applicant's ability in only one kind of aptitude.

**Speed tests** Test in which an applicant is asked to correctly complete as many items as possible in a specific amount of time.

**Strong Inventory Interest (SII)** A popular interest inventory used to help people choose careers.

**Subjective scoring** A method of scoring psychological tests in which people scoring the test rely more on their own judgment than on scoring guides, and high scoring agreement is unlikely.

**Thematic Apperception Test (TAT)** A projective personality test in which test takers are shown pictures and asked to tell a story about the picture.

**Thin-layer chromatography** A method of analyzing urine specimens for drugs that is performed by hand and requires a great deal of analyst skill.

**Uniform Guidelines** Federal guidelines that are used to guide an employer in establishing fair selection methods.

**Urbanity** A category referring to social skills and refinement, one of the five dimensions in the trait approach to scoring letters of recommendation.

**Vertical percentage method** The method for scoring weighted application blanks in which the percentage of unsuccessful employees responding in a particular way is subtracted from the percentage of successful employees responding in the same way.

**Vigor** A category referring to energy, one of the five dimensions in the trait approach to scoring letters of recommendation.

**Vocational counseling** The process of helping an individual choose and prepare for the most suitable career.

**Voice stress analyzer** An electronic test that is intended to determine honesty by measuring an individual's voice changes that occur after being asked questions.

**Weighted application blank (WAB)** A method of selection involving application blanks that contain questions that research has shown will predict job performance.

**Wonderlic Personnel Test** The mental ability test that is most commonly used in industry.

**Work sample** A method of selecting employees in which an applicant is asked to perform samples of actual job-related tasks.

# 7

# EVALUATING EMPLOYEE PERFORMANCE

Have you ever received a grade that you did not think was fair? Perhaps you had an 89.6 and the instructor would not "round up" to an A, or the test contained questions that had nothing to do with the class. If so, you were probably upset with the way in which your professor appraised your performance. In this chapter, we will discuss the process of evaluating and appraising employee performance, which is similar to evaluating a student's.

The process can be divided into several interrelated steps. The first step is to determine the reasons an organization evaluates employee performance (Cleveland, Murphy, & Williams, 1989). This is important because the various performance-appraisal techniques are appropriate for some purposes but not others. For example, a performance-appraisal method that we will discuss—the forced-choice rating scale—is excellent for determining compensation but terrible for training purposes.

Once the reasons for performance evaluation have been established, the second step is to identify relevant evaluation criteria. Criteria are ways of describing employee success. For example, it might be decided that attendance, quality of work, and safety are the three most important criteria for a successful employee.

After relevant criteria are chosen, the third step is to choose and create methods for measuring the criteria. That is, how can we measure attendance, quality, and safety? Although this step is important, the choice of instruments is not as important as *how* the results of the evaluations are actually used (Hodap, 1986).

The fourth step in the process is to explain the system to employees and supervisors and to elicit their suggestions and comments. At this point, a training program for supervisors should be established on how to evaluate performance. It is imperative to provide supervisors with the necessary time and incentives to take the performance-appraisal process seriously. This can be accomplished in such ways as including performance-appraisal duties in supervisor job descriptions and making part of a supervisor's own performance evaluation dependent upon how well she evaluates her employees. For example, 20% of the performance-evaluation scores for supervisors working for Salt Lake City are based on their efforts in evaluating employee performance.

The fifth step is the actual evaluation of employee performance using the instrument chosen and created in the second step. This step includes the observation and cognitive processing of behaviors, the recording or remembering of behaviors, and the actual evaluation of these behaviors. As we will see throughout this chapter, distortion and error frequently occur at this stage.

The final step is the **performance-appraisal review,** during which the supervisor formally communicates the results of the appraisal to the employee. During this time, employees explain why their performance might have been poor, and employees and supervisors discuss what steps will be taken to improve future performance. The performance-appraisal review will be discussed in greater depth toward the end of this chapter. An example of the performance-appraisal process used by the state of Wyoming is shown in Figure 7.1. As you can see from the figure, the performance-appraisal process can be complicated and must be carefully thought out.

## REASONS FOR EVALUATING EMPLOYEE PERFORMANCE

### COMPENSATION

As mentioned in Chapter 3, a job's worth is determined by many factors, including the degree of responsibility and level of education required to perform the job. But the difference in compensation between two individuals

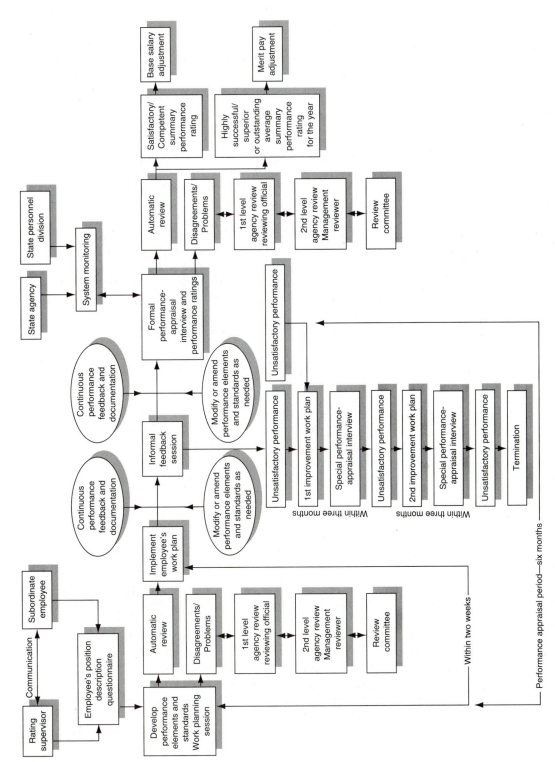

**Figure 7.1** An example of a performance-appraisal system

Source: Reprinted with permission of the Personnel Division, State of Wyoming.

within the same job is a function of both tenure and job performance. That is, it would not seem fair to pay a poorly performing employee the same amount as an excellently performing one. Thus, one important reason for evaluating employee performance is to provide a fair basis on which to determine an employee's salary.

## PROMOTIONS

Another reason for evaluating performance is to determine which employees will be promoted. Although it would seem only fair to promote the best employee, this does not often occur. For example, the policy in some organizations is to promote employees with the most seniority. This is especially true of organizations whose employees belong to unions. Even though promoting employees on the basis of performance or tenure seems fair, it may not always be smart. The best employee at one level is not always the best at the next level. Promoting the best or most senior employee often results in the so-called **Peter Principle**—the promotion of employees until they reach their highest level of incompetence. If performance evaluations are used to promote employees, care should be taken to ensure that the employee is evaluated well on the job dimensions that are similar to the new position's dimensions.

For example, the five important job dimensions of a salesperson might be sales, communication skills, accuracy of paperwork, client rapport, and responsibility. The four important job dimensions of sales manager would be communication skills, accuracy of paperwork, motivational ability, and employee rapport. The salesperson with the highest scores on the overlapping dimensions, which in this case are communication skills and accuracy of paperwork, should be the one promoted. Sales volume might not even be used as a factor in promotion.

## EMPLOYEE TRAINING AND FEEDBACK

By far, the most important use of performance evaluation is to improve employee performance by providing them feedback about what they are doing right and wrong. Even though employee training should be an ongoing process (see Chapter 8), the semiannual performance-appraisal review is an excellent time to meet with employees to discuss their strengths and weaknesses. But more importantly, it is the time to determine how weaknesses can be corrected. This process is thoroughly discussed later in the chapter.

Another use of performance appraisal data is in training-needs analysis, which will be discussed in greater detail in Chapter 8. If many employees score poorly on a performance-appraisal dimension, an increase or change in training is probably necessary for all employees. If only a few employees have low scores, training at an individual level is indicated. Thus, performance appraisal can provide useful information about an organization's strengths and weaknesses.

## PERSONNEL RESEARCH

A final reason for evaluating employees is for personnel research. As discussed in previous chapters, employment tests must be validated, and one way this can be done is by correlating test scores with some measure of job performance. To do this, however, an accurate and reliable measure of job performance must be available.

The same is true in evaluating the effectiveness of training programs. To determine effectiveness, an accurate measure of performance must be available for use in determining whether performance increases as a result of training.

Although not the most important reason for evaluating employee performance, personnel research is still important, especially in organizations where union contracts forbid the use of performance evaluations in personnel decisions. In those situations, performance evaluations are still needed for effective personnel research.

# THE PERFORMANCE-APPRAISAL PROCESS

## DECIDING WHO WILL EVALUATE PERFORMANCE

Traditionally, employee performance has been evaluated solely by supervisors. Recently, however, organizations have realized that supervisors see only certain aspects of an employee's behavior. For example, as shown in Figure 7.2, a branch manager might observe only 30% of a teller's work behavior; the rest is observed by customers, peers, and support staff in other parts of the bank. Furthermore, the teller might behave very differently around her supervisor than around other people. Consequently, to obtain an accurate view of the teller's performance, these other sources should provide feedback. The buzzword for using multiple sources to appraise performance is **360-degree feedback** (Hoffman, 1995). Sources of relevant information about employee performance include: supervisors, peers, subordinates, customers, and self-appraisal.

### Supervisors

By far the most common type of performance appraisal is the supervisor rating. In fact, Lacho, Stearns, and Villere (1979) estimated that 95% of all performance appraisals are conducted using supervisors' ratings of performance. Supervisors are best able to evaluate the extent to which an employee contributes to the overall success of the organization. Though supervisors may not see every minute of an employee's behavior, they do see the end result. A supervisor may not actually see a teller sign-up customers for Visa cards but will review the daily sales totals. Likewise, a professor

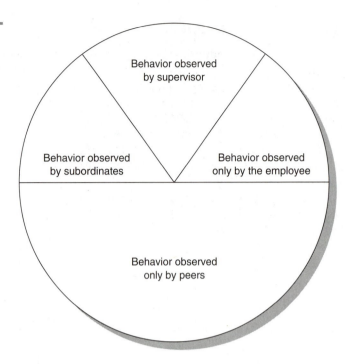

**Figure 7.2**
Who observes employee performance?

Behavior observed by supervisor

Behavior observed by subordinates

Behavior observed only by the employee

Behavior observed only by peers

does not see a student actually research and write a paper but infers the levels of these behaviors by viewing the results — the finished term paper.

### Peers

While supervisors see the *results* of an employee's efforts, peers often see the actual *behavior*. Peer ratings usually come from employees who work directly with an employee; a bank teller could be rated by other bank tellers. However, other employees in the organization, those who often come in contact with the employee, can also provide useful information. For example, our teller could be rated by employees from the loan support or Visa Card departments.

Research has shown that peer ratings are fairly reliable only when the peers who make the ratings are similar to and well acquainted with the employees being rated (Landy & Guion, 1970; Mumford, 1983). Most importantly, peer ratings have been successful in predicting the future success of promoted employees; they also tend to correlate highly with supervisor ratings (Cederbloom, 1989). But even though peer ratings appear promising, few organizations use them (DeNisi, Randolph, & Blencoe, 1983; Lazer & Wikstrom, 1977). One reason could be that peer ratings are lenient when used for evaluation purposes but not when they are only used to provide feedback (Farh, Cannella, & Bedeian, 1991).

Research suggests certain employees are more lenient in their peer ratings than are other employees. Saavedra and Kwun (1993) found that high performers evaluate their peers more strictly than do low performers. This difference in ratings is probably because employees compare others to themselves. Thus, the average employee does not appear impressive to a high performer but may be a less-productive employee.

### Subordinates

Subordinate feedback is an important component of 360-degree feedback as subordinates can provide a very different view about a supervisor's behavior (Whetstone, 1994). However, with the exception of students rating teachers, formal methods are neither common nor well regarded by managers (McEvoy, 1990; McEvoy, 1988). Subordinate ratings can be difficult to obtain because employees fear a backlash if they unfavorably rate their supervisor. For example, when the supervisors at one mental health facility gave poor performance ratings to their boss, each was reprimanded for having the audacity to rate the boss poorly. After such a brow beating, what do you think is the probability the subordinates will be honest again in the future? However, subordinates' feedback can be encouraged if supervisors appear open to employee comments (Baumgartner, 1994). Interestingly, subordinate ratings correlate highly with upper-management ratings of supervisors' performance (Furnham & Stringfield, 1994; Riggio & Cole, 1992). Recent research indicates that subordinate feedback can increase managerial performance, especially that of poorly performing managers (Atwater, Roush, & Fischthal, 1995; Smither et al., 1995).

### Customers

Though it would be unlikely that an organization would ask customers to fill-out a performance appraisal instrument on an employee, organizations do value customer feedback. Informally, customers provide feedback on employee performance by filing complaints or complimenting a manager about one of her employees. Formally, customers provide feedback by completing evaluation cards such as that shown in Figure 7.3.

Organizations also seek customer feedback in the form of *secret shoppers* — current customers who have been enlisted by a company to periodically evaluate the service they receive. In exchange for their ratings, secret shoppers get a few dollars and a free meal. For years, I have been "employed" by a national marketing company to eat at local restaurants and secretly complete a rating of the quality of food and service. The fee is only $4 per visit plus reimbursement for the meal, but it is a fun experience.

### Self-Appraisal

Allowing an employee to evaluate her own behavior and performance is a technique used by 12% of a sample of organizations (Lazer & Wikstrom, 1977). Research on self-appraisal, however, has found what we might expect to find: employee self-appraisals tend to suffer from leniency (Holzbach, 1978; Meyer, 1980) and correlate moderately (.29) with actual performance (Mabe & West, 1982) and poorly with subordinate ratings (London & Wohlers, 1991).

**Figure 7.3**
Customer evalua-
tion card

---

**McBurger Queen Restaurants**

Dear Customer:

We value your business and strive to make
each of your visits a dining pleasure.  To
help us reach our goal, we would appreciate
your completing this card and placing it in
our suggestion box on your way out.

1. Was your food cooked properly?     Y  N
2. Was your server friendly?          Y  N
3. Was your server efficient?         Y  N
4. Do you plan to return?             Y  N

5. Who was your server? _____

**Comments:**

_____
_____
_____
_____

---

The leniency found in the self-ratings of U.S. workers may not generalize to other countries. Farh, Dobbins, and Cheng (1991) found that the self-
ratings of Taiwanese workers suffered from modesty rather than leniency.
However, Furnham and Stringfield (1994) and Yu and Murphy (1993) found
leniency in the self-ratings of Chinese employees. Further research is still
needed to investigate potential cultural differences in self-ratings.

Self-appraisals of performance appear to be most accurate when the
purpose of the self-appraisal is for either research or use in performance-
appraisal review interviews rather than for such administrative purposes as
raises or promotions (Bassett & Meyer, 1968), employees understand the
performance-appraisal system (Williams & Levy, 1992), and employees believe an objective record of their performance is available with which the supervisor can compare the self-appraisal (Farh & Werbel, 1986).

## DEVELOPING THE PERFORMANCE-APPRAISAL INSTRUMENT

As mentioned earlier in the chapter, the choice of the criteria and method
used to measure the criteria are important (Lance, Teachout, & Donnelly,
1992). An excellent example of this importance comes from a study of the
relationship between age and job performance. Using meta-analysis, Waldman and Avolio (1986) found a correlation of .27 between age and objective

**Table 7.1** Example of a trait-focused evaluation system

| Please rate the employee on the extent to which he/she is: | Low | | | | High |
|---|---|---|---|---|---|
| Friendly | 1 | 2 | 3 | 4 | 5 |
| Dependable | 1 | 2 | 3 | 4 | 5 |
| Creative | 1 | 2 | 3 | 4 | 5 |
| Trustworthy | 1 | 2 | 3 | 4 | 5 |
| Reliable | 1 | 2 | 3 | 4 | 5 |
| Cooperative | 1 | 2 | 3 | 4 | 5 |
| Assertive | 1 | 2 | 3 | 4 | 5 |

measures of job performance for 13 studies covering 40 separate samples. The correlation between age and supervisor ratings, however, was −.14. Thus, using the latter ratings would lead to the conclusion that older workers do not perform as well as younger workers. But using actual performance as the criterion leads to the opposite conclusion: older workers performed better than younger workers.

Industrial psychologists have spent considerable effort in developing different methods for evaluating performance because each has its advantages and disadvantages. The human resource professional must choose the method that is most appropriate for the organization's needs. However, prior to developing the actual performance-appraisal instrument, two important decisions must be made: the focus of the performance-appraisal instrument and the type of rating scale that will be used. A performance-appraisal instrument can focus on traits, behaviors, or results.

### Trait-Focused Performance-Appraisal Systems

As shown in Table 7.1, a trait-focused system concentrates on employees' attributes such as their dependability, assertiveness, and friendliness. Though commonly used, trait-focused performance-appraisal instruments are not a good idea for two reasons. First, they are illegal and will not survive a court challenge. Courts have consistently ruled that performance-appraisal systems must be behavioral. Second, even if they were not illegal, trait-focused instruments should not be used because they provide poor feedback and thus will not result in employee development and growth. For example, think of a performance-review meeting in which the supervisor tells an employee that she received low ratings on responsibility and friendliness. Because traits are personal, the employee is likely to become defensive. Furthermore, the employee will want specific examples the supervisor may not have available. The only developmental advice the supervisor can offer would be to "be more responsible and friendly." Such advice is not specific enough for the employee to change her behavior.

**Figure 7.4**
A graphic rating scale

| Initiative | Poor | 1 | 2 | 3 | 4 | 5 | Excellent |
|---|---|---|---|---|---|---|---|
| Cooperation | Poor | 1 | 2 | 3 | 4 | 5 | Excellent |
| Dependability | Poor | 1 | 2 | 3 | 4 | 5 | Excellent |

### Behavior-Focused Performance-Appraisal Systems

While trait-focused instruments concentrate on who an employee *is,* behavior-focused instruments focus on what an employee *does.* That is, instead of rating a bank teller on her friendliness, supervisors using a behavior-focused instrument would rate the teller on such specific behaviors as "properly greets each customer," "knows customers' names," and "thanks customer after each transaction." The obvious advantage to a behavior-focused system is the increased amount of specific feedback that can be given to each employee. Further, the focus on behavior rather than traits not only reduces employee defensiveness, but reduces potential legal problems. Several methods are used for rating behavior.

**Graphic Rating Scales**   The most common scale for rating behavior is the **graphic rating scale.** An example is shown in Figure 7.4. As you can see, such scales are fairly simple, with five to seven points accompanied by words such as "excellent" and "poor" anchoring the ends of the scale.

The obvious advantage to graphic rating scales is their ease of construction and use, but they have been criticized because of their susceptibility to rating errors such as halo and leniency, which are discussed later in this chapter (Kingstrom & Bass, 1981). To minimize or prevent these problems, other rating methods have been devised.

**Behaviorally Anchored Rating Scales**   To reduce the rating problems associated with graphic rating scales, Smith and Kendall (1963) developed **Behaviorally Anchored Rating Scales (BARS).** As shown in Figure 7.5, BARS use critical incidents (samples of behavior) to formally provide meaning to the numbers on a rating scale. Although BARS are time-consuming to construct, the process (shown in Appendix 7A) is not overly complicated.

To use the scale when actually rating performance, the supervisor compares the incidents she has recorded for each employee to the incidents on each scale. This can be done in one of two ways. The most accurate (and the most time-consuming) method compares each of the recorded incidents to the anchors and records the value of the incident on the scale that most closely resembles the recorded incident. This is done for each recorded incident. The value for each incident is summed and divided by the total number of incidents recorded for that dimension; this yields an average incident value, which is the employee's rating for that particular job dimension.

In the second method (easier, but probably less accurate), all of the recorded incidents are read to obtain a general impression of each em-

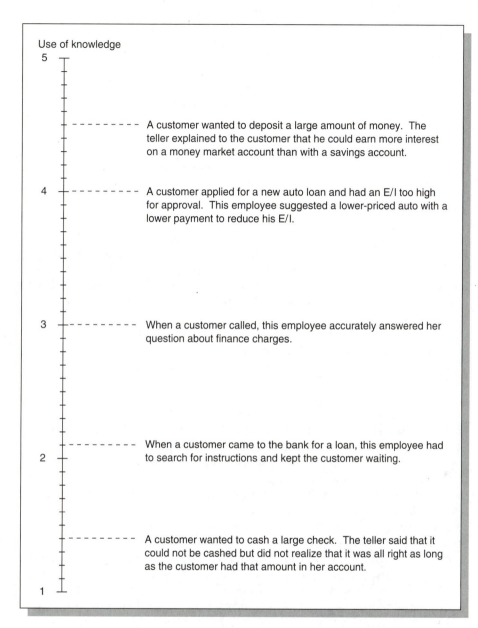

Use of knowledge

5 —

A customer wanted to deposit a large amount of money. The teller explained to the customer that he could earn more interest on a money market account than with a savings account.

4 —

A customer applied for a new auto loan and had an E/I too high for approval. This employee suggested a lower-priced auto with a lower payment to reduce his E/I.

3 —

When a customer called, this employee accurately answered her question about finance charges.

2 —

When a customer came to the bank for a loan, this employee had to search for instructions and kept the customer waiting.

A customer wanted to cash a large check. The teller said that it could not be cashed but did not realize that it was all right as long as the customer had that amount in her account.

1 —

**Figure 7.5**
Example of behaviorally anchored rating scale (BARS)

ployee. This general impression is compared to the incidents that anchor each scale point. The scale point next to the incident that most closely resembles the general impression gained from the incidents then becomes an employee's score for that dimension.

The third way to use BARS (and the least recommended) is to use the incidents contained in the BARS to arrive at a rating of the employee without recording actual incidents. Instead, the BARS are only used to provide meaning to the five scale points.

**Figure 7.6**
Forced-choice
rating scale

**Directions:** In each of the following items, check the one statement that is *most like* the teller being rated and the one statement that is *least like* the teller being rated.

|  | Most | Least |  |
|---|---|---|---|
| 1. a) | _____ | _____ | Teller is always on time (neutral). |
| b) | _____ | _____ | Teller is never short at end of day (poor). |
| c) | _____ | _____ | Teller smiles at each customer (excellent). |
| | | | |
| 2. a) | _____ | _____ | Teller usually cross-sells (excellent). |
| b) | _____ | _____ | Teller keeps work area neat and orderly (poor). |
| c) | _____ | _____ | Teller is friendly to other employees (neutral). |

**Forced-Choice Rating Scales**   One problem with BARS is that supervisors often do not use the anchors when rating employees. Instead, they choose a point on the scale and then quickly glance to see which anchor is associated with the number. Because of this tendency, BARS do not often reduce leniency in ratings.

To overcome this problem, **forced-choice rating scales** have been developed. These scales use critical incidents and relevant job behaviors as do BARS, but the scale points are hidden. An example of a forced-choice rating scale is shown in Figure 7.6.

In using the forced-choice scale to evaluate employee performance, the supervisor chooses the behavior in each item that appears most typical of that performed by a given employee. The supervisor's choices then are scored by a member of the personnel department to yield the employee's rating on each dimension. The scores on each of the dimensions can be summed to form an overall rating.

As shown in Appendix 7B, the development of forced-choice rating scales is a long and complicated process, which partly explains why they are not commonly used. However, this method of evaluation does have its advantages. For example, because the supervisor must choose behaviors without knowing "the key," common rating errors such as leniency and halo are less likely. Consequently, performance evaluations should be more accurate.

But the disadvantages of the forced-choice rating scale probably outweigh its advantages. First, evaluations on forced-choice scales can be "faked." A supervisor who wants to give an employee a high rating need only think about an excellent employee when evaluating the employee in question. Second, supervisors often object to forced-choice scales because the key is kept secret. Not only does this secrecy deprive a supervisor of any control over the rating process, but it can be seen by supervisors as a lack of trust in their abilities to evaluate their employees. Most importantly, however, because the key must be kept secret, forced-choice scales make feedback almost impossible. Thus, they should be used only when the major goal of the performance-appraisal system is accurate employee evaluation for purposes such as promotion and salary increases.

**Figure 7.7**
Mixed-standard
scale

**Directions:** Place a "+" after the statement if the typical behavior of the teller is usually better than that represented in the statement, a "0" if the typical behavior of the teller is about the same as that represented in the statement, and a "–" if the typical behavior of the teller is worse than that represented in the statement.

Rating

1. Teller constantly argues with other employees (P). _____
2. Teller smiles at customers (A). _____
3. Teller asks customers how their families are doing (E). _____
4. Teller helps other employees when possible (A). _____
5. Teller is always friendly to and talks with (E) other employees. _____
6. Teller asks customers what they want (P). _____

Items 1, 4, and 5 are from the Employee Relations Dimension.
Items 2, 3, and 6 are from the Customer Relations Dimension.

**Mixed-Standard Scales** To overcome some of the problems of forced-choice rating scales, Blanz and Ghiselli (1972) developed **mixed-standard scales,** an example of which is shown in Figure 7.7. Mixed-standard scales are developed by having employees rate job behaviors and critical incidents on the extent to which they represent various levels of job performance. For each job dimension, a behavior or incident is chosen that represents excellent performance, average performance, and poor performance. These behaviors are then shuffled and the end results look similar to those shown in Figure 7.7.

To evaluate an employee, a supervisor reads each behavior and places a plus (+) next to it when a particular employee's behavior is usually better than the behavior listed, a zero (0) if the employee's behavior is about the same as the behavior listed, or a minus (–) if the employee's behavior is usually worse than the behavior listed. To arrive at a score for each scale, the supervisor uses a chart like the one shown in Table 7.2. An overall score can be obtained by summing the scores from each of the scales.

Although mixed-standard scales are less complicated than forced-choice scales, they also have their drawbacks. The most important is that supervisors often make what are called "logical rating errors." For example, it would make no sense for a supervisor to rate an employee as better than the example of excellent performance or worse than the example of poor performance. Yet these types of errors are common. Logical rating errors can still be scored by using the revised scoring method developed by Saal (1979) (see Table 7.3), but their existence alone casts doubt on the accuracy of the entire performance appraisal.

### Result-Focused Performance-Appraisal Systems

Result-focused systems concentrate on what an employee *accomplished* as a result of what she did. Result-focused systems are tempting because they

**Table 7.2** Original scoring system for mixed-standard scales

|  | Statement Type | | Dimension Score |
|---|---|---|---|
| Good | Average | Poor | |
| + | + | + | 7 |
| 0 | + | + | 6 |
| – | + | + | 5 |
| – | 0 | + | 4 |
| – | – | + | 3 |
| – | – | 0 | 2 |
| – | – | – | 1 |

Source: Adapted from Blanz and Ghiselli (1972).

**Table 7.3** Revised scoring system for mixed-standard scales

|  | Statement Type | | Dimension Score |
|---|---|---|---|
| Good | Average | Poor | |
| + | + | + | 7 |
| 0 | + | + | 6 |
| + | + | 0 | 6 |
| + | 0 | + | 6 |
| – | + | + | 5 |
| + | + | – | 5 |
| + | 0 | 0 | 5 |
| + | – | + | 5 |
| 0 | + | 0 | 5 |
| 0 | 0 | + | 5 |
| – | + | + | 5 |
| – | 0 | + | 4 |
| + | 0 | – | 4 |
| + | – | 0 | 4 |
| 0 | + | – | 4 |
| 0 | 0 | 0 | 4 |
| 0 | – | + | 4 |
| – | + | 0 | 4 |
| – | – | + | 3 |
| + | – | – | 3 |
| 0 | 0 | – | 3 |
| 0 | – | 0 | 3 |
| – | + | – | 3 |
| – | – | + | 3 |
| – | 0 | 0 | 3 |
| – | – | 0 | 2 |
| 0 | – | – | 2 |
| – | 0 | – | 2 |
| – | – | – | 1 |

Source: Adapted from Saal (1979).

Care must be taken when using objective data to evaluate employee performance.

evaluate employees on their contribution to the bottom line: did their behavior on the job result in a tangible outcome for the organization (Planchy & Planchy, 1993)?

A problem with result-focused systems is that an employee can do everything asked of her by an organization and still not get the desired results due to factors beyond her control. In banking, a teller might not be successful in getting customers to sign-up for Visa Cards because the bank's interest rate is not competitive. In law enforcement, a police officer might not write many traffic citations because she patrols an area in which there are few cars. In retail, a salesperson has poor sales because of her geographic location. For example, two salespeople work in different locations. Bob Anderson sells an average of 120 air conditioners per month, while Fred Stone averages 93. Is this criterion free from contamination? Definitely not.

The number of sales is based not only on the skills of the salesperson, but also on factors such as the number of stores in the sales territory, the average temperature in the territory, and the relations between the previous salesperson and store owners. Thus, if we used only the number of sales, Bob Anderson would be considered our top salesperson. But if we take into account that sales are contaminated by the number of stores in the territory, we see that Bob Anderson sold 120 air conditioners in 50 possible stores, while Fred Stone sold 93 air conditioners in 10 stores. Thus, Bob Anderson sold an average of 2.4 air conditioners per store in an area with an average temperature of 93 degrees; Fred Stone sold an average of 9.3 air conditioners per store in an area with an average temperature of 80 degrees. By considering the potential areas of *contamination*, a different picture emerges of relative performance. As this example clearly shows, factors other than actual performance can affect criteria. Therefore, it is essential to identify as many sources of contamination as possible and to determine ways to adjust performance ratings to account for these contamination sources.

Result-focused systems use what is commonly called **objective,** or **hard,** criteria. Common types of hard criteria are quantity of work, quality of work, attendance, and safety.

**Quantity of Work**   Evaluation of a worker's performance in terms of **quantity** is obtained by simply counting the number of relevant job behaviors that take place. For example, we might judge a salesperson's performance by the number of units he sells, an assembly-line worker's performance by the number of bumpers she welds, or a police officer's performance by the number of arrests he makes. Even David Letterman is evaluated on the number of viewers who watch his show.

Although quantity measures appear to be objective measures of performance, they often are misleading. From our previous discussion of contamination, it should be readily apparent that many factors determine quantity of work other than an employee's ability and performance. Furthermore, for many people's jobs it might not be practical or possible to measure quantity. Computer programmers, doctors, and firefighters are examples.

**Quality of Work**   Another method to evaluate performance is by measuring the **quality** of the work that is done. Quality is usually measured in terms of **errors,** which are defined as deviations from a standard. Thus, to obtain a measure of quality, there must be a standard against which to compare an employee's work. For example, a seamstress's work quality would be judged by how it compares to a "model" shirt; a secretary's work quality produced would be judged by the number of typos (the standards being correctly spelled words); and a cook's quality might be judged by how the food resembles a standard as measured by size, temperature, and ingredient amounts.

Kentucky Fried Chicken evaluates the quality of its franchises' food by undercover inspectors. These inspectors purchase food, drive down the road, and, after parking, use a thermometer to see whether the food has been served at a standard acceptable temperature and a scale to determine whether the weight of the mashed potatoes is within the acceptable range.

For some jobs, measuring quality is not as difficult as with other jobs.

Note that the definition of an error is *any* deviation from a standard. Thus, errors can even be work quality that is higher than a standard. Why is this an error? Suppose a company manufactures shirts that are sold for $10. To keep down the manufacturing costs of its shirts, the company probably uses cheaper material and has its workers spend less time per shirt than does a company that manufactures $50 shirts. Thus, if an employee sews a shirt with 15 stitches per inch instead of the standard 10, the company will lose money because of higher quality!

When I was working my way through school, I held a summer job at an amusement park. The job involved wearing a pink and purple uniform and cooking prefabricated pizza. The standard for the large pepperoni pizza was two handfuls of cheese and 15 pieces of pepperoni. Now all pizza lovers recognize this to be a barren pizza. The cooks, therefore, tried to increase the pizza quality by tripling the number of pepperoni pieces. However, the management quickly explained to the young "gourmet chefs" that exceeding the standards was considered poor work performance, and employees who did so would be fired.

A similar situation developed at a factory that produced parts for telephones. Most of the employees were older and took great pride in their work quality and in the fact that their parts had the lowest percentage of errors in the company. They were told, however, that their quality was too high and that the parts were lasting so long that the company was not getting much repeat business. Quality errors can occur in many strange ways!

**Attendance**   A common method for objectively measuring one aspect of an employee's performance is by looking at attendance. (This will be discussed in greater detail in Chapter 13.) Attendance can be separated into three distinct criteria: absenteeism, tardiness, and tenure. Both absenteeism and tardiness have obvious implications for the performance-appraisal process. The weight that each has in the overall evaluation of the employee largely depends on the nature of the job.

Tenure as a criterion, however, is used mostly for research purposes when evaluating the success of selection decisions. For example, in a job such as cook at McDonald's, there is probably little difference among employees in the quantity and quality of hamburger or french fries that are cooked. But an employee might be considered a "success" if she stays with the company for at least four months and "unsuccessful" if she leaves before that time. In fact, the importance of tenure can be demonstrated by noting that several major fast-food restaurants and convenience stores have established bonus systems to reward long-tenure employees—that is, those who have worked for the company for at least six months. For each hour the employee works, the company places a specified amount of money into an account that can be used by the employee to pay such educational expenses as books and tuition.

**Safety**   Another method used to evaluate the success of an employee is safety. Obviously, employees who follow safety rules and who have no occupational accidents do not cost an organization as much money as those who break rules, equipment, and possibly their own bodies. As with tenure, safety is usually used for research purposes, but it also can be used for employment decisions such as promotions and bonuses.

### Scale Used to Rate Performance

Based on the discussion in the preceding pages, it is clear that most performance-appraisal instruments will focus on behavior. The next issue is what scale to use to rate performance on these behaviors. As shown in Table 7.4, employees can be rated in three ways: how they compared to other employees, the frequency with which they performed certain behav-

**Table 7.4**  Examples of three scales to measure behavior

Comparison to Other Employees
_____

Refers to customers by name
____ Much better than other tellers
____ Better than other tellers
____ The same as other tellers
____ Worse than other tellers
____ Much worse than other tellers

Frequency
_____

Refers to customers by name
____ Always
____ Almost always
____ Often
____ Seldom
____ Never

Extent to Which Organizational Expectations Were Met
_____

____ Greatly exceeds expectations
____ Exceeds expectations
____ Meets expectations
____ Falls slightly below expectations
____ Falls well below expectations


**Table 7.5**  Ranking method of evaluating performance

| Employee | Knowledge | Dependability | Quality | Total |
|----------|-----------|---------------|---------|-------|
| Clark    | 1         | 1             | 1       | 1.00  |
| Bailey   | 2         | 3             | 2       | 2.33  |
| Darden   | 3         | 2             | 3       | 2.67  |
| Shapiro  | 4         | 5             | 4       | 4.33  |
| Cochran  | 5         | 4             | 5       | 4.67  |

iors, and the extent to which the behaviors met the expectations of the employer.

**Comparisons to Other Employees**  To reduce leniency effects, employees can be compared with one another instead of rated individually on a scale. The easiest and most common of these methods is the **rank order.** In this approach, employees are ranked in order by their judged performance for each relevant dimension. As Table 7.5 shows, the ranks are then averaged across each dimension to yield an overall rank.

**Figure 7.8**

Example of paired comparison method

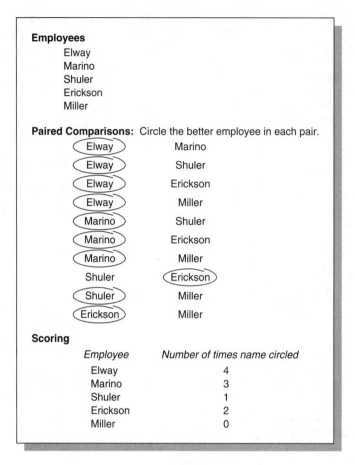

Rank orders are easily used when there are only a few employees to rank, but they become difficult to use with larger numbers. Ranking the top few and bottom few employees is relatively easy, but deciding which 2 of 50 employees should be placed at the 30th and 31st ranks is more difficult.

To make this process easier, **paired comparisons** can be used. This method involves comparing each possible pair of employees and choosing which one of each pair is the better employee. An example is shown in Figure 7.8. Even though comparing one pair of employees at a time is easier than simultaneously comparing a large number of employees, it does have its drawbacks. With large numbers of employees, the time necessary to make all of the comparisons becomes prohibitive. For example, to determine how many comparisons must be made, we can use the following formula:

$$\text{Number of comparisons} = \frac{n\,(n-1)}{2}$$

**Figure 7.9**
Forced-distribution method of performance appraisal

| Spelling | Tilly Stone | Griffith Hannah Basinger Close | Moore Hunt | Ryan |
|----------|-------------|-------------------------------|------------|------|
| 10% Terrible | 20% Poor | 40% Average | 20% Good | 10% Excellent |

where $n$ = the number of employees. Thus, if we have 10 employees to compare:

$$\text{Number of comparisons} = \frac{(10)(10-1)}{2} = \frac{(10)(9)}{2} = \frac{90}{2} = 45$$

Thus, we would need to make 45 comparisons for each performance dimension. Although this number is not too bad, evaluating 100 employees would result in 4,950 separate comparisons! And with five performance dimensions, some unfortunate supervisor would have to make almost 25,000 separate comparisons! Obviously, the supervisor would not favor such a task.

The final type of employee-comparison system is called the **forced-distribution** method. With this method, predetermined percentages of employees are placed into five categories as shown in Figure 7.9. This system is much easier to use than the other two employee-comparison methods, but it also has a drawback. To use the method, one must assume that employee performance is normally distributed, that is, that there are certain percentages of employees who are poor, average, and excellent. As we discussed in Chapter 4, employee performance probably is not normally distributed because of restriction of range. There probably are few terrible employees because they either were never hired or were quickly fired. Likewise, truly excellent employees probably have been promoted. Thus, employee performance is distributed in a nonnormal fashion.

Perhaps another way to look at this concept is by examining the grades given in a class. When students ask an instructor to "curve" a test, technically they are asking her to force their grades into a normal curve—that is, there will be approximately 10% As and 10% Fs. (Of course, what these students really are often asking for is extra points.)

Suppose that you are at the bottom of your class, yet you still have a 75% average on class exams. Do you deserve an F? What if you are the last person in the D category, and a student withdraws from the class with two weeks to go. To keep the distribution normal, you are given an F. Do you consider this fair?

Perhaps the greatest problem with all of the employee-comparison methods is that they do not provide information about how well an employee is actually doing. For example, even though every employee at a production plant might be doing an excellent job, someone has to be at the bottom. Thus, it might appear that one worker is doing a poor job (because she is last), when in fact she, and every other employee, is doing well.

**Frequency of Desired Behaviors**  As shown in Table 7.4, behaviors can be rated based on the frequency with which they occur. For example, we expect our production workers to follow safety guidelines. As part of our performance-appraisal system, supervisors are asked to decide whether their employees *always, almost always, often, seldom,* or *never* follow the rules. As you can imagine, it is often difficult for a supervisor to distinguish between levels such as *almost always* and *often.*

**Behavioral Observation Scales (BOS),** developed by Latham and Wexley (1977), are a more sophisticated method for measuring the frequency of desired behaviors. Even though BOS have no psychometric advantages over BARS (Bernardin & Kane, 1980), they are simpler to construct and easier to use (Latham, Fay, & Saari, 1979). BOS also provide high levels of feedback and are better than simple rating scales at motivating employees to change their behavior (Tziner, Kopelman, & Livnech, 1993).

The development of BOS are relatively straightforward. The first few steps are the same as with BARS: Critical incidents and behaviors are obtained from employees, the incidents are placed into categories, and each incident is rated as to the level of job performance that it represents.

As shown in Figure 7.10, the behaviors are then listed. Supervisors read each behavior on the list and use the following scale to find the frequency for an employee performing that specific behavior:

1 = Employee engaged in behavior less than 65% of the time

2 = Employee engaged in behavior 65–74% of the time

3 = Employee engaged in behavior 75–84% of the time

4 = Employee engaged in behavior 85–94% of the time

5 = Employee engaged in behavior 95–100% of the time

**Figure 7.10**
Behavioral observation scale (BOS)

**Job Knowledge**
1. _____  Is aware of current interest rates?
2. _____  Offers suggestions to customers about how they can make the most interest?
3. _____  Knows various strategies for converting IRAs?

**Employee Relations**
1. _____  Offers to help other employees when own workload is down?
2. _____  Praises other employees when they do well?

After each employee has been rated on each behavior, the scores from each item in each dimension are summed to give the dimension score. Dimension scores are then summed to yield an overall score. The greatest advantage to BOS is that a supervisor can show employees the *specific behaviors* that they currently do correctly and the specific behaviors that they should do to receive higher performance evaluations.

Because supervisors only conduct evaluations once every six months, BOS has been criticized for actually measuring only the *recall* of behaviors rather than measuring the actual *observation* of behaviors (Murphy, Martin, & Garcia, 1982). The importance of this distinction between recall and actual observation comes from research that has demonstrated that after some period of time, we cannot recall specific behaviors; instead, we "recall" behaviors that are consistent with sets of traits or **prototypes** that we attribute to employees (Feldman, 1981). That is, we assign certain traits or prototypes to employees; six months later, we recall behaviors that are consistent with those traits or prototypes. Furthermore, the closer an employee's behavior is to the prototype, the more accurate the performance evaluations (Mount & Thompson, 1987). Thus, as objective and behavioral as BOS appear, they may not be as accurate as initially believed because of cognitive processing distortions.

**Extent to Which Organizational Expectations Are Met**   As shown in Table 7.4, perhaps the best approach is to rate employees on the extent to which their behavior meets the expectations of the organization. Such an approach allows for high levels of feedback and can be applied to most types of employee behavior. Some behaviors, however, are not suitable for such a scale. Take for example the expectation that a police officer should always wear her seat belt. If she wears it all the time, she has *met* expectations (a rating of 3): there is no way to get a higher rating because one cannot wear a seat belt more often than always and thus can never exceed expectations.

## EVALUATION OF METHODS OF PERFORMANCE APPRAISAL

In the previous pages, several methods for evaluating employee performance have been discussed. Of course, we might now ask, "Is any one of these methods the best?" Probably not (Jacobs, Kafry, & Zedeck, 1980; Kingstrom & Bass, 1981; Schwab et al., 1975). Research has shown that more complicated techniques such as BARS, forced-choice rating scales, and mixed-standard scales are only occasionally superior to the inexpensive and uncomplicated graphic rating scale (Giffin, 1989; Guion & Gibson, 1988). In fact, behavioral anchors sometimes bias supervisors' ratings by forcing them to concentrate on specific behaviors (Murphy & Constans, 1987). And yet graphic rating scales are seldom superior to these more complicated rating methods.

Although the more complicated techniques are only slightly more psychometrically sound, they still have some advantages over graphic rating scales. Because employees are directly involved in creating techniques such as BARS, they tend to see performance-evaluation results as being more fair. Furthermore, many supervisors who make such ratings prefer many of the more complicated behavioral approaches (Dickenson & Zellinger, 1980). Finally, feedback from BARS may lead to greater increases in future performance than feedback from graphic rating scales (Hom, DeNisi, Kinicki, & Bannister, 1982).

### A NEW METHOD

As discussed above, a performance-appraisal instrument should be behaviorally focused and rated based on the extent to which the employee's behavior met the expectations of the employer. The format shown in Figure 7.11 represents a combination of the methods previously discussed in this chapter and meets the criteria of being behaviorally-focused and expectation-based.

A performance-appraisal instrument such as that depicted in Figure 7.11 is constructed by taking the task statements from a detailed job description (e.g., "types correspondence") and converting them into behavioral performance statements representing the level at which the behavior is expected to be performed (e.g., "correspondence is typed accurately and does not contain spelling or grammatical errors").

## USING THE APPRAISAL SYSTEM TO EVALUATE PERFORMANCE

### DOCUMENTING BEHAVIOR

After the actual performance-appraisal instrument has been created, the next step is to develop a system so that supervisors can document employees' behaviors as they occur. Such documentation is usually a written log consisting of **critical incidents**—formal accounts of excellent and poor employee performance that were observed by the supervisor. This documentation forces a supervisor to focus on employee behaviors rather than on traits and provides behavioral examples to use when reviewing performance ratings with employees.

Documentation helps supervisors recall behaviors when they are evaluating performance. Without documentation, instead of recalling all of an employee's behavior or at least a representative sample of behavior, supervisors tend to recall certain types of behaviors more than others. Supervisors tend to remember the following:

- **First impressions** Research from many areas of psychology indicates that we remember our first impression of someone (primacy effect) more than we remember later behaviors. Consequently, supervisors recall behaviors consistent with their first

**Use of Weapons and Vehicle**

**Definition of Dimension**

This dimension considers the possession and application of knowledge and skills required in the use of firearms and vehicle. This includes maintaining current skills, knowledge level, and certification(s). This also includes applying new knowledge or techniques to work activities. Equipment would include, but is not limited to, vehicles, batons/ASP, and OC spray.

A dimension rating of "3" indicates that there were no problems in this area during the performance rating period or that a minor problem was offset by other outstanding behavior. Ratings of "4" or "5" indicate the officer was especially adept at vehicle pursuits, marksmanship, and use of force (e.g., using the better of two appropriate alternatives) and/or acquired new knowledge above that expected of the typical patrol officer.

**Behavioral Elements**

Behaviors that can meet or exceed expectations
   _____ Effectively handled vehicle in pursuit or emergency response situations
   _____ Demonstrated marksmanship above minimum requirements

Behaviors that can only meet expectations
   _____ Weapons ratings are current and meet minimum requirements
   _____ Weapons were carried in an appropriate manner

Behaviors falling below expectations
   _____ Applied force when use of force was not justified
   _____ When force was justified, did not use appropriate type and/or amount
   _____ Vehicle was not operated in a safe manner or in accordance with Department policy
   _____ When weapons were used, reports were filed late and/or contained inaccurate information
   _____ Carried a weapon not issued and/or approved by the Department

**Dimension Rating**

   _____ 5 Performance could not realistically be better than that exhibited by this officer
   _____ 4 Officer's use of weapons and vehicle went beyond expectations
   _____ 3 Officer met expectations
   _____ 2 Minor problems occurred in this area
   _____ 1 Serious problems occurred; officer needs immediate and extensive improvement

**Comments**

_____

_____

_____

_____

_____

**Figure 7.11** Example of new behavioral format

impression of an employee, even though those first behaviors may not be representative of the employee's typical performance.

- **Recent behaviors**  In addition to first impressions, supervisors tend to recall the most recent behavior that occurred during the evaluation period.

- **Unusual or extreme behaviors**  Supervisors tend to remember unusual behaviors more than they remember common behaviors. For example, if an average performing police officer captures an important criminal, the officer's performance evaluations are likely to be inappropriately high. Likewise, a good officer who makes a terrible mistake is likely to receive inappropriately low ratings.

- **Behavior consistent with the supervisor's opinion**  Once we form an opinion of someone, we tend to look for behaviors that confirm that opinion. If a supervisor likes an employee, she will probably only recall behaviors consistent with that opinion. The opposite would be true for a supervisor who dislikes an employee. Once you get on someone's bad side, it is hard to get back off.

In addition to increasing the accuracy of performance ratings, documentation also helps an organization defend against legal actions taken against it by an employee who was terminated or denied a raise or promotion. As will be discussed later in this chapter, the courts closely examine the accuracy of the performance ratings upon which personnel decisions are based. Judges and juries are not likely to accept a supervisor's rating as proof of poor performance. Instead, they want to see proof of the behaviors that caused the supervisor to rate the employee poorly. Without documentation, employers will seldom win law suits filed against them (Rosen, 1992).

To use critical incidents to document performance, a supervisor maintains a log of all the critical behaviors she observes her employees performing. These behaviors are then used during the performance-appraisal review process to assign a rating for each employee. The log refreshes the supervisor's memory of her employees' performance and also provides justification for each performance rating. The use of logs to record behaviors not only provides an excellent source of documentation but also results in more accurate performance appraisals (Bernardin & Walter, 1977). This is especially true if the logs are organized by employee rather than maintained as only a random collection of incidents observed on the job (DeNisi, Robbins, & Cafferty, 1989).

A more formal method for using critical incidents in evaluating performance was developed by Flanagan and Burns (1955) for use by General Motors. Called the **Employee Performance Record,** this method consists of a two-color form similar to that shown in Figure 7.12. Half of the sheet is used to record examples of good behaviors, the other half to record examples of poor behaviors. On each side, there are columns for each of the relevant performance dimensions. Supervisors have a separate record for each employee and at the end of the day can record the observed behaviors.

**Figure 7.12**
Employee critical
behavior record

| Dimension | Type of Performance | |
| --- | --- | --- |
| | Poor | Excellent |
| Knowledge | | |
| Employee relations | | |
| Customer relations | | |
| Accuracy of work | | |

The advantage of this format is that supervisors are only allowed to record job-relevant behaviors. At the end of the performance-appraisal period (every six months), the supervisor has a record of job-relevant behaviors recorded in an organized fashion.

The Employee Performance Record had several positive effects for General Motors. The number of disciplinary warnings declined, suggestions in the company suggestion box increased, and productivity increased.

When the use of critical incidents was first announced, supervisors at General Motors were opposed, thinking it would take too much time. The actual time per day spent on recording the incidents, however, was only five minutes.

## APPRAISING PERFORMANCE

### Obtaining and Reviewing Objective Data

When it is time to appraise an employee's performance, a supervisor first should obtain and review any objective data that are relevant to an employee's behavior. For example, a police sergeant might review the numbers of tickets an officer wrote, arrests made, and citizen complaints received. A production supervisor might review the number of days an employee was absent, number of units she produced, and the tons of material that she wasted. These data, when combined with critical-incidents logs, provide a solid basis on which to rate an employee.

### Reading Critical-Incident Logs

After obtaining objective data, the supervisor should go back and read all of the critical incidents written for an employee. Reading these incidents should reduce the primacy, recency, and attention to unusual information errors.

### Completing the Rating Form

Once critical-incident logs have been read and objective data reviewed, the supervisor is ready to assign performance-appraisal ratings. While making these ratings, the supervisor must be careful not to make common rating errors.

### Rating Errors

**Distribution Errors**    A common type of error in evaluating employee performance involves the distribution of ratings on a rating scale; such errors are known as **distribution errors.** One kind of distribution error is called **leniency error** because certain raters tend to rate every employee at the upper end of the scale, regardless of the actual performance of the employee.

A related error is **central tendency error,** which results in a supervisor rating every employee in the middle of the scale. Still another error, **strictness error,** rates every employee at the low end of the scale.

These types of errors pose problems for an organization because two employees doing equal work will receive different ratings if one employee is supervised by a lenient rater and another by a strict rater. This problem can be eliminated partly by having several people rate each employee (Kane & Lawler, 1979), although this is not often feasible, especially in small branch offices with only one manager or supervisor.

**Halo Errors**    A **halo error** occurs when a rater allows either a single attribute or an overall impression of an individual to affect the ratings that she makes on each relevant job dimension. For example, a teacher might think that a student is highly articulate. Because of that, the teacher might rate the student as being intelligent and industrious when, in fact, the student's grades are below average. In this case, the instructor has allowed the student's articulateness to cloud her judgment of the student's other abilities. Halo effects occur especially when the rater has little knowledge of the job and is less familiar with the person being rated (Kozlowski, Kirsch, & Chao, 1986).

Usually, halo error is statistically determined by correlating the ratings for each dimension with those for the other dimensions. If they are highly correlated, halo error is often said to have occurred. But several industrial psychologists have argued that many times consistent ratings across several dimensions indicate not error but actual employee performance. Thus, a teacher who is rated highly in classroom teaching, ability to work with students, knowledge, and fairness of grading actually may excel in those things. But proponents of the halo-error explanation would argue that the instructor is friendly and so well liked by her students that she receives high ratings on the other dimensions when, in fact, she may not have shown a high level of knowledge in her subject matter.

Halo errors may or may not be a serious problem (Balzer & Sulsky, 1992), but they can be reduced by having supervisors rate each trait at separate times. That is, the supervisor might rate the employee on attendance one day and then rate him on dependability the next day (Cooper, 1981a, 1981b). Examples of halo, leniency, and strictness errors are shown in Figure 7.13.

**Proximity Errors**   **Proximity errors** occur when a rating made on one dimension affects the rating made on the dimension that immediately follows it on the rating scale. The difference between this error and halo error is in the cause of the error and the number of dimensions that are affected. With halo error, all dimensions are affected by an overall impression of the employee. With proximity error, only the dimensions physically located nearest a particular dimension on the rating scale are affected; the reason for the effect, in fact, *is* the close physical proximity of the dimension rather than an overall impression.

**Contrast Errors**   As you'll remember, we discussed the employment interview in Chapter 5. You learned that the performance rating one person receives can be influenced by the performance of a previously evaluated person. For example, a bank manager has six employees who are evaluated twice a year—on February 5 and again on August 5. The manager makes the evaluations in alphabetical order, starting with Joan Adams and then going to Frank Carr. Joan Adams is the best employee the bank has ever had, and she receives the highest possible rating on each dimension. After evaluating Adams, the manager then evaluates Carr. When compared to Adams, Carr is not nearly as effective an employee. Thus, Carr receives lower ratings than he might normally receive simply because he has been evaluated

**Figure 7.13**
Examples of rating errors

**Leniency Error**

| | Norm Nixon | | | | | | Walt Davis | | | | |
|---|---|---|---|---|---|---|---|---|---|---|---|
| Cooperation | 1 | 2 | 3 | 4 | (5) | Cooperation | 1 | 2 | 3 | 4 | (5) |
| Knowledge | 1 | 2 | 3 | 4 | (5) | Knowledge | 1 | 2 | 3 | 4 | (5) |
| Leadership | 1 | 2 | 3 | 4 | (5) | Leadership | 1 | 2 | 3 | 4 | (5) |

| | Earvin Johnson | | | | | | John Lucas | | | | |
|---|---|---|---|---|---|---|---|---|---|---|---|
| Cooperation | 1 | 2 | 3 | 4 | (5) | Cooperation | 1 | 2 | 3 | 4 | (5) |
| Knowledge | 1 | 2 | 3 | 4 | (5) | Knowledge | 1 | 2 | 3 | 4 | (5) |
| Leadership | 1 | 2 | 3 | 4 | (5) | Leadership | 1 | 2 | 3 | 4 | (5) |

**Strictness Error**

| | Norm Nixon | | | | | | Walt Davis | | | | |
|---|---|---|---|---|---|---|---|---|---|---|---|
| Cooperation | (1) | 2 | 3 | 4 | 5 | Cooperation | (1) | 2 | 3 | 4 | 5 |
| Knowledge | (1) | 2 | 3 | 4 | 5 | Knowledge | (1) | 2 | 3 | 4 | 5 |
| Leadership | (1) | 2 | 3 | 4 | 5 | Leadership | (1) | 2 | 3 | 4 | 5 |

| | Earvin Johnson | | | | | | John Lucas | | | | |
|---|---|---|---|---|---|---|---|---|---|---|---|
| Cooperation | (1) | 2 | 3 | 4 | 5 | Cooperation | (1) | 2 | 3 | 4 | 5 |
| Knowledge | (1) | 2 | 3 | 4 | 5 | Knowledge | (1) | 2 | 3 | 4 | 5 |
| Leadership | (1) | 2 | 3 | 4 | 5 | Leadership | (1) | 2 | 3 | 4 | 5 |

**Halo Error**

| | Norm Nixon | | | | | | Walt Davis | | | | |
|---|---|---|---|---|---|---|---|---|---|---|---|
| Cooperation | 1 | 2 | 3 | 4 | (5) | Cooperation | 1 | 2 | (3) | 4 | 5 |
| Knowledge | 1 | 2 | 3 | 4 | (5) | Knowledge | 1 | 2 | (3) | 4 | 5 |
| Leadership | 1 | 2 | 3 | 4 | (5) | Leadership | 1 | 2 | (3) | 4 | 5 |

| | Earvin Johnson | | | | | | John Lucas | | | | |
|---|---|---|---|---|---|---|---|---|---|---|---|
| Cooperation | 1 | 2 | 3 | 4 | (5) | Cooperation | (1) | 2 | 3 | 4 | 5 |
| Knowledge | 1 | 2 | 3 | 4 | (5) | Knowledge | (1) | 2 | 3 | 4 | 5 |
| Leadership | 1 | 2 | 3 | 4 | (5) | Leadership | (1) | 2 | 3 | 4 | 5 |

immediately after Adams. His performance has been contrasted to Adams's performance rather than to some objective standard.

Such **contrast errors** also can occur between separate performance evaluations of the same person. That is, the ratings received on one performance appraisal will affect the ratings made on an appraisal six months later. For example, an employee's performance during the first six months of the year is "excellent" and she receives outstanding performance ratings.

For some reason, the employee's actual behavior in the next six months is only "good." What type of performance ratings will she receive? Based on the results of a study by Murphy, Gannett, Herr, and Chen (1986), the answer probably is that her ratings will be less than "good." In contrast to her initial excellent performance, the employee's subsequent performance (which may indeed have been "good") appeared to be lower than it actually was.

Smither, Reilly, and Buda (1988) found that contrast effects occur only when the person making the evaluation actually sees the employee perform during both rating periods. Even if a new supervisor reads that an employee's previous evaluations were excellent but she observes poor performance by the employee, she will probably continue to give excellent ratings—even though the employee's performance deteriorated. Smither and his colleagues call this rating error **assimilation.**

### Training Raters to Reduce Errors

One way to reduce the number of rating errors is to train the people who will be making the performance evaluations (Spool, 1978). Research has indicated that training supervisors to become aware of the various rating errors and how to avoid them often increases accuracy (Smither,.Barry, & Reilly, 1989), reduces leniency and halo errors (Bernardin & Buckley, 1981; Fay & Latham, 1982), increases the validity of tests validated against the ratings (Pursell, Dossett, & Latham, 1980), and increases employee satisfaction with the ratings (Ivancevich, 1982). This is especially true when the training technique uses discussion, practice in rating, and feedback about rating accuracy rather than lecture (Smith, 1986). These training effects, however, are short-lived unless additional training and feedback are provided, and they can even reduce the accuracy of ratings by substituting new errors (Bernardin & Pence, 1980).

The effectiveness of rater training also is a function of training format. Raters who receive frame-of-reference training make fewer rating errors and recall more training information than do untrained raters or raters only receiving information about job-related behaviors (Athey & McIntyre, 1987; Sulsky & Day, 1992). **Frame-of-reference training** provides raters with job-related information, practice in rating, and examples of ratings made by experts as well as the rationale behind those expert ratings (Hauenstein & Foti, 1989; McIntyre, Smith, & Hassett, 1984).

### Sampling Problems

**Recency Effect**  Performance appraisals are typically conducted every six months, or biannually. The evaluation is designed to cover all of the behaviors that have taken place during the previous six months. Research has demonstrated, however, that recent behaviors are given more weight in the performance evaluation than behaviors that occurred during the first few months of the evaluation period. Such an effect penalizes workers who performed well during most of the period but trailed off toward the end, and it rewards workers who save their best work until just before the evaluation.

In baseball, the Los Angeles Dodgers had several poor seasons in which they lost many games early in the season, which eliminated them from pennant contention. But several players played well and produced great statistics during the final month of the season; the press called this period the "salary drive" as opposed to the "pennant drive." This suggests that the players may have been aware of the **recency effect.** They hoped that high performance before contracts were renewed would bring better evaluations and thus higher salaries for the next year.

**Infrequent Observation**   As shown in Figure 7.14, another problem that affects performance appraisals is that many managers or supervisors do not have the opportunity to observe a representative sample of employee behavior (Borman, 1978). **Infrequent observation** occurs for two reasons. First, managers are often so busy with their own work that they often have no time to "walk the floor" and observe their employees' behavior. Instead, they make inferences based on completed work or employee personality traits (Feldman, 1981). A good example involves a teacher who completes a reference form for a student. Reference forms commonly ask about characteristics such as the applicant's ability to cooperate or to get along with others. The teacher must base her evaluation on the term papers that she has seen and the student's test grades. Rarely does she have the opportunity to watch the student "get along with" or "cooperate with others." Instead, she surmises that because a group project was turned in on time and received an excellent grade, the student must have cooperated and gotten along well with other group members.

Employees often act differently around a supervisor than around other workers, which is the second reason why managers usually do not make candid observations. When the supervisor is absent, an employee may break rules, show up late, or work slowly. But when the boss is around, the employee becomes a model worker. In the eyes of the supervisor, the employee is doing an excellent job; the other workers, however, know better.

As discussed earlier in the chapter, this problem can be alleviated somewhat by having several raters evaluate the employee. Other raters can be other supervisors, fellow workers (peer ratings), and even customers. A meta-analysis conducted by Harris and Schaubroeck (1988) indicated that supervisor ratings on the average correlate .62 with peer ratings. Thus, even though the two groups tend to agree with one another, the agreement is certainly not perfect.

Unfortunately, ratings from these sources are often subject to more errors than the uninformed ratings made by a supervisor. For example, customers may complain about a worker even though she is following policy; and, a worker may provide low evaluations of her co-workers so  that she will receive a higher raise. Even with these problems, multiple raters remain a good idea.

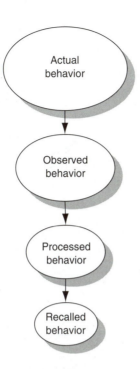

**Figure 7.14**
Information loss
in the performance-
appraisal process

*Cognitive Processing of Observed Behavior*

**Observation of Behavior**   As Figures 7.14 and 7.15 show, just because an employee's behavior is observed does not guarantee that it will be properly remembered or recalled during the performance-appraisal review. In fact, research (Cooper, 1981a; Feldman, 1981) indicates that raters recall those behaviors that are consistent with their general impression of an employee (a halo). And the greater the time interval between the actual behavior and the performance rating, the greater the probability that halo errors (Nathan & Lord, 1983) and distortion errors (Murphy, Martin, & Garcia, 1982) occur. Furthermore, raters who are familiar with the job being evaluated recall more judgments about performance but fewer behaviors than do raters who are unfamiliar with the job (Harriman & Kovach, 1987; Hauenstein, 1986).

But even though memory-based ratings lead to more distortion, in many circumstances they are more accurate than ratings made immediately after the behaviors occur (Murphy & Balzer, 1986). The reason for these increases in halo and accuracy is not yet clear. Supervisors perhaps realize that it will be a long interval between observation of employee behavior and the formal evaluation of that behavior and that they will be unable (without great effort or the use of log books) to remember specific behaviors. Thus, they form an overall impression of the employee and an overall impression of an ideal and a poor employee and evaluate the employee based on comparison with the ideal.

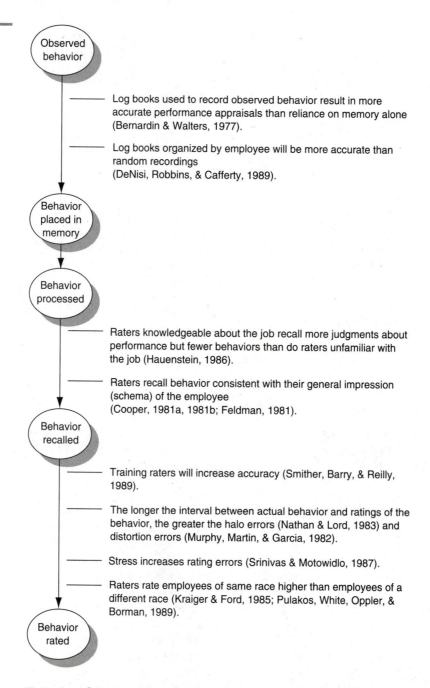

**Figure 7.15**
Factors affecting
information Loss

Observed behavior

Log books used to record observed behavior result in more accurate performance appraisals than reliance on memory alone (Bernardin & Walters, 1977).

Log books organized by employee will be more accurate than random recordings (DeNisi, Robbins, & Cafferty, 1989).

Behavior placed in memory

Behavior processed

Raters knowledgeable about the job recall more judgments about performance but fewer behaviors than do raters unfamiliar with the job (Hauenstein, 1986).

Raters recall behavior consistent with their general impression (schema) of the employee (Cooper, 1981a, 1981b; Feldman, 1981).

Behavior recalled

Training raters will increase accuracy (Smither, Barry, & Reilly, 1989).

The longer the interval between actual behavior and ratings of the behavior, the greater the halo errors (Nathan & Lord, 1983) and distortion errors (Murphy, Martin, & Garcia, 1982).

Stress increases rating errors (Srinivas & Motowidlo, 1987).

Raters rate employees of same race higher than employees of a different race (Kraiger & Ford, 1985; Pulakos, White, Oppler, & Borman, 1989).

Behavior rated

**Emotional State** The amount of **stress** under which a supervisor operates also affects performance ratings. Srinivas and Motowidlo (1987) found that raters who were placed in a stressful situation produced ratings with more errors than did raters who were not under stress. This finding is important because performance evaluations are often conducted hurriedly as supervisors evaluate employee performance so that they can return to their "real" work. Methods for reducing this problem will be discussed later in this chapter.

Raters who like the person being rated may be more lenient (Adams & DeLucca, 1987) and less accurate in rating employees than are raters who neither like nor dislike their employees (Cardy & Dobbins, 1986). But this does not mean that a person who is liked will always receive higher ratings than someone who is disliked. The rater may overcompensate in an effort to be "fair." The rater's feelings, or **affect,** toward an employee may interfere with the cognitive processing of actual performance information.

Research also has indicated that **racial bias** exists in performance evaluations. Kraiger and Ford (1985) conducted a meta-analysis of 74 studies and found that White raters gave higher performance ratings to White employees, and Black raters gave higher ratings to Black employees. Interestingly, this bias occurred only with studies involving real organizations—laboratory research seldom reveals racial bias in rating.

## COMMUNICATING APPRAISAL RESULTS TO EMPLOYEES

As was stated in the beginning of this chapter, the most important use of performance-evaluation data is to provide feedback to employees and to assess their strengths and weaknesses so that further training can be implemented. Although this feedback and training should be an ongoing process, the semiannual evaluation might be the best time to formally discuss employee performance. Furthermore, holding a formal review interview places the organization on better legal ground in the event of a lawsuit (Field & Holley, 1982).

Normally, in most organizations a supervisor spends a few minutes with employees every six months to *tell* them about the scores they received during the most recent evaluation period. This process is probably the norm because most managers do not like to judge others; because of this dislike, they try to complete the evaluation process as quickly as possible (McGregor, 1957; Rapp, 1978).

Furthermore, seldom does evaluating employees benefit the supervisor (Rapp, 1978; Whisler, 1958). The best scenario is to hear no complaints and the worst scenario is a lawsuit. In fact, one study demonstrated that dissatisfaction and a decrease in organizational commitment occurs even when an employee receives an evaluation that is "satisfactory" but not "outstanding" (Pearce & Porter, 1986). Finally, in the "tell and sell" approach to performance-appraisal interviews, a supervisor "tells" an employee everything she has done poorly and then "sells" her on the ways in which she can improve. This method, however, accomplishes little.

Research suggests that certain techniques can be used to make the performance-appraisal interview more effective: time, scheduling, and preparation.

### Prior to the Interview

**Allocating Time**   Both the supervisor and the employee must have time to prepare for the interview. Both should be allowed at least one hour to prepare before an interview and at least one hour for the interview itself.

**Scheduling the Interview**   The interview location should be in a neutral place that ensures privacy and allows the supervisor and employee to face one another without a desk between them as a communication barrier (King, 1984). Performance-appraisal review interviews should be scheduled at least once every six months for most employees and more often for new employees. Review interviews are commonly scheduled six months after an employee begins working for the organization. If this date comes at a bad time (such as during the Christmas season, a busy time for retail stores), the interview should be scheduled for a more convenient time.

**Preparing for the Interview**   While preparing for the interview, the supervisor should review the ratings she has assigned to the employee and the reasons for those ratings. This step is important because the quality of feedback given to employees will affect their satisfaction with the entire performance-appraisal process (Mount, 1983). Furthermore, employees perceive and react to the amount of time that a supervisor prepares for the interview (King, 1984).

Meanwhile, the employee should rate her own performance using the same format as the supervisor (Laumeyer & Beebe, 1988). The employee also should write down specific reasons and examples that support the ratings she gives herself.

### During the Interview

At the outset of the interview, the supervisor should communicate the following: (1) the role of performance appraisal—that making decisions about salary increases and terminations is not its only purpose; (2) how the performance appraisal was conducted; and (3) how the evaluation process was accomplished. It is advisable that the supervisor also communicate her own feelings about the performance-appraisal process (Kelly, 1984).

The review process is probably best begun with the employee communicating her own ratings and her justification for those ratings (King, 1984). Research indicates that employees who are actively involved in the interview from the start will be more satisfied with the results (Burke, Weitzel, & Weir, 1978; Maier, 1976).

The supervisor then communicates her ratings and the reasons for them. The supervisor should limit this communication to statements about behavior and performance rather than traits that are or are not possessed by the employee (Ilgen, Mitchell, & Fredrickson, 1981). Of course, it would be nice to provide only positive feedback because employees then are more satisfied with their reviews (Dipboye & dePontbriad, 1981) and often develop negative attitudes toward management if feedback is negative (Gabris & Mitchell, 1988). But few employees are perfect, and some negative feedback is inevitable. Because of this, positive feedback generally should be given first (Armentrout, 1993; Stone, Gueutal, & McIntosh, 1984) because employees will likely try to avoid negative feedback in order to maintain a positive self-image (Larson, 1989). Any major differences between the employee's self-ratings and those given by the supervisor should be discussed until both understand the differences.

The next step is perhaps the most important. Because few employees receive perfect evaluations, it is essential to discuss the reasons why an employee's performance is not considered to be perfect. The employee may lack some knowledge as to how to perform the job properly, may have been assigned too many duties, or may have outside problems that affect her work performance.

The supervisor's acknowledgement that there may be external reasons for an employee's poor performance can increase the employee's satisfaction with the review and allow her to perceive the feedback and evaluation as accurate and helpful. In addition, it will help the employee understand and appreciate the supervisor's perceptions (Bannister, 1986; Baron, 1988). Feedback should be candid, specific, and behavioral rather than personal (Hequet, 1994). Awareness and acknowledgement of external factors for performance is especially important because we have a tendency, called the *fundamental attribution error*, to attribute others' failure or poor performance to personal rather than situational factors.

Once the problems have been identified, the next and most difficult task is to find solutions to the problems (Nanry, 1988). What can the supervisor do to help? What can the organization do? What can the employee do? The idea here is that solutions to the problems result from joint effort. Too often, we attribute poor performance as being solely the fault of the employee, when, in fact, performance is affected by many factors (see Figure 7.16).

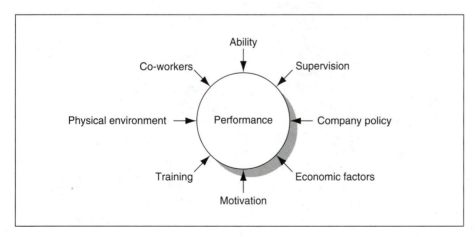

**Figure 7.16**
Factors affecting performance

At the conclusion of the interview, goals should be mutually set for future performance and behavior, and both supervisor and employee should understand how these goals will be met (Cederbloom, 1982). Goals and goal setting will be thoroughly discussed in Chapter 10. For now, however, keep in mind that goals should be concrete, reasonable (Brumback, 1988), and set by both employee and supervisor (Ivancevich, 1982).

## TERMINATING EMPLOYEES

As discussed in the preceding pages, the primary use of performance-appraisal is to provide feedback to employees about their behavior. Performance appraisals are also used to make positive personnel decisions such as raises and promotions. Unfortunately, there are times when managers have to terminate an employee's employment. Over the next few pages, we will discuss the legal aspects of terminating an employee.

### EMPLOYMENT-AT-WILL DOCTRINE

There is a big difference between terminating an employee in the public sector versus in the private sector. In the private sector, the **employment-at-will doctrine** in most states allows employers freedom to fire an employee without a reason—*at-will*. The idea behind employment at will is that because employees are free to quit their jobs at will, so too are organizations free to terminate an employee at will (Hilgert, 1988). However, there are some limitations to this doctrine.

- **State law**   Some states, such as California and New York, have laws that an employee can only be fired for cause—breaking a rule or an inability to perform.

- **Provisions of federal or state law**   Employees cannot be fired for reasons protected by federal or state law. For example, an employer could not fire an employee because she was a female, pregnant, non-White, or over the age of 40.

- **Public policy/interest**   Employers cannot terminate an employee for exercising a legal duty such as jury duty or refusing to violate the law or professional ethics. For example, a large savings and loan institution ordered one of its appraisers to appraise homes higher than their actual value so that its customers could qualify to finance property. Citing federal regulations and professional ethics against inflating property values, the employee refused the company order. After being terminated, the employee successfully filed a lawsuit claiming that he had been fired for refusing to violate the law and the ethical standards of his profession.

- **Contracts**   Obviously, if an individual employee has a signed employment contract stipulating a particular period of employment, an organization cannot fire the employee without cause. Likewise, unions enter into collective bargaining agreements (contracts) with employers that also limit or negate employment at will.

- **Implied contracts**  Employment at will is nullified if an employer implies that an employee "has a job for life" or can only be fired for certain reasons. For example, if an interviewer tells an applicant *"at this company, all you have to do is keep your nose clean to keep your job,"* the employer will not be able to terminate the employee for minor infractions or for poor performance.

- **Covenants of good faith and fair dealing**  Though employers are generally free to hire and fire at will, the courts have ruled that employers must still act in good faith and deal fairly with an employee (Buckley & Weitzel, 1988). These rulings have been based on an item in the Uniform Commercial Code that states "Every contract . . . imposes an obligation of good faith in its performance or enforcement," and the fact that courts consider employment decisions to be a form of contract.

To protect their right to use a policy of employment at will, most organizations include **employment-at-will statements,** such as that shown in Figure 7.17, in their job applications and employee handbooks (Hilgert, 1991). These statements usually holdup in court (Jenner, 1994), and employees seem not to challenge them (Hilgert, 1991).

## LEGAL REASONS
## FOR TERMINATING EMPLOYEES

In situations not covered by employment at will, there are only three reasons that an employee can be legally terminated: violation of company rules, inability to perform, and an economically caused reduction in force (layoffs).

### *Violation of Company Rules*

Courts consider five factors in determining the legality of a decision to terminate an employee for violating company rules. The first factor is that a rule against a particular behavior must actually exist. Though this may seem

I understand that, if employed, I have the right to end my employment with Taflinger Industries.  Likewise, I understand that my employment with Taflinger Industries is not for any definite period of time, and Taflinger Industries has the right to terminate my employment with or without cause and with or without notice. I understand that no representative of Taflinger Industries is authorized to imply any contract for permanent employment.

**Figure 7.17**
Sample employment-at-will statement

obvious, organizations often have "unwritten" rules governing employee behavior. These unwritten rules, however, will not hold-up in court. For example, a manufacturer fired an employee for wearing a gun under his jacket at work. The employee successfully appealed on the grounds that even though "common sense" would say that guns should not be brought to work, the company did not have a written rule against it.

If a rule exists, a company must prove that the employee knew the rule. Rules can be communicated orally during employee orientation and staff meetings and in writing in the handbooks, newsletters, bulletin boards, and paycheck stuffers. Rules communicated in handbooks are the most legally defensible. To prove that an employee knew a rule, organizations require employees to sign statements that they received information about the rule, read the rule, and understand the rule.

The third factor is the ability of the employer to prove that an employee actually violated the rule. Proof is accomplished through such means as witnesses, video recordings, and job samples. Human resource professionals almost have to be detectives—proving rule violations is often not easy. For example, two supervisors saw an employee stagger into work and could smell alcohol on her breath. She was terminated for violating the company rule against drinking. During her appeal of the termination, she claimed that she staggered because she had the flu and what the supervisors smelled was cough syrup rather than alcohol. The employee won the appeal. As a result of this case, the company now has an on-site nurse, and breathalyzer tests are administered to employees suspected of using alcohol at work.

The fourth factor considered by the courts is the extent to which the rule has been equally enforced (Segal, 1990). That is, if other employees violated the rule but were not terminated, terminating an employee for a particular rule violation may not be legal. This factor poses a dilemma for many organizations. Because courts look at consistency, lawyers advise organizations to fire any employee who violates a rule. To not fire a rule breaker sets a precedent making termination of future rule breakers more difficult. There are many times when a good employee breaks a rule, a situation that normally would result in termination. However, because the employee is highly valued, the organization does not want to fire the employee.

Such a situation occurred at a bank. In violation of a bank rule, a teller did not ask for the ID of a customer who cashed what turned out to be a forged check. The bank was torn as to what it should do. Because the employee was one of their best tellers, the bank did not want to fire her. However, not firing her in this case would increase the chance that they would lose a future lawsuit if they terminated another employee for doing the same thing. The bank's unusual decision was to terminate the employee, but it called a competitor, told it of the situation, and asked if it would hire her—which it did.

The fifth and final factor is the extent to which the punishment fits the crime. Employees in their probationary period (usually their first six months) can be immediately fired for a rule infraction. For more tenured employees, however, the organization must make a reasonable attempt to change the person's behavior through **progressive discipline.** The longer an employee has been with an organization, the greater the number of steps that must be taken to correct her behavior. Discipline can begin with something simple such as counseling or an oral warning, progress to a written warning or probation, and end with steps such as reductions in pay, demotions, or terminations.

For violations of some rules, progressive discipline is not always necessary. It is probably safe to say that an employer can terminate an employee who steals money or shoots someone at work.

### Inability to Perform

Employees also can be terminated for an inability to perform the job. To do so, though, an organization will need to prove that the employee could not perform the job, and that progressive discipline was taken to give the employee an opportunity to improve. For an employer to survive a court challenge to terminating a poor-performing employee, it must first demonstrate that there was a reasonable standard of performance that was communicated to the employee. The organization must next demonstrate that there was a documented failure to meet the standard. Such documentation can include critical-incident logs and work samples (for example, poorly typed letters for a secretary, improperly hemmed pants for a tailor).

A properly designed performance-appraisal system is the key to legally terminating an employee. Legal performance-appraisal systems (Smith, 1993)

- are based on a job analysis.
- have concrete, relevant standards that have been communicated to employees.
- involve multiple behavioral measures of performance.
- include several raters, each of whom has received training (Rosen, 1992).
- are standardized and formal.
- allow an employee to appeal.

### Reduction in Force (Layoff)

Employees can be terminated if it is in the best economic interests of an organization to do so. Reductions in force, more commonly called layoffs, have been used by the vast majority of Fortune 500 companies in the past decade (Byrne, 1994; Cameron, Freeman, & Mishra, 1991). In cases of large layoffs or plant closings, the Worker Adjustment and Retraining Notification Act (WARN) requires that organizations provide workers with at least 60 days notice. Though layoffs are designed to save money, research indicates that not only do force reductions have a devastating effect on employees (Leana

& Feldman, 1992), but they often do not result in the desired financial savings (Byrne, 1994).

## THE TERMINATION MEETING

### *Prior to the Meeting*

Once a decision has been made to terminate an employee, Connolly (1986) advises that certain steps should be taken to prepare for the meeting in which the decision will be communicated to the employee. The first step is to ensure that the legal process has been followed. For example, if an organization is about to terminate an employee for a rule violation, it must be sure that a rule actually existed, that the employee knew the rule, the organization has proof that the rule was violated, progressive discipline was used, and the rule was applied equally to all employees. An important responsibility for human resource professionals is to ensure that a termination decision is legally defensible.

The next step is to determine how much help, if any, the organization wants to offer the employee. Forms of help can include references, severance pay, and outplacement assistance. Usually, greater levels of help are given to employees who sign agreements not to sue the organization.

The final step is to schedule an appropriate place and time for the meeting to occur. The meeting should be held in a neutral, private location (DuBose, 1994). To avoid potential damage caused by a hostile reaction to the termination decision, the meeting should not be held in a supervisor's office. Rather than late on Friday afternoon, as is traditional, the meeting should take place on a Monday or Tuesday so that the employee has an opportunity to seek advice and the organization has a chance to talk to its employees (Rider, 1986). When a termination is made on a Friday afternoon, the employee is unable to contact sources of help over the weekend. Likewise, the terminated employee has all weekend to get on the phone to tell her side of the story to other employees while the organization must wait until Monday to refute the gossip.

### *During the Meeting*

During the meeting, the supervisor should get to the point about terminating the employee. The employee usually knows why she has been called in, and there is no reason to prolong the agony. The supervisor should rationally state the reasons for the decision, express gratitude for the employees efforts (if sincere), and offer whatever assistance the organization intends to provide (Howard, 1988). Administrative duties such as obtaining copies of keys and completing paperwork are then performed. Finally, the employee is asked to gather personal belongings and escorted out the door.

I realize the advice in the preceding paragraph may sound cold. However, terminating an employee is a difficult task, and there is little that can be done to make it pleasant. If you have ever ended a romantic relationship,

I think you will understand the feelings that go into terminating an employee. It is an emotional time, and the key is to be brief and professional (Pollan & Levine, 1994).

### After the Meeting

Once the meeting is over, the natural reaction of the supervisor is to feel guilty. To relieve some of this guilt, a supervisor should review the facts—she gave the employee every chance to improve, but the employee chose not to. A human resource professional for Valleydale Foods tells employees, *"Through your behavior, you fired yourself. I'm just completing the paperwork."*

When an employee is fired, other employees will be tense. Consequently, it is important to be honest with them about what happened; at the same time, negative statements about the terminated employee's character must be avoided.

## CHAPTER SUMMARY

This chapter discussed the performance-appraisal process, which typically has five steps: (1) determining the reasons for performance evaluation; (2) creating an instrument to evaluate performance; (3) explaining the system to those who will use it; (4) evaluating employee performance; and (5) reviewing the results of the evaluation with the employee.

The reasons for evaluating employee performance are not limited to compensation and promotion decisions. Evaluations also can be used for training, needs assessment, and personnel research.

The criteria used to evaluate employee performance must be job-related (relevant), free from outside sources of contamination, and congruent with the organization's goals. If ratings are used, care must be taken to prevent common rating errors such as leniency, central tendency, strictness, halo, proximity, contrast, recency, and infrequent observation of behavior. Training raters to avoid these errors will have only short-term benefits unless the training is repeated.

Employees can be evaluated in many ways. Objective criteria include work quantity, work quality, attendance, and safety. Subjective criteria include: employee-comparison methods of ranking, paired comparisons, and forced distribution; critical incidents; and rating scales such as Behaviorally Anchored Rating Scales (BARS), Behavioral Observation Scales (BOS), forced-choice rating scales, and mixed-standard scales.

After employees have been evaluated, it is essential that the supervisor discuss the evaluations. Important factors in the success of this discussion include scheduling the review to eliminate or minimize interruptions, letting the employee discuss her feelings and thoughts, and mutually setting goals for improvements in future performance.

At times, it is necessary to terminate an employee. In organizations not subject to the employment-at-will doctrine, employees can only be terminated for violating a company rule, inability to perform, or as part of a force reduction. The meeting to terminate the employee should be brief and professional. Care must be taken to protect the feelings of the supervisor and other employees.

# GLOSSARY

**Affect**   Feelings or emotions.

**Assimilation**   A type of rating error in which raters base their rating of an employee during one rating period on the ratings that they gave the employee in a previous rating period.

**Behavioral Observation Scales (BOS)**   A method of performance appraisal in which supervisors rate how often they have observed an employee perform a series of specific behaviors.

**Behaviorally Anchored Rating Scales (BARS)**   A method of performance appraisal involving the placement of benchmark behaviors next to each point on a graphic rating scale.

**Central tendency error**   A type of rating error in which a rater consistently rates all employees in the middle of the scale regardless of their actual levels of performance.

**Composite**   The combining of several different criterion scores into one score.

**Congruent**   The quality of being consistent or in agreement.

**Contamination**   The condition in which a criterion score is affected by things other than those under the control of the employee.

**Contrast error**   A type of rating error in which the rating of the performance level of one employee affects the ratings given to the next employee being rated.

**Critical incidents**   A method of performance appraisal in which the supervisor records employee behaviors that were observed on the job and rates the employee based on that record.

**Desirability**   The extent to which a trait or behavior is valued as being good in society.

**Distribution errors**   Rating errors in which a rater will use only a certain part of a rating scale when evaluating employee performance.

**Employee Performance Record**   A standardized use of the critical-incident technique developed at General Motors.

**Employment-at-will doctrine**   The opinion of courts in most states that employers have the right to hire and fire an employee at will and without any specific cause.

**Employment-at-will statements**   Statements in employment applications and company manuals reaffirming an organization's right to hire and fire at will.

**Errors**   Deviations from a standard of quality.

**Forced-choice rating scales**   A method of performance appraisal in which a supervisor is given several behaviors and is forced to choose which of the behaviors is most typical of the employee.

**Forced distribution**   A performance-appraisal method in which a predetermined percentage of employees are placed into a number of performance categories.

**Frame-of-reference training**   A method of training raters in which the rater is provided with job-related information, a chance to practice ratings, examples of ratings made by experts, and the rationale behind the expert ratings.

**Graphic rating scale**   A method of performance appraisal that involves rating employee performance on an interval or ratio scale.

**Halo error**   A type of rating error that occurs when raters allow either a single attribute or an overall impression of an individual to affect the ratings that they make on each relevant job dimension.

**Hard criteria**   Measures of work performance such as quantity and quality that are thought to be reliable and objective.

**Infrequent observation**   The idea that supervisors do not see most of an employee's behavior.

**Leniency error**   A type of rating error in which a rater consistently gives all employees high ratings, regardless of their actual levels of performance.

**Mixed Standard Scale**   A method of performance appraisal in which a supervisor reads the description of a specific behavior and then decides if the behavior of the employee is better than, equal to, or poorer than the behavior described.

**Multiple criteria**   Two or more separate criteria that are used as part of the performance-appraisal system.

**Paired comparison**   A form of ranking in which employees to be ranked are compared one pair at a time.

**Performance-appraisal review**   A meeting between a supervisor and a subordinate for the purpose of discussing performance-appraisal results.

**Peter Principle**   The idea that organizations tend to promote good employees until they reach the level at which they are not competent—in other words, their highest level of incompetence.

**Progressive discipline**   Providing employees with punishments of increasing severity in order to change behavior.

**Prototype**   The overall image that a supervisor has of an employee.

**Proximity error**   A type of rating error in which a rating made on one dimension influences the rating made on the dimension that immediately follows it on the rating scale.

**Quality**   A type of objective criteria used to measure job performance by comparing a job behavior with a standard.

**Quantity**   A type of objective criteria used to measure job performance by counting the number of relevant job behaviors that occur.

**Racial bias**   The tendency to give members of a particular race lower evaluation ratings than are justified by their actual performance, or to give members of one race lower ratings than members of another race.

**Rank order**   A method of performance appraisal in which employees are ranked in order from best to worst.

**Recency effect**   The tendency for supervisors to recall and place more weight on recent behaviors when they evaluate performance.

**Relevance**   The extent to which a criterion is related to the job.

**Reliability**   The extent to which criterion scores are stable and free from error.

**Soft criteria**   Measures of work performance such as supervisor ratings that require subjective judgment on the part of the rater.

**Standard deviation**   A statistic that indicates the variation of scores in a distribution.

**Stress**   Perceived psychological pressure.

**Strictness error**   A type of rating error in which a rater consistently gives all employees low ratings, regardless of their actual levels of performance.

**360-degree feedback**   A performance-appraisal system in which feedback is obtained from multiple sources such as supervisors, subordinates, and peers.

**Generation of Job Dimensions**   In the first step in BARS construction, the number and nature of job-related dimensions are determined. If a job analysis already has been conducted, the dimensions can be obtained from the job-analysis report. If for some reason a job analysis has not been conducted, a panel of some 20 job experts — the employees — is formed. This panel determines the important dimensions on which an employee's performance should be evaluated. If 15 to 20 employees are not available, several supervisors can meet and develop the job dimensions as a group (Shapira & Shirom, 1980). Usually, 5 to 10 dimensions are generated (Schwab, Heneman, & DeCotiis, 1975).

**Generation of Critical Incidents**   Once the relevant job dimensions have been iden-tified, employees are asked to generate examples of excellent, average, and poor behavior that they have seen for each dimension. Thus, if 5 dimensions have been identified, each employee is asked to generate 15 critical incidents — an excellent, an average, and a poor incident — for each of the 5 dimensions. If the organization is fairly small, employees may need to generate more than one example of the three types of behavior for each dimension.

**Sorting Incidents**   To make sure that the incidents written for each job dimension are actually examples of behavior for that dimension, three job experts independ-ently sort the incidents into each of the job dimensions. The dimension into which each incident has been sorted by each of the three sorters then is examined. If at least two sorters placed an incident in the same dimension, the incident becomes part of that dimension. But if each sorter has placed the incident in a different cate-gory, the incident is considered to be ambiguous and thus is discarded.

As discussed in Chapter 3, 3 sorters achieve results similar to those for 100 sorters. Many developers of BARS, however, use as many sorters as possible so that employ-ees have a part in developing the scales. If many employees are involved, a 60% level of sorter agreement should be used to determine whether an incident is part of a dimension.

**Rating Incidents**   Another group of job experts is given the incidents and asked to rate each one on a scale that can have from five to nine points as to the level of job performance that it represents (Bernardin, LaShells, Smith, & Alveres, 1976). The rat-ings from each rater for all of the incidents are then used to determine the mean rating and **standard deviation** for each incident (typically by computer).

**Choosing Incidents**   The goal of this step is to find one incident to represent each of the points on the scale for each dimension. To do so, the incidents whose mean ratings come closest to each of the scale points and whose standard deviations are small are kept. This procedure usually results in the retention of less than 50% of the incidents (Green, Sauser, Fagg, & Champion, 1981).

**Creating the Scale**   The incidents chosen in the previous step are then placed on a vertical scale such as that shown in Figure 7.5. Because the mean for each incident is unlikely to fall exactly on one of the scale points, they are often placed between the points, thus serving as anchors for future raters.

## Appendix 7B  Creating a Forced-Choice Rating Scale

To create a forced-choice rating scale, the first step is similar to that for BARS: Critical incidents and relevant job behaviors are generated. These incidents, of course, are only available when a job analysis has been conducted.

In the second step, employees rate all of the behaviors on the extent to which excellent employees perform them. After an approximately one-month interval, the employees again rate the items. This time, however, they rate the extent to which poor employees perform the behaviors. Finally, after another month, the employees again rate the behaviors, this time for their **desirability.**

In the third step, the actual items for the rating scale are created. This is done by computing the value for each behavior. These values are computed by subtracting the average rating given to each behavior that describes the poor employee from the average rating given to each behavior that describes the excellent employee. Behaviors with high positive values are considered to discriminate excellent from poor employees, items with high negative values are considered to discriminate poor from excellent employees, and behaviors with values near zero are considered neutral.

The next step in creating the items is to pick excellent, poor, and neutral behaviors that have similar desirability ratings. Thus, each rating item has three behaviors: One indicates excellent performance, one indicates poor performance, and one indicates neither excellent nor poor performance. Furthermore, all of the behaviors for an item have the same level of desirability. This process is repeated until several items have been constructed for each of the relevant job dimensions.

# 8

# DESIGNING AND EVALUATING TRAINING SYSTEMS

Employee performance can be improved in many ways. In Chapters 5 and 6, you learned that employee-selection procedures can bring higher employee performance. But as you also learned in Chapter 4, employee selection is not an effective way to improve productivity in situations where only a few applicants compete for a large number of openings or when a job involves only easily learned tasks.

When these situations are encountered, *training* rather than selection techniques must be emphasized (Kramm & Kramm, 1988). For example, I was once involved in a project designed to develop a selection system for intramural basketball officials. Although we were successful in finding a test that correlated significantly with referee performance, we ran into a problem with the selection ratio. The intramural department needed 35 referees each year, but only had 30 applicants. Thus, the selection test could not be used because the intramural department had to hire everyone who applied. The logical solution was to extensively train the referees who did apply.

This does not mean that training should be emphasized only when selection techniques are not appropriate. Instead, training should be used in conjunction with the selection systems discussed in Chapters 5 and 6 and with the motivational techniques that will be discussed in a later chapter.

**Training** is the "planned effort by an organization to facilitate the learning of job-related behavior on the part of its employees" (Wexley & Latham, 1991). These behaviors can include knowledge, skill, rules, concepts, and attitudes (Goldstein, 1993). Training is important for several reasons. As shown in the intramural example, organizations often have difficulty finding applicants with the necessary knowledge and skills to perform a job. Thus, training compensates for the inability to select desired applicants. Also, as discussed in Chapter 3, jobs change. Employees might have the necessary knowledge and skills one year, but have deficiencies by the next. Finally, no employee has the "complete package"—every technical and interpersonal knowledge and skill to be perfect: there is always room for improvement. The ultimate purpose of employee training is to increase an organization's profits.

Collectively, organizations realize the importance of training by spending more than $50 billion on it each year (Filipczak, 1994). Major organizations spend an average of 3.2% of their payroll on training—roughly $900 per employee (Kimmerline, 1993). Training managers earn an average of more than $70,000 a year, while the average annual salary for a corporate trainer is more than $39,000 (Langer, 1994). The job of a trainer is depicted in the employment profile of Mark Kremen.

# DETERMINING TRAINING NEEDS

Conducting a **needs analysis** is the first step in developing an employee training system (Schneier, Guthrie, & Olian, 1988). As its name implies, needs analysis is the process of determining the training needs for the organization. At times, however, this needs analysis will indicate that training may not be the solution to an organization's problems (Carr, 1994). As shown in Figure 8.1, three types of needs analysis are typically conducted: organizational analysis, task analysis, and person analysis (Sleezer, 1993).

## ORGANIZATIONAL ANALYSIS

The purpose of **organizational analysis** is to determine those organizational factors that either facilitate or inhibit training effectiveness. For example, an organization may view training important but may not have the

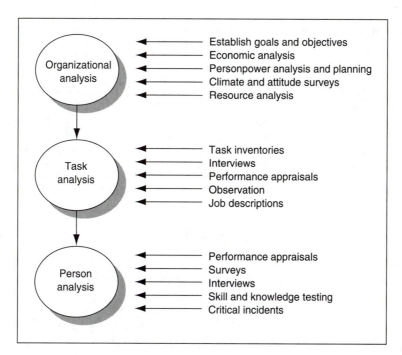

**Figure 8.1**
The needs-analysis process

Organizational analysis
- Establish goals and objectives
- Economic analysis
- Personpower analysis and planning
- Climate and attitude surveys
- Resource analysis

Task analysis
- Task inventories
- Interviews
- Performance appraisals
- Observation
- Job descriptions

Person analysis
- Performance appraisals
- Surveys
- Interviews
- Skill and knowledge testing
- Critical incidents

money to properly fund its training programs. Or an organization may not wish to spend money on training because employees leave the organization after a short period of time. Thus, training will only be effective if the organization is willing to provide a supportive climate for training, if it can afford an effective program, and if the goals of a program are consistent with those of the organization (Broadwell, 1993).

## TASK ANALYSIS

If the results of the organizational analysis indicate that a positive organizational climate for training exists, the next step is to conduct a **task analysis.** A task analysis involves using the job analysis methods discussed in Chapter 3 to obtain information about the job itself as well as the overall performance of the employees responsible for each of the tasks (Sims, Veres, & Heninger, 1989).

Part of this process is determining whether there is a training program for each important task. For example, the hypothetical bank depicted in Table 8.1 needs to develop training courses in dealing with difficult customers and in cross-selling.

Task analysis is important because training will only be effective if it addresses an area in which employees are weak. That is, if every employee in the organization is already proficient at using the computer system, providing

**Table 8.1**  Comparing task analysis results with training programs

| Task | How Task Is Learned |
| --- | --- |
| Answer customer questions about rates | Daily rate charts |
| Process customer transactions | Basic teller training |
| Calm irate customers | |
| Check loan applications for accuracy | Loan-processing course |
| Ask customers to complete VISA applications | |
| Input customer transactions into computer | Basic teller training |
| Answer customer questions about services | Basic teller training |

computer training probably would not greatly enhance performance. Likewise, if the organization is not aware of a particular training need and thus does not provide training in that area, employee performance will be less than optimal (Gent & Dell'Omo, 1989).

To determine training needs from a job description, all tasks, knowledge, and task-required skills are evaluated to determine whether each is covered in some aspect of training or selection. To illustrate, let's examine the job of a secretary. Obviously, tasks involving typing will be found throughout the job description. If we take just one of these tasks—typing internal memos—we can see that several knowledges and skills are involved: typing skills, knowledge of the company's word-processing package, knowledge of the computer used to do the word processing, and knowledge of the memo format used by the organization.

In all probability, the company will require a newly hired secretary who already possesses typing skills; thus, learning how to type will not be a training need. Knowledge of the word-processing program may or may not be required at the time of hire. If not required, then learning the program becomes a training need involving extensive training, while learning how to use a computer also becomes a training need (this training, however, should take only a short time). Finally, learning the memo format used by the organization is another training need but one with relatively little time required. With these needs in mind, the supervisor or the training officer must arrange for the new employee to receive the necessary training.

It is important that training needs arising from a task analysis be stated in the form of objectives (Mager, 1984). These objectives should concretely state

- what learners are expected to do,
- the conditions under which they are expected to do it, and
- the level at which they are expected to do it (Mager, 1984).

In other words, vague objectives such as "to be a better salesperson" should be replaced with specific objectives (Goldstein, 1993).

*Mark Kremen, M.S.*
*Training Officer*
*Sovereign Bank*

As training officer for Sovereign Bank, I am responsible for employee training and development throughout the New Jersey area. Sovereign is a very progressive bank. We continuously look for opportunities to merge with other banks. Therefore, Sovereign has lots of offices, and with lots of offices come lots of needs. It is extremely important for me to be able to identify the real need and to choose a solution for that need.

When you factor in such variables as time, money, and resources, identifying the real need and finding a solution becomes complex. For example, a manager came up to me and said, "Mark, I overheard a teller (we call them team members) being rude on the phone, and I would like this team member to attend a two-day customer-service training program as soon as possible." I asked the manager, "What was the reaction when you approached the team member with your concern?" The manager said, "I never approached her." Naturally, I have not heard from the manager again.

A powerful technique I use to help determine the needs of our organization is to ask appropriate open-ended questions. Because I use this technique, I often am viewed as an internal consultant working closely with all levels of the organization.

I'll set the stage for you by describing what is involved in a typical training session. Let's go back to the manager example. Suppose after talking with the manager and other team members, we decided to provide a training program on customer service for this individual and other team members. Because I provide training based on expectations and goals, I ask

management what they expect their team members to do differently after attending this training. I also ask how this training relates to Sovereign's critical success factors. For example, management may come to me and say, "I would like my team members to be friendlier toward customers." However, management and other team members may have different perceptions of what "friendly" is. I help them to develop expectations that are specific and measurable.

Once I have determined that a customer-service training program is the appropriate training, I can begin to develop a training session. First, I will need to choose a customer-service training program to use and that I can adjust in order to fit our needs. Coordinating and scheduling is a vital part of the development process. It is important that I identify the appropriate audience for the training session. Because of the group dynamics, I avoid mixing team members and their supervisors in the same class.

Timing is another important factor for the success of a training session. If the participants are not "ready" for the training, this will have a negative effect on the outcome. For example, when we merge with another bank, the new employees have such concerns as job security and learning the new computer system and other basic operational procedures. This would be an inappropriate time to schedule the customer-service training. However, providing them with training on our computer system would be more successful.

How a training program is facilitated can make the difference between a successful or unsuccessful program. It involves the understanding of the group dynamics among the participants. I stay aware of the pace of the session making sure it is not too fast or too slow. I ask many open-ended questions to help generate group discussion about the topic. Videos, flip charts, and skill practices are other resources I use to enrich the learning environment. I often find participants are very excited about their newly acquired skills, and I encourage them to keep that enthusiasm going once they return to their offices. I inform them that

*(continued)*

this training will be a waste of time unless they apply the skills they have learned. Someone once told me that the definition of insanity is "doing the same thing over and over again yet expecting different results."

Once the participants have completed the training, I solicit their feedback about the training. This helps me prepare for future classes. I also encourage the supervisors of the participants to help coach them with their new skills. This reinforces the learning that took

place and keeps them from avoiding the "insanity syndrome."

Finally, I follow-up with management to determine if their expectations have been met and if they can observe positive, measurable results from the training program. I constantly ask questions to identify the needs of Sovereign Bank and to help in the problem-solving process. The cycle never ends, and, believe it or not, I still have fun!

### PERSON ANALYSIS

The third and final step in the needs-analysis process is determining which employees need training and in which areas (McGehee & Thayer, 1961). **Person analysis** is based on the recognition that not every employee needs further training for every task performed. Thus, the purpose of person analysis is to use one or more of the following methods to determine the individual training needs for each employee: performance-appraisal scores, surveys, interviews, skill and knowledge tests, and critical incidents.

#### Performance-Appraisal Scores

Perhaps the easiest method of needs analysis is to use employees' **performance-appraisal scores.** Low ratings on a particular dimension for most employees may indicate that additional training in that dimension is needed. Conversely, if most employees score high on a particular dimension, relatively little training time is needed.

Table 8.2 provides an example of how performance-appraisal scores can be used. As can be seen, the employees as a whole need little training in loan processing or data entry, but they do need further training in cross-selling, customer relations, and keeping accurate teller drawers. But even though most employees can accurately process loans, Yamamoto needs further training in this area; both Kerrigan and Thomas probably can skip the training in teller drawer accuracy.

Although using performance-appraisal scores appears fairly easy as a method of needs-assessment, three problems can interfere with their use. First, as discussed in the previous chapter, several types of rating errors can reduce the accuracy of performance-appraisal scores. The most relevant here are leniency errors and strictness errors. If the performance-appraisal scores are consistently high because of leniency error, a human resource professional might incorrectly conclude that employees are proficient in a particular area and thus need no training. Likewise, consistently low scores

**Table 8.2** Using performance-appraisal scores for needs analysis

| Performance Dimension | Employee | | | | | Average |
|---|---|---|---|---|---|---|
| | Kerrigan | Witt | Hamil | Yamamoto | Thomas | |
| Cross-selling | 2 | 1 | 2 | 5 | 1 | 2.2 |
| Loan processing | 5 | 5 | 5 | 1 | 4 | 4.0 |
| Data input accuracy | 5 | 5 | 5 | 5 | 5 | 5.0 |
| Customer relations | 2 | 2 | 2 | 2 | 2 | 2.0 |
| Teller drawer accuracy | 5 | 3 | 1 | 2 | 5 | 3.2 |
| Average | 3.8 | 3.2 | 3.8 | 3.0 | 3.4 | |

might be interpreted as a need for training when, in fact, the actual cause of the low scores is rater error.

The second problem is that rarely are there situations in which all employees score either high or low on a dimension. Instead, it is more common for only a few employees to score poorly. In this case, a person examining the average performance-appraisal scores might conclude that training in a particular dimension is unnecessary. But that conclusion would be only partially correct. True, not everyone needs training in that dimension, but concluding that training should not be conducted would be incorrect. The correct interpretation is that training should be conducted for the few employees who scored low for that dimension.

Third, the current performance-appraisal system may not provide the type of information needed to conduct a training-needs analysis (Herbert & Doverspike, 1990). As discussed in Chapter 7, performance-appraisal systems must be specific to be useful.

### Surveys

Another common approach to determine training needs is designing and administering a survey that asks employees what knowledge and skills they believe should be included in future training (Brinkerhoff, 1986). **Surveys** offer several advantages. First, they eliminate the problems of performance-rating errors that we discussed previously. Second, employees often know best their own strengths and weaknesses. Thus, to determine what employees need, ask them (Graham & Mihal, 1986). Finally, training needs can be determined with surveys even when the organization has not previously made an effort to design an effective performance-appraisal system or adequate job descriptions.

As with any type of survey, training-needs surveys can be conducted in many ways. The most common method is a questionnaire that asks employees to list the areas in which they would like further or future training. Perhaps a better method was suggested by Graham and Mihal (1986): Provide a *list* of job-related tasks and knowledge and have the employees rate their need for training on each task and knowledge. The results of these ratings are given to supervisors who then "validate" the results. This process is used to determine whether the supervisors agree with their employees' perceptions and to prioritize training needs.

### Interviews

The third method of needs analysis is the interview, which is usually done with a selected number of employees. Interviews are not used as extensively as surveys, but they can yield even more in-depth answers to questions about training needs (Cline & Seibert, 1993). The main advantage of interviews is that employee feelings and attitudes are revealed more clearly than with the survey approach. The main disadvantage to interviews is that interview data are often difficult to quantify and analyze (Steadham, 1980).

### Skill and Knowledge Tests

The fourth way to determine training needs is with a **skill test** or a **knowledge test.** Some examples of areas that could be tested to determine training needs include knowledge of lending laws for loan officers, knowledge of company policy for new employees, free-throw shooting for basketball players, or the dreaded midterm exam for this course.

If all employees score poorly on these tests, training across the organization is indicated. If only a few employees score poorly, they are singled out for individual training. The greatest problem with using testing as a method to determine training needs is that relatively few tests are available for this purpose. An organization that wants to use this method will probably have to construct its own tests, and proper test construction is time-consuming and expensive.

### Critical Incidents

The fifth and final method for determining training needs is the Critical-Incident Technique (CIT) that was discussed in previous chapters. Although not a commonly used method, it will be discussed here because it is relatively easy to use, especially if a proper job analysis is available. To use this technique for needs assessment, **critical incidents** are sorted into dimensions and separated into examples of good and poor performance, as discussed in Chapter 3. Dimensions with many examples of poor performance are considered to be areas in which many employees are performing poorly and additional training is indicated (Glickman & Vallance, 1958).

## DEVELOPING A TRAINING PROGRAM

After training needs have been determined, the next step is to choose the most appropriate training method.

Organizations offer many different types of training and use different types of training methods. The best training programs use a variety of methods so that employees will understand the reasons for doing a certain task, how it should be done, and in what situations it should be done (Sims, Veres, & Heninger, 1989). In the following pages, several of these methods will be discussed.

## CLASSROOM INSTRUCTION

### Seminars

One of the most common training methods uses the lecture or **seminar** (Froiland, 1993). With this approach, either a member of the training staff or an outside consultant lectures to a few or many employees at one time. To save money, in-house staff are used when a training program will be presented many times and when the training staff has the time and expertise to deliver the training. A wide range of methods has been developed over the years. At one extreme, a trainer can speak to hundreds of employees and provide training by giving a particular amount and type of information. At the other extreme, a consultant can work with a small number of employees to help them improve such skills as interpersonal communication and conflict management (for example, dealing with angry customers).

Of course, the method used will depend on the type of information that employees need to know. If the purpose of the training is to convey

Lecture is a common training method.

information to new employees about building locations and company policy, then a lecture conducted by a training staff member is appropriate. If the purpose of training, however, is to teach a complicated skill, the seminar should be conducted by an expert and the audience limited to relatively few employees. For example, at the AT&T plant in the New River Valley (Fairlawn, Virginia), seminars on problem solving are conducted by the training staff, communication-skills seminars by an outside consultant, and seminars on the principles of electronics by a local community college instructor. In many locations, employees can receive college credit for certain training programs (Forsyth & Galloway, 1988).

Seminars work best when they begin with some sort of **icebreaker** (Dahmer, 1992). Icebreakers range from asking trainees to introduce the person next to them to a scavenger hunt in which trainees are given a list of questions (e.g., Who likes baseball? Who has a daughter?) and asked to mingle with the other trainees to obtain answers to the questions. Icebreakers are important because they loosen-up a group, build a sense of trust and group spirit, and help focus attention on training.

Tens of thousands of consultants around the country offer seminars to industry. In fact, almost 10,000 consultants annually use seminar materials provided by one company alone, Performax Systems International. Thus, many types of seminars are conducted by a wide variety of consultants. Needs analysis, however, must be used to determine whether such seminars are actually necessary. Sam Miller, personnel director for Roanoke Electric Steel Company (Roanoke, Virginia), has commented that he receives an average of two brochures every day advertising various seminars. Even though a seminar may sound interesting, it should be used only if it directly relates to some aspect of the job or to the people doing the job. For example, a seminar on communication skills may sound interesting, but it probably would not improve a coil winder's performance, but a seminar on electronics might. Likewise, a seminar on personal money management may not relate to the coil winder's job, but it might be useful if it solves outside problems that affect his job performance or attendance.

As with college lectures, many activities can take place within a seminar, including lecture, the use of learning aids such as slides and videotapes, discussion, and question-and-answer periods. Again, the choice of activities depends on the task or skill to be taught. If the skill is complicated, such as operating a machine or dealing with an angry customer, lecture alone will not be enough. The seminar should also include some type of practice or role play. If the information is not complicated but involves visual material such as building locations, flow charts, or diagrams, visual aids such as slides should be added to the lecture. If the material covered is not comprehensive or if the feelings of the employees toward the material are important, then discussion should be included. Discussion not only helps to further learning, but it also allows employees to feel that their opinions are important. As we will see in the discussion of quality circles, discussion often results in valuable ideas that can save a company money.

Another consideration is the use of films or videotapes in place of lectures. About 90% of all organizations use videotapes as part of their training programs (Rae, 1994). Videos have a clear economic advantage over live lecture only when the lecture is to be repeated several times. A consultant-conducted seminar usually costs around $150 an hour plus expenses, while most videotapes can be purchased for $200 to $600. Thus, a two-hour video-tape will pay for itself if used only two or three times.

Apparently, this economic advantage does not decrease training effectiveness—80% of research has found that videotapes are at least as effective as live lectures (Schramm, 1962). Perhaps one reason for their effectiveness is that videos ensure consistency in both the presentation of material and the control of the image received by the trainee (O'Grady & Matthews, 1987). That is, if a lecturer describes an object such as a graph or piece of machinery, each trainee develops his or her own image of the object. Thus, to describe objects or procedures, videotapes are appropriate substitutes for or additions to the lecture method (Storer, 1986). One example of a popular training video used in industry is the *You Are, What You Were, When* series created by psychologist Morris Massey. The tapes deal with the development of values and touch on topics such as why older workers value money and loyalty more than do younger workers. The six tapes in the series cost approximately $500 each. The series is used by thousands of organizations every year to increase workers' understanding of themselves and other workers.

Listening to lectures and watching videos can indeed be boring, but research has indicated that lecture is still an effective training method (Goldstein, 1993; Miner, 1963). Many trainers, however, do not consider lecture to be an effective training technique (Carroll, Paine, & Ivancevich, 1972).

### Programmed Instruction

One disadvantage of the lecture method is that all employees must be taught at the same pace. This is unfortunate because some employees are brighter or more experienced than others and will be bored if a lecture moves too slowly. Other employees, however, will become frustrated if a lecture goes too quickly. Thus, to allow employees to learn the material at their own pace, programmed instruction can be used.

**Programmed instruction** can be delivered in one of three ways. In the oldest method, each employee is provided with a step-by-step booklet that provides the material to be learned as well as a series of exams that measure the employee's knowledge of the material. If employees do not pass the test at the end of each unit, they must reread the material and retake the test until they pass. In this way, employees study at their own pace, and the exams ensure that employees understand the material.

The second method also uses booklets but has the answers printed in a special latent ink. The employee reads and answers a question and then uses a felt-tipped, latent-image developer pen to uncover "hidden" feedback about the correctness of the chosen answer. With this technique, not only does the employee receive immediate feedback, but the trainer also has a written record of the answers given and the progress made by each employee (Parsons, 1986).

The third method of programmed instruction uses computers. This is most commonly called **Computer-Assisted Instruction (CAI)** and is used by approximately 44% of all organizations (Rae, 1994). CAI uses the same learning principles as programmed instruction: The only real difference is the manner in which the material and tests are delivered. With CAI, an employee studies at a computer terminal at his own pace. At the end of the material, the computer poses a series of questions to the employee. If the employee does not answer enough questions correctly, the computer informs the employee about the areas in which he needs help and returns him to the appropriate material.

Programmed instruction is effective because it takes advantage of several important learning principles (King, 1986). First, learning is *self-paced*—that is, each trainee proceeds at his own pace. You have probably been in classes in which the lecturer went too quickly and in others in which the lecturer went too slowly. When the presentation speed of the material does not parallel the comprehension speed of the learner, frustration occurs and the material will not be learned as well as it might.

Second, each trainee is *actively involved* in the learning. This contrasts sharply with the lecture method, where the employee might sit through two hours of lecture without being actively involved. Think of your favorite classes: The instructor probably allowed you to become involved and actually do things. (That is why some of the chapters in the text are so detailed. By making the text inclusive and complete, your instructor can spend class time on projects instead of straight lecture.)

Finally, programmed instruction presents information in *small units* or chunks because learning smaller amounts of material is easier than learning larger amounts. The use of small chunks is based on the principle of **massed** versus **distributed practice,** which will be discussed later in this chapter. To demonstrate this point, think of the exam for this class. Would your score on the test be higher if you read and reviewed one chapter each week or if you waited until the night before the test to read five chapters? (The answer is obvious, and hopefully you did not answer the question from experience!)

A recent advance in programmed instruction known as **interactive video** adds a video machine to the computer. With interactive video, the employee sees a videotaped situation on a television screen. At the end of each situation, the employee chooses his response to the situation, and the computer selects a video that shows what would happen based on the employee's response (Packer, 1988). In 1990, interactive video was being used by more than 21% of U.S. organizations (Rae, 1994). On the down side, interactive video is more expensive and less adaptable than other types of program instruction.

In general, programmed instruction has been a successful training method. Research has indicated that its greatest advantage is that it is quicker than many other methods and achieves higher levels of immediate learning (Nash, Muczyk, & Vettori, 1971). Furthermore, a meta-analysis by Manson (1989) concluded that programmed instruction can lead to improved performance at relatively low cost.

The training program used by Life of Virginia (Richmond, Virginia) is a good example. One problem encountered by the company was that more than 1,000 sales agents were spread over 140 offices throughout the country. Thus, to conduct a training program that would be both effective and practical, consultants Williams and Streit (1986) used sales experts to create seven training modules: marketing and asking for referrals, calling for appointments, interviews, preparing the insurance recommendation, presenting the recommendation, delivering the insurance policy, and periodic review. Each module contained a 5- to 10-page reading assignment, a written exercise on the reading, a videotape showing models performing the appropriate behaviors, a situational problem, and a series of questions to be answered by each insurance agent. Agents study at their own pace, taking between two and four weeks per module. This training program resulted in a 25% annual increase in sales and a 10% decrease in turnover.

Similar success was found at Federal Express. Because Federal Express has over 700 locations, costs for sending trainers to each location were high. As a solution to this high cost, Federal Express placed over 1,200 interactive video units at their 700 locations. This change from live seminars to interactive video reduced training expenses, reduced customer-contact training time from 32 to 8 hours, and resulted in the company receiving several awards for its innovative program (Wilson, 1994).

### Case Studies

Another type of classroom training exercise, which is used by 42% of all U.S. organizations, is the **case study.** Case studies are similar to leaderless group discussions and situational interview problems (which were discussed in Chapters 4 and 5) and are the best training method for teaching problem-solving skills (Niemeyer, 1995; Newstrom, 1980). With this method, the members of a small group each read a case, which is either a real or hypothetical situation that might be encountered on the job. The group then discusses the case, identifies possible solutions, evaluates the advantages and disadvantages of each solution, and arrives at what it thinks is the best solution to the problem.

For case studies to be most successful, the cases should be taken from actual situations (Inguagiato, 1993). For example, to make their case study more realistic, Andrews and Noel (1986) had General Electric employees in New York use actual information about a problem within the company. Trainees not only discussed the problem but interviewed employees to gather more information. This use of a **living case** was found to be superior to the typical case study: Not only was the problem relevant, but the solution could actually be used, thus providing an incentive for the trainees to take the training program seriously.

In addition to being realistic, case studies should be interesting. They are best when written in the form of a story, contain dialogue between the characters, use realistic details, are descriptive, are easy to follow, contain all information necessary to solve the problem, and are difficult enough to be challenging (Owenby, 1992).

### Critical Incidents

In Chapter 3 we discussed CIT as a job-analysis method, and in Chapter 7 we discussed how these incidents could be used for performance-appraisal purposes. Critical incidents also can be used for training in two ways. In the simpler of the two methods, the critical incidents obtained from a job analysis are compiled in a notebook that is read by each employee, who is able to study actual examples of good and poor performance.

The second method involves taking the first method a step further. The critical incidents are converted into situations, which is similar to the situational interview discussed in Chapter 5. The employee reads each situation and is given four possible responses. After the employee chooses a response, he is told whether the choice is correct and why the choice was or was not correct (O'Brien & Plooij, 1977). The technique is ideally suited for use with computers, but it also can be used in booklet form.

## SAMPLE JOB PERFORMANCE

### Simulation

**Simulation** exercises allow the trainee to work with equipment and in an environment similar to the work environment. The exercises offer the advantage of allowing the trainee to work under actual working conditions without the consequences of mistakes (Lierman, 1994). For example, using a cash register or taking a customer's order is easy to learn. But they are much more difficult tasks with a long line of angry customers or irritable co-workers. Simulation exercises allow the trainee to feel such pressure but without actually affecting the organization's performance.

Like all training methods, simulation exercises come in many different forms. Some, such as airline simulators, are extremely expensive and complex to use, but others, such as a simulated restaurant counter, are relatively inexpensive. In fact, a good example of an inexpensive simulation exercise is that used by nurses to teach diabetics how to administer their insulin shots—the patients practice by injecting water into oranges. Situational exercises from assessment centers are also commonly used in employee training and development. The majority of simulations involve training in oral communication, planning, and decision making (Keel, Cochran, Arnett, & Arnold, 1989).

Whatever the method used, a simulation exercise can only be effective if it physically and psychologically simulates actual job conditions. For example, dummy simulators are a standard part of cardiopulmonary resuscitation (CPR) training provided by the American Red Cross. People practice CPR on the dummies, which simulate the human body and also provide feedback on pressure and location of chest compressions. However, although the use of these CPR simulators is probably better than lecture alone, there is some concern that the dummies do not adequately simulate the feel of the human chest. Even worse, practicing CPR on a dummy in front of fellow employees does not have the pressure or environment that is often encountered in an actual emergency.

Despite the fact that most simulators do not exactly replicate actual physical and psychological job conditions, they are still better than using only lecture or actual practice. That is, training a pilot is cheaper on a simulator than on a passenger jet, and it is safer for a medical student to practice on a pig rather than on a sick patient. Rapid advances in **virtual reality** technology hold tremendous promise for trainers (Lierman, 1994). The day that we can exactly simulate real working conditions may not be far away.

### Role Playing

The use of **role play** allows the trainee to perform necessary interpersonal skills by acting out simulated roles. For example, when conducting seminars in assertiveness training, psychologist Curt McKee has his audience participate as actors in predetermined situations. The participants are given a problem situation and are told to use what they have learned about assertiveness to confront the individuals involved in each situation.

Role plays are useful in teaching customer service.

Role playing is used in many types of training situations, from supervisors practicing performance-appraisal reviews to sales clerks taking customer orders. One interesting variation of role playing has an employee playing the role of "the other person." For example, a supervisor might play the role of an employee or a sales clerk might play the role of a customer who is frustrated with recently purchased merchandise. In this way, the employee can better understand the reasoning and feelings of the people with whom he works. This method is one of the best for learning interpersonal skills (Carroll et al., 1972; Newstrom, 1980).

Though role plays allow employees to practice what is being taught, they are not for everyone. Many employees feel uneasy and embarrassed about being required to "act." This reluctance can be reduced to some extent by using warm-up exercises and praising employees after they participate (Swink, 1993).

### Modeling

Also called *social learning,* **modeling** is a vitally important method of learning. As the method's name implies, employees learn by watching how other employees perform, or model, a behavior.

A formal training technique known as *behavior modeling* is used in a controlled setting, with employees observing proper work behavior and then practicing the behavior they observe. This technique will be discussed following the discussion of modeling.

Modeling as a learning technique is astoundingly pervasive. Think of how you first learned a sport such as baseball. You probably learned your batting stance by watching a favorite player. Why do you dress the way you do? Mostly because you model the way your peers and idols dress. We are most likely to learn through modeling when we are unsure about how to behave. For example, in our first days on a new job, we watch how others act. Do they take only the allotted time on breaks? Do they treat customers politely? Do they pay attention to their work? We learn how to behave at work by watching others so that we will fit in. A theory of job satisfaction that will be discussed in Chapter 10 hypothesizes that we even decide how satisfied we will be in our job by matching our level of job satisfaction with the levels exhibited by other employees.

As with operant conditioning, modeling is most effective under certain conditions. These conditions mainly involve characteristics of the employee whose behavior is being duplicated and the characteristics of the person attempting to model that performance.

**Characteristics of the Model**   Of course, we do not model everyone else's behavior. Instead, we tend to model the behavior of people who are *similar* to us, who are *successful,* and who have *status.* For example, if we are deciding what new clothes to purchase, who would we model? If male, would we pick Candace Bergen or Bill Clinton? After all, both have status and have been successful. No, instead we would look for someone who is more similar to us both in gender and age.

Likewise, if we are going to model our batting stance after someone, who would it be? Almost certainly, we would choose someone in the major leagues because of their status and success. But which player would it be? It would not be one of the worst players in either league. Instead, we probably would choose someone such as Will Clark, Frank Thomas, or another successful player. Finally, which successful player would it be? It would probably be the successful player who is most similar to us in terms of race, hair color, home town, position, and so on.

This raises an important point about models in industry. If it is true that we tend to look for models who are similar to us, then for modeling to be effective, the appropriate role models for employees should be similar to them in significant ways. This is why it is essential that a school faculty have minority, female, and male teachers, that a company have minority, female, and male managers, and that television shows portray all types of people in different occupational roles.

**Characteristics of the Observer**   For an employee to model another's behavior, three conditions are necessary. First, the employee must observe the behavior of other employees. All the role models in the world will be unable to effect a behavioral change in an employee if the employee pays no attention to the role model.

Second, the employee must be able to *retain* the information that is being modeled. Have you ever watched a person dance and then later tried the dance yourself? For most of us it is difficult to do if there are many steps to remember. Thus, even though we might have been paying close attention, there were too many behaviors to recall or retain. That is why training techniques that use modeling concentrate on only a few behaviors at a time.

Finally, the employee must have the ability or skill to *reproduce* the behavior that is seen. For example, I have watched the summer Olympics ever since I was a child. During the games, I have seen weightlifters lift more than 400 pounds. But even though I have paid attention to their technique and can remember how they lift, I still cannot lift 400 pounds because I do not possess the strength to reproduce the behavior I have observed. Instead, I must be content with watching the Olympics and performing 12-ounce Budweiser curls.

To use a work example, suppose that a new employee observes a veteran employee winding coils. If the new employee does not have the proper dexterity, technique alone will not allow the employee to be as successful as the veteran. Thus, it is important to limit the scope of the behaviors being modeled so that they are at a skill level that can be reproduced by the observing employee.

### Behavior Modeling

One of the most successful training methods is **behavior modeling,** which is similar to role playing except trainees role play ideal behavior rather than the behavior they might normally perform. The behavior modeling technique begins first with a discussion of a problem, why it occurred, and the employee behaviors necessary to correct the problem. Next, employees view a videotape of another employee who correctly solves a problem involving a customer who returns a jacket that he claims was torn when purchased and wants to return it. The trainee takes notes during the tape and is given an opportunity to ask questions.

After viewing the tape, trainees rehearse the solution to the problem in the way that the employee solved it on the videotape; they then receive feedback on their performance (Mann & Decker, 1984). Employees also play the role of the "other" person so that they will gain the same insight they would have by role-play training. By this procedure, employees will already have had experience in dealing with the problem in the proper way when they encounter the same situation on the job. In other words, positive transfer of learning will have occurred.

Of course, for behavior modeling to be successful, the videotapes must represent commonly encountered problems and situations—thus demonstrating the importance of a thorough job analysis. By observing and interviewing employees and by collecting critical incidents, the necessary problems and situations can be obtained. An important and related issue is whether employees should be trained on specific situational skills or on generic skills that will cover any situation (Hultman, 1986). For example, a specific situational skill would be handling a bank customer who is angry about a bounced check. The related generic skill would be calming *any* angry customer. Obviously, generic skills are more difficult to teach and require the modeling of many different types of behavior in many different situations.

Another issue involves the number and types of models that are viewed in the training video. Russ-Eft and Zucchelli (1987) conducted a study at Zenger-Miller, Inc. (Cupertino, California), in which employees viewed either one or two models. If the employees saw two models, they saw either two models performing correct behaviors or one model performing correctly and the other performing incorrectly. The study results indicated that viewing two models increased training performance more than viewing one, but the addition of a negative model was no more effective in increasing training performance than two positive models. When the proper procedures are followed, behavior modeling can significantly increase employee performance (Meyer & Raich, 1983; Sorcher & Spence, 1982).

### Job Rotation

Another excellent on-the-job training method is **job rotation** where an employee performs several different jobs within an organization. Job rotation is especially popular for managerial training because it allows a manager trainee to experience and understand most if not all of the jobs within the organization that his subordinates will perform.

Kroger and Wal-Mart train their assistant managers as clerks, stockers, and baggers prior to promotion to manager. Allstate trains its manager trainees in a similar fashion by having them spend a few months in sales, underwriting, personnel, cash control, and marketing. With job rotation, these organizations believe their managers will perform better by understanding more clearly how each employee performs his job.

Job rotation is also commonly used to train nonmanagerial employees. Aside from increasing employee awareness, the main advantage of job rotation is that it allows for both lateral transfers within an organization and greater flexibility in replacing absent workers. For example, if two bank tellers are ill, an employee who normally approves loans is able to temporarily take over the tellers' tasks.

Another advantage, which will be discussed in greater detail in another chapter, is that job rotation can also improve job satisfaction by reducing the boredom that often comes with a task-repetitive job (Wilbur, 1993). Job rotation works best if a corporate trainer is assigned to supervise employees throughout the duration of their rotations (Nadler, 1993). Such a situation provides more stability than would occur if the employee had a different supervisor for each rotation.

An interesting innovation in training is taking job rotation outside the organization and encouraging employees to volunteer for worthwhile charities and nonprofit organizations (Caudron, 1994). For example, GATX Capitol employees helped renovate a daycare center, EDS employees helped clean a local beach, and Helene Curtis employees raised funds to battle AIDS. The United Way takes advantage of corporate volunteerism through its "Loaned Executive" program in which organizations "lend" their executives to the United Way to help raise funds.

Employers report that volunteerism increases morale while also increasing employee communication, time management, and planning skills. Added benefits include increased respect for diversity, self-esteem, and social obligation (Caudron, 1994).

## INFORMAL ON-THE-JOB TRAINING

### Apprentice Training

**Apprentice training** is used by more than 50,000 people annually and is typically found in craft and building trades such as carpentry and plumbing. With apprentice training, an individual usually takes 144 hours of formal classroom work each year and then works with an expert for several (usually four) years to learn a particular trade and perhaps become eligible to join a trade union. Although apprenticeships are usually formal agreements between labor and management and are regulated by the U.S. Department of Labor's Bureau of Apprenticeship and Training as well as by state agencies, apprenticeships can also be less formal.

For example, an apprentice working with a plumber will initially help the plumber by carrying supplies, picking up parts from suppliers, and holding tools. But with time, the apprentice is taught the necessary knowledge and skills for plumbing. When the apprenticeship is complete, the apprentice can start his own business.

Apprenticeships are good for both the apprentice and the expert. The apprentice learns a valuable trade, and the expert or the organization gets

Apprenticeships can provide excellent training opportunities.

inexpensive labor—usually one-half the cost of expert labor. This is why apprenticeships have become more popular over the last few decades. Despite this increased popularity, however, some researchers have criticized apprenticeship programs for two major reasons. First, the emphasis during the apprenticeship often is on the production of work as opposed to teaching new skills to the apprentice (Strauss, 1967). Second, unions use apprenticeships to restrict entry into their trades, which results both in inflated wages caused by high demand and a lower supply of workers and unfair minority hiring practices (Strauss, 1971). Employers often shun apprenticeships for fear that the apprentice will become a competitor or join a competing company (Budman, 1994).

### Coaching

**Coaching** is another popular method of training new employees. With coaching, a new employee is assigned to an experienced employee who is told to "show the kid the ropes." Coaching can be highly effective, allowing the new employee the chance to learn from a job expert. After all, who knows a job better than a person who has mastered it for several years? Furthermore, new employees report that such coaches are more empathic and knowledgeable than trainers who are assigned to orient new employees (Comer, 1989).

Coaching, however, has its own problems. First, good workers are not necessarily good trainers, and good trainers are not necessarily good workers (Rae, 1994). Being able to do a job is not the same as explaining it. Sports provide good examples of this point. The best coaches often have been terrible players. Charlie Lau was one of the most successful and best respected batting coaches of all time, yet as a player he hit just .255 over 11 seasons. Ted Williams, arguably the best hitter ever in baseball, was a bust as a manager. (Perhaps this explains the sports joke that "those who can't do—teach, and those who can't teach, teach P.E.")

This is not to say, of course, that excellent employees or players will never be good teachers or coaches. For example, in the world of sports we have seen such successful basketball players as Bill Russell and John Wooden become excellent coaches. In education, we see successful people leave industry to become fine educators. The key is to find a way to identify those workers who will be good coaches or trainers. One solution has been to establish "train-the-trainer" programs in which future trainers or coaches are taught the skills they will need to train other employees.

A second problem with coaching is that it diminishes the expert's productivity (Wexley & Latham, 1981). That is, while the expert shows the new employee how to do the job, his own production declines. If he is on a bonus system, he may lose money as his production declines, as will the organization if the experienced employee is an outstanding worker. As one solution to this problem, the organization can reward workers who do well in training new employees.

Many organizations such as Pitney-Bowes have also adopted **pass-through programs** in which experienced workers are temporarily assigned to the training department. These workers are taught training techniques and then spend several months training new employees before resuming their old jobs (Geber, 1987).

Mentoring is a form of coaching that has recently received much attention. A **mentor** is a veteran in the organization who takes a special interest in a new employee and helps him to not only adjust to the job, but also to advance in the organization. Typically, mentors are older and at least one level or position above the employee being mentored. As with coaching, not all employees make good mentors, thus both the mentor and the employee to be mentored must be carefully chosen and matched (Mendleson, Barnes, & Horn, 1989).

### Performance Appraisal

As discussed in Chapter 7, one of the major uses for employee-performance evaluation is training. One excellent method of on-the-job training is when a

Training often comes from informal mentoring.

supervisor meets with an employee to discuss his strengths and weaknesses on the job. Once the weaknesses have been identified, the supervisor and employee can determine what training methods would best help the employee to improve his job knowledge or skill.

But using performance appraisal for both training and determining raises and promotions can be difficult. As pointed out by Kirkpatrick (1986), three factors account for this difficulty. First, the focus on salary administration is on *past* behavior, while the focus for training is on *future* behavior. Second, performance appraisal for salary administration often is subjective and emotional, while such appraisal for training is objective and unemotional. Finally, salary administration looks at overall performance while training looks at detailed performance. Because of these differences, Kirkpatrick (1986) suggests the use of two separate performance-appraisal systems in an organization—one for salary administration and the other for training.

## CONDUCTING THE TRAINING PROGRAM

Once a training method has been chosen, the next step is to actually conduct the training. In order for training to be most successful, attention must be focused on two issues: *transfer of training* and *massed practice versus distributed practice*.

## TRANSFER OF TRAINING

Research in learning indicates that the more similar the training situation is to the actual job situation, the more effective the training will be; in other words, the **transfer of training** will be greater. This principle is extremely important when a training program is being chosen or designed (Garavaglia, 1993). For example, if a restaurant is training its employees how to wait on tables, the training will be more effective if the employees can practice in an environment that is similar to that encountered when they actually work. This realism might even include "customers" complaining and changing their orders.

Another way to increase *positive* transfer of training is by having the trainee practice the desired behavior as much as possible. Such practice is especially important for tasks that will not be performed on a daily basis after training has been completed. For example, if a firefighter is learning to perform CPR, he must overlearn the task through constant practice. This **overlearning** is essential because it may be months before the firefighter will practice what he has learned. In contrast, once our coil winder learns a task during training, it is time for him to move to another task. Overlearning is not necessary for the coil winder because he will perform the task every hour once training has been completed. (The term *overlearning* does not have the same meaning in training that it has on most college campuses. In training, overlearning means practicing a task even after it has been successfully learned. Many students, however, think of overlearning as the negative consequence of "studying too hard." Although it is commonly believed that one can study too hard and "over learn" the material, research does not support this. Therefore, no one will be hurt by studying a little longer. In fact, a meta-analysis by Driskell, Willis, and Cooper [1992] indicated that overlearning significantly increases retention of training material.)

Finally, to further increase the transfer of training, practice in as many different situations as possible should be provided. For example, we might have our coil winder wind coils as fast as possible, wind them slowly, and wind them in various sizes. In this way, the employee will be better able to deal with any changes that occur in the job.

For information learned in training to transfer to behavior on the job, employees must be allowed to apply what they have learned (Ford, Quinones, Sego, & Sorra, 1992). Employees are more likely to be given opportunities to perform what they have learned if their supervisor perceives them as competent and the organizational climate is supportive (Baldwin & Ford, 1988; Ford et al., 1992). Though this seems obvious, research indicates that employers are neither supportive nor do they provide opportunities to apply what is learned—especially if the training is in the form of employees going to school to work on degrees (Posner, Hall, & Munson, 1991).

## MASSED PRACTICE VERSUS DISTRIBUTED PRACTICE

The best example of the principle of **massed practice versus distributed practice** is studying for exams. If we *distribute* the reading over several days, the material is relatively easy to learn. But if we wait until the night before the test to read three chapters—that is, *mass* the reading—we will not retain much at all.

As alluded to earlier in the discussion of modeling, material learned in training should be presented in small, easily remembered chunks (distributed). If too much training occurs at one time (massed), employees probably will not be able to concentrate on nor remember all that is being taught (Wexley & Latham, 1991).

# ENCOURAGING THE USE OF TRAINING MATERIAL

### GOAL SETTING

The use of knowledge and skills learned in training can be encouraged by having employees set goals (Goldstein, 1993). For example, tellers at a credit union received two days of training on cross-selling new products. This training included information about new loans and loan rates, types of retirement accounts, alternative savings plans, and the advantages to using a new "premium" credit card. Each teller might set a goal of daily asking four credit union members if they would like information about one of the new products. Goal setting works best when goals are individually set by each employee, are concrete rather than vague, and are high enough to be challenging but not so difficult as to be impossible. A more comprehensive discussion of goal setting is found in Chapter 12.

In addition to setting goals, employees should be given some choice about the training programs in which they are going to participate. Baldwin, Magjuka, and Loher (1991) found that employees given a choice about training programs were more motivated than employees not given a choice. Employees given a choice, but then not given the program they chose, were the least motivated.

### FEEDBACK

Learning is enhanced when **feedback** is provided on the employee's training progress. With some tasks, feedback occurs naturally. For example, in baseball, a batter receives feedback on his swing by seeing how hard and far the ball travels.

For other tasks, however, judging the correctness of a behavior without feedback is difficult. For example, if you write a term paper for this class and get a C, your next term paper will probably not improve unless you have been provided feedback about what was right and wrong with the previous paper.

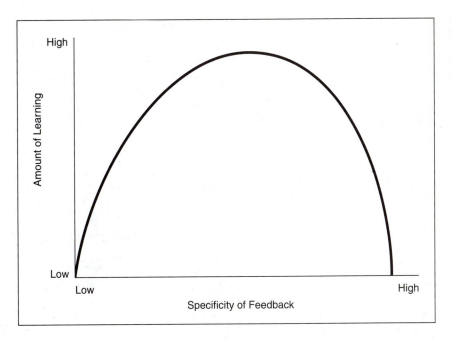

**Figure 8.2**
Relationship between feedback specificity and amount of learning

Source: Adapted from Blum and Naylor (1968).

The same is true for training in industry. Our coil winder needs feedback early in the training process to know if the winding is tight enough, if there is an easier way to wind the coil, or if the winding is equally distributed on the coil. A balance, however, must be maintained between giving too little or too much feedback. As shown in Figure 8.2, the employee will not learn if too little feedback is given. However, too much or overly detailed feedback causes frustration and the employee will not learn at an optimal level (Blum & Naylor, 1968).

A final consideration for feedback concerns what type to give. Research and common sense agree that positive feedback should be given when an employee correctly performs a task during training. Praise provides an incentive to continue correct behavior. But if an employee is not performing a task correctly, should he receive **negative feedback**? Probably, even though negative feedback is more complicated than positive feedback. For negative feedback to be most effective, it should be provided by a trustworthy and knowledgeable supervisor or trainer to employees who are concerned about performing the task correctly (Ilgen, Fisher, & Taylor, 1979).

## INCENTIVES FOR LEARNING

One principle of learning borrowed from operant conditioning is that no employee will be motivated to learn without some incentive. That is, a coil winder who is taking a course in electronics will probably not study and learn unless he can see how that knowledge will improve his performance enough to result in a desirable outcome such as a salary increase or chance of promotion.

One incentive for learning is **skill-based pay,** which is used by 40% of major U.S. organizations (Lawler, Chang, & Ledford, 1993). With skill-based pay, an employee participates in a training program that is designed to increase a particular skill an employee needs to be either promoted or to receive a pay raise. For example, employees who are currently in the position of Printer III must learn to set their own type before they can be promoted to Printer II. The employees must be able to demonstrate their mastery of the newly taught skill rather than just attend training sessions. Similarly, in situations where promotion is not possible, pay increases alone are given to employees who master new skills.

At Federal Express, each year employees are required to watch eight hours of interactive video training on customer-contact. Employees must score 90% on exams given on this material in order to pass. Ten percent of the employees' performance review (salary increase) is then based on their test scores (Wilson, 1994).

Skill-based pay not only provides incentives for employees to successfully complete training, but also results in increased savings for an organization. For example, a General Foods plant in Kansas found a 92% decrease in its quality-reject rate and a 33% decrease in fixed-overhead costs after introducing a skill-based pay program (Feuer, 1987b).

The principles of **operant conditioning** are important in the learning and training process. Also called **behavior modification,** operant conditioning is based on the premise that humans learn to behave in ways that result in favorable outcomes, and resist behavior that results in unfavorable outcomes (Skinner, 1938; 1969).

Thus, if an employee is rewarded for certain types of behavior, the probability increases that he will continue to perform those behaviors. Likewise, if an employee is punished for certain types of behaviors, the probability decreases that he will perform those behaviors. Finally, if an employee is neither reinforced nor punished for a behavior, he will try other behaviors until he finds one that is reinforced.

Although the basic principles of operant conditioning are fairly simple, additional factors can modify the effectiveness of both reward and punishment.

### Timing of the Consequence

Research indicates that a *reinforcer* or a *punisher* is most effective if it occurs soon after the performance of the behavior. Unfortunately, if the **timing of the consequence** is too long after a particular behavior, the effectiveness of operant conditioning in both training and other attempts to improve performance will be hindered. For example, a restaurant employee learning how to wait on tables performs many behaviors in the course of serving a customer. A tip is usually left by the customer after the meal, which provides immediate feedback about the employee's performance. However, if the tip is small, the employee is not sure which particular behavior caused the customers' displeasure. Likewise, if the tip is large, the employee is unsure which particular behavior or behaviors initiated the large tip. Consequently, timing of the consequence by itself may not be enough to change behavior.

### Contingency of Consequence

If it is not possible to immediately reward or punish a behavior, it should at least be made clear which behaviors brought reward or punishment. To return to our example of the waiter, if he is told the reason for the size of his tip, he will be better able to change his behavior. Have you ever given a waiter or waitress a large tip even though the service was terrible? Most of us have. In so doing, however, the waiter or waitress is reinforced for poor performance and has no incentive to improve unless poor performance has its own consequence. In a similar fashion, if the waiter had done an outstanding job but received a small tip, the probability of his repeating his outstanding performance is reduced.

The point of these examples is that reward and punishment must be made contingent on performance; the **contingency of consequences** must be clear if learning is to occur. If the reward or punishment cannot be administered immediately, the employee must be told the purpose of the consequence so that the link between behavior and outcome is clear.

### Type of Consequence

The *type* of consequence is an important issue that will be discussed in Chapter 10. It is obvious that different types of people like different types of rewards. For example, some employees value awards or praise, while others value money. Thus, for a reward to be effective, it must have value to an employee.

The same is true of punishment. Threatening an employee with a three-day suspension will only be effective if he needs the money or doesn't like being off from work; yelling at an employee will only be effective if the employee does not like being yelled at; and threatening not to promote an employee will only be effective if the employee values promotions and perceives he has a reasonable chance of being promoted.

## EVALUATION OF TRAINING RESULTS

As discussed in Chapter 1, one important characteristic of industrial psychology is its reliance on research. Evaluating training results is a good example of this reliance. Because training programs can be costly in both time and money, it is essential that the I/O psychologist evaluate a training program to know whether it significantly increases performance or effects positive changes in behavior. A recent survey of training directors, however, found that 90% claimed that even though they believed the evaluation of training to be important, they did not conduct evaluations because their organizations did not require them (Bell & Kerr, 1987).

## RESEARCH DESIGNS FOR EVALUATION

There are many ways to evaluate the effectiveness of a training program, and two factors differentiate the various methods. The first involves *practicality*, and the second is concerned with *experimental rigor*. Although scientifically rigorous research designs are preferred, their use is not always possible. And yet a practical research design without scientific rigor yields little confidence in research findings.

The most simple and most practical of research designs implements a training program and then determines whether significant change is seen in performance or job knowledge. To use this method, performance or job knowledge must be measured twice. The first measurement, a **pretest,** is taken before the implementation of training. The second measurement, a **posttest,** is taken after the training program is complete. A diagram of this simple design is as follows:

Pretest → Posttest

Although this method is fairly simple, its findings are difficult to interpret for several reasons. First, there is no **control group** against which the results can be compared. That is, suppose a significant difference in performance is seen between the pretest and the posttest. If a training program has occurred between the two tests, it would be tempting to credit the training for the increase. The increase, however, may have resulted from other factors such as changes in machinery, changes in motivation caused by non-training factors, or changes in managerial style or philosophy.

Likewise, suppose no significant increase in performance is observed between pretest and posttest. The natural conclusion might be that the training program did not work. Without a control group, that interpretation is not necessarily correct. The same changes noted above for an increase may have caused a decrease in performance in this second case. Thus, it is possible that the training program actually did increase performance but other factors reduced it, which resulted in no net gain in performance from training.

To overcome these problems, a control group should be used. For training purposes, a control group consists of employees who will be tested and treated in the same manner as the experimental group except that they will not receive training. The control group will be subject to the same policy, machinery, and economic conditions as the employees in the experimental group who receive training. The diagram for this design looks like this:

Experimental group:   Pretest → Training → Posttest
Control group:             Pretest                   Posttest

The advantage of this second design is that it allows a researcher to look at the training effect after controlling for outside factors. For example, after going through a training program, employees at R. R. Donnelley & Sons increased their annual commissions by $22,000, and the company increased profits by $34 million. The company was obviously pleased but was worried that the increased performance could have been due to something other than training. So, it compared the results to a control group of employees that had not received training. The commissions of the control employees increased by $7,000 over the same period. Thus the net effect of the training was still sizable — $15,000 per employee — but not as high as the $22,000 originally thought. The control group allowed the company to control for such factors as increased sales agent experience and new company promotions (Montebello & Haga, 1994).

Even though this design is an improvement on the first, it too has its drawbacks. First, except for training manipulation, it is almost impossible to treat a control group in an identical manner to the experimental group. Control groups often consist of workers at other plants or in other shifts at the same plant. Such groups are used because there often is no alternative. But the fact that they are in different environments reduces confidence in the research findings.

Even if employees in the same plant on the same shift can be randomly split into control and experimental groups, problems will still exist. The most glaring of these involves the possibility that because the two groups are close to one another, the training effect for the experimental group will spill over to the control group. Employees in the control group also may resent not being chosen for training. This resentment alone may lead to a decrease in performance by employees in the control group. Finally, it is possible that the untrained employees will pressure the newly trained employees to revert to the "old way" of doing things (Spitzer, 1986).

With both of the above designs, the pretest itself presents a problem. That is, the mere taking of a test may itself lead to increases in performance. Because of this, a rather complicated method, called the **Solomon Four Groups Design,** can be used (Campbell & Stanley, 1963). With this design, one group will undergo training but will not take the pretest, a second group will undergo training but will take the pretest, a third group will neither undergo training nor take the pretest, and a fourth group will not undergo training but will take the pretest. The diagram for this design is as follows:

| Group 1: | | Training → Posttest |
|---|---|---|
| Group 2: | Pretest → | Training → Posttest |
| Group 3: | Pretest | Posttest |
| Group 4: | | Posttest |

This design allows a researcher to control not only for outside effects, but also for any pretest effect. This is the most scientifically rigorous of the research designs used to evaluate training, but even it has a serious drawback: it is often not practical. That is, four groups of employees must be used, two of which do not receive training. Thus, to use this design at one organization or plant, ideally a relatively large number of employees must be available and kept from discussing the training with one another.

## EVALUATION CRITERIA

### Content Validity

Even though all of the designs suffer from problems with practicality or scientific rigor, training effects should still be evaluated in the best possible way given each particular situation. At times, the only way that training can be evaluated is by comparing training content with the knowledge, skills, and abilities required to perform a job. In other words, the **content validity** of the training can be examined. For example, if a job analysis indicates that a knowledge of electronic circuitry is necessary to perform a job, then a seminar that is designed to teach this knowledge would have content validity. Although content analysis may ensure that a training program is job related, it still does not indicate whether a particular training method is effective. But if a training program is content-valid and is conducted by a professional trainer who can *document* previous success with the method in other organizations, it may be a safe assumption that the training program will be successful. Keep in mind, however, that making such an assumption is only acceptable when actually evaluating the effect of training is not possible because there are too few employees.

### Employee Reactions

Another way to evaluate training is by determining **employee reactions** to the training. Thus, when directly measuring training effects is not possible, trainee reactions can be used. Employee reactions are important because employees will not have confidence in the training and will not be motivated to use it if they do not like the training process. However, even though positive employee reactions are necessary for training to be successful, they may not indicate changes in knowledge or performance (Alliger & Janak, 1989). In fact, trainee reactions constitute the lowest level of training evaluation (Birnbrauer, 1987), and can often be misleading. For example, most seminars conducted by outside consultants are informative and well presented, so employee reactions are almost always positive, even though the training may not actually affect knowledge or future performance (Alliger & Janak, 1989).

### Employee Learning

Instead of using employee reactions as the criterion in evaluating training performance, actual **employee learning** usually can be measured (Bell & Kerr, 1987). That is, if a training program is designed to increase employee knowledge of communication techniques, then creating a test to determine whether an employee actually learned is possible. The measurements that will be used for the pretest and posttest, as with selection tests, must be both reliable and valid. Thus, if the purpose of a training program is to increase job knowledge, an appropriate job-knowledge test must be constructed or purchased. A trainer can spend a great deal of time creating a training program and evaluating its effectiveness, but the whole training effort will be wasted if the measure used to evaluate effectiveness is no good. At times, reliable and valid measures of training effectiveness are difficult to obtain. Perhaps a good example of this is seen with the human relations seminars that are common to training programs (Buzzotta, 1986). Typically, an outside consultant conducts a seminar on a topic such as "better communication skills" or "calming irate customers." A seminar may run from two hours to two days in length. Once completed, however, it is important to measure the effectiveness of the seminar training. But how will it be measured?

### Application of Training

Another criterion for evaluating the effectiveness of training is to determine the degree of **application of training,** or the extent to which employees actually can use the learned material (Geber, 1995), which can be done by testing. But even if an employee remembers the training, this does not mean he can or will use the information. Learning and memorizing new material is one thing, and applying it is another.

### Bottom-Line Measures

The final criterion that can be used to evaluate a training program's effectiveness is a **bottom-line measure.** That is, did the organization actually save money as a result of the training program? As an example, imagine that a bank trains its tellers to cross-sell Visa cards. The tellers rate the training session as being enjoyable, all of the employees pass a test on sales techniques, and sales attempts increase by 30%. The bottom-line approach would then ask the question, "If we spent $5,000 training the tellers, how much more revenue was brought in as a result of the training?" If the answer to the question is more than the amount spent on training (called *return on investment*, or ROI), then the program would be considered a success (Shelton & Alliger, 1993).

## CHAPTER SUMMARY

In this chapter, we examined three major steps to training: conducting a needs assessment, developing training programs, and evaluating their effectiveness.

Needs analysis or assessment is the process of determining an organization's training needs. The most common needs-analysis methods are performance-appraisal scores, task analyses, surveys, interviews with employees and supervisors, skill and knowledge tests, and critical incidents.

After needs analysis has identified areas that require attention, training programs are chosen to meet those needs. To be most effective, these training programs should account for several important principles of human learning. For example, operant-conditioning principles state that people will learn if they are rewarded for doing so. The learning is increased if the reward for learning follows soon after the training program and if the reward is one desired by the employee.

People also learn the behavior of others through modeling. We especially model the behavior of those who are similar to us, are successful in what they do, and who have status. Our ability to model the behavior of others is a consequence of our paying attention to the model, having the opportunity to retain the information that was modeled, and having the physical and mental ability to reproduce the modeled behavior.

Training also will be most effective if the training program is similar to the actual work that will be performed (transfer of training), if the training takes place over time (distributed practice), if we receive feedback on our progress, and if there is an incentive for learning.

Training methods take many forms. Classroom learning techniques include seminars, audio-visual aids, programmed instruction, case studies, and critical incidents. Sample job-performance techniques include simulation, role playing, behavior modeling, and job rotation. Informal training techniques include apprentice training, coaching, and performance appraisal.

Once the training programs have been designed and the actual training has been conducted, the training program's effectiveness must be evaluated. In addition to employees' reactions to the training, it is essential to measure actual changes in job performance.

## GLOSSARY

**Application of training**  Measurement of the effectiveness of training by determining the extent to which employees apply the material taught in a training program.

**Apprentice training**  A training program, usually found in the craft and building trades, in which employees combine formal course work with formal on-the-job training.

**Association**  The idea that two events that occur at the same time are seen as belonging together.

**Behavior modeling**  A training technique in which employees observe correct behavior, practice that behavior, and then receive feedback about their performance.

**Behavior modification**  The application of learning principles for the purpose of improving human behavior (see also *operant conditioning*).

**Bottom-line measure**  Evaluation of a training program by determining if the organization actually saved money as a result of the program.

**Case study**  A training technique in which employees, usually in a group, are presented with a real or hypothetical workplace problem and are asked to propose the best solution.

**Classical conditioning**  Learning through association or the close occurrence of two events.

**Coaching**   A method of training in which a new employee receives on-the-job guidance from an experienced employee.

**Computer-Assisted Instruction (CAI)**   A type of programmed instruction presented through a computer.

**Content validity**   The extent to which the topics in a training program are consistent with the knowledge, skills, and abilities identified in a job analysis.

**Contingency of the consequence**   The extent to which a reward or punishment is based on the performance of a particular behavior.

**Control group**   A group of employees who do not receive a particular type of training so that their performance can be compared to that of employees who do receive training.

**Critical incidents**   Examples of good and bad employee behavior observed to have occurred on the job.

**Distributed practice**   Learning a few things at a time.

**Employee learning**   Evaluating the effectiveness of a training program by measuring how much employees learned from the training program.

**Employee reactions**   A method of evaluating training in which employees are asked their opinions of a training program.

**Feedback**   Providing employees with specific information about how well they are performing a task or series of tasks.

**Interactive video**   A training technique in which an employee is presented with a videotaped situation and is asked to respond to the situation and then receives feedback based on the response.

**Job rotation**   A method of training in which employees perform a variety of jobs within an organization.

**Knowledge test**   A test that measures the level of an employee's knowledge about a job-related topic.

**Living case**   A case study based on a real situation rather than a hypothetical one.

**Massed practice**   Learning many things at one time.

**Mentor**   An experienced employee who advises and looks out for a new employee.

**Modeling**   Learning through watching and imitating the behavior of others.

**Needs analysis**   The process of determining the training needs of an organization.

**Negative feedback**   Telling employees what they are doing incorrectly in order to improve their performance of a task.

**Operant conditioning**   A type of learning based on the idea that humans learn to behave in ways that will result in favorable outcomes and learn not to behave in ways that result in unfavorable outcomes.

**Organizational analysis**   The process of determining the organizational factors that will either facilitate or inhibit training effectiveness.

**Overlearning**   Practicing a task even after it has been mastered in order to retain learning.

**Pass-through programs**   A formal method of coaching in which excellent employees spend a period of time in the training department learning training techniques and training employees.

**Performance-appraisal score**   A rating representing some aspect of an employee's work performance.

**Person analysis**   The process of identifying the employees who need training and determining the areas in which each individual employee needs to be trained.

**Posttest**   A measure of job performance or knowledge taken after a training program has been completed.

**Pretest**   A measure of job performance or knowledge taken before the implementation of a training program.

**Programmed instruction**   A training method in which employees learn information at their own pace.

**Role play**   A training technique in which employees act out simulated roles.

**Seminar**   A method of training in which a trainer using lectures or discussions trains several employees at one time.

**Simulation**   A training exercise in which employees practice job-related behavior under conditions similar to those actually found on the job.

**Skill-based pay**   Compensating an employee who participates in a training program designed to increase a particular job-related skill.

**Skill test**   A test that measures an employee's level of some job-related skill.

**Solomon Four Groups Design**   An extensive method of evaluating the effectiveness of training with the use of pretests, posttests, and control groups.

**Surveys**   Questionnaires asking employees about the areas in which they feel they need training.

**Task analysis**   The process of identifying the tasks for which employees need to be trained.

**Timing of the consequence**   The amount of time between the performance of a behavior and the reward or punishment that follows the behavior.

**Training**   A planned effort by an organization to facilitate the learning of job-related behavior on the part of its employees.

**Transfer of training**   The extent to which behavior learned in training will be performed on the job.

# 9
# LEADERSHIP

Imagine a company with thousands of workers that has seen sales drop in each of the past five years. The president of the company steps down and a new president is installed. Several years later, the company makes a profit and everyone hails the new president as the reason for the improvement.

Also imagine a football team with a winning record in each of the last ten years. The team's coach leaves for another school and the team loses the majority of its games in the next few years.

In both of these examples, a new leader took over. In the first example, the organization became more successful, whereas in the other example it declined. How much of the organization's performance can be attributed to the leader? If the leader *was* the major cause of the changes in performance, why was one leader successful and the other a failure? These types of questions will be addressed in this chapter.

# THEORIES OF LEADERSHIP

Many different theories about leadership have been developed over the last few decades. Although none of the theories tells the whole story about leadership, each has received at least some empirical support. Understanding the theories and research behind leadership is important because the theory that company executives believe about leadership will, for the most part, determine how an organization selects or develops its managers.

For example, if we believe that certain people are born leaders because of their personal traits (leadership trait theories), then managers should be selected based on their scores on certain tests. But if we believe that leadership consists of specific skills or behaviors (leader behavior theories), then theoretically we should be able to train any employee to become an outstanding leader. If we believe that good leadership is the result of an interaction between certain types of behaviors and particular aspects of the situation (situational leadership theory), then we might choose certain types of people to be leaders at any given time, or we might teach a leader how to adapt her behavior to meet the situation.

The following pages provide brief explanations of the most popular leadership theories. When reading about each theory, think about what the theory would imply about the selection or development of leaders for an organization. In addition, think of how you manage and the type of leader you wish to be.

### TRAIT THEORIES

**Trait theories** are based on the idea that personal traits or characteristics play an important role in the leadership process. Trait theories have concentrated on three aspects of leadership: leader emergence, leader performance, and leader characteristics.

#### Leader Emergence

**Leader emergence** is the idea that leaders possess traits or characteristics different from nonleaders. That is, this theory would say that leaders such as Ronald Reagan, John Kennedy, Adolph Hitler, Martin Luther King, Jr. and Elizabeth Dole share similar traits that your neighbor or a cook at McDonald's do not. If you use your school as an example, this theory would predict that the students in your student government would be different than students who do not participate in leadership activities.

Almost 100 traits have been identified in studies as differentiating leaders from nonleaders, some of which are listed in Table 9.1. But only three traits—intelligence, dominance, and masculinity—have been commonly found to relate to leader emergence. Even then, the relationship between these traits and leader emergence is not especially strong (Kenny & Zaccaro, 1983; Lord, De Vader, & Alliger, 1986). Thus, the preponderance of research

**Table 9.1** Important characteristics for effective leadership

| Personal Characteristics | Physical Characteristics |
| --- | --- |
| Adaptable | Athletic |
| Assertive | Attractive |
| Charismatic | Tall |
| Creative | |
| Decisive | |
| Dominant | |
| Energetic | |
| Extraverted | |
| Friendly | |
| Honest | |
| Intelligent | |
| Masculine | |
| Outgoing | |
| Self-confident | |
| Wise | |

suggests that trait theories are not good predictors of leader emergence (Bird, 1940; Stogdill, 1948). More recently, research indicates that males emerge as leaders more often than do females, and high self-monitors (people who change their behavior based on the social situation) emerge as leaders more often than low self-monitors (Dobbins, Long, Dedrick, & Clemons, 1990; Kent & Moss, 1990).

These findings are especially perplexing because anecdotal evidence suggests that leadership behavior has some stability. To illustrate this point, think of a friend whom you consider to be a leader. In all probability, that person is a leader in many situations. That is, she might influence a group of friends about what movie to see, she might make decisions about what time everyone should meet for dinner, and she might take charge when playing sports. Conversely, you probably have a friend who has never assumed a leadership role in his life. Thus, it appears that some people consistently emerge as leaders in a variety of situations, whereas others who share these characteristics never emerge as leaders (Kenny & Zaccaro, 1983; Sabini, 1995).

### Leader Performance

In contrast to leader emergence, which deals with the likelihood that a person will *become* a leader, **leader performance** involves the idea that excellent leaders possess certain traits that poor leaders do not. For example, an excellent leader might be intelligent, assertive, friendly, and independent, while a poor leader might be shy, aloof, and calm. The idea behind trait theories certainly is appealing, but research indicates that only two traits —

intelligence and interpersonal adjustment—have consistently been related to leadership performance (Heslin & Dunphy, 1964).

An interesting extension of the trait theory of leader performance suggests that certain traits are necessary requirements for leadership excellence, but they do not guarantee it (Simonton, 1979). Instead, leadership excellence is a function of the right person being in the right place at the right time. The fact that one person with certain traits becomes an excellent leader while another with the same traits flounders may be no more than the result of timing and chance.

For example, Lyndon Johnson and Martin Luther King, Jr. were considered successful leaders because of their strong influence on improving civil rights. But other people prior to the 1960s had the same thoughts, ambitions, and skills as King and Johnson yet they did not become successful civil rights leaders perhaps because the time was not right.

**Needs**   A specific trait theory that has received recent support pertains to a leader's **need for power, need for achievement,** and **need for affiliation.** Research by McClelland and Burnham (1976) and McClelland and Boyatzis (1982) has demonstrated that high-performance managers have a **leadership motive pattern,** which is a high need for power and a low need for affiliation. The need is not for personal power, but for organizational power.

This pattern of needs is thought to be important because it implies that an effective leader should be concerned more with results than with being liked. A leader who needs to be liked by her subordinates will have a tough time making decisions. A decision to make employees work overtime, for example, may be necessary for the organization's survival, but it will probably be unpopular with employees. A leader with high affiliation needs may decide that being liked is more important than being successful, causing conflict with her decision.

This theory would also explain why internal promotions often do not work. Consider, for example, a person who worked for six years as a loan officer. She and ten co-workers often went drinking together after work and away on weekends. But one day she was promoted to manager and now had to lead the same people with whom she was friends. The friendships and her need to be liked hindered the new manager from giving orders and disciplining her employees. When she tried to separate herself from her friends, she was quickly thought of as being too good for her friends—a tough situation with no apparent solution according to this theory.

This does not mean a leader should not be friendly and care about subordinates. But a successful leader will not place her need to be liked above the goals of the organization. President Richard Nixon was thought to have a high need for being liked. He would often make a tough decision and then apologize for it because he wanted to be liked by both the public and the press.

Needs for power, achievement, and affiliation can be measured through various psychological tests. The most commonly used is the **Thematic**

**Apperception Test (TAT).** The TAT is a projective test in which a person is shown a series of pictures and asked to tell a story about what is happening in each picture. The stories are then analyzed by a trained psychologist who identifies the needs themes that are contained in the stories. Obviously, this technique is time-consuming and requires a great deal of training.

Another commonly used measure is the **Job Choice Exercise (JCE)** developed by Stahl and Harrell (1982). With the JCE, a subject reads descriptions of jobs that involve varying degrees of power, achievement, and affiliation needs and then rates how desirable he finds each particular job. These ratings are then subjected to a complicated scoring procedure that uses regression analysis to reveal scores on the three need categories.

**Adaptability**  Another trait theory was proposed by Foster (1989) who believes that good leaders need to possess only one stable trait: *adaptability*. Thus, good leaders will constantly change their behaviors to meet the demands of the situation or the person with whom the leader is dealing. (This thinking also has been echoed by Cohen and Bradford, 1990.) Support for this theory comes from a study by Caldwell and O'Reilly (1982) who found field representatives who dealt with many different types of people were more effective if they were high self-monitors. High self-monitors are sensitive to social cues and are able and willing to adapt their behavior to fit a particular situation. Similar results were found by Zaccaro, Foti, and Kenny (1991).

### Unsuccessful Leaders

In a departure from research to identify characteristics of successful leaders, Hogan (1989) attempted to identify traits of unsuccessful leaders. Hogan was interested in investigating poor leaders because both empirical research as well as anecdotal accounts indicate that most employees report that one of the greatest sources of stress in their jobs is their supervisors' poor performance, strange behavior, or both. This idea should come as no surprise: You can probably quickly recall many examples of poor performance or strange behavior with current or former supervisors.

**Lack of Training**  Based on years of research, Hogan (1989) concluded that poor leadership behavior has three major causes. The first is a *lack of leadership training* given to supervisors. The armed forces are among the few organizations that require supervisors to complete leadership training before taking charge of groups of people. The norm for most organizations, however, is either to promote a current employee or hire a new employee and place her directly into a leadership role. If training is ever provided, it is usually after the promotion and well after the supervisor has begun supervising. The serious consequences of this lack of training can best be understood if we imagine allowing doctors to perform surgery without training or allowing truck drivers to drive the highways without first learning how to drive.

**Cognitive Deficiencies**   The second cause of poor leadership stems from *cognitive deficiencies*. Hogan (1989) believes that poor leaders are unable to learn from experience and are unable to think strategically (that is, to plan ahead). They consistently make the same mistakes and do not plan ahead.

The manager of a local convenience store that I frequent is an example of a person who does not learn from his mistakes. The manager did not give employees their work schedules until one or two days before they had to work. The employees complained because the hours always changed, and they could not schedule their personal, family, and social lives. But the manager continued to do it his way and most of the employees quit. Eight years later, he still does it his way, and his employees still leave at a high rate.

**Personality**   The third, and perhaps most important, source of poor leadership behavior involves the *personality* of the leader. Hogan (1989) believes that many unsuccessful leaders are insecure and adopt one of three personality types: the paranoid/passive-aggressive, the high-likability floater, and the narcissist.

The source of insecurity for leaders who are paranoid, passive-aggressive, or both is some incident in their lives in which they felt betrayed. This *paranoid/passive-aggressive* leader has deeply rooted, but perhaps unconscious, resentment and anger. On the surface, these leaders are charming, quiet people who often compliment their subordinates and fellow workers. But they resent the successes of others and are likely to act against subordinates in a passive-aggressive manner; that is, on the surface they appear to be supportive, but underneath they may desire to undermine their employees' effectiveness.

The type of leader who is insecure and seldom causes trouble is known as a *high-likability floater*. This person goes along with the group, is friendly to everyone, and never challenges anyone's ideas. Thus, he or she travels through life with many friends and no enemies. The reason they have no enemies is because they never do anything, challenge anyone, or stand up for the rights of their employees. These leaders will be promoted and never fired because even though they make no great performance advances, they are well liked. Their employees have high morale but show relatively low performance.

*Narcissists* are leaders who overcome their insecurity by overconfidence. They like to be the center of attention, promote their own accomplishments, and take most if not all of the credit for the successes of their group—but they avoid all blame for failure.

### Leader Characteristics

The third aspect of leadership theory uses a **sociological approach** and is involved with identifying characteristics of leaders; it does not, however, involve comparing these characteristics to those of nonleaders or unsuccessful leaders. Although this line of research has little usefulness to human resource managers, it has had some interesting findings. For example, Presidents Franklin Roosevelt, Kennedy, and Reagan had high needs for power; Presidents Harding, Truman, and Nixon had high needs for affiliation; and Presidents Wilson, Hoover, and Carter had high needs for achievement (Winter, 1988).

## BEHAVIOR THEORIES

Behavior theories focus on what a leader *does* as opposed to what she *is*. Trait and behavior theories at first appear to be the same, but there is a subtle, yet very important, difference. Behavior theories suggest that a leader is able to successfully compensate for a particular trait weakness. For example, a leader may possess the trait of shyness and not truly want to communicate with other people. She knows, however, that talking to others is an important part of her job, so she says hello to her employees when she arrives at work, and at least once a day, she stops and talks with each employee. Thus, our leader has the trait of shyness although her behavior is not shy.

### Consideration and Initiating Structure

The most well-known behavior theory of leadership resulted from a series of studies at Ohio State University in the early 1950s. After years of research, the investigators identified two main behavioral elements in leadership—consideration and initiating structure (Fleishman, Harris, & Burtt, 1955).

**Consideration** is the degree to which a leader acts in a warm and supportive manner and shows concern for her subordinates. Examples of such behavior would include consulting subordinates before making decisions, praising their work, asking about their families, and not looking over their shoulders.

**Initiating structure** is the degree to which a leader defines and structures her own role and those of her subordinates to attain the group's formal goals. Examples of initiating-structure behaviors include setting goals, making decisions without consulting the group, rewarding and punishing subordinates based on their productivity, and giving orders.

A leader's tendency to use either consideration or initiating-structure behaviors can be measured by several instruments, but the most popular are the **Leadership Opinion Questionnaire (LOQ)** and the **Leader Behavior Description Questionnaire (LBDQ).** The LOQ is filled out by supervisors or leaders who desire to know their own behavioral style. The LBDQ is completed by subordinates to provide a picture of how they perceive their leader's behavior. A meta-analysis by Eagly and Johnson (1990) indicates that females are more likely to use a consideration style and less likely to use an initiating-structure style than are males.

Research on the effectiveness of consideration and initiating-structure leadership styles has brought interesting findings. As shown in Figure 9.1, leaders who score high in consideration tend to have satisfied employees, while leaders who score high in initiating structure tend to have productive employees. Leaders scoring high in both have satisfied and productive

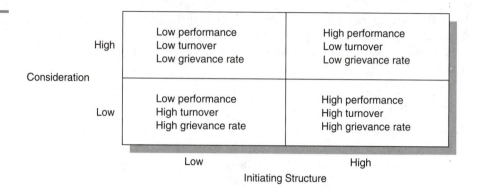

**Figure 9.1**
Consequences of two Ohio State leadership styles

|  | Low performance<br>Low turnover<br>Low grievance rate | High performance<br>Low turnover<br>Low grievance rate |
|---|---|---|
| **High**<br>Consideration<br>**Low** | Low performance<br>High turnover<br>High grievance rate | High performance<br>High turnover<br>High grievance rate |

Low                                    High
Initiating Structure

employees, while leaders scoring low in both tend to have unhappy and unproductive employees (Korman, 1966; Fleishman & Harris, 1962).

The above results certainly make sense, but other research indicates that the relationship between consideration and initiating structure is more complex than was first thought. Several studies have shown that variables such as leader experience and knowledge as well as external variables such as time pressures and work importance tend to moderate the relationship between consideration scores and satisfaction and between initiating-structure scores and subordinate performance.

### Theory X and Theory Y

A theory similar to that just described was developed by Douglas McGregor (1967). McGregor believes that leaders operate from one of two theories. **Theory X leaders** see their employees as lazy, extrinsically motivated, wanting security, undisciplined, and shirking responsibility. Because of these assumptions, Theory X leaders tend to manage or lead by giving directives, setting goals, and making decisions without consulting their subordinates.

**Theory Y leaders,** on the other hand, believe that employees are intrinsically motivated, seek responsibility, are self-controlled, and do not necessarily dislike work. Because of these assumptions, a Theory Y leader involves employees in the decision-making process and uses a more hands-off approach to leadership.

### Managerial Grid

A third theory that essentially divides leaders into task or person orientations is the **managerial grid,** which was developed by Blake and Mouton (1984). In managerial-grid theory, leadership style is measured through a leadership test. As shown in Figure 9.2, there are five main leadership styles: impoverished, country club, task-centered, team, and middle-of-the-road.

**Impoverished Leadership**   The **impoverished** type of leader accepts almost any decision made by the group. She is concerned with neither production nor the feelings and well-being of her subordinates.

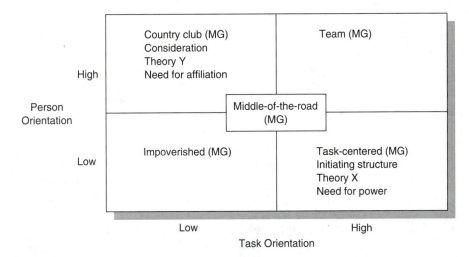

**Figure 9.2**
Relationship between managerial grid (MG) and other task/person behavior theories

The figure shows a grid with Person Orientation (High/Low) on the vertical axis and Task Orientation (Low/High) on the horizontal axis.

- Top-left: Country club (MG), Consideration, Theory Y, Need for affiliation
- Top-right: Team (MG)
- Center: Middle-of-the-road (MG)
- Bottom-left: Impoverished (MG)
- Bottom-right: Task-centered (MG), Initiating structure, Theory X, Need for power

**Country Club Leadership**   The **country club** leader has a high concern for the feelings of his subordinates but little concern for productivity. Such a leader will go out of his way to keep from making his subordinates unhappy.

**Task-Centered Leadership**   **Task-centered** leaders are concerned solely with production. The worth of a subordinate is measured according to how well she accomplishes an assigned task. Task-centered leaders give orders, do not ask for advice, and do not want discussion or subordinate input.

**Team Leadership**   **Team** leaders reflect the ideal of leadership styles, combining a concern with production with a concern for the welfare of subordinates. Such a leader makes decisions herself when she is able and asks for the advice of subordinates when necessary.

**Middle-of-the-Road Leadership**   **Middle-of-the-road** leaders have a balanced approach to task and people concerns. The difference between middle-of-the-road leaders and team leaders, however, is one of degree. Team leaders are high in both task and people orientation, while middle-of-the-road leaders are moderate in both orientations.

## SITUATIONAL THEORIES

As already indicated, the effectiveness of leadership behavior often depends on the particular situation in which the leader finds herself. In the past few decades, several theories have emerged that seek to explain the situational nature of leadership.

### Fiedler's Contingency Model

The most well-known and controversial of the situational theories was developed by Fred Fiedler in the mid-1960s (Fiedler, 1967). Fiedler believed that an individual's leadership style is the result of a lifetime of experiences and thus is extremely difficult to change. **Fiedler's Contingency Model** holds that any individual's leadership style is only effective in certain situations. The way to increase leader effectiveness, then, is to help a person understand her style of leadership and learn how to manipulate a situation so that the two match. To help a person understand her leadership style, Fiedler developed the **Least-Preferred Co-worker (LPC) Scale.**

To complete the LPC Scale, a leader identifies the subordinate or employee with whom she would least want to work. She then rates that person on several semantic differential scales that range from nice to nasty and friendly to unfriendly. The higher the leader rates her least-preferred co-worker, the higher the LPC score. This score is then compared to the favorableness of the situation to determine leader effectiveness. Low-scoring LPC leaders tend to be task-oriented, while high-scoring LPC leaders tend to be more concerned with interpersonal relations (Fiedler, 1978; Rice, 1978).

The favorableness of a situation is determined by three variables. The first is **task structuredness.** Structured tasks have goals that are clearly stated and known by group members, have only a few correct solutions to a problem, and can be completed in only a few ways. The more structured the task, the more favorable the situation.

The second variable is **leader position power.** That is, the greater the position or legitimate power of the leader, the more favorable the situation. Thus, a group or organizational setting in which there is no assigned leader is not considered to be a favorable leadership situation.

The third variable is **leader-member relations.** The more that subordinates like their leader, the more favorable the situation. The leader-member relationship is considered the most important of the three variables.

As shown in Figure 9.3, the relationship between LPC scores and group performance is complex. Basically, low-scoring LPC leaders (those who rate their least-preferred co-worker low) function best in situations that are either favorable or unfavorable, while high-scoring LPC leaders function best when the situation is only of moderate favorability.

In spite of psychometric problems with the LPC Scale (Kennedy, Houston, Korsgaard, & Gallo, 1987; Stewart & Latham, 1986), research generally has supported Fiedler's theory. Strube and Garcia (1981) conducted a meta-analysis of 145 independent studies that investigated Fiedler's model as well as 33 of Fiedler's own studies and concluded that the ideas were well supported by the research. Schriesheim, Tepper, and Tetrault (1994) found support for the general predictions of leader behavior but not for some of the specific predictions.

Fiedler's training program, called **Leader Match,** has also been supported by research (Strube & Garcia, 1981). This program is based on Fiedler's belief that an individual's leadership style is not easily changed. Thus, to improve their abilities, leaders learn through four-hour workshops how to diagnose situations and then change these situations to fit their particular leadership styles (Csoka & Bons, 1978). Leader Match is probably the

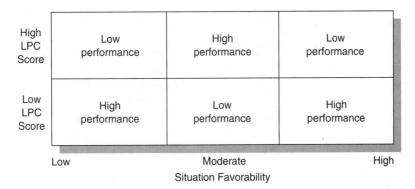

**Figure 9.3**
Relationship between LPC scores and group success

| | Low | Moderate | High |
|---|---|---|---|
| **High LPC Score** | Low performance | High performance | Low performance |
| **Low LPC Score** | High performance | Low performance | High performance |

Situation Favorability

only training program in the country concentrating on changing the situation rather than the leader.

### IMPACT Theory

A more recent situational theory, known as **IMPACT theory,** was developed by Geier, Downey, and Johnson (1980) who believe that each leader is one of six behavioral types. Each type is only effective in a particular situation, or in what the researchers call an *organizational climate.* As shown in Table 9.2, the six styles are similar to the five bases of power suggested by French and Raven (1959; also Raven, 1965). The six IMPACT styles and their appropriate climates, according to Geier et al. are *informational, magnetic, position, affiliation, coercive,* and *tactical.*

**Informational Style**   The leader who has an **informational style** provides information in a climate of **ignorance,** where important information is missing from the group. For example, if a car containing four college professors and a mechanic broke down on the side of the road, who would become the leader? Almost certainly it would be the mechanic because she would probably be the one who had the most knowledge or information needed to solve the problem.

In recent years in the U.S. Senate, Sam Nunn has become one of the most powerful and respected congressional leaders. He became powerful because of his expertise in defense matters, an area that was important and that few in Congress knew much about. Thus, Nunn used an informational style in a climate of ignorance to become a powerful leader.

**Magnetic Style**   A leader with a **magnetic style** leads through energy and optimism and is only effective in a climate of **despair,** which is characterized by low morale. Ronald Reagan is perhaps the best example of a magnetic leader. As president, he was optimistic and well liked, even by people who may not have agreed with him politically. He was elected at a time when the national mood was depressed because of high inflation, high unemployment, and the Iran hostage situation. The chances of successful

**Table 9.2**  Comparison of IMPACT styles and bases of power

| IMPACT Style (Geier et al.) | Base of Power (French & Raven) |
| --- | --- |
| Informational | Expert |
| Magnetic | Referent |
| Position | Legitimate |
| Affiliation | Coercive/Reward |
| Coercive | |
| Tactical | |

leadership increase in a situation of general despair when a magnetic or charismatic individual assumes control (Latham, 1983).

**Position Style**   A person who uses the **position style** leads by virtue of the power inherent in that position. Such a person might lead through such statements as, "As your captain, I am ordering you to do it," or "Because I am your mother—that's why." Individuals who use a position style will only be effective in climates of **instability.** This style is especially effective during corporate mergers, particularly when people are not sure what actions to take. However, often questions arise about a leader's legitimate scope of power (Yukl, 1989).

**Affiliation Style**   A person with an **affiliation style** leads by liking and caring about others. This style is similar to that of consideration as defined by the Ohio State studies. A leader using affiliation will be most effective in a climate of **anxiety** or when worry predominates. Former President Jimmy Carter is an excellent example of the affiliation style. Carter was elected president shortly after the Watergate affair when many voters were worried that they could not trust politicians or their government. Carter campaigned successfully with statements such as "I care" and "I'm not part of that Washington crowd."

**Coercive Style**   A person using the **coercive style** leads by controlling reward and punishment and is most effective in a climate of **crisis.** Such a leader will often use statements such as "Do it or you're fired," or "If you can get the package there on time, I will have a little something for you." This style is typical in war. If soldiers disobey an order, an officer can have them shot. Conversely, if soldiers behave with bravery and distinction, an officer can reward them with a medal or promotion.

Support for the situational appropriateness of coercive styles of leadership was found by Mulder, de Jong, Koppelaar, and Verhage (1986) when they studied the behavior of bankers whose leadership styles had been measured by the Influence Analysis Questionnaire. Mulder and his colleagues found that in crisis situations, bankers tend to use more formal and coercive types of leadership than in noncrisis situations.

**Tactical Style**   A leader with a **tactical style** leads through the use of strategy and is most effective in a climate of **disorganization.** A good example is a class that breaks into small groups to complete an assignment. Ideally, every student knows the material well enough to complete the assignment, but normally there is a limited amount of time and too much work to do. The person who becomes the leader is the one who is best able to organize the group.

**Becoming an Effective Leader According to IMPACT Theory**   If IMPACT theory is correct, a person can become an effective leader by one of several methods. The first is by finding a climate that is consistent with her behavioral style. This method, however, involves either a great deal of luck or a lot of patience, requiring the leader to be in the right place at the right time.

In the second method, the leader changes her style to meet a particular climate (Suedfeld & Rank, 1976). That is, if the climate is one of ignorance, the individual changes her behavior and uses information to lead. On the other hand, if the climate is one of despair, she becomes more outgoing and positive. Thus, a person who is willing to adapt her behavior and who has the ability to perform each of the six leadership styles should be an effective leader.

Although there is continual debate about whether a person can be trained to be a leader, a study by Manz and Sims (1986) suggests that leaders *can indeed* be taught different styles of leadership. Manz and Sims used a behavioral modeling approach to successfully teach 40 leaders how to use positive-reward behavior, reprimand behavior, and goal-setting behavior. Thus, those who are willing to use different leadership styles can learn the necessary skills and behaviors through training programs.

The third method by which a person can become an effective leader is to change followers' perception of the climate so that the perception matches the leader's behavioral style. This tactic is common in politics in which each candidate tries to convince the voting public that he or she is the best person for an office.

The fourth method by which a leader can become effective is by actually changing the climate itself rather than simply changing followers' perceptions of the climate. Obviously, this is difficult to do, but it is the strategy advocated in Fiedler's Leader Match training. Such a strategy is difficult but can be successful.

### Path-Goal Theory

House (1971) believes that a leader's behavior will be accepted by subordinates only to the extent to which the behavior helps the subordinates achieve their goals. Thus, a leader will only be successful if her subordinates perceive her as working with them to meet certain goals and if those goals offer a favorable outcome for the subordinates.

Because the needs of subordinates change with each new situation, a supervisor must adjust her behavior to meet the needs of her subordinates.

That is, in some situations subordinates need a leader to be directive and to set goals; in others, they already know what to do and only need emotional support.

According to House's **path-goal theory,** a leader can adopt one of four behavioral leadership styles to handle each situation: instrumental, supportive, participative, and achievement-oriented.

The **instrumental** style calls for planning, organizing, and controlling the activities of employees. The **supportive** leader shows concerns for employees, the **participative** leader shares information with employees and lets them participate in decision making, and the leader who uses the **achievement-oriented** style sets challenging goals and rewards increases in performance.

Each style will only work in certain situations and depends on subordinates' abilities and the extent to which the task is structured. In general, the higher the level of subordinate ability, the less directive the leader should be. Likewise, the more unstructured the situation, the more directive the leader should be (Schriesheim & DeNisi, 1981).

House and Mitchell (1974) further advise that, to be effective, a leader should:

- Recognize the needs of subordinates and work to satisfy those needs,
- Reward subordinates who reach their goals,
- Help subordinates identify the best paths to take in reaching particular goals, and
- Clear those paths so that employees can reach their goals.

Path-goal theory is intuitively appealing because it gives a manager direct advice about how to behave in certain situations. Furthermore, because it is behavior-based rather than trait-based, the theory could be used in training. Research thus far, however, has not supported application of this theory (Hammer & Dachler, 1975; Schriesheim & Schriesheim, 1980). Thus, if path-goal theory is to have real impact, it will need further revision.

### Vertical Dyad Linkage Theory

**Vertical dyad linkage (VDL)** theory was developed by Dansereau, Graen, and Haga (1974) and is a unique situational theory that makes good intuitive sense. The situational theories discussed earlier concentrate on interactions between leaders and situations. VDL theory, however, concentrates on the interactions between leaders and subordinates. The theory takes its name from the relationship between two people (a *dyad*), the position of the leader above the subordinate (*vertical*), and their interrelated behavior (*linkage*).

VDL theory states that leaders develop different roles with different subordinates and thus act differently with different subordinates. Dansereau and his colleagues believed that subordinates fall into one of two groups: the *in-group* or the *out-group.*

In-group subordinates are those who have developed trusting, friendly relationships with the leader. As a result, the leader deals with in-group members by allowing them to participate in decisions and by rarely disciplining them. Out-group subordinates are treated differently than those in the in-group and are more likely to be given direct orders and have less say about how affairs are conducted.

In general, research on VDL theory has been supportive (Graen & Scheismann, 1978; Scandura, Graen, & Novak, 1986; Vecchio, Griffeth, & Hom, 1986; Wakabayashi & Graen, 1984). There are, however, relationships between leaders and subordinates that probably can be categorized into types other than in-group and out-group. Thus, further research is needed into the relationship between leaders and subordinates.

### Situational Leadership Theory

Another theory, which focuses on the relationship between leader and follower, is the **situational leadership theory** developed by Hersey and Blanchard (1988). Hersey and Blanchard postulate that a leader typically uses one of four behavioral styles: delegating, directing, supporting, and coaching. Although these styles are not much different from the styles of the previously mentioned theories, situational leadership theory does suggest that a leader must adapt her behavior not only to situation and climate, but also to followers' characteristics.

Hersey and Blanchard termed the most important follower characteristic *follower readiness,* or the ability and willingness to perform a particular task. The degree of follower readiness can be measured by either the manager's rating form or the self-rating form developed by Hersey and Blanchard. Scores from these forms place followers into one of four categories, or readiness (R) levels:

R1: Unable and unwilling or insecure

R2: Unable but willing or confident

R3: Able but unwilling or insecure

R4: Able and willing or confident

As shown in Figure 9.4, for R1 followers, the most effective leader behavior is the *directing approach*. That is, the leader directs the follower by telling her what to do and how to do it. A *coaching approach* should be used with R2 followers because they are willing to do the work but are not sure *how* to do it. Leaders using this approach explain and clarify how work should be done. R3 followers are given plenty of emotional support as well as opportunities for two-way communication. This approach is successful because these followers already know what to do but are not sure whether they *want* to do it. R4 followers are most productive and happy when a delegating leadership style is used. These followers are both willing and able to perform the task. Thus, the only real job for the leader is to delegate specific tasks to subordinates and then let them complete those tasks with minimal supervision or guidance.

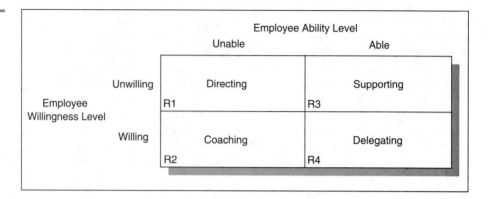

Under this theory, effective leaders first diagnose the competency and motivation levels of employees for each goal or series of tasks and then adapt their leadership style to fit the employee's level. As the employee makes developmental progress, the leader changes her style and becomes less directive. It is important for leaders to discuss this strategy with each employee so that employees will understand why they are being treated a particular way (Blanchard, Zigarmi, & Zigarmi, 1985).

As with many theories of leadership, situational leadership theory has excellent intuitive appeal and has been successful in some organizational applications (Gumpert & Hambleton, 1979) but not others (Goodson, McGee, & Cashman, 1989; Norris & Vecchio, 1992). Unfortunately, however, until more research is available and revisions to the theory made, it is difficult to determine its long-term effectiveness (Nicholls, 1985).

## SPECIFIC BEHAVIORAL THEORIES

Another way to think about leadership is that excellent leaders possess specific behaviors or skills that poor leaders do not. After observing thousands of leaders in a variety of situations, Yukl (1982), Carter (1952), Hemphill and Coons (1950), and Gibbs (1969) have proposed a behavioral "theory." According to these researchers, leaders do the following:

1. Initiate ideas
2. Informally interact with subordinates
3. Stand up for and support subordinates
4. Take responsibility
5. Develop a group atmosphere
6. Organize and structure work
7. Communicate formally with subordinates
8. Reward and punish subordinates
9. Set goals

10. Make decisions

11. Train and develop employee skills

12. Solve problems

13. Generate enthusiasm

This theory is not particularly exciting and is the least described in textbooks, but it is the way that leadership is most often practiced in industry. If this theory is true, then leadership is something learned; if the specific behaviors and skills important for effective leadership can be identified, then almost anyone can be trained to become an effective leader. Many examples of such training programs are currently in use.

The city of San Diego has its own management academy that provides interested employees with the skills necessary to become managers. On weeknights and weekends, employees learn skills such as oral communication, report writing, decision making, conflict management, and performance appraisal. After an employee is trained and tested in each of these important skill areas, he or she receives a certificate of completion. Even though graduates of the management academy are not promised managerial positions, more often than not they are the employees who are promoted.

If you have ever attended a leadership conference, you probably have noticed that the training involved specific leadership skills such as time management, goal setting, persuasion, and communication. Such an agenda typifies the idea that leadership consists of specific and learnable skills and behaviors.

Although it is beyond the scope of this text to discuss each of the behaviors and skills listed in Table 9.3, we will discuss some of the best-known specific behavioral theories as well as some specific leadership skills.

**Table 9.3**  Specific behaviors taught in leadership training programs

Communication skills
Decision-making skills
Delegation
Discipline
Motivation
Persuasion
Public speaking
Reward and punishment
Running a meeting
Stress management
Team building
Time management
Training techniques
Understanding people
Writing

### Leadership Through Decision Making: The Vroom-Yetton Model

Decision making is a specific behavior or skill that is important for a leader to possess. Vroom and Yetton (1973), however, pointed out that previous research has shown that only in certain situations are decisions best made by the leader; in other situations, decisions are best made with the participation of a leader's subordinates, colleagues, or both. Because of this situational aspect to decision making, Vroom and Yetton believe that leadership performance can be improved by teaching leaders to become better decision makers. To aid this process, Vroom and Yetton developed a decision tree to help leaders decide when decisions should be made alone and when they should be made with the help of others.

Of course, developing a chart that would tell a leader what to do in every possible situation would be impossible. But the **Vroom-Yetton Model** does provide a flowchart that can tell a leader what *process* to go through to make a decision in a particular situation. As Figure 9.5 shows, the answers to seven important diagnostic questions will determine how such a decision should be made.

**Importance of Decision Quality**  The first concern when making a decision is whether one decision will be better than another. For example, if a supervisor is trying to decide whether to sign a letter with blue ink or black ink, her decision probably will not make any difference to the company.

Effective managers allow employees to participate in relevant decisions.

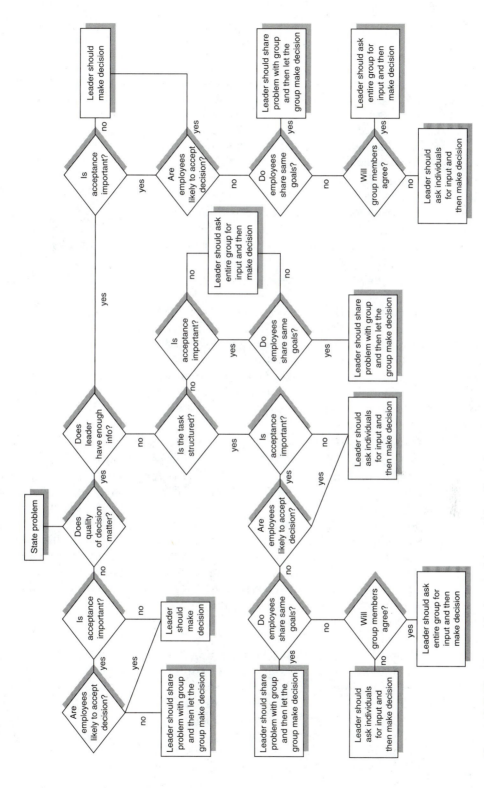

**Figure 9.5** The Vroom-Yetton decision-making flowchart

Thus, the importance of the decision quality is low, and little time or effort should be spent making it.

**Leader Knowledge of Problem Area**  The second concern of decision making involves the extent to which the leader has sufficient information to make the decision alone. If she does, then consultation with others is only desired if she wants her subordinates to feel involved. If the leader lacks sufficient knowledge to make a decision, consultation is essential. For example, it would be difficult for a manager to select a benefit package without first asking her employees about the type of benefits they need.

**Structure of the Problem**  The third concern involves the extent to which a leader knows what information is needed and how it can be obtained—that is, the problem's structure. If the leader does not know how to obtain this information, the decision-making process will require other people, and the decision will take longer to reach.

**Importance of Decision Acceptance**  The fourth decision-making concern involves the degree to which it is important that the decision is accepted by others. For example, for a supervisor to decide what hours each employee will work, it is important the employees agree with and have input into the decision-making process. But if the supervisor is deciding what she wants for lunch, whether other people agree with or have input into the decision is not important (unless, of course, the choices involve onions or garlic).

**Probability of Decision Acceptance**  The fifth decision-making concern is subordinate acceptance. If the leader feels she can make the decision herself but that acceptance of the decision is important, she must determine whether her subordinates will accept it. If the leader is popular and powerful, they undoubtedly will accept and follow the decision. But if the leader is not popular, not powerful, or both, she will probably want help from her subordinates and colleagues in making the decision—even though she has the ability to make the decision herself. This is why leaders often ask subordinates and colleagues for their opinions. The leader may already know what she will decide, but gaining the support of others by eliciting opinions and comments increases the chances that they will accept her decision when she announces it.

**Subordinate Trust and Motivation**  The sixth concern of the decision-making process is the extent to which subordinates are motivated to achieve the organizational goals and thus can be trusted to make decisions that will help the organization. For example, suppose that the leader needs both information and acceptance from her subordinates. As shown in Figure 9.5, in such a situation she would need input from her subordinates. But if the subordinates were motivated to help themselves more than the organization (for example, with work schedules, salary, or affirmative action), then the leader must use their input when making the decision, although she still must make the decision herself.

**Probability of Subordinate Conflict**  The final concern of the decision-making process involves the amount of conflict that is likely among the subordinates when various solutions to the problem are considered. If there are many possible solutions and the employees are likely to disagree about which is best, the leader would be served best by gathering information from employees and then, as in the previous situation, making the decision herself.

**Decision-Making Strategies Using the Vroom-Yetton Model**  Answering the questions in the flowchart shown in Figure 9.5 will lead to one of five possible decision-making strategies, which are called Autocratic I, Autocratic II, Consultative I, Consultative II, and Group I.

With the *Autocratic I* decision-making strategy, the leader uses the available information to make the decision without consulting her subordinates. This is an effective strategy when the leader has the necessary information, and acceptance by the group is either not important or is likely to occur regardless of the decision.

With the *Autocratic II* strategy, the leader obtains the necessary information from her subordinates and then makes her own decision. The leader may or may not tell the subordinates about the nature of the problem. The purpose of this strategy is for the leader to obtain information she needs to make a decision even though acceptance of the solution by the group is not important.

The leader using the *Consultative I* strategy shares the problem on an individual basis with some or all of her subordinates. After receiving their input, the leader makes a decision that may or may not be consistent with the thinking of the group. This strategy is especially useful in situations in which it is important for the group to accept the decision but the group members may not agree regarding the best decision.

The leader using the *Consultative II* strategy shares the problem with her subordinates as a group. After receiving the group's input, the leader makes a decision that may or may not be acceptable to the group. This strategy is used when acceptance of the decision by the group is important and the individual group members are likely to agree with one another about the best solution.

With the *Group I* strategy, the leader shares the problem with the group and lets the group reach a solution. The role of the leader is merely to assist in the decision-making process. This strategy is effective when group acceptance of the decision is important and when the group can be trusted to arrive at a decision that is consistent with the goals of the organization.

Although relatively little research has been conducted on the Vroom-Yetton model, the results of a few studies have been encouraging. For example, Field and House (1990) and Jago and Vroom (1977) found that managers who used the decision-making strategy recommended by the model had better quality decisions than managers who used decision-making strategies that the model would not have recommended. Similar results were found by Brown and Finstuen (1993) with military officers and Paul and Ebadi (1989) with sales managers.

### *Leadership Through Contact: Management by Walking Around*

Management by walking around (MBWA) is another popular specific behavioral theory. This one holds that leaders and managers are most effective when they are out of their offices, walking around, and meeting with and talking to employees and customers about their needs and progress. Many industry leaders such as Sam Walton of Wal-Mart have adopted this approach with great success.

In an interesting series of studies by Komaki and her associates (Komaki, 1986; Komaki, Zlotnick, & Jensen, 1986), the behavior of bank managers was observed to determine the differences between effective and ineffective managers. The results of the investigations indicated that the main difference between the two was that effective managers spent more time walking around and monitoring the behavior and performance of their employees. Empirical evidence thus seems to support the MBWA concept.

Many managers prefer a more direct, hands-on leadership style.

## Leadership Through Power

Another strategy that leaders often use is management by power. Power is important to a leader because as it increases, so does the leader's potential to influence others. Leaders who have power are able to obtain more resources, dictate policy, and advance farther in an organization than those who have little or no power.

Earlier in this chapter, French and Raven's bases of power were alluded to in terms of their relationships to Geier et al.'s IMPACT theory. French and Raven (1959; Raven, 1992) identified five basic types of power: expert, legitimate, reward, coercive, and referent.

**Expert Power**  As mentioned earlier in the chapter, in certain situations, leaders who know something useful—that is, have expert knowledge—will have power. But there are two requirements for **expert power.** First, the knowledge must be something that others in an organization need. In a university's psychology department, a researcher with an excellent grasp of statistics has power over those who do not. Similarly, a soldier who knows how to get around the military bureaucracy has more power than those who only know how to follow established channels and procedures. Second, others must be aware that the leader knows something. Information is only powerful if other people know that the leader has it or if the leader uses it (Benzinger, 1982).

**Legitimate Power**  Leaders obtain **legitimate power** on the basis of their positions. For example, a sergeant has power over a corporal, a vice-president has power over a supervisor, and a coach has power over players on a football team. Leaders with legitimate power are best able to get employees to comply with their decisions (Rahim & Afza, 1993) but have low follower satisfaction (Rahim, 1989).

**Reward and Coercive Powers**  Leaders also have power to the extent that they can reward and punish others. **Reward power** involves having control over the obvious—salary increases, bonuses, or promotions—and the subtle—praise or more favorable work assignments.

For a leader to have **coercive power,** it is important that others believe she is willing to use her ability to punish; she cannot maintain coercive power if employees believe she is bluffing. Punishment includes such actions as being fired or not being promoted and the more subtle actions of being given a "cold shoulder."

**Referent Power**  Another source of power for a leader may lie in the positive feelings that others hold for her. Leaders who are well liked can influence others even in the absence of reward and coercive power. Leaders can obtain such **referent power** by complimenting others, doing favors, and generally being friendly and supportive (Kipnis, Schmidt, & Wilkinson, 1980). Employees of leaders with referent power are most committed to their organizations and satisfied with their jobs (Rahim & Afza, 1993).

### Leadership Through Vision: Transformational Leadership

While most leadership theories concentrate on the short-term relationships between leaders and subordinates (Howell & Avolio, 1993), **transformational leadership** focuses on long-term goals (Bass, 1990; Howell & Avolio, 1993). Transformational leaders are often labeled as being visionary, charismatic, and inspirational. They lead by developing a vision, changing organizations to fit this vision, and motivating employees to reach the vision or long-term goal. Transformational leaders are confident, have a need to influence others, and hold a strong attitude that their beliefs and ideas are correct (Bryman, 1992). They innovate, challenge the status quo, focus on people, are flexible, look to the future, carefully analyze problems, and trust their intuition (Bennis, 1989; Nanus, 1992; Yukl, 1994). One study, however, failed to find any relationship between these personal characteristics and transformational leadership (Dubinsky, Yammarino, & Jolson, 1995).

Yukl (1994) offers the following guidelines for transformational leadership:

- Develop a clear and appealing vision
- Develop a strategy for attaining the vision
- Articulate and promote the vision
- Act confident and optimistic
- Express confidence in followers
- Use early success in small steps to build confidence
- Celebrate successes
- Use dramatic, symbolic actions to emphasize key values
- Lead by example
- Create, modify, or eliminate such cultural forms as symbols, slogans, and ceremonies

### Leadership Through Persuasion

The ability to persuade others is a commonly needed leadership skill. Supervisors often need to persuade upper-level managers that a new program will work; politicians need to persuade fellow politicians to vote a particular way; and public relations executives often want to persuade the public to change its perception of an organization or a product. Two important aspects of persuasion—the communicator and the message—will be briefly discussed.

**Persuasion by Communication**  Considerable research indicates that people who have certain characteristics—expertise, trustworthiness, and attractiveness—can communicate through persuasion more easily than people who lack these characteristics.

*Expertise*  Research has found that, in general, a leader who either has or is perceived as having **expertise** about a topic will be more persuasive

The ability to persuade is an important leadership characteristic.

than a leader who does not (Maddux & Rogers, 1980; Wilson & Sherrell, 1993). Thus, for leaders to persuade their followers, they must be the most knowledgeable about their common interest. In many high-tech fields, technical knowledge is an essential characteristic for a leader. If, however, those who are to be persuaded also are knowledgeable about a topic, the leader's expertise plays a smaller role (Rhine & Severance, 1970).

*Trustworthiness* Another leader characteristic important in persuasion is **trustworthiness.** Used car salespeople, for example, have difficulty persuading customers to buy cars because customers do not trust them. And in many corporations, management is distrusted by its employees and thus may have trouble convincing union members, especially, that the organization does not have the money available to grant raises. When being persuaded, then, people look not only at the expertise of the persuader but also at her motives.

To improve her trustworthiness, a leader can do several things. First, she can occasionally argue against what appears to be her own self-interest

(Walster, Aronson, & Abrahams, 1966). For example, she can sometimes tell her employees not to work as hard or she can disagree with other managers. In doing so, she will not appear to be one-sided.

A leader also can communicate to those she hopes to persuade that not only is she similar to them (Dembroski, Lasater, & Ramirez, 1978) but also that her goals are the same as theirs (Cantor, Alfonso, & Zillman, 1976). For example, a manager trying to increase her department budget can explain to the vice-president that her goal includes saving the company money, but to do so she needs a larger recruiting budget so that better quality employees can be hired.

*Attractiveness*   Chapter 5 briefly observed that attractive people tend to receive higher interview scores than do unattractive people. **Attractiveness** has the same effect with persuasion: attractive people are more persuasive than unattractive people (Chaiken, 1979; DeBono, 1992). This is why television commercials generally use attractive people and why attractive politicians are considered to be ideal candidates.

**The Message**   In addition to the leader's personal attributes, the type of message that is presented also has a role in persuasion.

*Message Discrepancy*   Suppose that you are representing a group of employees in a labor negotiation. The employees currently are paid $8 per hour, but you think they deserve $10 per hour. What strategy would best achieve an increase to $10? Would it be to ask for $20 an hour and hope that management will actually give you more than $10? Or would the best strategy be honesty—that is, ask for exactly what you want—$10 per hour? Or would the best strategy be to ask for $13 an hour so that you appear reasonable but still have room to negotiate when management offers $8.50 an hour?

According to persuasion research, the third choice would be best. Ask for more than you want and then back down during negotiations (Jaccard, 1981; Cialindi, 1985). Asking for too much, or making an argument that is too far away from the other side's, will diminish your credibility. Asking for the amount you actually desire leaves no room for negotiation.

*One-Sided versus Two-Sided Arguments*   Another question that arises concerning the persuasive message is whether giving only one side of an argument is better than giving both sides. The answer is, it depends. If the person being persuaded already is positive about an idea, it is usually better to argue only one side of an issue. If, however, the other person disagrees with the reasoning, it is better to argue both sides (Sawyer, 1973). When the other side is presented, the other person's perspective is acknowledged as legitimate and understood. But after the other side of the issue has been argued, it can be refuted and the favored side can then be reargued. If you know that an opponent will bring up negative information about you or your position, it is better to bring it up yourself (Williams, Bourgeois, & Croyle, 1993).

*Threats*   The threat is another method of persuasion that a leader can use when appropriate. For a threat to be effective, however, the person being persuaded must actually believe that it will be carried out—that is, that the consequences of not complying are undesirable and inevitable (Tedeschi, Bonoma, & Schlenker, 1972).

For example, a supervisor tells an employee that she will be fired if she does not work overtime. For the threat to be effective, the employee must believe that the supervisor has both the authority and the willingness to fire her. Even then, the threat will only be effective if the employee values her job.

Threats certainly can be effective in persuasion, but they also can have negative consequences. Few people like being threatened, and many will resent the person who makes the threat (Heilman, 1974; Rubin & Lewecki, 1973). Some may even so react against the threat that they do the opposite of what the leader wants (Brehm, 1966).

## LEADERSHIP: WHERE ARE WE TODAY?

Most of this chapter has described leadership theories. Of course, when several theories address the same topic, the question comes to mind, which of the theories are true? The answer probably is that each is somewhat true and that the best "theory" about leadership is some combination.

As Figure 9.6 shows, if we combine all of the theories discussed in this chapter, leadership emerges as a set of interactions: between a leader's traits and skills, between a situation's demands and characteristics, and between followers' needs and characteristics. Thus, certain people will be effective leaders in certain situations when particular types of people are followers. Unfortunately, we are not yet at the stage where we can determine the exact matches that result in the best leadership. But it is probably safe to make the following assumptions:

1. Because different situations require different leadership styles and skills, individuals who have a wide variety of relevant skills will be best able to be effective leaders in a larger variety of situations. That is, a person who only has excellent planning skills will only be an effective leader in situations that require planning. But a leader who has excellent skills in planning, persuasion, people, goal setting, and motivation will be able to lead in many different types of situations.

   The advice that follows from this assumption is obvious. As Table 9.4 shows, an individual interested in becoming an effective leader should obtain as many leadership skills as possible. By attending leadership conferences, taking college courses, and gaining a variety of experiences, a leader can gain most of these skills.

**Figure 9.6**
Effective leadership: interaction of leader, situation, and follower characteristics

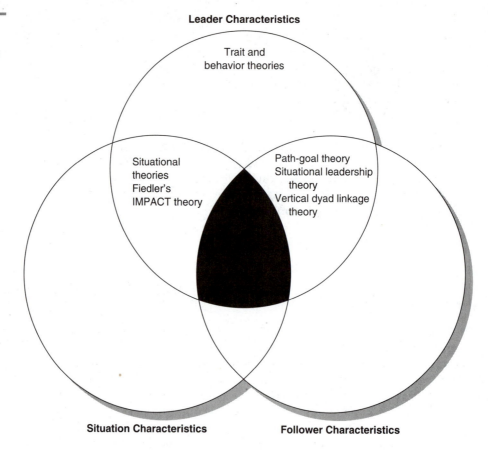

**Leader Characteristics**

Trait and behavior theories

Situational theories Fiedler's IMPACT theory

Path-goal theory Situational leadership theory Vertical dyad linkage theory

**Situation Characteristics**

**Follower Characteristics**

**Table 9.4** Effective leadership skills

| Leadership Skill | Information | Direction | Empathy/Support | Motivation | Persuasion |
|---|---|---|---|---|---|
| Decision making | | X | | | |
| Goal setting | | X | | | |
| Persuasion | X | X | | X | X |
| Team building | | | X | X | |
| Stress management | | | X | | |
| Friendliness | | | X | X | |
| Empathy | | | X | | |
| Energy | | | | X | |
| Time management | | X | | | |
| Technical knowledge | X | | | | |
| Intelligence | X | X | | | |

*Requirements of the Situation/Follower*

**Walter L. Pierce Jr., M.S.**
**District Manager**
**Liberty National Life**

My first job out of graduate school was personnel manager for a small poultry company in the Shenandoah Valley of Virginia. This was a dream come true for me because I thought it was exactly what I had wanted to do upon finishing school. I had performed a practicum in the personnel department of a Fortune 500 company and loved the work. I was the first personnel manager this company had ever had and was responsible for designing and implementing practically every human resource management function in a new plant. My major accomplishments included staffing the plant, designing and implementing a salary administration program, conducting research and validation of a weighted applicant blank, and creating and editing an employee newsletter. Even though I was gaining great experience and had a great opportunity to advance with this company, I left after 11 months. I was disillusioned with company politics, and I could see a limited income potential.

My next job was as personnel officer with a Fortune 500 transportation company. I worked for this corporation for three and a half years and was transferred to Atlanta, Georgia. My major duties and accomplishments included selecting professional and blue-collar applicants in a 21-state area, selecting management trainees through college recruiting, performing internal promotional evaluations of employees utilizing various aptitude and behavioral instruments, instructing management performance appraisal workshops, and performing research on testing and selection methods. It was exciting working as a mid-level manager for a company with 40,000 employees, but I quickly

learned that company politics were once again heavily involved in personnel decisions. At this time I finally realized that as an employee of a company there would always be a limit on the amount of income I could earn. I made a painful decision and decided to leave the human resource management field.

I had a close personal friend who was very successful in the insurance business and had arranged for me to start with his company right away. I quickly found that selling insurance is probably the highest paid hard work and the lowest paid easy work that I could have possibly found. I have always been a very positive individual and was successful in tripling my previous income in my first year. I had reached one of my goals: I was in business for myself. The beginning of my second year I was promoted to the position of sales manager in which I was responsible for recruiting and training a small sales force. In my third year I was promoted to district manager and once again realized I was working as a human resource manager. This time, however, I did not have to deal with politics, and I had unlimited income potential.

As a district manager with Liberty National I am heavily involved in practically every area of human resource management. My most important function is recruiting—turnover is particularly high in the insurance industry. I do a great deal of observational recruiting and use many centers of influence. My company utilizes a test that helps to select those individuals with the highest aptitude. Selecting the correct individual is of extreme importance to my company because of the large compensation package and benefits we provide. My average agent who worked in my office at least one year earned $47,852 in 1994.

Training, counseling, and labor relations are the next most important functions of a district manager. Liberty National Managers spend a great deal of time educating and field training agents. I use the KASH formula (Knowledge, Attitude, Skills, Habits) when training new agents. The insurance business is tough, so counseling is an ongoing activity for most managers. I do a great deal of recognition on a

*(continued)*

2. Because individuals have different needs and personalities, leaders who are able to adapt their interpersonal styles to fit the needs of followers will be better leaders than those who stick to just one behavioral style. It is much easier for a leader to adapt her style to fit the individual needs of her followers than for 30 people with different needs and styles to adapt their behavior to fit their leader's needs and style.

3. Because a leader must use different skills in different situations and act differently with different followers, it is important that she be able to understand the needs of the situation, the follower, or both and then behave accordingly. Thus, leaders who accurately recognize situational and follower needs will be more effective than those who are unable to distinguish one situation from another.

## CHAPTER SUMMARY

This chapter has discussed several leadership theories. The earliest theory, the trait theory, postulates that people who become leaders (leader emergence) and people who are effective leaders (leader performance) possess certain traits that nonleaders or unsuccessful leaders do not. Research, however, has not supported this theory well.

Behavior theories state that certain leader behaviors are needed for effective leadership. The Ohio State studies suggest that leader behavior can be placed into the categories of consideration and initiating structure. McGregor categorizes leader behavior according to whether it conforms to Theory X or Theory Y. Theory X leaders are task-oriented, whereas Theory Y leaders are person-oriented. Managerial grid theory places leadership behavior into one of five categories: country club, impoverished, task-centered, team, and middle-of-the-road.

The third type of theory discussed were situational theories. These theories are based on the assumption that certain leader behaviors will only be effective in certain situations. Examples discussed were Fiedler's contingency theory, IMPACT theory, path-goal theory, and vertical dyad linkage theory.

The final types of leadership discussed were those from the specific behavioral and skill theories. This set of theories states that effective leaders possess specific skills such as persuasion, motivation, and decision making. Ineffective leaders do not. The skills discussed in this section included decision making, walking around, power, and persuasion.

## GLOSSARY

**Achievement-oriented style**   In path-goal theory, a leadership style in which the leader sets challenging goals and rewards achievement.

**Affiliation style**   A leadership style in which the individual leads by caring about others and is most effective in a climate of anxiety.

**Anxiety**   An organizational climate in which worry predominates.

**Attractiveness**   The extent to which a leader is appealing to look at.

**Coercive power**   Leadership power that comes from the leader's capacity to punish others.

**Coercive style**   A leadership style in which the individual leads by controlling reward and punishment and is most effective in a climate of crisis.

**Consideration**   The degree to which a leader acts in a warm and supportive manner toward his or her subordinates.

**Country club leadership**   A style of leadership in which the leader is concerned about the well-being of employees but is not task oriented.

**Crisis**   A critical time or climate for an organization in which the outcome of a decision has extreme consequences.

**Despair**   An organizational climate characterized by low morale.

**Disorganization**   A climate in which the organization has the necessary knowledge and resources but does not know how to efficiently use the knowledge or the resources.

**Expertise**   The amount of knowledge or skill possessed by a leader.

**Expert power**   The idea that a person who has knowledge also has power.

**Fiedler's Contingency Model**   A theory of leadership that states that leadership effectiveness is dependent on the interaction between the leader and the situation.

**Ignorance**   An organizational climate in which important information is not available.

**IMPACT Theory**   A leadership theory that divides leadership into six styles (informational, magnetic, position, affiliation, coercive, and tactical); each style will only be effective in one of six organizational climates.

**Impoverished leadership**   A style of leadership in which the leader is concerned with neither productivity nor the well-being of employees.

**Informational style**   A style of leadership in which the leader leads through knowledge and information in a climate of ignorance.

**Initiating structure**   The extent to which a leader defines and structures his or her role and the roles of his or her subordinates.

**Instability**   An organizational climate in which people are not sure what to do.

**Instrumental style**   In path-goal theory, a leadership style in which the leader plans and organizes the activities of employees.

**Job Choice Exercise (JCE)**   An objective test that is used to measure various need levels.

**Leader Behavior Description Questionnaires (LBDQ)**   A test used to measure perceptions of a leader's style by his or her subordinates.

**Leader emergence**   A part of trait theory that postulates that certain types of people will become leaders and certain types will not.

**Leader Match**   A training program that teaches leaders how to change situations so that they are consistent with their leadership styles.

**Leader-member relations**   The variable in Fiedler's Contingency Model that refers to the extent to which subordinates like a leader.

**Leader performance**   A part of trait theory that postulates that certain types of people will be better leaders than will other types of people.

**Leader position power**   The variable in Fiedler's Contingency Model that refers to the extent to which a leader, by the nature of his or her position, has the power to reward and punish subordinates.

**Leadership motive pattern**   The name for a pattern of needs in which a leader has a high need for power and a low need for affiliation.

**Leadership Opinion Questionnaire (LOQ)**   A test used to measure a leader's self-perception of his or her leadership style.

**Least-Preferred Co-worker (LPC) Scale**   A test used in conjunction with Fiedler's Contingency Model to reveal leadership style and effectiveness.

**Legitimate power**   The power that an individual has because of his or her elected or appointed position.

**Magnetic style**   A style of leadership in which the leader has influence because of his or her charismatic personality; is effective in a climate of despair.

**Managerial grid**   A measure of leadership that classifies a leader into one of five leadership styles.

**Middle-of-the-road leadership**   A leadership style reflecting an approach that balances people and task orientation.

**Need for achievement**   According to trait theory, the extent to which a person desires to be successful.

**Need for affiliation**   According to trait theory, the extent to which a person desires to be around other people.

**Need for power**   According to trait theory, the extent to which a person desires to be in control of other people.

**Participative style**   In path-goal theory, a leadership style in which the leader allows employees to participate in decisions.

**Path-goal theory**   A theory of leadership that states that leaders will be effective if their behavior helps subordinates achieve relevant goals.

**Position style**   A leadership style in which the leader influences others by virtue of his or her appointed or elected authority; is effective in a climate of instability.

**Referent power**   Leadership power that exists when followers can identify with a leader and the leader's goals.

**Reward power**   Leadership power that exists to the extent that the leader has the ability and authority to provide rewards.

**Situational leadership theory**   A theory of leadership that states that effective leaders must adapt their style of leadership to fit both the situation and the followers.

**Sociological approach**   A study of leadership that focuses on the identification of characteristics possessed by leaders.

**Supportive style**   In path-goal theory, a leadership style in which the leader shows concern for employees.

**Tactical style**   A leadership style in which a person leads through organization and strategy and is most effective in a climate of disorganization.

**Task-centered leadership**   A leadership style in which the leader is more concerned with productivity than with employee well-being.

**Task structuredness**   The variable in Fiedler's Contingency Model that refers to the extent to which tasks have clear goals and problems can be solved.

**Team leadership**   A leadership style in which the leader is concerned with both productivity and employee well-being.

**Thematic Apperception Test (TAT)**   A projective test that is used to measure various need levels.

**Theory X leaders**   Leaders who believe that employees are extrinsically motivated and thus lead by giving directives and setting goals.

**Theory Y leaders**   Leaders who believe that employees are intrinsically motivated and thus lead with a "hands-off" or participative approach.

**Trait theory**   A type of leadership theory based on the idea that personal characteristics determine leader emergence and leader performance.

**Transformational Leadership**   Visionary leadership in which the leader changes the nature and goals of an organization.

**Trustworthiness**   The extent to which a leader is believed and trusted by his or her followers.

**Vertical dyad linkage (VDL) theory**   A leadership theory that concentrates on the interaction between the leader and his or her subordinates.

**Vroom-Yetton Model**   A theory of leadership that concentrates on helping a leader choose how to make a decision.

# 10

# GROUP BEHAVIOR
# AND CONFLICT

With few exceptions, most employee behavior takes place in groups. Fire-

fighters work together when fighting a fire, managers make decisions in

committee meetings, and bank tellers work together to deal with customers.

Because employees tend to work in groups, it is important for a manager or

a leader to understand group dynamics. This understanding is especially im-

portant in light of the increased use of teams by organizations in the 1990s

(Filipczak, 1994).

# DEFINITION OF A GROUP

Perhaps the first place to begin our discussion of group behavior is defining what constitutes a group. For a collection of people to be called a group, the following four criteria must be met (Gordon, 1983): (1) The members of the group must see themselves as a unit; (2) the group must provide rewards to its members; (3) anything that happens to one member of the group affects every other member; and (4) the members of the group must share a common goal.

## MULTIPLE MEMBERS

The first criterion is that the group must have multiple members. Obviously, one person does not constitute a group. Therefore, at least two people are necessary to form a group. Usually we refer to two people as a dyad, three people as a triad, and 4 to 20 people as a small group (Forsyth, 1990). To be considered a group these two or more people must also see themselves as a unit. Thus, three individuals walking down the sidewalk would only be considered a group if they know one another and are together. Eight separate customers shopping at a store would also not be considered a group.

## GROUP REWARDS

The second group criterion is that membership must be rewarding for each individual in the group. We will discuss shortly the reasons people join groups, but for now it is important to remember that people will only join or form a group if it provides some form of reward.

To demonstrate this point, imagine four students studying for an exam. If the four study in separate rooms and do not share information, they are not a group. But take the same four people and put them at one desk in the library. If each person studies the book separately and never communicates with the other three, then the four still will not be a group because none of the individuals is rewarded by the others. But if none of the four would have otherwise studied independently, then the four students would be considered a group because being together was rewarding. Even though they did not talk with one another during their time in the library, the fact that they were together provided the structure for each of them to study.

## CORRESPONDING EFFECTS

The third group criterion is an event that affects one group member should affect all group members. That is, if something significant happens to one person and does not affect any of the other people gathered with her, then the collection of people cannot be considered a group. This criterion is called **corresponding effects.** For example, five bank tellers work side by side; one teller becomes ill and goes home. If the activities of the other four

change as a result of the one teller leaving, the five might be considered a group. But if the activities of the four do not change after the one teller leaves, then the tellers cannot be considered a group.

## COMMON GOALS

The fourth and final criterion is that all members must share a **common goal.** In the teller example, if the goal of one of the tellers is to meet only young, single customers, while the goal of another teller is to serve as many customers as possible, the tellers are not considered to be a group because they work in different ways and for different reasons.

Why do we care if a collection of people meets the technical definition of a group? The answer lies within your ability to change employee performance. Over the course of this chapter, you will learn many factors affecting group performance. If you apply what you learn, you will be effective in changing performance only if the collection of individuals is actually a *group*.

## REASONS FOR JOINING GROUPS

### AFFILIATION

**Affiliation** involves our need to be with other people. Thus, one reason that people join groups is to be near and talk to other people. Research has demonstrated that our need for affiliation is very strong. Mayo (1946), for example, found that employees at a textile plant who worked separately from other employees were not as satisfied with their jobs as were employees at the same plant who had the opportunity to work with others. Likewise, Burling, Lentz, and Wilson (1956) found that turnover in a hospital could be reduced by assigning maids who worked alone to work in teams.

Perhaps the most interesting demonstrations of the strength of the human affiliation need come from the writings of Schein (1956) and Naughton (1975). These researchers were interested in the reasons why American prisoners of war (POWs) in World War II behaved so differently from those in the Korean and Vietnam conflicts. POWs in World War II made more escape attempts, suffered fewer deaths, and provided information less frequently to the enemy than did their counterparts in Korea and Vietnam.

Although the American public attributed the differences to a postwar decline in the American character (Hampton, Summer, & Webber, 1978), both Schein and Naughton pointed out the differences from a perspective of group dynamics. In World War II, the POWs were kept in groups that remained together for long periods of time. Thus, these men were able to receive emotional support from one another, they could work together to plan escapes, they were able to hear what each POW said to the enemy, and they knew about and supported a strong group norm about not talking to the enemy.

In the two Asian conflicts, the situations were entirely different. Rather than living in groups, these POWs were isolated and not allowed to communicate with one another. Naughton (1975) reports that the men were so in need of contact and communication with others that they scraped their cell walls to make noise and establish contact and informal communication with one another. This behavior is similar to that reported by hostages held in Beirut and Syria.

These examples, as well as research studies, indicate that people often perform better and are usually more satisfied with their work when in groups. If people are not allowed the opportunity for affiliation, they make attempts to secure at least minimal contact. When even minimal contact is not possible, morale and perhaps even the will to live are lessened.

Of course, people are not equal in their desire or need to affiliate with others (Smart, 1965). For example, computer programmers have lower needs and desires to affiliate than people in many other occupations. This point is especially interesting because a trend in the computer-programming industry is to place programmers and analysts into groups to debug programs and solve problems (Shneiderman, 1980). Although research is not yet available on the effects of such grouping, putting such strong individualists into groups does not sound like a promising idea. However, people with a high need for affiliation perform better in groups than alone (Klein & Pridemore, 1992).

## IDENTIFICATION

Another reason why we join groups is our desire for **identification** with some group or cause. There are many examples of this need to identify with others. In the 1960s and 1970s, young men wore their hair long; although some thought it attractive and comfortable, many others grew long hair because it helped them identify with other males of their generation and separated them from adult males of previous generations. Many of us still know someone who wears his hair long and refers to the 1960s and 1970s, thus identifying himself with an earlier period. In the 1980s and 1990s, so-called punk and grunge styles of hair and clothes were worn by students in much the same way that long hair and tie-dyed shirts were worn by people in the 1960s. But each was separating himself from a more conservative majority and identifying with a more liberal or radical group.

Around your school you may notice that many students wear T-shirts with logos or messages. Students wearing *Boyz to Men,* Los Angeles Dodgers, or *Sail Florida* shirts are all identifying with particular groups and thus making statements about themselves.

A study by Cialindi and his associates (Cialindi, Borden, Thorne, Walker, Freeman, & Sloane, 1976) investigated clothing as a means of identification. At several universities, Cialindi et al. observed the number of students who wore school-related clothing such as T-shirts and sweatshirts on the Monday following a school football game. They found that following a football victory, many more students wore school-related clothing than on Mondays following football losses. In a second study, Cialindi et al. also asked students who won the football game. As we might expect, when the football team won, the students answered by saying, "We won." When the team lost, the students answered by saying, "They lost." Based on these two studies, Cialindi called this identification process "basking in reflected glory."

Another example of the identification process comes from a major manufacturing plant in Virginia. Several months before union contract talks began, the company gave each employee several nice shirts with the company name printed on the front. The company did this because it had previously noticed that in the months before contract negotiations began, the employees began to wear more union caps and shirts. The company believed that this clothing helped increase the employees' level of identification with the union. To counter this effect, the company hoped that its shirts would influence the negotiation process. Although we cannot determine the exact effect of this strategy, that year was the only one in a decade that union members did not strike.

## EMOTIONAL SUPPORT

We also join groups to obtain emotional support. Alcoholics Anonymous and Weight Watchers are good examples of groups that provide emotional support for their members.

## ASSISTANCE OR HELP

People often join groups to obtain assistance or help. For example, students having problems with an algebra class might form a study group.

## COMMON INTERESTS

People often join groups because they share a common interest (Greenberg & Baron, 1995). At school, students joining a geology club share an interest in geology, students joining a fraternity share an interest in socializing, and students joining a service club such as Circle K or Alpha Phi Omega share an interest in helping people.

It is an interesting side note that most campus clubs that are based on common academic interests such as a psychology club or a Latin club are usually smaller and less active than other campus groups. Apparently, college students have many needs, and common academic interests are usually not as strong as the social needs that are satisfied by the Greek organizations. For example, a service club on the Radford University campus was having difficulty attracting members, so several advisors suggested that it increase its number of social activities to attract people who had both community service and social needs. This slight change in activities increased membership from 15 to 45.

## COMMON GOALS

People who join political parties are examples of people in pursuit of a common goal. These people may also share common interests, but their primary purpose is to get a particular person or members of a particular party elected to office.

## PHYSICAL PROXIMITY

One especially strong reason that a person might join a particular group, especially if the group is informal, is physical proximity (Forsyth, 1990). That is, people tend to form groups with people who either live or work nearby. For example, think of the intramural teams on your campus. Most teams consist of students who live in the same dorms or have classes together. At work, employees tend to form groups that consist of those who work in the same general area. As we will discuss in greater detail in a later chapter, some employees seek close physical proximity to people in power hoping they will become part of an elite group.

## ASSIGNMENT

In the workplace, employees are often assigned to groups rather than joining them voluntarily. For example, a new employee might be assigned to a department with five other employees, all of whom are asked to work together as a team. Other examples might include employees assigned to committees or quality improvement teams.

## GROUP COHESIVENESS

**Group cohesiveness** is the extent to which group members like and trust one another. In general, the more cohesive the group, the greater its productivity (Mullen & Copper, 1994), decision quality (Mullen, Anthony, Salas, & Driskell, 1994), member satisfaction (Brawley, Carron, & Widmeyer, 1993; Deluga & Winters, 1991), and member interaction (Shaw & Shaw, 1962). Research has demonstrated that cohesive work groups perform best in such areas as safety (Speroff & Kerr, 1952), turnover and absenteeism (Van Zelt, 1952), and job satisfaction (Zander, 1982). Furthermore, cohesive baseball and volleyball teams tend to win more games than do less cohesive teams (Bird, 1977; Long, 1982).

In its 1989 strike against Pittston Coal Co., the United Mine Workers union realized the importance of cohesiveness and identification needs by adopting a unique strategy. Each union member as well as his or her family members and supportive friends wore camouflage shirts and fatigues as a sign of unity. Every time a miner looked around him, he saw others dressed like him. The union members thus developed a sense of unity and cohesiveness that helped them last through a lengthy strike. Groups such as the Boy Scouts and the Guardian Angels also wear uniforms to increase group cohesiveness.

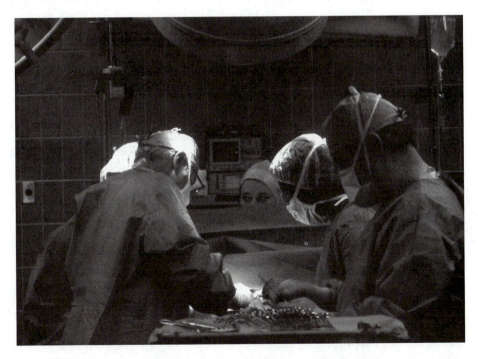

Group cohesiveness is essential for many jobs.

But cohesiveness can also lower group performance, especially in a work setting. When employees become too cohesive, they often lose sight of organizational goals. For example, it is common for restaurant employees to put the needs of other employees above those of their customers. Similarly, police departments tend to be highly cohesive—so much so that anyone who is not a police officer is considered an outsider, which can make community relations difficult.

Although the majority of research supports the conclusion that cohesiveness results in better group performance, it is not always necessary to have cohesion to have high group performance. For example, the Oakland As in the early 1970s and the New York Yankees in the mid-1970s were baseball teams that won championships despite constant fighting among the players.

Research has also demonstrated that employees in cohesive work groups will conform to a norm of lower production even though they are capable of higher performance (Forsyth, 1990; Roethlisberger & Dickson, 1939). An excellent example of this conformity to a group norm involved the Hollywood division of the Los Angeles Police Department in the early 1980s. Many of the division's officers and detectives were extensively involved in property crimes. They would break into various retail stores and radio that they were responding to the ringing burglar alarms. They then placed the stolen goods in their car trunks and proceeded as if they were investigating the break-ins. The officers later met at specific locations to hide and sell the stolen goods. Officers who did not participate in the crimes saw the merchandise and knew what was going on, but they did not report the offenders. Instead, they put their loyalty to their fellow officers above their loyalty to the city or the police department.

### Group Homogeneity

The homogeneity of a group is the extent to which its members are similar. A homogeneous group contains members who are similar in some or most ways, whereas a heterogeneous group contains members who are more different than alike. An important question for a leader to consider when developing a group is which composition, homogeneous or heterogeneous, will lead to the best group performance. Many research studies have sought to answer this question, but only mixed results have been found with some studies finding homogeneous groups most effective and others finding heterogeneous groups most effective. For example, Hoffman (1959) found groups with homogeneous personalities to be superior in a laboratory task, while Aamodt and Kimbrough (1982) found groups with heterogeneous personalities to be superior for solving a laboratory problem. Likewise, Klein and Christiansen (1969) found heterogeneous basketball teams to be best, while Vander Velden (1971) found that homogeneous basketball teams performed better than heterogeneous teams.

Neufeldt, Kimbrough, and Stadelmaier (1983) sought to explain these mixed results by predicting that certain types of groups would do better with certain types of tasks. Neufeldt and his colleagues thus had homogeneous and heterogeneous groups each perform several different tasks. Though they expected the homogeneous groups to perform better on simple tasks and the heterogeneous groups to perform better on more complex tasks, Neufeldt et al. instead found that the type of task did not moderate the relationship between group composition and performance.

Aamodt, Kimbrough, and Alexander (1983) then hypothesized that previous research yielded mixed results because the compositions of the best-performing groups were actually somewhere between completely homogeneous and completely heterogeneous. These authors thus labeled them **slightly heterogeneous groups.**

To test their hypothesis, Aamodt and his colleagues separated 202 NCAA Division I basketball teams into three categories based on the racial composition of the starting five players. Heterogeneous groups were teams with three Whites and two Blacks or two Blacks and three Whites (3-2), homogeneous groups had five Blacks or five Whites (5-0), and slightly heterogeneous groups had either four Blacks and one White or four Whites and one Black (4-1). The study results supported the notion that slightly heterogeneous groups were superior—they won 60% of their games. Both heterogeneous and homogeneous teams won about 53% of their games (all winning percentages are above 50% because Division I teams played and usually beat many non-Division I teams).

These results were later supported by a study that divided contestants on the television game show *Family Feud* into the same three groups as described above but with gender rather than race as the variable. The results indicated that the slightly heterogeneous teams won more money than the other two group types. The slightly heterogeneous families won an average of $330, heterogeneous families an average of $278, and homogeneous families an average of $254. A meta-analysis by Aamodt, Freeman, and Carneal (1992) found support for the superiority of slightly-heterogeneous groups.

Thus this research appears to support the conclusion that the best working groups consist primarily of people who are similar but with a dissimilar person adding tension and a different vantage point. But it is not yet clear which variable is most important in terms of determining group composition. That is, variables in previous research have included race, gender, personality, intelligence, attitudes, and background. Thus, a group might be homogeneous in terms of race but heterogeneous in gender. More research is needed to clarify this issue. Though it appears that slightly heterogeneous groups result in the highest levels of performance, research indicates that homogeneous groups result in the greatest member satisfaction and lowest amount of turnover (Aamodt, Freeman, & Carneal, 1992; Jackson, Brett, Sessa, Cooper, Julin, & Peyronnin, 1991).

### Stability of Membership

The greater the **stability** of the group, the greater the cohesiveness. Thus, groups whose members remain in the group for long periods of time are more cohesive and perform better than groups that have high turnover

(Argote, Insko, Yovetich & Romero, 1995). A good example again can be found on a college campus. At most colleges, fraternities and sororities usually are the most active organizations and have high levels of performance, while professional clubs and honorary societies such as Psi Chi and Lambda Alpha Beta tend to be the least active. Why is this? Certainly, it cannot be the abilities of the memberships—honorary societies have more intelligent members than most fraternities and sororities. Instead, the answer might be in the stabilities of the groups. Students tend to join Greek organizations in their freshman or sophomore years, while students tend to join professional clubs in their junior year and honorary societies in their senior year, often to help "pad" their résumés. The Greek organizations thus have more stable memberships than the other organizations.

### *Isolation*

Physical **isolation** is another variable that tends to increase a group's cohesiveness. Groups that are isolated or located away from other groups tend to be highly cohesive. A good example is the New River Valley (Virginia) branch of the AT&T Credit Union. The credit union has 10 branches, most

Physically isolated groups are usually very cohesive.

located within a few miles of one another and within a few miles of the main branch in Winston-Salem, North Carolina. The New River Valley branch is 100 miles from the next closest branch; physically and psychologically, the branch is isolated from the main part of the organization. The New River Valley branch, however, is the only one to have no turnover in five years. It also is the branch where the employees are most cohesive.

### Outside Pressure

Groups who are pressured by outside forces also tend to become highly cohesive. To some degree, this response to **outside pressure** can be explained by the phenomenon of *psychological reactance* (Brehm, 1966). When we believe that someone is trying to intentionally influence us to take some particular action, we often react and do the opposite (Van Leeuwen, Frizzell, & Nail, 1987). Consider, for example, a teenaged dating couple. As the boy arrives to pick up his date, the girl's father notices the young man's beard and Harley-Davidson motorcycle and forbids his daughter to go out. Before this order, the daughter may not have been especially interested in the boy, but after being told she cannot go on the date, she reacts by liking the boy more.

On a larger scale, such reactions are commonly seen in labor negotiations. Company managements and unions tend to disagree with and criticize one another. But often such criticism backfires—attacking another group may serve to strengthen that group. In fact, if a company or group wants to increase the cohesiveness of its membership, it can artificially create pressure and attribute it to another group. This tactic involves building a *straw man*—an opponent who does not actually exist but to whom negative statements about the group can be charged (Schweitzer, 1979).

### Group Size

Groups are most cohesive and perform best when **group size** is small. Studies have shown that large groups have less coordination and lower morale (Frank & Anderson, 1971), are less active (Indik, 1965), less cohesive (Carron, 1990), and more critical (Valacich, Dennis, & Nunamaker, 1992) than smaller groups. In fact, research suggests that groups perform best (Manners, 1975) and have greater member satisfaction (Hackman & Vidmar, 1970) when they consist of approximately five members. Thus, a large organization probably works best when it is divided into smaller groups and committees, and work groups are limited to approximately five people.

This does not mean, however, that small groups are always best. Although small groups usually increase cohesiveness, high performance is only seen with certain types of tasks. **Additive tasks** are those for which the group's performance is equal to the sum of the performances by each group member. **Conjunctive tasks** are tasks for which the group's performance depends on the least effective group member. **Disjunctive tasks** are those on which the group's performance is based on the most talented group member. Examples of the three task types are shown in Table 10.1. Large groups are thought to perform best on disjunctive and additive tasks

**Table 10.1**  Examples of task types

| Task Type | Group Activity |
|---|---|
| Additive | Typing pool |
| | Relay race |
| | Bowling team |
| | Car washing |
| Disjunctive | Problem solving |
| | Brainstorming |
| | Golf tournament |
| Conjunctive | Assembly line |
| | Hiking |

(Littlepage, 1991), while small groups perform best on conjunctive tasks (Frank & Anderson, 1971; Steiner, 1972).

The addition of more members has its greatest effect when the group is small. This idea was first investigated by Latane (1981) when he formulated **social impact theory.** Imagine a four-person committee studying safety problems at work. If the group is stable and cohesive, adding a fifth person may be disruptive. But in a factory of 3,000 employees, the hiring of one new employee is not likely to change the complexion of the company. This is why sport experts have observed that a single great player can turn around a poor basketball team—as occurred with Bill Walton and the Portland Trailblazers, Kareem Abdul-Jabbar and the Milwaukee Bucks, and Shaquille O'Neil with the Orlando Magic—but not a football or baseball team.

More recent research indicates that groups working over a computer behave differently than groups working face-to-face. When computers are used, large groups appear to perform best and have the most satisfied members (Dennis, Valacich, & Nunamaker, 1990; Valacich, Dennis, & Connolly, 1994; Valacich, Dennis, & Nunamaker, 1992).

### Group Status

The higher the group's status, the greater its cohesiveness. This is an important point: A group can be made more cohesive by increasing **group status.** The group does not actually have to *have* high status, but it is more important that its members *believe* they have high status.

Again, look around campus and notice the methods used by various groups to artificially increase their status. On our campus, one fraternity advertises itself as the "Porsche of fraternities," while another claims to be the "fraternity of distinction." Of course, there is little difference between the actual status and performance of most organizations, so effective leaders try to increase the cohesiveness of group members by claiming high status—and it apparently works.

One way that leaders can increase their groups' status is by increasing the perception that the groups are difficult to join but that, once in, members will find that the groups' activities are special. In most high schools, "two-a-day" practices are typical during the week before football practice begins. During this period, each prospective team member is worked close to exhaustion. Coaches have such "hell weeks" to increase team status and thus its cohesion and performance. Obviously, a player cannot get into shape in a week, so the purpose of two-a-day practices is not conditioning—it is to build the status of the group members who survive the week. A similar approach is taken by the Marine Corps. By its tough basic training, the Corps builds the status of its enlistees so that Marines and non-Marines alike will believe that the Corps consists of just a "few good men."

Fraternities and sororities are also notorious for hazing during their pledge weeks. Aside from the illegality and cruelty of this behavior, hazing serves the purpose of increasing the effort required for a potential member to join, thus increasing the group's cohesiveness and status. Football players, Marines, and fraternity or sorority members are not likely to quit a group that they have worked so hard to join.

## COMMUNICATION STRUCTURE

Another variable that can affect a group's performance is its **communication structure** or network. For a group to perform successfully, it is essential that there be good communication among members. As shown in Figure 10.1, a variety of communication networks can be used by small groups alone; even more complex networks are possible with larger groups. Each network has its advantages and disadvantages, but the best networks depend on the situations and goals of their groups. For example, if the goals of fraternities and singles clubs are to allow the members to get to know one another, then a centralized structure is less conducive than a completely open one. Conversely, if the goal of a group is to solve a problem as quickly as possible,

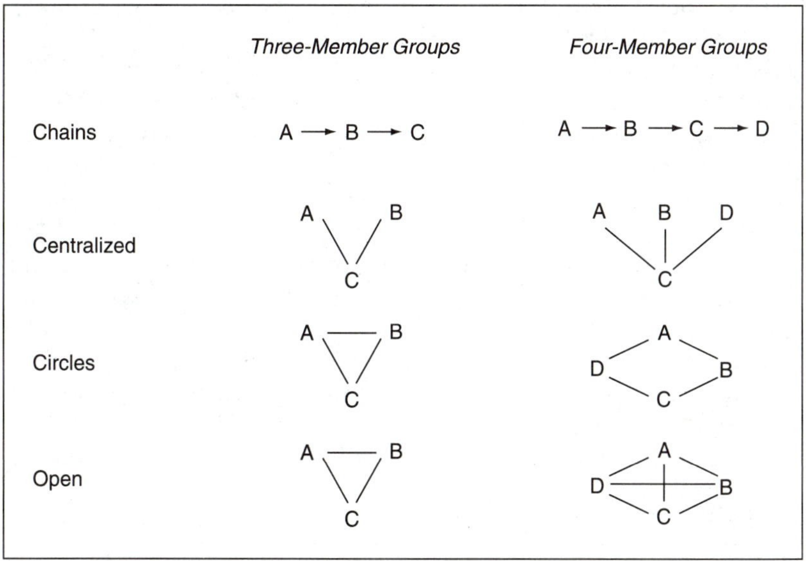

**Figure 10.1**
Possible communication networks for small groups

then the centralized network would be the best structure. A good leader thus carefully chooses the communication network that best facilitates the goals of the group.

## GROUP ROLES

Another factor that affects the performance of a group is the extent to which its members assume different roles. For a group to be successful, its members' roles must fall into one of three categories: task-oriented, maintenance-oriented, and individual (Benne & Sheets, 1948). Task-oriented roles involve behaviors such as offering new ideas, coordinating activities, and finding new information; maintenance-oriented roles involve encouraging cohesiveness and participation; and individual roles include blocking group activities, calling attention to one's self, and avoiding group interaction. Individual roles seldom result in higher group productivity.

Group members will often naturally assume these roles based on their individual personalities and experiences, although sometimes leaders must assign roles to certain individuals. For example, if a leader notices that every group member is filling a task-oriented role, he may either recruit a new group member or assign a current member to fill a maintenance role.

## PRESENCE OF OTHERS

### Social Facilitation and Inhibition

In 1898, researcher N. Triplett noticed that cyclists rode faster when competing against other cyclists than when competing against a clock. Intrigued by this observation, Triplett conducted a study in which children completed a task either alone or while competing against other children. As expected, Triplett found that children who worked against others completed their tasks faster than did children who worked alone.

Since that first study, psychologists have studied what we now call *social facilitation* and *social inhibition*. **Social facilitation** involves the positive effects of the presence of others on an individual's behavior; **social inhibition** involves the negative effects of others' presence. Social facilitation and social inhibition can be further delineated by *audience effects* and *coaction*.

**Audience Effects**    The phenomenon of **audience effects** takes place when a group of people passively watches an individual. An example would be a sporting event held in an arena.

The strength of the effect of having an audience present is a function of at least three factors. Latane (1981) hypothesized these factors to be an audience's size, its physical proximity to the person or group, and its status. Thus, groups are most likely to be affected by large audiences of experts who are physically close to the group (Jackson, 1986; Tanford & Penrod, 1984).

**Table 10.2** Tasks affected by social facilitation and social inhibition

| Skill Level | Facilitation: Increased Performance | Inhibition: Decreased Performance |
|---|---|---|
| Well learned | Bicycle racing | — |
| | Pool shooting | — |
| | Simple mathematics | — |
| | Ant nest building | — |
| | Cockroaches running | — |
| Novice | — | Pool shooting |
| | — | Learning nonsense syllables |
| | — | Completing a maze |
| | — | Complex mathematics |
| | — | Cockroaches turning |

**Coaction**   The effect on behavior when two or more people are performing the same task in the presence of one another is called **coaction.** Examples would be two runners competing against each other without a crowd present or two mail clerks sorting envelopes in the same room. Two studies provide interesting examples of coaction. In the first study, Sommer, Wynes, and Brinkley (1992) found that when people shopped in groups, they spent more time in a store and purchased more goods than when alone. In the second study, de Castro and Brewer (1992) discovered that meals eaten in large groups are 75% larger than those eaten when alone.

**Explaining Social Facilitation Effects**   More than 200 studies of social facilitation have indicated that performance does not always increase in the presence of others. Performance will increase only when the task being performed is easy or well learned; performance will decrease when the task is difficult or not well learned (Bond & Titus, 1983; Zajonc, 1965). Social facilitation and coaction effects occur not only with humans, but also with cockroaches running a maze (Zajonc, Heingartner, & Herman, 1969), chickens eating food (Tolman, 1968), and ants building nests (Chen, 1937). See Table 10.2 for research examples.

   Although researchers have not agreed on the exact reason for these findings, four explanations have each received some empirical support. The first explanation holds that the **mere presence** of others naturally produces arousal (Zajonc, 1980). This arousal or increase in energy helps an individual perform well-learned tasks but hinders him on poorly learned or unpracticed tasks.

   The second explanation states that a coacting audience provides a means for **comparison.** If an individual is working on a task with another individual, he can directly compare his performance to the other person's (Seta, 1982). In some jobs, this comparison effect may increase competition and production quantity, while in other jobs, comparison effects may cause employees to slow down to be in line with the working norm.

The third explanation—**evaluation apprehension**—hypothesizes that judgment by others causes the differential effects of social facilitation (Cottrell, 1972). That is, individuals are aware that the presence of others can be rewarding (for example, when a crowd cheers) or punishing (when a crowd boos). Thus, on well-learned tasks, the individual knows that he normally performs well and thus expects a rewarding experience when in the presence of others. When the task is not well learned, however, the individual may believe that he will not perform well and will be embarrassed, and thus he performs even worse than if he were alone.

One example of this phenomenon was seen in an experiment by Michaels, Blommel, Brocato, Linkous, and Rowe (1982). Michaels and his colleagues observed students shooting pool and found that good players increased their shot accuracy from 71% to 80% when watched by an audience, while poor players' accuracy decreased from 36% to 25% when they were watched. In another study, Thombs, Beck, and Mahoney (1993) found high intensity drinkers were more likely than low intensity drinkers to drink in social situations.

The evaluation-apprehension explanation has special application to industry and training settings. Imagine a waiter who must carry five plates of food to a table. For a new waiter, this is not a well-learned task, and in the presence of others he is likely to be anxious. When the lack of practice in carrying plates is combined with a large restaurant crowd, the chance of an accident increases. So what is the solution? The waiter should practice carrying several plates before the restaurant opens.

Evaluation apprehension also occurs when performance is being monitored electronically rather than in-person (Aiello & Svec, 1993). Thus, supervisors who remotely monitor employee performance over a computer must be aware of the potential effects on performance.

The fourth explanation proposes that the presence of others is **distracting** to the individual who is trying to perform a task (Sanders, 1981). On well-learned tasks, the individual is able to perform despite the distraction because the behaviors are almost automatic. On a novel or complicated task, however, the distraction caused by other peoples' presence keeps the individual from concentrating and learning the task. For example, Baxter, Manstead, Stradling, and Campbell (1990) found that drivers with passengers were less likely to signal than were drivers without anyone else in the car.

An example that demonstrates the effects emphasized by both the evaluation-apprehension and distraction theories is that of coaching children in sports. In a typical Little League practice, one coach must teach an 8-year old how to bat while 10 other children stand in the field and wait for a ball to be hit to them. Each time the child at the plate fails to hit the ball the others tease him. After a while, the children in the field are bored and begin to throw rocks and talk with one another. What is the probability of success in teaching this child to hit under these circumstances? For the coach to be successful, he must teach the child alone and away from other children.

Social facilitation effects also have been examined in the sports world by investigating the advantage that a team might have by playing its game at home. In general, having a home crowd behind a team increases the probability of its winning; this is especially true with indoor sports (Schwartz & Barsky, 1977). The effect increases immediately after a crowd cheers a play or boos a referee's decision (Greer, 1983).

### Social Loafing

While the social facilitation and social inhibition theory explains increases and decreases in performance when others are present and either watching the individual or working with them, the **social loafing** theory considers the effect on individual performance when people work together on a task. Social loafing was first investigated in a study by Ringleman (reported in Moede, 1927), whose subjects singly pulled as hard as possible on a rope while he measured their exerted force. Ringleman then had his subjects perform the task in pairs. He expected the force exerted by two subjects to be approximately twice that exerted by a single subject, but to his surprise he found that both subjects exerted less force than when they worked alone.

Social loafing can occur when people work in groups.

More recent research has supported the theory and has found that social loafing occurs with many tasks. For example, one study found that restaurant customers tipped about 19% of the bill when they dined alone, 16% of the bill when they dined with another person, and 13% when they dined with five others (Latane, 1981). This explains why tips, or gratuities, often are automatically added to a bill when six or more people dine at a table.

Although it is clear that social loafing occurs, especially in poor performers (Hardy & Crace, 1991), it is not clear *why* it occurs. One theory is that because group members realize their individual efforts will not be noticed, there is little chance of individual reward. A second theory, called the *free-rider theory* (Kerr & Bruun, 1983), postulates that when things are going well, a group member realizes that his effort is not necessary and thus he does not work as hard as he would if he were alone. If this explanation is true, social loafing should only occur when a group project is going well.

The third theory, called the *sucker-effect theory* (Kerr, 1983; Robbins, 1995), hypothesizes that social loafing occurs when a group member notices that other group members are not working hard and thus are "playing him for a sucker." To avoid this situation, the individual lowers his work performance to match those of the other members. This theory, however, does not explain the loafing of other members.

Social loafing is an important variable to keep in mind: having employees work together on a project may not be as productive as having them work individually. Fortunately, social loafing can be reduced by identifying individual performance and providing feedback to each worker on how hard he works when rated against some goal or standard (Williams, Harkins, & Latane, 1981), punishing those who loaf (Miles & Greenberg, 1993), and rewarding those who achieve (Shepperd, 1993).

## INDIVIDUAL DOMINANCE

Another variable that can affect group performance is **individual dominance** by a leader or single group member. If the leader or group member has an accurate solution to a problem the group is trying to solve, the group will probably perform at a high level. But if the leader or group member has an inaccurate solution, he will lead the group astray, and it will perform poorly.

## GROUPTHINK

The term **groupthink** was coined by Janis (1972) after studying the disastrous Bay of Pigs invasion of 1961. The Bay of Pigs was the Cuban landing site for 1,400 Cuban exiles who sought to overthrow the government of Fidel Castro. The plan called for the U.S. Navy and Air Force to covertly protect the invasion force and its supply ships. The invaders, however, were met unexpectedly by 20,000 Cuban troops and were quickly killed or captured. The help promised by the U.S. government never developed. Janis (1972) proposed the concept of groupthink to explain how some of the nation's brightest men could hatch such an ill-conceived plan.

With groupthink, members become so cohesive and likeminded that they make poor decisions despite contrary information that might reasonably lead them to another decision. Groupthink most often occurs when the group:

- Is cohesive (Bernthal & Insko, 1993)
- Is insulated from qualified outsiders
- Has an illusion of invulnerability, infallibility, or both
- Believes that it is morally superior to its adversaries
- Is under great pressure to conform
- Has a leader who promotes a favorite solution
- Has gatekeepers who keep information from other group members

Groupthink can be reduced in several ways. First, the group leader should not state his own position or beliefs until late in the decision-making process. Second, the leader should promote open discussion and encourage group members to speak. Third, a group or committee can be separated into subgroups to increase the chance of disagreement. Finally, one group member can be assigned the job of **devil's advocate**—one who questions and disagrees with the group. Though groupthink is commonly written about, a comprehensive evaluation of it by Aldag and Fuller (1993) has questioned its validity as a phenomenon as well as its negative effect.

## INDIVIDUAL VERSUS GROUP PERFORMANCE

An important decision a leader must make is when to assign tasks to individuals and when to assign tasks to groups or committees. This decision should be based both on the type of task and the outcome desired. If the *quality* of the task is most important, it should be assigned to a group or committee. Research has shown that groups generally produce higher quality results than do individuals (Kanekar, 1987; Lorge, Fox, Davitz, & Brenner, 1958). Group superiority in performance probably is due to the fact that a group encourages its members to work on a task more seriously, provides emotional support, and provides a broader knowledge base (Maier, 1976).

If the task involves *creating* ideas, individuals should be asked to independently create ideas and then meet as a group. Although **brainstorming** is a commonly used technique, it is not an effective one. In brainstorming, group members are encouraged to say aloud any and all ideas that come to mind and are not allowed to comment on the ideas until all have been given.

When research compares a brainstorming group's creativity with that of a single individual, the brainstorming group will almost always be more creative. However, when comparing the number and quality of ideas created by individual group members to the quality and number of ideas created jointly by the group in a brainstorming session, ideas of the individuals are more creative than the group (Diehl & Stroebe, 1987; Dunnette, Campbell, & Jaastad, 1963; Lamm & Trommsdorff, 1973).

If the task involves *taking chances* or *being risky,* then the task should be assigned to a group or committee. Although showing somewhat mixed results, research has generally shown that groups make more decisions that require risk than do individuals (Clark, 1971; Johnson & Andrews, 1971). This increased riskiness is thought in part to be due to group polarization, the tendency for group members to shift their beliefs to a more extreme version of what they already believe individually (Greenberg & Baron, 1995). In a particularly interesting piece of research, Cromwell, Marks, Olson, and Avary (1991) found that burglars committed more crimes when working as part of a group than when working alone.

An example of increased group riskiness comes from a brokerage firm that was interested in getting its brokers to make riskier but higher yielding investments. A consulting firm was asked to develop a way to select such brokers. Using its knowledge of group dynamics, the consulting firm told the brokerage company that it could obtain better results by having its brokers make investment decisions in groups rather than individually. Implementing this suggestion, the company later reported that its brokers were indeed making riskier investments.

# GROUP CONFLICT

As discussed early in this chapter, there are many reasons for joining groups and many factors that influence group performance. When individuals work together in groups, however, there is always potential for conflict.

Conflict can keep people from working together, lessen productivity, spread to other areas, and increase turnover. This does not mean that conflict is always bad, however. In fact, moderate conflict often produces higher group performance than either low or high levels of conflict (Brown, 1983). The energy resulting from moderate levels of conflict can stimulate new ideas and increase friendly competition (Litterer, 1966). Furthermore, moderate conflict can reduce the risk of much larger conflicts.

## TYPES OF CONFLICT

### Interpersonal Conflict

Within an organization, employees can be in conflict with one another over many things. Two employees competing for a promotion, a new desk, or the opportunity to talk with the boss are all examples of interpersonal conflict. Although interpersonal conflict is usually the result of the factors that will soon be discussed, it can also result from an individual's play for power or need for conflict (Berne, 1964).

When a person is in conflict with another, he can usually respond with one of five styles (Thomas, 1970). With the **avoiding style,** he chooses to ignore the conflict and hopes that the conflict will resolve itself. When conflicts are minor and infrequent, this style may be fine, but obviously it is not the best way to handle every type of conflict.

When a person is so intent on settling a conflict that he gives in and risks hurting himself, he has adopted the **accommodating style.** People who use this style when the stakes are high are usually viewed as cooperative but weak. I observed an example of this style at a self-serve gas station. Two drivers parked their cars next to the same pump at roughly the same time. Both drivers got out of their cars and simultaneously reached for the only pump. Obviously, one person had to give in to avoid conflict and would have to wait five minutes longer than the other. Yet one driver quickly told the other to "go ahead." Why did this person so quickly accede to the other? Probably because he has an accommodating reaction to potential conflict, and, in this case, the stakes were low.

A person with a **forcing style** handles conflict in a win-lose fashion and does what it takes to win with little regard for the other person. This style can be effective in winning, but it also can damage relations so badly that other conflicts will result.

An individual with a **collaborative style** wants to win but also wants to see the other person win. These people seek win-win solutions — that is, ways in which both sides get what they want. This style is probably the best to use whenever possible (Burke, 1970).

The final strategy is the **compromising style.** The user of this style adopts give-and-take tactics that allow each side to get some of what it wants but not everything it wants. A person's method of dealing with conflict at work can be measured by the Rahim organizational conflict inventory II (Rahim & Magner, 1995). The inventory places an individual into one of five styles similar to those just mentioned.

### Individual–Group Conflict

Conflict can also occur between an individual and a group just as easily as between two individuals. **Individual–group conflict** usually occurs when the individual's needs are different from the group's needs, goals, or norms. For example, a Marine might want more independence than the Corps will give him, a basketball player might want to shoot when the team needs him to rebound missed shots, a faculty member might be more interested in teaching when his university wants him to publish, and a store employee might be more interested in customer relations when the store wants him to concentrate on sales.

### Group–Group Conflict

The third type of conflict occurs between two or more groups. In academia, such **group–group conflict** occurs annually as departments fight for budget allocations and space. In industry, company divisions often conflict for the same reasons. A good example of group–group conflict occurred between two branches of the same bank located in the same town. The branches not only competed with other banks for customers, but also with each other. To make matters worse, the two branches were to be consolidated, so their staffs were involved in even more conflict as they tried to establish who would be in charge of the new and unified branch.

## CAUSES OF CONFLICT

### Competition for Resources

In the marketplace, when customer demand exceeds product supply, prices increase. Similarly, in groups, when demand for a resource exceeds its supply, conflict occurs. This often occurs in organizations, especially when there is not enough money, space, personnel, or equipment to satisfy the needs of every person or every group (Smith & Mackie, 1995).

A good example of this cause of conflict, **competition for resources,** occurs annually when Congress decides on the nation's budget. With only limited tax revenues and many worthy programs, tough choices must be made. But often instead of working together to solve the country's problems, our representatives come into conflict over whose favorite programs will be funded.

Another example of this competition occurs in colleges and universities across the country. There are probably few universities where parking and office spaces are not a problem. Faculty and students argue about who gets the parking places, and once that argument is settled, seniors and juniors argue over what is left.

I once belonged to an organization that initially had no conflict over resources because there were none to fight over. There were no extra offices, no equipment, and no supplies. Organization members even had to supply their own paper! After several years, however, the organization received a large amount of money and a new building with plenty of space. But as expected, conflict increased. Everyone wanted more space, their own computers, and so on. What had once been a very cohesive group was now one characterized by conflict because of competition for new resources.

### Task Interdependence

Another cause of conflict, **task interdependence,** comes when the performance of some group members depends on the performance of other group members (Pfeffer & Salancik, 1978). For example, a group is assigned to present a research report. The person who is assigned to type the report cannot do his job unless he can read what others have written, the person assigned to write the conclusion cannot do so until others have written their sections, and no member of the group is finished until every member has completed his or her assignment.

Conflict caused by task interdependence is especially likely when two groups who rely on each other have conflicting goals. For example, the production department in a factory wants to turn out a high volume of goods, while the quality control department wants the goods to be of high quality. Neither department can do its job without the help of the other, and yet a production department with high quality goals probably will have lower quality standards than those desired by quality control. By insisting on high quality, the quality control department is forcing the production department to slow down. When this happens, conflict is likely to occur.

### Jurisdictional Ambiguity

A third cause of conflict, **jurisdictional ambiguity,** is found when geographical boundaries or lines of authority are unclear. When lines of authority are not clear, conflict is most likely to result when new situations and relationships develop (Deutsch, 1973). A good example was seen in an organization that was changing from typewriters to computers that could use word-processing software. Before the change, the head of the secretarial department was in charge of selecting and purchasing all the secretarial equipment and the head of the data-processing department was responsible for selecting and purchasing all of the organization's computer equipment. Conflict developed when the new machines being used by the secretaries were considered computer equipment and thus came under the purview of the data-processing department. The two department heads waged a "turf battle" to determine who would have authority for the word-processing equipment.

On an international level, jurisdictional ambiguity is a cause for many wars and conflicts. For example, in the early 1990s Iraq invaded Kuwait under the pretense that Kuwait actually belonged to Iraq, and in the 1980s, England and Argentina fought over who had the right to the Falkland Islands.

### Communication Barriers

**Communication barriers** are the fourth cause of conflict. The barriers to interpersonal communication can be *physical,* such as separate locations on different floors or in different buildings; *cultural,* such as different languages or different customs; or *psychological,* such as different styles or personalities. An in-depth discussion of the communication process can be found in Chapter 11.

### Personality

A fifth cause of conflict are the **personalities** of people involved in conflict. Such conflict is often the result of two incompatible personalities who must work together. For example, a person who is very quality oriented will probably have conflicts with a person who is very quantity oriented. Likewise, a "big picture" person is likely to have conflicts with a "nuts and bolts" person.

Though it is probably true that most of the conflict that can be attributed to personality is the result of incompatible personalities, it is also very true that certain people are generally more difficult to work with than others. For example, research has revealed that people who are dogmatic and authoritarian and who have low self-esteem are involved in conflict more often than open-minded people who feel good about themselves.

Though there has been little research investigating "difficult people" who are most likely to cause conflict, a fair amount has been written about the topic in the popular press. For example, Bernstein and Rozen (1992) describe in great detail three types of *Neanderthals at Work*—rebels, believers, and competitors—and how conflict with each can be managed.

The most commonly referred to classification of difficult people was developed by Bramson (1981) and enhanced by Brinkman and Kirschner (1994). Brinkman and Kirschner (1994) postulate that abnormally high needs for control, perfection, approval, or attention form the basis for the difficult personality.

People with high needs for control are obsessed with completing a task and take great pride in getting a job done quickly. The *Tank* gets things done quickly by giving orders, being pushy, yelling, and at times being too aggressive. The *Sniper* controls people by using sarcasm, embarrassment, and humiliation. The *Know-It-All* controls others by dominating conversations, not listening to others' ideas, and rejecting arguments counter to his position.

People with high needs for perfection are obsessed with completing a task correctly. They seldom seem satisfied with anyone or any idea. *Whiners* constantly complain about the situation but never try to change it. The *No Person* believes that nothing will ever work and thus disagrees with every suggestion or idea. The *Nothing Person* responds to difficult situations by doing and saying nothing; they simply give up or retreat.

People with high needs for approval are obsessed with being liked. Their behavior is often centered on gaining approval rather than completing a task correctly or quickly. The *Yes Person* agrees to everything and as a result, often agrees to do so much that he cannot keep his commitments. The *Yes Person* seldom provides others feedback because he is afraid of someone getting mad at him. The *Maybe Person* avoids conflicts by never taking a stand on any issue. He delays making decisions, seldom offers opinions, and seldom commits to any course of action.

People with high needs for attention are obsessed with being appreciated. They behave in a manner that will get them noticed. When he doesn't feel appreciated, the *Grenade* throws a tantrum; he yells, swears, rants, and raves. The *Friendly Sniper* gets attention by poking fun at others. Unlike the *Sniper*, the *Friendly Sniper's* aim is to get attention rather than control. The *Think-They-Know-It-All* exaggerates, lies, and gives unwanted advice to gain attention.

Do you recognize any of these people? A summary of how to deal with each type of difficult person can be found in Table 10.3.

## REACTIONS TO CONFLICT

When conflict does occur, people respond in several common ways (Blake, Shepard, & Mouton, 1964). While some are better responses than others, each of the following is appropriate in certain situations: withdrawal, winning at all costs, persuasion, smoothing and conciliation, negotiation and bargaining, cooperative problem solving, and third-party intervention.

### Withdrawal

When conflict occurs, **withdrawal** from the situation is one of the easiest ways to handle it. A person can leave a difficult marriage by divorce, an employee can avoid a work conflict by quitting the organization, or a manager can avoid a turf battle by letting another manager win. Even though withdrawal can make one feel better, often it only postpones conflict rather than prevents it.

### Winning at All Costs

A second reaction to conflict is adopting what has been called a *win-lose* mentality in which the goal is to win a conflict and cause another person to lose (Johnson & Johnson, 1975). This strategy of **winning at all costs** occurs especially when a person regards his side as correct; the other person is regarded as the enemy whose side is incorrect.

This reaction often occurs when each side needs a victory to gain or retain status. Union-management conflicts provide good examples of this need for status. For a union to survive, its members must perceive it as being useful. Thus, during contract negotiations, union leadership must force management to "give in," or it runs the risk of losing status with its membership.

But the problem with putting status on the line is that it makes backing down to resolve a conflict very difficult. As a conflict escalates, each side "digs in" and becomes less willing to compromise. Unless one side has the resources to clearly win, the win-at-all-costs reaction is likely to prolong conflict. Thus, this strategy is only appropriate if the position holder is actually correct and if winning the conflict is more important than the probable damage to future relationships.

### Persuasion

It is possible to resolve conflict without taking a win-at-all-costs strategy. If one side in a conflict is convinced that it is right, it can seek to "win" by solving the conflict through techniques of **persuasion.** This can be done by providing the other side with factual evidence on a position's correctness,

**Table 10.3** Types of difficult people

| Type | Need | Obsession | Description | Best Way to Handle |
|------|------|-----------|-------------|--------------------|
| Tank | Control | Task Completion | Pushes, yells, gives orders, intimidates | Don't counterattack or offer excuses, hold your ground. |
| Sniper | Control | Task Completion | Uses sarcasm, criticizes, humiliates others | Call them on their sarcasm and have them explain what was really behind their comment. |
| Know-It-All | Control | Task Completion | Dominates conversations, doesn't listen | Acknowledge their knowledge, make your statements appear as if they are in agreement. |
| Whiner | Perfection | Task Quality | Constantly complains | Focus their complaints on specifics and solutions. |
| No Person | Perfection | Task Quality | Disagrees with everything | Don't rush them or argue; acknowledge their good intentions. |
| Nothing Person | Perfection | Task Quality | Doesn't do anything | Be patient and ask them open-ended questions. |
| Yes Person | Approval | Being Liked | Agrees to everything | Talk honestly and let the person know it is safe to disagree with you. |
| Maybe Person | Approval | Being Liked | Won't commit or make a decision | Help them learn a decision-making system, and then reassure about the decisions they make. |
| Grenade | Attention | Being Appreciated | Throws tantrums | Don't show anger, acknowledge their complaint, and give them a chance to cool down. |
| Friendly Sniper | Attention | Being Appreciated | Uses jokes to pick on people | Give them attention when they are not making fun of you. |
| Think-They-Know-It-All | Attention | Being Appreciated | Exaggerates, lies, gives advice | Give them attention and ask them for specifics; don't embarrass them. |

discrediting the opponent's position, and pointing out how the proposal will benefit the other side.

### Smoothing and Conciliation

An effective way to end conflict, or to at least limit its damage, is by using tactics of **smoothing and conciliation.** These tactics involve expressing a desire for cooperation, offering compliments, avoiding negative interaction, emphasizing the similarities of two groups, and pointing out common philosophies.

Osgood (1966) believes that one key to resolving conflict is to reduce tension and increase trust between two parties. This can be accomplished by stating an intention to reduce tension, publicly announcing what steps will be taken to reduce tension, inviting the other side also to take action to reduce tension, and making sure that each initiative offered is unambiguous. By taking these steps early on, minor conflict can be resolved quickly and serious conflict can be resolved through negotiation.

### Negotiation and Bargaining

Most conflicts are resolved through some form of compromise so that a solution benefits both sides (Forsyth, 1990; Seitz & Modica, 1980). Thus, a good way to handle conflict is by **negotiation and bargaining.** That is, the most important points are negotiated and less important points are given up. This process usually begins with each side making an offer that asks for much more than it really wants. For example, union leaders might demand $10 an hour while management offers $5 an hour. Each side understands what the other is doing, so the union might lower its demand to $9 and management might raise its offer to $6. This process continues until an acceptable compromise has been reached.

An *acceptable compromise* is one that will fall within the settlement range for both sides (Schatzki, 1981). According to Schatzki, a settlement range is between the **least acceptable result (LAR)** and the **maximum supportable position (MSP)** for each side. The LAR is the lowest settlement that a person is willing to accept; it must be realistic and satisfy the person's actual needs. The MSP is the best possible settlement that a person can ask for and still reasonably support with facts and logic. A short-order cook's proposal for $30 an hour would not be reasonably supportable and thus would not be a proper MSP.

As shown in Figure 10.2, negotiations usually begin with each side offering its MSP as an opening bid. The actual negotiating territory is the area between both sides' LARs. Each side then bargains for a settlement closest to its own MSP and the other's LAR. The final settlement will be a function of the skill of each negotiator as well as time pressures. Such pressures may be exerted by customers who cannot wait for a settlement or union members who cannot financially afford prolonged negotiations.

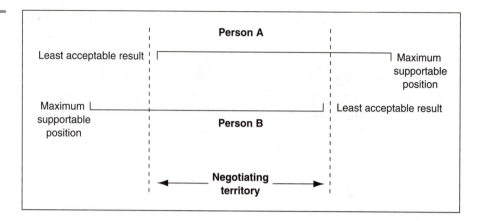

**Figure 10.2**
Negotiating territory and conflict resolution

Seitz and Modica (1980) have suggested four indicators that tell when negotiations are coming to an end so that each side can prepare its final offer:

1. The number of counter-arguments is reduced.
2. The positions of the two sides appear closer together.
3. The other side talks about final arrangements.
4. The other side appears willing to begin putting things in writing.

Although this conflict-resolution strategy appears to be the best approach to take, it often is not. Sometimes, compromise results in a bad solution. For example, if Congress wants to include $100 million in the federal budget to construct a new nuclear-power plant and the president wants to budget only $50 million, then the two are likely to agree on a median figure such as $75 million. But if the project cannot be completed for less than $100 million, then the compromise may waste millions of dollars that could be spent elsewhere.

### Cooperative Problem Solving

Another conflict-resolution strategy is for two sides to jointly arrive at a solution. A good example of **cooperative problem solving** is when the president of an organization forms a task force or committee with representatives from all of the departments or divisions that will be affected by the solution. Together these representatives work to define the problem, identify possible solutions, and arrive at the best solution.

### Third-Party Intervention

If conflict cannot be resolved by the parties involved, it is often a good idea to bring in outside help—that is, ask for **third-party intervention.** This outside help usually is provided through arbitration or mediation.

**Deborah K. Hedrick, EdD,
LPC, NCC, SPHR
Employee Relations
Director
Carilion Health System**

I work for the second largest health-care system in Virginia. We have over 8,000 employees in the system. The System has 12 hospitals and over 15 health-care related businesses. Most of the hospitals and businesses are located in southwest Virginia.

My title, employee relations director, only describes a portion of my responsibilities. Human resources generalist, advocate, and counselor are probably more accurate descriptions of the way I function. Just as there is a string of letters after my name, I utilize all of my skills, education, and professional experiences to provide a variety of services to my company.

I knew when I joined the company five years ago that these would be interesting times as the corporate structure was new and we were embarking upon new territory in many ways. To be a part of a team developing a corporate human resources presence is an exciting endeavor and a great learning experience. I also realized after a short time here that there were many views of what my job was or might be. I must admit that due to my love of variety and change I have encouraged the evolution of my job and have avoided having it defined in narrow terms.

I came into human resources through the back door. I gained most of my HR knowledge on the job, but utilized my education and other work experiences as transferable skills.

As employee relations director for the company, I have corporate responsibility for development, communications, and maintenance of policies, such as our problem-solving process (grievance procedure) and corrective-action (disciplinary action) procedures. Some of my major projects have been the development and dissemination of human resources policies and procedures, an HR policy and procedures manual, and an employee handbook. I also have been responsible for employee satisfaction surveys and the goal-setting processes that result from these activities. Because of my education and counseling experience, I get a lot of requests from managers and employees throughout the system for conflict resolution, team building, management development, training on policies, and consultation and training on supervision issues and techniques. From the corporate perspective, when I deal with conflict it may be between affiliates or departments within affiliates over policies and procedures.

One of my other corporate hats is as human resource liaison or consultant for the outlying hospitals. Calls can vary from someone wanting to discuss a termination or investigate a harassment complaint to a managed affiliate wanting my input on their employee handbook. This role has recently resulted in my being appointed interim human resources director for our Psychiatric Hospital. Yes, I currently have two 60-hour-a-week jobs in the company.

In our Roanoke-based non-hospital affiliates, which have over 1400 employees, I provide operational assistance in conflict resolution and policy interpretation. I sometimes function as a mediator for employees and managers depending upon the issue at hand. Conflict can be between employees or between employees and management. Occasionally, a whole work unit will be in conflict and ask for assistance. The simplest and most typical calls I get are over interpretations of policies from both managers and employees. Other more difficult issues I deal with are those where there have been allegations of discrimination or sexual or other forms of harassment. In all cases listening and analytical skills are needed to determine what the "real" issues are and to facilitate those involved in developing acceptable solutions.

*(continued)*

While life gets hectic every now and then, I can honestly say that working in human resources has been one of the most rewarding careers I have had. As a career counselor, I always felt that people should have a passion for their work. After all, we spend a great deal of time at work. Being in human resources gives me the opportunity to help others not only find joy in their jobs, but to move beyond that in providing employees with an environment of respect and equity.

**Arbitration**   With **arbitration,** a neutral third party listens to both sides' arguments and then makes a decision. Within an organization, this neutral party is often the manager of the two employees in conflict (Katz & Kahn, 1978). Arbitration decisions can be either *binding* or *nonbinding.* If the decision is binding, the two sides have agreed to abide by the arbitrator's decision regardless of how displeased one or both sides may be with that decision. If the decision is nonbinding, then one or both sides can reject an unfavorable decision. Even though arbitration can end conflicts quickly, usually neither side is as satisfied with the outcome as they would be had they settled the conflict themselves (Stagner & Rosen, 1965).

Some research even suggests performance may drop (Sommers, 1983) and turnover increase (Bretz & Thomas, 1992) as a result of an arbitrator's decision. As you might imagine, an individual's performance is most likely to drop after losing and most likely to increase after winning an arbitration hearing (Hauenstein & Lord, 1989).

**Mediation**   With **mediation,** a neutral third party is asked to work with both sides to reach a mutually agreeable solution to the conflict. The job of a mediator usually is not to make a decision for the groups, but rather to facilitate the solution process. Mediators are most useful when two parties do not like one another (Kressel & Pruitt, 1985), and they provide the best results when both sides consider them to be competent and trustworthy (Rubin & Brown, 1975).

## CHAPTER SUMMARY

Chapter 10 has provided an in-depth discussion of both group dynamics and group conflict. Groups were defined as consisting of multiple members who perceive themselves as a unit and who share a common goal or goals.

We also discussed the many reasons why people join groups. These reasons include a need for affiliation, a need to identify with success, a need for emotional support, a need for assistance, common goals, physical proximity, and assignment. Groups can be successful in attracting members only if they satisfy important needs.

Not all groups are successful in terms of survival and performance. Some of the factors that influence a group's success include its level of cohesiveness, the composition of its membership, the stability of the membership, and the group's size, status, and communication structure. We saw, for example, how being in the presence of others in a group can increase performance through social facilitation or decrease performance through both social inhibition, social loafing, and groupthink.

Conflict can occur when people work in groups. Such conflict can occur between two people, between a person and a group, or between two groups. Conflict usually results from factors such as competition for resources, task interdependence, jurisdictional ambiguity, communication barriers, and personality.

When conflict occurs, people or groups can react in several ways. They can ignore the conflict through withdrawal, try to win at all costs, try to persuade the other side to resolve the conflict in their favor, use smoothing and conciliation to end the conflict, bargain for an agreement, or ask for third-party help.

# GLOSSARY

**Accommodating style**   The conflict style of a person who tends to respond to conflict by giving in to the other person.

**Additive tasks**   Tasks for which the group's performance is equal to the sum of the performances of each group member.

**Affiliation**   The need to be with other people.

**Arbitration**   A method of resolving conflicts in which a neutral third party is asked to choose which side is correct.

**Audience effects**   The effect on behavior when one or more people passively watch the behavior of another person.

**Avoiding style**   The conflict style of a person who reacts to conflict by pretending that it does not exist.

**Brainstorming**   A technique in which ideas are generated by people in a group setting.

**Coaction**   The effect on behavior when two or more people are performing the same task in the presence of each other.

**Collaborative style**   The conflict style of a person who wants a conflict resolved in such a way that both sides get what they want.

**Common goal**   An aim or purpose shared by members of a group.

**Communication barriers**   Physical, cultural, and psychological obstacles that interfere with successful communication and create a source of conflict.

**Communication structure**   The manner in which members of a group communicate with one another.

**Comparison**   The effect when an individual working on a task compares his performance with the performance of another person performing the same task.

**Competition for resources** A cause of conflict that occurs when the demand for resources is greater than the resources available.

**Compromising style** A style of resolving conflicts in which an individual allows each side to get some of what it wants.

**Conjunctive tasks** Tasks for which the group's performance is dependent on the performance of the least effective group member.

**Cooperative problem solving** A method of resolving conflict in which two sides get together to discuss a problem and arrive at a solution.

**Corresponding effects** An event that affects one member of a group will affect the other group members.

**Devil's advocate** A group member who intentionally provides an opposing opinion to that expressed by the leader or the majority of the group.

**Disjunctive tasks** Tasks for which the performance of a group is based on the performance of its most talented member.

**Distracting** The idea that social inhibition occurs because the presence of others provides a distraction that interferes with concentration.

**Evaluation apprehension** The idea that a person performing a task becomes aroused because he or she is concerned that others are evaluating his or her performance.

**Forcing style** The conflict style of a person who responds to conflict by always trying to win.

**Group cohesiveness** The extent to which members of a group like and trust one another.

**Group–group conflict** Conflict between two or more groups.

**Group size** The number of members in a group.

**Group status** The esteem in which the group is held by people not in the group.

**Groupthink** A state of mind in which a group is so concerned about group cohesiveness that it ignores important information.

**Heterogeneous groups** Groups whose members share few similarities.

**Homogeneous groups** Groups whose members share the same characteristics.

**Identification** The need to associate ourselves with the image associated with other people, groups, or objects.

**Individual dominance** When one member of a group dominates the group.

**Individual–group conflict** Conflict between an individual and the other members of a group.

**Interpersonal conflict** Conflict between two people.

**Isolation** The degree of physical distance of a group from other groups.

**Jurisdictional ambiguity** Conflict caused by a disagreement about geographical territory or lines of authority.

**Least acceptable result (LAR)** The lowest settlement that a person is willing to accept in a negotiated agreement.

**Maximum supportable position (MSP)** The highest possible settlement that a person could reasonably ask for and still maintain credibility in negotiating an agreement.

**Mediation** A method of resolving conflict in which a neutral third party is asked to help the two sides reach an agreement.

**Mere presence**   The theory that states that the mere presence of others naturally produces arousal and thus may affect performance.

**Negotiation and bargaining**   A method of resolving conflict in which two sides use verbal skill and strategy to reach an agreement.

**Outside pressure**   The amount of psychological pressure placed on a group by people who are not members of the group.

**Personality**   Relatively stable traits possessed by an individual.

**Persuasion**   A method of resolving conflict in which one side uses facts to convince the other side that the first side's position is correct.

**Slightly heterogeneous groups**   Groups in which a few group members have different characteristics from the rest of the group.

**Smoothing and conciliation**   Resolving a conflict by cooperating with and praising the opponent.

**Social facilitation**   The positive effects that occur when a person performs a task in the presence of others.

**Social impact theory**   A theory that states that the addition of a group member has the greatest effect on group behavior when the size of the group is small.

**Social inhibition**   The negative effects that occur when a person performs a task in the presence of others.

**Social loafing**   The fact that individuals in a group often exert less individual effort than they would if they were not in a group.

**Stability**   The extent to which the membership of a group remains consistent over time.

**Task interdependence**   A potential source of conflict that arises when the completion of a task by one person affects the completion of a task by another person.

**Third-party intervention**   When a neutral party is asked to help resolve a conflict.

**Winning at all costs**   An approach to handling conflict in which one side seeks to win regardless of the damage to the other side.

**Withdrawal**   An approach to handling conflict in which one of the parties removes himself or herself from the situation in order to avoid the conflict.

# 11
# COMMUNICATION

Picture the following situations:

- A male employee cannot understand why he was reprimanded for referring to female employees as the "girls in the office."

- A supervisor has tried everything to communicate with her employees but they still seem lost.

- Customers don't like Sheila because she appears cold and aloof though she is actually a very caring person.

- A supervisor is frustrated because her employees never read the notices posted on the bulletin board in the break room.

All four situations represent common communication problems. This chapter looks at ways in which employees communicate within an organization, problems in the communication process, and ways in which communication can be improved. We begin our discussion by examining the types of communication that occur within an organization.

# TYPES OF ORGANIZATIONAL COMMUNICATION

### UPWARD COMMUNICATION

**Upward communication** is that of subordinate messages to superiors or employees communicating to managers. Of course, in ideal upward communication employees speak directly to management in an "open door" policy environment. Such a policy, however, is often not practical for several reasons. Perhaps the most important reason involves the potential volume of communication if every employee communicated with a specific manager. Direct upward communication also may not be workable because employees often feel threatened by managers and may not be willing to openly communicate bad news or complaints. This is especially true of employees who have strong aspirations for promotion (Read, 1962) and for organizations that have distinct status levels (Hage, 1974).

To minimize the number of different people communicating with the top executive, many organizations utilize **serial communication.** With serial communication, the message is relayed from an employee to her supervisor, who relays it to her supervisor, who relays it to her supervisor, and so on until the message reaches the top. Although this type of upward communication relieves the top executive of excessive demands, it suffers several serious drawbacks.

The first is that the message's content and tone change as it moves from person to person. As will be discussed later in the chapter, messages are seldom received the way they were sent—especially if the message is being passed verbally from person to person.

The second drawback to serial communication is that bad news and complaints are seldom relayed. Rosen and Tesser (1970) have labeled this the **MUM (minimize unpleasant messages) effect.** The MUM effect negatively affects the organization by keeping important information from reaching the upper levels. But for an employee, the MUM effect is an excellent survival strategy—no one wants to be the bearer of bad news.

Serial communication's third drawback, especially with informal communication channels, is that it is less effective the farther away two people are from one another. That is, a supervisor is more likely to pass along a message to another supervisor if the two are in close physical **proximity.** It is unlikely, therefore, that an informal message originating with an employee at a plant in Atlanta will reach another employee at the corporate office in Phoenix. The importance of physical proximity cannot be overstated. In fact, a major source of power often comes from being physically near an executive. Seasoned executives have been known to place rising executives in distant offices to reduce their potential power. And going to lunch with those in power has long been recognized as a means of obtaining new information and increased power.

As one would imagine, proximity does not play a role when messages are communicated electronically using e-mail (Valacich, Paranka, George, &

Nunamaker, 1993). Thus, e-mail may reduce the power of proximity when communication is formal.

Because of these problems with serial communication, organizations use several other methods to facilitate upward communication. One method, the **attitude survey,** is usually conducted annually by an outside consultant who administers a questionnaire asking employees to rate their opinions on factors such as satisfaction with pay, working conditions, and supervisors. Employees are also given the opportunity to list complaints or suggestions that they want management to read. The consultant then tabulates the responses and reports the findings to management.

Although attitude surveys are commonly used, they are useful only if an organization takes the results seriously. If an organization finds that its employees are unhappy and does nothing to address the problem areas, the survey results will not be beneficial. Furthermore, an organization should share survey results with employees (Rosen, 1987).

If survey results are to be shared, then management must share *all* of them. While proposing a project to a local police department, I encountered a great deal of hostility from many of the senior officers. After a little probing, the officers revealed that several years earlier they had completed an attitude survey for the city. A few months later, the results were made public, and the city cited five main complaints by the officers and promised that action would be taken to solve these problems. The officers were happy until they realized that none of their complaints about pay and working conditions were included in the report—the city was ignoring them. The officers became so resentful and mistrustful of consultants and management that they vowed never again to participate in a project.

Another method for facilitating upward communication is the **suggestion box** or **complaint box.** Theoretically, these two boxes should be the same, but a box asking for suggestions is not as likely to get complaints as a box specifically labeled "complaints," and vice versa. The biggest advantage of these boxes is that they allow employees to immediately communicate their feelings. With attitude surveys, of course, employee thoughts are communicated only once or twice a year. In large organizations, to save money, surveys are sent to a random sample rather than to all employees.

For these boxes to be beneficial, management must respond to the suggestions and complaints in a timely manner. Management can respond to every suggestion or complaint by placing it on a bulletin board along with management's response. In this way, employees receive feedback about their ideas, which further encourages other employees to use the boxes to communicate.

Some organizations take employee suggestions quite seriously and reward employees who provide useful ideas. Hercules, Inc., for example, provides cash awards up to $10,000 for employees who suggest money-saving ideas, and Ingersoll-Rand gives plaques to employees who submit cost-saving ideas that are ultimately adopted by the company.

The use of a **liaison** or an **ombudsperson** is another method that can increase upward communication. Both are responsible for taking employee complaints and suggestions and personally working with management to find solutions. The advantage of this system is that the ombudsperson is neutral and works for a solution that is acceptable to both employees and management. Furthermore, the ombudsperson is typically supervised at the vice-presidential level, so she is not concerned about being fired if she steps on a few toes while looking for a solution.

As good as it is, the ombudsperson method is often not used because organizations do not want the expense of an employee who does not produce. To overcome this problem, Moore Tool Company in Springdale, Arkansas, started its "Red Shirt" program in which selected senior employees wear red shirts that identify them as informal ombudspeople. If an employee has a problem, she can seek help from a Red Shirt who has authority to help find a solution. This system not only opens communication channels, but it also provides job enrichment for an employee who works at an otherwise boring job.

In organizations that have their employees represented by unions, the job of the ombudsperson is typically handled by the **union steward.** But management-union relationships are often adversarial, so the union steward has a difficult time solving problems because she is not perceived by management or union members as being neutral.

## DOWNWARD COMMUNICATION

**Downward communication** is that of superior to subordinate or management to employees. Such communication can be accomplished in many ways. One of the most common methods, of course, is the memorandum or *memo*. Memos have the advantage of providing detailed information to a large number of people in a short period of time. With the widespread use of photocopy machines, however, employees (especially office workers) now receive so many memos that they often do not read them. In fact, the executive of a major company once stated that he never read a memo when it first came to him. Instead, he believed that if the message were really important, the person would talk to him about it later. Although such an attitude probably is not a good one, it does underscore the excessive use of memos and their diminishing effectiveness in communication.

Another method of downward communication is the *telephone call*. In the past, this method was appropriate only when the message was short and when only a few people needed to receive the communication. But with the advent of conference calls, the number of people who can be reached by this method has certainly increased. Furthermore, telephone calls were previously appropriate only for messages that did not involve detail. But the facsimile, or fax, machine now allows detailed sketches or numbers to be sent to people in different locations in a matter of seconds, and these then can be discussed by telephone. It also has been shown that phone calls, even when long distance, can be less expensive than most memos or letters (Fulger, 1977).

One limitation of phone calls, of course, is that nonverbal cues are not available. Thus, a major portion of the message is often not communicated. For important calls, however, video-enhanced teleconferencing can now be used. In fact, many organizations save interview expenses by having job applicants across the company participate in such teleconferences, which allow both parties to see one another.

In the 1990s many memos and telephone calls have been replaced with **e-mail** and **voice mail** (sophisticated phone answering systems). Voice mail and e-mail are primarily used to exchange general information, ask questions, and exchange *timely* information (Rice, 1993). The ability to easily document the sending and receiving of e-mail gives it an advantage over voice mail in many situations (Reinsch & Beswick, 1990). The advantages to e-mail and voice mail include a reduction in the use and filing of paper and time saved by avoiding "small talk" when communicating a short message by phone.

On the downside, voice mail often results in "phone tag," and both e-mail and voice mail reduce opportunities for personal contact. In fact, Carillon Health Care Systems recently got rid of its voice mail system because employees and customers were tired of getting answering machines and wanted to talk to "a real person."

The **bulletin board** is yet another method of downward communication. The next time you visit a company, look around for bulletin boards. You will see them everywhere. Their main use, however, is to communicate nonwork-related opportunities such as scholarships, optional meetings, and items for sale. Important information is seldom seen because the bulletin board is not the appropriate place to post a change of policy or procedure. Still, bulletin boards have the advantage of low cost and wide exposure to both employees and visitors. This is especially true if the boards are placed in high traffic areas such as outside restrooms and cafeterias or near time clocks. Electronic bulletin boards allow the display of even more current information.

Instead of the bulletin board, the **company manual** is the place for posting important changes in policy or procedure. This manual contains all the rules under which employees must operate. Most manuals are written in highly technical language, although they should be written in a less technical style to encourage employees to read them as well as to make them easier to understand. Furthermore, the contents of these manuals are considered binding contracts by courts, so the manuals must be updated each time a policy changes. This usually is done by sending updated pages to employees so that they can replace older material with newer. To make this process easier, many organizations punch binder holes in the pages to facilitate their replacement.

The typical company manual is hundreds of pages long, so it is not surprising that many employees do not want to read them. To reduce length problems, most organizations have two types of company manuals. The first, called a *policy manual,* is very specific and lengthy, containing all of the rules and policies under which the organization operates. The second type, usually known as the *employee handbook,* is much shorter and contains only the most essential policies and rules as well as general summaries of less important rules.

An example that supports the need for two manuals involved security guards at a manufacturing plant. The security guards were paid minimum wage and had an average tenure of about three months before quitting. The company became concerned for two reasons. First, three months was not enough time for the guards to learn all of the policies in the 300-page emergency procedures manual. Second, the manual was written by an engineer, and none of the security guards was able to understand the writing. The organization thus had I/O graduate student interns develop a short, easy-to-read procedure manual that could be read and understood in a day or two. Tips for effective manual writing as developed by Reddout (1987) are shown in Table 11.1

Management must communicate with employees to train and motivate them effectively. Thus, the effectiveness of company policy and the attainment of company goals are to a large extent determined by the way in which the policy and goals are communicated and the extent to which the organizational communication system meets each of the following four conditions (Neuner, Keeling, & Kallaus, 1972):

**Table 11.1** Tips for effective manual writing

| Avoid Using | Instead Use |
|---|---|
| *Abstract and general words:* | *Concrete and specific words:* |
| Office equipment | Typewriter |
| Vehicle | Truck |
| Several | Six |
| Writing implement | Pen |
| *Formal words:* | *Common words:* |
| Utilize | Use |
| Facilitate | Help |
| Optimal | Best |
| Remainder | Rest |
| Competencies | Skills |
| *Phrases:* | *Single words:* |
| Perform the calculation | Calculate |
| Until such time as | Until |
| For the reason that | Because |
| Should it prove to be true | If |
| For the purpose of | For |

Source: Adapted from "Manual Writing Made Easier," by D. J. Reddout, 1987, *Training and Development Journal, 41*(4), 68. Copyright 1987, American Society for Training and Development. Reprinted with permission.

1. Information must be easy to access.
2. Information must be current.
3. Information must be sent economically.
4. Information must be accurate.

## HORIZONTAL COMMUNICATION

The third direction of organizational communication is **horizontal communication.** As the name implies, this is communication among employees at the same level and can involve job-related information as well as informal information. Often, informal information is transmitted through the **grapevine,** a term that can be traced back to the Civil War when loosely hung telegraph wires resembled grapevines. The communication across these lines was often distorted. Because unofficial employee communication is also thought to be distorted, the term has become synonymous with an informal communication network (Davis, 1977). Grapevines are common because they provide employees with information, power, and entertainment (Laing, 1993).

Davis (1953) studied the grapevine and established the existence of four grapevine patterns: single strand, gossip, probability, and cluster. As Figure 11.1 shows, in the **single strand** grapevine, Jones passes a message

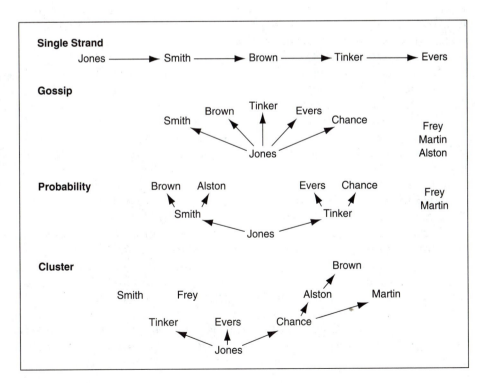

**Figure 11.1**
Grapevine patterns

to Smith who passes the message to Brown, and so on until the message is either received by everyone or someone "breaks the chain." This pattern is similar to the children's game of "telephone." In the **gossip** grapevine, Jones passes the message only to a select group of people. Notice that with this pattern, only one person passes the message along and not everyone has a chance to receive, or will receive, the message. In the **probability** grapevine, Jones tells the message to a few other employees and they in turn randomly pass the message along to other employees. In the **cluster grapevine**, Jones tells only a few select employees who in turn tell a few select others.

Research on the grapevine has supported several of Davis' (1953) findings. Sutton and Porter (1968) studied 79 employees in a state tax office and reached several interesting conclusions. They found that employees could be placed into one of three categories. **Isolates** were employees who received less than half of the information, **liaisons** were employees who both received most of the information and passed it to others, and **dead-enders** were those who heard most of the information but seldom passed it on to other employees.

Managers tended to be liaisons because they had heard 97% of the grapevine information and most of the time passed this information on. Nonmanagerial employees heard 56% of the grapevine information but seldom passed it on. Only 10% of nonmanagerial employees were liaisons; 57% were dead-enders and 33% were isolates.

Although most people consider the grapevine to be inaccurate, research has shown that information in the grapevine often contains a great deal of truth (Zaremba, 1988). Walton (1961) found that 82% of the information transmitted across the grapevine in one company was accurate. Such a statistic, however, can be misleading. Consider the following hypothetical example: A message travels through the grapevine that "the personnel director will fire 25 people on Monday morning at 9 o'clock." The truth, however, is that the personnel director will *hire* 25 people on Monday morning at 9 A.M. Thus, even though four out of five parts of the message, 80%, are correct, the grapevine message paints a picture quite different from reality.

Not to be confused with the grapevine, **rumor** is poorly substantiated information that is transmitted across the grapevine. Usually, rumor will occur when the available information is both interesting and ambiguous (Allport & Postman, 1947). Rumor and gossip are often ways in which employees can relieve stress (Mishra, 1990) and respond to perceived organizational wrongs in a nonaggressive way (Tucker, 1993).

Certainly not all horizontal communication is informal. Employees at the same level often exchange job-related information on such topics as customers and clients, the status of projects, and information necessary to complete a particular task. To increase the amount of job-related horizontal communication, many organizations have adopted the practice of self-managed work groups (Overman, 1994).

For example, at Columbia Gas Development in Houston, 12-person drilling teams were formed. The team approach greatly increased communication between geologists, engineers, and other staff members who were previously located in separate departments. As another example, the use of teams at Meridian Insurance in Indianapolis increased communication and efficiency so much that a 29-step process for handling paperwork was reduced to 4 steps.

## INTERPERSONAL COMMUNICATION

**Interpersonal communication** involves the exchange of a message across a communication channel from one person to another. As shown in Figure 11.2, the interpersonal communication process begins with a sender encoding and transmitting a message across a communication channel (memo, orally, nonverbally) and ends with another person (the receiver) receiving and decoding the message. Although this seems like a simple process, there are three main problem areas where things can go wrong and interfere with the message's accurate transmission or reception.

### PROBLEM AREA 1: INTENDED MESSAGE VERSUS MESSAGE SENT

For effective communication, the sender must know what she wants to say and how she wants to say it. Interpersonal communication problems can occur when the message a person sends is not the message she intended to say. There are three solutions to this problem: thinking about what you want to communicate, practicing what you want to communicate, and learning better communication skills.

#### *Thinking About What You Want to Communicate*

Often the reason we don't say what we mean is because we are not really sure what we want to say. For example, think of using the drive-through window at a fast-food restaurant. As soon as you stop, but before you have a chance to read the menu board, a voice booms, *Can I take your order?* You intelligently reply something such as, *uhhhhhhh, could you hang-on a*

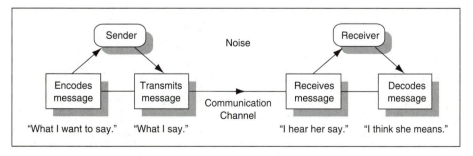

**Figure 11.2**
The interpersonal communication process

*minute,* and then quickly try to place an order as the pressure builds. As you drive off, you realize that you did not really order what you wanted.

Does this scenario sound familiar? If so, you are not alone. Foster and his colleagues (1988) found that many fast-food restaurant customers have so little time to think about their order that they make ordering mistakes. Foster et al. (1988) found that placing a menu sign before the ordering station gave customers more time to think about their orders, which decreased average ordering time from 28 seconds to 6 seconds and ordering errors from 29% to 4%.

As another example, think about calling a friend and unexpectedly getting an answering machine. Have you ever left a message in which the first few sentences sounded reasonably intelligent? Did the first sentence again begin with *uhhhhhhhhh*? Or, have you ever made a call expecting to get an answering machine and instead had an actual person answer the phone? These examples show the importance of thinking about what you want to communicate.

### Practice What You Want to Communicate

Even though you may know what you want to say, communication errors can occur if you do not actually say what you mean. Thus, when communication is important, it should be practiced. Just as consultants practice before giving a training talk and actors rehearse prior to a performance, you too need to practice what you want to say in important situations. Perhaps you can remember practicing how you were going to ask a person out on a date: changing the tone of your voice, altering your first line, or thinking of topics to discuss so that you would appear spontaneous.

### Learn Better Communication Skills

Even if you know what you want to say and how you want to say it, communication errors can still occur if you do not have the proper communication skills. It is essential to take courses in public speaking, writing, and interpersonal communication so that you will be better prepared to communicate effectively.

### PROBLEM AREA 2: MESSAGE SENT VERSUS MESSAGE RECEIVED

Even though an individual knows what she wants to say and says it exactly as she planned, as shown in Figure 11.3, there are many factors that affect how that message is received.

### The Actual Words Used

A particular word may mean one thing in one situation but something else in another. Take the word *fine* as an example. If I told you that you had *fine jewelry,* you would probably take the statement as a compliment. If the word

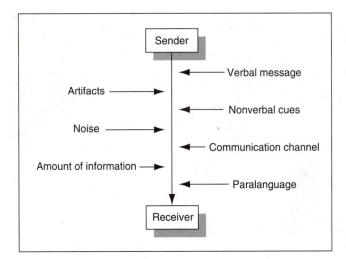

**Figure 11.3**
Factors affecting the message sent versus the message received

were used to describe the weather—*the weather here in Virginia is just fine*—it would still have a positive connotation. However, if a spouse asks, *How was the dinner I cooked?* or, *How did you like our evening of romance?*, an answer of *fine* will probably result in death.

A particular word may also mean one thing to one person and something different to another. For example, a 60-year-old man with a rural background may use the word *girl* as a synonym for *female*. He may not understand why the females at work get upset when he refers to them as the "girls in the office." When I conduct training sessions for police officers, we discuss how such words as *boy, son,* and *pretty little lady* can be emotionally charged and should thus be avoided.

Words or phrases that are vague also can cause problems. For example, you need a set of data by the end of the day, so you tell your assistant that you need the data immediately. At the end of the day, however, the data are not there. The next morning, the employee proudly brings you the data that she has compiled in "less than a day" and is confused about why you are angry. In this example, you encoded the message as, *I need it by five o'clock,* you transmitted the message as, *I need it immediately,* and the employee decoded it as, *She needs it tomorrow.*

If someone told you, "I won't be gone long," when would you expect them back? When I ask this question of my classes or seminar audiences, the answers usually range from ten minutes to three hours. Interestingly, at one seminar I conducted, a woman responded that her husband said that very phrase and came back four days later.

As the above examples demonstrate, it is important to be concrete in the words we use. Why then are we often vague in the way we communicate? One reason is that we want to avoid confrontations. If a husband tells his spouse that he will be gone for four hours, he may know that she will object. By being vague, he avoids the initial confrontation and hopes that she will

Males and females often have different communication styles.

not notice how long he has actually been gone—a common ploy but one that never seems to work.

Another reason for vagueness is that it gives us a chance to "test the water" and see what a person's initial reaction might be before we say what we really want. Asking someone out on a date is a perfect example. Instead of being direct and saying "Do you want to go out this Friday," we often say something such as, "So, what are you up to this weekend?" If the response is positive, we become a bit more bold.

Gender is another factor related to the use of words. As shown in Table 11.2, Deborah Tannen (1986; 1990) believes that men and women speak very different languages and have different communication styles. By understanding these differences, communication in the workplace as well as in the home can be drastically improved.

Based on our above discussion, communication can be improved by choosing our words carefully and asking, "How might the other person interpret what I am about to say." If I use the word *girl,* will anyone be upset? If so, what word could I use that is better?

### Communication Channel

Problems in communication can occur as a result of the **channel** through which the message is transmitted. Information can be communicated a variety of ways such as orally, nonverbally, through a second party, or through a written medium such as a letter or memo. The same message can be interpreted in different ways based on the channel that was used to communi-

**Table 11.2** Gender differences in communication

| Men | Women |
|---|---|
| Talk about events | Talk about daily life |
| Tell the main point | Provide details |
| Are more direct | Are more indirect |
| Use "uh-huh" to agree | Use "uh-huh" to listen |
| Are comfortable with silence | Are less comfortable with silence |
| Concentrate on the words spoken | Concentrate on meta-messages |
| Sidetrack unpleasant topics | Focus on unpleasant topics |

Adapted from (Tannen 1986, 1990)

cate it. For example, an employee being reprimanded will receive the message very differently if it were communicated in a memo rather than face-to-face. An employee who gives the "cold-shoulder" to another employee will receive a different response than if she had yelled at the employee or discussed the anger with her.

Another example of the channel's importance would be that of a supervisor criticizing an employee in front of other employees. The employee might be so embarrassed and angered that the criticism was made in front of others that she would not hear the message's content. Again, the transmission of a message through an inappropriate channel interferes with the message's meaning and accurate interpretation.

### Noise

The **noise** surrounding a transmission channel can also affect the way in which a message is received. Noise can be defined as any interference that affects proper reception of a message. An obvious example is *actual* noise, such as the sound of a subway interfering with conversation. Other examples are the appropriateness of the channel, the reputation of the person sending the message, and other information being received at the same time.

### Nonverbal Cues

Much of what we communicate is conveyed nonverbally. Our words often say one thing, while our actions say another. For example, a supervisor may tell an employee that she is interested in hearing her opinions, while at the same time she is frowning and looking out the window. The verbal message from the supervisor may be "I care," but the nonverbal message is "I'm bored." Which message will the employee pay attention to? Most likely, it will be the nonverbal, even though nonverbal cues often lead to incorrect impressions (Malandro & Barker, 1983). Nonverbal cues can be divided into five categories (Costley & Todd, 1987): body language, paralanguage, use of space, use of time, and artifacts.

**Body Language**   The ways in which we move and position our bodies — our *body language* — communicates much to other people. For example:

- When one's body faces another person, often this is interpreted as a sign of liking, whereas a person's body turned away from another is interpreted as a sign of dislike or disinterest (Clore, Wiggins, & Itkin, 1975).

- Making eye contact implies interest. In a casual conversation, increased eye contact is interpreted as a sign of liking, in a bar it might be a sign of flirting, while on a football field it may be interpreted as a sign of aggression. Lack of eye contact can mean many things including disinterest, discomfort, or embarrassment (Taylor, Peplau, & Sears, 1994). A person who makes eye contact while speaking but not while listening is often perceived as being powerful or dominant.

- Raising or lowering the head or the shoulders may indicate superiority or inferiority, respectively.

- Touching someone usually indicates liking, friendship, or nurturance (Brehm & Kassin, 1993). In fact, one study has shown that a waitress who touches her customers will receive a larger tip than one who does not touch (Crusco & Wetzel, 1984). Another study found that library clerks who briefly touched patrons as they were being handed books were rated by the patrons as being better employees than clerks who did not touch (Fisher, Rytting, & Heslin, 1976). Men initiate contact more often than females (Major, Schmidlin, & Williams, 1990).

Fleeting facial expressions and changes in voice pitch and eye contact can indicate that a person is lying (DePaulo, Stone, & Lassiter, 1985; Frick, 1985; Knapp, 1978). In fact, voice cues are more accurate than facial expressions when determining deception (DePaulo, Zuckerman, & Rosenthal, 1980). Thus, at times it might be advantageous to interview a job applicant or an employee by telephone rather than in person.

As one might expect, gender differences occur in the use of nonverbal cues. For example, Dolin and Booth-Butterfield (1993) found that females use nonverbal cues such as head nodding to show attention more often than do males. In social situations, females touch, smile, and make eye contact more than males (DePaulo, 1992).

Research has shown that body language can affect employee behavior. For example, Forbes and Jackson (1980) found that effective use of nonverbal cues resulted in a greater probability of being hired for a job. Similarly, Rasmussen (1984) found that the use of nonverbal cues during an interview will help if the applicant gives the correct answer to an interview question but will hurt the applicant if an incorrect answer is given.

Though body language can be a useful source of information, it is important to understand that the same nonverbal cue can mean different things in different situations and cultures. So, be careful, and try not to read too much into a particular nonverbal cue.

**Use of Space**  The way in which people make use of space can also provide nonverbal cues about their feelings and personalities. Dominant people or those who have authority are given more space by others and at the same time take space from others. For example, people stand farther away from such status figures as executives and police officers (and even college professors) and stand in an office doorway rather than directly enter such a person's office. These same status figures, however, often move closer as a show of power. Police officers are taught that moving in close is one method of intimidating a person.

On the other hand, status figures also increase space to establish differences between themselves and the people with whom they are dealing. A common form of this use of distance is for an executive to place a desk between herself and another person. An interesting story is told by a sports agent who was negotiating a player's contract with George Steinbrenner, owner of the New York Yankees baseball club. When the agent arrived at Steinbrenner's office, he noticed that Steinbrenner sat at one end of a long desk. At the other end was a small chair in which the agent was to sit. Recognizing the spatial arrangement to be a power play, the agent moved his chair next to Steinbrenner's. As the story goes, the Yankee owner was so rattled by this ploy that the agent was able to negotiate an excellent contract for his player client.

The following example also illustrates how the use of space can enhance a person's status by adding an image of importance. Recently, the psychology building at Radford University was renovated, and with efficient use of attic space, every faculty member was given an office. Students who visited during office hours had been accustomed to faculty members sharing offices. Many of these students commented on how important a psychology faculty member must be to receive his or her own office. (Of course, we never told them that we all had our own offices and that faculty members in other departments would also soon have their own.)

The way an office is furnished also communicates a lot about that person. As mentioned earlier, certain desk placements indicate openness and power; visitors and subordinates prefer not to sit before a desk that serves as a barrier (Davis, 1984). People whose offices are untidy are perceived as being busy, while people whose offices contain plants are perceived as caring and concerned.

Four major spatial distance zones have been recognized and defined (Hall, 1963): intimacy, personal distance, social distance, and public distance.

The **intimacy zone** extends from physical contact to 18 inches away from a person and is usually reserved for close relationships such as dates, spouses, and family. When this zone is entered by strangers in such situations as crowded elevators, we generally feel uncomfortable and nervous. The **personal distance zone** ranges from 18 inches to 4 feet away from a person and is the distance usually reserved for friends and acquaintances. The **social distance zone** is from 4 to 12 feet away and is the distance typically observed when dealing with businesspeople and strangers. Finally, the **public distance zone** ranges from 12 to 25 feet away and is characteristic of such large group interactions as lectures and seminars.

**Use of Time**   The way in which people make use of time is another element of nonverbal communication. If an employee is supposed to meet with a supervisor at 1 P.M. and the supervisor shows up at 1:10, the supervisor is communicating an attitude about the employee, the importance of the meeting, or both. Tardiness is more readily accepted from a higher-status person than from a lower-status person. Dean Smith, the great basketball coach at the University of North Carolina, suspends any player who is even a minute late for a practice because he believes that tardiness is a sign of arrogance and works against the team concept.

In a similar fashion, before a meeting a supervisor sets aside 30 minutes and tells others that she is not to be disturbed because she is in conference. A definitive message thus is conveyed, one that is likely to prevent constant interruptions by telephone calls or people stopping by to say hello because they saw an open door.

### Paralanguage

**Paralanguage** involves the way in which something is said and consists of variables such as tone, tempo, volume, number and duration of pauses, and rate of speech. A message that is spoken quickly will be perceived differently than one that is spoken slowly. In fact, research (Pearce & Conklin, 1971) has shown that people with fast speech rates are perceived as more intelligent than people with slow rates of speech. People who use many "uh-hums," "ers," and "ahs" are also considered less intelligent. Men with high-pitched voices are considered to be weak, while females with high-pitched voices are considered to be petite.

Simple changes in the tone used to communicate a message can change the entire meaning of the message. To demonstrate this point, consider the sentence, "I didn't say Bill stole your car." At first reading, it does not seem unusual, but what does it actually mean? As Table 11.3 shows, if we emphasize the first word, *I*, the implication is that *someone else* said, "Bill stole your car." But if we emphasize the word *Bill*, the meaning changes to "Someone else stole your car." And so on. Thus, a simple written message can be interpreted in seven different ways. As we can see, the message might have been better sent orally.

### Artifacts

A final element of nonverbal communication concerns the objects, or **artifacts,** a person wears or with which she surrounds herself. A person who wears bright and colorful clothes is perceived differently than a person who wears such conservative colors as white or gray. Similarly, the man-

**Table 11.3**   Inflection changes and meaning

| Inflected Sentences | Meaning |
| --- | --- |
| **I** did not say Bill stole your car. | **Someone else** said Bill stole your car. |
| I **did not** say Bill stole your car. | I **deny** I said Bill stole your car. |
| I did not **say** Bill stole your car. | I **implied** that Bill stole your car. |
| I did not say **Bill** stole your car. | **Someone else** stole your car. |
| I did not say Bill **stole** your car. | He **borrowed** your car. |
| I did not say Bill stole **your** car. | Bill stole **someone else's** car. |
| I did not say Bill stole your **car.** | Bill stole **something else** of yours. |

ager who places all of her awards on her office wall, the executive with a large and expensive chair, and the student who carries a briefcase rather than a book bag are all making nonverbal statements about themselves.

### Amount of Information

The amount of information contained in a message can affect the accuracy with which it is received. When a message contains more information than we can hold in memory, the information becomes leveled, sharpened, and assimilated. For example, suppose a friend told you the following message over the phone:

> John Atoms was an employee for Mell South Corporation. He came to work one day wearing a brown shirt, plaid pants, white socks, and dark shows and appeared to be intoxicated. He leaned forward, barfed all over the floor, and then passed out. He was obviously intoxicated. This occurred about 9:30 in the morning on a Tuesday. He had worked for the company for 13 years, and thus they didn't want to fire him, but they had to do something. The company decided to suspend him for new days and place him on probation. They were especially sensitive to his problems because he was on his eighth marriage.

What would the story sound like if you passed it on to a friend? When you **level** some of the information, unimportant details are removed. For example, information about the color of the employee's shirt and socks would probably not be passed along to the next person. When you **sharpen** the information, interesting and unusual information is kept. In the example here, the employee's "barfing" and his eight marriages would probably be the story's main focus as it is passed from you to your friend. When you **assimilate** the information, it is modified to fit your existing beliefs and knowledge. Most of us have never heard the last name *Atoms,* but we probably have known someone named *Adams.* Likewise, *Mell South* would be told as *Bell South, dark shows* as *dark shoes,* and *new days* as *a few days.* You would probably use the word *drunk* rather than *intoxicated.*

**Reactions to Communication Overload**   With many jobs, communication overload can occur when an employee receives more communication than she can handle. When an employee is overloaded, she can adapt or adjust in one of several ways to reduce the stress (Miller, 1960): through omission, error, queuing, escape, using a gatekeeper, or using multiple channels.

***Omission*** One way to manage communication overload is **omission:** a conscious decision not to process certain types of information. For example, a busy supervisor may let the phone ring without answering it so that she can finish her paperwork. Although this technique can work if the overload is temporary, it will be ineffective if the employee misses an important communication.

***Error*** In the **error** type of response, the employee attempts to deal with every message he receives. But in so doing, each processed message includes reception error. The processing errors are not intentional but result from processing more than can be handled.

Perhaps a good example of this would be a student who has two hours in which to study four chapters for a test. A student using the error method would attempt to read and memorize all four chapters in two hours. Obviously, her test score will probably indicate that even though she did all of her reading, much of it was not remembered or remembered correctly.

The probability of error occurring can be reduced in two ways. First, the message can be made **redundant.** That is, after communicating an important message over the telephone, it is a good idea to write a memo to the other person summarizing the major points of the conversation. Furthermore, after sending an important memo, it is wise to call its recipient to ensure that the memo was not only received but also read.

Communication overload can cause high levels of employee stress.

**Figure 11.4**
Example of a signature memo

DATE:   June 21, 1995

TO:     All Department Managers
        _DS_ Donald Shula
        _TL_ Thomas Landry
        ____ Patrick Reilly
        ____ William Daly
        ____ William Walsh

FROM:   William Walsh

        Attached is a copy of last month's productivity report.  Please look it over
        carefully, initial that you have read it, and then send it to the next manager
        on the list.

Second, error can be reduced by having the recipient *verify* the message. This can be done by asking the person to repeat the message or acknowledge that she has read and understood it. For example, after a customer has placed an order at the drive-through window of a fast-food restaurant, the employee repeats the order to the customer to make sure that she heard it correctly. (Of course, with the poor quality intercoms used by such places, most people still cannot understand the employee.) In a second example of verification, this time verifying the receipt of a message, a single copy of a memo is sent to several different people. As shown in Figure 11.4, the person who heads the list reads the memo, puts her initials next to her name, and sends the memo to the next person on the list.

*Queuing*  Another method of dealing with communication overload is **queuing**—placing the work into a *queue*, or waiting line. The order of the queue can be based on such variables as the message's importance, timeliness, or sender. For example, a memo sent by the company president will probably be placed near or at the beginning of the queue, as would an emergency phone message. On the other hand, a message to return the phone call of a salesperson most likely would go at the end of the queue.

With this method of handling communication overload, all of the work will usually get done. Queues are only effective, however, if the communication overload is temporary. If the employee is constantly overloaded, she will never reach the work at the end of the queue.

*Escape*  If communication overload is prolonged, a common employee response is to **escape,** which usually takes the form of absenteeism and, ultimately, resignation. This response certainly is not beneficial to an organization, but it can be beneficial to an employee if it protects her mental and physical health by relieving stress.

An example of the escape response is often seen with students who withdraw from college courses. A student may enroll in six classes and realize after two months that she does not have enough time to do all of the reading and writing required for six classes. Rather than choosing the error or omission strategies, both of which would result in lower grades, the student withdraws from one of her classes to reduce her overload.

*Use of a Gatekeeper*  A response to communication overload used by many executives is the use of a **gatekeeper,** a person who screens potential communication and allows only the most important to go through. Receptionists and secretaries are the most obvious examples of gatekeepers.

*Use of Multiple Channels*  The final coping response to communication overload is the use of **multiple channels.** With this strategy, an organization reduces the amount of communication going to one person by directing some of it to another. For example, in a small restaurant all of the problems that involve customers, employees, finances, and vendors are handled by the owner. But as the business grows, the owner may not be able to handle all of the communication and thus may hire others to deal with finances (a bookkeeper) and vendors (an assistant manager).

Knowing and understanding this list of responses to communication overload is important. When communication overload occurs, employees will react in ways that reduce the increased stress. Some of these strategies (omission, error, escape) result in negative consequences for the organization. Thus, the organization must recognize when overload occurs and aggressively adopt an acceptable strategy to deal with it.

## PROBLEM AREA 3: MESSAGE RECEIVED VERSUS MESSAGE INTERPRETED

Even though a person knows what she wants to say, says it the way she wants, and another individual properly receives the intended message, its meaning can change based on the way in which the receiver interprets the message that was received. As shown in Figure 11.5, this interpretation is affected by a variety of factors such as listening skills, listening style, emotional state, cognitive ability, personality, and personal biases.

### Listening Skills

Listening is probably the most important communication skill that a supervisor should master. In a study of managers, Nichols and Stevens (1957) found that 70% of the white-collar workday is spent communicating. Of that, 9% is spent writing, 16% is spent reading, 30% is spent speaking, and 45% is spent listening. Thus, a manager spends more time listening than in any other single activity. This is an important point for two reasons.

First, our formal education in high school and college does not prepare us for managerial communication. We are required to take English courses to improve our reading and writing and are usually required to take one speech course to improve our oral communication skills—but we spend lit-

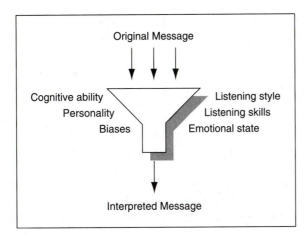

**Figure 11.5**
Factors affecting the message received versus the message interpreted

tle, if any, time learning how to listen. Thus, the amount of time spent in college on various types of communication is inversely related to the actual amount of time spent by managers on the job.

Second, listening effectiveness is poor. It has been estimated that, immediately after a meeting, we retain only 50% of the material we have heard, and only 25% of the material is retained 48 hours later (Nichols & Stevens, 1957). Although much of this loss can be attributed to poor memory practices, some is the result of poor listening habits.

### Styles of Listening

What can be done to increase listening effectiveness? Perhaps the most important thing we can do is to recognize that every person has a particular listening style that serves as a communication filter. Geier and Downey (1980) have developed a test, the **Attitudinal Listening Profile System,** to measure an employee's listening style. Their theory postulates six main styles of listening: leisure, inclusive, stylistic, technical, empathic, and nonconforming.

**Leisure** **Leisure listening** is the listening style that is practiced by "good-time" people who listen only for words that indicate pleasure. For example, as a student, a leisure listener will pay attention only when the teacher is interesting and tells jokes. As an employee, she is the last one to "hear" that employees are needed to work overtime.

**Inclusive** **Inclusive listening** is the style of the person who listens for the main ideas behind any communication. In an hour-long meeting full of details and facts about a decline in sales, the only information that this type of listener will "hear" is the main point that sales are down and that things better improve. This listening style can be an advantage in allowing the listener to cut through a jungle of detail, but it can be a disadvantage when detail is important.

**Stylistic**   **Stylistic listening** is practiced by the person who listens to the *way* communication is spoken. Stylistic listeners will not listen unless the speaker's style is appropriate, or the speaker "looks the part," or both. For example, when speaking to a stylistic listener, a lecturer on finance will find an attentive ear only if she wears a nice suit. After all, this listener reasons, if the lecturer cannot afford a nice suit, why listen to what she has to say about investing money? Similarly, if the speaker says that an event will be fun, she must *sound* as if she means it. And if an employee calls in sick to a manager who is a stylistic listener, she had better "sound" sick.

**Technical**   **Technical listening** is the style practiced by the "Jack Webb" of the listening world—she wants just the facts. The technical listener hears and retains large amounts of detail—but she does not hear the *meaning* of those details. Using the example of the meeting in which employees are told that sales have decreased, the technical listener will hear and remember that sales last year were 12.3% higher than this year, that profits are down by 21%, and that six employees will probably be laid off—but she will miss the point that, unless sales improve, she could be one of those six.

**Empathic**   The user of **empathic listening** tunes in to the feelings of the speaker and, of the six listening types, is the most likely to pay attention to nonverbal cues. Thus, an empathic listener will listen to an employee complain about her boss, and is the only one of the six types of listeners who will not only pay attention, but also understand that the employee's complaints indicate true frustration and unhappiness.

**Nonconforming**   In **nonconforming listening,** the listener attends only to information that is consistent with her way of thinking. If the nonconforming listener does not agree with a speaker, she will not listen to what the speaker says. Furthermore, the nonconforming listener will pay attention only to those people whom she considers to be strong or have authority.

### How Listening Styles Affect Communication

The following example will demonstrate the importance of the six listening styles in a work setting. Suppose that an employee approaches a supervisor and tells him that she has a temperature of 106 degrees. How would each of the six listeners react?

The leisure listener would pay little attention to the employee because she does not like to hear about unpleasant things, and illness certainly is not pleasant. The inclusive listener would probably tell a story about when she had a high temperature, thinking that the topic of conversation was fever. You may have friends who often say things that are not related to your conversation; as this example points out, they are probably inclusive listeners who mistake the main points of a conversation. In this case, the employee is communicating that she does not feel well; she is not discussing "temperatures I have had."

The stylistic listener would pay attention only if the employee sounded and looked ill. You may have also called a professor or a date and tried to sound ill in order to cancel an appointment or date. Few people actually sound ill, even when they are, but we understand the importance of style in listening and behave accordingly.

The technical listener would hear every word but would not realize their meaning. That is, ten minutes later when another employee asks whether Sue is sick, the supervisor would respond, "She didn't say. She has a temperature of 106, but I'm not sure how she is feeling."

The nonconforming listener would pay little attention to the employee. After all, if she actually had a temperature of 106 degrees, she would be dead, and because she is not dead, she must be lying. Of course, the employee has exaggerated her temperature because she is emphasizing the point that she is sick. But the nonconforming listener would not "hear" anything once an initial statement is incorrect.

In this example, the empathic listener would be the only one who would understand the real point of the communication. The employee is mentioning her temperature because she does not feel well and wants to go home.

Understanding each of the six styles can make communication more effective in two ways. First, becoming aware of one's own style allows a person to understand the filter that she uses when listening to others. For example, a student who uses a leisure style may need to recognize that if she only listens to lectures that she finds interesting, she probably will miss a lot of important information. She might want to learn how to concentrate on lectures even when they are boring. Second, understanding the six styles can lead to better communication with others. For example, when speaking to an inclusive listener, we must either write down relevant details that we want her to remember or have her repeat the details. Otherwise, the inclusive listener will remember only the main point: "I know that there is a party tonight, but I'm not sure when or where." On the other hand, when we speak to a technical listener, it is important to tell her what the details mean. For example, if you tell a technical listener there will be a party at your house on Thursday at 8 P.M., you should also add that she is invited, or she will only understand that there is a party and not that she has been invited.

Of course, the million dollar question is, "How can we tell what style of listener is listening to us?" The best way might be to test the listener on the Attitudinal Listening Profile mentioned earlier, but this is hardly practical. The most practical method is using the persons' speaking style as an indicator of listening style. If the person usually mentions how she feels about things, she is probably an empathic listener, but if she speaks with a lot of detail, she is probably a technical listener.

Someone speaking to a group, of course, must relate to all styles of listeners. The best communicators thus will have something for everyone. A good instructor will provide jokes and humorous stories for leisure listeners, use an outline format and provide main points for inclusive listeners, provide specific facts and details for technical listeners, discuss her feelings about the topic for empathic listeners, have good speaking skills and

**Table 11.4**  Ten keys to effective listening

| Keys | The Bad Listener | The Good Listener |
|---|---|---|
| 1. Find areas of interest. | Tunes out dry subjects. | Opportunitizes; asks "What's in it for me?" |
| 2. Judge content, not delivery. | Tunes out if delivery is poor. | Judges content, skips over delivery errors. |
| 3. Hold your fire. | Tends to enter into argument. | Doesn't judge until comprehension is complete. |
| 4. Listen for ideas. | Listens for facts. | Listens for central themes. |
| 5. Be flexible. | Takes intensive notes using only one system. | Takes fewer notes. Uses 4–5 different systems, depending on speaker. |
| 6. Work at listening. | Shows no energy output. Attention is faked. | Works hard, exhibits active body state. |
| 7. Resist distractions. | Is distracted easily. | Fights or avoids distractions, tolerates bad habits, knows how to concentrate. |
| 8. Exercise your mind. | Resists difficult expository material; seeks light, recreational material. | Uses heavier material as exercise for the mind. |
| 9. Keep your mind open. | Reacts to emotional words. | Interprets color words; does not get hung up on them. |
| 10. Capitalize on fact that *thought* is faster than speech. | Tends to daydream with slow speakers. | Challenges, anticipates, mentally summarizes, weighs the evidence, listens between lines to tone of voice. |

Source: Adapted from Steil, L.K. (1980). Prepared by Dr. Lyman K. Steil for the Sperry Corporation. Reprinted with permission of Dr. Steil and Unisys Corporation.

appropriate dress for stylistic listeners, and be confident and accurate for nonconforming listeners.

**Tips for Effective Listening**  In addition to understanding the way in which our listening style serves as a filter, we can improve our listening effectiveness in many other ways. The best tips that I have seen are in a booklet prepared for the Sperry Corporation by Steil (1980). These tips are shown in Table 11.4.

Other authors also have offered tips for more effective listening. For example, Davis (1967) provides the following suggestions:

1. Stop talking.

2. Put the speaker at ease.

3. Show the speaker that you want to listen.

4. Remove distractions.

5. Empathize with the speaker.

6. Be patient.

7. Hold your temper.

8. Go easy on argument and criticism.

9. Ask questions.

10. Stop talking.

De Mare (1968) further suggests:

1. Establish an agreeable atmosphere (put the speaker at ease).

2. Be prepared to hear the other person through on her own terms.

3. Be prepared on the subject to be discussed.

4. Evaluate the speaker, and make allowances for circumstances.

5. Avoid getting mentally sidetracked when subjects are not central to the issue or touch on sore points.

6. Listen for and summarize basic ideas.

7. Restate the substance of what you have heard to the speaker.

Golen (1990) found that bad listeners are lazy, opinionated, insincere, bored, inattentive, and have closed minds.

### Emotional State

The interpretation of a message can certainly be affected by the receiver's emotional state. When we are mad, anxious, depressed, elated, or upset, we do not think as clearly as when our moods are more moderate. Think of the last time you had an argument with someone. How rational and intelligent was your conversation? After the argument was over, did both of you re-member what was said in the same way?

Likewise, have you ever attended a class when your mind was some-where else? My guess is that neither your attention span nor your compre-hension of the material were as high as normal.

### Cognitive Ability

Cognitive ability is another factor that can affect the way in which a re-ceived message is interpreted. That is, a person can receive a message ex-actly as it was sent yet not be able to understand it. For example, have you ever attended a class where you had no idea what the professor was talking about? You heard her words and saw her diagrams but the message still made no sense. Likewise, have you ever told a great pun only to be disap-pointed that the person on the receiving end of the joke did not understand it? If so, then you have first-hand experience in understanding how cogni-tive ability can affect the way in which information is interpreted.

### Bias

Our biases obviously affect our ability to interpret information that is received. For example, we can hate a political candidate so much we can refuse to process any of the positive information we hear about the candidate. We do, however, process every piece of information that is consistent with our opinion.


# IMPROVING EMPLOYEE COMMUNICATION SKILLS

Organizations are always looking for employees with excellent communication skills. The difficulty in finding such employees was recently exemplified by the experience of a national insurance company. The company was having difficulty with a position that required employees to respond to customer complaints. The company had hired expensive consultants to teach its employees how to write effective letters, but performance had not improved. The company then constructed sample letters so that an employee could read a customer complaint, find a standard response form, and add a few personal lines. This also did not work. Finally, the company tried using a standardized writing test before hiring its employees. Although the test showed significant prediction for the performance of Black employees, it did not predict the performance of White employees. This case of single-group validity made the test risky to use. Thus, the question remains: How can an organization increase the communication skills of its employees?


## INTERPERSONAL COMMUNICATION SKILLS

One of the most common methods used to increase interpersonal communication skills is the training workshop conducted by an outside consultant. Although a large number of consultants lead communication workshops, research generally has indicated that such workshops bring only short-term improvement in skills.

An exception to this general failure to produce long-term improvements was reported by Freston and Lease (1987) from their work with Questar Corporation in Salt Lake City. As the personnel manager at Questar, Freston believed that the organization's managers were not properly trained in communication. Questar thus hired Lease as a communications consultant and together Freston and Lease designed a new training program that included seminars on awareness, nonverbal communication, assertiveness, and listening. In addition to the seminars, Freston and Lease also utilized role playing and group discussion. The revised training program brought more positive attitudes for supervisors as well as increased performance quality in tasks such as performance appraisal and training.

## WRITTEN COMMUNICATION SKILLS

Attempts to improve the quality of written communication have generally taken two paths. One approach concentrates on improving the writer's skills, and the other concentrates on making material easier to read.

### Improved Writing

It is difficult for an organization to overcome an employee's lack of formal training in writing (or change bad writing habits). Several consulting firms, however, specialize in the improvement of employee writing by teaching employees the most important concepts of writing. Dumaine (1987) and Fey (1987) believe that to improve writing, employees must learn certain basic concepts. For example, an employee needs to analyze her audience. If a written communication is intended for people with only a high school education, then the readability must be kept at that level. If the intended audience is a busy executive, the message must be kept short. A list of strategies for effective business writing can be found in Figure 11.6.

### Readability

Written communication can break down when material is too difficult for many employees to read. For example, research has shown that Federal Aviation Administration (FAA) regulations and many airline company–pilots' association agreements are too difficult for pilots to read (Blumenfeld, 1985). The Position Analysis Questionnaire, the job-analysis instrument discussed earlier in this book, is also too difficult for most job incumbents to

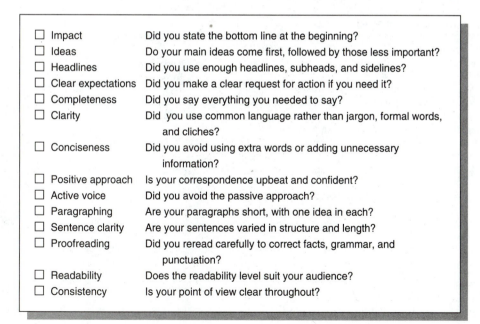

| | |
|---|---|
| ☐ Impact | Did you state the bottom line at the beginning? |
| ☐ Ideas | Do your main ideas come first, followed by those less important? |
| ☐ Headlines | Did you use enough headlines, subheads, and sidelines? |
| ☐ Clear expectations | Did you make a clear request for action if you need it? |
| ☐ Completeness | Did you say everything you needed to say? |
| ☐ Clarity | Did you use common language rather than jargon, formal words, and cliches? |
| ☐ Conciseness | Did you avoid using extra words or adding unnecessary information? |
| ☐ Positive approach | Is your correspondence upbeat and confident? |
| ☐ Active voice | Did you avoid the passive approach? |
| ☐ Paragraphing | Are your paragraphs short, with one idea in each? |
| ☐ Sentence clarity | Are your sentences varied in structure and length? |
| ☐ Proofreading | Did you reread carefully to correct facts, grammar, and punctuation? |
| ☐ Readability | Does the readability level suit your audience? |
| ☐ Consistency | Is your point of view clear throughout? |

**Figure 11.6**
Checklist for effective business writing

Source: From "Strategic Writing for Trainers," by D. Dumaine, 1987, *Training and Development Journal, 47*(1), 60. Used with permission.

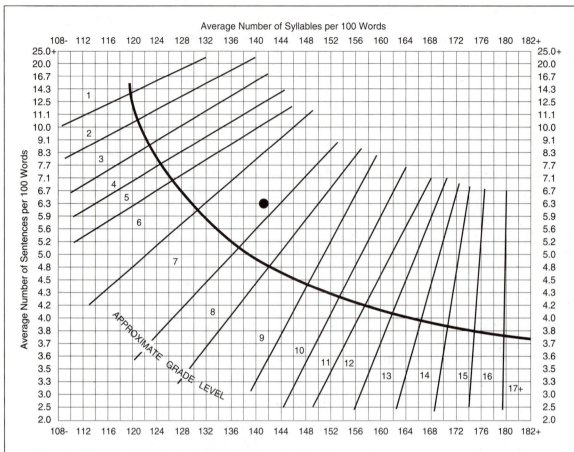

Average Number of Syllables per 100 Words

**Expanded Directions for Working Readability Graph**
1. Randomly select three sample passages and count out exactly 100 words each, beginning with the beginning of a sentence. Do count proper nouns, initializations, and numerals.
2. Count the number of sentences in the 100 words, estimating length of the fraction of the last sentence to the nearest one-tenth.
3. Count the total number of syllables in the 100-word passage. If you don't have a hand counter available, simply put a mark above every syllable over one in each word. Then when you get to the end of the passage, count the number of marks and add 100. Small calculators can also be used as counters by pushing numeral 1, then pushing the + sign for each word or syllable when counting.
4. Enter graph with *average* sentence length and *average* number of syllables; plot dot where the two lines intersect. Area where dot is plotted will give you the approximate grade level.
5. If a great deal of variability is found in syllable count or sentence count, putting more samples into the average is desirable.
6. A word is defined as a group of symbols with a space on either side; thus *Joe, IRA, 1945,* and *&* are each one word.
7. A syllable is defined as a phonetic syllable. Generally, there are as many syllables as vowel sounds. For example, *stopped* is one syllable and *wanted* is two syllables. When counting syllables for numerals and initializations, count one syllable for each symbol. For example, *1945* is four syllables, *IRA* is three syllables, and *&* is one syllable.

**Figure 11.7** Graph for estimating readability—extended

read (Ash & Edgell, 1975). Thus, providing employees with important material to read will be an effective communication form only if the employees can understand what is written.

To ensure that employees will be able to understand written material, several readability indexes are available. When using such an index, an organization analyzes the material to be read and then compares its readability level with the typical education of the employees who will read the document. For example, if most employees have high school degrees and have not been to college, the document should be written at less than a 12th-grade level.

Each index uses a slightly different formula or method. For example, the **Fry Readability Graph** (Fry, 1977) uses the average number of syllables per word and the average length of sentences to determine readability (see Figure 11.7). **The Flesch Index** (Flesch, 1948) uses the average sentence length and number of syllables per 100 words; the **FOG Index** (Gunning, 1964) uses the number of words per sentence and the number of three-syllable words per 100; and the **Dale-Chall Index** (Dale & Chall, 1948) uses the number of words that are not included in a list of words known by 80% of fourth graders.

All of the readability indexes show reasonable reliability and correlate highly with one another (Blumenfeld & Justice, 1975; Forbes & Cottle, 1953). (The readability levels of selected publications are shown in Table 11.5.) As we can see from these indexes, an easily read document has short sentences, uses simple rather than complicated words, and uses common rather than unusual words.

Specialized indexes also have been introduced by both Flesch (1948), who measures the human-interest level of reading material, and Tysinger and Pitchford (1988), who developed a method for determining the readability of trait-based psychological tests. Many word-processing packages (such as Microsoft Word) now contain readability indexes that make writing to a particular audience level easier.

**Table 11.5**  Readability levels of selected publications

| Document | Readability Level |
| --- | --- |
| FAA regulations | Graduate Student |
| Position Analysis Questionnaire | College Graduate |
| *Air Line Pilot* magazine | College Student |
| Study of Values | 12th Grade |
| *Time* magazine | 11th Grade |
| *Newsweek* | 11th Grade |
| *Reader's Digest* | 10th Grade |
| Otis Employment Test | 9th Grade |
| *Ladies' Home Journal* | 8th Grade |
| Most comic books | 6th Grade |
| Minnesota Multiple Personality Inventory | 6th Grade |

*Ge Ge Beall, M.S., PHR*
*Human Resources*
*Consultant*
*Personnel Research*
*Associates*

As a general human resource consultant, I provide a variety of HR services to clients of all shapes and sizes. One of the best things about my job is the variety of work, which can include most of the topics in your text. For example, some of my recent work has included conducting training seminars, working on the design of a performance-appraisal system, and providing career advice.

One of my favorite jobs is conducting seminars; in particular, communication seminars. While businesses may have a wide variety of industry-specific problems, communication is something they all have in common. Whether a company provides a service or manufactures a product, communication is fundamental to their success. You only have to look at the nearest picket line of striking miners, baseball players, teachers, or other employee groups to get an idea of how devastating a breakdown in communication can be. Having employees refuse to work is probably the most serious communication problem an organization can have. However, as you know yourself, a communication problem does not have to be this monumental in scope to have an effect on you. In fact, for nearly all of us, the most bothersome dilemmas center around communication problems with our boss, co-workers, family members, or significant others. Since these are the problems that affect people the most, my company tends to gear our seminars more toward interpersonal communication rather than organizational communication.

One focus is on teaching people to understand others and their differences. During our lives, we have been told time and time again that every individual is unique; however, we tend to forget this when someone doesn't react the way we expect (i.e., "our way"). During the seminars, we look at a variety of things that help shape us into the people we are such as school size, friends, health, genetics, personality, urban versus rural upbringing, TV, and other variables. We also take a personality test and discuss the differences within the group. We spend a lot of time just talking about ourselves and our experiences. The hope is that insight will promote understanding or, at the very least, tolerance of our differences.

Another focus is on understanding the communication process itself. There are so many places that communication can break down, it's amazing that we can get anyone to understand anything we have to say. In the seminars, we look at how things such as choice of words, the communication channel, nonverbal cues, paralanguage, and gender differences affect our messages.

Communication is also a very important component of the employee motivation seminars we teach to managers. It is surprising how many managers want employees to be motivated, yet are unaware of how their own communication style can affect this. There is a joke about treating employees like mushrooms (i.e., keeping them in the dark). Unfortunately, this still seems to be fairly common in industry. To some managers, information is a form of power, and they don't want to share it. Other managers are just not sure how or what type of information to share.

Keeping employees informed of company circumstances is important, but even more important is letting employees know what is expected of them. Believe it or not, I have heard many HR staff members say that it is not that uncommon for managers to let an employee do something wrong or miss an important job function for months, waiting for the yearly performance review to let them know. Not only do most employees need and want ongoing feedback, but companies cannot afford months of inadequate performance.

We also talk about the value of asking employees for their ideas. Companies are constantly looking for ways to improve. So, what is one of the best sources for ideas? The employees who actually perform the jobs. Managers have to learn to encourage and ask for ideas because, as you know yourself, not everyone feels comfortable speaking up.

Strengthening the business with employee ideas, correcting problems as they develop, and reducing employee turnover are just a few of the benefits of good communication. Managers who are effective communicators can do more than create a positive work environment, they can improve the company's bottom line.

Teaching communication seminars is so much fun! Since communication is such a universal topic, people have no problem coming up with examples and tell all kinds of stories on themselves, spouses, co-workers, and bosses.

By the way, if you are thinking of becoming a trainer, remember good trainers don't simply spit information at participants; they interact with them. As a trainer, you've got to know your material, entertain, move, listen, and be sincere. People are so used to the rapid-fire scene changes provided by TV that they cannot tolerate a stagnant "talking head" reading scripted notes from behind a podium. This is especially true with the younger members of the workforce.

Probably one of the best things you can do to improve your teaching ability or presentation style is to take an acting class. Not only can it help you with movement, voice, and diction, but it can also help you loosen up physically and emotionally by tapping into your creativity and spontaneity. And, since acting requires you to "become" other people, it helps you to empathize and understand the feelings of others, which is a huge plus for anyone who has to get information across to a diverse group.

## CHAPTER SUMMARY

This chapter began by discussing the importance of organizational communication, which can take several directions. *Upward communication* moves from employees to management and utilizes methods such as serial communication, attitude surveys, suggestion boxes, and ombudspeople. *Downward communication* moves from management to employees and utilizes methods such as telephone calls, memos, voice mail, e-mail, bulletin boards, and company manuals. *Horizontal communication* is communication between people at the same level of an organization and includes rumor, the grapevine, and work groups.

The chapter then discussed interpersonal communication by explaining the communication process and three major problem areas. The first problem area involved the intended message versus the message actually sent.

The second problem area involved the message sent versus the message received. Concerns in this second problem area included the actual words used in the message, the communication channel, noise, nonverbal cues (such as body language, use of space, use of time), artifacts, and the amount of information.

In discussing this second problem area, we learned that although effective communication is essential, too much can cause *communication overload*. When such overload occurs, employees can react by using one or more of several strategies, including omission, error, queuing, escape, use of a gatekeeper, and use of multiple channels.

The third problem area involved the message received versus the message interpreted. We learned that interpersonal communication can be improved with more effective listening skills, understanding the six different styles of listening (leisure, inclusive, stylistic, technical, empathic, and nonconforming), and considering the emotional state, cognitive ability, and personal biases of the sender and the receiver.

The chapter concluded by demonstrating that written communication can be improved by learning better writing skills and by writing organizational documents at a reading level that matches the reading level of most employees.

# GLOSSARY

**Assimilated**  A description of a message in which the information has been modified to fit the existing beliefs and knowledge of the person sending the message before it is passed on to another person.

**Attitude survey**  A form of upward communication in which a survey is conducted to determine employee attitudes about an organization.

**Attitudinal Listening Profile System**  A test developed by Geier and Downey that measures individual listening styles.

**Bulletin board**  A method of downward communication in which informal or relatively unimportant written information is posted in a public place.

**Channel**  The medium by which a communication is transmitted.

**Cluster**  A pattern of grapevine communication in which a message is passed to a select group of people who each in turn pass the message to a few select others.

**Company manual**  Also called a policy manual, a book containing formal company rules and regulations.

**Complaint box**  A form of upward communication in which employees are asked to place their complaints in a box.

**Dale-Chall Index**  A method of determining the readability level of written material.

**Dead-enders**  Employees who receive much grapevine information but who seldom pass it on to others.

**Downward communication**  Communication within an organization in which the direction of communication is from management to employees.

**Empathic listening**  The listening style of a person who listens for the feelings of the speaker.

**Error**  A type of response to communication overload that involves processing all information but processing some of it incorrectly.

**Escape**  A response to communication overload in which the employee leaves the organization to reduce the stress.

**Flesch Index**  A method of determining the readability level of written material.

**FOG Index**  A method of determining the readability level of written material.

**Fry Readability Graph**  A method of determining the readability level of written material.

**Gatekeeper**  A person who screens potential communication for someone else and allows only the most important information to pass through.

**Gossip**  A pattern of grapevine communication in which a message is passed to only a select group of individuals.

**Grapevine**  An unofficial, informal communication network.

**Horizontal communication**  Communication between employees at the same level in an organization.

**Inclusive listening**  The listening style of a person who listens only for the main points of a communication.

**Interpersonal communication**  Communication between two individuals.

**Intimacy zone**  A distance zone within 18 inches of a person where only people with a close relationship to the person are allowed to enter.

**Intraorganizational communication**  Communication within an organization.

**Intrapersonal communication**  Communication that takes place within an individual.

**Isolate**  An employee who receives less than half of all grapevine information.

**Leisure listening**  The listening style of a person who listens only for interesting information.

**Leveled**  A description of a message from which unimportant information details have been removed before the message is passed from one person to another.

**Liaison**  A person who acts as an intermediary between employees and management; or the type of employee who both sends and receives most grapevine information.

**Multiple channels**  A strategy for coping with communication overload in which an organization reduces the amount of communication going to one person by directing some of it to another person.

**MUM (minimize unpleasant messages) effect**  The idea that people prefer not to pass on unpleasant information, with the result that important information is not always communicated.

**Noise**  Any variable concerning or affecting the channel that interferes with the proper reception of a message.

**Nonconforming listener**  The listening style of a person who listens only to information that is consistent with her way of thinking.

**Ombudsperson**  A person who investigates employees' complaints and solves problems.

**Omission**  A response to communication overload that involves the conscious decision not to process certain types of information.

**Personal distance zone**  A distance zone from 18 inches to four feet from a person that is usually reserved for friends and acquaintances.

**Probability**  A pattern of grapevine communication in which a message is passed randomly among all employees.

**Proximity**  Physical distance between people.

**Public distance zone**  A distance zone greater than 12 feet from a person that is typical of the interpersonal space allowed for social interactions such as large group lectures.

**Queuing** A method of coping with communication overload that involves organizing work into an order in which it will be handled.

**Rumor** Poorly substantiated information that is passed along the grapevine.

**Serial communication** Communication passed consecutively from one person to another.

**Sharpened** A description of a message in which interesting and unusual information has been kept in the message when it is passed from one person to another.

**Single strand** A pattern of grapevine communication in which a message is passed in a chain-like fashion from one person to the next person until the chain is broken.

**Social distance zone** An interpersonal distance zone from 4 to 12 feet from a person that is typically used for business and for interacting with strangers.

**Stylistic listening** The listening style of a person who listens to the way in which words are spoken.

**Suggestion box** A form of upward communication in which employees are asked to place their suggestions in a box.

**Technical listening** The listening style of a person who listens for facts and details.

**Union steward** An employee who serves as a liaison between unionized employees and management.

**Upward communication** Communication within an organization in which the direction of communication is from employees up to management.

# 12
# EMPLOYEE MOTIVATION AND SATISFACTION

After an organization has selected and trained its employees, it is important that employees are both motivated by and satisfied with their jobs. Industrial psychologists generally define work **motivation** as the force that drives a worker to perform well. Ability and skill determine whether a worked *can* do the job, but motivation determines whether the worker *will* do it properly. Although actually testing the relationship between motivation and performance is difficult, researchers generally agree that increased worker motivation results in increased job performance.

The same may not be true of **job satisfaction**—the attitude an employee has toward his job. As shown in Table 12.1, research has shown that job satisfaction is only marginally related to an employee's attendance (Hackett, 1989), tenure, commitment to the organization (Tett & Meyer, 1993), and job performance (Iaffaldano & Muchinsky, 1985).

In this chapter, we will explore several theories that seek to explain why workers are satisfied with and motivated by their jobs. None of the theories completely and accurately explains job satisfaction and motivation, but each is valuable in that it suggests ways to increase employee performance and satisfaction. Thus, even though a theory itself may not be completely supported by research, the resulting suggestions have generally led to increased performance or longer tenure. This is an important point because most textbooks have separate chapters for motivation and satisfaction. In this text, the two are combined—not because motivation and satisfaction are the same construct, but because the suggestions that result from these theories can be applied to increase both satisfaction and motivation.

It is important to understand that the relation between satisfaction and motivation is complex. To combine the two or treat them as completely unrelated would not be accurate. This complexity becomes even more evident when examining the nature of job satisfaction. Historically, we have studied global job satisfaction—our overall level of job satisfaction. However, in the past few decades, researchers have come to realize that satisfaction has many *facets*. That is, we might be satisfied with the tasks we perform and the pay we receive but not with our supervisor or our co-workers. In research, the results found when studying global satisfaction are not always consistent with those found when studying facet satisfaction.

**Table 12.1** Meta-analysis results of the relationship between job satisfaction and performance, turnover, absenteeism, and commitment

| Satisfaction | Performance[a] | Turnover[b] | Absenteeism | | Commitment[b] |
| | | | Frequency[c] | Duration[c] | |
| --- | --- | --- | --- | --- | --- |
| **Facet** | | | | | |
| Pay | .06 | | −.08 | −.07 | |
| Supervision | .19 | | −.13 | −.08 | |
| Co-workers | .12 | | −.07 | −.07 | |
| Work | .21 | | −.21 | −.14 | |
| Promotion opportunities | .15 | | −.09 | −.07 | |
| **Type** | | | | | |
| Intrinsic | .23 | | −.25 | −.01 | |
| Extrinsic | .18 | | −.24 | −.21 | |
| **Overall satisfaction** | .19 | −.25 | −.15 | −.23 | .70 |

[a] Iaffaldano and Muchnisky (1985)
[b] Tett and Meyer (1993)
[c] Hackett (1989)

**Needs theories** postulate that job satisfaction is determined by how well the job or the organization is able to satisfy certain employee needs such as safety and recognition. Although needs theories have brought beneficial ways of looking at employee behavior, they have generally been criticized as being untestable and involving wants rather than needs.

## MASLOW'S NEEDS HIERARCHY

Perhaps the most famous theory of satisfaction and motivation was developed by Abraham Maslow (1954). Maslow believed that employees would be satisfied with their jobs at any given point in time if certain needs were met. As Figure 12.1 shows, Maslow believed that people have five major types of needs and that these needs are hierarchical—that is, lower-level needs must be satisfied before an employee will be concerned with the next level of needs. It is helpful to look at a **hierarchy** as if it were a staircase that is climbed one step at a time until the top is reached. The same is true of Maslow's hierarchy. Each level is taken one step at a time, and a higher-level need cannot be reached until a lower-level need is satisfied. In Maslow's hierarchy, the five major needs are biological, safety, social, ego, and self-actualization.

### Basic Biological Needs

Maslow thought that an individual first seeks to satisfy **basic biological needs** for food, air, water, and shelter. In our case, an individual who does not have a job, is homeless, and is on the verge of starvation will be satisfied with any job as long as it provides for these basic needs. When asked how well they enjoy their job, people at this level might reply, *I can't complain, it pays the bills.*

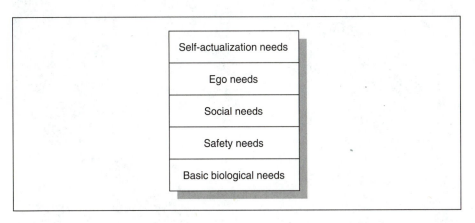

**Figure 12.1**
Maslow's Hierarchy
of Needs

- Self-actualization needs
- Ego needs
- Social needs
- Safety needs
- Basic biological needs

### Safety Needs

After basic biological needs have been met, a job that merely provides food and shelter will no longer be satisfying. Employees then become concerned about meeting their **safety needs.** That is, they may work in an unsafe coal mine to earn enough money to ensure their family's survival, but once their family has food and shelter, they will remain satisfied with their jobs only if the workplace is safe.

Safety needs have been expanded to include psychological as well as physical safety. Psychological safety—often referred to as job security—can certainly affect job satisfaction. For example, public sector employees often list job security as a main benefit to their jobs—a benefit so strong that they will stay in lower paying public sector jobs rather than take higher paying, yet less secure, jobs in the private sector.

### Social Needs

Once these first two need levels have been met, employees will remain satisfied with their jobs only when their social needs have been met. **Social needs** involve working with others, developing friendships, and feeling needed. Organizations attempt to satisfy their employees' social needs in a variety of ways. Company cafeterias provide workers the place and opportunity to socialize and meet other employees, company picnics allow families to meet one another, and company sports programs such as bowling teams and softball games provide opportunities for employees to play together in a neutral environment.

Satisfaction at work can result in increased life satisfaction.

It is important that an organization make a conscious effort to satisfy these social needs when a job itself does not encourage social activity. For example, with a job such as that of a janitor or a night watchman, the employee will encounter few other people while working. Thus, the chance of making new friends is small.

### Ego Needs

When social needs have been satisfied, employees concentrate next on meeting their **ego needs.** These are needs for recognition and success, and an organization can help to satisfy them through praise, awards, promotions, salary increases, and publicity. Ego needs can be satisfied in many ways. For example, Johnny Carson has commented that the most prestigious sign at NBC is not the salary of the television star or producer, but rather whether the person has his or her own parking place. Likewise, many organizations use furniture to help satisfy ego needs. The higher the employee's position, the better his office furniture. Similarly, at one engineering firm in Louisville, Kentucky, engineers are not allowed to mount their diplomas or awards on the wall until they receive their professional certification.

### Self-Actualization Needs

Even when an employee has friends, has earned awards, and is making a relatively high salary, he may not be completely satisfied with his job: His **self-actualization needs** might not have been satisfied yet. These needs are the fifth and final level of Maslow's needs hierarchy (the top level in Figure 12.1). Self-actualization might be best defined by the U.S. Army's recruiting slogan, "Be all that you can be." An employee striving for self-actualization wants to reach his potential in every task. Thus, an employee who has worked with the same machine for 20 years may become dissatisfied with his job. He has accomplished all that can be accomplished with that particular machine and now searches for a new challenge. If none is available, he may become dissatisfied.

With some jobs, satisfying self-actualization needs is easy. For example, a college professor always has new research to conduct, new classes to teach, and new clients to consult. Thus, the variety of tasks and the new problems that are encountered provide a constant challenge that can lead to higher job satisfaction.

Other jobs, however, may not satisfy self-actualization needs. A good example is an employee who welds parts on an assembly line. For 8 hours a day, 40 hours a week, he performs only one task. Boredom and the realization that the job will never change begin to set in. It is no wonder that the employee becomes dissatisfied.

**Rotation, Enlargement, and Enrichment**  To help satisfy self-actualization needs, several changes can be made. The easiest and most common are **job rotation, job enlargement,** and **job enrichment.** With job rotation and job enlargement, an employee learns how to use several different machines or conduct several different tasks within an organization. With job rotation, the employee is given the same number of tasks to do at one time, but the tasks change from time to time. With job enlargement, an employee is given more tasks to do at one time.

A job can be enlarged in two ways: knowledge used and tasks performed. With knowledge enlargement, employees are allowed to make more complex decisions. With task enlargement, they are given more tasks of the same difficulty level to perform. As one might imagine, job satisfaction increases with knowledge enlargement and decreases with task enlargement (Campion & McClelland, 1993).

Job rotation and job enlargement accomplish two main objectives. First, they challenge employees by requiring them to learn to operate several different machines or perform several different tasks. Thus, once employees have mastered one task or machine, they can work toward mastering another. Second, job rotation helps to alleviate boredom by allowing an employee to change tasks. Thus, if an employee welds parts one day, assembles bumpers on another, and tightens screws on a third, the boredom caused by performing the same task every day should be reduced.

Perhaps an even better way to satisfy self-actualization needs is through job enrichment. The main difference between job rotation and job enrichment is that with the former, an employee performs different tasks, and with job enrichment, the employee assumes more responsibility over the tasks (Ford, 1973).

In their **Job-Characteristics Model,** Hackman and Oldham (1975; 1976) theorize that enriched jobs will be the most satisfying. Enriched jobs allow a variety of skills to be used, allow an employee to complete an entire task (such as process a loan application from start to finish) rather than parts of a task, involve tasks that have meaning or importance, allow employees to make decisions, and provide feedback about performance. Hackman and Oldham developed the **Job Diagnostic Survey** to measure the extent to which these characteristics are present in a given job.

If we look again at the job of college professor, job enrichment is clearly an inherent part of the job. That is, the professor decides what he will research and what he will teach in a particular course. This authority to make decisions about one's own work leads to higher job satisfaction.

With an assembly line worker, however, responsibility is something that must be added because the employee has minimal control over the way a job is done. After all, bumpers must be assembled in the same way each time and welded to the same place. So what can be done to enrich the typical factory worker's job?

One method is to give workers more responsibility over their jobs. For example, when an employee first begins working for a company, his work is checked by a quality control inspector. After the employee has been with the company long enough for the first four needs levels to be satisfied, the employee is given responsibility for checking his own quality. Likewise, more control can be given to the employee about where and when he will eat lunch, when he will take vacation time, or how fast he will accomplish his work. At one Kaiser Aluminum production plant, for example, time clocks were removed so that the workers could assume more responsibility for their performance by keeping track of their own hours.

It may seem strange to suggest that allowing an employee to make such trivial decisions as lunch times will result in higher job satisfaction. But research has shown that allowing residents in a nursing home to make such decisions resulted in lower death rates as did allowing them to own pets (Langer & Rodin, 1976; Schulz, 1976). Thus, it is not farfetched to think that allowing control even in limited areas can increase one's level of job satisfaction.

Even when increased decision-making responsibilities are not possible, job-enrichment ideas can still be implemented. For example, many organizations have or work with credit unions whose credit committees and boards of directors consist of company employees. These committees and boards provide excellent opportunities to increase employees' decision-making powers even though the decisions are not directly related to their jobs.

Another method to increase the level of job enrichment is by showing employees that their jobs have meaning and that they are meeting some worthwhile goal through their work (Hackman & Oldham, 1975). At some automobile factories, for example, this is accomplished by having employees work in teams to build cars. Instead of an employee performing a single task all day, he does several tasks, as do the other employees in his group. Thus, at the end of the day, the employee can see a completed car that he has had a major role in building.

A plant that manufactured transformers provides another example. The training department realized that even though employees spent 8 hours a day manufacturing the product, few understood what it did, who used it, and what would happen if it were not manufactured correctly. To correct this problem, the employees participated in a training session in which they were shown how the transformer was used, who used it, and the consequences that resulted from poor manufacturing.

The final method for increasing employees' self-actualization needs that we will discuss here is the use of **self-directed teams** or **quality circles.** With quality circles, employees meet as a group and make decisions about such quality-enhancing factors as the music played in the work area, the speed of the assembly line, and how to reduce waste. Quality circles are especially effective in increasing employees' job satisfaction when there is little or no chance for advancement. They allow employees to have more control and responsibility.

In an extensive review of the literature, Wagner (1994) concluded that allowing employees to participate in making decisions results in small, but significant, increases in performance and job satisfaction. Arthur (1994) found lower turnover in steel mills that allowed employees to make decisions on their own than in steel mills with a more controlling style.

Though team approaches are popular, there is considerable debate about their effectiveness. Most quality improvement programs using a team approach fail to provide the desired results (Zemke, 1993).

### Evaluation of Maslow's Theory

Although Maslow's needs theory makes good intuitive sense, is popular with managers and marketing analysts, and its general components have withstood the test of time, research has generally not supported its more technical aspects (Wahba & Bridwell, 1976). Perhaps the biggest problem with the theory concerns the number of levels. Although Maslow believed there are five needs levels, research has failed to support that number and suggests instead that there may only be two or three levels (Aldefer, 1972; Lawler & Suttle, 1972; Mitchell & Mougdill, 1976).

A second problem with the theory is that some people do not progress up the hierarchy as Maslow suggests they do. That is, most people move up from the basic biological needs level to safety needs to social needs and so on. Some people, however, have been known to skip levels. For example, bungee jumpers obviously skip the safety needs level and go straight to satisfying their ego needs. Thus when exceptions to the hierarchical structure occur, the theory loses support.

Another problem is that the theory predicts that once the needs at one level are satisfied, the next needs level should become most important. Research, however, has shown that this does not necessarily happen (Salancik & Pfeffer, 1977).

Even if Maslow's theory has not been supported by research, it may still be useful. Some of the theory's specific assertions may not be true, but it still provides guidelines that organizations can follow to increase job satisfaction. Providing recognition, enrichment, and a safe workplace *do* increase employee satisfaction. The validity of these suggestions is probably why Maslow's theory still is widely used by human resource professionals even though it is not popular with academicians and researchers who prefer more complicated models.

## ERG THEORY

Because of the technical problems with Maslow's hierarchy, Aldefer (1972) developed a needs theory that has only three levels. As shown in Figure 12.2, the three levels are existence, relatedness, and growth—hence the name **ERG Theory.** Research by Wanous and Zwany (1977) has supported Aldefer's proposed number of levels.

**Figure 12.2**
ERG Theory
Dimensions

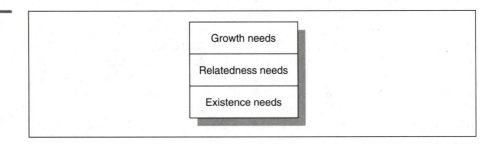

Other than the number of levels, the major difference between Maslow's theory and ERG theory is that Aldefer suggests that a person can skip levels. By allowing for such movement, Aldefer has removed one of the biggest problems with Maslow's theory.

Furthermore, Aldefer's theory explains why a higher level sometimes does not become more important once a lower level need has been satisfied. Aldefer believes that for jobs in many organizations, advancement to the next level is not possible because of such factors as company policy or the nature of the job. Thus, the path to the next level is blocked, and the employee becomes frustrated and places more importance on the previous level. Perhaps that is why some unions demand more money and benefits for their members rather than job enrichment. They realize that the jobs will always be tedious and that little can be done to improve them. Thus, the previous needs level becomes more important. This idea has received at least some empirical support (Hall & Nougaim, 1968; Salancik & Pfeffer, 1977).

## TWO-FACTOR THEORY

Another needs theory, which reduces the number of levels to two, was developed by Herzberg (1966). As shown in Table 12.2 and Figure 12.3, Herzberg's **two-factor theory** suggests that job-related factors can be divided into two categories: motivators and hygiene factors. **Hygiene factors** are those job-related elements that result from but do not involve the job itself. For example, pay and benefits are consequences of work but do not involve the work itself. Similarly, making new friends may result from going to work, but they also are not directly involved with the tasks and duties of the job.

**Motivators** are job elements that *do* concern actual tasks and duties. Examples of motivators would be the level of responsibility, the amount of job control, and the interest that the work holds for the employee. Herzberg believes that hygiene factors are necessary but not sufficient for

**Table 12.2**   Examples from Herzberg's Two-Factor Theory

| Hygiene Factors | Motivators |
| --- | --- |
| Pay | Responsibility |
| Security | Growth |
| Co-workers | Challenge |
| Working conditions | Stimulation |
| Company policy | Independence |
| Work schedule | Variety |
| Supervisors | Achievement |
|  | Control |
|  | Interesting work |

**Figure 12.3**
Comparison of the
Herzberg, Maslow,
and ERG theories

| Maslow | ERG | Herzberg |
|---|---|---|
| Self-actualization | Growth | Motivators |
| Ego | | |
| Social | Relatedness | Hygiene factors |
| Safety | Existence | |
| Physical | | |

job satisfaction and motivation. That is, if a hygiene factor is not present at an adequate level (for example, the pay is too low), the employee will be dissatisfied. But if all hygiene factors are represented adequately, the employee's level of satisfaction will only be neutral. Only the presence of both motivators and hygiene factors can bring job satisfaction and motivation.

Thus, an employee who is paid a lot of money but has no control or responsibility over his job will probably be neither satisfied nor dissatisfied. But an employee who is not paid enough *will* be dissatisfied even though he might have tremendous control and responsibility over his job. Finally, an employee who is paid well and has control and responsibility will probably be satisfied.

Two-factor theory focuses on the issue of **intrinsic** versus **extrinsic** satisfaction and motivation. When we are intrinsically motivated, we are satisfied with the job and motivated to perform well because we enjoy performing the actual tasks. When we are extrinsically motivated, we don't particularly enjoy the tasks but are motivated to perform well in order to receive some type of reward, avoid negative consequences, or both (Deci & Ryan, 1985). People who are intrinsically motivated don't need external rewards such as pay or praise. In fact, being paid for something we enjoy reduces our satisfaction and intrinsic motivation (Mossholder, 1980). Individual orientations toward intrinsic and extrinsic motivation can be measured by the **Works-Preference Inventory** (Amabile, Hill, Hennessey, & Tighe, 1994).

Again, Herzberg's is one of those theories that makes sense but has not received strong research support. In general, researchers have criticized the theory because of the methods used to develop the two factors as well as the fact that few research studies have replicated the findings obtained by Herzberg and his colleagues (Hinrichs & Mischkind, 1967; King, 1970).

## MCCLELLAND'S NEEDS THEORY

The final needs theory that we will discuss was developed by McClelland (1961) and suggests that differences between individuals stem from the relationship between a job and each employee's level of satisfaction or motivation. McClelland believes that employees differ in their needs for achievement, affiliation, and power.

Employees who have a strong **need for achievement** desire jobs that are challenging and over which they have some control, whereas employees who have minimal achievement needs are more satisfied when jobs involve little challenge and have a high probability of success. In contrast, employees who have a strong **need for affiliation** prefer working with and helping other people. These types of employees are found more often in people-oriented service jobs than in management or administration (Smither & Lindgren, 1978). Finally, employees who have a strong **need for power** have a desire to influence others rather than simply be successful.

Research has shown that employees who have a strong need for power and achievement often make the best managers (McClelland & Burnham, 1976; Stahl, 1983), and those employees who are motivated most by their affiliation needs will probably make the worst managers.

These needs are measured by one of two tests. The first and most popular is the **Thematic Apperception Test (TAT),** which was discussed briefly in Chapter 9. With the TAT, an employee is shown a series of pictures and then asked to tell a story about each one. From the responses, a psychologist identifies the degree to which each theme of power, affiliation, and achievement is present in the stories.

The problem with the TAT is that it is time-consuming and must be administered by a psychologist trained in its use. To avoid these problems, Stahl (1983) developed a more objective and less expensive paper-and-pencil test that measures the same three needs. Although this test has not yet become popular, research seems to indicate that it is as reliable and valid a measure as the TAT (Stahl, 1983).

# DISCREPANCY THEORIES

Theories in this category postulate that our satisfaction with a job is determined by the discrepancy between what we *want, value,* and *expect* and what the job actually provides (Lawler, 1973; Locke, 1969). For example, if you enjoy working with people but your job involves working with data, you are not likely to be satisfied with your job. Likewise, if you value helping others, yet your job involves selling things people don't really need, you will probably be dissatisfied with your job.

Potential discrepancies between employee wants and values and job requirements serve as the basis for career assessment and guidance programs. In these programs, employees are administered a battery of interest, ability,

**Heather King, M.A.**
**Director;**
**Assessment Plus, Inc.**

I work for a management consulting firm that specializes in organizational surveys and leadership development. Most of the work we do involves using surveys to help organizations and individuals identify their strengths and developmental areas.

As director, I am an external consultant to management, and work primarily with HR professionals and top managers of organizations. Specifically, I manage organizational survey projects, which involves working closely with clients to develop and administer the survey. I also manage a clerical staff and subcontractors, provide clients with status reports on their project, compile and analyze survey results, provide feedback to clients, and work with them to develop feedback and follow-up strategies to their survey results.

We use surveys to measure several different aspects of jobs, including job satisfaction. There are many components of job satisfaction, and we try to measure those that are most meaningful to the company and its employees. Our surveys are tailored to meet the individual needs of each client. Typically, items cover a wide range of areas such as amount of authority and decision-making ability, teamwork, communication, pay and benefits, supervisory effectiveness, employee involvement, morale, customer-service issues, and identification and accountability with work.

There are several ways to develop a survey: focus groups, item banks, one-on-one interviews, and meetings with management. We typically develop surveys through meetings with management. In these meetings, they tell us the types of issues they want to target in the survey, then we recommend some items for their use. These items are ones that we have used before or develop to meet their specific needs. Items can also be generated in management meetings, where the managers in the meeting develop several items, then rank them in order of importance.

The use of focus groups is a widely used and excellent way to target issues in an organization. This process involves meeting with small groups of employees to talk about broad issues (i.e., factors affecting job satisfaction), good and bad aspects of working for the company, the company's values, and characteristics of the culture. This information is used to choose or develop survey items. Items also can be developed by the group, then ranked in order of importance.

One-on-one interviews are used in the same fashion as focus groups: to identify broad areas of concern. A structured interview is used, and employees answer the questions and talk about areas they feel are important.

Many organizations use "off-the-shelf" surveys that are already developed to measure such areas as job satisfaction. These surveys typically allow the company to compare its results with those of other organizations. Also, some firms keep a database of items. Companies who use these items in their surveys can compare their results with those of other companies.

Surveys come in several formats, perhaps the most common of which is the paper-and-pencil form. We sometimes use a scannable survey if there is a large number of recipients, because it is a quicker and more cost-effective means of entering the data. Surveys also can be entered directly into a computer, faxed, or completed over a telephone.

Most of our surveys have a list of categories (i.e., gender, race, department, length of service). We use these categories to present the survey information in a way that will be most meaningful to management. We try to include as few categories as possible, so that people do not feel that their individual responses could be traced back to them. Most of our surveys contain at least one open-ended question, and anywhere from 5 to 100 closed items with a four- or five-point scale such as "agree/disagree."

## Employment Profile

Communication regarding the survey is very important. Employees need to know when the survey is coming and what its purpose is. They also need to know how and when the results will be reported and used. A cover letter from the top manager in the company is sometimes included that provides employees with this information.

Once the survey is developed, I will coach the client in administration procedures. Most of our clients use the paper-and-pencil format, which is administered in groups, picked up at a central location, handed out, or sent through the mail. Regardless of the administration procedure, I emphasize the importance of confidentiality. We ask that the employee's name not be placed anywhere on the survey and, if possible, not on the envelope. I also ask that the survey not be attached to something that has the employee's name on it. If the survey is administered in groups, each person should be provided with an envelope in which they can seal their survey and drop in a central location. Employees who take our surveys are given, or have access to, envelopes that are pre-paid with our address on it that they can drop in the mail.

As the surveys are received, the data are entered (or scanned), and comments are transcribed verbatim. We usually sort the comments and data by some or all of the categories listed on the survey. Most of the time, we will only report an individual group's response if there are at least five people. Our clients usually receive a report with overall company results, one that includes a comparison of all the individual department results, and a separate report for each department.

After the results are compiled, I usually write a narrative summary of the results, which includes a brief background about the survey, overall findings, and recommendations for improvement. I highlight the company's strengths that were identified by the survey, as well as opportunities for improvement.

I give most of my clients feedback over the phone. During this conversation, I highlight strengths and opportunities for improvement and discuss with them why they feel the results turned out they way they did. We also talk about providing feedback, developing action plans, and following up on the survey.

Clients are encouraged to provide employees with some sort of feedback as quickly as possible. For larger organizations, this may involve summarizing the findings in a newsletter; while in smaller organizations, employee meetings are typically conducted. After the top manager reviews the survey results, he or she will meet with the executive staff. In this meeting, the results are presented and discussed, areas for improvement are targeted (I recommend choosing one to three areas), and an action plan is developed. A meeting is then held for all employees to give them feedback. The results are presented, and areas for improvement are shared. Feedback meetings are then conducted with smaller groups (usually departments). These meetings are used as an exchange of information, and employees talk in detail about the issues identified in the survey. One to three areas for the group/department are usually targeted for improvement, and an action plan for dealing with these issues is developed.

One of the most important stages in the survey process is follow-up. After action plans are developed and implemented, I encourage the client to follow-up periodically to see if and where there have been improvements. Informal follow-up can be easily done on a monthly basis by asking people (either in a meeting or one-on-one) how they think the company/department is doing in a particular area. Formal follow-up can be done using a very short survey that measures how things have changed in the last few months. Follow-up gives the company an opportunity to "market" their efforts to employees, find out if changes in action plans are necessary, and redirect their efforts as needed.

In the past, our clients have conducted surveys every two or three years, but recently they have done surveys every quarter, semi-annually, or once per year. More frequent surveying allows companies to target particular issues and find out how they are doing in areas in which they have made changes. Surveys are a valuable means of gathering a large amount of data from a large number of employees in a relatively short period of time, and they are an excellent tool for measuring job satisfaction.

**Table 12.3** Commonly used vocational interest and values tests

| Vocational Interests |
| --- |
| Aamodt Vocational Interest Survey (AVIS) |
| Career Assessment Inventory |
| COPS Interest Inventory |
| Jackson Vocational Interest Survey |
| Kuder Occupational Interest Survey |
| Ohio Vocational Interest Survey (OVIS) |
| Self-Directed Search (SDS) |
| Strong Interest Inventory (SII) |

| Work Values |
| --- |
| Career Orientation Placement and Evaluation Survey (COPES) |
| Study of Values |
| Survey of Interpersonal Values |
| Work Environment Preference Schedule |
| Work Values Inventory |

and values tests. The results of these tests are then used to match the employee to jobs with compatible requirements. A list of commonly used interest and work values tests can be found in Table 12.3.

In addition to wants and values, a discrepancy between what an employee expected a job to be like and the reality of the job can affect satisfaction. For example, a recruiter tells an applicant how much fun employees have at a particular company and about the "unlimited potential" for advancement. After three months on the job, however, the employee has yet to experience the fun and can't find any signs of potential advancement opportunities. Because his expectations have not been met, the employee will probably feel dissatisfied.

As you can guess from this example, it is important that applicants be given a **realistic job preview** (a concept that you no doubt remember from Chapter 5). Though being honest about the negative aspects of a job may reduce the applicant pool, it decreases the chances of hiring a person who will later become dissatisfied. A good example of this comes from an employee who works for a public mental health agency. Prior to accepting her current job, she had worked in the public sector for ten years in a variety of administrative positions. She was excited about her new opportunity because it was a newly created position with what appeared to be excellent opportunities for personal growth. After a year, however, it became clear that the position was clerical, had no opportunity for advancement, and the most important decision she could make involved whether to order pizza or sandwiches for executive meetings. As you can imagine, she was deeply disappointed and angry at having been mislead. Her level of job satisfaction is now at an all-time personal low, and she is seeking other, more professional, opportunities.

A more recent theory of job satisfaction suggests that certain types of people will generally be satisfied and motivated regardless of the type of job they hold (Weaver, 1978). This idea also makes intuitive sense. We all know people who constantly complain and whine about every job they have, and we also know people who are motivated and enthusiastic about their every job or task.

One such personality theory of work motivation was developed by Wherry and South (1977), who used a 70-item test to measure a person's general level of work motivation. The results of their investigation provided support for the notion that levels of work motivation may be fairly stable across people and jobs.

Similar results were obtained for job satisfaction measures in a study by Dubin and Champoux (1977). This study indicated that some people have a job-oriented focus of life and that these people are happier in their jobs than people without this focus. Orpen (1978) also found a small but positive correlation between satisfaction with work and satisfaction with life.

Judge and Watanabe (1993) and Tait, Padgett, and Baldwin (1989) have expanded the idea that job satisfaction is consistent across time and jobs. These researchers found evidence that job satisfaction is significantly correlated ($r = .44$) with life satisfaction. Thus, people happy in life tend to be happy in their jobs and vice versa.

Significant correlations were found by Staw and Ross (1985) between the job-satisfaction levels of employees in 1969 and in 1971 ($r = .33$), by Judge and Watanabe (1993) between job-satisfaction levels of employees in 1972 and 1977 ($r = .37$), and by Staw, Bell, and Clausen (1986) between adolescent and adult levels of satisfaction. These studies have been interpreted as providing support for the hypothesis that job satisfaction might be at least partially affected by personality traits.

An interesting and controversial study by Arvey, Bouchard, Segal, and Abraham (1989) suggested that job satisfaction may not only be fairly stable across jobs but may also be genetically determined. Arvey and his colleagues arrived at this conclusion by comparing the levels of job satisfaction of 34 sets of identical twins who were separated from each other at an early age.

If job satisfaction is purely environmental, then there should be no significant correlation between levels of job satisfaction for identical twins who were raised in different environments and who were now working at different types of jobs. But if identical twins have similar levels of job satisfaction despite being reared apart and despite working at dissimilar jobs, then a genetic predisposition for job satisfaction would be likely.

Based on their analysis, Arvey and his colleagues found that approximately 30% of job satisfaction appears to be explainable by genetic factors. Thus, one way to increase the overall level of job satisfaction in an organization would be to hire only those applicants who show high levels of overall job and life satisfaction. Because these findings are controversial and have received some criticism (Cropanzano & James, 1990), more research is needed before firm conclusions can be drawn.

# COGNITIVE THEORIES

### EQUITY THEORY

Equity theory was developed by Adams (1965) and is based on the premise that our levels of job satisfaction and motivation are related to how fairly we believe we are treated in comparison with others. If we believe we are treated unfairly, we attempt to change our beliefs or behaviors until the situation appears to be fair. Three components are involved in this perception of fairness: inputs, outputs, and input-output ratio.

**Inputs** are those personal elements that we put into our jobs. Obvious elements are time, effort, education, and experience. Less obvious elements include money spent on child care and distance driven to work.

**Outputs** are those elements that we receive from our jobs. A list of obvious outputs includes pay, benefits, challenge, and responsibility. Less obvious outputs are benefits such as friends and office furnishings.

According to the theory, each employee subconsciously lists all his outputs and inputs and then computes an **input-output ratio** by dividing output value by input value. By itself, this ratio is not especially useful. But each employee then computes the input-output ratios for other employees and to previous work experiences and then compares them to his own. If his ratio is lower than those of others, he becomes dissatisfied and thus is motivated to make the ratios equal in one or more ways.

First, the employee can seek greater outputs by such means as asking for a raise or for more responsibility. Second, the employee can make the ratio more equal by reducing his inputs. Thus, he might not work as hard or he might reduce his attendance.

A less practical way of equalizing the ratios would be changing the ratios of other employees. For example, an employee might try to get another employee to work harder and thus increase that employee's inputs. Or he might try to reduce the outputs of another employee by withholding friendship or finding a way to reduce the other employee's bonuses. Fortunately, however, strategies to equalize input-output ratios seldom involve reducing others' outputs. Employees can also restore equity by rationalizing the input-output ratio differences, changing the person to whom they are comparing themselves, or leaving the organization.

In general, research has supported the idea that our job satisfaction decreases when our input-output ratios are lower than others'. Research on this was conducted by Lord and Hohenfeld (1979) and Hauenstein and Lord (1989) with major league baseball players. Players who either had their salary cut during their first year of free agency or had lost an arbitration case performed at lower levels the following year. Thus, players who thought that their output (salary) was too low, responded by reducing their inputs (performance).

In an interesting study, O'Reilly and Puffer (1989) found that employees' satisfaction and motivation increased when co-workers received appropriate sanctions for their behavior. That is, when a high-performing group member was rewarded or a poor performing group member was punished, the satisfaction and motivation of the group increased.

The degree of inequity that an employee feels when underpaid appears to be a function of whether the employee chose the actions that resulted in underpayment (Cropanzano & Folger, 1989). That is, if an employee chooses to work harder than others who are paid the same, he will not feel cheated, but if he is pressured into working harder for the same pay, he will be unhappy.

An interesting prediction from this theory is a situation in which an employee's input-output ratio is *higher* than the ratios of others. Because the theory is based on equity, the prediction would be that the employee would still strive for equal ratios by either increasing his inputs or decreasing his outputs. In other words, he would either work harder or ask to be paid less. In fact, research has indicated that employees often do respond to being "overpaid" by working harder (Adams & Rosenbaum, 1962; Pritchard, Dunnette, & Jorgenson, 1972). But feelings of inequity caused by being overpaid do not last long and probably do not produce long-term changes in behavior (Carrell & Dittrich, 1978).

One of the greatest problems with this theory is that despite its rational sense, it is difficult to implement. That is, based on this theory, the best way to keep employees satisfied is to treat them all fairly, which would entail paying the most to those employees who contributed the most. Although few of us would disagree with this approach, it is difficult to implement for several reasons. The first reason is *practicality*. An organization certainly can control such variables as salary, hours worked, and benefits, but it cannot easily control other variables such as how far an employee lives from work or the number of friends an employee makes on the job. The second reason that equity is difficult to achieve is that the employee's *perception* of inputs and outputs determines equity, not *actual* inputs and outputs. For example, two students of equal ability receive the same grade on an exam. One student knows that he studied 10 hours for the exam but never saw the other student in the library. He may feel that the scores are unfair because he studied harder than but received the same grade as the student whom he never saw study. Of course, the other student may have studied 20 hours while at work but the other student would not know that. In this case, the student's perception of input level may not match reality.

Thus, it is important that employees base their judgments on factual information. Of course, this may be easier said than done. Although one way to do this would be by open and public information on salaries, many organizations keep such information confidential and even include statements in their employee manuals that forbid employees from divulging their salaries to one another. Such policies, however, encourage employees to speculate about how much other people make. This speculation usually results in employees thinking the worst and believing that others make more than they do. Thus, it is probably in the best interests of an organization to make salaries and performance information available to all employees, although each employee's permission must be obtained before such information is released.

Even if an organization were able to maintain complete internal equity, employees would then compare their ratios with those of employees from other organizations. The problem with such comparisons is that an organization has little or no control over another's policies. Furthermore, perceptions of wages and benefits at other organizations most likely will be more distorted than internal perceptions. Thus, even if equity theory were completely accurate, maintaining a high level of employee satisfaction would still be difficult.

## EXPECTANCY THEORY

The second cognitive theory that focuses on worker motivation is **expectancy theory,** which was first proposed by Vroom (1964) and then modified by others, including Porter and Lawler (1968). This theory has three components, the definitions of which vary with each modification of the theory. The following definitions, however, are combinations of those suggested by others and make the theory easier to understand:

- *Expectancy (E):* The perceived relationship between the amount of effort an employee puts in and the resulting outcome.
- *Instrumentality (I):* The extent to which the outcome of a worker's performance, if noticed, results in a particular consequence.
- *Valence (V):* The extent to which an employee values a particular consequence.

To understand or predict an employee's level of motivation, these components are used in the following formula:

$$\text{Motivation} = E\,(I \times V)$$

Thus, all possible outcomes of a behavior are determined, the valence of each is multiplied by the probability that it occurs at a particular performance level, and then the sum of these products is multiplied by the expectancy of an employee putting in the effort to attain the necessary level of performance. As can be seen from this formula, the higher the score on each component, the greater the employee's motivation. To expound on this, let us examine each component in more detail.

In terms of *expectancy,* if an employee believes that no matter how hard he works, he will never reach the necessary level of performance, then his motivation will probably be low. For *instrumentality,* the employee will be motivated only if his behavior results in some specific consequence. That is, if the employee works extra hours, he expects to be rewarded, or if he is inexcusably absent from work, he expects to be punished. For a behavior to have a desired consequence, two events must occur. First, the employee's behavior must be noticed. If the employee believes that he is able to attain the necessary level of performance but that his performance will not be noticed, then his level of motivation will be low. Second, noticed behavior must be rewarded. If no rewards are available, then, again, motivation will be low. As will be discussed in greater detail later in this chapter, if appropriate behavior does not have positive consequences or if inappropriate behavior does not have negative consequences, then the probability that a worker will continue undesired behaviors increases, and the probability that an employee will continue desired behaviors decreases. For *valence*, if an employee is rewarded, then the reward must be something that the employee values. If good performance is rewarded by an award, then the employee will be motivated only if he values awards. Likewise, if we punish an employee by suspending him, then the punishment will be effective only if the employee needs the money. If he does not particularly like his job and would rather spend a few days at the lake, the suspension will obviously not be effective.

This theory can be used to analyze a situation experienced by a bank in Virginia. Concerned that the bank's tellers were averaging only three new Visa customers each month, the management sought to increase the number of Visa applications taken by each teller. To do so, the tellers were expected to ask each customer if he or she had a Visa Card. If not, the tellers were to give them applications. The tellers would receive $5 extra per month each if they increased the number of new Visa customers per month to 25.

The program was a flop, much to management's surprise. Applying expectancy theory, however, would have led an I/O psychologist to predict the program's lack of success. First, let us look at the expectancy component. If the tellers currently averaged only 3 new Visa customers each month, they probably did not believe that, even working harder, they would be able to generate 25 new customers. Thus, the expectancy probability for the program was low.

Second, most tellers probably did not place much value on an extra $5 per month, so the valence component also was low. Thus, with two of three components having low values, the program was destined to fail from the start. The bank later reduced the monthly number of new Visa cards to 10 and increased the teller reward to $20. These simple changes brought the desired increase in new Visa customers.

In addition to predicting employee effort, expectancy theory has been applied successfully to predict speeding drivers and cheating by students. To demonstrate this last behavior, imagine the typical examination in a typical college class. First, look at the expectancy component. We might ask what the probability is for catching a cheater. Students who cheat most likely believe that it is very low. To determine the instrumentality component, we might ask what the probability is for some negative consequence if a cheater is caught. In many universities, the probability of getting caught is low. Furthermore, not only is it difficult to prove that a student cheated, but if the student is caught and it's the student's first offense, punishment usually results in no more than a few days' suspension. Finally, we examine the valence component. Even if a student *is* caught and suspended, how terrible would that be? For many students, a few days of vacation may not seem so terrible. Thus, when combining the three components, we should not be surprised that cheating often occurs.

Expectancy theory also can be used to suggest ways to change employee motivation. As we saw with the bank, motivation was increased by making the performance standard more reasonable and increasing the value of the consequence. Similarly, if we wanted to apply the theory to decrease cheating, we should increase the probability of catching cheaters, make convicting a person who has cheated easier, and make the consequences for cheating more severe.

Although expectancy theory is an interesting and useful method of predicting and increasing employee motivation, some researchers have also criticized it. The major criticism involves the components equation. As it is now written, all of the components are multiplied. Some researchers have questioned whether the addition of some components would be more appropriate than their multiplication (Schmidt, 1973). That is, when the components are multiplied, a zero in any component would result in a prediction of zero motivation, even when ratings in the other components are high.

A second criticism involves the values that are assigned to each component (Ilgen, Nebeker, & Pritchard, 1981). Research has indicated that even though valence and instrumentality can be reliably measured (Mitchell, 1974), the theory is most predictive when people behave rationally (Stahl & Harrell, 1981), which they often do not, and have an internal locus of control (Lied & Pritchard, 1976), which may not always be the case. Despite problems with the equation, however, the theory is still one of the most useful for predicting employee behavior.

## CONSISTENCY THEORY

The third theory that explains work motivation was developed by Korman (1970, 1976) and concerns the relationship between the employee's level of **self-esteem** and job performance. According to this theory, there is a positive correlation between the two. Furthermore, employees with high self-esteem desire to perform at high levels, and employees with low self-esteem desire to perform at low levels.

There are three types of self-esteem. **Chronic self-esteem** is a person's overall feeling about himself. **Situational self-esteem** is a person's feeling about himself in a particular situation such as operating a machine or talking to other people. **Socially influenced self-esteem** is how a person feels about himself based on the expectations of others. All three types of self-esteem are important to job performance. Research indicates that employees with high self-esteem rate the quality of their work higher than do employees with low self-esteem (Farh & Dobbins, 1989; Levy, 1993).

If this theory is true, an employee's performance can be improved by increasing his self-esteem. But increasing self-esteem, especially chronic self-esteem, is difficult, although it is typically attempted in two ways. In the first, employees are given insights into their strengths. This is usually done in workshops or sensitivity groups. It is thought that these insights raise self-esteem by showing the employee he has several strengths and is a good person.

In the second method, an employee is given a task so easy that he will almost certainly succeed. It is thought that this success increases self-esteem, which should increase performance, then further increase self-esteem, then further increase performance, and so on. This method is based loosely on the principle of **self-fulfilling prophecy,** which states that an individual will perform as well or as poorly as he expects to perform. In other words, if he believes he is intelligent, he should do well on tests. If he thinks he is dumb, he should do poorly.

Research has certainly supported the concept of self-fulfilling prophecy. Rosenthal (1968) has demonstrated that our expectations of others' performance lead us to treat them differently. That is, if we think that someone will do a poor job, we will probably treat them in ways that bring that result. Thus, when an employee becomes aware of others' expectations and matches his own with them, he will perform in a manner that is consistent with those expectations (Oz & Eden, 1994).

Sandler (1986) believes that our expectations are communicated to employees through nonverbal cues such as head tilting or eyebrow raising and through more overt behaviors such as providing low-expectation employees with less feedback, worse facilities, and less praise than high-expectation employees. He also believes that employees are quick to pick up on these cues. Along with Korman (1970) and Rosenthal (1968), Sandler believes that employees then adjust their behaviors to be consistent with our expectations and in a way that is self-sustaining.

Research on consistency theory has brought mixed results. Laboratory studies have generally supported the theory: Subjects who were led to believe that they would perform well on a task did so, and subjects who were led to believe that they would do poorly on a task also did so (Greenhaus & Badin, 1974). The theory, however, has been criticized by Dipboye (1977), who believes that factors other than self-esteem, such as the need to achieve or the need to enhance oneself, can explain the same results.

But given that consistency theory does have some reasonable research support, the next concern is how it can be used to increase employee performance. If employees do indeed respond to their managers' expectations, then it becomes reasonable to predict that managers who communicate positive and optimistic feelings to their employees will lead employees to perform at higher levels.

Another set of theories hypothesizes that workers are only motivated when they are *rewarded* for excellent performance. **Behavioral theories** predict many of the same behaviors as do cognitive theories, but there is a difference in *how* these behaviors are predicted. Behavioral theories only focus on overt employee behavior, whereas cognitive theories focus on employees' decision-making processes.

## OPERANT CONDITIONING

Perhaps the most influential behavioral theory is operant conditioning, which we briefly discussed in Chapter 7. Essentially, operant conditioning principles state that an employee will continue to do those behaviors for which he is reinforced. Thus, if an employee is rewarded for not making errors, he is more likely to produce high quality work. If the employee is rewarded for the amount of work done, he will place less emphasis on quality and try to increase his quantity. Finally, if an employee is not rewarded for any behavior, he will search for behaviors that will be rewarded. Unfortunately, these might include absenteeism (which is rewarded by going fishing) or carelessness (which is rewarded by spending more time with friends).

Obviously, it is important to reward employees for productive work behavior. But different employees like different types of rewards, which is why supervisors should have access to and be trained to administer different types of reinforcers. For example, some employees can be rewarded with praise, others with awards, some with interesting work, and still others with money (Filipczak, 1993).

The use of money to motivate better worker performance has again become popular (Schuster & Zingheim, 1992). As shown in Figure 12.4, a compensation plan should include base pay and a benefit package to provide employees with security, salary adjustments to cover such conditions as undesirable shifts and geographic areas with high costs of living and variable pay to provide an incentive to perform better. Though incentive systems often result in higher levels of performance, when designed poorly, they can result in such negative outcomes as increased stress, decreased health, and decreased safety (Schleifer & Amick, 1989; Schleifer & Okogbaa, 1990). Incentive pay can be given for either individual performance or group performance.

### Individual Incentive Plans

Individual-based incentive plans are designed to make high levels of individual performance financially worthwhile. Individual incentives help reduce such group problems as social loafing, which was discussed in Chapter 10. Two main problems are associated with individual incentive plans. The first is the difficulty in measuring individual performance. Not only are objective measures difficult to find, but supervisors are reluctant to evaluate employ-

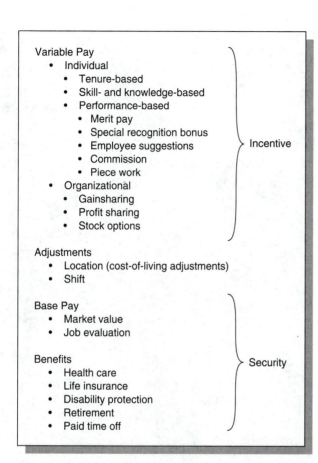

**Figure 12.4**
Components of a compensation plan

Variable Pay
- Individual
  - Tenure-based
  - Skill- and knowledge-based
  - Performance-based
    - Merit pay
    - Special recognition bonus
    - Employee suggestions
    - Commission
    - Piece work
- Organizational
  - Gainsharing
  - Profit sharing
  - Stock options

} Incentive

Adjustments
- Location (cost-of-living adjustments)
- Shift

Base Pay
- Market value
- Job evaluation

Benefits
- Health care
- Life insurance
- Disability protection
- Retirement
- Paid time off

} Security

ees, especially when the outcome will determine the amount of money an employee will receive (Schuster & Zingheim, 1992). The second problem is that individual incentive plans can foster competition among employees. Though competition is not always bad, it is seldom consistent with the recent trend toward a team approach to work. When done right, however, team environments and individual incentive programs can coexist and result in high levels of employee performance (Steers & Porter, 1991). The two most common individual incentive plans are **pay-for-performance** and **merit pay.**

**Pay for Performance**   Also called *earnings-at-risk (EAR)* plans, pay-for-performance plans pay employees according to how much they individually produce. Simple pay-for-performance systems with which you are probably familiar include commission and piece work.

The first step in creating more complicated pay-for-performance plans is to determine the average or standard amount of production. For example, the average number of envelopes sorted by mail clerks might be 300 per hour. The next step is to determine the desired average amount of pay. We might decide that, on average, our mail clerks should earn $9 an hour. We

Money is seldom the main determinant of job satisfaction.

then compute the piece rate by dividing hourly wage by number of envelopes sorted (9/300), which is .03. Thus, each correctly sorted envelope is worth three cents. If a mail clerk is good and sorts 400 envelopes per hour, he will make $12 per hour. If our clerk is not a good worker and can sort only 200 pieces per hour, he makes $6 per hour. To protect workers from the effects of external factors, minimum-wage laws ensure that even the worst employee will make enough money to survive. As suggested in Figure 12.4, most organizations provide a base salary to ensure employees will have at least minimum financial security.

Union National Bank in Little Rock, Arkansas, has had tremendous success by paying its workers for the number of customers they serve, the number of new customers gained, the amount of time taken to balance accounts at the end of the day, and so on. The bank's pay-for-performance program has resulted in the average employee making 25% more in take-home pay, and the bank itself has almost doubled its profits.

Nucor in Charlotte, North Carolina, is another company that has used a pay-for-performance plan. By paying its steelworkers for the amount of work they do, Nucor has seen productivity more than double and its workers make more than $30,000 per year while the industry average is some $27,000. Though pay-for-performance plans appear to be successful for both the employee and the employer, some research suggests that employees are not satisfied with such plans (Brown & Huber, 1992).

**Merit Pay**   The major distinction between merit pay and pay-for-performance is that merit-pay systems base their incentives on performance-appraisal scores rather than on such objective performance measures as sales and productivity. Thus, merit pay is a potentially good technique for jobs in which productivity is difficult to measure.

The actual link between performance-appraisal scores and the amount of merit pay received by an employee varies greatly around the United States. In the state of Virginia's merit-pay system, employees' performance-appraisal scores at each office are ranked, and the top 30% of employees each receive a $1,000 annual bonus.

In the merit-pay system used by one nonprofit mental health agency, each employee's performance-appraisal rating is divided by the total number of performance points possible, and this percentage is then multiplied by the maximum 3% merit increase that can be received by an employee. With this system, an employee must receive a perfect rating to receive the full 3% increase. Most employees receive between 2% and 2.5%.

The merit-pay system used by a California public transit system is similar to that used by the mental health agency with the exception that the merit increase becomes part of an employee's base salary for the next pay period. Thus, increases are perpetuated each year, unlike the mental health system's one-time reward.

Research on merit pay has brought mixed reviews. Some research has shown that employees like the idea of merit pay, but other research has found that it is not popular with all employees, and many employees do not consider the merit ratings to be fair (Hills, Scott, Markham, & Vest, 1987; Wisdom & Patzig, 1987). Employees are most satisfied with merit pay if they help develop the system (Gilchrist & White, 1990).

One of merit pay's biggest problems is that increases are based on subjective performance appraisals. Aware of this, some supervisors will inflate performance-appraisal scores to increase their employees' pay and thus more positive employee feelings about the supervisors. Managers have also been known to inflate performance-appraisal ratings when they believe the base salaries for certain positions are too low.

Another problem with merit pay is that its availability or amount often changes with each fiscal year. Thus, excellent performance one year might result in a large bonus, while the same performance another year might bring no bonus at all. This is especially true in the public sector. Thus, for merit pay to be successful, funding must be consistently available, and information about its availability and amount should be shared with employees (Wisdom & Patzig, 1987).

### Organizational Incentives

The idea behind organizational-based incentive plans is to get employees to participate in the success or failure of the organization (Schuster & Zingheim, 1992). Rather than encouraging individual competition, these plans reward employees for reaching group goals. The problems with group incentive plans are that they can encourage social loafing and can get so complicated that they become difficult to explain to employees.

**Profit Sharing**   Profit sharing was developed in the United States by Albert Gallatin way back in 1794 (Henderson, 1994). As its name implies, profit-sharing programs provide employees with a percentage of *profits* above a certain amount. For example, in addition to their base salary, employees might receive 50% of the profits a company makes above 6%. Organizations will usually not share the initial 5% or so of profits because that money is needed for research and development and as a safety net for unprofitable years. The profits to be shared can be paid directly to employees as a bonus (cash plans) or placed into the employees' retirement fund (deferred plans). Profit sharing will only motivate employees if they understand the link between performance and profits and believe that the company has a reasonable chance of making a profit.

**Gainsharing**   A related plan, known as **gainsharing,** uses pay incentives based on *improvement* in organizational performance. Though the first gainsharing program was developed in 1935 by the Nunn-Bush Shoe Company in Milwaukee, gainsharing has only become popular in the last two decades (Gowen, 1990). About 15% of large organizations have gainsharing programs. Gainsharing programs consist of two elements: a cooperative/participative management philosophy and a group-based formula (Hanlon & Taylor, 1992).

The typical gainsharing program works as follows. First, the company monitors performance measures over some period of time to derive a **baseline.** Then, productivity goals above the baseline are set, and the employees are told that they will receive bonuses for each period that the goal is reached. To make goal setting more effective, constant feedback is provided to employees on how current performance is in relation to the goal. At the end of each reporting period, bonuses are paid based on how well the group did.

An excellent example of a successful gainsharing program can be found at the Dana Spicer Heavy Axle Division facility in Ohio (Hatcher, Ross, & Ross, 1987). Employees at the Dana plant receive a financial bonus when productivity surpasses the baseline. The gainsharing program has dramatically increased the number of employee suggestions, product quality, and productivity. Employees' bonuses average 14% above their normal pay each month, with year-end bonuses between 11% and 16%.

In general, gainsharing plans seem to be effective. A review of gainsharing studies indicates improvements in productivity, increased employee and union satisfaction, and declines in absenteeism (Gowen, 1990). As with any incentive plan, gainsharing is most effective when employees are formally involved in their design and operation (Bullock & Tubbs, 1990) and there is not a long delay between performance and the financial payoff (Mawhinney & Gowen, 1990).

**Stock Options**   Stock options represent the most complicated organizational incentive plan. With stock options, employees are annually offered company stock at a set price—usually well below market value. Employees then have the option of purchasing the discounted stock in the company. The idea behind this plan is that as a company does well, the value of its stock increases as does the employee's profit. For example, suppose that AT&T stock is selling for $55 per share. The company gives employees the option of purchasing the stock for $50 per share. Ten years later, the stock is worth $75 per share and the employee realizes a $25-per-share profit. However, if the stock had fallen from $55 to $45, the employee would realize a $5 per share decrease ($50 purchase price–$45 selling price).

Stock options allow employees to share in the long-term success of an organization. At times, they may not be good motivators because employees have trouble understanding the concept of stock and the incentive (profit made on the selling of stock) is psychologically well removed from day-to-day performance.

### Premack Principle

Another reinforcement technique stems from the **Premack Principle** (Premack, 1963), which states that reinforcement is relative, and a supervisor can reinforce an employee with something that on the surface does not appear to be a reinforcer. The best way to explain this principle is to construct a **reinforcement hierarchy** on which an employee lists his preferences for a variety of reinforcers.

As Figure 12.5 shows, our hypothetical employee most desires money and time off from work and least desires typesetting and cleaning the press. Our employee can enjoy and do a better job of cleaning his press if we give him money for each time he properly completes the task, but such a reward system can become expensive. Thus, according to the Premack Principle, we can get our employee to properly clean his press by allowing him to do one of the activities he likes more than cleaning. From his reinforcement hierarchy, we can see that he ranked throwing out oily rags as more enjoyable because he can take a short break by walking outdoors to the disposal area. Thus, all we need for a reward is to let him dispose of the rags.

The Premack Principle may sound silly, but think of the reinforcers you have used to reward yourself for studying. After reading a certain number of pages, you might allow yourself a trip to the water fountain. Certainly, getting a drink of water is hardly anyone's idea of a good time, but it may be more interesting than studying and so can become a reinforcer to increase studying.

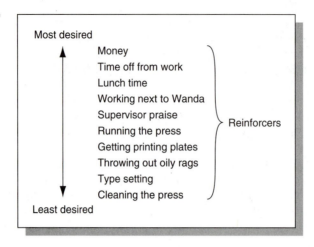

**Figure 12.5**
Example of a reinforcement hierarchy

Most desired

Money
Time off from work
Lunch time
Working next to Wanda
Supervisor praise } Reinforcers
Running the press
Getting printing plates
Throwing out oily rags
Type setting
Cleaning the press

Least desired

Even though operant conditioning has been successful in improving motivation and performance, a note of caution comes from Deci (1972), who believes that for some people and some jobs, work is intrinsically motivating. That is, people are motivated because they enjoy working, not because they are being rewarded. A reasonable body of research, much of it conducted by Deci himself, demonstrates that paying a person for the amount of work done will reduce the degree to which he enjoys performing the task. Thus, when financial incentives are no longer available, the employee will be less motivated to work than before rewards were used.

### Goal Setting

To further increase the effectiveness of reinforcement, goal setting should be used. With **goal setting,** each employee is given a goal, which might be a particular quality level, a certain quantity of output, or a combination of the two. For goal setting to be most successful, the goals themselves should possess certain qualities.

First, they should be *concrete* and *specific* (Terborg, 1977; Wood, Mento, and Locke, 1987). A goal such as, "I will produce as many as I can," will not be as effective as, "I will print 5,000 pages in the next hour." The more specific the goal, the greater the productivity. To underscore this point, we will use an example involving push-ups. If a person says that he will "do as many push-ups as I can," does that mean he will do as many as he can until he tires? Or does it mean he will do as many as he can before he begins to sweat? Or does it mean he will do as many as he did the last time? The problem with such a goal is its ambiguity and lack of specific guidelines. Setting more specific subgoals can also improve performance (Klawsky, 1990).

Second, a properly set goal is high but reasonable (Locke, 1968; Locke & Latham, 1990). If an employee regularly prints 5,000 pages an hour and sets a goal of 4,000 pages, performance is certainly not going to increase. Conversely, if the goal becomes 20,000 pages, it will also not be effective because the employee will quickly realize that he cannot meet the goal and will quit trying.

A good example of goals set too high comes from the academic retention program at Radford University. This program is designed to help special students who are having academic trouble and whose G.P.A.s have fallen below that needed to stay in school. The program involves tutoring, study skills, and goal setting. Although it has generally been a success, many students fail to improve their academic performances. A brief investigation revealed that the goal-setting process was one of the reasons for these failures. Students were allowed to set their own G.P.A. goals for the semester—and students with G.P.A.s of 1.0 were setting goals of 4.0! Obviously, none of the students was able to reach this goal. The problem typically came when a student did poorly on his first test, and his chance for an A in a class was gone, as was his chance for a 4.0 G.P.A. for the semester. Because their goals could not be attained, the students felt they had failed and quit trying.

Until fairly recently, it was generally thought that a goal will lead to the greatest increase in productivity if it is set at least in part by the employee. That is, although performance will increase if the supervisor sets the employee's goal, it will increase even more if the employee participates. However, several meta-analyses have indicated that participating in goal setting does not increase performance (Mento, Steel, & Karren, 1987; Tubbs, 1986).

The first goal-setting study that caught the interest of industrial psychologists was conducted by Latham and Blades (1975). Their study was brought about because truck drivers at a logging mill were not completely filling their trucks before making deliveries. Empty space in the trucks obviously cost the company money. To increase each delivery's load, the drivers were given specific weight goals and were told that they would be neither punished for missing the goal nor rewarded for reaching it. A significant increase in the average load per delivery resulted. Although this is the most celebrated study, goal setting has been shown to be effective in a wide variety of situations.

### Feedback

To further increase the effectiveness of reinforcement and goal setting, feedback should be provided to the employee on his progress in reaching his goal (Locke & Latham, 1990). Feedback can include verbally telling an employee how he is doing, placing a chart on a wall, or displaying a certain color of light when the employee's work pace will result in goal attainment and a different color of light when the pace is too slow to reach the goal.

An excellent example of the use of feedback comes from Domino's Pizza. Each month, the average delivery and service times for each store are printed as "box scores" in *The Pepperoni Press,* the company's newsletter (Feuer, 1987). These box scores provide each store with feedback on how it compares with other stores. This feedback is one reason why Domino's is the world's fastest-growing fast-food outlet.

## SOCIAL LEARNING THEORY

A second behavioral theory postulates that employees observe the levels of motivation and satisfaction of other employees and then model those levels. Thus, if an organization's older employees work hard and talk positively about their jobs and their employer, new employees will model this behavior and be both productive and satisfied. The reverse is also true: If veteran employees work slowly and complain about their jobs, so will new employees.

To test this theory, Weiss and Shaw (1979) had subjects view training videos in which assembly line workers made either positive or negative comments about their jobs. After viewing a videotape, each subject was given an opportunity to perform the job. The study found that those subjects who had seen the positive tape enjoyed the task more than did subjects who viewed the negative tape.

This theory has not yet been heavily researched, but it certainly makes intuitive sense. Think of courses you have taken in which one student participated more than anyone else. After a while, the student's level of participation probably decreased to be more in line with the rest of the class. In work as in school, social pressures force a person to behave in ways that are consistent with the norm, even though the person may privately believe something different (Nail, 1986).

## INTEGRATION OF THEORIES

In this chapter, we discussed many theories of job satisfaction and work motivation. The question you must be asking (other than when does this chapter end?) is how then do we motivate and satisfy employees? Unfortunately the answer to this question is complex and depends on a variety of factors. We can, however, use the theories to design an organizational climate that is more conducive to motivation and satisfaction than the typical climate.

### JOB SATISFACTION

As shown in Figure 12.6, individual difference theories say that each of us brings to a job an initial tendency to be satisfied with life and its various aspects such as work. A person with a low tendency toward satisfaction might *start* a job with only 6 hypothetical satisfaction points, a person with a neutral tendency might start with 10 hypothetical points, and a person with a high tendency might bring 14.

For example, research indicates that in addition to genetics, such traits as internal locus of control (Stout, Slocum, & Cron, 1987; Surrette & Harlow, 1992), Type A behavior, patience/tolerance (Bluen, Barling, & Burns, 1990), and social trust (Liou, Sylvia, & Brunk, 1990) are related to our ten-

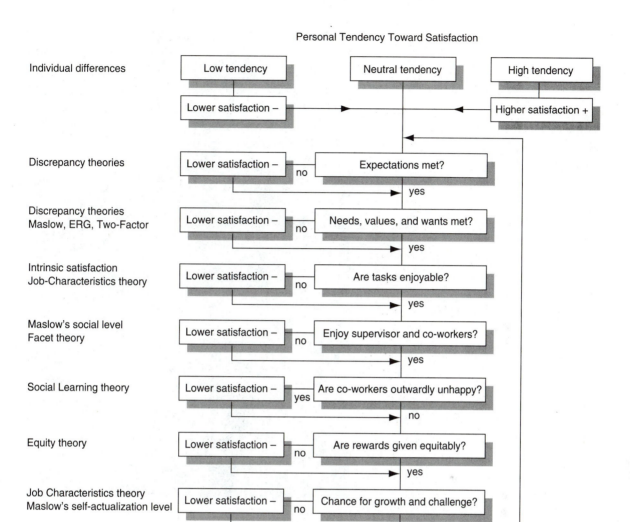

**Figure 12.6** Integrating job-satisfaction theories

dency to be satisfied with work. Demographically, males and females are equally satisfied with work, Whites are more satisfied than Blacks, and older workers are more satisfied than younger workers (Rhodes, 1983).

Surrette and Harlow (1992) found that people will be most satisfied with a job if they had the *option to choose* that job from other alternatives rather than the job being their only choice. Once people are employed at a job, however, they are most satisfied when they don't have other career alternatives (Pond & Geyer, 1987).

Many jobs are
not intrinsically
satisfying.

During our years at work, certain events and conditions occur that can
add to or decrease our initial level of satisfaction that was due to personal
predispositions.

According to discrepancy, Maslow's, ERG, McClelland's, and Herzberg's
theories, we will remain satisfied with our job if it meets our various needs,
wants, expectations, and values. As we discussed previously in the chapter,
individuals vary greatly on their needs for such things as achievement, status, safety, and social contact. Thus, not every job can satisfy the needs of
every employee during every period of their lives. By being aware of employee needs, however, we can select the employees whose needs are consistent with the requirements and characteristics of the job.

According to the intrinsic satisfaction theory and Job Characteristics
Theory, we will be more satisfied with our jobs if the tasks themselves are
enjoyable to perform. What makes a task enjoyable varies across individuals. For some, working on a computer is fun, whereas for others, nothing

could be more boring. Many people enjoy such things as making decisions, solving conflicts, and seeing a project through from start to finish, whereas others don't.

Overall satisfaction can be affected by our satisfaction with individual facets of the job. For example, an incompetent boss, terrible co-workers, low pay, or limited opportunities for advancement can lessen overall job satisfaction. Even trivial things can lessen job satisfaction. I once worked at a job where the vending machines never worked, and supplies such as paper and pens often were not available. These factors were irritants for most employees—enough so to lessen job satisfaction but certainly not enough to make any of us *dissatisfied* with the job.

According to social learning theory, we will be more satisfied if our co-workers are satisfied. If everyone else is whining and complaining, it is difficult to be the only person at work who loves his job. No matter how much we intrinsically like our work, equity theory predicts we will become dissatisfied if rewards and punishments are not given equitably. If you work harder than a co-worker, yet he receives a bigger raise, you are less likely to be satisfied even though money may not be the reason you are working. Based on Job Characteristics Theory and Maslow's level of self-actualization, lack of opportunity for growth, challenge, variety, autonomy, and advancement will decrease satisfaction in many people. The results of these factors are summed to indicate an employee's current level of satisfaction. As conditions change, so will the level of satisfaction.

## WORK MOTIVATION

As shown in Figure 12.7, people come to a job with a predisposition toward motivation. That is, some people, such as those with high self-esteem, are generally more motivated than others. From goal-setting theory, we find that employees who have, understand, and agree to goals will be more motivated than those without goals or with unclear goals. From expectancy theory and goal-setting theory, we know that the goals must be challenging but reasonable. From operant learning and expectancy theories, it is clear that extrinsically motivated people will be more motivated if behavior results in a reward. From these same two theories plus discrepancy theory, the needs theories, and the Premack Principle, we know that the rewards must have value to the employee in order to be motivating. Because different people value different rewards, care must be taken to ensure that a variety of rewards are available. From equity theory, we know that rewards that are valued will only be motivating if they are given in an equitable way. As discussed previously in the chapter, *perceptions* of equity are as important as the *reality* of equity. Social learning theory tells us that if some employees are motivated, there is an increased probability that others will model their behavior and be motivated. The results of these factors are summed to indicate an employee's current level of motivation. As conditions change, so will the motivation level.

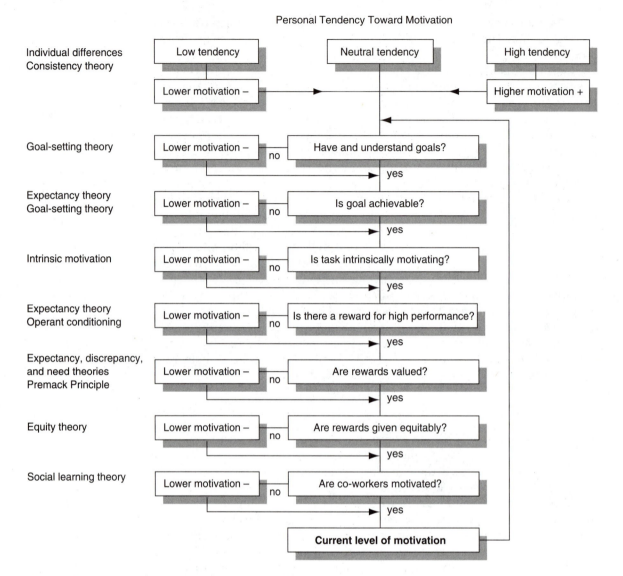

**Figure 12.7** Integrating work motivation theories

## MEASURING JOB SATISFACTION

This chapter has discussed several theories that seek to explain job satisfaction. But one important issue that remains is how an employee's level of job satisfaction is determined. Generally, it is measured by one of several different paper-and-pencil tests.

One of the first methods for measuring job satisfaction was developed by Kunin (1955) and is called the **Faces Scale** (a simulation is shown in Fig-

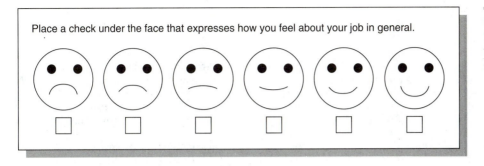

**Figure 12.8**
Simulation of faces scale of job satisfaction

Place a check under the face that expresses how you feel about your job in general.

ure 12.8). Although the scale is easy to use, it is no longer commonly administered partly because it lacks sufficient detail.

The scale most commonly used today is the **Job Descriptive Index (JDI)** (See Figure 12.9). The JDI was developed by Smith, Kendall, and Hulin (1969) and consists of a series of job-related adjectives and statements that are rated by employees. The scales yield scores on five dimensions of job satisfaction: supervision, pay, promotional opportunities, co-workers, and the work itself.

A similar measure of job satisfaction is the **Minnesota Satisfaction Questionnaire (MSQ),** which was developed by Weiss, Dawis, England, and Lofquist (1967). The MSQ, the short form of which is shown in Figure 12.10, contains 100 items that yield scores on 20 scales.

The fact that the JDI has 5 scales and the MSQ 20 underscores the point that job satisfaction is not easy to measure. This is especially true when one considers that employees' responses on the JDI are not highly correlated with their responses on the MSQ (Gillet & Schwab, 1975).

Because both JDI and the MSQ measure specific aspects of job satisfaction, Ironson, Smith, Brannick, Gibson, and Paul (1989) recently developed the **Job-in-General (JIG) Scale.** The JIG is useful when an organization wants to measure the overall level of job satisfaction rather than specific aspects of job satisfaction. In the 1990s, job satisfaction is most commonly measured by custom-designed employee surveys. These surveys typically contain 80 to 100 items and are used by over 70 percent of all organizations (Paul & Bracken, 1995).

## CHAPTER SUMMARY

This chapter began with a discussion of the definitions and interrelationships of job satisfaction and motivation. This discussion concluded that satisfaction is moderately related to turnover and absenteeism, slightly related to performance, and very much related to organizational commitment.

We then discussed several theories about the factors related to employee motivation and job satisfaction. The first set of theories—needs theories—

Think of your present work. What is it like most of the time? In the blank beside each word given below, write

<u>Y</u>  for "Yes" if it describes your work
<u>N</u>  for "No" if it does NOT describe it
<u>?</u>  if you cannot decide

Think of the pay you get now. How well does each of the following words describe your present pay? In the blank beside each word, put

<u>Y</u>  if it describes your pay
<u>N</u>  for "No" if it does NOT describe it
<u>?</u>  if you cannot decide

Think of the opportunities for promotion that you have now. How well does each of the following words describe these? In the blank beside each word put

<u>Y</u>  for "Yes" if it describes your opportunities for promotion
<u>N</u>  for "No" if it does NOT describe them
<u>?</u>  if you cannot decide

*Work on Present Job*

____ Routine
____ Satisfying
____ Good
____ On your feet

*Present Pay*

____ Income adequate for normal expenses
____ Insecure
____ Less than I deserve
____ Highly paid

*Opportunities for Promotion*

____ Promotion on ability
____ Dead-end job
____ Unfair promotion policy
____ Regular promotions

Think of the kind of supervision that you get on your job. How well does each of the following words describe this supervision? In the blank beside each word below, put

<u>Y</u>  if it describes the supervision you get on your job
<u>N</u>  if it does NOT describe it
<u>?</u>  if you cannot decide

Think of the majority of the people that you work with now or the people you meet in connection with your work. How well does each of the following words describe these people? In the blank beside each word below, put

<u>Y</u>  if it describes the people you work with
<u>N</u>  if it does NOT describe them
<u>?</u>  if you cannot decide

*Supervision on Present Job*

____ Impolite
____ Praises good work
____ Influential
____ Doesn't supervise enough

*People on Your Present Job*

____ Boring
____ Responsible
____ Intelligent
____ Talk too much

**Figure 12.9** Sample items from the job descriptive index

Source: *The measurement of satisfaction in work and retirement,* by P. C. Smith, L. M. Kendall, & C. L. Hulin, 1969; Chicago: Rand McNally. The Job Descriptive Index is copyrighted by Bowling Green State University. The complete forms, scoring key, instructions, and norms can be requested from Dr. Patricia C. Smith, Department of Psychology, Bowling Green State University, Bowling Green, Ohio 43403. Used by permission of the authors.

*Ask yourself:* How **satisfied** am I with this aspect of my job?

**Very Sat.** *means I am very satisfied with this aspect of my job.*

**Sat.** *means I am satisfied with this aspect of my job.*

**N** *means I can't decide whether I am satisfied or not with this aspect of my job.*

**Dissat.** *means I am dissatisfied with this aspect of my job.*

**Very Dissat.** *means I am very dissatisfied with this aspect of my job.*

| On my present job, this is how I feel about... | Very Dissat. | Dissat. | N | Sat. | Very Sat. |
|---|---|---|---|---|---|
| 1. Being able to keep busy all the time | ☐ | ☐ | ☐ | ☐ | ☐ |
| 2. The chance to work alone on the job | ☐ | ☐ | ☐ | ☐ | ☐ |
| 3. The chance to do different things from time to time | ☐ | ☐ | ☐ | ☐ | ☐ |
| 4. The chance to be "somebody" in the community | ☐ | ☐ | ☐ | ☐ | ☐ |
| 5. The way my boss handles employees | ☐ | ☐ | ☐ | ☐ | ☐ |
| 6. The competence of my supervisor in making decisions | ☐ | ☐ | ☐ | ☐ | ☐ |
| 7. Being able to do things that don't go against my conscience | ☐ | ☐ | ☐ | ☐ | ☐ |
| 8. The way my job provides for steady employment | ☐ | ☐ | ☐ | ☐ | ☐ |
| 9. The chance to do things for other people | ☐ | ☐ | ☐ | ☐ | ☐ |
| 10. The chance to tell people what to do | ☐ | ☐ | ☐ | ☐ | ☐ |
| 11. The chance to do something that makes use of my abilities | ☐ | ☐ | ☐ | ☐ | ☐ |
| 12. The way company policies are put into practice | ☐ | ☐ | ☐ | ☐ | ☐ |
| 13. My pay and the amount of work I do | ☐ | ☐ | ☐ | ☐ | ☐ |
| 14. The chances for advancement on this job | ☐ | ☐ | ☐ | ☐ | ☐ |
| 15. The freedom to use my own judgment | ☐ | ☐ | ☐ | ☐ | ☐ |
| 16. The chance to try my own methods of doing the job | ☐ | ☐ | ☐ | ☐ | ☐ |
| 17. The working conditions | ☐ | ☐ | ☐ | ☐ | ☐ |
| 18. The way my co-workers get along with each other | ☐ | ☐ | ☐ | ☐ | ☐ |
| 19. The praise I get for doing a good job | ☐ | ☐ | ☐ | ☐ | ☐ |
| 20. The feeling of accomplishment I get from the job | ☐ | ☐ | ☐ | ☐ | ☐ |
| | Very Dissat. | Dissat. | N | Sat. | Very Sat. |

**Figure 12.10** Minnesota Satisfaction Questionnaire short form

Source: *Minnesota Satisfaction Questionnaire* (short form), copyright 1967, Vocational Psychological Research, University of Minnesota. Used by permission.

postulates that job satisfaction is determined by how well an organization is able to satisfy its employees' needs. Maslow proposed that we have five needs (basic biological, safety, social, ego, and self-actualization), Aldefer proposed (in his ERG theory) that we have three needs (existence, relatedness, and growth), Herzberg proposed that we seek to satisfy two basic types of needs or factors (hygiene and motivators), and McClelland proposed that we have three important needs (achievement, power, and affiliation).

The second type of theory discussed is the individual difference theory, which postulates that certain types of people are predisposed to be satisfied with their jobs while others are predisposed to be dissatisfied.

The third set of theories postulates that motivation and satisfaction are the result of cognitive factors. Equity theory states that our level of satisfaction and perhaps effort is based on a comparison of what we put into our jobs (inputs) and what we get from our jobs (outputs) with the inputs and outputs of others. If the input-output ratio does not match those of others, inequity results.

Expectancy theory states that our level of motivation is a function of three factors: expectancy, instrumentality, and valence. To be motivated to work hard, we must believe that we can perform a job, that we will be rewarded for our performance, and that the reward is something desirable.

Consistency theory states that our performance level is consistent with our level of self-esteem. If we have low self-esteem, we will perform at a low level, while if we have high self-esteem, we will perform at a high level.

The fourth set of theories — behavioral theories — postulates that we will exert effort if we are rewarded for doing so. The main theories in this category are operant conditioning and social learning theory. The discussion on behavioral theories included the use of incentives to motivate employees.

After a discussion of the research and theories of job satisfaction and motivation, two charts were presented to help integrate the theories.

The chapter concluded by discussing ways in which job satisfaction can be measured. The most common method is by using job-satisfaction scales. These include the Faces Scale, the Job Descriptive Index (JDI), the Minnesota Satisfaction Questionnaire (MSQ), and the Job in General (JIG) Scale.

# GLOSSARY

**Baseline**   The level of productivity before the implementation of a gainsharing plan.

**Basic biological needs**   The first step in Maslow's needs hierarchy, which concerns survival needs such as those for food, air, and water.

**Chronic self-esteem**   The positive or negative way in which a person views himself or herself as a whole.

**Ego needs**   The fourth step in Maslow's needs hierarchy, which concerns the individual's need for recognition and success.

**ERG Theory**   Aldefer's needs theory that describes three levels of satisfaction: existence, relatedness, and growth.

**Expectancy**   In expectancy theory, the perceived probability that a particular amount of effort will result in a particular level of performance.

**Extrinsic**   Nonpersonal factors such as pay, co-workers, and opportunities for advancement that affect our levels of job satisfaction and work motivation.

**Faces Scale**   A measure of job satisfaction in which raters place a mark under a facial expression that is most similar to the way they feel about their jobs.

**Gainsharing**   A group incentive system in which employees are paid a bonus based on improvements in group productivity.

**Goal setting**   A method of increasing performance in which employees are given specific performance goals to aim for.

**Hierarchy**   A system arranged by rank.

**Hygiene factors**   In Herzberg's two-factor theory, job-related elements that result from but do not involve the job itself.

**Input-output Ratio**   The ratio of how much employees believe they put into their jobs to how much they believe they get from their jobs.

**Inputs**   In equity theory, the elements that employees put into their jobs.

**Instrumentality**   In expectancy theory, the perceived probability that a particular level of performance will result in a particular consequence.

**Intrinsic**   The degree to which we are satsfied by a job or motivated to perform in the absence of such external factors as pay, promotion, and co-workers.

**Job-characteristics theory**   The theory proposed by Hackman and Oldham that suggests that certain characteristics of a job will make the job more or less satisfying, depending on the particular needs of the worker.

**Job Descriptive Index (JDI)**   A measure of job satisfaction that yields scores on five dimensions.

**Job Diagnostic Survey (JDS)**   A measure of the extent to which a job provides opportunities for growth, autonomy, and meaning.

**Job enlargement**   A system in which employees are given more tasks to perform at the same time.

**Job enrichment**   A system in which employees are given more responsibility over the tasks and decisions related to their jobs.

**Job-in-General (JIG) Scale**   A measure of the overall level of job satisfaction.

**Job rotation**   A system in which employees are given the opportunity to perform several different jobs in an organization.

**Job satisfaction**   The attitude employees have toward their jobs.

**Merit pay**   An incentive plan in which employees receive pay bonuses based on performance-appraisal scores.

**Minnesota Satisfaction Questionnaire (MSQ)**   A measure of job satisfaction that yields scores on 20 dimensions.

**Motivation**   The force that drives an employee to perform well.

**Motivators**   In Herzberg's two-factor theory, elements of a job that concern the actual duties performed by the employee.

**Need for achievement**   The extent to which a person desires to master a task.

**Need for affiliation**   The extent to which a person desires to be around other people.

**Need for power**   The extent to which a person desires to have influence over other people.

**Needs theory**   A theory based on the idea that employees will be satisfied with jobs that satisfy their needs.

**Outputs**   In equity theory, the things that employees get from their jobs.

**Pay for performance**   A system in which employees are paid based on how much they individually produce.

**Premack Principle**   The idea that reinforcement is relative both within an individual and between individuals.

**Quality circles**   Employee groups that meet to propose changes that will improve productivity and the quality of work life.

**Reinforcement hierarchy**   A rank-ordered list of reinforcers for an individual.

**Safety needs**   The second step in Maslow's hierarchy, concerning the need for security, stability, and physical safety.

**Self-actualization needs**   The fifth step in Maslow's needs hierarchy, which concerns the need to realize one's potential.

**Self-directed teams**   See *quality circles.*

**Self-esteem**   The positive or negative way in which people view themselves.

**Self-fulfilling prophecy**   The idea that people behave in ways consistent with their self-image.

**Situational self-esteem**   The positive or negative way in which people view themselves in a particular situation.

**Socially influenced self-esteem**   The positive or negative way in which people view themselves based on the expectations of others.

**Social needs**   The third step in Maslow's needs hierarchy, which concerns the need to interact with other people.

**Thematic Apperception Test (TAT)**   A projective test that is designed to measure various need levels.

**Two-factor theory**   Herzberg's needs theory that postulates that two factors are involved in job satisfaction: hygiene factors and motivators.

**Valence**   In expectancy theory, the perceived desirability of a consequence that results from a particular level of performance.

**Work-Preference Inventory**   A measure of an individual's orientation toward intrinsic and extrinsic motivation.

# 13

# WORKING CONDITIONS AND ABSENTEEISM

In previous chapters you learned that employee performance can be improved through proper selection and training programs, effective organizational communication, and state-of-the-art incentive and participation systems. In this chapter, you will learn that performance and satisfaction are also affected by such working conditions as work schedules, noise, temperature, office design, technology, absenteeism policies, and safety.

Today, most employees work eight hours a day, five days a week. Usually, the workdays are Monday through Friday, and the work times are from 8 A.M. to 5 P.M. with an hour break for lunch. But these have not always been the typical work hours. In the late eighteenth century, it was common for employees to work 14 to 16 hours a day, 6 days per week. By the early to mid-nineteenth century, there was a movement to reduce working hours to a maximum of 10 per day. This reduction was opposed by many religious organizations, which feared the trouble that supposedly would be caused by people with idle time. But by 1950, the 5-day, 40-hour work week was fairly standard.

## COMPRESSED WORK WEEKS

Although the vast majority of people still work 8 hours a day, 5 days a week, there is a trend toward working fewer days a week but more hours per day. These deviations from the typical 5-day work week are called **compressed work weeks** and usually involve an employee working either 10 hours a day for 4 days or 12 hours a day for 3 days.

The first formal use of a compressed work schedule was in 1940 when both the Mobil Oil and Gulf Oil companies had their truck drivers work 10 hours a day for 4 days and then take 3 days off. The "explosion" in organizations that used compressed schedules came in the early 1970s after Riva Poor (1970) published the first book on the topic. The number of organizations using such schedules jumped from 40 in 1970 to 3,000 by 1973 (Kopelman, 1986).

The potential advantages of compressed work schedules are obvious. From the employees' perspective, they get more vacation days, can spend more time with their families, have increased opportunities to moonlight, and have reduced commuting costs and times. Furthermore, if both parents have different compressed schedules, child-care costs are greatly reduced.

Because it appears obvious that the employee's nonwork-related life will improve with a compressed schedule, the important question becomes, What is the effect of a compressed schedule on an employee's performance at work? Most people answer that a worker will be more tired causing more mistakes and accidents.

The research thus far, however, does not support such speculation. Although research generally indicates that workers do feel moderately more fatigued, their work behavior and work attitudes generally *improve* once a compressed work schedule has been adopted. In a recent meta-analysis, Moores (1990) identified 186 different articles on compressed schedules; 51 were studies, but only 15 were empirically valid enough to be analyzed. Based on these 15 studies, Moores concluded that compressed schedules generally bring a moderate reduction in absenteeism, a small increase in productivity, a large increase in job satisfaction, and a moderate increase in fa-

**Table 13.1** Effect sizes for compressed work schedules

| Criterion | Number of Studies | Mean Effect Size |
|---|---|---|
| Absenteeism | 5 | −.44 |
| Fatigue | 1 | .35 |
| Productivity | 8 | .25 |
| Satisfaction | 5 | .73 |

Source: Adapted with permission from Moores (1990).

tigue. Furthermore, based on 3,800 employees in 6 studies, Moores (1990) concluded that almost 90% of employees who worked compressed schedules are satisfied with them. The exact effect sizes from Moores' meta-analysis are shown in Table 13.1.

More recently, Williamson, Gower, and Clarke (1994) found that employees who work 12-hour shifts were healthier than those working 8-hour shifts. There were no measurable differences in productivity and turnover. Duchon, Keran, and Smith (1994) found even more positive results with underground mine workers. Mine workers changing from an 8-hour to a 12-hour shift reported higher satisfaction, improved sleep, and no negative health or performance changes. The effects of compressed work schedules are more pronounced with white-collar jobs than with blue-collar jobs.

In addition to these empirically verified benefits to employees, an organization that adopts compressed work schedules may realize other advantages. Perhaps the greatest of these is the reduction in start-up and cleanup times that are associated with many jobs. For example, a printer spends considerable time inking and setting up a press before beginning work. At the end of the day, the printer must also spend time cleaning the press and putting supplies away. If these beginning and ending activities together take an hour, then at least an hour a week can be saved if the printer works four days rather than five. Extended across a year and multiplied by the number of employees in a company, such savings can be substantial.

## FLEXIBLE WORK HOURS

A second and increasingly popular alternative work schedule involves flexible work hours and is called **flextime.** Flextime originated in West Germany as a way to alleviate traffic problems by staggering the hours that people worked. The plan then spread to North America, where it was used first in Canada and then in the United States in the mid-1970s. Some form of flextime is formally offered by 48% of organizations and informally by another 38% (Austin, 1994).

According to Thornburg (1994), organizations use flexible hours to:

1. Accommodate employees' family responsibilities
2. Attract employees when the available qualified work force is small

3. Comply with transportation and air-quality regulations

4. Satisfy customer demands for 24-hour-a-day services

With flextime, employees are given greater control over the hours they work. This increase in control and flexibility appears to have many advantages for employees. First, an employee can take care of personal tasks such as going to the doctor, picking up children from school, and even sleeping in. Furthermore, as discussed in Chapter 12, this increased control should enrich the employee's job, thus resulting, theoretically, in increased job satisfaction.

Flextime can be arranged in many ways, but all share the same three basic components: bandwidth, core hours, and flexible hours. As shown in Figure 13.1, the **bandwidth** is the total number of potential hours available for work each day. For example, an employee can work her 8 hours anytime in the 12-hour bandwidth between 6 A.M. and 6 P.M.

**Core hours** are those that everyone must work and typically consist of the hours during which an organization is busiest with its outside contacts. For example, a restaurant might have core hours between 11 A.M. and 1 P.M. to cover its lunchtime business, while a bank might have core hours from 12 noon to 1 P.M. and from 5 P.M. to 6 P.M. to cover the periods of highest customer volume.

Finally, **flexible hours** are those that remain in the bandwidth and in which the employee has a choice of working. For example, if the bandwidth is the 12-hour period from 6 A.M. to 6 P.M. and the core hours are from 9 A.M. to 12 noon, then the employee can schedule the remaining six hours (including her lunch hour) anywhere from 6 A.M. to 9 A.M. and from 12 noon to 6 P.M. The actual degree to which these hours are truly flexible depends on the specific flextime program that is used by the organization.

The most flexible of these schedules is called **gliding time.** With this system, an employee can choose her own hours without advance notice or scheduling. Employees can come and go as they please as long as they work 8 hours each day and 40 hours each week. Such a flexible schedule, however, will work only where it is not necessary to always have an employee working, such as in typing or accounting. In an organization such as a retail store or a restaurant, such a system would mean that at any given time,

**Figure 13.1**
Diagram of a bank's flextime arrangement

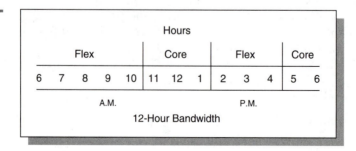

**Table 13.2** Meta-analysis of flextime studies

| Variable | Effects Observed | | |
| --- | --- | --- | --- |
| | Positive | None | Negative |
| Absenteeism | 47 | 6 | 1 |
| Leave usage | 4 | 3 | 1 |
| Family/leisure time | 21 | 0 | 0 |
| Organizational costs | 6 | 5 | 5 |
| Overtime pay | 9 | 1 | 0 |
| Productivity | 51 | 8 | 2 |
| Satisfaction | 43 | 0 | 0 |
| Transportation ease | 23 | 0 | 0 |
| Turnover | 8 | 0 | 0 |

Source: Adapted with permission from Estes (1990).

**Table 13.3** Effect sizes for flextime programs

| Variable | Number of Studies | Mean Effect Size |
| --- | --- | --- |
| Absenteeism | 10 | −.59 |
| Family/leisure time | 3 | .23 |
| Leave usage | 13 | −.15 |
| Productivity | 29 | .19 |
| Role conflict | 2 | −.48 |
| Satisfaction | 9 | .27 |

Source: Adapted with permission from Estes (1990).

there may not be *any* employee present, which, of course, is probably not the best way to conduct a business.

Most flexible working schedules are categorized as **flexitour** or **modified flexitour,** with the employee enjoying greater flexibility in working hours although the hours must be scheduled in advance. With a flexitour system, the employee must submit a schedule on a weekly, biweekly, or monthly basis, depending on the organization. In a modified flexitour, the employee must schedule her hours in advance but can change these hours on a daily basis with some advance notice.

Understandably, flexible working schedules are not only popular with employees but also beneficial to organizations. Estes (1990) conducted a meta-analysis of more than 60 studies and found that flextime resulted in less absenteeism, less overtime, higher job satisfaction, less role conflict, and a slight increase in productivity (see Tables 13.2 and 13.3). These effects were strongest for smaller organizations and for those organizations in which employees shared limited physical resources such as space and equipment.

## PEAK-TIME PAY

A third alternative work schedule is **peak-time pay.** With peak-time pay, certain employees are encouraged to work only part-time but are paid at a higher hourly rate for those hours than employees who work full-time. Thus, an employee will make more per hour than her full-time counterpart, although she will make less money per day.

The concept of peak-time pay came from the banking and fast food industries, both of which face unique problems (Mahlin & Charles, 1984). Both types of organizations need to be open during the entire day yet have only approximately 4 hours per day that are busy. For example, a McDonald's restaurant might need 20 employees to cover its lunch-time crowd but need only 2 employees from 2 P.M. until 5 P.M., at which time the dinner crowd begins for another 2-hour peak period. Rather than paying 20 employees to sit around for most of the day, it would be better to have 15 employees work for 3 hours a day during peak time and only 5 employees work the full 8 hours.

Unfortunately, few people want to work only 3 hours a day at $5 per hour. And those who would be willing, such as students, are often not available during the most crucial hours. Thus, with peak-time pay, 15 people may be paid $7 or $8 per hour to work only the 3 peak hours. Thus, the employee makes a reasonable amount of money per day, and the organization still saves money over what it would have spent had its employees worked the entire 8 hours.

## JOB SHARING

A fourth alternative working schedule—**job sharing**—involves two employees who share their work hours. Rather than one person working 40 hours each week, two employees combine their hours so that they total 40. At first glance, job sharing may seem to be little more than part-time work. There are, however, big psychological, if not administrative, differences.

First, part-time work usually involves lower-level jobs such as those found in the retail and restaurant industries. But job sharing allows people in such complex occupations as teaching and accounting to enjoy the advantages of fewer work hours.

Second, with part-time work, the performance of one employee rarely affects the performance of another. That is, the work completed by two part-time employees results from two separate jobs. But with job sharing, the work may be done by two different employees who share one job title and one position. Poor quality work by one employee must be corrected by the other.

From a psychological standpoint, the main difference between job sharing and part-time employment is the level of employee commitment, both to the organization and to the other employee. Job-sharing programs are targeted at employees who have family responsibilities. Thus, an organization can attract a highly qualified employee who would not be able to work full-time.

Furthermore, an increasing trend is for husbands and wives in similar professions to share the same position. One such situation recently occurred with a high school teaching position: the wife teaches three morning classes while her husband takes care of their two children; the husband then teaches three afternoon classes while his wife cares for their children.

## WORK AT HOME

The fifth and final alternative work schedule is **work at home.** With this schedule, the employee works at home rather than at the workplace. Although homework has recently received increased attention, it is certainly not a new concept. For more than a century, women have sewn garments at home and then sold them to factories for piece-rate prices. Today, with the increase in computers, other types of work can also be done in the home.

With many types of homework, work is completed with little or no contact with a central office or factory. With **telecommuting,** however, an employee uses a computer and modem at home to electronically interact with a

Working at home can save commuting time.

central office. Telecommuting is ideal for such tasks as computer programming, data entry, and telemarketing. About 6% of the nation's employees telecommute (Barnes, 1994). Telecommuters feel more social support and less isolation than do their more traditional work-at-home counterparts (Trent, Smith, & Wood, 1994).

A new concept in telecommuting is the neighborhood "telebusiness center." At these centers, employees from a variety of organizations share office space close to their homes but are connected electronically to their respective organizations (Verespes, 1994).

For telecommuting to be effective, employees must want to work at home, have the ability to work independently, be dependable, and possess good communication skills (Barnes, 1994; Weiss, 1994). Supervisors of telecommuters must define what they expect, plan and communicate schedules, and determine how often they expect telecommuters to contact the office.

Homework has many advantages for both the employee and the employer. For the employee, it offers the opportunity to avoid or minimize child-care and commuting costs while allowing flexibility and comfort in working conditions. For the employer, money is saved on both office space and utilities.

Unfortunately, there is little empirical research investigating the consequences of telecommuting. However, anecdotal evidence has been very positive. For example, Weiss (1994) reports the following telecommuting success stories:

- Bell Atlantic reported that 27% of its managers increased their performance ratings.
- JC Penney and American Express reported substantial decreases in absenteeism costs.
- Metropolitan Life found decreases in turnover.
- Pacific Bell saved $400,000 in office space costs.

But with the advantages come certain disadvantages, which is why most unions oppose homework (Brennan, 1994). First, it is difficult for a union to organize workers whey they are scattered in many locations. Second, it is difficult for the government to enforce safety and fair treatment standards when employees are not in a central location. Finally, employees cannot be easily supervised with homework. Unfortunately, the actual evaluation of the merits of homework will have to wait until more research has been conducted. Until then, homework sounds like a promising idea when used with controls and checks to ensure employee safety and fair treatment.

## SHIFT WORK

Even though most people work from 8 or 9 A.M. to 5 P.M. , approximately 25% of all employees work evening or late night shifts due to economic and safety factors. Police officers and nurses must work around the clock because neither crime nor illness stops at 5 P.M., retail employees must work

**Table 13.4**  Effects of working evening and late night shifts

| Factor | Improved | No Change | Deteriorated |
|--------|----------|-----------|--------------|
| Physical health | | | Akerstedt & Torsvall (1978) |
| | | | Colligan, Forckt, & Tasto (1970) |
| | | | Dunham (1977) |
| | | | Frese & Semmer (1986) |
| | | | Meers, Maasen, & Verhaegen (1978) |
| | | | Mott, Mann, McLoughlin, & Warwick (1965) |
| | | | Wolinsky (1982) |
| Performance | | | Malaviya & Ganesh (1977) |
| | | | Mott et al. (1965) |
| | | | Wyatt & Mariott (1953) |
| Attendance | | Gannon, Norland, & Robeson (1983) | Colligan et al. (1970) |
| | | | Jamal (1981) |
| | | | Nicholson, Jackson, & Howes (1978) |
| Fatigue | | | Wedderburn (1978) |
| Social and family life | | | Akerstedt & Torsvall (1978) |
| | | | Bast (1960) |
| | | | Dunham (1977) |
| | | | Jamal (1981) |
| | | | Ulrich (1957) |
| | | | Wedderburn (1978) |
| | | | Wyatt & Mariott (1953) |
| Mental health | | | Colligan et al. (1979) |
| | | | Jamal (1981) |
| | | | Wedderburn (1978) |
| Job satisfaction | | Dunham (1977) | Frost & Jamal (1979) |
| | | | Jamal (1981) |

late hours to accommodate when most people are able to shop, and factory workers work these shifts because it allows one plant to be three times as productive if it can operate around the clock.

Because **shift work** is necessary and affects approximately 25% of all employees, research has attempted to identify its effects and ways to reduce any negative effects. As Table 13.4 shows, research clearly indicates that working evening ("swing") and late night ("graveyard") shifts have many physical, mental, and work-related effects.

These negative effects are thought to occur because of disruptions in the **circadian rhythm,** the 24-hour cycles of physiological functions that are maintained by every person. For example, most people sleep at night and eat in the morning, at noon, and in the evening. Although there are individual differences in the exact times for eating and sleeping, people generally follow the same pattern. Working evening and late night shifts disrupts this pattern and often causes digestive, appetite, and sleeping problems.

Many of the psychological and social effects of shift work are caused by the incompatibility of an employees' schedule with the schedules of other people. That is, a person who works nights and sleeps mornings may be ready to socialize in the afternoon. Unfortunately, fewer people are around. And when the family is active, the employee is sleeping and thus requires quiet.

As Figure 13.2 shows, many factors influence the degree to which shift work will affect an employee. For example, an employee with a family is affected more than a single employee because the employee must adjust her sleeping schedule to those of others in the household (Smith & Folkard, 1993). Other important factors are uniqueness of shift, whether a shift is fixed or rotating, frequency of rotation, and individual differences.

### Uniqueness of Shift

The social effects of shift work can be greatly reduced if other organizations in the geographical area also use other shifts. The higher the percentage of organizations with shifts, the greater the number of stores and restaurants that are open during the evening and the greater the number of other people available with whom to socialize. Shift work especially affects male workers who pattern their schedule around leisure concerns; females tend to adjust their schedules to domestic concerns (Chambers, 1986).

### Fixed versus Rotating Shifts

Shifts can be either fixed or rotated. With **fixed shifts,** separate groups of employees permanently work the day shift, swing shift, and night shift. **Rotating shifts** are those in which an employee rotates through all three shifts, working the day shift for a while, then switching to the swing shift, then working the night shift, and so on.

**Figure 13.2**
Factors influencing shift work effects

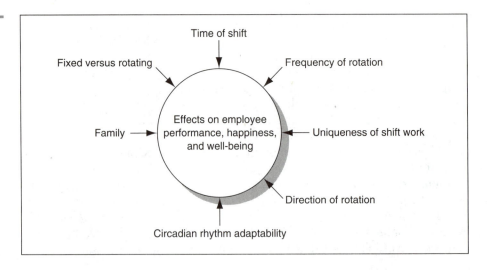

The rationale for rotating shifts is that the negative effects of working swing or night shifts can be lessened if each employee is allowed to work the day shift part of the time. With fixed shifts, even though two-thirds of all workers will have hours that are not compatible with their circadian rhythms, staying permanently on the same shifts will allow them to physically adjust better than if they change shifts, especially when considering that about two days are needed to adjust to each shift change.

Research on shift rotation has strongly suggested that fixed shifts result in fewer physical and psychological problems than do rotating shifts (Frese & Okonek, 1984; Jamal & Jamal, 1982; Verhaegen, Cober, de Smedt, & Dirkx, 1987). For example, Jamal (1981) found that employees on fixed shifts had less absenteeism and tardiness, greater job satisfaction and social participation, and better mental health than did their counterparts working rotating shifts. In a convincing review of the literature on night shifts, Wilkinson (1992) concluded that fixed shifts were superior to rotating shifts.

### Frequency of Rotation

As the preceding discussion concludes, fixed shifts are better than rotating shifts. At times, however, shifts must be rotated because employees who feel stuck on swing and night shifts insist on having the opportunity to work days. In such situations, the frequency of the shift rotation must be considered. That is, should the rotation occur daily, weekly, monthly (and so on)?

Research on this point has been sparse and has not provided a clear and obvious solution. Both Williamson and Sanderson (1986) and Knauth and Kiesswetter (1987) studied changes from seven-day to three-day rotations and found the faster rotating shifts to result in fewer sleep and eating difficulties. Frese and Semmer (1986), however, found no such effect after controlling for the amount of on-the-job stress. Furthermore, the first two studies comparing the two had relatively fast rotations. Research is still needed that compares slower rotations of at least one month with the faster rotations before the effects of rotation frequency can be clarified. If shifts are to be rotated, the rotation should be clockwise with later starting times for the morning shift (Barton & Folkard, 1993; Knauth, 1993). Rest periods of at least two days between shift rotations can lessen the negative effects of the rotations (Totterdell, Spelten, Smith, Barton, & Folkard, 1995).

### Individual Differences

The final factor concerning the effects of shift work involves individual differences in employees. Obviously, not all employees will react to shift work in the same way because of the differences in their biological time clocks. In fact, we have all known people who claimed to be "night people" or those who "prefer the morning." These individual differences in time preference are called chronotype (Greenwood, 1994).

Several questionnaires have been developed to distinguish so-called morning people from evening people. Perhaps the best of these was developed by Smith, Reilly, and Midkiff (1988), which contains the 13 most reliable and valid questions from 3 other available scales (Reilly & Smith, 1988). Such a questionnaire can be used to select and place employees into their optimal shifts or students into their optimal class schedules (Guthrie, Ash, & Bendapuli, 1995). Introverts tend to be "morning people" more so than extroverts (Harma, 1993). Males adapt to shiftwork better than do females, and shiftwork affects older workers more than younger workers (Oginska, Pokorski, & Oginski, 1993).

## ISSUES RELATED TO WORK SCHEDULES

### Child Care

With the increasing number of dual-income and single-parent families, the number of organizations involved with child care also has increased. A small sample of these organizations is shown in Table 13.5. Organizational child-care programs usually fall into one of three categories: on-site care, voucher systems, and referral services. In the first category, an organization such as First Union Bank will build an **on-site child-care facility.** Such a

**Table 13.5** Organizations with progressive child-care programs

| Organization | Location |
| --- | --- |
| Abt Associates | Cambridge, MA |
| American West Airlines | Phoenix, AZ |
| Apple Computer | Cupertino, CA |
| Campbell Soup Co. | Camden, NJ |
| Community Hospital of the Roanoke Valley | Roanoke, VA |
| Corning | Corning, NY |
| First National Bank of Atlanta | Atlanta, GA |
| First Union Bank | Roanoke, VA |
| Georgia Baptist Medical Center | Atlanta, GA |
| Greenville News-Piedmont | Greenville, SC |
| Halmode Apparel | Roanoke, VA |
| Hill, Holliday, & Connors | Boston, MA |
| Hoffman–La Roche Pharmaceuticals | Nutley, NJ |
| Intermedics Int. | Freeport, TX |
| Merck & Co. | Rahway, NJ |
| Nyloncraft, Inc. | Mishawaka, IN |
| PCA International | Matthews, NC |
| Proctor and Gamble | Cincinnati, OH |
| Prudential | Woodbridge, NJ |
| Red Rope | Bristol, PA |
| Roanoke Memorial Hospital | Roanoke, VA |
| St. Albans Hospital | Radford, VA |
| Spartanburg General Hospital | Spartanburg, SC |
| Stride Rite | Boston, MA |
| Syntex | Palo Alto, CA |
| Zale Corp. | Dallas, TX |

facility allows a parent to save commuting time because a separate stop at a child-care center is avoided; this also permits the parent to visit the child during breaks.

Some organizations fully fund the cost of child care, whereas others charge the employee the going rate. There are advantages both to the employee and the organization that pays the full cost of child enrolled in its facility. For example, the child-care cost can be used as a benefit, meaning that neither the employee nor the organization will have to pay taxes on the amount. Of course, tax laws may eventually change the situation, but until that time, calculating child care as an employee benefit is financially rewarding for both the employee and the organization.

Although the employee response to such on-site programs has been overwhelmingly positive, on-site centers cost about $100,000 to start and more than $2,000 per child to maintain (Fooner, 1986). Because of such high costs, it is important to determine whether these centers are cost effective by reducing such phenomena as employee turnover and absenteeism. Unfortunately, there is little empirical research available to answer this question (Johnson, 1990).

Positive evidence has been provided from three sources: Intermedics, in Freeport, Texas, reported a 23% decrease in turnover and absenteeism, Scott and Markham (1982) reported an average decrease of 19% in absenteeism for organizations that established on-site centers, and Tioga Sportswear in New Jersey found a 50% decrease in turnover (LaMarre & Thompson, 1984). Negative evidence has been provided by Miller (1984), who reviewed published studies and concluded that providing child-care may not have the effects that it was initially thought to have. Still, child-care centers will probably have their greatest effect on organizations with high percentages of young, married female workers.

A second avenue that can be taken with child care is to provide employees with *vouchers* to be used with private daycare centers. For example, the San Antonio, Texas, branch of Levi Strauss provides a $100 monthly voucher for employees making less than $32,000. NationsBank offers a similar program. From the perspective of the organization, **voucher systems** alleviate both the high start-up costs and the high costs of liability insurance associated with on-site centers. From an employee's perspective, this approach reduces the cost of private child care.

Unfortunately, for several reasons this approach probably does not reduce employee turnover or absenteeism. First, an employee must still leave work to visit a sick child or to attend parent conferences. Second, most private child-care centers operate from 7 A.M. until 6 P.M. Thus, employees who work swing or night shifts are not helped. Finally, quality child care is not available in many areas. Some corporations, such as the Fayetteville, Arkansas, branch of Levi Strauss, donate large sums of money to local child-care centers to expand hours or services (Harris, 1993). Others, such as Time Warner, provide backup child-care services for children who are ill.

The final avenue taken by organizations is to provide a **referral service** to quality child-care centers. This approach has been taken by both IBM and

Digital Corp. Although this is certainly a useful service, nothing about it would suggest that it would reduce either absenteeism or turnover.

Hallmark Cards, Inc. is an excellent example of a company with progressive child-care and family benefits. Hallmark allows employees to take six months of unpaid maternity and paternity leave, reimburses employees up to $5,000 for the cost of adopting a child, helps employees locate care for children and aged parents, provides care for mildly ill children, holds parenting seminars, and provides alternative care arrangements for children out of school during holidays, inclement weather, or teacher work days (Matthes, 1993).

### Moonlighting

Another interesting problem involving work hours is seen with employees working more than one job, or **moonlighting.** For example, an employee might work the day shift as a machine operator for Ford Motor Co. and then work the night shift as a store clerk for a 7–11 convenience store. People moonlight for obvious reasons: they want or need to earn extra money, and they enjoy the second job (Baba & Jamal, 1992). Somewhere between 5% and 17% of American employees work more than one job (Baba & Jamal, 1992), and this rate goes as high as 30% in highly skilled fields such as data processing (Lasden, 1983). These high percentages of moonlighting employees raise concerns about the effects of extra work on performance and absenteeism for these employees' primary jobs.

As with child care, few studies so far have investigated the effects of moonlighting. Jamal (1981) and Jamal and Crawford (1984) surveyed more than 400 workers at six organizations and found that moonlighters were no different than nonmoonlighters in terms of mental health, quality of life, job performance, and intention to leave their companies. But moonlighters did miss about one day more of work per year than did nonmoonlighters.

Neither Arcuri and Lester (1990), Miller and Sniderman (1974), nor Mott, Mann, McLoughlin, and Warwick (1965) found any negative effects for moonlighting. In fact, Mott et al. (1965) found that moonlighters were better adjusted and more active in the community than were their non-moonlighting counterparts.

## WORK ENVIRONMENT

### NOISE

If you have ever been upset when someone played their stereo too loudly while you were studying, then you can understand why psychologists are interested in studying the effects of workplace noise. If the "obvious" were true, we could start and end our discussion of noise by stating that high levels of noise reduce performance and make workers unhappy. But as Figure 13.3 shows, the relationship between noise and worker behavior is much more complicated than we might first think.

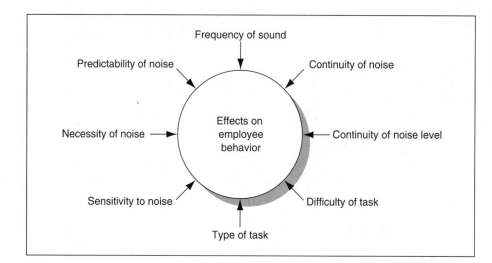

**Figure 13.3**
Factors determining possible noise effects

To understand this relationship, we must first realize that not all noise is the same. Two sounds with the same level of loudness can have different *frequencies*. For example, the sound of a tug boat whistle is much lower in frequency than a train whistle. Lower frequencies do not affect employee performance as much as higher frequencies.

Furthermore, sounds that have the same frequency, intensity, and loudness can differ in their *pleasantness*. For example, noise levels at rock concerts and nightclubs are certainly loud, yet some of us enjoy the sound enough to pay money to hear it. We would probably not pay money to hear a jet engine producing the same sound levels as a rock concert.

This effect can be seen with an employee who listens to music through headphones at work. The noise level of the music is often greater than that of the machines in the environment but is considered to be more pleasant. Keep in mind, however, that even though the music may be more interesting than the machine noise, the noise level has the same potential effects: Hearing loss can occur just as easily from music as it can from factory noise.

Noises also differ in whether they are continuous or intermittent. Constant noise has less effect on employee behavior, and so environments with steady noise levels are not as disrupting as those in which either noise frequency or intensity changes (Teichner, Arees, & Reilly, 1963; Vernon & Warner, 1932).

Another factor that affects the relationship between noise and employee behavior is the *type* and *difficulty of the task*. Noise affects difficult tasks or those that involve cognitive and perceptual skills more than it affects less difficult tasks or those that involve physical performance (Cohen & Weinstein, 1981).

*Individual differences* in people also determine the degree to which noise will affect performance. Weinstein (1978) examined individual differences in noise sensitivity in college students and found that noise-sensitive students had lower academic performance, were less comfortable in the presence of others, and became more disturbed than their less noise-sensitive peers. Melamed, Harari, and Green (1993) found that Type A personalities' blood pressure and heart rate increased under conditions of high noise but not under conditions of low noise.

The effect of noise also depends on the *reason* for and *familiarity* of the noise. When certain noises cannot be avoided—for example, the sound of an office typewriter—they are less irritating than unnecessary noises such as an employee talking too loudly or a roommate playing a stereo at full volume.

Likewise, familiar noise is less irritating than unfamiliar noise, probably for two reasons. First, a familiar noise is less distracting or meaningful than one that we hear for the first time. For example, the regular passing of a train outside an office produces less distracting noise than a suddenly dropped glass. Even though the train is louder, it is expected and familiar and thus not as distracting. Soldiers with war experience have often reported they were able to sleep through artillery explosions but would awaken instantly at the sounds of snapped twigs or close footsteps.

Familiar sounds may also be less distracting because our hearing loses sensitivity to loud sounds. For example, on first entering a factory, the noise levels are often very high and distracting. After a few minutes, however, the noise is less noticeable because we have become temporarily less sensitive to it.

Finally, noise affects certain *types* of employee behaviors in different ways. Noise is more likely to decrease the quality of performance rather than its quantity (Broadbent & Little, 1960), cause people to walk faster and make less eye contact (Korte & Grant, 1980), decrease job satisfaction (Sundstrom et al., 1994), and decrease performance on cognitive tasks (Cohen & Weinstein, 1981). But perhaps the greatest effects of noise are not on performance, but on employee health and morale.

As Table 13.6 shows, research indicates that in addition to hearing loss, continued exposure to high levels of noise (measured in decibels) can raise blood pressure (Burns, 1979), increase worker illness (Cohen, 1972), cause people to be less helpful (Fisher, Bell, & Baum, 1984), and produce more aggression and irritability (Donnerstein & Wilson, 1976).

Noise also causes people to narrow their focus of attention so that they concentrate only on the most important stimuli. In one experiment, Korte and Grant (1980) placed unusual objects and people along the sidewalk of a busy shopping district, including a woman wearing a large pink hat and a bouquet of brightly colored balloons tied to a lamp post. Korte and Grant then asked shoppers if they had seen anything unusual and read them a list of the unusual people and things they could have seen.

The study results indicated that when traffic noise was high, only 35% of the shoppers noticed the items compared to more than 50% when the noise was low. Although such narrowing of attention may decrease the performance levels of employees for whom it is important to notice many stimuli (for example, police officers or safety inspectors), it may help the performance of employees who need only focus on a few different stimuli (Broadbent, 1971).

**Table 13.6**  Effects of noise at different levels

| Cause of Noise | Loudness of Noise (in decibels) | Effect of Noise |
|---|---|---|
| Rocket launch | 180 | |
| | 170 | |
| | 160 | |
| | 150 | |
| Gunshot blast | 140 | |
| Jet takeoff | 130 | Brief exposure can result in permanent deafness (Trahiotis & Robinson, 1979) |
| | 125 | |
| Disco | 120 | |
| Riveting machine | 115 | Maximum legal exposure to noise |
| Power lawn mower | 110 | A person cannot speak over a sound at this level |
| | 105 | |
| Textile-weaving plant | 100 | Blood pressure increases (Burns, 1979) |
| Food blender | 95 | Cognitive performance is reduced (Hockey, 1970) |
| | | Employees report more illness and somatic complaints (Cohen, 1972) |
| | 93 | Angry people become more aggressive (Baron, 1977) |
| | | Driving performance decreases (Finkelman, Zeitlin, Filippi, & Friend, 1977) |
| City traffic | 90 | Legal acceptable noise limit for eight-hour day |
| Computer card verifier | 85 | Helping behavior decreases (Mathews & Canon, 1975) |
| Train (100 feet away) | 80 | Reaction time decreases by 3% (Lahtela, Niemi, Kunsela, & Hypen, 1986) |
| Car | 75 | |
| Noisy restaurant | 70 | Telephone use is difficult |
| | 68 | Reduced detection of grammatical errors during proofreading (Weinstein, 1977) |
| | 65 | Hearing loss can occur in sensitive individuals |
| Normal speech | 60 | |
| | 50 | |
| Normal noise at home | 40 | |
| Soft whisper | 30 | |
| | 20 | |
| Breathing | 10 | |
| | 0 | |

## Noise Reduction

Given that noise affects employee morale, health, and perhaps performance, employers have attempted to solve or minimize the problem of noise by several methods. One method sets legal time limits on the exposure to noise at different decibel levels. These time limits are shown in Table 13.7. A second method is to change the environment by using carpeting and acoustically treated ceilings (Sundstrom et al., 1994).

**Table 13.7**  Maximum legal exposure to noise

| Hours of Exposure | Maximum Noise Level (in decibels) |
| --- | --- |
| 8 | 90 |
| 7 | 91 |
| 6 | 92 |
| 5 | 93 |
| 4 | 95 |
| 3 | 97 |
| 2 | 100 |
| 1.5 | 102 |
| 1 | 105 |
| 0.5 | 110 |
| 0.25 | 115 |

A third method reduces the amount of unwanted noise that reaches an employee. Examples include having employees wear protective ear plugs and muffs or work in soundproof areas away from the sources of noise. Although these methods may limit the effects on employee health, they may also decrease performance in jobs that require detection of or attention to certain types of noise (Mershon & Lin, 1987).

Another method uses engineering technology to reduce the actual amount of noise emitted. For example, rubber pads on typewriters reduce noise by reducing vibration, laser technology greatly reduces the noise from dot-matrix and thimble printers, and belt drives instead of gears reduce the noise made by many types of machines. In one study, using *white noise*, such as air flow from ventilation systems to mask office noise improved performance on a cognitive task. However, the white-noise group still performed worse than the no-noise group (Loewen & Suedfeld, 1992).

The above discussion has concentrated on the potential harmful effects of noise, but noise also can be beneficial in the working environment, especially as a warning method. For example, loud noises alert workers that a forklift is backing up, loud whistles tell workers when it is time to go home, and alarms tell workers when a machine has malfunctioned.

### Music

One intriguing method for enhancing worker performance and morale has been the use of music during work. The rationale is that music will help reduce the periods of boredom and keep employees alert. More than 10,000 organizations have music played for their employees and customers by subscribing to Muzak (more commonly known as elevator music).

Rather than playing any type of music, Muzak is highly specific, playing 486 soft instrumental songs per day, each selected so that it can be heard but not be distracting. Furthermore, the music is played in 15-minute programs, with the music at the beginning of the program less stimulating than that played toward the end of the program (is any of Muzak stimulating?).

Although use of music is popular, questions still remain about its effectiveness. In general, research has shown that employees enjoy listening to music at work and believe that they are more productive because of it (Newman, Hunt, & Rhodes, 1966). But little well-conducted research is available that has tested the actual effects of music on productivity. The little research that is available, however, has generally been favorable (Fox, 1971). For example, a Japanese study found that worker fatigue was reduced by 32% (Wokoun, 1980), and Muzak's own research shows a 17% increase in factory productivity, a 13% increase in clerical performance, and a 53% decrease in turnover by airline reservation agents. Furthermore, research has demonstrated that the presence of fast music causes customers in a restaurant to eat faster (Roballey & Gardner, 1986), while the presence of slow music causes supermarket customers to spend 38% more money (Milliman, 1986). Thus, music might indeed make working conditions better.

Much more research is necessary, however, because the relationship between music and performance probably depends on several factors. One is undoubtedly the type of music being played. Muzak uses a specific type and sequence of music that it believes is best. But employees often listen to classical, jazz, rock, and country music through their own headphones. What effects do these types of music have? And what if an employee does not like the music being played?

Another issue that needs further investigation is the relationship between music and task type. Music might increase performance in manual tasks that require little thinking, but it is doubtful that the same would hold true for complex tasks involving focused mental effort (Gilmer & Deci, 1977; Uhrbrock, 1961). Contrary to what one might expect from this discussion, Wentworth (1991) found no effect for music with mentally retarded production workers.

## TEMPERATURE

Another important concern in the working environment is the effect of temperature on employee performance and health. This is an important issue because many jobs such as those in construction and in the steel industry involve working in intense heat, whereas others such as rescue squads and meat-packing plants often involve working in extreme cold.

Perhaps the best place to begin a discussion of the effects of temperature is by describing how the human body tries to maintain an ideal temperature. When body temperature is above normal, we cool down in one of two ways. The first is through **radiation,** with the excess heat radiating away from the body. The second way is by **evaporation,** or by sweating away excess heat.

When body temperature is below normal, blood vessels constrict. Although this process helps protect against cold, it also produces numbness by reducing circulation. That is why our feet and hands are the first parts of the body to feel numb when we are cold. Police officers working a beat can often be seen stomping their feet in cold temperatures to stimulate circulation.

**Table 13.8** Effective temperature as a function of air temperature and humidity

| Humidity (%) | Air Temperature (°F) | | | | | |
|---|---|---|---|---|---|---|
| | 41 | 50 | 59 | 68 | 77 | 86 |
| 100 | 39 | 52 | 64 | 78 | 96 | 120 |
| 80 | 39 | 52 | 63 | 75 | 90 | 111 |
| 60 | 40 | 51 | 62 | 73 | 86 | 102 |
| 40 | 40 | 51 | 61 | 72 | 83 | 96 |
| 20 | 41 | 50 | 60 | 70 | 81 | 91 |
| 0 | 41 | 50 | 59 | 68 | 77 | 86 |

We must next understand how different factors affect what is called the **effective temperature,** or how hot or cold our environment feels to us. In theory, effective temperature has four components—air temperature, humidity, airflow, and temperature of objects in the environment—but it is usually computed by considering only air temperature and humidity. Note that effective temperature is more than simple air temperature. A 90-degree day in a Nevada desert feels cooler than a 90-degree day in a Georgia swamp. As Table 13.8 shows, the higher the humidity, the warmer the air temperature feels, and thus the higher the effective temperature.

Many jobs, such as those in the steel and construction industries, involve working in intense heat, which can affect employee performance and health.

In addition to humidity, airflow is also important. We all can probably recall the feeling of relief from a breeze coming off a lake or off the ocean. The air temperature probably did not change, but discomfort decreased along with the effective temperature. Likewise, we might recall a "biting wind" that made a winter day seem so cold.

Finally, the effective temperature is affected by the heat that radiates from other objects in the environment. For example, the field-level temperature of outdoor sports stadiums that use artificial turf is usually much higher than the air temperature in the stands. The reason is that heat radiates from the artificial turf. Other examples of this radiation effect include how much hotter it feels when sitting with a group of people than when sitting alone or how much hotter it feels when lying on the sand at the beach than when sitting up.

I can remember many summer days in Los Angeles when the air temperature was already more than 100 degrees and the heat radiating from a sidewalk added another 15 degrees, which made walking extremely uncomfortable. Similarly, a manager who thinks that her outdoor salespeople will be fine in an 85-degree temperature must also account for the effective temperature caused by radiating heat. An air temperature of 85 degrees above a concrete sidewalk is not the same as 85 degrees above a dirt road.

Both air temperature and humidity interact with the body's ability to cool down through radiation and evaporation. When air temperature is higher than body temperature, we are unable to radiate heat. When humidity is high, it is more difficult to lose body heat through evaporation. Thus, high air temperature and high humidity make the body's natural cooling system less effective.

The relevant question here, of course, is what happens when the effective temperature in the working environment is high or low? As shown in Figure 13.4, the answer is that performance usually deteriorates. The degree of

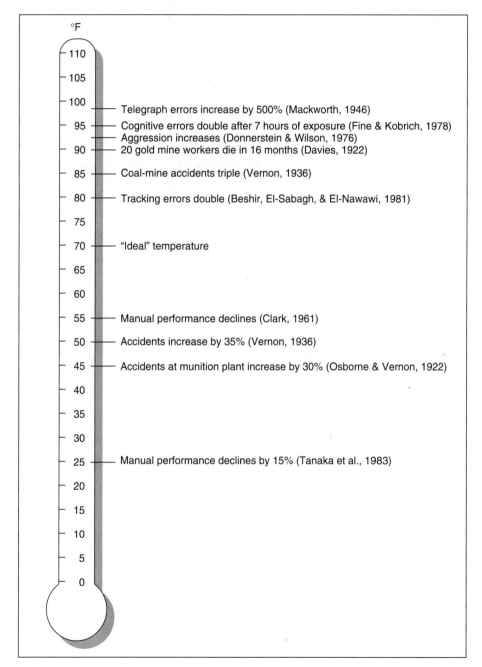

**Figure 13.4**
Effects of various temperatures (°F) on employee behavior

°F
- 110
- 105
- 100 — Telegraph errors increase by 500% (Mackworth, 1946)
- 95 — Cognitive errors double after 7 hours of exposure (Fine & Kobrich, 1978)
   — Aggression increases (Donnerstein & Wilson, 1976)
- 90 — 20 gold mine workers die in 16 months (Davies, 1922)
- 85 — Coal-mine accidents triple (Vernon, 1936)
- 80 — Tracking errors double (Beshir, El-Sabagh, & El-Nawawi, 1981)
- 75
- 70 — "Ideal" temperature
- 65
- 60
- 55 — Manual performance declines (Clark, 1961)
- 50 — Accidents increase by 35% (Vernon, 1936)
- 45 — Accidents at munition plant increase by 30% (Osborne & Vernon, 1922)
- 40
- 35
- 30
- 25 — Manual performance declines by 15% (Tanaka et al., 1983)
- 20
- 15
- 10
- 5
- 0

deterioration, however, depends on several factors, including the type of task, the workload, and the number and frequency of rest periods that are allowed.

### Effects on Tasks

Research indicates that high effective temperatures can affect performance on cognitive, physical, and perceptual tasks. For example, Fine and Kobrick (1978) found that after 7 hours of exposure to 95-degree temperatures with 88% humidity, employees made twice as many errors on a cognitive task than did a control group that worked in a moderate temperature of 75 degrees with 25% humidity.

Beshir, El-Sabagh, and El-Nawawi (1981) also investigated the effects of heat exposure on a perceptual tracking task. Beshir and his colleagues found that subjects' performance did not greatly decrease after working 90 minutes at 68 degrees. At 86 degrees, however, performance decreased significantly within 30 minutes.

While employee comfort and performance is important, heat can also affect the performance of machines and equipment. For example, a California printing and bookbinding company ran into interesting problems that involved airflow in one of its plants. The facility had many different types of printing presses as well as binders that required the melting of glue chips. As you can imagine, the heat from summer air, binding machines, and employees' bodies combined to make working conditions uncomfortable. To solve this problem, the managers decided to increase the airflow by opening all of the plant's doors and windows and thus let ocean breezes cool the plant. Unfortunately, the increased airflow not only cooled the plant and made the employees more comfortable, but it also caused the mechanical collating machines to malfunction. The collating machines use sensors that warn their operators when too many or too few sheets of paper have been picked up. The breezes ruffled the sheets and thus set off the sensors. The increased airflow may have made the employees more comfortable and productive, but it reduced the equipment's productivity. Because the potential output of the collating machines was much greater than the outputs of the individual employees, the windows were closed. As a result, the employees became irritable, but overall productivity increased.

A similar case occurred at a knitting mill whose owners discovered that yarn tended to snap when humidity was low. Therefore, they made no attempt to dehumidify the air. Unfortunately for the millworkers, the high humidity made working conditions uncomfortable. Thus, a decision had to be made as to the ideal humidity level that would keep the employees happy and productive without causing the yarn to snap. So, the humidity level was slightly lowered.

A final example of the differential effects of temperature comes from baseball. When temperatures are high, players are uncomfortable and pitchers tire more quickly than when temperatures are moderate. But the hotter air allows a baseball to travel farther, and there are often more home runs. Thus, the higher temperatures negatively affect pitchers but positively affect batters.

Some jobs involve working in high levels of heat.

### Effects Related to Workload

High temperatures obviously most affect work performance when work-loads are heavy. That is, an effective temperature of 95 degrees would quickly affect a person using a sledgehammer but take longer to affect a person pulling weeds. However, even exposure to moderate levels of heat while performing "light" repetitive-motion work can be dangerous. In a study of female laundry workers, Brabant (1992) found increases in discomfort and cardiac strain—results that were not immediately dangerous but had the potential for future health problems.

### Rest Periods

Temperature will have the greatest effect on performance when work activity is continuous. With rest breaks, the effects of either heat or cold can be greatly reduced. For example, most people can work for approximately

120 minutes at 90 degrees without impaired performance. At 100 degrees, however, the maximum time for continued performance is approximately 30 minutes; after that time, performance deteriorates (Wing, 1965). Thus, in temperatures of 90 degrees, rest breaks scheduled at a maximum of two hours apart will help keep performance (and the employee) from deteriorating. At 100 degrees, rest breaks must occur at intervals of less than 30 minutes.

An interesting problem developed at a large amusement park when its employees were exposed to summer heat. The park had several employees dress in theme costumes, which we will call gnomes to protect the park's reputation. The thick and heavy gnome costumes were worn even during summer when temperatures were almost always in the 90s and 100s. The job of each costumed employee was to walk around the park and greet customers, especially children. Problems, however, began when children punched the gnomes and knocked them over (a rolling gnome was actually a fairly funny sight). Normally, the gnomes kept their sense of humor and laughed, but after an hour in costume in 100 degree temperatures, they sometimes lost their humor and began punching back. And when they were not hitting children, the gnomes were passing out from the heat. Obviously, something had to be done. To solve the problem, the park's management had the gnomes work four-hour shifts instead of eight. As we might expect from the above discussion, this solution was ineffective. Why? Because the outside temperature was 100 degrees and the effective temperature inside the costumes was at least 20 degrees higher. At such high temperatures, continuous activity brought decreased performance in less than 30 minutes. The solution that worked, of course, was to have the gnomes work for 20 minutes and then take short breaks in an air-conditioned room, thus taking advantage of what we know about exposure limits to heat as well as frequency of breaks.

## COMPUTERS

There is little doubt that the increased use of computers over the last two decades has greatly changed the work environment. Word-processing programs allow material to be typed faster and without spelling errors, statistical programs and spreadsheets make research and accounting duties easier, and desktop-publishing systems allow material to be attractively produced at a fraction of the cost of using a professional typesetter. But with the improvements in efficiency and quality come certain problems. Perhaps the most publicized are the perceived hazards of using computer terminals and keyboards and the "fear" of computers.

### *Monitors*

In the last few years, employees who use computers have complained about health problems. These complaints have even been voiced by students, half of whom believe that computer monitors are dangerous (Trinkaus, 1986). As listed in Table 13.9, these complaints have ranged from simple fatigue to increased numbers of miscarriages suffered by pregnant employees.

**Table 13.9** Research showing problems from VDT use

| Study | Finding |
| --- | --- |
| Mason (1984) | VDT users have 550% more vision-related complaints |
| Rice (1983) | 33% of VDT users are anxious, 5% show symptoms of nausea, high blood pressure, and dizziness |
| DeGroot and Kamphois (1983) | VDT users report increased eye strain, migraine headaches, and back problems |
| Dainoff, Happ, and Crane (1981) | VDT users complain about sore arms, sore backs, and headaches |
| Harris (1981) | Increased eye strain, migraines, and back problems |
| Smith, Cohen, and Stammerjohn (1981) | Increased strain, boredom, work load and back pains |
| Savage (1988) | High percentages of miscarriages for women using VDTs |
| Nussbaum (1980) | VDT typists report twice as much fatigue |
| Gunnarson and Ostberg (1977) | Increased monotony and loss of control for VDT users |

Even though employees may report such symptoms, it is unclear how accurate the reports are. For example, Dainoff, Happ, and Crane (1981) believe that the symptoms result from increased stress brought on by the lack of control an employee feels when using a computer as well as by the increased amount of work that can be done on the computer. Thus, the computer itself does not cause problems, but the loss of control and increased work load does.

Research by the National Research Council (1983) has indicated that while computer use may cause eye strain, it does not result in permanent eye damage. Furthermore, eye strain can be greatly reduced by eliminating the glare from the terminal screens. This can be done in several ways, including changing the angle of the screen to limit light reflection, using hoods to screen the terminal from overhead light, using antiglare screens, and changing the lighting in the room in which the terminal is located.

Eye strain also can be reduced by using large screens with good resolution. Early computer screens tended to be small and had print that was difficult to read. Although many different screen colors are available, research has shown no advantage of one color over another. The best color is simply a matter of individual preference, indicating that the employee who will use the screen should be the one to pick the color. For the most part, concerns about screen color have become moot as most employees work with monitors capable of displaying a vast array of colors.

Many of the other physical symptoms reported by computer users are caused by poorly designed workstations (Overman, 1990). Employees often use the same desk and chair for both their computers and their typing, writing, and other work. Kroemer and Price (1982) and Grandjean, Hunting, and Pidermann (1983) have conducted extensive research on the optimal design of a computer workstation and how a computer user should sit. For example, the optimal elbow angle when using a computer is 99 degrees, with a 104-degree trunk incline. Obviously, few users are going to measure their elbow angles, but they can be trained to sit in a particular way and be provided with equipment such as detachable keyboards and adjustable tables. These ergonomic changes probably will greatly reduce the problems of computer use.

### Keyboards

As a result of the amount of work employees perform on computers, the number of hand and wrist injuries has greatly increased over the last decade. The most common of these repetitive-stress injuries (RSI) are carpal-tunnel syndrome (CTS) and tendinitis (an affliction that I developed while writing this book). Repetitive-stress injuries annually cost employers over $20 billion in workers' compensation claims and absenteeism (Heilbroner, 1993). RSIs caused by computer use are the result of physical stress placed on the tendons and nerves that pass through a tunnel connecting the wrists and hands. The normal stress associated with repeated finger and hand movements is complicated by the awkward angle in which keyboard users must hold their wrists. Early symptoms of RSI include numbness and tingling in the hands and forearms. Later stages involve pain severe enough to make opening a door or holding a pen difficult if not impossible.

Treatments for carpal-tunnel syndrome include taking anti-inflammatants, wearing wrist braces, and surgery (over 100,000 are performed annually). The healing process can take up to six months at a cost per case of $29,000 in medical expenses and lost wages (Heilbroner, 1993). Many RSIs can be prevented by learning ergonomically proper keyboard techniques, performing warm-up exercises, using wrist rests and special keyboards, taking breaks, and stopping work when numbness or pain begins. Barnes (1994) suggests that keyboards should stand between 23 and 29 inches from the floor

Use of computers can cause repetitive stress injuries.

(depending on employee height) and the top of the keys should be no higher than 2 to 2.5 inches above the work surface.

### Fear of Computers

Another problem with the use of computers in the workplace is that many employees, especially older ones, are afraid of them (DeLoughry, 1993; Martin, 1973). Again, it is not clear whether employees are actually frightened by the computers themselves or of some aspect of their required use. Galagan (1983) believes that the fear reported by new users is actually a fear that they will damage the computer. This is analogous to a person who will not pick up an expensive piece of crystal in a store. The shopper obviously does not have a fear of crystal, but fears dropping this particular piece.

On the basis of hundreds of interviews, Zuboff (1982) believes that the fear of computers is really a fear of change. Employees fear that computers will limit their control, make their jobs boring, and perhaps take away their jobs (Kalimo & Leppanen, 1985). This might also explain the increased reluctance of older employees who have used typewriters or accounting ledgers for decades and simply do not want to change. Finally, Brod (1985) believes that many people fear technology, not computers. That is, regardless of whether the new equipment is a computer, a photocopy machine, or a complicated washing machine, these people will be afraid.

To test these three hypotheses of fear, Reardon (1986) had students work on either a computer or a complicated tape recorder to test their fear of computers against their fear of technology. Furthermore, the subjects either had or did not have previous experience with the piece of equipment so that their fear of computers could be tested against their fear of change. Finally, the subjects were told either that they had to be careful because the computer or the tape recorder was sensitive and easily damaged or that it was indestructible—this tested their fear of computers against their fear of causing damage.

Reardon's study results supported the proposition that fear of computers really is fear of technology—and that computers themselves do not necessarily produce fear or anxiety. Thus, the best way to introduce computers or new technology to employees is through training, which includes information on not only the use of new equipment but also its consequences (Cirillo, 1983; Shneiderman, 1980).

## OFFICE DESIGN

### LANDSCAPED OFFICES

In the past decade or so, many organizations have adopted what is called an "open" or "landscaped" office design (Martinez, 1990). Originally developed by furniture manufacturers in Germany, the design uses large, open office areas without walls. Individual work units are separated by such items as

**Table 13.10**   Effects of landscaped office environments

| Study | Employee Effects |
| --- | --- |
| Brookes and Kaplan (1972) Davis (1984) | Increased socialization |
| Allen and Gertsberger (1973) | Increased communication |
| | Decreased construction costs |
| | Decreased relocation costs |
| | Decreased lighting and electrical costs |
| | Decreased office attractiveness |
| Sundstrom, Burt, and Kamp (1980) | Decreased privacy |
| | Decreased productivity |
| | Decreased satisfaction |
| Oldham and Brass (1979) | Decreased motivation |
| | Decreased satisfaction |
| | Decreased concentration |
| | Increased noise |

plants, bookcases, and desks. The idea behind this design is that without the physical barriers of walls, employees will communicate better with one another and be easier to supervise and help.

There are three common designs for open or landscaped offices (Martinez, 1990). In a *freestanding design* (also called a bullpen design), all desks are placed in a large area that is completely open. With *uniform plans,* desks are placed at uniform distances and are separated by panels into cubicle areas. *Free-form work stations* use a combination of designs so that the different needs of each worker can be accommodated.

The landscaped office may be appealing, but as Table 13.10 shows, the research has not generally been especially supportive. Landscaped offices can increase contact and communication and are less expensive than regular offices, but they can often lessen productivity and job satisfaction (Sundstrom, Town, Rice, Osborn, & Brill, 1994). In a study of over 500 employees in 14 organizations, O'Neill (1994) found that storage space and the ability to adjust or control one's office space were the best predictors of satisfaction with work space. Variables such as partition type, panel height, and square footage were not related to satisfaction or performance.

## OFFICE FURNITURE

Given that private offices are more common than, and probably superior to, open office environments, research has sought to determine the factors that affect the placement and perception of furniture within the private office. In particular, this research has concentrated on visitors' perceptions of certain office characteristics as well as on the personalities of office occupants.

Research on visitors' perceptions of certain office characteristics has brought several interesting but not necessarily surprising findings. One line

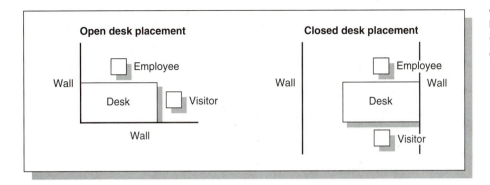

**Figure 13.5**
Open and closed desk placements

of research examined the perceptions of visitors to offices that used either open or closed desk arrangements. As shown in Figure 13.5, an **open desk arrangement** faces a desk against a wall so that a visitor can sit next to or adjacent to the person who sits behind the desk. A **closed desk arrangement** places a desk so that a visitor must sit across from the person behind the desk.

Visitors to offices that use open rather than closed desk arrangements perceive the offices to be more comfortable and their occupants as friendlier and more trustworthy, open, interested, and extroverted (Campbell, 1979; McElroy, Morrow, & Wall, 1983; Widgery & Stackpole, 1972). Conversely, visitors rate people with messy offices as being active and busy, those with clean offices as being organized and introverted, and those with organized offices (lots of papers placed in stacks) as being active and achievement-oriented (McElroy, Morrow, & Wall, 1983; Morrow & McElroy, 1981). Finally, visitors rate offices with plants and posters as more comfortable, inviting, and hospitable than offices without plants and posters (Campbell, 1979).

This line of research is not only interesting, but also important. A supervisor with a messy office and a closed desk arrangement is sending the message that she does not want to be bothered. This may not be her intended message, but it is the one that is perceived by her subordinates. Thus, a manager who wants to be more open and improve communication with her employees might start by changing the appearance of her office.

With research indicating that people make judgments about others based on their offices, the next logical step is to determine whether people with different types of offices actually have different types of personalities. Limited research, in fact, does seem to show that the appearance of an office provides insight into the personality of the occupant.

McElroy, Morrow, and Ackerman (1983) looked at the personalities of faculty members who had open desk arrangements and those who had closed desk arrangements, and found that those with open desk arrangements were more extroverted and people-oriented than their closed desk counterparts. Furthermore, faculty members who used open desk arrangements had lower external locus of control and scored higher on the Least-Preferred Co-worker (LPC) Scale, which was discussed in Chapter 9.

In another study, Zweigenhaft (1976) compared desk placement using several variables and found that older, higher-status faculty members used closed desk arrangements more than did younger members. Even more interesting was the finding that faculty members who used closed desk arrangements were also evaluated less favorably in the classroom. Thus, desk placement was able to partially predict the effectiveness of a faculty member, providing support for the idea that different types of people arrange their offices in different ways.

In a study of personnel managers, Cochran, Kopitzke, and Miller (1984) compared the office characteristics used by managers with their personality. Cochran et al. found that dominant, achievement-oriented managers did not decorate their offices with anything other than standard furniture; outgoing managers had photographs of their vacations to remind them of good times and clocks to let them know when it was quitting time; introverted managers had plants and paintings so that their office would remind them of home; and organized managers had cartoons to show that even though they were neat and compulsive, they also had a sense of humor.

The presence of windows is another factor that seems to affect the way in which an office is decorated. Heerwagen and Orians (1986) examined the way in which people decorated both windowed and windowless offices and found that occupants of windowless offices used twice as many decorative items such as posters, pictures, and paintings. Not surprisingly, the posters in windowless offices contained more landscapes and fewer cityscapes than did offices with windows.

## WORKPLACE VIOLENCE

In the past few years, the issue of workplace violence has received considerable interest. This interest stems from research indicating that 17% of fatal workplace deaths are homicides (Moore & Kondrasuk, 1994). Homicide represents 12% of fatal workplace injuries among men and 42% of the fatal workplace injuries among women. Furthermore, 10% of employees in a given year are threatened with or victimized by workplace violence. The gender differences in workplace violence can be explained by the fact that men traditionally work in higher risk occupations such as mining that have high levels of fatalities caused by such other means as driving and construction accidents (Thornburg, 1993).

Though these figures are certainly attention getting, from a human resource perspective, these figures can be misleading. Though the exact numbers are not available, a relatively small portion of the homicides were committed by current or former employees. Incidents of workplace violence can be placed into one of three categories. The first category is violence against an employee occurring as a result of a *crime* being committed. The most common examples are employees assaulted during the commission of a robbery. In fact, taxi drivers and convenience store clerks are the two occupations most susceptible to workplace violence (working the graveyard shift at a 7–11 store may have more than chronological meaning).

The second category is violence against law enforcement officers (such as police officers, sheriffs, FBI agents) or security guards while they are in the *line of duty*. Law enforcement officers have a homicide rate of 9.3 per 100,000 employees while the rate for security guards is 3.6 per 100,000. The average for all workers is 0.7 per 100,000.

The third and final category is violence against an employee or supervisor as an act of *anger* or *vengeance* by another employee, a customer, or a jilted lover. It is this category of violence that most involves human resource professionals and has captured the imagination of the public. The majority of this type of violence (54%) is committed by employees against other employees. However, annually 13,000 acts of violence and 31 homicides are committed by husbands and lovers against women in the workplace (Miller, 1995).

Employee violence against other employees is usually the result of interpersonal disagreements. For example, an employee of Prescolite, Inc. in Arkansas killed one co-worker and wounded seven others because the employee was upset that he was being harassed by his co-workers.

However, employees can be assaulted when co-workers take out their anger on a supervisor. For example,

- In 1994, a Tulsa, Oklahoma, Wendy's employee, angry because his boss asked him to start work early, fired 12 shots from a .380-caliber handgun, wounding his supervisor and five other employees.

- In 1988, an employee in a Micropure Plant in California killed two and wounded four employees because he was frustrated with his job.

Thirteen percent of workplace violence incidents involve employees seeking revenge against a supervisor as a result of being fired, laid off, or subject to some form of negative personnel action. For example,

- After being fired, Paul Calden killed three supervisors at Firemen's Fund Insurance before shooting himself.

- Fernando Ruiz shot his supervisor at Dahn's Fresh Herbs in Houston after his boss threatened to fire him.

- Larry Hansel used a 12-gauge shotgun to kill two company executives who he believed were responsible for his being fired.

## PERPETRATORS OF WORKPLACE VIOLENCE

Research on workplace violence by employees reveals a fairly consistent pattern. Perpetrators tend to be male (80%), between the ages of 20 and 50 (usually in their 40s), have their self-esteem tied to their job, are fond of violent films and TV shows, are fascinated by guns, have ready access to guns, often subscribe to *Soldier of Fortune,* and are usually described as loners (Dietz, 1994). Psychologically they are often classified as suffering from paranoid disorders. About 15% are suffering severe stress due to family problems, 8% are suffering from other severe sources of stress, and another 10% have severe substance-abuse problems (Trenn, 1993).

## REDUCING WORKPLACE VIOLENCE

Acts of workplace violence cannot completely be eliminated but they can be reduced through security measures, employee screening, and management awareness (Dietz, 1994).

### Security Measures

Increased security measures can decrease the probability of workplace violence. These measures can include such physical changes as adding surveillance cameras, silent alarms, bright external lighting, bulletproof barriers, sophisticated lock systems, and security guards; making high-risk areas more visible; and using drop safes and posting signs stating that only limited cash is kept on the premises. Staffing changes can include increasing the number of staff on duty; closing during the higher risk late-night and early morning hours; and training employees how to deal with robberies, conflicts, and angry customers.

### Employee Screening

Though increased security measures are primarily aimed at reducing workplace violence resulting from other crimes such as robbery, they can also aid in reducing violence caused by current and former employees. Another method of reducing violence committed by current and former employees is to use psychological tests, reference checks, and background checks to screen applicants for violence potential.

Background and reference checks can provide information about an applicant's history of violence (Tonowski, 1993). These checks are important because employees who engage in workplace violence are chronically disgruntled, have a history of causing trouble, and frequently change jobs. Dietz (1994) provides two interesting examples. An applicant at a California maintenance company was hired in spite of a history of domestic violence and burglary convictions. He later set fire to a bookkeeper who wouldn't give him his pay check. Another organization was sued because an employee who had killed a co-worker was rehired by the same company in an effort to employ ex-cons. After a short period on the job, the employee killed another co-worker. It is important to note that ex-cons cannot categorically be denied employment. An organization must take into account the length of time that has passed since the crime was committed, the seriousness of the crime, and the relevance of the crime to the job in question.

*Teige McShane, M.A.*
*Human Resources*
*Manager*
*Perdue Farms, Inc.*

Perdue Farms, Inc., is the third largest poultry processing company in the country, with both national and international sales. Its processing plants are primarily in the South and mid-Atlantic regions. I am a human resources manager at one of those facilities in Virginia. My responsibilities include employment, wage and hour administration, benefits administration, training, policies, employee relations, and medical and safety.

The areas of medical and safety are particularly important because the facility operates 24 hours a day in a labor- and machine-intensive environment. I work closely with members of my own staff as well as with other department managers to implement and maintain a safety process that is broad in scope yet with a single goal of providing a safe, healthy, and productive environment. Each human resources manager at Perdue is responsible for ensuring compliance in a number of areas.

One of these areas is legal compliance to OSHA's (Occupational Safety and Health Administration) written programs such as LOTO, Confined Space Entry, Hazardous Communication, Emergency Action Planning, and Process Safety Management. With each written program there must also be training, auditing, and enforcement documentation. These written programs represent the minimum training that all covered employers are legally required to provide in order to set the stage for an effective safety process. However, to achieve an effective safety process, an employer must go far beyond the minimum training. The program must be communicated and integrated into the work environment so that it becomes a part of each affected job's process. Many manufacturing sites have met disaster by failing to do this. Moreover, programs fail when there is no follow-up training or enforcement documentation, which can lead a written program to follow a course of noncompliance. Rarely do employers choose to ignore the legal requirements of the written programs. When this does occur, accidents and injuries may result, which can put a company out of business and subject management and owners to criminal charges.

Another area of compliance comes with the voluminous regulations and standards from OSHA that must be met in the manufacturing environment. Sometimes these regulations and standards conflict with those of other government regulatory agencies. For example, one person working with one piece of equipment can have over 20 applicable standards, and those standards may change throughout the course of the day's work depending on the nature of the work performed. I have been through several OSHA inspections, and not only are these standards inspected for, but the person performing the job is taken aside and quizzed about them. An employer can be fined up to $70,000 by OSHA for each willful safety violation.

The medical department can have a great impact on the safety process and usually comes under equal scrutiny by OSHA. Medical departments are staffed with an RN and an LPN working during both production shifts. The medical department is responsible for ensuring consistent and uniform quality treatment of injuries and illnesses. The department also initiates and promotes wellness programs. Additionally, there is considerable documentation required in the treatment of injuries and illnesses. Documentation is provided to the state for statistical tracking and to OSHA for their 200 log. In short, the medical department helps to facilitate the safety process.

Perdue has been extremely proactive in the area of safety—its senior management and executives are committed to making this so. For this reason, Perdue Farms, Inc., has one of the best safety records in the industry.

Psychological tests such as the MMPI and a variety of integrity tests discussed in Chapter 6 can potentially predict violence in people without histories of violence. However, an empirical link between scores on these tests and workplace violence has yet to be made (Tonowski, 1993). Care must also be taken as the Americans with Disabilities Act (ADA) provides limitations to the use of tests designed to determine psychological problems.

### Management Awareness

Workplace violence can be greatly reduced by making managers aware of high-risk situations and then empowering them to take immediate action. Most experts on workplace violence (for example, Dietz, 1994; Turner, 1994) believe that *berserkers*—employees who "go crazy" and shoot people—give indications that they are going to commit future violence. Such indications include threats, acts of violence, comments about wanting to get even, excessive talk of guns, and comments about famous serial and mass murderers. In one survey, 50% of human resource practitioners who had incidents of workplace violence in their organizations observed warning signs prior to the incident (Trenn, 1993).

Take, for example, Thomas McIlvane, a fired postal worker who shot eight postal employees, killing four. Prior to a union hearing appealing his termination, he stated that if he lost his grievance he would make a shooting incident in Oklahoma that took the lives of 14 postal workers "look like a tea party." As another example, prior to being fired and then killing his supervisors, Larry Hansel was reprimanded for excessively talking about a postal worker who killed two co-workers in Escondido, California (Graham, 1991).

Janik and Hagness (1994) advise a "zero tolerance" for threats and violence. That is, one act and the employee is terminated (fired, not killed). Dietz (1994) suggests that anyone who makes others feel uncomfortable is potential trouble. Turner (1994) suggests that employees whose behavior makes others feel scared should be screened for violence potential. This screening includes interviews with co-workers and supervisors as well as meetings with a clinical psychologist. From these interviews and meetings, Turner and his associates place the employee into one of five risk categories:

1. High violence potential, qualified for arrest/hospitalization
2. High violence potential, does not qualify for arrest/hospitalization
3. Insufficient evidence for violence potential but sufficient evidence for *intentional* infliction of emotional distress upon co-workers
4. Insufficient evidence for violence potential but sufficient evidence for *unintentional* infliction of emotional distress upon co-workers
5. Insufficient evidence for violence potential and insufficient evidence for infliction of emotional distress upon co-workers

The potential for workplace violence also can be reduced through careful handling of terminations and layoffs. If you recall, in Chapter 7 we discussed specific ways to fairly evaluate and terminate employees. In addition to these techniques, free voluntary counseling should be made available to all employees; especially those exhibiting emotional, interpersonal, or discipline problems (Mantell & Albrecht, 1994).

## ABSENTEEISM

A problem faced by many organizations is employee absenteeism—2% of the workforce is absent each day. Although 2% may not seem like much, absenteeism costs employers billions of dollars a year in lost productivity. Understanding absenteeism is important as it is correlated with turnover ($r = .23$) and thought to be a warning sign of intended turnover (Mitra, Jenkins, & Gupta, 1992). However, before an organization spends time and money trying to stop absenteeism, it must first understand the theories of why people miss work. That is, punishment will reduce absenteeism only if people make conscious decisions about attending. Likewise, wellness programs will only increase attendance if absenteeism is mostly the result of illness. Employees miss work for several reasons.

### NO CONSEQUENCES FOR ATTENDING OR MISSING WORK

The **decision-making theory** about absenteeism essentially holds that employees make a decision each day as to whether they will or will not attend work. Although the decision-making process is not clearly understood, it probably includes weighing the consequences of going to work against the consequences of not going. If this theory is true, absenteeism can be reduced by increasing the advantages of going to work and increasing the disadvantages of not going. Based on decision-making theory, attendance can be increased in several ways.

#### Rewards for Attending

Attendance can be increased through the use of financial incentives, time off, and recognition programs.

**Financial Incentives** Financial-incentive programs use money to reward employees for achieving certain levels of attendance. One of these programs, **well pay,** involves paying employees for their unused sick leave. For example, an employee who uses only four of her allowed six days would receive money for the remaining two. The amount of the payment varies among organizations: some reward the employee by paying the equivalent of her daily salary while others might split the savings by paying the employee an amount equal to half her daily salary for each unused sick day.

A second method provides a financial bonus to employees who attain a certain level of attendance. With this method, an employee with perfect attendance over a year might receive a $1,000 bonus, and an employee who misses five days might receive $300, while an employee who misses ten days receives nothing.

A meta-analysis conducted by Johnson (1990) found that well pay and financial incentives showed excellent results. But the effectiveness of incentive plans is based on such factors as the size of the incentive, the nature of the incentive, and the time that elapses between attending and being rewarded.

A third financial incentive method is to use **games** to reward employees who attend work. There are many examples. One company used poker as its game, giving a playing card each day to employees who attended. At the end of the week, employees with five cards compared the value of their hands, and the winning employee would be given a prize such as dinner for two at the best restaurant in town or a gas barbecue grill. Although some studies have reported success in using such games, the meta-analysis conducted by Johnson (1990) found that the mean effect size for games was close to zero.

**Time Off**　Another approach is the paid-time-off program (PTO) or paid-leave bank (PLB). With this type of program, vacation, personal, holiday, and sick days are combined into one category—paid time off. For example, in a traditional system, an employee might be given 10 vacation days, 3 personal days, 5 holidays, and 10 days of sick leave for a total of 28 days. With a PTO, the employee might be given 23 days of paid time off with another 5 days placed into an account for a catastrophic illness. An employee who is seldom sick has more days to use for vacation, is protected in case of a long-term illness, and the organization saves money by reducing the total number of normal sick days (Markowich, 1994).

One variation of time-off programs gives unused sick time back to the employee for later use as vacation time. A neighbor of mine works for a hospital and has not missed a day of work in five years. As a consequence, she now has three months' extra vacation time, which she plans to spend with her newborn son.

**Recognition Programs**　One other way that we can make work attendance more rewarding is through recognition and praise. Formal recognition programs provide employees with such recognition as perfect attendance certificates, coffee mugs, plaques, lapel pins, and watches. In an award-winning study, Scott, Markham, and Robers (1985) directly compared recognition with other techniques such as incentives and discipline. The results of their investigation supported the effectiveness of recognition, as did Johnson's meta-analysis (Table 13.11).

**Table 13.11** Reducing absenteeism: effect sizes of various methods

| Method | Number of Studies | Effect Size |
|---|---|---|
| Well pay | 4 | .86 |
| Flextime | 10 | .59 |
| Compressed work schedules | 5 | .44 |
| Discipline | 12 | .36 |
| Recognition | 6 | .30 |
| Wellness programs | 6 | .18 |
| Financial incentives | 7 | .17 |
| Games | 6 | .08 |

Source: Adapted from Johnson (1990). Used with permission.

### Discipline for Not Attending

Absenteeism can be reduced by punishing or disciplining employees who miss work. Discipline can range from giving a warning or a less popular work assignment to firing the employee. As shown in Table 13.11, discipline works fairly well, especially when combined with some positive reinforcement for attending.

## UNCLEAR POLICY AND POOR RECORD KEEPING

Another way to increase the negative consequences of missing work is through policy and record keeping. Most organizations measure absenteeism by counting the number of days missed, or *frequency*. Perhaps a better method would be to record the number of *instances* of absenteeism rather than the number of days. For example, instead of giving employees 12 days of sick leave, they are given 3 or 4 instances of absenteeism. Missing 1 day or 3 consecutive days each count as one instance of absenteeism.

As shown in Figure 13.6, the number of days missed and the instances of absenteeism often yield different results. By decreasing the number of times that a person can miss, the odds increase that the employee will utilize sick leave only for actual illness. These odds can be further increased by requiring a doctor's excuse for missing work.

Absenteeism can be decreased by setting attendance goals and providing feedback on how well the employees are reaching those goals. An interesting study by Harrison and Shaffer (1994) found that almost 90% of employees think their attendance is above average and estimate the typical absenteeism of their co-workers at a level two times higher than the actual figures. Similar results were found by Johns (1994). Thus, one reason employees miss work is that they incorrectly believe their attendance is at a higher level than their co-workers'. Providing feedback to employees about how their attendance compares to their co-workers and to desired levels may increase attendance.

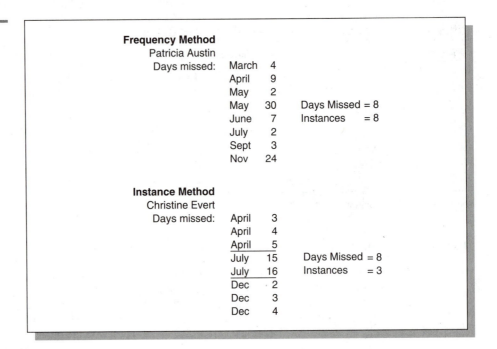

**Figure 13.6**
Frequency and instance methods of measuring absenteeism

**Frequency Method**
Patricia Austin
Days missed:

| | | |
|---|---|---|
| March | 4 | |
| April | 9 | |
| May | 2 | |
| May | 30 | Days Missed = 8 |
| June | 7 | Instances    = 8 |
| July | 2 | |
| Sept | 3 | |
| Nov | 24 | |

**Instance Method**
Christine Evert
Days missed:

| | | |
|---|---|---|
| April | 3 | |
| April | 4 | |
| April | 5 | |
| July | 15 | Days Missed = 8 |
| July | 16 | Instances    = 3 |
| Dec | 2 | |
| Dec | 3 | |
| Dec | 4 | |

## ADJUSTMENT TO WORK STRESS

Absenteeism can be reduced by removing the negative factors employees associate with going to work. One of the most important factors is *stress*. The greater the job stress, the greater the probability that most people will want to skip work. One form of stress is boredom, and it is easy to understand why a person would avoid attending a boring job or class.

Personal problems with other employees or with management constitute another reason for wanting to avoid work. If the employee feels she is not liked or will be verbally abused, it should come as no surprise that she would want to avoid dealing with her fellow employees or supervisors. Finally, employees might miss work to avoid physical dangers involved with work such as dealing with hazardous chemicals.

To increase attendance, then, the negative factors cited above must be eliminated. The first step in this elimination, of course, is to become aware of the negative factors that bother employees. These can be determined by asking supervisors or by employee questionnaires. After the problems are known, it is important that management diligently work to eliminate the identified problems from the workplace. Applying what you have learned in Chapter 12 will go a long way toward reducing absenteeism.

## ILLNESS AND PERSONAL PROBLEMS

Another obvious reason why employees miss work is illness. No data are available to indicate the percentage of absenteeism in industry that results from illness, but a study conducted with college students provides some insight. Kovach, Surrette, and Whitcomb (1988) asked more than 500 general psychology students to anonymously provide the reason for each day of class they missed. Less than 30% of the missed days were the result of illness!

However strong its effect, illness is a leading cause of missed work. The question, of course, is whether illness-induced absenteeism can be reduced. The answer is not as clear as we would like, but most indications are that organizational wellness programs involving exercise, stress reduction, smoking cessation, and improved nutrition seem to help. In a meta-analysis of the small number of available studies, Bonner (1990) found that the mean effect size for wellness programs in reducing absenteeism was .18, a fairly small effect. Results found by Erfurt, Foote, and Heirich (1992) did not support the effectiveness of wellness programs in reducing health problems.

Other sources of absenteeism are personal problems such as divorce and alcoholism. Industry, however, can reduce the effects from these factors in two ways. First, factors in the workplace that contribute to family problems and stress can be eliminated or reduced. These factors or variables include extensive employee travel, overtime, fatigue, and job-related stress. Second, some form of **Employee Assistance Program (EAP)** can be implemented. EAPs use professional counselors to deal with employee problems. An employee with a problem can either choose to see a counselor on her own or be recommended by her supervisor. Some large organizations have their own EAP counselors, but most use private agencies, which are often run through local hospitals.

The motivation for EAPs may be good, but little if any empirical evidence supports their effectiveness. Still, many organizations have used EAPs and have been quite pleased with them. Independently operated EAPs typically claim a 3-to-1 return on the dollars invested through increased productivity and reduced absenteeism and turnover.

## INDIVIDUAL DIFFERENCES

One interesting theory of absenteeism postulates that one reason people miss work is the result of a particular set of personality traits they possess. That is, certain types of people are more likely to miss work than are other types. In fact, in one study, only 25% of the employees were responsible for all of the unavoidable absenteeism (Dalton & Mesch, 1991).

Although little research has been conducted on this theory, Kovach, Surrette, and Whitcomb (1988) did find that the best predictor of student attendance in general psychology courses was the tendency of compulsive, rule-oriented behavior. If more research supports this theory, then a new strategy for increasing employee attendance might be to screen out people during the selection stage who have a tendency to miss work.

## UNIQUE EVENTS

Many times an individual will miss work because of events or conditions that are beyond management's control. One study estimated that 40% of absenteeism is unavoidable (Dalton & Mesch, 1991). For example, bad weather is one reason why absenteeism is higher in the Northeast than in the South. Although an organization can do little to control weather, the accessibility of the plant or office can be considered in the decision of where to locate. In fact, this is one reason why many organizations have started in or moved to the so-called Sunbelt in the last two decades. Organizations may also want to offer some type of shuttle service for their employees to avoid not only weather problems but also any resulting mechanical failures of employees' automobiles.

Bad weather can certainly be a legitimate reason for an employee to miss work, but one study found that job satisfaction best predicted attendance on days with poor weather. That is, in good weather, most employees attended, but in inclement weather, only those employees with high job satisfaction attended. Thus, even in bad weather, the degree to which the employee likes her job will help to determine her attendance. As the late industrial psychologist Dan Johnson has asked: "How come we hear about employees not being able to get to work and students not being able to attend class because of bad weather, yet we don't ever hear about an employee or a student who can't get home because of bad weather?" It certainly makes one think!

## CHAPTER SUMMARY

Rather than working the traditional 8 hours per day, 5 days each week, an employee can work one of several alternative work schedules. Compressed work schedules involve working 40 hours over a 3- or 4-day period rather than the traditional 5-day period, while flextime schedules allow employees to select their own hours. Research indicates that both compressed work schedules and flextime increase job satisfaction and decrease absenteeism. Other alternative schedules include peak-time pay, job sharing, and homework.

Many employees work traditional 5-day, 40-hour work weeks but do so during swing and night shifts. Although these shifts often are economically necessary, research indicates that shift work has negative effects on physical health, performance, and leisure time. Factors that modify how shift work will affect an employee include family, the uniqueness of the shift, whether the shift is fixed or rotating, and the frequency of the rotation.

In addition to schedules, such influences as noise and temperature also can affect employee behavior. Noise can reduce job performance and satisfaction depending on its frequency, pleasantness, purpose, familiarity, and continuity as well as the type of task being performed. Temperature will affect work behavior depending on the type of task being performed, the workload, and the number and length of rest periods that are allowed.

The effects of computers also were discussed in this chapter. Computers increase eye strain and levels of stress, although the latter probably results from the loss of control one feels when working with a computer as well as a fear of technology. Eye strain can be corrected through the proper design and construction of computer workstations.

The office environment is another factor that can affect work behavior. Private offices are superior to open or landscaped offices. An interesting finding is that the way in which a person decorates his office not only indicates his personality, but also affects the behavior of office visitors.

Workplace violence has recently received considerable attention. Homicides represent 17% of fatal workplace death. These homicides are the result of employees killed during the commission of a crime, law enforcement officials being killed in the line of duty, and employees being killed as an act of anger or vengeance. Workplace violence can be reduced through increased security measures, employee screening, and management awareness.

A major problem faced by most organizations is that of employee absenteeism. Decreases in absenteeism can be accomplished by increasing the reasons that an employee has for going to work (well pay, bonuses, games), increasing the negative consequences of missing work (discipline, better record keeping), and decreasing the negative consequences of attending work (reducing stress, boredom, and personal problems).

# GLOSSARY

**Bandwidth**   The total number of potential work hours available each day.

**Circadian rhythm**   A 24-hour cycle of physiological functions that are maintained by every person.

**Closed desk arrangement**   An office arranged so that a visitor sits across from the person behind the desk.

**Compressed work weeks**   Work schedules in which 40 hours are worked in less than the traditional five-day work week.

**Core hours**   The hours in a flextime schedule during which every employee must work.

**Decision-making theory**   A theory about absenteeism that holds that employees daily make a conscious decision about whether to attend work.

**Effective temperature**   The combination of air temperature, humidity, air flow, and heat radiation that determines how hot or cold the environment feels.

**Employee Assistance Program (EAP)**   A program designed to help employees overcome alcohol, drug, and psychological problems.

**Evaporation**   One way our bodies maintain a normal temperature, in which perspiration reduces excess heat.

**Financial bonus**   A method of absenteeism control in which employees who meet an attendance standard are given a cash reward.

**Fixed shift**   A shift schedule in which employees never change the shifts that they work.

**Flexible hours**   The part of a flextime schedule in which employees may choose which hours to work.

**Flexitour**  A flextime schedule in which employees have flexibility in scheduling but must schedule their work hours at least a week in advance.

**Flextime**  A work schedule that allows employees to choose their own work hours.

**Games**  An absenteeism control method in which games such as poker and bingo are used to reward employee attendance.

**Gliding time**  A flextime schedule in which employees can choose their own hours without any advance notice or scheduling.

**Job sharing**  A work schedule in which two employees share one job by splitting the work hours.

**Modified flexitour**  A flextime schedule in which employees have flexibility in scheduling but must schedule their work hours a day in advance.

**Moonlighting**  Working more than one job.

**On-site child-care facility**  A child-care center that is located on the site of the organization employing the parent.

**Open desk arrangement**  An office arranged so that a visitor can sit adjacent to rather than across from the person behind the desk.

**Peak-time pay**  A system in which part-time employees who work only during peak hours are paid at a higher hourly rate.

**Radiation**  One way our bodies maintain a normal temperature, by the emission of heat waves.

**Referral service**  A system of child care in which an employer maintains a list of certified child-care centers that can be used by its employees.

**Rotating shift**  A shift schedule in which employees periodically change the shifts that they work.

**Voucher system**  A system of child care in which an organization pays all or some of its employees' child-care costs at private child-care centers by providing the employees with vouchers.

**Well pay**  A method of absenteeism control in which employees are paid for their unused sick leave.

**Work at home**  A system in which employees work at home rather than in an organization's building.

# REFERENCES

Aamodt, M. G. (1986, June). *Validity of expert advice regarding the employment interview.* Paper presented at the 10th Annual Meeting of International Personnel Management Association—Assessment Council, San Francisco, CA.

Aamodt, M. G., Bryan, D. A., & Whitcomb, A. J. (1993). Predicting performance with letters of recommendation. *Public Personnel Management, 22*(1), 81–90.

Aamodt, M. G., & Carr, K. (1988). Relationship between recruitment source and employee behavior. *Proceedings of the 12th Annual Meeting of International Personnel Management Association,* 143–146.

Aamodt, M. G., Dwight, S., & Michals, J. (1994). *Reliability and validity of the trait approach to letters of recommendation.* Paper presented at the annual meeting of the International Personnel Management Association—Assessment Council, Charleston, SC.

Aamodt, M. G., Freeman, D. M., & Carneal, D. H. (1992). *Effects of group homogeneity on group performance: Two studies and a meta-analysis.* Paper presented at the annual meeting of the Virginia Psychological Association, Roanoke, VA.

Aamodt, M. G., Johnson, D. L., & Freeman, D. M. (1992). *Estimating future adverse impact using selection ratios and group differences in test scores.* Paper presented at the annual meeting of the International Personnel Management Association—Assessment Council, Baltimore, MD.

Aamodt, M. G., & Kimbrough, W. W. (1982). Validity considerations in acceptance of Personal Profile System interpretations. *Educational and Psychological Measurement, 42,* 625–628.

Aamodt, M. G., & Kimbrough, W. W. (1985). Comparison of four methods for weighing multiple predictors. *Educational and Psychological Measurement, 45,* 477–482.

Aamodt, M. G., Kimbrough, W. W., & Alexander, C. J. (1983). A preliminary investigation of the relationship between team racial heterogeneity and team performance in college basketball. *Journal of Sports Sciences, 1,* 131–133.

Aamodt, M. G., Kimbrough, W. W., Keller, R. J., & Crawford, K. (1982). Relationship between sex, race, and job performance level and the generation of critical incidents. *Educational and Psychological Research, 2,* 227–234.

Aamodt, M. G., & McShane, T. (1992). A meta-analytic investigation of the effect of various test item characteristics on test scores and test completion times. *Public Personnel Management, 21*(2), 151–160.

Aamodt, M. G., & Peggans, D. (1988). Tactfully rejecting job applicants. *Personnel Administrator, 33,* 58–60.

Aamodt, M. G., & Pierce, W. L. (1987). Comparison of the rare response and vertical percent methods of scoring the biographical information blank. *Educational and Psychological Measurement, 47,* 505–511.

Aamodt, M. G., Reardon, C., & Kimbrough, W. W. (1986). The Critical Incident Technique revisited. *Journal of Police and Criminal Psychology, 2,* 48–59.

Aamodt, M. G., VanMarter, J., Pearson, M. & Martin, J. E. (1993). *Increasing the effectiveness of situational interviews.* Paper presented at the annual meeting of the International Personnel Management Association—Assessment Council, Sacramento, CA.

Adair, B., & Pollen, D. (1985, September 23). No! No! A thousand times no: The declining art of the rejection letter. *The Washington Post,* p. C–5.

Adams, J. S. (1965). Inequity in social change. In L. Berkowitz (Ed.), *Advances in experimental social psychology* (Vol. 2), (pp. 267–299). New York: Academic Press.

Adams, J. S., & Rosenbaum, W. B. (1962). The relationship of worker productivity to cognitive dissonance about wage inequities. *Journal of Applied Psychology, 46,* 161–164.

Adams, L., & DeLucca, J. (1987). Effect of confidentiality and likability in performance evaluations. *Proceedings of the 8th Annual Graduate Conference on Industrial/Organizational Psychology and Organizational Behavior,* 183–184.

Aiello, J. R., & Svec, C. M. (1993). Computer monitoring of work performance: Extending the social facilitation framework to electronic presence. *Journal of Applied Social Psychology, 23*(7), 537–548.

Akerstedt, T., & Torsvall, L. (1978). Experimental changes in shift schedules: Their effects on well-being. *Ergonomics, 21,* 849–856.

Aldag, R. J., & Fuller, S. R. (1993). Beyond fiasco: A reappraisal of the groupthink phenomenon and a new model of group decision processes. *Psychological Bulletin, 113*(3), 533–552.

Aldefer, C. P. (1972). *Existence, relatedness, and growth: Human needs in organizational settings.* New York: Free Press.

Allen, T. J., & Gertsberger, P. C. (1973). A field experiment to improve communications in a product engineering department: The nonterritorial office. *Human Factors, 15,* 487–498.

Alliger, G. M., & Janak, E. A. (1989). Kirkpatrick's levels of training criteria: Thirty years later. *Personnel Psychology, 42,* 331–342.

Allport, G. W., & Postman, L. (1947). *The psychology of rumor.* New York: Holt, Rinehart & Winston.

Allred, S. (1995). An overview of the Family and Medical Leave Act of 1983. *Public Personnel Management, 24*(1), 67–73.

Amabile, T. M., Hill, K. G., Hennessey, B. A., & Tighe, E. M. (1994). The Work Preference Inventory: Assessing intrinsic and extrinsic motivational orientations. *Journal of Personality and Social Psychology, 66*(5), 950–967.

Amalfitano, J. G., & Kalt, N. C. (1977). Effects of eye contact on the evaluation of job applicants. *Journal of Employment Counseling, 14,* 46–48.

Ammerman, H. L. (1965). *A model of junior officer jobs for use in developing task inventories.* HumPRO Technical Report 65–10. Alexandria, VA: Human Resources Research Organization.

Anastasi, A. (1988). *Psychological testing.* New York: Macmillan.

Anderson, N. H. (1965). Adding versus averaging as a stimulus combination rule in impression formation. *Journal of Experimental Psychology, 70,* 394–400.

Andrews, E. S., & Noel, J. J. (1986). Adding life to the case study method. *Training and Development Journal, 40*(2), 28–33.

Arcuri, A. E., & Lester, D. (1990). Moonlighting and stress in police oficers. *Psychological Reports, 66,* 350.

Armentrout, B. W. (1993). Eight keys to effective performance appraisal. *HR Focus, 70*(4), 13.

Arthur, J. B. (1994). Effects of human resource systems on manufacturing performance and turnover. *Academy of Management Journal, 37*(3), 670–687.

Arvey, R. D. (1979). *Fairness in selecting employees.* Reading, MA: Addison-Wesley.

Arvey, R. D., & Begalla, M. E. (1975). Analyzing the homemaker job using the PAQ. *Journal of Applied Psychology, 60,* 513–517.

Arvey, R. D., Bouchard, T. J., Segal, N. L., & Abraham, L. M. (1989). Job satisfaction: Environmental and genetic components. *Journal of Applied Psychology, 74,* 187–192.

Arvey, R. D., & Campion, J. E. (1982). The employment interview: A summary and review of recent research. *Personnel Psychology, 35,* 281–327.

Arvey, R. D., Davis, G. A., McGowen, S. L., & Dipboye, R. L. (1982). Potential sources of bias in job analytic processes. *Academy of Management Journal, 25,* 618–629.

Arvey, R. D., Gordon, M., Massengill, D., & Mussio, S. (1975). Differential report rates of minority and majority job candidates due to time lags between selection procedures. *Personnel Psychology, 38,* 175–180.

Arvey, R. D., Nutting, S. M., & Landon, T. E. (1992). Validation strategies for physical ability testing in police and fire settings. *Public Personnel Management, 21*(3), 301–312.

Ash, R. A., & Edgell, S. A. (1975). A note on the readability of the Position Analysis Questionnaire (PAQ). *Journal of Applied Psychology, 60,* 765–766.

Ash, R. A., & Levine, E. L. (1980). A framework for evaluating job analysis methods. *Personnel, 57*(6), 53–59.

Asher, J. J., & Sciarrino, J. A. (1974). Realistic work sample tests: A review. *Personnel Psychology, 27,* 519–533.

Asquith, N., & Feld, D. E. (1993). *Employment testing manual: 1993 cumulative supplement.* Boston: Warren, Gorham, and Lamont.

Athey, T. R., & McIntyre, R. M. (1987). Effect of rater training on rater accuracy: Levels of processing theory and social facilitation perspectives. *Journal of Applied Psychology, 72,* 567–572.

Atwater, L., Roush, P., & Fischthal, A. (1995). The influence of upward feedback on self- and follower ratings of leadership. *Personnel Psychology, 48,* 35–60.

Austin, N. K. (1994). How managers manage flexibility. *Working Woman, 7,* 19–20.

Baba, V. V., & Jamal, M. (1992). How much do we really know about moonlighters? *Public Personnel Management, 21*(1), 65–73.

Babbie, E. (1992). *The practice of social research.* Belmont, CA: Wadsworth Publishing.

Baldwin, T. T., & Ford, J. K. (1988). Transfer of training: A review and directions for future research. *Personnel Psychology, 41,* 63–105.

Baldwin, T. T., Magjuka, R. J., & Loher, B. T. (1991). The perils of participation: Effects of choice of training on trainee motivation and learning. *Personnel Psychology, 44,* 51–65.

Balzer, W. K., & Howard, A. (1994). 1993 profile of division 14 members: Noteworthy trends. *The Industrial-Organizational Psychologist, 31*(3), 95–97.

Balzer, W. K., & Sulsky, L. M. (1992). Halo and performance appraisal research: A critical examination. *Journal of Applied Psychology, 77*(6), 971–986.

Banks, M. H., Jackson, P. R., Stafford, E. M., & Warr, P. B. (1983). The Job Components Inventory and the analysis of jobs requiring limited skill. *Personnel Psychology, 36,* 57–66.

Banks, M. H., & Miller, R. L. (1984). Reliability and convergent validity of the Job Components Inventory. *Journal of Occupational Psychology, 57,* 181–184.

Bannister, B. D. (1986). Performance outcome feedback and attributional feedback: Interactive effects on recipient responses. *Journal of Applied Psychology, 71,* 203–210.

Bargerstock, A. S. (1989). Establish a direct mail recruitment program. *Recruitment Today, 2*(3), 52–56.

Barnes, K. (1994a). Is your office ergonomically correct? *HR Focus, 71*(6), 17.

Barnes, K. (1994b). Tips for managing telecommuters. *HR Focus, 71*(11), 9–10.

Baron, R. A. (1977). *Human aggression.* New York: Plenum.

Baron, R. A. (1983). Sweet smell of success: The impact of pleasant artificial scents on evaluations of job applicants. *Journal of Applied Psychology, 68,* 709–713.

Baron, R. A. (1988). Negative effects of destructive criticism: Impact on conflict, self-efficacy, and task performance. *Journal of Applied Psychology, 73,* 199–207.

Barr, S. H., & Hitt, M. A. (1986). A comparison of selection decision models in manager versus student samples. *Personnel Psychology, 39,* 599–617.

Barton, J., & Folkard, S. (1993). Advancing versus delaying shift systems. *Ergonomics, 36*(1), 59–64.

Barton, M. (1993). National origin discrimination claims rising. *HR News,* (12), 5.

Bass, B. M. (1990). *Bass & Stogdill's handbook of leadership: Theory, research, and application* (3rd ed.). New York: Free Press.

Bassett, G. A., & Meyer, H. H. (1968). Performance appraisal based upon self-review. *Personnel Psychology, 21,* 421–430.

Bast, G. H. (1960). *Ploegenarbeid in de industry.* Arnheim: Contract groepvuoering productiviteit Van Loghum Slaterus. Cited by P. E. Mott, *Shift work.* (1965). Ann Arbor, MI: University of Michigan Press.

Baumgartner, J. (1994). Give it to me straight. *Training & Development Journal, 48*(6), 49–51.

Baxter, J. C., Brock, B., Hill, P. C., & Rozelle, R. M. (1981). Letters of recommendation: A question of value. *Journal of Applied Psychology, 66,* 296–301.

Baxter, J. S., Manstead, A. S., Stradling, S. G., & Campbell, K. A. (1990). Social facilitation and driving behavior. *British Journal of Psychology, 81*(3), 351–360.

Beall, G. E. (1991). Validity of the weighted application blank across four job criterion. *Applied H.R.M. Research, 2*(1), 18–26.

Beason, G., & Belt, J. R. (1976). Verifying applicants' backgrounds. *Personnel Journal, 55,* 345–348.

Becker, T. E., & Colquitt, A. L. (1992). Potential versus actual faking of a biodata form: An analysis along several dimensions of item type. *Personnel Psychology, 45,* 389–406.

Bell, J. D., & Kerr, D. L. (1987). Measuring training results: Key to managerial commitment. *Training and Development Journal, 41*(1), 70–73.

Bender, J. M. (1973). What is "typical" of assessment centers? *Personnel, 50*(6), 50–57.

Benge, E. J., Burk, S. L., & Hay, E. N. (1941). *Manual of job evaluation.* New York: Harper & Row.

Benne, K. D., & Sheets, P. (1948). Functional roles of group members. *Journal of Social Issues, 4*(2), 41–49.

Bennis, W. (1989). *On becoming a leader.* Reading, MA: Addison-Wesley.

Ben-Shakhar, G., Bar-Hillel, M., Bilu, Y., Ben-Abba, E., & Flug, A. (1986). Can graphology predict occupational success? Two empirical studies and some methodological ruminations. *Journal of Applied Psychology, 71,* 645–653.

Benzinger, K. (1982, May–June). The powerful woman. *Hospital Forum,* pp. 15–20.

Bernard Hodes Advertising. (1985). *Employee referral policies and programs.* New York: Doyle Dane Bernbach Advertising.

Bernardin, H. J., & Buckley, M. R. (1981). Strategies in rater training. *Academy of Management Review, 6,* 205–242.

Bernardin, H. J., & Kane, J. S. (1980). A second look at behavioral observation scales. *Personnel Psychology, 33,* 809–814.

Bernardin, H. J., LaShells, M. B., Smith, P. C., & Alvares, K. M. (1976). Behavioral expectation scales: Effects of developmental procedures and formats. *Journal of Applied Psychology, 61,* 75–79.

Bernardin, H. J., & Pence, E. C. (1980). Effects of rater training: Creating new response sets and decreasing accuracy. *Journal of Applied Psychology, 65,* 60–66.

Bernardin, H. J., & Walters, C. S. (1977). Effects of rater training and diary-keeping on psychometric error in ratings. *Journal of Applied Psychology, 62,* 64–69.

Berne, E. (1964). *Games people play.* New York: Grove Press.

Bernstein, A. J., & Rozen, S. C. (1992). *Neanderthals at work.* New York: Ballantine Books.

Bernthal, P. R., & Insko, C. A. (1993). Cohesiveness without groupthink: The interactive effects of social and task cohesion. *Group and Organization Management, 18*(1), 66–87.

Beshir, M. Y., El-Sabagh, A. S., & El-Nawawi, M. A. (1981). Time on task effect on tracking performance under heat stress. *Ergonomics, 24,* 95–102.

Biddle, R. E. (1993). How to set cutoff scores for knowledge tests used in promotion, training, certification, and licensing. *Public Personnel Management, 22*(1), 63–79.

Biegeleisen, J. I. (1994). *Make your job interview a success* (4th ed.). Englewood Cliffs, NJ: Prentice Hall.

Bird, A. (1977). Team structure and success as related to cohesiveness and leadership. *Journal of Social Psychology, 103,* 217–223.

Bird, C. (1940). *Social psychology.* New York: Appleton-Century-Crofts.

Birnbrauer, H. (1987). Evaluation techniques that work. *Training and Development Journal, 41*(1), 53–55.

Blake, R. R., & Mouton, J. S. (1984). *The managerial grid III.* Houston: Gulf Publishing.

Blake, R. R., Shephard, H., & Mouton, J. S. (1964). *Managing intergroup conflict in industry.* Houston: Gulf Publishing.

Blanchard, K. H., Zigarmi, P., & Zigarmi, D. (1985). *Leadership and the one minute manager.* New York: William Morrow and Company.

Blanz, F., & Ghiselli, E. E. (1972). The mixed standard scale: A new rating system. *Personnel Psychology, 25,* 185–200.

Bloch, G. D. (1995). Avoiding liability for sexual harassment. *HRMagazine, 40*(4), 91–97.

Bluen, S. D., Barling, J., & Burns, W. (1990). Predicting sales performance, job satisfaction, and depression using the Achievement Strivings and Impatience-Irritability dimensions of Type A behavior. *Journal of Applied Psychology, 75,* 212–216.

Blum, M. L., & Naylor, J. C. (1968). *Industrial psychology.* New York: Harper & Row.

Blumenfeld, W. S. (1985). Appropriateness of readability of a Federal Aviation Agency regulation, a flight crew manual, and a company pilot labor agreement for an airline's pilots. *Perceptual and Motor Skills, 61,* 1189–1190.

Blumenfeld, W. S., & Justice, B. M. (1975). Six replicated investigations of the relationship between Flesch and Gunning readability indices. *Perceptual and Motor Skills, 40,* 110.

Bolles, R. N. (1995). *What color is your parachute.* Berkeley, CA: Ten Speed Press.

Bond, C. F., & Titus, L. J. (1983). Social facilitation: A meta-analysis of 241 studies. *Psychological Bulletin, 94,* 265–292.

Bonjean, C. M., Hill, R. J., & McLemore, S. D. (1967). *Sociological measurement: An inventory of scales and indices.* San Francisco: Chandler.

Bonner, D. (1990). Effectiveness of wellness programs in industry. *Applied H.R.M. Research, 1*(2), 32–37.

Bonner, J. J. (1993). *Measurement of résumé content preference.* Unpublished master's thesis, Radford University, Radford, VA.

Borman, W. C. (1978). Exploring upper limits of reliability and validity in job performance ratings. *Journal of Applied Psychology, 63,* 135–144.

Boudreau, J. W. (1983). Economic considerations in estimating the utility of human resource productivity improvement programs. *Personnel Psychology, 36,* 551–576.

Brabant, C. (1992). Heat exposure standards and women's work: Equitable or debatable? *Women and Health, 18*(3), 119–130.

Bradburn, W. J., & Villar, P. (1992). Adverse impact resulting from the use of clerical tests: A meta-analysis. *Applied H.R.M. Research, 3*(1), 65–72.

Bramson, R. (1981). *Coping with difficult people.* New York: Anchor Press.

Brawley, L. R., Carron, A. V., & Widmeyer, W. N. (1993). The influence of the group and its cohesiveness on perceptions of group goal-related variables. *Journal of Sport and Exercise Psychology, 15*(3), 245–260.

Breaugh, J. A. (1981). Relationships between recruitment sources and employee performance, absenteeism, and work attitudes. *Academy of Management Journal, 24,* 261–267.

Breaugh, J. A., & Mann, R. B. (1984). Recruiting source effects: A test of two alternative explanations. *Journal of Occupational Psychology, 57,* 261–267.

Brehm, J. W. (1966). *A theory of psychological reactance.* New York: Academic Press.

Brehm, S. S., & Kassin, S. M. (1993). *Social psychology* (2nd ed.). Boston, MA: Houghton Mifflin.

Brennan, J. (1994). New outlaws? *Forbes, 151*(4), 70.

Bretz, R. D., & Thomas, S. L. (1992). Perceived equity, motivation, and final offer arbitration. *Journal of Applied Psychology, 77*(3), 280–287.

Brigham, T. A. (1989). On the importance of recognizing the difference between experiments and correlation studies. *American Psychologist, 44*(7), 1053–1061.

Brinkerhoff, R. O. (1986). Expanding needs analysis. *Training and Development Journal, 40*(2), 64–65.

Brinkman, R., & Kirschner, R. (1994). *Dealing with people you can't stand.* New York: McGraw-Hill.

Broadbent, D. E. (1971). *Decision and stress.* New York: Academic Press.

Broadbent, D. E., & Little, E. A. (1960). Effect of noise reduction in a work situation. *Occupational Psychology, 343,* 133–140.

Broadwell, M. M. (1993). Seven steps to building better training. *Training, 30*(10), 75–81.

Brod, C. (1985). How to deal with technostress. *Office Administration and Automation, 28*(8), 46–47.

Brookes, M. J., & Kaplan, A. (1972). The office environment: Space planning and effective behavior. *Human Factors, 14,* 373–391.

Broussard, R. D., & Brannen, D. E. (1986). Credential distortions: Personnel practitioners give their views. *Personnel Administrator, 31*(6), 129–145.

Brown, D. L. (1993). Target stores settle out of court in Sorona v. Dayton Hudson. *The Industrial Organizational Psychologist, 31*(2), 88–89.

Brown, K. A., & Huber, V. L. (1992). Lowering floors and raising ceilings: A longitudinal assessment of the effects of an earnings-at-risk plan on pay performance. *Personnel Psychology, 45*(2), 279–311.

Brown, L. D. (1983). *Managing conflict at organizational interfaces.* Reading, MA: Addison-Wesley.

Brown, S. H. (1978). Long-term validity of a personal history item scoring procedure. *Journal of Applied Psychology, 63,* 673–676.

Brown, W. F., & Finsteun, K. (1993). The use of participation in decision making: A consideration of the Vroom-Yetton and Vroom-Jago normative models. *Journal of Behavioral Decision Making, 6*(3), 207–219.

Browning, R. C. (1968). Validity of reference ratings from previous employers. *Personnel Psychology, 21,* 389–393.

Brumback, G. B. (1986, June). *Performance appraisal in a time capsule.* Address to the 10th Annual Meeting of International Personnel Management Association—Assessment Council, San Francisco, CA.

Brumback, G. B. (1988). Some ideas, issues, and predictions about performance management. *Public Personnel Management, 17,* 387–402.

Bryan, D. A. (1992). Differences in trait interpretations between black and white professionals when evaluating letters of recommendation. *Applied H.R.M. Research, 3*(2), 130–161.

Bryman, A. (1992). *Charisma & leadership.* London: Sage Publications.

Bucalo, J. P. (1983). Good advertising can be more effective than other recruitment tools. *Personnel Administrator, 28,* 73–79.

Buchner, L. M. (1990). Increases in interrater reliability of situational interviews as a function of the number of benchmark answers. *Applied H.R.M. Research, 1*(2), 27–31.

Buckley, M. R., & Eder, R. W. (1989). The first impression. *Personnel Administrator, 34*(5), 72–74.

Buckley, M. R., & Weitzel, W. (1988). Employing at will. *Personnel Administrator, 33*(8), 78–81.

Budman, M. (1994). Apprentices begin apprenticing in the U.S. *Across the Board, 31*(1), 36–37.

Bullock, R. J., & Tubbs, M. E. (1990). A case meta-analysis of gainsharing plans as organization development interventions. *Journal of Applied Behavioral Science, 26*(3), 383–404.

Burke, R. J. (1970). Methods of resolving superior-subordinate conflict: The constructive use of subordinate difference and disagreement. *Organizational Behavior and Human Performance, 5,* 393–411.

Burke, R. J., Weitzel, W., & Weir, T. (1978). Characteristics of effective employee performance review and development interviews. *Personnel Psychology, 31,* 903–919.

Burling, T., Lentz, E., & Wilson, R. (1956). *To give and take in hospitals.* New York: Putnam.

Burnett, J. J., & Dunne, P. M. (1986). An appraisal of the use of student subjects in marketing research. *Journal of Business Research, 14*(4), 329–343.

Burns, W. (1979). Physiological effects of noise. In C. M. Harris (Ed.), *Handbook of noise control* (pp. 15-1–15-23). New York: McGraw-Hill.

Buros, O. K. (1975a). *Personality tests and reviews II.* Highland Park, NJ: Gryphon Press.

Buros, O. K. (1975b). *Vocational tests and reviews.* Highland Park, NJ: Gryphon Press.

Buzzotta, V. R. (1986). Does "people skills" training really work? *Training, 23*(8), 59–60.

Byrne, D. (1971). *The attraction paradigm.* New York: Academic Press.

Byrne, J. A. (1994, May 9). The pain of downsizing. *Business Week,* 60–69.

Caldwell, D. F., & O'Reilly, C. A. (1982). Boundary spanning and individual performance: The impact of self-monitoring. *Journal of Applied Psychology, 67,* 124–127.

Caldwell, D. F., & Spivey, W. A. (1983). The relationship between recruiting source and employee success: An analysis by race. *Personnel Psychology, 36,* 67–72.

Cameron, K. S., Freeman, S. J., & Mishra, A. (1991). Best practices in white-collar downsizings: Managing contradictions. *Academy of Management Executive, 5,* 57–73.

Campbell, D. E. (1979). Interior office design and visitor response. *Journal of Applied Psychology, 64,* 648–653.

Campbell, D. T., & Stanley, J. C. (1963). *Experimental and quasi-experimental designs in research.* Chicago: Rand McNally.

Campbell, J. C. (1983). *Using job descriptions to increase job performance.* Nashville, TN: James C. Campbell & Associates.

Campion, J. E., Greener, J., & Wernli, S. (1973). Work observation versus recall in developing behavioral examples for rating scales. *Journal of Applied Psychology, 58,* 286–288.

Campion, M. A., & McClelland, C. L. (1993). Follow-up and extension of the interdisciplinary costs and benefits of enlarged jobs. *Journal of Applied Psychology, 78*(3), 339–351.

Campion, M. A., Pursell, E. D., & Brown, B. K. (1988). Structured interviewing: Raising the psychometric properties of the employment interview. *Personnel Psychology, 41,* 25–42.

Cantor, J., Alfonso, H., & Zillman, D. (1976). The persuasive effectiveness of the peer appeal and a communicator's first-hand experience. *Communication Research, 3,* 293–310.

Cardy, R. L., & Dobbins, G. H. (1986). Affect and appraisal accuracy: Liking as an integral dimension in evaluating performance. *Journal of Applied Psychology, 71,* 672–678.

Carlson, R. E. (1970). Effects of applicant sample on ratings of valid information in an employment setting. *Journal of Applied Psychology, 54,* 217–222.

Carr, C. (1994). How to improve performance. *Training & Development, 48*(7), 35–37.

Carrell, M. R., & Dittrich, J. E. (1978). Equity theory: The recent literature, methodological considerations, and new directions. *Academy of Management Review, 3,* 202–210.

Carroll, S. J., & Nash, A. N. (1972). Effectiveness of a forced-choice reference check. *Personnel Administration, 35,* 42–146.

Carroll, S. J., Paine, F. T., & Ivancevich, J. J. (1972). The relative effectiveness of training methods: Expert opinion and research. *Personnel Psychology, 25,* 495–510.

Carron, A. V. (1990). Group size in sport and physical activity: Social psychological and performance consequences. *International Journal of Sport Psychology, 21*(4), 286–304.

Carter, J. H. (1952). Military leadership. *Military Review, 32,* 14–18.

Cascio, W. F. (1987, April). *Utility analysis and strategic management.* Paper presented at 8th Annual Conference in Industrial/Organizational Psychology and Organizational Behavior, Knoxville, TN.

Cascio, W. F., Alexander, R. A., & Barrett, G. V. (1988). Setting cutoff scores: Legal, psychometric, and professional issues and guidelines. *Personnel Psychology, 41,* 1–24.

Cascio, W. F., Outtz, J., Zedeck, S., & Goldstein, J. L. (1991). Statistical implications of six methods of test score use in personnel selection. *Human Performance, 4*(4), 233–264.

Cascio, W. F., & Phillips, N. F. (1979). Performance testing: A rose among thorns. *Personnel Psychology, 32,* 751–756.

Cash, T. E., Gillen, B., & Burns, D. S. (1977). Sexism and "beautyism" in personnel consultants' decision making. *Journal of Applied Psychology, 62,* 361–370.

Caudron, S. (1994). Volunteer efforts offer low cost training options. *Personnel Journal, 73*(6), 38–44.

Ceci, S. J., & Peters, D. (1984). Letters of reference: A naturalistic study of the effects of confidentiality. *American Psychologist, 39,* 29–31.

Cederbloom, D. (1982). The performance appraisal interview: A review, implications, and suggestions. *Academy of Management Review, 7,* 219–227.

Cederbloom, D. (1989). Peer and supervisor evaluations: An underused promotion method used for law enforcement. *Proceedings of 13th Annual Meeting of International Personnel Management Association — Assessment Council.*

Cederbloom, D., Pence, E. C., & Johnson, D. L. (1984). Making I/O psychology useful: The personnel administrator's view. *The Industrial/Organizational Psychologist, 21*(3), 9–17.

Cellar, D. F., Curtis, J. R., Kohlepp, K., Poczapski, P., & Mohiuddin, S. (1989). The effects of rater training, job analysis format and congruence of training on job evaluation ratings. *Journal of Business and Psychology, 3*(4), 387–401.

Chaiken, S. (1979). Communicator physical attractiveness and persuasion. *Journal of Personality and Social Psychology, 33,* 1387–1397.

Chambers, D. A. (1986). The constraints of work and domestic schedules on women's leisure. *Leisure Studies, 5,* 309–325.

Chauran, T. (1989). Taking Texas on the road. *Recruitment Today, 2*(2), 48–52.

Chen, S. C. (1937). Social modification of the activity of ants in nest-building. *Physiological Zoology, 10,* 420–436.

Church, A. H. (1993). Estimating the effect of incentives on mail survey response rates: A meta-analysis. *Public Opinion Quarterly, 57*(1), 62–79.

Cialindi, R. B. (1985). *Influence: Science and practice.* Glenview, IL: Scott, Foresman.

Cialindi, R. B., Borden, R., Thorne, A., Walker, M., Freeman, S., & Sloane, L. T. (1976). Basking in reflected glory: Three (football) field studies. *Journal of Personality and Social Psychology, 34,* 366–375.

Cirillo, C. J. (1983). Office ergonomics: Coping with causes of stress in the automated workplace. *Management Review, 25,* 38–39.

Clark, R. D. (1971). Group-induced shift toward risk: A critical appraisal. *Psychological Bulletin, 76,* 251–271.

Clark, R. E. (1961). *The limiting hand skin temperature for unaffected manual performance in the cold.* Natick, MA: Quartermaster Research and Engineering Command, Technical Report EP-147.

Cleveland, J. N., Murphy, K. R., & Williams, R. E. (1989). Multiple uses of performance appraisal: Prevalance and correlates. *Journal of Applied Psychology, 74,* 130–135.

Cline, E. B., & Seibert, P. S. (1993). Help for first time needs assessors. *Training and Development, 47*(5), 99–101.

Clore, G. L., Wiggins, N. H., & Itkin, S. (1975). Gain and loss in attraction: Attributions from nonverbal behavior. *Journal of Personality and Social Psychology, 31,* 706–712.

Cochran, A., Kopitzke, K., & Miller, D. (1984). Relationship between interviewer personality and interior office characteristics. *Proceedings of the 5th Annual Graduate Student Conference in Industrial/Organizational Psychology and Organizational Behavior.*

Cohen, A. (1972, September). *The role of psychology in improving worker safety and health under the Worker Safety and Health Act.* Paper presented at the annual meeting of the American Psychological Association, Honolulu, HI.

Cohen, A. R., & Bradford, D. L. (1990). *Influence without authority.* New York: John Wiley & Sons.

Cohen, J. (1977). *Statistical power analysis for the behavioral sciences.* New York: Academic Press.

Cohen, S., & Weinstein, N. (1981). Nonauditory effects of noise on behavior and health. *Journal of Personality and Social Psychology, 37,* 36–70.

Cohen, S. L. (1980). Pre-packaged vs. tailor made: The assessment center debate. *Personnel Journal, 59*(12), 989–991.

Colligan, M. J., Frockt, I. J., & Tasto, D. L. (1970). Frequency of sickness absence and worksite clinic visits among nurses as a function of shift. *Applied Ergonomics, 10,* 79–85.

Comer, D. R. (1989). Peers as providers. *Personnel Administrator, 34*(5), 84–86.

Connolly, P. M. (1986). Clearing the deadwood. *Training & Development Journal, 40*(1), 58–60.

Conoley, J. C., & Kramer, J. J. (1989). *The tenth mental measurements yearbook.* Lincoln, NB: University of Nebraska Press.

Converse, J. M., & Presser, S. (1986). *Survey questions: Handcrafting the structured questionnaire.* Newbury Park, CA: Sage.

Cooper, W. H. (1981a). Ubiquitous halo. *Psychological Bulletin, 90,* 218–244.

Cooper, W. H. (1981b). Conceptual similarity as a source of illusory halo in job performance ratings. *Journal of Applied Psychology, 66,* 302–307.

Cornelius, E. T., Carron, T. J., & Collins, M. N. (1979). Job analysis models and job classification. *Personnel Psychology, 32,* 693–708.

Cornelius, E. T., & Hakel, M. D. (1978). *A study to develop an improved enlisted performance evaluation system for the U.S. Coast Guard.* Washington, DC: Department of Transportation.

Cornelius, E. T., Hakel, M. D., & Sackett, P. R. (1979). A methodological approach to job classification for performance appraisal purposes. *Personnel Psychology, 32,* 283–297.

Costley, D. L., & Todd, R. (1987). *Human relations in organizations.* St. Paul, MN: West Publishing.

Cottrell, N. B. (1972). Social facilitation. In C. G. McClintock (Ed.), *Experimental social psychology* (pp. 185–236). New York: Holt, Rinehart & Winston.

Cowan, G., & Kasen, J. H. (1984). Form of reference: Sex differences in letters of recommendation. *Journal of Personality and Social Psychology, 46,* 636–645.

Cromwell, P. F., Marks, A., Olson, J. N., & Avary, D. W. (1991). Group effects on decision-making by burglars. *Psychological Reports, 69*(2), 579–588.

Cronbach, L. J. (1951). Coefficient alpha and the internal structure of tests. *Psychometrika, 16,* 297–334.

Cropanzano, R., & Folger, R. (1989). Referent cognitions and task decision autonomy: Beyond equity theory. *Journal of Applied Psychology, 74,* 293–299.

Cropanzano, R., & James, K. (1990). Some methodological considerations for the behavioral genetic analysis of work attitudes. *Journal of Applied Psychology, 75,* 433–439.

Crosby, M. M. (1990, April). *Social desirability and biodata: Predicting sales success.* Poster presented at the Annual Conference of the Society for Industrial and Organizational Psychology, Miami Beach, FL.

Crusco, A. H., & Wetzel, C. G. (1984). The midas touch: The effects of interpersonal touch on restaurant tipping. *Personality and Social Psychology Bulletin, 10,* 512–517.

Csoka, L. S., & Bons, P. M. (1978). Manipulating the situation to fit the leader's style: Two validation studies of leader match. *Journal of Applied Psychology, 63,* 295–300.

Cureton, E. E. (1965). Reliability and validity: Basic assumptions and experimental designs. *Educational and Psychological Measurement, 25,* 327–346.

Currer-Briggs, N. (1971). *Handwriting analysis in business: The use of graphology in personnel selection.* New York: John Wiley & Sons.

Dahmer, B. (1992). Kinder, gentler icebreakers. *Training and Development Journal, 46*(8), 47–49.

Dainoff, M. F., Happ, A., & Crane, P. (1981). Visual fatigue and occupational stress in VDT operators. *Human Factors, 23,* 420–437.

Dale, E., & Chall, J. S. (1948). A formula for predicting readability. *Educational Research Bulletin, 27,* 37–54.

Dalton, D. R., & Mesch, D. J. (1991). On the extent and reduction of avoidable absenteeism: An assessment of absence policy provisions. *Journal of Applied Psychology, 76*(6), 810–817.

Daniel, D. (1990). Validity of a standardized reference checklist. *Applied H.R.M. Research, 1*(2), 51–66.

Daniel, S. (1987). Strength and endurance testing. *Personnel Journal, 66*(6), 112.

Dansereau, F., Graen, G., & Haga, W. J. (1974). *A vertical dyad linkage approach to leadership within the formal organization.* Unpublished report, State University of New York, Buffalo.

Davies, E. (1922). *Transactions of the Institute of Mining Engineering, 63,* 326.

Davis, K. (1953). Management communication and the grapevine. *Harvard Business Review, 31*(5), 43–59.

Davis, K. (1967). *The dynamics of organizational behavior.* New York: McGraw-Hill.

Davis, K. (1977). *Human behavior at work.* New York: McGraw-Hill.

Davis, T. R. (1984). The influence of the physical environment in offices. *Academy of Management Review, 9,* 271–283.

Day, D. V., & Silverman, S. B. (1989). Personality and job performance: Evidence of incremental validity. *Personnel Psychology, 42,* 25–36.

DeBono, K. G. (1992). Pleasant scents and persuasion: An information processing approach. *Journal of Applied Social Psychology, 22*(11), 910–919.

de Castro, J. M., & Brewer, E. M. (1992). The amount eaten in meals by humans is a power function of the number of people present. *Physiology and Behavior, 51*(1), 121–125.

Deci, E. L. (1972). The effects of contingent and noncontingent rewards and controls on intrinsic motivation. *Organizational Behavior and Human Performance, 8,* 217–229.

Deci, E. L., & Ryan, R. M. (1985). *Intrinsic motivation and self-determination in human behavior.* New York: Plenum Press.

Decker, P. J., & Cornelius, E. T. (1979). A note on recruiting sources and job survival rates. *Journal of Applied Psychology, 64,* 463–464.

DeGroot, J. P., & Kamphois, A. (1983). Eyestrain in VDT users: Physical correlates and long-term effects. *Human Factors, 25,* 409–413.

Del Gaizo, E. (1984). Proof that supervisory training works. *Training and Development Journal, 38*(3), 30–31.

DeLong, B., & St. Clair, S. (1990). An analysis of recruiting strategies in public and private organizations. *Applied H.R.M. Research, 1*(2), 43–50.

DeLoughry, T. J. (1993). Two researchers say 'technophobia' may afflict millions of students. *The Chronicle of Higher Education, 39*(34), 25–26.

Deluga, R. J., & Winters, J. J. (1991). Why the aggravation? Reasons students become resident assistants. *Journal of College Student Development, 32*(6) , 546–552.

De Mare, G. (1968). *Communicating for leadership—A guide for executives.* New York: Ronald Press.

Dembroski, T. M., Lasater, T. M., & Ramirez, A. (1978). Communicator similarity, fear arousing communications, and compliance with health care recommendations. *Journal of Applied Social Psychology, 8,* 254–269.

DeNisi, A. S., Cornelius, E. T., & Blencoe, A. G. (1987). Further investigation of common knowledge effects of job analysis ratings. *Journal of Applied Psychology, 72,* 262–268.

DeNisi, A. S., Randolph, W. A., & Blencoe, A. G. (1983). Potential problems with peer ratings. *Academy of Management Journal, 26,* 457–464.

DeNisi, A. S., Robbins, T., & Cafferty, T. P. (1989). Organization of information used for performance appraisals: Role of diary-keeping. *Journal of Applied Psychology, 74,* 124–129.

DePaulo, B. M. (1992). Nonverbal behavior and self-presentation. *Psychological Bulletin, 111,* 203–243.

DePaulo, B. M., Stone, J. L., & Lassiter, G. D. (1985). Deceiving and detecting deceit. In B. R. Schlenker (Ed.), *The self and social life* (pp. 323–370). New York: McGraw-Hill.

DePaulo, B. M., Zuckerman, M., & Rosenthal, A. R. (1980). Detecting deception: Modality effects. In L. Wheeler (Ed.), *The review of personality and social psychology.* Beverly Hills, CA: Sage Publications.

Dessler, G. (1984). *Personnel management.* Reston, VA: Reston Publishing.

Deutsch, M. (1973). *The resolution of conflict.* New Haven, CT: Yale University Press.

Dickenson, T. L., & Zellinger, P. M. (1980). A comparison of the behaviorally anchored rating and mixed standard scale format. *Journal of Applied Psychology, 65,* 147–154.

Dickson, D. H., & Kelly, I. W. (1985). The "Barnum Effect" in personality assessment: A review of the literature. *Psychological Reports, 57,* 367–382.

Diehl, M., & Stroebe, W. (1987). Productivity loss in brainstorming groups: Toward the solution of a riddle. *Journal of Personality and Social Psychology, 53,* 497–509.

Dietz, P. E. (1994). *Overview of workplace violence.* Seminar presented to the society of human resource management, Roanoke, VA.

Dipboye, R. L. (1977). A critical review of Korman's self-consistency theory of work motivation and occupational choice. *Organizational Behavior and Human Performance, 18,* 108–126.

Dipboye, R. L., & dePontbriad, R. (1981). Correlates of employee reactions to performance appraisals and appraisal systems. *Journal of Applied Psychology, 66,* 248–251.

Dipboye, R. L., Fromkin, H. L., & Wilback, K. (1975). Relative importance of applicant sex, attractiveness and scholastic standing in evaluation of job applicant résumés. *Journal of Applied Psychology, 60,* 39–43.

Dipboye, R. L., Stramler, C. S., & Fontenelle, G. A. (1984). The effects of the application on recall of information from the interview. *Academy of Management Journal, 27,* 561–575.

Dobbins, G. H., Long, W. S., Dedrick, E. J., & Clemons, T. C. (1990). The role of self-monitoring and gender on leader emergence: A laboratory and field study. *Journal of Management, 16*(3), 609–618.

Dolin, D. J., & Booth-Butterfield, M. (1993). Reach out and touch someone: Analysis of nonverbal comforting responses. *Communication Quarterly, 41*(4), 383–393.

Donnerstein, E., & Wilson, D. W. (1976). Effects of noise and perceived control on ongoing and subsequent aggressive behavior. *Journal of Personality and Social Psychology, 34,* 774–781.

Donnoe, W. (1986, June). *Implications of validity generalization and utility analysis in job knowledge testing.* Paper presented at 10th Annual Meeting of International Personnel Management Association—Assessment Council, San Francisco, CA.

Dougherty, T. W., Ebert, R. J., & Callender, J. C. (1986). Policy capturing in the employment interview. *Journal of Applied Psychology, 71,* 9–15.

Douglas, J. A., Feld, D. E., & Asquith, N. (1989). *Employment testing manual.* Boston: Warren, Gorham & Lamont.

Driskell, J. E., Willis, R. P., & Copper, C. (1992). Effect of overlearning on retention. *Journal of Applied Psychology, 77*(5), 615–623.

Dubin, R., & Champoux, J. E. (1977). Central life theory and job satisfaction. *Organizational Behavior and Human Performance, 18,* 366–377.

Dubinsky, A. J., Yammarino, F. J., & Jolson, M. A. (1995). An examination of linkages between personal characteristics and dimensions of transformational leadership. *Journal of Business and Psychology, 9*(3), 315–355.

Dubose, C. (1994). Breaking the bad news. *HRMagazine, 39*(4), 62–64.

Duchon, J. C., Keran, C. M., & Smith, T. J. (1994). Extended workdays in an underground mine: A work performance analysis. *Human Factors, 36*(2), 258–268.

Dumaine, D. (1987). Strategic writing for trainers. *Training and Development Journal, 47*(1), 57–60.

Dunham, R. B. (1977). Shiftwork: A review and theoretical analysis. *Academy of Management Review, 2,* 626–634.

Dunnette, M. D., Campbell, J. D., & Jaastad, K. (1963). The effects of group participation on brainstorming effectiveness of two industrial samples. *Journal of Applied Psychology, 47,* 30–37.

Eagly, A. H., & Johnson, B. T. (1990). Gender and leadership style: A meta-analysis. *Psychological Bulletin, 108*(2), 233–256.

Egler, T. D. (1995). Five myths about sexual harassment. *HRMagazine, 40*(1), 27–30.

Ekeberg, S., Switzer, F., & Siegfried, W. D. (1991). *What do you do with a master's degree in I/O Psychology.* Symposium conducted at the 6th Annual Conference of the Society for Industrial and Organizational Psychology, St. Louis, MO.

Ellis, R. A. & Taylor, S. M. (1983). Role of self-esteem within the job search process. *Journal of Applied Psychology, 68,* 632–640.

England, G. W. (1971). *Development and use of weighted application blanks.* Minneapolis: University of Minnesota Industrial Relations Center.

Erffmeyer, E. S., & Mendel, R. M. (1990). Master's level training in industrial/organizational psychology: A case of the perceived relevance of graduate training. *Professional Psychology: Research and Practice, 21*(5), 405–408.

Erfurt, J. C., Foote, A., & Heirich, M. A. (1992). The cost-effectiveness of worksite wellness programs for hypertension control, weight loss, smoking cessation, and exercise. *Personnel Psychology, 45*(1), 5–28.

Estes, R. (1990) Effects of Flexi-time: A meta-analytic review. *Applied H.R.M. Research, 1*(1), 15–18.

Fahr, J., Cannella, A. A., & Bedeian, A. G. (1991). Peer ratings: The impact of purpose on rating quality and user acceptance. *Group and Organization Studies, 16*(4), 367–386.

Fahr, J., & Dobbins, G. H. (1989). Effects of self-esteem on leniency bias in self-reports of performance: A structural equation model analysis. *Personnel Psychology, 42*(4), 835–850.

Fahr, J., Dobbins, G. H., & Cheng, B. S. (1991). Cultural relativity in action: A comparison of self-ratings made by Chinese and U.S. workers. *Personnel Psychology, 44*(1), 129–147.

Fahr, J., & Werbel, J. D. (1986). Effects of purpose of the appraisal and expectation of validation on self-appraisal leniency. *Journal of Applied Psychology, 71,* 527–529.

Faley, R. J., Kleiman, L. S., & Lengnick-Hall, M. L. (1984). Age discrimination and personnel psychology: A review and synthesis of the legal literature with implications for future research. *Personnel Psychology, 37,* 327–350.

Faloona, D., Henson, C., Jahn, M., & Snyder, A. (1985). Effect of paper type and color on personnel managers' evaluation of résumés. *Proceedings of the 6th Annual Graduate Conference in Industrial/Organizational Psychology and Organizational Behavior,* 97–98.

Farr, J. L. (1973). Response requirements and primacy-recency effects in a simulated selection interview. *Journal of Applied Psychology, 57,* 228–233.

Farr, J. L., & York, C. M. (1975). Amount of information and primacy-recency effects in recruitment decision. *Personnel Psychology, 28,* 233–238.

Fay, C. H., & Latham, G. P. (1982). Effects of training and rating scales on rating errors. *Personnel Psychology, 35,* 105–116.

Feldman, D. C. (1986). The MBA-ing of Ph.D. education. *The Industrial/Organizational Psychologist, 23*(4), 43–46.

Feldman, J. (1981). Beyond attribution theory: Cognitive processes in performance appraisal. *Journal of Applied Psychology, 66,* 127–148.

Feuer, D. (1987a). Paying for knowledge. *Training, 24*(5), 57–66.

Feuer, D. (1987b). Domino's Pizza: Training for fast times. *Training, 24*(7), 25–30.

Fey, C. (1987). Engineering good writing. *Training, 24*(3), 49–54.

Fiedler, F. E. (1967). *A theory of leadership effectiveness.* New York: McGraw-Hill.

Fiedler, F. H. (1978). Recent developments in research on the contingency model. In L. Berkowitz (Ed.), *Group processes* (pp. 207–223). New York: Academic Press.

Field, H. S., & Holley, W. H. (1982). The relationship of performance appraisal system characteristics to verdicts in selected employment discrimination cases. *Academy of Management Journal, 25,* 392–406.

Field, R. H., & House, R. J. (1990). A test of the Vroom-Yetton model using manager and subordinate reports. *Journal of Applied Psychology, 75*(3), 362–366.

Filipczak, B. (1993). Why no one likes your incentive program. *Training, 30*(5), 19–25.

Filipczak, B. (1994). 1994 industry report. *Training, 31*(10), 29–64.

Fine, B. J., & Kobrick, J. L. (1978). Effects of altitude and heat on complex cognitive tasks. *Human Factors, 20,* 115–122.

Fine, S. A. (1955). What is occupational information? *Personnel and Guidance Journal, 33,* 504–509.

Fine, S. A., & Wiley, W. W. (1971). *An introduction to functional job analysis.* Washington, DC: W. E. Upjohn Institute for Employment Research.

Finkelman, J. M., Zeitlin, L. R., Filippi, J. A., & Friend, M. A. (1977). Noise and driver performance. *Journal of Applied Psychology, 62,* 713–718.

Fisher, J. D., Bell, P. N., & Baum, A. (1984). *Environmental psychology.* New York: Holt, Rinehart & Winston.

Fisher, J. D., Rytting, M., & Heslin, R. (1976). Hands touching hands: Affective and evaluative effects of an interpersonal touch. *Sociometry, 39,* 416–421.

Flanagan, J. C. (1954). The critical incident technique. *Psychological Bulletin, 51,* 327–358.

Flanagan, J. C., & Burns, R. K. (1955). The employee performance record: A new appraisal and development tool. *Harvard Business Review, 33,* 95–102.

Fleishman, E. A. (1979). Evaluating physical abilities required by jobs. *Personnel Administrator, 23*(6), 82.

Fleishman, E. A., & Harris, E. F. (1962). Patterns of leadership behavior related to grievances and turnover. *Personnel Psychology, 15*, 43–56.

Fleishman, E. A., Harris, E. F., & Burtt, H. E. (1955). *Leadership and supervision in industry.* Columbus: Ohio State University Press.

Fleishman, E. A., & Reilly, M. E. (1992). *Administrator's guide F-JAS.* Palo Alto, CA: Consulting Psychologists Press.

Flesch, R. (1948). A new readability yardstick. *Journal of Applied Psychology, 32*, 221–233.

Fooner, A. (1986, October). Six good solutions for child care. *Working Woman,* 173.

Forbes, F. W., & Cottle, W. C. (1953). A new method for determining readability of standardized tests. *Journal of Applied Psychology, 37*, 185–190.

Forbes, R. J., & Jackson, P. R. (1980). Non-verbal behaviour and the outcome of selection interviews. *Journal of Occupational Psychology, 53*, 65–72.

Ford, J. K., Quinones, M. A., Sego, D. J., & Sorra, J. S. (1992). Factors affecting the opportunity to perform trained tasks on the job. *Personnel Psychology, 45*, 511–527.

Ford, R. (1973). Job enrichment lessons at AT&T. *Harvard Business Review, 73*, 96–106.

Forst, J. K. (1987). Factors affecting the evaluation of administrator competence. *Proceedings of 8th Annual Graduate Conference in Industrial/Organizational Psychology and Organizational Behavior,* 165–166.

Forsyth, D. R. (1990). *Group dynamics* (2nd ed.). Monterey, CA: Brooks/Cole.

Forsyth, S., & Galloway, S. (1988). Linking college credit with in-house training. *Personnel Administrator, 33*(11), 78–79.

Forsythe, S., Drake, M. F., & Cox, C. E. (1985). Influence of applicant's dress on interviewer's selection decisions. *Journal of Applied Psychology, 70*, 374–378.

Foster, M. (1989). *Relationship between self-monitoring, personality and supervisor performance.* Unpublished master's thesis, University of Georgia, Athens.

Foster, M. (1990). A closer look at the relationship between interviewer-interviewee similarity and ratings in a selection interview. *Applied H.R.M. Research, 1*(1), 23–26.

Foster, R. S., Aamodt, M. G., Bodenmiller, J. A., Rodgers, J. G., Kovach, R. C., & Bryan, R. A. (1988). Effect of menu sign position on customer ordering times and number of food-ordering errors. *Environment and Behavior, 20*(2), 200–210.

Fox, J. G. (1971). Background music and industrial productivity: A review. *Applied Ergonomics, 2*, 70–73.

Frank, C. L., & Hackman, J. R. (1975). Effects of interviewer-interviewee similarity on interviewer objectivity in college admissions interviews. *Journal of Applied Psychology, 60*, 356–360.

Frank, F., & Anderson, L. R. (1971). Effects of task and group size upon group productivity and member satisfaction. *Sociometry, 34*, 135–149.

French, J. R. P., & Raven, B. H. (1959). The bases of social power. In D. Cartwright (Ed.), *Studies in social power* (pp. 150–167). Ann Arbor: University of Michigan Press.

Frese, M., & Okonek, K. (1984). Reasons to leave shiftwork and psychological and psychosomatic complaints of former shiftworkers. *Journal of Applied Psychology, 69*, 509–514.

Frese, M., & Semmer, N. (1986). Shiftwork, stress, and psychosomatic complaints: A comparison between workers in different shiftwork schedules, non-shiftworkers, and former shiftworkers. *Ergonomics, 29*, 99–114.

Freston, N. P., & Lease, J. E. (1987). Communication skills training for selected supervisors. *Training and Development Journal, 41*(7), 67–70.

Frick, R. W. (1985). Communicating emotion: The role of prosodic features. *Psychological Bulletin, 97*, 412–429.

Friedman, L., & Harvey, R. J. (1986). Can raters with reduced job descriptive information provide accurate Position Analysis Questionnaire (PAQ) ratings? *Personnel Psychology, 39*, 779–789.

Frizzell, M. L. (1989). The placement of I/O master's degree graduates. *Proceedings of the 10th Annual Graduate Conference in Industrial/Organizational Psychology and Organizational Behavior.*

Froiland, P. (1993). Who's getting trained? *Training, 30*(10), 53–60.

Frost, P. J., & Jamal, M. (1979). Shift work, attitudes and reported behaviors: Some associations between individual characteristics and hours of work and leisure. *Journal of Applied Psychology, 64*, 77–81.

Fry, E. (1977). Fry's Readability Graph: Clarifications, validity, and extension to level 17. *Journal of Reading, 21*, 243–252.

Fulger, R. (1977). Which costs less — the phone or the letter? *Management World, 6*, 13–14.

Furnham, A., & Stringfield, P. (1994). Congruence of self and subordinate ratings of managerial practices as a correlate of superior evaluation. *Journal of Occupational and Organizational Psychology, 67*(1), 57–67.

Fyock, C. D. (1988). New ways to say "help wanted." *Personnel Administrator, 33*, 100.

Gabris, G. T., & Mitchell, K. (1988). The impact of merit raise scores on employee attitudes: The Matthew effect of performance appraisal. *Public Personnel Management, 17*, 369–386.

Gael, S. (1983). *Job analysis: A guide to assessing work activities.* San Francisco: Jossey-Bass.

Galagan, P. (1983). Treating computer anxiety with training. *Training and Development Journal, 37*, 57–60.

Gandy, J. A., & Dye, D. A. (1989). Development and initial validation of a biodata inventory in a merit system context. *Proceedings of 13th Annual Meeting of International Personnel Management Association — Assessment Council,* 138–142.

Garavaglia, P. L. (1993). How to ensure transfer of training. *Training and Development, 47*(10), 63–68.

Gaugler, B. B., Rosenthal, D. B., Thornton, G. C., & Bentson, C. (1987). Meta-analysis of assessment center validity. *Journal of Applied Psychology, 72*, 493–511.

Geber, B. (1987). Who should do the sales training? *Training, 24*(5), 69–76.

Geber, B. (1995). Does training make a difference? Prove it. *Training, 32*(3), 27–34.

Geier, J. G., & Downey, D. E. (1980). *Attitudinal Listening Profile System.* Minneapolis, MN: Performax Systems International.

Geier, J. G., Downey, D. E., & Johnson, J. B. (1980). *Climate Impact Profile.* Minneapolis, MN: Performax Systems International.

Gent, M. J., & Dell'Omo, G. G. (1989). The needs assessment solution. *Personnel Administrator, 34*(7), 82–84.

Ghiselli, E. E. (1966). *The validity of occupational tests.* New York: John Wiley & Sons.

Ghiselli, E. E. (1973). The validity of aptitude tests in personnel selection. *Personnel Psychology, 26*, 461–477.

Gibbs, C. A. (1969). Leadership. In G. Lindzey & E. Aronson (Eds.), *Handbook of social psychology* (pp. 205–282). Reading, MA: Addison-Wesley.

Giffin, M. E. (1989). Personnel research on testing, selection, and performance appraisal. *Public Personnel Management, 18*, 127–137.

Gilchrist, J. A., & White, K. D. (1990). Policy development and satisfaction with merit pay: A field study in a university setting. *College Student Journal, 24*(3), 249–254.

Gillet, B., & Schwab, D. P. (1975). Convergent and discriminant validities of corresponding Job Descriptive Index and Minnesota Satisfaction Questionnaire scales. *Journal of Applied Psychology, 60*, 313–317.

Gilliland, S. (1993). The perceived fairness of selection systems: An organizational justice perspective. *Academy of Management Review, 18*, 694–734.

Gilmer, B. V. H., & Deci, E. L. (1977). *Industrial and organizational psychology.* New York: McGraw-Hill.

Gilmore, D. C. (1989). Applicant perceptions of simulated behavior description interviews. *Journal of Business and Psychology, 3*, 279–288.

Gilmore, D. C., Beehr, T. A., & Love, K. G. (1986). Effects of applicant sex, applicant physical attractiveness, type of rater and type of job on interview decisions. *Journal of Occupational Psychology, 59*, 103–109.

Glickman, A. S., & Vallance, T. R. (1958). Curriculum assessment with critical incidents. *Journal of Applied Psychology, 42*, 329–335.

Glueck, W. F. (1973). Recruiters and executives: How do they affect job choice? *Journal of College Placement, 34*, 77–78.

Goldman, B. A., & Busch, J. C. (1978). *Directory of unpublished experimental measures* (Vol. 2). New York: Human Sciences Press.

Goldman, B. A., & Busch, J. C. (1982). *Directory of unpublished experimental measures* (Vol. 3). New York: Human Sciences Press.

Goldman, B. A., & Osborne, W. L. (1985). *Directory of unpublished experimental measures* (Vol. 4). New York: Human Sciences Press.

Goldman, B. A., & Saunders, J. L. (1974). *Directory of unpublished experimental measures* (Vol. 1). New York: Behavioral Publishers.

Goldstein, I. L. (1971). The application blank: How honest are the responses? *Journal of Applied Psychology, 55*, 491–492.

Goldstein, I. L. (1993). *Training in organizations* (3rd ed.). Pacific Grove, CA: Brooks/Cole.

Golen, S. (1990). A factor analysis of barriers to effective listening. *Journal of Business Communication, 27*, 25–36.

Golightly, C., Huffman, D., & Byrne, D. (1972). Liking and loaning. *Journal of Applied Psychology, 56*, 521–523.

Goodale, J. G. (1992). *One to one: Interviewing, selecting, appraising, and counseling employees.* Englewood Cliffs, NJ: Prentice-Hall.

Goodson, J. R., McGee, G. W., & Cashman, J. F. (1989). Situational leadership theory: A test of leadership prescriptions. *Group and Organization Studies, 14*(4), 446–461.

Gordon, J. R. (1983). *A diagnostic approach to organizational behavior.* Boston: Allyn & Bacon.

Gordon, M. E., Slade, L. A., & Schmitt, H. (1986). The "science of the sophomore" revisited: From conjecture to empiricism. *Academy of Management Review, 11*, 191–207.

Gousie, L. J. (1993). Interview structure and interviewer prejudice as factors in the evaluation and selection of minority and nonminority applicants. *Applied H.R.M. Research, 4*(1), 1–13.

Gowen, C. R. (1990). Gainsharing programs: An overview of history and research. *Journal of Organizational Behavior Management, 11*(2), 77–99.

Graen, G., & Scheimann, W. (1978). Leader member agreement: A vertical dyad linkage approach. *Journal of Applied Psychology, 63*, 206–212.

Graham, J. K., & Mihal, W. L. (1986). Can your management development needs surveys be trusted? *Training and Development Journal, 40*(3), 38–42.

Graham, J. P. (1991). Disgruntled employees—ticking time bombs? *Security Management,* 83–85.

Grandjean, E., Hunting, W., & Pidermann, M. (1983). VDT workstation design: Preferred settings and their effects. *Human Factors, 25*, 161–175.

Green, S. B., Sauser, W. I., Fagg, F. N., & Champion, C. H. (1981). Shortcut methods for deriving behaviorally anchored rating scales. *Educational and Psychological Measurement, 41*, 761–775.

Green, S. B., & Stutzman, T. (1986). An evaluation of methods to select respondents to structured job-analysis questionnaires. *Personnel Psychology, 39*, 543–564.

Greenberg, J., & Baron, R. A. (1995). *Behavior in organizations* (5th ed.). Englewood Cliffs, NJ: Prentice Hall.

Greenhaus, J. H., & Badin, I. J. (1974). Self-esteem, performance, and satisfaction: Some tests of a theory. *Journal of Applied Psychology, 59,*722–726.

Greenwood, K. M. (1994). Long-term stability and psychometric properties of the composite scale of morningness. *Ergonomics, 37*(2), 377–383.

Greer, D. L. (1983). Spectator booing and the home advantage: A study of social influence in the basketball arena. *Social Psychology Quarterly, 46,* 252–261.

Griffiths, R. F., & McDaniel, Q. P. (1993). Predictors of police asaults. *Journal of Police and Criminal Psychology, 9*(1), 5–9.

Guion, R. N., & Gibson, W. M. (1988). Personnel selection and placement. *Annual Review of Psychology, 39,* 349–374.

Gumpert, R. A., & Hambleton, R. K. (1979). Situational leadership: How Xerox managers fine-tune managerial styles to employee maturity and task needs. *Management Review, 12,* 9.

Gunnarson, E., & Ostberg, O. (1977). *Physical and psychological working environment in a terminal-based data system.* Research Report No. 35. Stockholm: National Board of Occupational Safety and Health.

Gunning, R. (1964). *How to take the FOG out of writing.* Chicago: Dartnell Corp.

Guthrie, J. P., Ash, R. A., & Bendapudi, V. (1995). Additional validity evidence for a measure of morningness. *Journal of Applied Psychology, 80*(1), 186–190.

Guzzo, R. A., Jette, R. D., & Katzell, R. A. (1985). The effects of psychologically based intervention programs on worker productivity: A meta-analysis. *Personnel Psychology, 38,* 275–291.

Hackett, R. D. (1989). Work attitudes and employee absenteeism: A synthesis of the literature. *Journal of Occupational Psychology, 62*(3), 235–248.

Hackman, J. R., & Oldham, G. R. (1975). Development of the job diagnostic survey. *Journal of Applied Psychology, 60,* 159–170.

Hackman, J. R., & Oldham, G. R. (1976). Motivation through the design of work: Test of a theory. *Organizational Behavior and Human Performance, 16,* 250–279.

Hackman, R., & Vidmar, N. (1970). Effects of size and task type on group performance and member reactions. *Sociometry, 33,* 37–54.

Hage, J. (1974). *Communication and organizational control: Cybernetics in health and welfare settings.* New York: Wiley & Sons.

Hakel, M. D., Ohnesorge, J. P., & Dunnette, M. D. (1970). Interviewer evaluations of job applicants' résumés as a function of the qualifications of the immediately preceding applicant: An examination of contrast effects. *Journal of Applied Psychology, 54,* 27–30.

Halcrow, A. (1989). You're in good hands with direct mail. *Recruitment Today, 2*(1), 21–23.

Hall, D. T., & Nougaim, K. E. (1968). An examination of Maslow's need hierarchy in an organizational setting. *Organizational Behavior and Human Performance, 3,* 12–35.

Hall, E. T. A. (1963). A system for the notation of promemic behavior. *American Anthropologist, 65,* 1003–1026.

Hammer, T. H., & Dachler, H. P. (1975). A test of some assumptions underlying the path goal model of supervision: Some suggested conceptual modifications. *Organizational Behavior and Human Performance, 14,* 60–75.

Hampton, D. R., Summer, C. E., & Webber, R. A. (1978). *Organizational behavior and the practice of management.* Glenview, IL: Scott, Foresman.

Hanlon, S. C., & Taylor, R. R. (1992). How does gainsharing work? Some preliminary answers following application in a service organization. *Applied H.R.M. Research, 3*(2), 73–91.

Hardy, C. J., & Crace, R. K. (1991). The effects of task structure and teammate competence on social loafing. *Journal of Sport and Exercise Psychology, 13*(4), 372–381.

Harma, M. (1993). Individual differences in tolerance to shiftwork: A review. *Ergonomics, 36*(1), 101–109.

Harper, D. C. (1988). An Rx for the RN shortage. *Recruitment Today, 1*(2), 18–26.

Harriman, T. S., & Kovach, R. (1987). The effects of job familiarity on the recall of performance information. *Proceedings of the 8th Annual Graduate Conference in Industrial/Organizational Psychology and Organizational Behavior,* 49–50.

Harris, D. (1993). Big business takes on child care. *Working Woman, 6,* 50–56.

Harris, M. (1981). *America now.* New York: Simon & Schuster.

Harris, M. M., & Schaubroeck, J. (1988). A meta-analysis of self-supervisor, self-peer, and peer-supervisor ratings. *Personnel Psychology, 41,* 43–62.

Harrison, D. A., & Shaffer, M. A. (1994). Comparative examinations of self-reports and perceived absenteeism norms: Wading through Lake Wobegon. *Journal of Applied Psychology, 79*(2), 240–256.

Harrison, K. (1986). Validity of a weighted application blank in predicting tenure of mental health counselors. *Proceedings of the 7th Annual Graduate Conference in Industrial/Organizational Psychology and Organizational Behavior.*

Harvey, R. J., Friedman, L., Hakel, M. D., & Cornelius, E. J. (1988). Dimensionality of the Job Element Inventory, a simplified worker-oriented job analysis questionnaire. *Journal of Applied Psychology, 73,* 639–646.

Hatcher, L., Ross, T. L., & Ross, R. A. (1987). Gainsharing: Living up to its name. *Personnel Administrator, 32*(6), 154–164.

Hattie, J., & Cooksey, R. W. (1984). Procedures for assessing the validities of tests using the "known-groups" method. *Applied Psychological Measurement, 8,* 295–305.

Hauenstein, N. M. A. (1986). *A process approach to ratings: The effects of ability and level of processing on encoding, retrieval, and rating outcomes.* Unpublished doctoral dissertation, University of Akron, Akron, OH.

Hauenstein, N. M. A., & Foti, R. J. (1989). From laboratory to practice: Neglected issues in implementing frame-of-reference rater training. *Personnel Psychology, 42,* 359–378.

Hauenstein, N. M. A., & Lord, R. G. (1989). The effects of final-offer arbitration on the performance of major league baseball players: A test of equity theory. *Human Performance, 2*(3), 147–165.

Heerwagen, J. H., & Orians, G. H. (1986). Adaptations to windowlessness: A study of the use of visual decor in windowed and windowless offices. *Environment & Behavior, 18,* 604–622.

Heilbroner, D. (1993). The handling of an epidemic. *Working Woman, 2,* 60–65.

Heilman, M. E. (1974). Threats and promises: Reputational consequences and transfer of credibility. *Journal of Experimental Social Psychology, 10,* 310–324.

Heilman, M. E., Block, C. J., & Lucas, J. A. (1992). Presumed incompetent? Stigmatization and affirmative action efforts. *Journal of Applied Psychology, 77*(4), 536–544.

Heilman, M. E., Kaplow, S. R., Amato, M. G., & Stathatos, P. (1993). When similarity is a liability: Effects of sex-based preferential selection on reactions to like-sex and different-sex others. *Journal of Applied Psychology, 78*(6), 917–927.

Heilman, M. E., Lucas, J. A., & Kaplow, S. R. (1990). Self-derogating consequences of preferential selection: The moderating role of initial self-confidence. *Organizational Behavior and Human Decision Processes, 46,* 202–216.

Heilman, M. E., & Saruwaturi, L. R. (1979). When beauty is beastly: The effect of appearance and sex on evaluations of job applicants for managerial and nonmanagerial jobs. *Organizational Behavior and Human Performance, 23,* 360–372.

Helmreich, R. L., Sawin, L. L., & Carsrud, A. L. (1986). The honeymoon effect in job performance: Temporal increases in the predictive power of achievement motivation. *Journal of Applied Psychology, 71,* 185–188.

Hemphill, J. K., & Coons, A. E. (1950). *Leader behavior description.* Columbus: Personnel Research Board, Ohio State University.

Henderson, R. I. (1994). *Compensation management: Rewarding performance.* Englewood Cliffs, NJ: Prentice Hall.

Hequet, M. (1994). Giving good feedback. *Training, 31*(9), 72–77.

Herbert, G. P., & Doverspike, D. (1990). Performance appraisal in the training needs analysis process: A review and critique. *Public Personnel Management, 19*(3), 253–270.

Hersey, P., & Blanchard, K. H. (1988). *Management of organizational behavior* (5th ed.). Englewood Cliffs, NJ: Prentice-Hall.

Herzberg, F. (1966). *Work and the nature of man.* Cleveland: World Publishing.

Heslin, R., & Dunphy, D. (1964). Three dimensions of member satisfaction in small groups. *Human Relations, 17,* 99–112.

Hilgert, R. L. (1988). How at-will statements hurt employees. *Personnel Journal, 57*(2), 75–76.

Hills, F. S. (1987). *Compensation and decision making.* New York: Dryden Press.

Hills, F. S., Scott, K. D., Markham, S. E., & Vest, M. J. (1987). Merit pay: Just or unjust desserts. *Personnel Administrator, 32*(9), 53–59.

Hinrichs, J. R., & Mischkind, L. A. (1967). Empirical and theoretical limitations of the two-factor hypothesis of job satisfaction. *Journal of Applied Psychology, 51,* 191–200.

Hockey, G. R. (1970). Signal probability and spatial locations as possible bases for increased selectivity in noise. *Quarterly Journal of Experimental Psychology, 22,* 37–42.

Hodap, R. (1986, June). *The State of Wyoming performance appraisal system.* Paper presented at the 10th Annual Meeting of International Personnel Management Association—Assessment Council, San Francisco, CA.

Hoff Macan, T., Avedon, M., & Paese, M. (1994). *The effects of applicants' reactions to cognitive ability tests and an assessment center.* Paper presented at the 9th Annual Conference of the Society for Industrial and Organizational Psychology, Nashville, TN.

Hoffman, L. R. (1959). Homogeneity of member personality and its effect on group problem solving. *Journal of Abnormal and Social Psychology, 58,* 27–32.

Hoffman, R. (1995). Ten reasons you should be using 360-degree feedback. *HRMagazine, 40*(4), 82–85.

Hogan, J., & Quigley, A. (1994). Effects of preparing for physical ability tests. *Public Personnel Management, 23*(1), 85–104.

Hogan, R. (1989, June). *The darker side of charisma.* Paper presented at the 13th Annual Meeting of International Personnel Management Association—Assessment Council, Orlando, FL.

Hollmann, T. D. (1972). Employment interviewers' errors in processing positive and negative information. *Journal of Applied Psychology, 56,* 130–134.

Holzbach, R. L. (1978). Rater bias in performance ratings: Supervisor, self- and peer ratings. *Journal of Applied Psychology, 63,* 579–588.

Hom, P. W., DeNisi, A. S., Kinicki, A. J., & Bannister, B. D. (1982). Effectiveness of performance feedback from behaviorally anchored rating scales. *Journal of Applied Psychology, 67,* 568–576.

Hoover, L. T. (1992). Trends in police physical ability selection testing. *Public Personnel Management, 21*(1), 29–40.

Hopkins, J. T. (1980). The top twelve questions for employment agency interviews. *Personnel Journal, 59*(5), 379–381.

House, R. J. (1971). A path-goal theory of leader effectiveness. *Administrative Science Quarterly, 9,* 321–332.

House, R. J., & Mitchell, T. R. (1974, Autumn). Path-goal theory of leadership. *Journal of Contemporary Business, 3,* 81–98.

Howard, C. G. (1988). Strategic guidelines for terminating employees. *Personnel Administrator, 33*(4), 106–109.

Howard, G. S., & Dailey, P. R. (1979). Response-shift bias: A source of contamination of self-report measures. *Journal of Applied Psychology, 64*, 144–150.

Howell, J. M., & Avolio, B. J. (1993). Transformational leadership, transactional leadership, locus of control, and support of innovation: Key predictors of consolidated-business-unit performance. *Journal of Applied Psychology, 78*(6), 891–902.

Huegli, J. M., & Tschirgia, H. D. (1975). Monitoring the employment interview. *Journal of College Placement, 39*, 37–39.

Huffcutt, A. I., & Arthur, W. (1994). Hunter and Hunter (1984) revisited: Interview validity for entry-level jobs. *Journal of Applied Psychology, 79*(2), 184–190.

Hughes, J. F., Dunn, J. F., & Baxter, B. (1956). The validity of selection instruments under operating conditions. *Personnel Psychology, 9*, 321–324.

Hultman, K. E. (1986). Behavior modeling for results. *Training and Development Journal, 40*(12), 60–63.

Hunter, J. E., & Hunter, R. F. (1984). Validity and utility of alternative predictors of job performance. *Psychological Bulletin, 96*(1), 72–98.

Hunter, J. E., & Schmidt, F. L. (1982). Fitting people to jobs: The impact of personnel selection on national productivity. In M. D. Dunnette & E. D. Fleishman (Eds.), *Human performance and productivity, Vol. 1: Human capacity assessment* (pp. 233–284). Hillsdale, NJ: Erlbaum.

Hunter, J. E., & Schmidt, F. L. (1983). Quantifying the effects of psychological interventions on employee job performance and work-force productivity. *American Psychologist, 38*, 473–478.

Iaffaldano, M. T., & Muchinsky, P. M. (1985). Job satisfaction and job performance: A meta-analysis. *Psychological Bulletin, 97*, 251–273.

Ilaw, M. (1985). Reading between the lines. *Black Enterprise, 15*, 95–96.

Ilgen, D. R., Fisher, C. D., & Taylor, M. S. (1979). Consequences of individual feedback on behavior in organizations. *Journal of Applied Psychology, 64*, 349–371.

Ilgen, D. R., Mitchell, T. R., & Fredrickson, J. W. (1981). Poor performers: Supervisors' and subordinates' responses. *Organizational Behavior and Human Performance, 27*, 386–410.

Ilgen, D. R., Nebeker, D. M., & Pritchard, R. D. (1981). Expectancy theory measures: An empirical comparison in an experimental simulation. *Organizational Behavior and Human Performance, 28*, 189–223.

Indik, B. P. (1965). Organization size and member participation: Some empirical tests of alternate explanations. *Human Relations, 15*, 339–350.

Inguagiato, R. J. (1993). Case studies: Let's get real. *Training and Development, 47*(10), 20–24.

Insko, C. A., Yovetich, N., & Romero, A. A. (1995). Group learning curves: The effects of turnover and task complexity on group performance. *Journal of Applied Social Psychology, 25*(6), 512–529.

Ironson, G. H., Smith, P. C., Brannick, M. T., Gibson, W. M., & Paul, K. B. (1989). Construction of a Job in General Scale: A comparison of global, composite, and specific measures. *Journal of Applied Psychology, 74*, 193–200.

Ivancevich, J. M. (1982). Subordinates' reactions to performance appraisal interviews: A test of feedback and goal-setting techniques. *Journal of Applied Psychology, 67*, 581–587.

Jaccard, J. (1981). Toward theories of persuasion and belief change. *Journal of Personality and Social Psychology, 40*, 260–269.

Jackson, D. E., O'Dell, J. W., & Olson, D. (1982). Acceptance of bogus personality interpretations: Face validity reconsidered. *Journal of Clinical Psychology, 38*, 588–592.

Jackson, J. M. (1986). In search of social impact theory: Comment on Mullen. *Journal of Personality and Social Psychology, 50*, 511–513.

Jackson, S. E., Brett, J. F., Sessa, V. T., Cooper, D. M., Julin, J. A., & Peyronnin, K. (1991). Some differences make a difference: Individual dissimilarity and group homogeneity as correlates of recruitment, promotions, and turnover. *Journal of Applied Psychology, 76*(5), 675–689.

Jacobs, R., Kafry, D., & Zedeck, S. (1980). Expectations of behaviorally anchored rating scales. *Personnel Psychology, 33*, 595–640.

Jago, A. G., & Vroom, V. H. (1977). Hierarchical level and leadership style. *Organizational Behavior and Human Performance, 18*, 131–145.

Jamal, M. (1981). Shift work related to job attitudes, social participation, and withdrawal behavior: A study of nurses and industrial workers. *Personnel Psychology, 34*, 535–547.

Jamal, M. (1988). Is moonlighting mired in myth? *Personnel Journal, 67*(5), 48–53.

Jamal, M., & Crawford, R. L. (1984). Consequences of extended work hours: A comparison of moonlighters, overtimers, and modal employees. *Human Resource Management, 4*, 18–23.

Jamal, M., & Jamal, S. M. (1982). Work and nonwork experiences of employees on fixed and rotating shifts: An empirical assessment. *Journal of Vocational Behavior, 20*, 282–293.

Janik, J., & Hagness, W. (1994, October). *Firing under fire.* Paper presented at the 23rd Annual Meeting of the Society of Police and Criminal Psychology, Madison, WI.

Janis, I. L. (1972). *Victims of groupthink.* New York: Houghton Mifflin.

Jansen, A. (1973). *Validation of graphological judgments: An experimental study.* The Hague, Netherlands: Mouton.

Janz, T. (1982). Initial comparisons of patterned behavior description interviews versus unstructured interviews. *Journal of Applied Psychology, 67*(5), 577–580.

Janz, T., Hellervik, L., & Gilmore, D. C. (1986). *Behavior description interviewing.* Boston, MA: Allyn & Bacon.

Jaques, E. (1961). *Equitable payment.* New York: John Wiley & Sons.

Jenner, L. (1994). Employment-at-will liability: How protected are you? *HR Focus, 71*(3), 11.

Johns, G. (1994). Absenteeism estimates by employees and managers: Divergent perspectives and self-serving perceptions. *Journal of Applied Psychology, 79*(2), 229–239.

Johnson, D. L., & Andrews, I. R. (1971). The risky-shift hypothesis tested with consumer products as stimuli. *Journal of Personality and Social Psychology, 30*, 382–385.

Johnson, D. L., & King, J. (1988, August). *Judgment of experts' decisions when using high technology.* Paper presented at the annual meeting of the American Psychological Association, Atlanta, GA.

Johnson, D. W., & Johnson, F. P. (1975). *Jointing together: Group theory and group skills.* Englewood Cliffs, NJ: Prentice-Hall.

Johnson, L. (1990). *Employer supported child care: What are the effects?* Unpublished master's thesis, Radford University, Radford, VA.

Johnson, T. L. (1990). A meta-analytic review of absenteeism control methods. *Applied H.R.M. Research, 1*(1), 23–26.

Jones, A. P., Main, D. S., Butler, M. C., & Johnson, L. A. (1982). Narrative job descriptions as potential sources of job analysis ratings. *Personnel Psychology, 35*, 813–828.

Jones, J. J., & DeCotiis, T. A. (1969). Job analysis: National survey findings. *Personnel Journal, 48*, 805–819.

Jones, J. W., & Terris, W. (1989). After the polygraph ban. *Recruitment Today, 2*(2), 24–31.

Judge, T. A., & Watanabe, S. (1993). Another look at the job satisfaction-life satisfaction relationship. *Journal of Applied Psychology, 78*(6), 939–948.

Kaiser, P., & Brull, H. (1987, June). *I hate it when that happens.* Paper presented at the 11th Annual Meeting of the International Personnel Management Association — Assessment Council, Philadelphia, PA.

Kalimo, R., & Leppanen, A. (1985). Feedback from video display terminals, performance control and stress in text preparation in the printing industry. *Journal of Occupational Psychology, 58*, 27–38.

Kaman, V. S., & Bentson, C. (1988). Role play simulations for employee selection: Design and implementation. *Public Personnel Management, 17*, 1–8.

Kane, J. S., & Lawler, E. E. (1979). Performance appraisal effectiveness: Its assessment and determinants. In B. M. Staw (Ed.), *Research in organizational behavior, Vol. 1* (pp. 425–478). Greenwich, CT: JAI Press.

Kanekar, S. (1987). Individual versus group performance: A selective review of experimental studies. *Irish Journal of Psychology, 8*(1), 9–19.

Kaplan, A. B., Aamodt, M. A., & Wilk, D. (1991). The relationship between advertising variables and applicant responses to newspaper recruitment advertisements. *Journal of Business and Psychology, 5*(3), 383–395.

Katz, D., & Kahn, R. L. (1978). *The social psychology of organizations.* New York: John Wiley & Sons.

Katzell, R. A., & Dyer, F. J. (1977). Differential validity revived. *Journal of Applied Psychology, 62*, 137–145.

Keel, S. B., Cochran, D. S., Arnett, K., & Arnold, D. R. (1989). AC's are not just for the big guys. *Personnel Administrator, 34*(5), 98–101.

Keenan, A. (1978). Selection interview outcomes in relation to interviewer training and experience. *Journal of Social Psychology, 106*, 249–260.

Keinan, G. A., & Barak, A. (1984). Reliability and validity of graphological assessment in the selection process of military officers. *Perceptual and Motor Skills, 58*, 811–821.

Kelly, C. M. (1984, January). Reasonable performance appraisals. *Training and Development Journal, 38*, 79–82.

Kennedy, J. K., Houston, J. M., Korsgaard, M. A., & Gallo, D. D. (1987). Construct space of the Least Preferred Coworker (LPC) Scale. *Educational and Psychological Measurement, 47*(3), 807–814.

Kenny, D. A., & Zaccaro, S. J. (1983). An estimate of variance due to traits in leadership. *Journal of Applied Psychology, 68*, 678–685.

Kent, R. L., & Moss, S. E. (1990). Self-monitoring as a predictor of leader emergence. *Psychological Reports, 66*(3), 875–881.

Kerr, N. L. (1983). Motivation loss in small groups: A social dilemma analysis. *Journal of Personality and Social Psychology, 45*, 819–828.

Kerr, N. L., & Bruun, S. E. (1983). Dependability of member effort and group motivation loss: Free-rider effects. *Journal of Personality and Social Psychology, 44*, 78–94.

Kimmerline, G. (1993). Gathering best practices. *Training and Development, 47*(9), 29–36.

King, J. (1986). Computer based instruction. In L. Donaldson & E. E. Scannell (Eds.), *Human resource development: The new trainer's guide* (pp. 79–85). Reading, MA: Addison-Wesley.

King, N. (1970). Clarification and evaluation of the two-factor theory of job satisfaction. *Psychological Bulletin, 74*, 18–31.

King, P. (1984). *Performance planning and appraisal.* New York: McGraw-Hill.

Kingstrom, P. O., & Bass, A. R. (1981). A critical analysis of studies comparing behaviorally anchored rating scales (BARS) and other rating formats. *Personnel Psychology, 34*, 263–289.

Kipnis, D., Schmidt, S., & Wilkinson, I. (1980). Intraorganizational influence tactics: Exploration in getting one's way. *Journal of Applied Psychology, 65*, 440–452.

Kirkpatrick, D. L. (1986). Performance appraisal: When two jobs are too many. *Training, 23*(3), 65–68.

Klawsky, J. D. (1990). The effect of subgoals on commitment and task performance. *Proceedings of the 11th Annual Graduate Conference in Industrial/Organizational Psychology and Organizational Behavior.*

Kleiman, L. S., & Faley, R. H. (1978). Assessing content validity: Standards set by the court. *Personnel Psychology, 31*, 701–713.

Kleiman, L. S., & White, C. S. (1991). Reference checking: A field survey of SHRM professionals. *Applied H.R.M. Research, 2*(2), 84–95.

Klein, J. D., & Pridemore, D. R. (1992). Effects of cooperative learning and need for affiliation on performance, time on task, and satisfaction. *Educational Technology Research and Development, 40*(4), 39–47.

Klein, M., & Christiansen, G. (1969). Group composition, group structure, and group effectiveness of basketball teams. In J. W. Loy & G. S. Kenyon (Eds.), *Sport, culture, and society* (pp. 397–428). Toronto: Macmillan.

Klimoski, R. J., & Rafaeli, A. (1983). Inferring personal qualities through handwriting analysis. *Journal of Occupational Psychology, 56*, 191–202.

Klimoski, R. J., & Strickland, W. J. (1977). Assessment centers—validity or merely prescient? *Personal Psychology, 30*, 353–361.

Kluger, A. N., & Colella, A. (1993). Beyond the mean bias: The effect of warning against faking on biodata item variances. *Personnel Psychology, 46*, 763–780.

Knapp, M. L. (1978). *Nonverbal communication in human interaction.* New York: Holt, Rinehart & Winston.

Knauth, P. (1993). The design of shift systems. *Ergonomics, 36*(11), 15–28.

Knauth, P., & Kiesswetter, E. (1987). A change from weekly to quicker shift rotations: A field study of discontinuous three-shift workers. *Ergonomics, 30*, 1311–1321.

Knouse, S. B. (1983). The letter of recommendation: Specificity and favorability of information. *Personnel Psychology, 36*, 331–341.

Komaki, J. L. (1986). Toward effective supervision: An operant analysis and comparison of managers at work. *Journal of Applied Psychology, 71*, 270–279.

Komaki, J. L., Zlotnick, S., & Jensen, M. (1986). Development of an operant-based taxonomy and observational index of supervisory behavior. *Journal of Applied Psychology, 71*, 260–269.

Kopelman, R. E. (1986). *Managing producitivity in organizations.* New York: McGraw-Hill.

Koppes, L. L. (1991). I/O psychology master's-level training: Reality and legitimacy in search of recognition. *The Industrial and Organizational Psychologist, 29*(2), 59–67.

Korman, A. K. (1966). Consideration, initiating structure, and organzational criteria: A review. *Personnel Psychology, 19*, 349–361.

Korman, A. K. (1970). Toward a hypothesis of work behavior. *Journal of Applied Psychology, 54*, 31–41.

Korman, A. K. (1976). Hypothesis of work behavior revisited and an extension. *Academy of Management Review, 1*, 50–63.

Korte, C., & Grant, R. (1980). Traffic noise, environmental awareness, and pedestrian behavior. *Environment & Behavior, 12*, 408–420.

Kosidiak, J. G. (1987). DACUM: An alternative job analysis tool. *Personnel, 64*(3), 14–21.

Kovach, R., Surrette, M. A., & Whitcomb, A. J. (1988, January). *Contextual, student, and instructor factors involved in college student absenteeism.* Paper presented at the 10th Annual National Institute on the Teaching of Psychology, St. Petersburg, FL.

Kozlowski, S. W., Kirsch, M. P., & Chao, G. T. (1986). Job knowledge, ratee familiarity, conceptual similarity and halo error: An exploration. *Journal of Applied Psychology, 71*, 45–49.

Kraiger, K., & Ford, J. K. (1985). A meta-analysis of ratee race effects. *Journal of Applied Psychology, 70*, 56–65.

Kramer, J. J., & Conoley, J. C. (1992). *The eleventh mental measurements yearbook.* Lincoln, NE: University of Nebraska-Lincoln.

Kramm, K. R., & Kramm, D. A. (1988). Having the competitive edge. *Personnel Administrator, 33*(10), 88–92.

Kravitz, D. A., & Platania, J. (1993). Attitudes and beliefs about affirmative action: Effects of target and of respondent sex and ethnicity. *Journal of Applied Psychology, 78*(6), 928–938.

Kressel, K., & Pruitt, D. G. (1985). Themes on the mediation of social conflict. *Journal of Social Issues, 41*, 179–198.

Kroemer, K. H. E., & Price, D. L. (1982). Ergonomics in the office: Comfortable work stations allow maximum productivity. *Industrial Engineering, 14*(7), 24–32.

Kryger, B. R., & Shikiar, R. (1978). Sexual discrimination in the use of letters of recommendation: A case of reverse discrimination. *Journal of Applied Psychology, 63*(3), 309–314.

Kuder, G. F., & Richardson, M. W. (1937). The theory of estimation of test reliability. *Psychometrika, 2*, 151–160.

Kunin, T. (1955). The construction of a new type of attitude measure. *Personnel Psychology, 8*, 65–78.

Lacho, K. J., Stearns, G. K., & Villere, M. R. (1979). A study of employee appraisal systems of major cities in the United States. *Public Personnel Management, 8*, 111–125.

Lahtela, K., Niemi, P., Kunsela, V., & Hypen, K. (1986). Noise and visual choice reaction time. *Scandinavian Journal of Psychology, 27*, 52–57.

Laing, M. (1993). Gossip: Does it play a role in the socialization of nurses? *Journal of Nursing Scholarship, 25*(1), 37–41.

LaMarre, S. E., & Thompson, K. (1984). Industry sponsored day care. *Personnel Administrator, 29*(2), 53–65.

Lamm, H., & Trommsdorff, G. (1973). Group versus individual performance on tasks requiring ideational proficiency (brainstorming): A review. *European Journal of Social Psychology, 3*, 361–388.

Lance, L. E., Teachout, M. S., & Donnelly, T. M. (1992). Specification of the criterion construct spare: An application of hierarchical confirmatory factor analysis. *Journal of Applied Psychology, 77*(4), 437–453.

Landy, F. J., & Bates, F. (1973). Another look at contrast effects in the employment interview. *Journal of Applied Psychology, 58*, 141–144.

Landy, F. J., & Guion, R. M. (1970). Development of scales for the measurement of work motivation. *Organizational Behavior and Human Performance, 5,* 93–103.

Landy, F. J., & Vasey, J. (1991). Job analysis: The composition of SME samples. *Personnel Psychology, 44,* 27–50.

Langdale, J. A., & Weitz, J. (1973). Estimating the influence of job information on interviewer agreement. *Journal of Applied Psychology, 57,* 23–27.

Langer, E. J., & Rodin, J. (1976). The effects of choice and enhanced personal responsibility for the aged: A field experiment in an institutional setting. *Journal of Personality and Social Psychology, 34,* 191–198.

Langer, S. (1994). Incomes inch up. *Personnel Journal, 30*(1), 67–71.

Larson, J. R. (1989). The dynamic interplay between employees' feedback seeking strategies and supervisors' delivery of performance feedback. *Academy of Management Review, 14,* 408–422.

Lasden, M. (1983). Moonlighting: A double standard? *Computer Decisions, 15*(3), 83–92.

Latane, B. (1981). The psychology of social impact. *American Psychologist, 36,* 343–356.

Latham, G. P., & Blades, J. J. (1975). The practical significance of Locke's theory of goal setting. *Journal of Applied Psychology, 60,* 122–124.

Latham, G. P., Fay, C. H., & Saari, L. M. (1979). The development of behavioral observation scales for appraising the performance of foremen. *Personnel Psychology, 32,* 299–311.

Latham, G. P., & Saari, L. M. (1984). Do people do what they say: Further studies on the situational interview. *Journal of Applied Psychology, 69,* 569–573.

Latham, G. P., Saari, L. M., Pursell, E. D., & Campion, M. A. (1980). The situational interview. *Journal of Applied Psychology, 65,* 422–427.

Latham, G. P., & Wexley, K. N. (1977). Behavioral observation scales for performance appraisal purposes. *Personnel Psychology, 30,* 225–268.

Latham, G. P., & Whyte, G. (1994). The futility of utility analysis. *Personnel Psychology, 47,* 31–46.

Latham, V. M. (1983). Charismatic leadership: A review and proposed model. *Proceedings of the 4th Annual Graduate Conference in Industrial/Organizational Psychology and Organizational Behavior.*

Laumeyer, J., & Beebe, T. (1988). Employees and their appraisals. *Personnel Administrator, 33*(12), 76–80.

Lawler, E. E. (1973). *Motivation in work organizations.* Belmont, CA: Brooks/Cole.

Lawler, E. E., Chang, L., & Ledford, G. E. (1993). Who uses skillbased pay and why. *Compensation and Benefits Review, 25*(2), 22–27.

Lawler, E. E., & Suttle, J. L. (1972). A causal correlational test of the need hierarchy concept. *Organizational Behavior and Human Performance, 7,* 265–287.

Lawshe, C. H., Bolda, R. A., Brune, R. L., & Auclair, G. (1958). Expectancy charts II: Their theoretical development. *Personnel Psychology, 11,* 545–559.

Lazer, R. I., & Wikstrom, W. S. (1977). *Appraising managerial performance.* New York: The Conference Board.

Leana, C. R., & Feldman, D. C. (1992). *Coping with job loss.* New York: Lexington Books.

Ledvinka, J., & Schoenfeldt, L. F. (1978). Legal developments in employment testing: Albemarle and beyond. *Personnel Psychology, 31,* 1–13.

Lee, J. A., Moreno, K. E., & Sympson, J. R. (1986). The effects of test administration on test performance. *Educational and Psychological Measurement, 46,* 467–474.

Levine, E. L. (1983). *Everything you always wanted to know about job analysis.* Tampa, FL: Mariner Publishing.

Levine, E. L., Ash, R. A., & Bennett, N. (1980). Exploratory comparison study of four job analysis methods. *Journal of Applied Psychology, 65,* 524–535.

Levine, E. L., Ash, R. A., Hall, H., & Sistrunk, F. (1983). Evaluation of job analysis methods by experienced job analysts. *Academy of Management Journal, 26,* 339–348.

Levin-Epstein, M. D. (1987). *Primer of equal employment opportunity.* Washington, DC: Bureau of National Affairs.

Levy, P. E. (1993). Self-appraisal and attributions: A test of a model. *Journal of Management, 19*(1), 51–62.

Lied, T. L., & Pritchard, R. D. (1976). Relationship between personality variables and components of the expectancy-valence model. *Journal of Applied Psychology, 61,* 463–467.

Lierman, B. (1994). How to develop a training simulation. *Training and Development, 48*(2), 50–52.

Lin, T. R., & Adrian, N. (1993). *Preliminary validation findings of a multi-method, multi-dimension structured interview for supervisory personnel.* Paper presented at the annual meeting of the International Personnel Management Association—Assessment Council, Sacramento, CA.

Lin, T. R., Petersen, B. C., & Manligas, C. L. (1987, June). *Rater and ratee race effects in the structured selection interview: A field study.* Paper presented at the 11th Annual Meeting of the International Personnel Management Association—Assessment Council, Philadelphia, PA.

Liou, K. T., Sylvia, R. D., & Brunk, G. (1990). Non-work factors and job satisfaction revisited. *Human Relations, 43,* 77–86.

Litterer, J. A. (1966). Conflict in organizations: A reexamination. *Academy of Management Journal, 9,* 178–186.

Littlepage, G. E. (1991). Effects of group size and task characteristics on group performance: A test of Steiner's model. *Personality and Social Psychology Bulletin, 17*(4), 449–456.

Locke, E. A. (1968). Toward a theory of task motivation and incentives. *Organizational Behavior and Human Performance, 3,* 157–189.

Locke, E. A. (1969). What is job satisfaction? *Organizational Behavior and Human Performance, 4,* 309–336.

Locke, E. A., & Latham, G. P. (1990). *A theory of goal setting and task performance.* Englewood Cliffs, NJ: Prentice-Hall.

Lockowandt, O. (1976). Present status of the investigation of handwriting psychology as a diagnostic method. *JSAS Catalog of Selected Documents, 6*(4), MS No. 11172.

Loewen, L. J., & Suedfeld, P. (1992) Cognitive arousal effects of masking office noise. *Environment and Behavior, 24*(3), 381–395.

London, M., & Wohlers, A. J. (1991). Agreement between subordinate and self-ratings in upward feedback. *Personnel Psychology, 44,* 375–390.

Long, G. (1982). *Cohesiveness of high school baseball teams.* Unpublished master's thesis, Southern Illinois University, Carbondale, IL.

Lopez, F. E., Rockmore, B. W., & Kesselman, G. A. (1980). The development of an integrated career planning program at Gulf Power Company. *Personnel Administrator, 25*(10), 21–29.

Lopez, F. M., Kesselman, G. A., & Lopez, F. E. (1981). An empirical test of a trait-oriented job analysis technique. *Personnel Psychology, 34,* 479–502.

LoPresto, R. L., Mitcham, D. E.,& Ripley, D. E. (1985). *Reference checking handbook.* Alexandria, VA: American Society for Personnel Administration.

Lord, R. G., De Vader, C. L., & Alliger, G. M. (1986). A meta-analysis of the relation between personality traits and leadership perceptions: An application of validity generalization procedures. *Journal of Applied Psychology, 71,* 402–410.

Lord, R. G., & Hohenfeld, J. A. (1979). Longitudinal field assessment of equity effects in the performance of major league baseball players. *Journal of Applied Psychology, 64,* 19–26.

Lorge, I., Fox, D., Davitz, J., & Brenner, M. (1958). A survey of studies contrasting the quality of group performance versus individual performance. *Psychological Bulletin, 55,* 337–372.

Lounsbury, J. W., Bobrow, W., & Jensen, J. B. (1989). Attitudes toward employment testing: Scale development, correlates, and "known group" validation. *Professional Psychology: Research and Practice, 20*(5), 340–349.

Love, K. G., Bishop, R. C., & Scionti, C. (1991). Responsive bias in job analysis ratings: Relation between ratings of task liking and task characteristics. *Psychological Reports, 68,* 1113–1144.

Lowe, R. H. (1993). Master's programs in industrial/organizational psychology: Current status and a call for action. *Professional Psychology: Research and Practice, 24*(1) 27–34.

Maas, S. B. (1965). Patterned scaled expectation interview. *Journal of Applied Psychology, 49,* 431–433.

Mabe, P. A., & West, S. G. (1982). Validity of self-evaluation of ability: A review and meta-analysis. *Journal of Applied Psychology, 67,* 280–296.

Machungwa, P. D., & Schmitt, N. (1983). Work motivation in a developing country. *Journal of Applied Psychology, 68,* 31–42.

Mackworth, N. H. (1946). Effects of heat on wireless telegraphy operators hearing and receiving Morse messages. *British Journal of Industrial Medicine, 3,* 145.

Maddux, J. E., & Rogers, R. W. (1980). Effects of source expertness, physical attractiveness, and supporting arguments on persuasion: A case of brains over beauty. *Journal of Personality and Social Psychology, 39,* 235–244.

Mager, R. F. (1984). *Preparing institutional objectives.* Belmont, CA: Pitman Learning.

Mahlin, S. J., & Charles, J. (1984). Peak-time pay for part-time work. *Personnel, 63*(11), 60–65.

Maier, N. R. F. (1976). *The appraisal interview.* La Jolla, CA: University Associates.

Major, B., Schmidlin, A. M., & Williams, L. (1990). General patterns in social touch: The impact on setting and age. *Journal of Personality and Social Psychology, 58,* 634–643.

Malandro, L. A., & Barker, L. L. (1983). *Nonverbal communication.* Reading, MA: Addison-Wesley.

Malaviya, P., & Ganesh, K. (1977). Individual differences in productivity across type of work shift. *Journal of Applied Psychology, 62,* 527–528.

Mann, K.O. (1965). Characteristics of job evaluation programs. *Personnel Administration, 28,* 45–57.

Mann, R. B., & Decker, P. J. (1984). The effect of key behavior distinctiveness on generation and recall in behavior modeling training. *Academy of Management Journal, 27,* 900–910.

Manners, G. E. (1975). Another look at group size, group problem solving, and member consensus. *Academy of Management Journal, 18,* 715–724.

Manson, T. (1989). The effectiveness of computer based training in organizational settings: A meta-analysis. *Proceedings of the 10th Annual Meeting of Graduate Conference in Industrial/Organizational Psychology and Organizational Behavior.*

Mantell, M., & Albrecht, S. (1994). *Ticking bombs: Defusing violence in the workplace.* New York: Business and Irwin.

Manz, C. C., & Sims, H. P. (1986). Beyond limitation: Complex behavioral and affective linkages resulting from exposure to leadership training models. *Journal of Applied Psychology, 71,* 571–578.

Markowich, M. M. (1994). Re-engineering sick pay. *HR Focus, 71*(4), 12–13.

Martin, C. L., & Nagao, D. H. (1989). Some effects of computerized interviewing on job applicant responses. *Journal of Applied Psychology, 74,* 72–80.

Martin, J. (1983). *Design of man-computer dialogues.* New York: AMACOM.

Martin, J. E. (1993). The effect of providing choices on the validity of a situational interview for resident assistants. *Applied H.R.M. Research, 4*(1), 69–77.

Martin, J. E., & Andrews, C. (1992). The effect of situational interview format on applicant interview scores. *Proceedings of the Annual Graduate Conference in Industrial/Organizational Psychology and Organizational Behavior.*

Martinez, M. N. (1990). In search of a productive design. *HRMagazine, 35*(2), 36–39.

Martinez, M. N. (1994). FMLA: Headache or opportunity? *HRMagazine, 39*(2), 42–45.

Maslow, A. H. (1954). *Motivation and personality.* New York: Harper & Row.

Maslow, A. H. (1970). *Motivation and personality* (2nd ed.). New York: Harper & Row.

Mason, N. A., & Belt, J. A. (1986). The costs and strategies of recruitment advertising. *Journal of Management, 12*(3), 425–432.

Mason, R. M. (1984). Ergonomics: The human and the machine. *Library Journal, 15,* 331–332.

Mathews, K. E., & Canon, L. K. (1975). Environmental noise level as a determinant of helping behavior. *Journal of Personality and Social Psychology, 32,* 571–577.

Matthes, K. (1993). Greeting from Hallmark. *HR Focus, 70*(8), 12–13.

Maurer, S. D., & Fay, C. (1988). Effect of situational interviews, conventional structured interviews, and training on interview rating agreement: An experimental analysis. *Personnel Psychology, 41,* 329–344.

Mawhinney, T. C., & Gowen, C. R. (1990). Gainsharing and the law of effect as the matching law: A theoretical framework. *Journal of Organizational Behavior Management, 11*(2), 61–75.

Mayfield, E. C. (1964). The selection interview: A reevaluation of published research. *Personnel Psychology, 17,* 239–260.

Mayfield, E. C., Brown, S. H., & Hamstra, B. W. (1980). Selection interviewing in the life insurance industry: An update of research and practice. *Personnel Psychology, 33,* 725–739.

Mayo, E. (1946). *The human problems of an industrial civilization.* Cambridge, MA: Harvard University Press.

McClelland, D. C. (1961). *The achieving society.* Princeton, NJ: Van Nostrand.

McClelland, D. C., & Boyatzis, R. E. (1982). Leadership motive pattern and long-term success in management. *Journal of Applied Psychology, 67,* 737–743.

McClelland, D. C., & Burnham, D. H. (1976). Power is the great motivator. *Harvard Business Review, 54*(2), 102–104.

McCormick, E. J. (1979). *Job analysis: Methods and applications.* New York: AMACOM.

McCormick, E.J., Jeanneret, P. R., & Mecham, R. C. (1969). *Position Analysis Questionnaire.* West Lafayette, IN: Purdue Research Foundation.

McCormick, E. J., Jeanneret, P. R., & Mecham, R. C. (1972). A study of job characteristics and job dimensions as based on the Position Analysis Questionnaire (PAQ). *Journal of Applied Psychology, 56,* 347–368.

McDaniel, L. (1995). Group assessments produce better hires. *HRMagazine, 40*(4), 56–61.

McDaniel, M. A., Whetzel, D. L., Schmidt, F. L., & Maurer, S. D. (1994). The validity of employment interviews: A comprehensive review and meta-analysis. *Journal of Applied Psychology, 79*(4), 599–616.

McDaniel, Q., & Johnson, D. L. (1992). The effectiveness of electronic résumé databases. *Applied H.R.M. Research, 3*(2), 162–169.

McElroy, J. C., Morrow, P. C., & Ackerman, R. J. (1983). Personality and interior office design: Exploring the accuracy of visitor attributions. *Journal of Applied Psychology, 68,* 541–544.

McElroy, J. C., Morrow, P. C., & Wall, L. C. (1983). Generalizing impact of object language to other audiences: Peer response to office design. *Psychological Reports, 53,* 315–332.

McEvoy, G. M. (1988). Evaluating the boss. *Personnel Administrator, 33*(9), 115–120.

McEvoy, G. M. (1990). Public sector managers' reactions to appraisals by subordinates. *Public Personnel Management, 19*(2), 201–212.

McGehee, W., & Thayer, P. W. (1961). *Training in business and industry.* New York: Wiley.

McGregor, D. (1957). An uneasy look at performance appraisal. *Harvard Business Review, 35,* 89–94.

McGregor, D. (1967). *The professional manager.* New York: McGraw-Hill.

McIntyre, R., Smith, D., & Hassett, C. (1984). Accuracy of performance ratings as affected by rater training and perceived purpose of training. *Journal of Applied Psychology, 69,* 147–156.

McShane, T. D. (1993). Effect of nonverbal cues and verbal first impressions in unstructured and situational interview settings. *Applied H.R.M. Research, 4*(2), 137–150.

Meehan, B.T. (1994, January 16). Ice star, bodyguard a pair who didn't fit in. *Roanoke Times and World News,* pp. A1, A8.

Meehl, P. E. (1965). See over sign: The first good example. *Journal of Experimental Research in Personality, 1,* 27–32.

Meers, A., Maasen, A., & Verhaagen, P. (1978). Subjective health after six months and after four years of shift work. *Ergonomics, 21,* 857–859.

Mehrabian, A. (1965). Communication length as an index of communicator attitude. *Psychological Reports, 17,* 519–522.

Melamed, S., Harari, G., & Green, M. S. (1993). Type A behavior, tension, and ambulatory cardiovascular reactivity in workers exposed to noise stress. *Psychosomatic Medicine, 55*(2), 185–193.

Mellor, E. F. (1984, June). Investigating the differences in weekly earnings of women and men. *Monthly Labor Review,* pp. 17–28.

Mendleson, J. L., Barnes, A. K., & Horn, G. (1989). The guiding light to corporate culture. *Personnel Administrator, 34*(7), 70–71.

Mento, A. J. (1980). *A review of assessment center research.* Washington, DC: U.S. Office of Personnel Management.

Mento, A. J., Steel, R. P., & Karren, R. J. (1987). A meta-analytic study of the effects of goal setting on task performance: 1966–1984. *Organizational Behavior and Human Decision Processes, 39,* 52–83.

Mershon, D. H., & Lin, L. (1987). Directional localization in high ambient noise with and without the use of hearing protectors. *Ergonomics, 30,* 1161–1173.

Meyer, H. H. (1980). Self-appraisal of job performance. *Personnel Psychology, 33,* 291–296.

Meyer, H. H., & Raich, M. S. (1983). An objective evaluation of a behavior modeling training program. *Personnel Psychology, 36,* 755–761.

Michaels, J. W., Blommel, J. M., Brocato, R. M., Linkous, R. A., & Rowe, J. S. (1982). Social facilitation and inhibition in a natural setting. *Replications in Social Psychology, 2,* 21–24.

Mijares, T. C. (1993). Selecting police personnel for tactical assignments: Considerations for female officers. *Applied H.R.M. Research, 4*(2), 94–101.

Miles, J. A., & Greenberg, J. (1993). Using punishment threats to attenuate social loafing effects among swimmers. *Organizational Behavior and Human Decision Processes, 56*(2), 246–265.

Miller, G. W., & Sniderman, M. S. (1974). Multijobholding of Wichita public school teachers. *Public Personnel Management, 3,* 392–402.

Miller, J. (1995). Domestic violence: Tips for employers. *IPMA News,* January, page 19.

Miller, J. G. (1960). Information input, overload, and psychopathology. *American Journal of Psychiatry, 116,* 695–704.

Miller, K. I., & Monge, P. D. (1986). Participation, satisfaction, and productivity: A meta-analytic review. *Academy of Management Journal, 29*(4), 727–753.

Miller, T. I. (1984). Effects of employee-sponsored day care on employee absenteeism, turnover, productivity, recruitment or job satisfaction: What is claimed and what is known. *Personnel Psychology, 37,* 277–289.

Miller, R. K., & Van Rybroek, G. J. (1988). Internship letters of recommendation: Where are the other 90%? *Professional Psychology: Research and Practice, 19*(1), 115–117.

Milliman, R. E. (1986). The influence of background music on the behavior of restaurant patrons. *Journal of Consumer Research, 13,* 290–296.

Miner, J. B. (1963). Evidence regarding the value of a management course based on behavioral science subject matter. *The Journal of Business of the University of Chicago, 36,* 325–335.

Mishra, J. (1990). Managing the grapevine. *Public Personnel Management, 19*(2), 213–226.

Mitchell, J. V. (1983). *Tests in print III.* Lincoln, NE: University of Nebraska Press.

Mitchell, M. B. (1985). *Ninth mental measurements yearbook.* Lincoln, NE: University of Nebraska Press.

Mitchell, T. R. (1974). Expectancy models of job satisfaction, occupational preference, and effort: A theoretical, methodological, and empirical approach. *Psychological Bulletin, 81,* 1053–1077.

Mitchell, T. R. (1985). An evaluation of the validity of correlational research conducted in organizations. *Academy of Management Review, 10,* 192–205.

Mitchell, V. F., & Mougdill, P. (1976). Measurement of Maslow's need hierarchy. *Organizational Behavior and Human Performance, 16,* 334–349.

Mitra, A., Jenkins, G. D., & Gupta, N. (1992). A meta-analytic review of the relationship between absence and turnover. *Journal of Applied Psychology, 77*(6), 879–889.

Moede, W. (1927). Die Richtlinien der Leistungs-Psychologie. *Industrielle Psychotechnik, 4,* 193–207.

Molloy, J. T. (1975). *Dress for success.* New York: Warner Books.

Molloy, J. T. (1978). *The woman's dress for success book.* New York: Warner Books.

Montebello, H. R., & Haga, M. (1994). To justify training, test, test again. *Personnel Journal, 30*(1), 83–87.

Moore, H., & Kondrasuk, J. (1994, March). Threat of violence demands HR attention. *HR News,* 8–9.

Moores, J. (1990). A meta-analytic review of the effects of compressed work schedules. *Applied H.R.M. Research, 1*(1), 12–18.

Morrow, P. C., & McElroy, J. C. (1981). Interior office design and visitor response: A constructive replication. Journal of Applied Psychology, 66, 646–650.

Morse, C. S. (1988). Employer liability for negligent hiring and retention of employees. *PAR Employment Law Update, 5*(1), 1–4.

Mosel, J. N., & Goheen, H. W. (1952). Agreement among replies to an employment recommendation questionnaire. *American Psychologist, 7,* 365–366.

Mosel, J. N., & Goheen, H. W. (1958). The validity of the Employment Recommendation Questionnairé in personnel selection: Skilled traders. *Personnel Psychology, 11,* 481–490.

Mossholder, K. W. (1980). Effects of externally mediated goal setting on intrinsic motivation: A laboratory experiment. *Journal of Applied Psychology, 65*(2), 202–210.

Motowidlo, S. J., Carter, G. W., Dunnette, M. D., Tippins, N., Werner, S., Burnett, J. R., & Vaughan, M. J. (1992). Studies of the structured behavioral interview. *Journal of Applied Psychology, 77*(5), 571–587.

Mott, P. E., Mann, F. C., McLoughlin, Q., & Warwick, D. P. (1965). *Shift work.* Ann Arbor: University of Michigan Press.

Moulton, D. A. (1994). *Effects of organizational policies and training on sexual harassment.* Unpublished master's thesis, Radford University, Radford, VA.

Mount, M. K. (1983). Comparisons of managerial and employee satisfaction with a performance appraisal system. *Personnel Psychology, 36,* 99–110.

Mount, M. K., & Ellis, R. A. (1989). Sources of bias in job evaluation: A review and critique of research. *Journal of Social Issues, 45*(4), 153–167.

Mount, M. K., & Thompson, D. E. (1987). Cognitive categorization and quality of performance ratings. *Journal of Applied Psychology, 72*, 240–246.

Moynahan, B. (1993). Creating harassment-free work zones. *Training and Development, 47*, 67–70.

Muchinsky, P. M. (1979). The use of reference reports in personnel selection: A review and evaluation. *Journal of Occupational Psychology, 52*, 287–297.

Muchinsky, P. M., & Tuttle, M. L. (1979). Employee turnover: An empirical and methodological assessment. *Journal of Vocational Behavior, 14*, 43–77.

Mulder, M., de Jong, R. D., Koppelaar, L., & Verhage, J. (1986). Power, situation, and leaders' effectiveness: An organizational field study. *Journal of Applied Psychology, 71*, 566–570.

Mullen, B., Anthony, T., Salas, E., & Driskell, J. E. (1994). Group cohesiveness and quality of decision making: An integration of the groupthink hypothesis. *Small Group Research, 25*(2), 189–204.

Mullen, B., & Copper, C. (1994). The relation between group cohesiveness and performance: An integration. *Psychological Bulletin, 115*(2), 210–227.

Mullins, W. C. (1986). *A note on the efficacy of the spurious nature of relational causation.* Paper presented at the annual meeting of the Society of Police and Criminal Psychology, Little Rock, AR.

Mullins, W. C., & Kimbrough, W. W. (1988). Group composition as a determinant of job analysis outcomes. *Journal of Applied Psychology, 73*, 657–664.

Mumford, M. D. (1983). Social comparison theory and the evaluation of peer evaluations: A review and some applied implications. *Personnel Psychology, 36*, 867–881.

Munsterberg, H. (1913). *Psychology of industrial efficiency.* Boston: Houghton Mifflin.

Murphy, K. R. (1993). *Honesty in the workplace.* Pacific Grove, CA: Brooks/Cole.

Murphy, K. R., & Blazer, W. K.(1986). Systematic distortions in memory-based bahavior ratings and performance evaluations: Consequences for rating accuracy. *Journal of Applied Psychology, 71*, 39–44.

Murphy, K. R., & Constans, J. I. (1987). Behavioral anchors as a source of bias in rating. *Journal of Applied Psychology, 72*, 573–577.

Murphy, K. R., Gannett, B. A., Herr, B. M., & Chen, J. A. (1986). Effects of subsequent performance on evaluations of previous performance. *Journal of Applied Psychology, 71*, 427–431.

Murphy, K. R., Martin, C., & Garcia, M. (1982). Do behavioral observation scales measure observation? *Journal of Applied Psychology, 67*, 562–567.

Myers, J. H., & Errett, W. (1959). The problem of preselection in weighted application blank studies. *Journal of Applied Psychology, 43*, 94–95.

Nadler, P. (1993). How to start job-rotation training on the right track. *American Banker, 158*(12), 7.

Nail, P. R. (1986). Toward an integration of some models and theories of social response. *Psychological Bulletin, 100*(2), 190–206.

Nanry, C. (1988). Performance linked training. *Public Personnel Management, 17*, 457–463.

Nanus, R. (1992). *Visionary leadership.* San Francisco: Jossey-Bass.

Nash, A. N., & Carroll, S. J. (1970). A hard look at the reference check: Its modest worth can be improved. *Business Horizons, 13*, 43–49.

Nash, A. N., Muczyk, J. P., & Vettori, F. L. (1971). The relative practical effectiveness of programmed instruction. *Personnel Psychology, 24*, 397–418.

Nathan, B., & Lord, R. (1983). Cognitive categorization and dimensional schemata: A process approach to the study of halo in performance ratings. *Journal of Applied Psychology, 68*, 102–114.

National Research Council. (1983). *Video displays, work, and vision.* Washington, DC: National Academy Press.

Naughton, R. J. (1975). Motivational factors of American prisoners of war in Vietnam. *Naval War College Review, 27*(4), 2–14.

Naughton, T. J. (1988). Effect of female-linked job titles on job evaluation ratings. *Journal of Management, 14*(4), 567–578.

Neufeldt, D., Kimbrough, W. W., & Stadelmaier, M. F. (1983, April). *Relationship between group composition and task type on group problem solving ability.* Paper presented at the 11th Annual Graduation Conference in Personality and Social Psychology, Norman, OK.

Neuner, J., Keeling, L., & Kallaus, N. (1972). *Administrative office management.* Cincinnati, OH: Southwestern Publishing.

Newman, R. L., Hunt, D. L., & Rhodes, F. (1966). Effects of noise on productivity in a skateboard factory. *Journal of Applied Psychology, 50*, 493–496.

Newstrom, J. W. (1980). Evaluating the effectiveness of training methods. *Personnel Administrator, 25*, 55–60.

Nicholls, J. R., (1985). A new approach to situational leadership. *Leadership and Organization Development Journal, 6*(4), 2–7.

Nichols, R. G., & Stevens, L. A. (1957). *Are you listening?* New York: McGraw-Hill.

Nicholson, N., Jackson, P., & Howes, G. (1978). Shiftwork and absence: A study of temporal trends. *Journal of Occupational Psychology, 51*, 127–137.

Niebuhr, R. E., & Oswald, S. L. (1992). The impact of workgroup composition and other work unit/victim characteristics on perceptions of sexual harassment. *Applied H.R.M. Research, 3*, 30–47.

Niemyer, E. S. (1995). The case for case studies. *Training and Development, 49*(1), 50–52.

Norris, W. R., & Vecchio, R. P. (1992). Situational leadership theory: A replication. *Group and Organization Management, 17*(3), 331–342.

Norton, T. W. (1987). *Personnel marketplace*. New York: Fidelifacts.

Nowack, K. M. (1993). 360-degree feedback: The whole story. *Training and Development Journal, 47*(1), 69–72.

Nussbaum, K. (1980). *Race against time*. Cleveland, OH: National Association of Office Workers.

O'Brien, G. E., & Plooij, D. (1977). Comparison of programmed and prose culture training upon attitudes and knowledge. *Journal of Applied Psychology, 62*, 499–505.

O'Connor, E. J., Wexley, K. N., & Alexander, R. A. (1975). Single group validity: Fact or fallacy? *Journal of Applied Psychology, 60*, 352–355.

O'Grady, T., & Matthews, M. (1987). Video: Through the eyes of the trainee. *Training, 24*(7), 57–59.

O'Meara, D. P. (1994). Personality tests raise questions of legality and effectiveness. *HRMagazine, 39*(1), 97–100.

O'Neill, M. J. (1994). Work space adjustability, storage, and enclosure as predictors of employee reactions and performance. *Environment and Behavior, 26*(4), 504–526.

O'Reilly, C. A., & Puffer, S. M. (1989). The impact of rewards and punishments in a social context: A laboratory and field experiment. *Journal of Occupational Psychology, 62*(1), 41–53.

Oginska, H., Pokorski, J., & Oginski, A. (1993). Gender, aging, and shiftwork intolerance. *Ergonomics, 36*(1), 161–168.

Oldham, G. R., & Brass, D. J. (1979). Employee reactions to an open-plan office: A naturally occurring quasi-experiment. *Administrative Science Quarterly, 24*, 267–284.

Oliphant, V. N., & Alexander, E. R. (1982). Reactions to résumés as a function of résumé determinateness, applicant characteristics, and sex of raters. *Personnel Psychology, 35*, 829–842.

Ones, D. S., Viswesvaran, C., & Schmidt, F. L. (1993). Comprehensive meta-analysis of integrity test validities: Findings for personnel selection and theories of job performance. *Journal of Applied Psychology, 78*(4), 679–703.

Orpen, C. (1978). Work and nonwork satisfaction: A causal-correlational analysis. *Journal of Applied Psychology, 63*, 530–532.

Osborne, E. E., & Vernon, H. M. (1972). The influence of temperature and other conditions on the frequency of industrial accidents. Cited in Harrell, T. W. (1958). *Industrial Psychology*. New York: Rinehart & Co.

Osgood, C. (1966). *Perspective in foreign policy*. Palo Alto, CA: Pacific Books.

Overman, S. (1990). Prescriptions for a healthier office. *HRMagazine, 35*(2), 30–34.

Overman, S. (1994). Teams score on the bottom line. *HRMagazine, 39*(5), 82–84.

Overman, S. (1995). Bizarre questions aren't the answer. *HRMagazine, 40*(5), 72–76.

Owenby, P. H. (1992). Making case studies come alive. *Training, 29*(1), 43–46.

Oz, S., & Eden, D. (1994). Restraining the Golem: Boosting performance by changing the interpretation of low scores. *Journal of Applied Psychology, 79*(5), 744–754.

Pace, L. A., & Schoenfeldt, L. F. (1977). Legal concerns in use of weighted applications. *Personnel Psychology, 30*, 159–166.

Packer, A. (1988). America's new learning technology. *Personnel Administrator, 33*(9), 62–132.

Padgett, V. R. (1989). Empirical validation of firefighter vision standards. *Proceedings of 13th Annual Meeting of International Personnel Management Association— Assessment Council*.

Parsons, F. W. (1986). Inexpensive interactive video training. *Training and Development Journal, 40*(9), 38–39.

Patrick, J., & Moore, A. K. (1985). Development and reliability of a job analysis technique. *Journal of Occupational Psychology, 58*, 149–158.

Patterson, J. (1976). *Interpreting handwriting*. New York: McKay.

Paul, K. B., & Bracken, D. W. (1995). Everything you always wanted to know about employee surveys. *Training & Development, 49*(1), 45–49.

Paul, R. J., & Ebadi, Y. M. (1989). Leadership decision making in a service organization: A field test of the Vroom-Yetton model. *Journal of Occupational Psychology, 62*(3), 201–211.

Pearce, J. L., & Porter, L. W. (1986). Employee responses to formal performance appraisal feedback. *Journal of Applied Psychology, 71*, 211–218.

Pearce, W. B., & Conklin, F. (1971). Nonverbal vocalic communication and perceptions of a speaker. *Speech Monographs, 38*, 235–241.

Peggans, D., Chandra, L., & McAlarnis, C. (1986). Managers' perceptions of the appropriateness of I/O psychology and M.B.A. coursework. *Proceedings of the 7th Annual Graduate Conference in Industrial/Organizational Psychology and Organizational Behavior*.

Pendleton, C. S. (1986). Drug abuse strategies for business. *Security Management, 8*, 75.

Peres, S. H., & Garcia, J. R. (1962). Validity and dimensions of descriptive adjectives used in reference letters for engineering applicants. *Personnel Psychology, 15*, 279–286.

Peter, L. J., & Hull, R. (1969). *The Peter principle: Why things go wrong*. New York: Morrow.

Petrocelli, W., & Repa, B. K. (1992). *Sexual harassment on the job*. Berkeley: Nolo Press.

Pfeffer, J., & Salancik, G. (1978). *The external control of organizations*. New York: Harper & Row.

Phillips, A. P., & Dipboye, R. L. (1989). Correlational tests of predictions from a process model of the interview. *Journal of Applied Psychology, 74*, 41–52.

Pibal, D. C. (1985). Criteria for effective résumés as perceived by personnel directors. *Personnel Administrator, 30*(5), 119–123.

Pinneau, S. R. (1961). *Changes in intelligence quotients from infancy to maturity.* Boston: Houghton Mifflin.

Planchy, R. J., & Planchy, S. J. (1993). Focus on results, not behavior. *Personnel Journal, 72*(3), 28–30.

Platt, H. A. (1994). Nonsexual harassment claims hit HR's desk. *HRMagazine, 39*(3), 29–34.

Pollan, S. M., & Levine, M. (1994). Firing an employee. *Working Woman, 19*(8), 55.

Pond, S. B., & Geyer, P. D. (1987). Employee age as a moderator or the relationship between perceived work alternatives and job satisfaction. *Journal of Applied Psychology, 72,* 552–557.

Poor, R. (1970). *4 days, 40 hours.* Cambridge, MA: Bursk and Poor Publishing.

Porter, L. W., & Lawler, E. E. (1968). *Managerial attitudes and performance.* Homewood, IL: Dorsey.

Posner, B. Z., Hall, J. L., & Munson, J. M. (1991). A first look at the benefits of educational benefits programs. *Applied H.R.M. Research, 2*(2), 128–152.

Powell, G. N. (1991). Applicant reactions to the initial employment interview: Exploring theoretical and methodological issues. *Personnel Psychology, 44,* 67–83.

Premack, D. (1963). Prediction of the comparative reinforcement values of running and drinking. *Science, 139,* 1062–1063.

Premack, S. L., & Wanous, J. P. (1985). A meta-analysis of realistic job preview experiments. *Journal of Applied Psychology, 70,* 706–719.

Prien, E. P. (1977). The function of job analysis in content validation. *Personnel Psychology, 30,* 167–174.

Primoff, E. S. (1975). *How to prepare and conduct job element examinations.* Washington, DC: U.S. Civil Service Commission.

Pritchard, R. D., Dunnette, M. D., & Jorgenson, D. O. (1972). Effects of perceptions of equity and inequity on worker performance and satisfaction. *Journal of Applied Psychology, 56,* 75–94.

Pulakos, E. D., White, L. A., Oppler, S. H., & Borman, W. C. (1989). Examination of race and sex effects on performance ratings. *Journal of Applied Psychology, 74,* 770–780.

Pursell, E. D., Campion, M. A., & Gaylord, S. R. (1980). Structured interviewing and avoiding selection problems. *Personnel Journal, 59*(11), 907–912.

Pursell, E. D., Dossett, D. L., & Latham, G. P. (1980). Obtaining valid predictors by minimizing rating errors in the criterion. *Personnel Psychology, 33,* 91–96.

Quaglieri, P. L. (1982). A note on variations in recruiting information obtained through different sources. *Journal of Occupational Psychology, 55,* 53–55.

Quinn, J. F., & Petrick, J. A. (1993). Emerging strategic human resource challenges in managing accent discrimination and ethnic diversity. *Applied H.R.M. Research, 4*(2), 79–93.

Rae, L. (1994). Choose your method. *Training and Development, 48*(4), 19–25.

Rafaeli, A., & Klimoski, R. J. (1983). Predicting sales success through handwriting analysis: An evaluation of the effects of training and handwriting sample content. *Journal of Applied Psychology, 68,* 212–217.

Rahim, M. A. (1989). Relationships of leader power to compliance and satisfaction with supervision: Evidence from a national sample of managers. *Journal of Management, 15*(4), 545–556.

Rahim, M. A., & Afza, M. (1993). Leader power, commitment, satisfaction, compliance, and propensity to leave a job among U.S. accountants. *Journal of Social Psychology, 133*(5), 611–625.

Rahim, M. A., & Magner, N. R. (1995). Confirmatory factor analysis of the styles of handling interpersonal conflict: First-order factor model and its invariance across groups. *Journal of Applied Psychology, 80*(1), 122–132.

Rand, T., & Wexley, K. N. (1975). Demonstration of the effect "similar to me" in simulated employment interviews. *Psychological Reports, 26,* 535–544.

Range, L. M., Menyhert, A., Walsh, M. L., Hardin, K. N., Craddock, A., & Ellis, J. B. (1991). Letters of recommendation: Perspectives, recommendations, and ethics. *Professional Psychology: Research and Practice, 22*(5), 389–392.

Rapp, B. (1978, May). You asked for it—but did you get it? *Public Management,* pp. 8–11.

Rasmussen, K. G. (1984). Nonverbal behavior, verbal behavior, résumé credentials, and selection interview outcomes. *Journal of Applied Psychology, 69,* 551–556.

Rassenfoss, S. E., & Kraut, A. I. (1988). Survey of personnel research departments. *The Industrial/Organizational Psychologist, 25*(4), 31–37.

Raven, B. H. (1965). Social influence and power. In I. D. Steiner & M. Fishbein (Eds.), *Current studies in social psychology* (pp. 371–382). New York: Holt, Rinehart & Winston.

Raven, B. H. (1992). A power/interaction model of interpersonal influence: French and Raven thirty years later. *Journal of Social Behavior and Personality, 7*(2), 217–244.

Rawlinson, H. (1988). What do your classified ads say about you? *Recruitment Today, 1,* 47–52.

Raza, S. M., & Carpenter, B. N. (1987). A model of hiring decisions in real employment interviews. *Journal of Applied Psychology, 72,* 596–603.

Read, W. (1962). Upward communication in industrial hierarchies. *Human Relations, 15,* 3–16.

Reardon, C. E. (1986). *Effect of equipment type, fear of damaging equipment, and novelty of equipment on anxiety of computer terminal users.* Unpublished master's thesis, Radford University, Radford, VA.

Reddout, D. J. (1987). Manual writing made easier. *Training and Development Journal, 41*(4), 66–68.

Reilly, C. E., & Smith, C. (1988). Effects of shiftwork and psychometric evaluation of shiftworker selection instruments. *Proceedings of the 9th Annual Graduate Conference in Industrial/Organizational Psychology and Organizational Behavior.*

Reilly, R. R., & Chao, G. T. (1983). Validity and fairness of some alternative employee selection procedures. *Personnel Psychology, 35*, 1–62.

Reinsch, N. L., & Beswick, R. W. (1990). Voice mail versus conventional channels: A cost minimization analysis of individuals' preferences. *Academy of Management Journal, 33*(4), 801–816.

Reynolds, A. H. (1979). The reliability of a scored oral interview for police officers. *Public Personnel Management, 8*, 324–328.

Rhine, R. J., & Severance, L. J. (1970). Ego-involvement, discrepancy, source credibility, and attitude change. *Journal of Personality and Social Psychology, 16*, 175–190.

Rhodes, S. R. (1983). Age-related differences in work attitudes and behavior: A review and conceptual analysis. *Psychological Bulletin, 93*, 328–367.

Rice, B. (1983). Curbing cyberphobia. *Psychology Today, 8*, 79.

Rice, R. E. (1993). Media appropriateness: Using social presence theory to compare traditional and new organizational media. *Human Communication Research, 19*(4) 451–484.

Rice, R. W. (1978). Psychometric properties of the esteem for least preferred co-worker (LPC) scale. *Academy of Management Review, 3*, 106–118.

Rider, C. P. (1986). Honing your axe-wielding skills. *Training and Development Journal, 40*(6), 6.

Riggio, R. E., & Cole, E. J. (1992). Agreement between subordinate and superior ratings of supervisory performance and effects on self and subordinate satisfaction. *Journal of Occupational and Organizational Psychology, 65*, 137–158.

Roballey, T. C., & Gardner, E. (1986). Eat to the beat. *Psychology Today, 20*(2), 16.

Robbins, T. L. (1995). Social loafing on cognitive tasks: An examination of the "sucker effect." *Journal of Business and Psychology, 9*(3), 337–345.

Roberts, D. C., & Lozada-Larsen, S. R. (1994). *The impact of assessment on applicant attitudes about organizations.* Paper presented at the annual meeting of the International Personnel Management Association—Assessment Council, Charleston, SC.

Robertson, I. T., & Kandola, R. S. (1982). Work sample tests: Validity, adverse impact, and applicant reaction. *Journal of Occupational Psychology, 55*, 171–183.

Robinson, D. D. (1981). Content-oriented personnel selection in a small business setting. *Personnel Psychology, 34*, 77–87.

Robinson, J. P., Athanasious, R., & Head, K. B. (1969). *Measurements of occupational attitudes and occupational characteristics.* Ann Arbor, MI: Institute for Social Research.

Robinson, R. K., Allen, B. M., & Abraham, Y. T. (1992). Affirmative action plans in the 1990's: A double edged sword? *Public Personnel Management, 21*(2), 261–272.

Robinson, R. K., Allen, B. M., Franklin, G. M., & Duhan, D. L. (1993). Sexual harassment in the workplace: A review of the legal rights and responsibilities of all parties. *Public Personnel Management, 22*(1), 123–135.

Roethlisberger, F., & Dickson, W. (1939). *Management and the worker.* Cambridge, MA: Harvard University Press.

Rohmert, W., & Landau, K. (1983). *A new technique for job analysis.* New York: Taylor & Francis.

Rose, G. L., & Andiappan, P. (1978). Sex effects on managerial hiring decisions. *Academy of Management Journal, 21*, 104–112.

Rosen, D. J. (1992). Appraisals can make or break your court case. *Personnel Journal, 71*(11), 113–116.

Rosen, N. (1987). Employee attitude surveys: What managers should know. *Training and Development Journal, 41*(11), 50–52.

Rosen, S., & Tesser, A. (1970). Reluctance to communicate undesirable information: The MUM effect. *Sociometry, 33*, 253–263.

Rosen, T. H. (1987). Identification of substance abusers in the workplace. *Public Personnel Management, 16*(3), 197–208.

Rosenthal, R. (1968). *Pygmalion in the classroom.* New York: Holt, Rinehart & Winston.

Ross, J. D. (1979). A current review of public sector assessment centers: Cause for concern. *Public Personnel Management, 8*, 41–46.

Rothstein, H. R., & McDaniel, M. A. (1992). Differential validity by sex in employment settings. *Journal of Business and Psychology, 7*(1), 45–62.

Rothstein, H. R., Schmidt, F. L., Erwin, F. W., Owens, W. A., & Sparks, C. P. (1990). Biographical data in employment selection: Can validities be made generalizable? *Journal of Applied Psychology, 75*, 175–184.

Rouleau, E. J., & Krain, B. F. (1975). Using job analysis to design selection procedures. *Public Personnel Management, 4*, 300–304.

Rowe, P. M. (1989). Unfavorable information and interview decisions. In R. W. Eder & G. R. Ferris (Eds.), *The employment interview* (pp. 77–89). Newbury Park, CA: Sage Publications.

Rubin, J. Z., & Brown, B. R. (1975). *The social psychology of bargaining and negotiation.* New York: Academic Press.

Rubin, J. Z., & Lewecki, R. J. (1973). A three-factor experimental analysis of promises and threats. *Journal of Applied Social Psychology, 3*, 240–257.

Rupert, G. (1989). Employee referrals as a source of recruitment and job performance. *Proceedings of the 10th Annual Graduate Conference in Industrial/Organizational Psychology and Organizational Behavior.*

Rushton, J. P. (1995). Construct validity, censorship, and the genetics of race. *American Psychologist, 50*(1), 40–41.

Russ-Eft, D., & Zucchelli, L. (1987). When wrong is all right. *Training and Development Journal, 41*(11), 78–79.

Russell, C. J., Colella, A., & Bobko, P. (1993). Expanding the context of utility: The strategic impact of personnel selection. *Personnel Psychology, 46*, 781–801.

Ryan, A. M., & Lasek, M. (1991). Negligent hiring and defamation: Areas of liability related to pre-employment inquiries. *Personnel Psychology, 44*, 293–319.

Rynes, S. L., Bretz, R. D., & Gerhart, B. (1991). The importance of recruitment in job choice: A different way of looking. *Personnel Psychology, 44*(3), 487–520.

Rynes, S., & Connerley, M. (1993). Applicant reactions to alternative selection procedures. *Journal of Business and Psychology, 7*, 261–277.

Rynes, S. L., & Miller, H. E. (1983). Recruiter and job influences on candidates for employment. *Journal of Applied Psychology, 68*, 147–154.

Rynes, S. L., Weber, C. L., & Milkovich, G. T. (1989). Effects of market survey rates, job evaluation, and job gender on job pay. *Journal of Applied Psychology, 74*(1), 114–123.

Saal, F. E. (1979). Mixed standard rating scale: A consistent system for numerically coding inconsistent response combinations. *Journal of Applied Psychology, 64*, 422–428.

Saavedra, R., & Kwun, S. K. (1993). Peer evaluation in self-managing work groups. *Journal of Applied Psychology, 78*(3), 450–462.

Sabini, J. (1995). *Social psychology* (2nd. ed.). New York: Norton.

Sackett, P. R., Burris, L. R., & Callahan, C. (1989). Integrity testing for personnel selection: An update. *Personnel Psychology, 42*, 491–528.

Sackett, P. R., & Roth, L. (1991). A Monte Carlo examination of banding and rank order methods of test score use in personnel selection. *Human Performance, 4*(4), 279–295.

Sadri, G., & Robertson, I. T. (1993). Self-efficacy and work-related behavior: A review and meta-analysis. *Applied Psychology: An International Review, 42*(2), 139–152.

Salancik, G., & Pfeffer, J. (1977). An examination of need-satisfaction models of job satisfaction and job attitudes. *Administrative Science Quarterly, 22*, 427–456.

Sanchez, J. I., & Fraser, S. L. (1992). On the choice of scales for task analysis. *Journal of Applied Psychology, 77*, 545–553.

Sanchez, J. I., & Levine, E. L. (1989). Determining important tasks within jobs: A policy-capturing approach. *Journal of Applied Psychology, 74*, 336–342.

Sanders, G. S. (1981) Driven by distraction: An integrative review of social facilitation theory and research. *Journal of Experimental Social Psychology, 17*, 227–251.

Sandler, L. (1986). Self-fulfilling prophecy: Better management by magic. *Training, 23*, 60–64.

Savage, J. I. (1988). Study refires VDT safety debate: Shows link between heavy use and miscarriages. *Computerworld, 22*(6), 1–2.

Sawyer, A. (1973). The effects of repetition or refutational and supportive advertising appeals. *Journal of Marketing Research, 10*, 23–33.

Scandura, T. A., Graen, G. B., & Novak, M. A. (1986). When managers decide not to decide autocratically: An investigation of leader-member exchange and decision influence. *Journal of Applied Psychology, 71*, 579–584.

Schatzki, M. (1981). *Negotiation.* New York: Signet.

Schein, E. (1956). The Chinese indoctrination program for prisoners of war. *Psychiatry, 19*, 149–177.

Schippmann, J. S., Prien, E. P., & Katz, J. A. (1990). Reliability and validity of in-basket performance measures. *Personnel Psychology, 43*, 837–859.

Schippmann, J. S., Schmitt, S. D., & Hawthorne, S. L. (1992). I/O work roles: PhD vs. masters level practitioners. *The Industrial-Organizational Psychologist, 29*(4), 35–39.

Schleifer, L. M., & Amick, B. C. (1989). System response time and method of pay: Stress effects in computer-based tasks. *International Journal of Human Computer Interaction, 1*(1), 23–39.

Schleifer, L. M., & Okogbaa, O. G.(1990). System response time and method of pay: Cardiovascular stress effects in computer-based tasks. *Ergonomics, 33*(12), 1495–1509.

Schmidt, F. L. (1971). The relative efficiency of regression and simple unit predictor weights in applied differential psychology. *Educational and Psychological Measurement, 31*, 699–714.

Schmidt, F. L. (1973). Implications of a measurement problem for expectancy theory research. *Organizational Behavior and Human Performance, 10*, 243–251.

Schmidt, F. L. (1988). The problem of group differences in ability test scores in employment selection. *Journal of Vocational Behavior, 33*(3), 272–292.

Schmidt, F. L. (1991). Why all banding procedures in personnel selection are logically flawed. *Human Performance, 4*, 265–277.

Schmidt, F. L., Gast-Rosenberg, I., & Hunter, J. E. (1980). Validity generalization results for computer programmers. *Journal of Applied Psychology, 65*, 643–661.

Schmidt, F. L., Greenthal, A. L., Hunter, J. E., Berner, J. G., & Seaton, F. W. (1977). Job sample vs. paper and pencil trades and technical tests: Adverse impact and examinee attitudes. *Personnel Psychology, 30*, 187–197.

Schmidt, F. L., & Hunter, J. E. (1978). Moderator research and the law of small numbers. *Personnel Psychology, 31*, 215–232.

Schmidt, F. L., & Hunter, J. E. (1981). Employment testing: Old theories and new research. *American Psychologist, 36*, 1128–1137.

Schmidt, F. L., Hunter, J. E., Pearlman, K., & Hirsh, H. R. (1985). Forty questions about validity generalization and meta-analysis. *Personnel Psychology, 38*, 697–798.

Schmitt, N., & Cohen, S. A. (1989). Internal analyses of task ratings by job incumbents. *Journal of Applied Psychology, 74*, 96–104.

Schmitt, N., Coyle, B. W., & Rauschenberger, J. (1977). A Monte Carlo evaluation of three formula estimates of cross-validated multiple correlation. *Psychological Bulletin, 84*, 751–758.

Schmitt, N., Gooding, R. Z., Noe, R. A., & Kirsch, M. (1984). Meta-analysis of validity studies published between 1964 and 1982 and the investigation of study characteristics. *Personnel Pyschology, 37,* 407–421.

Schmitt, N., Schneider, J. R., & Cohen, S. A. (1990). Factors affecting validity of a regionally administered assessment center. *Personnel Psychology, 43,* 1–12.

Schneier, C. E., Guthrie, J. P., & Olian, J. D. (1988). A practical approach to conducting and using the training needs assessment. *Public Personnel Management, 17,* 191–205.

Schramm, W. (1962). Learning from instructional television. *Review of Educational Research, 32,* 156–157.

Schriesheim, C. A., & DeNisi, A. S. (1981). Task dimensions as moderators of the effects of instrumental leadership: A two-sample replicated test of path-goal leadership theory. *Journal of Applied Psychology, 66,* 589–597.

Schriesheim, C. A., Tepper, B. J., & Tetrault, L. A. (1994). Least preferred co-worker score, situational control, and leadership effectiveness: A meta-analysis of contingency model performance predictions. *Journal of Applied Psychology, 79*(4), 561–573.

Schriesheim, J. F., & Schriesheim, C. A. (1980). A test of the path-goal theory of leadership and some suggested directions for future research. *Personnel Psychology, 33,* 349–370.

Schulz, R. (1976). Effects of control and predictability on the physical and psychological well-being of the institutionalized aged. *Journal of Personality and Social Psychology, 33,* 563–573.

Schuster, J. R., & Zingheim, P. K. (1992). *The new pay.* New York: Lexington Books.

Schwab, D. P. (1982). Recruiting and organizational participation. In K. M. Rowland & G. R. Farris (Eds.), *Personnel management.* Boston, MA: Allyn & Bacon.

Schwab, D. P., & Heneman, H. G. (1969). Relationship between interview structure and inter-interviewer reliability in an employment situation. *Journal of Applied Psychology, 53,* 214–217.

Schwab, D. P., Heneman, H. G., & DeCotiis, T. A. (1975). Behaviorally anchored rating scales: A review of the literature. *Personnel Psychology, 28,* 549–562.

Schwartz, B., & Barsky, S. (1977). The home advantage. *Social Forces, 55,* 641–666.

Schweitzer, S. C. (1979). *Winning with deception and bluff.* Englewood Cliffs, NJ: Prentice-Hall.

Scott, D., & Markham, S. (1982). Absenteeism control methods: A survey of practice and results. *Personnel Administrator, 27*(6), 73–84.

Scott, K. D., Markham, S. E., & Robers, R. W. (1985). Rewarding good attendance: A comparative study of positive ways to reduce absenteeism. *Personnel Administrator, 30,* 72–75.

Scott, W. D. (1903). *The theory of advertising.* Boston: Small Maynard.

Sears, D. O. (1986). College sophomores in the laboratory: Influences of a narrow data base on social psychology's view of human nature. *Journal of Personality and Social Psychology, 51*(3), 515–530.

Segal, J. A. (1990). Follow the yellow brick road. *HRMagazine, 35*(2), 83–86.

Seitz, D. D., & Modica, A. J. (1980). *Negotiating your way to success.* New York: Mentor.

Serlin, R. C., & Lapsley, D. K. (1985). Rationality in psychological research: The good-enough principle. *American Psychologist, 40,* 73–83.

Seta, J. J. (1982). The impact of comparison processes on coactor's task performance. *Journal of Personality and Social Psychology, 42,* 281–291.

Shaffer, D. R., & Tomarelli, M. (1981). Bias in the ivory tower: An unintended consequence of the Buckley Amendment for graduate admissions. *Journal of Applied Psychology, 66,* 7–11.

Shaffer, G. S., Saunders, V., & Owens, W. A. (1986). Additional evidence for the accuracy of biographical data: Long-term retest and observer ratings. *Personnel Psychology, 39*(4), 791–809.

Shapira, Z., & Shirom, A. (1980). New issues in the use of behaviorally anchored rating scales: Level of analysis, the effects of incident frequency, and external validation. *Journal of Applied Psychology, 65,* 517–523.

Shaw, M. E., & Shaw, I. M. (1962). Some effects of social grouping upon learning in a second grade classroom. *Journal of Social Psychology, 57,* 453–458.

Shelton, S., & Alliger, G. (1993). Who's afraid of Level 4 evaluations? *Training and Development, 43*(6), 43–46.

Shepperd, J. A. (1993). Productivity loss in performance groups: A motivation analysis. *Psychological Bulletin, 113*(1), 67–81.

Shetzer, L., & Stackman, R. (1991). The career path component in realistic job previews: A meta-analysis and proposed integration. *Applied H.R.M. Research, 2*(2), 153–169.

Shneiderman, B. (1980). *Software psychology.* Cambridge, MA: Winthrop.

Sieber, J. E., & Saks, M. J. (1989). A census of subject pool characteristics and policies. *American Psychologist, 44*(7), 1053–1061.

Sieling, M. S. (1984). Staffing patterns prominent in female-male earnings gap. *Monthly Labor Review, 107*(6), 29–30.

Silva, J. M., & Jacobs, R. R. (1993). Performance as a function of increased minority hiring. *Journal of Applied Psychology, 78*(4), 591–601.

Simonton, D. K. (1979). Multiple discovery and invention: Zeitgeist, genius, or chance? *Journal of Personality and Social Psychology, 37,* 1603–1616.

Sims, R. R., Veres, J. G., & Heninger, S. M. (1989). Training for competence. *Public Personnel Management, 18,* 101–107.

Skinner, B. F. (1938). *The behavior of organizations.* New York: Appleton.

Skinner, B. F. (1969). *Contingencies of reinforcement.* New York: Appleton-Century-Crofts.

Sleezer, C. M. (1993). Tried and true performance analysis. *Training and Development, 47*(11), 52–54.

Smart, R. (1965). Social group membership, leadership, and birth order. *Journal of Social Psychology, 67,* 221–225.

Smith, B. N., Hornsby, J. S., Benson, P. G., & Wesolowski, M. (1989). What is in a name: The impact of job titles on job evaluation results. *Journal of Business and Psychology, 3*(3), 341–351.

Smith, C., Reilly, C., & Midkiff, K. (1988, August). *Psychometric evaluation of circadian rhythm questionnaires with suggestions for improvement.* Paper presented at the annual meeting of the American Psychological Association, Atlanta, GA.

Smith, D. E. (1986). Training programs for performance appraisal: A review. *Academy of Management Review, 11,* 22–40.

Smith, E. R., & Mackie, D. M. (1995). *Social psychology.* New York: Worth.

Smith, J. E., & Hakel, M. D. (1979). Convergence among data sources, response bias, and reliability and validity of a structured job analysis questionnaire. *Personnel Psychology, 32,* 677–692.

Smith, L., & Folkard, S. (1993). The perceptions and feelings of shiftworkers' partners. *Ergonomics, 36*(1), 299–305.

Smith, M. J., Cohen, B. G., & Stammerjohn, L. W. (1981). An investigation of health complaints and job stress in video display operations. *Human Factors, 23*(4), 387–400.

Smith, M. L. (1993). Defensible performance appraisals. *Journal of Management in Engineering, 9*(2), 128–135.

Smith, P. C., & Kendall, L. M. (1963). Retranslating expectations: An approach to the construction of unambiguous anchors for rating scales. *Journal of Applied Psychology, 47,* 149–155.

Smith, P. C., Kendall, L. M., & Hulin, C. L. (1969). *The measurement of satisfaction in work and retirement.* Chicago: Rand McNally.

Smith, P. L., Smits, S. J., & Hoy, F. (1992). Human resource policies in small firms: Linkages to employee satisfaction. *Applied H.R.M. Research, 3*(1), 1–19.

Smith, R. E. (1993). *Psychology.* Minneapolis-St. Paul, MN: West Publishing.

Smither, J. W., Barry, S. R., & Reilly, R. R. (1989). An investigation of the validity of expert true score estimates in appraisal research. *Journal of Applied Psychology, 74,* 143–151.

Smither, J. W., London, M., Vasilopoulos, N. L., Reilly, R. R., Millsap, R. E., & Salvemini, N. (1995). An examination of an upward feedback program over time. *Personnel Psychology, 48,* 1–34.

Smither, J. W., Reilly, R. R., & Buda, R. (1988). Effect of prior performance information on ratings of recent performance: Contrast versus assimilation revisited. *Journal of Applied Psychology, 73,* 487–496.

Smither, J. W., Reilly, R. R., Millsap, R. E., Pearlman, K., & Stoffey, R. W. (1993). Applicant reactions to selection procedures. *Personnel Psychology, 46,* 49–76.

Smither, R., & Lindgren, H. C. (1978). Salary, age, sex, and need for achievement in bank employees. *Psychological Reports, 42,* 334.

Smothers, R. (1993, January 31). Settlement commits Shoney's to affirmative action plan. *Roanoke Times and World News,* p. B6.

Snyman, J., Aamodt, M. G., Johnson, D. L., & Frantzve, J. (1991). Pre-employment paper-and-pencil testing: A quantitative review. *Journal of Police and Criminal Psychology, 7*(2), 11–25.

Society for Industrial and Organizational Psychology. (1986). *Graduate training programs in I/O psychology and organizational behavior.* College Park, MD: Author.

Sollie, D., & Sollie, W. (1993, October). *Non-lethal weapons: An implementation study.* Paper presented at the annual meeting of the Society of Police and Criminal Psychology, New Orleans, LA.

Sommer, R., Wynes, M., & Brinkley, G. (1992). Social facilitation effects in shopping behavior. *Environment and Behavior, 24*(3), 285–297.

Sonnemann, U., & Kernan, J. (1962). Handwriting analysis—a valid selection tool? *Personnel, 39,* 8–14.

Sorcher, M., & Spence, R. (1982). The Interface Project: Behavior modeling as social technology in South Africa. *Personnel Psychology, 35,* 557–581.

Speroff, B., & Kerr, W. (1952). Steel mill "hot strip" accidents and interpersonal desirability values. *Journal of Clinical Psychology, 8,* 89–91.

Spitzer, D. (1986). Five keys to successful training. *Training, 23*(6), 37–39.

Spock, G., & Stevens, S. (1985). A test of Anderson's averaging versus adding model on résumé evaluations. *Proceedings of the 6th Annual Graduate Conference in Industrial/Organizational Psychology and Organizational Behavior,* 95–96.

Spool, M. D. (1978). Training programs for observers of behavior: A review. *Personnel Psychology, 31,* 853–888.

Springbett, B. M. (1958). Factors affecting the final decision in the employment interview. *Canadian Journal of Psychology, 12,* 13–22.

Srinivas, S., & Motowidlo, S. J. (1987). Effects of rater's stress on the dispersion and favorability of performance ratings. *Journal of Applied Psychology, 72,* 247–251.

Stafford, E. M., Jackson, P. R., & Banks, M. H. (1984). An empirical study of occupational families in the youth labor market. *Journal of Occupational Psychology, 57,* 141–155.

Stagner, R., & Rosen, H. (1965). *Psychology of union-management relations.* Monterey, CA: Brooks/Cole.

Stahl, M. J. (1983). Achievement, power, and managerial motivation: Selecting managerial talent with the job choice exercise. *Personnel Psychology, 36,* 775–789.

Stahl, M. J., & Harrell, A. M. (1981). Modeling effort decisions with behavioral decision theory: Toward an individual differences model of expectancy theory. *Organizational Behavior and Human Performance, 27,* 303–325.

Stahl, M. J.,& Harrell, A. M. (1982). Evolution and validation of a behavioral decision theory measurement approach to achievement, power, and affiliation. *Journal of Applied Psychology, 67,* 744–751.

Staw, B. M., Bell, N. E., & Clausen, J. A. (1986). The dispositional approach to job attitudes: A lifetime longitudinal test. *Administrative Science Quarterly, 31,* 56–77.

Staw, B. M., & Ross, J. (1985). Stability in the midst of change: A dispositional approach to job attitudes. *Journal of Applied Psychology, 70,* 469–480.

Steadham, S. V. (1980). Learning to select a needs assessment strategy. *Training and Development Journal, 30*(1), 56–61.

Steers, R. M., & Porter, L. W. (1991). *Motivation and work behavior* (4th ed). New York: McGraw-Hill.

Steil, L. K. (1980). *Your personal listening profile.* Great Neck, NY: Sperry Corp.

Steiner, I. D. (1972). *Group process and productivity.* New York: Academic Press.

Stewart, D. W., & Latham, D. R. (1986). On some psychometric properties of Fiedler's contingency model of leadership. *Small Group Behavior, 17*(1), 83–94.

Stewart, R., Ellenburg, G., Hicks, L., Kremen, M., & Daniel, M. (1990). Employee references as a recruitment source. *Applied H.R.M. Research, 1*(1), 1–3.

Stogdill, R. M. (1948). Personal factors associated with leadership. *Journal of Psychology, 23,* 36–71.

Stokes, G. S., Hogan, J. B., & Snell, A. F. (1993). Comparability of incumbent and applicant samples for the development of biodata keys: The influence of social desirability. *Personnel Psychology, 46,* 739–762.

Stone, D. L., Gueutal, H. G., & McIntosh, B. (1984). The effects of feedback sequence and expertise of the rater on performance feedback accuracy. *Personnel Psychology, 37,* 487–506.

Storer, T. S. (1986). Technical training by videotape. *Training, 23*(7), 27–30.

Stout, S. K., Slocum, J. W., & Cron, W. L. (1987). Career transitions of superiors and subordinates. *Journal of Vocational Behavior, 30,* 124–137.

Strauss, G. (1967). Related instruction: Basic problems and issues. In *Research in apprentice training.* Madison: University of Wisconsin, Center for Vocational and Technical Education.

Strauss, G. (1971). *Union policies and the admission of apprenticeships.* Reprint No. 357. Berkeley: University of California Press.

Strube, M. J., & Garcia, J. E. (1981). A meta-analytic investigation of Fiedler's contingency model of leadership effectiveness. *Psychological Bulletin, 90,* 307–321.

Suedfeld, P., & Rank, A. D. (1976). Revolutionary leaders: Long-term success as a function of changes in conceptual complexity. *Journal of Personality and Social Psychology, 34,* 169–178.

Sulsky, L. M., & Day, D. V. (1992). Frame-of-reference training and cognitive categorization: An empirical investigation of rater memory issues. *Journal of Applied Psychology, 77*(4), 501–511.

Sundstrom, E., Burt, R. E., & Kamp, D. (1980). Privacy at work: Architectural correlates of job satisfaction and job performance. *Academy of Management Journal, 23,* 101–117.

Sundstrom, E., Town, J. P., Rice, R. W., Osborn, D. P., & Brill, M. (1994). Office noise, satisfaction, and perfomance. *Environment and Behavior, 26*(2), 195–222.

Surrette, M. A. (1993, October). *Can gender ever be a BFOQ in the selection of law enforcement personnel: An analysis of legal decisions.* Paper presented at the annual meeting of the Society of Police and Criminal Psychology, New Orleans, LA.

Surrette, M. A. (1995, June). The selection and placement of corrections officers: *The legality of gender as a BFOQ.* Paper presented at the annual meeting of the International Personnel Management Association Assessment Council, New Orleans.

Surrette, M. A., Aamodt, M. G., & Johnson, D. L. (1990). Effect analyst training and amount of available information on job analysis ratings. *Journal of Business and Psychology, 4,* 439–451.

Surrette, M. A., & Harlow, L. L. (1992). Level of satisfaction and commitment to a decisional choice as mediated by locus of control. *Applied H.R.M. Research, 3*(2), 92–113.

Sutton, H. W., & Porter, L. W. (1968). A study of the grapevine in a governmental organization. *Personnel Psychology, 21,* 223–230.

Swaroff, P. G., Bass, A. R., & Barclay, L. A. (1985). Recruiting sources: Another look. *Journal of Applied Psychology, 70,* 720–728.

Sweetland, R. C., & Keyser, D. J. (1983). *Tests.* Kansas City, MO: Test Corp. of America.

Swink, D. F. (1993). Role-play your way to learning. *Training and Development, 47*(5), 91–97.

Tait, M., Padgett, M. Y., & Baldwin, T. T. (1989). Job and life satisfaction: A reexamination of the strength of the relationship and gender effects as a function of the date of the study. *Journal of Applied Psychology, 74,* 502–507.

Tanaka, M., Tochihara, Y., Yamazaki, S., Ohnaka, T., & Yoshida, K. (1983). Thermal reaction and manual performance during cold exposure while wearing cold-protective clothing. *Ergonomics, 26,* 141–149.

Tanford, S., & Penrod, S. (1984). Social influence model: A formal integration of research on majority and minority influence processes. *Psychological Bulletin, 95,* 189–225.

Tannen, D. (1986). *That's not what I meant!* New York: Ballantine Books.

Tannen, D. (1990). *You just don't understand: Women and men in conversation.* New York: Ballantine Books.

Taylor, H. C., & Russell, J. T. (1939). The relationship of validity coefficients to the practical effectiveness of tests in selection: Discussion and tables. *Journal of Applied Psychology, 23,* 565–578.

Taylor, L. R. (1978). Empirically derived job families as a foundation for the study of validity generalization. Study 1. The construction of job families based on the component and overall dimensions of the PAQ. *Personnel Psychology, 31,* 325–340.

Taylor, M. S., & Schmidt, D. W. (1983). A process-oriented investigation of recruitment source effectiveness. *Personnel Psychology, 36,* 343–354.

Taylor, S. E., Peplau, L. A., & Sears, D. D. (1994). *Social psychology* (8th ed.). Englewood Cliffs: Prentice Hall.

Tedeschi, J. T., Bonoma, T. V., & Schlenker, B. R. (1972). Influence, decision, and compliance. In J. T. Tedeschi (Ed.), *The social influence process* (pp. 346–418). Chicago: Aldine-Atherton.

Teichner, W. H., Arees, E., & Reilly, R. (1963). Noise and human performance. *Ergonomics, 6,* 83–97.

Telenson, P. A., Alexander, R. A., & Barrett, G. V. (1983). Scoring the biographical information blank: A comparison of three weighting techniques. *Applied Psychological Measurement, 7,* 73–80.

Terborg, J. R. (1977). Validation and extension of an individual differences model of work performance. *Organizational Behavior and Human Performance, 18,* 188–216.

Terpstra, D. E., & Rozell, E. J. (1993). Relationship of staffing practices to organzational level measures of performance. *Personnel Psychology, 46,* 27–48.

Tett, R. P., Jackson, D. N., & Rothstein, M. (1991). Personality measures as predictors of job performance: A meta-analytic review. *Personnel Psychology, 44,* 703–742.

Tett, R. P., & Meyer, J. P. (1993). Job satisfaction, organizational commitment, turnover intention, and turnover: Path analyses based on meta-analytic findings. *Personnel Psychology, 46*(2), 259–293.

Thayer, P. W. (1988). Some things non-I/O psychologists should know about I/O psychology. *The Industrial/Organizational Psychologist, 26*(1), 55–65.

Thomas, K. W. (1970). Conflict and conflict management. In M. D. Dunnette (Ed.), *Handbook of industrial and organizational psychology.* Chicago: Rand McNally.

Thombs, D. L., Beck, K. H., & Mahoney, C. A. (1993). Effects of social context and gender on drinking patterns of young adults. *Journal of Counseling Psychology, 40*(1), 115–119.

Thompson, D. E., & Thompson, T. A. (1982). Court standards for job analysis in test validation. *Personnel Psychology, 35,* 865–874.

Thornburg, L. (1993). When violence hits business. *HRMagazine, 38*(7), 40–45.

Thornburg, L. (1994). Change comes slowly. *HRMagazine, 39*(2), 46–49.

Thornton, G. (1993). The effect of selection practices on applicants' perceptions of organizational characteristics. In H. Schuler, J. Farr, & M. Smith (Eds.), *Personnel selection and assessment: Individual and organizational perspectives.* Hillsdale, NJ: Erlbaum.

Tolman, C. W. (1968). The role of the companion in social facilitation of animal bahavior. In E. C. Simmel, R. A. Hoppe, & G. A. Milton (Eds.), *Social facilitation and initiative behavior* (pp. 33–54). Boston: Allyn & Bacon.

Tonowski, R. F. (1993). Assessing a violent situation: Violence and personnel assessment practices in the U.S. Postal Service. *IPMAAC News,* September, 3–5.

Toth, C. (1993). Effect of résumé format on applicant selection for a job interview. *Applied H.R.M. Research, 4*(2), 115–125.

Totterdell, P., Spelten, E., Smith, L., Barton, J., & Folkard, S. (1995). Recovery from work shifts: How long does it take? *Journal of Applied Psychology, 80*(1), 43–57.

Trahiotis, C., & Robinson, D. E. (1979). Auditory psychophysics. *Annual Review of Psychology, 30,* 31–61.

Trenn, K. (1993, December). Third of survey respondents report violent episodes. *HR News,* 2–4.

Trent, J. T., Smith, A. L., & Wood, D. L. (1994). Telecommuting: Stress and social support. *Psychological Reports, 74,* 1312–1314.

Trinkaus, J. W. (1986). Perceived hazard of video display terminals: An informal look. *Perceptual and Motor Skills, 62,* 118.

Triplett, N. (1988). The dynamogenic factors in pacemaking and competition. *American Journal of Psychology, 9,* 507–533.

Tubbs, M. E. (1986). Goal setting: A meta-analytic examination of the empirical evidence. *Journal of Applied Psychology, 71,* 474–483.

Tucker, J. (1993). Everyday forms of employee resistance. *Sociological Forum, 8*(1), 25–45.

Turner, J. T. (1994, October). *Violence in the work place: First line of defense.* Paper presented at the 23rd Annual Meeting of the Society of Police and Criminal Psychology, Madison, WI.

Twomey, D. P. (1986). *A concise guide to employment law.* Cincinnati, OH: Southwestern Publishing.

Tysinger, A., & Pitchford, L. (1988, April). *A readability index for trait based psychological tests.* Paper presented at the 9th Annual Graduate Conference in Industrial/Organizational Psychology and Organizational Behavior, Toledo, OH.

Tziner, A., Kopelman, R. E., & Livnech, N. (1993). Effects of performance appraisal format on perceived goal characteristics, appraisal process satisfaction, and changes in rated job performance: A field experiment. *The Journal of Psychology, 127*(3), 281–292.

Uhrbrock, R. S. (1961). Music on the job: Its influence on worker morale and production. *Personnel Psychology, 14,* 9–38.

Ulrich, E. (1957). Zur frage der belastung des arbeitenden menschen durch nacht-und schicktarbeit. *Psychologische Rundschar, 8*, 42–61.

Ulrich, L., & Trumbo, D. (1965). The selection interview since 1949. *Psychological Bulletin, 63*, 100–116.

U.S. Department of Labor. (1989, April). *News.* Washington, DC: Author.

Valacich, J. S., Dennis, A. R., & Connolly, T. (1994). Idea generation in computer-based groups: A new ending to an old story. *Organizational Behavior and Human Decision Processes, 57*(3), 448–467.

Valacich, J. S., Dennis, A. R., & Nunamaker, J. F. (1992). Group size and anonymity effects on computer-mediated idea generation. *Small Group Research, 23*(1), 49–73.

Valacich, J. S., Paranka, D., George, J. F., & Nunamaker, J. F. (1993). Communication concurrency and the new media: A new dimension for media richness. *Communication Research, 20*(2), 249–276.

Vander Velden, L. (1971). *Relationships among member, team, and situational variables and basketball team success.* Unpublished doctoral dissertation, University of Wisconsin, Madison, WI.

Van Leeuwen, M., Frizzell, M. D., & Nail, P. R. (1987, April). *An examination of gender differences in response to threatening communications.* Paper presented at the annual meeting of the Oklahoma Psychological Association, Oklahoma City, OK.

Van Zelt, R. H. (1952). Sociometrically selected work teams increase production. *Personnel Psychology, 5*, 175–186.

Vecchio, R. P., Griffeth, R. W., & Hom, P. W. (1986). The predictive utility of the vertical dyad linkage approach. *Journal of Social Psychology, 126*(5), 617–625.

Veglahn, P. A. (1989). Drug testing that clears the arbitration hurdle. *Personnel Administrator, 34*(2), 62–64.

Veres, J. G., Green, S. B., & Boyles, W. R. (1991). Racial differences on job analysis questionnaires: An empirical study. *Public Personnel Management, 20*(2), 135–144.

Verespes, M. A. (1994). The anytime, anyplace workplace. *Industry Week, 243*(13), 37–40.

Verhaegen, P., Cober, R., de Smedt, M., & Dirkx, J. (1987). The adaptation of night nurses to different work schedules. *Ergonomics, 30*, 1301–1309.

Vernon, H. M. (1936). *Accidents and their prevention.* London: Cambridge University Press.

Vernon, H. M., & Warner, C. G. (1932). Objective and subjective tests for noise. *Personnel Journal, 11*, 141–149.

Vroom, V., & Yetton, P. W. (1973). *Leadership and decision making.* Pittsburgh, PA: University of Pittsburgh Press.

Vroom, V. H. (1964). *Work and motivation.* New York: John Wiley & Sons.

Wagner, J. A. (1994). Participation effects on performance and satisfaction: A reconsideration of research evidence. *Academy of Management Review, 19*(2), 312–330.

Wahba, M. A., & Bridwell, L. T. (1976). Maslow reconsidered: A review of research on the need of hierarchy theory. *Organizational Behavior and Human Performance, 15*, 212–240.

Wainer, H. (1976). Estimating coefficients in linear models: It don't make no nevermind. *Psychological Bulletin, 83*, 213–217.

Wakabayashi, M., & Graen, G. B. (1984). The Japanese career progress study: A seven-year follow-up. *Journal of Applied Psychology, 69*, 603–614.

Waldman, D. A., & Avolio, B. J. (1986). A meta-analysis of age differences in job performance. *Journal of Applied Psychology, 71*, 33–38.

Walster, E., Aronson, E., & Abrahams, D. (1966). On increasing the persuasiveness of a low prestige communicator. *Journal of Experimental Social Psychology, 2*, 325–342.

Walton, E. (1961). How efficient is the grapevine? *Personnel, 28*, 45–49.

Wanous, J. P. (1980). *Organizational entry: Recruitment, selection, and socialization of newcomers.* Reading, MA: Addison-Wesley.

Wanous, J. P., & Zwany, A. (1977). A cross-sectional test of need hierarchy theory. *Organizational Behavior and Human Performance, 18*, 78–97.

Ward, E. A. (1989). Field study of job knowledge, job satisfaction, intention to turnover, and ratings of simulated performance. *Psychological Reports, 64*, 179–188.

Weaver, C. N. (1978). Job satisfaction as a component of happiness among males and females. *Personnel Psychology, 31*, 831–840.

Webster, E. D. (1964). *Decision making in the employment interview.* Montreal: Eagle.

Wedderburn, A. A. (1978). Some suggestions for increasing the usefulness of psychological and sociological studies of shiftwork. *Ergonomics, 21*, 827–833.

Weekley, J. A., & Gier, J. A. (1987). Reliability and validity of the situational interview for a sales position. *Journal of Applied Psychology, 72*, 484–487.

Weins, A. N., Jackson, R. H., Manaugh, T. S., & Matarazzo, J. D. (1969). Communication length as an index of communicator attitude: A replication. *Journal of Applied Psychology, 53*, 264–266.

Weinstein, N. D. (1977). Noise and intellectual performance: A confirmation and extension. *Journal of Applied Psychology, 62*, 104–107.

Weinstein, N. D. (1978). A longitudinal study in a college dormitory. *Journal of Applied Psychology, 63*, 458–466.

Weiss, H. M., Dawis, R. V., England, G. W., & Lofquist, L. H. (1967). *Manual for the Minnesota Satisfaction Questionnaire.* Minneapolis, MN: University of Minnesota, Industrial Relations Center.

Weiss, H. M., & Shaw, J. B. (1979). Social influences on judgments about tasks. *Organizational Behavior and Human Performance, 24*, 126–140.

Weiss, J. M. (1994). Telecommuting boosts employee output. *HRMagazine, 39*(2), 51–53.

Wentworth, R. (1991). The effects of music and distracting noise on the productivity of workers with mental retardation. *Journal of Music Therapy, 28*(1), 40–47.

Wernimont, P. F. (1962). Re-evaluation of a weighted application blank for office personnel. *Journal of Applied Psychology, 46,* 417–419.

Wexley, K. N., & Latham, G. A. (1991). *Developing and training human resources in organizations* (2nd ed.). New York: Harper Collins.

Wexley, K. N., Sanders, R. E., & Yukl, G. A. (1973). Training interviewers to eliminate contrast effects in employment interviews. *Journal of Applied Psychology, 57,* 233–236.

Wexley, K. N., Yukl, G. A., Kovacs, S. Z., & Sanders, R. E. (1972). Importance of contrast effects in employment interviews. *Journal of Applied Psychology, 56,* 45–48.

Whelchel, B. D. (1985). Use of performance tests to select craft apprentices. *Personnel Journal, 65*(7), 65–69.

Wherry, R. J., & South, J. C. (1977). A worker motivation scale. *Personnel Psychology, 30,* 613–636.

Whetstone, T. S. (1994). Subordinates evaluate supervisory and administrative performance. *The Police Chief, 61*(6), 57–62.

Whisler, T. L. (1958). Performance appraisal and the organization man. *Journal of Business, 31,* 19–27.

Whitcomb, A., & Bryan, D. (1988, April). Validity of the Peres and Garcia method of scoring letters of recommendation. *Proceedings of the 9th Annual Graduate Conference in Industrial/Organizational Psychology and Organizational Behavior.*

Widgery, R., & Stackpole, C. (1972). Desk position, interviewee anxiety, and interviewer credibility: An example of cognitive balance in a dyad. *Journal of Counseling Psychology, 19,* 173–177.

Wiesner, W. H., & Cronshaw, S. F. (1988). A meta-analytic investigation of the impact of interview format and degree of structure on the validity of the employment interview. *Journal of Occupational Psychology, 61,* 275–290.

Wilbur, L. P. (1993). The value of on-the-job rotation. *Supervisory Management, 38*(11), 6.

Wilkinson, R. T. (1992). How fast should the night shift rotate? *Ergonomics, 35*(12), 1425–1446.

Williams, J. R., & Levy, P. E. (1992). The effects of perceived system knowledge on the agreement between self-ratings and supervisor ratings. *Personnel Psychology, 45,* 835–847.

Williams, K. D., Bourgeois, M. J., & Croyle, R. T. (1993). The effects of stealing thunder in criminal and civil trials. *Law and Human Behavior, 17*(6), 597–609.

Williams, K. D., Harkins, S., & Latane, B. (1981). Identifiability as a deterrent to social loafing: Two cheering experiments. *Journal of Personality and Social Psychology, 40,* 303–311.

Williams, R., & Garris, T. S. (1991). A second look at situation wanted advertisements. *Applied H.R.M. Research, 2*(1), 33–37.

Williams, S. W., & Streit, T. (1986). Learner-driven sales training at Life of Virginia. *Training, 23*(2), 65–68.

Williamson, A. M., Gower, C. G. I., & Clarke, B. C. (1994). Changing the hours of shift work: A comparison of 8- and 12-hour shift rosters in a group of computer operators. *Ergonomics, 37*(2), 287–298.

Williamson, A. M., & Sanderson, J. W. (1986). Changing the speed of shift rotation: A field study. *Ergonomics, 29,* 1085–1089.

Willihnganz, M. A., & Myers, L. S. (1993). Effects of time of day on interview performance. *Public Personnel Management, 22*(4), 545–550.

Willis, S. C., Miller, T. A., & Huff, G. (1991). Situation-wanted advertisements: A means for obtaining job inquiries and offers. *Applied H.R.M. Research, 2*(1), 27–32.

Wilson, E. J., & Sherrell, D. L. (1993). Source effects in communication and persuasion research: A meta-analysis of effect size. *Journal of the Academy of Marketing Science, 21*(2), 101–112.

Wilson, M. A., & Harvey, R. J. (1990). The value of relative-time-spent ratings in task-oriented job analysis. *Journal of Business and Psychology, 4*(4), 453–461.

Wilson, W. (1994). Video training and testing supports customer service goals. *Personnel Journal, 30*(10), 47–51.

Wing, J. F. (1965). Upper tolerance limits for unimpaired mental performance. *Aerospace Medicine, 36,* 960–964.

Winter, D. G. (1988). What makes Jesse run? *Psychology Today, 22*(6), 20–24.

Wisdom, B., & Patzig, D. (1987). Does your organization have the right climate for merit? *Public Personnel Management, 16,* 127–133.

Wokoun, W. (1980). *A study of fatigue in industry.* New York: Muzak Board of Scientific Advisors.

Wolinsky, J. (1982). Beat the clock. *APA Monitor, 13,* 12.

Wood, R. F., Mento, A. J., & Locke, E. A. (1987). Task complexity as a moderator of goal effects: A meta-analysis. *Journal of Applied Psychology, 72,* 416–425.

Wooten, W. (1993). Using knowledge, skill and ability (KSA) data to identify career pathing opportunities: An application of job analysis to internal manpower planning. *Public Personnel Management, 22*(4), 551–563.

Wright, P. M., Lichtenfels, P. A., & Pursell, E. D. (1989). The structured interview: Additional studies and a meta-analysis. *Journal of Occupational Psychology, 62,* 191–199.

Wyatt, S., & Marriot, R. (1953). Night work and shift changes. *British Journal of Industrial Medicine, 10,* 164–177.

Yager, E. (1980). When new hires don't make the grade: The case for assessment centers. *Personnel Journal, 59*(5), 387–390.

Yammarino, F. J., Skinner, S. J., & Childers, T. L. (1991). Understanding mail survey response behavior: A meta-analysis. *Public Opinion Quarterly, 55*(4), 613–639.

Yoder, D. (1962). *Personnel management and industrial relations* (5th ed.). Englewood Cliffs, NJ: Prentice-Hall.

Yoder, D., & Heneman, H. G. (1979). *Motivation and commitment: Wage and salary administration.* Washington, DC: American Society for Personnel Administration.

Young, D. M., & Beier, E. G. (1977). The role of applicant nonverbal communication in the employment interview. *Journal of Employment Counseling, 14,* 154–165.

Yu, J., & Murphy, K. (1993). Modesty bias in self-ratings or performance: A test of the cultural relating hypothesis. *Personnel Psychology, 46*(2), 357–363.

Yukl, G. (1982, April). *Innovations in research on leader behavior.* Paper presented at the annual meeting of the Eastern Academy of Management, Baltimore, MD.

Yukl, G. A. (1989). *Leadership in organizations.* Englewood Cliffs, NJ: Prentice-Hall.

Yukl, G. A. (1994). *Leadership in organizations* (3rd ed.) Englewood Cliffs, NJ: Prentice Hall.

Zaccaro, S. J., Foti, R. J., & Kenny, D. A. (1991). Self-monitoring and trait-based variance in leadership: An investigation of leader flexibility across multiple group situations. *Journal of Applied Psychology, 76*(2), 308–315.

Zajonc, R. B. (1965). Social facilitation. *Science, 149,* 269–274.

Zajonc, R. B. (1980). Compressence. In P. B. Paulus (Ed.), *Psychology of group influence.* Hillsdale, NJ: Erlbaum.

Zajonc, R. B., Heingartner, A., & Herman, E. M. (1969). Social enhancement and impairment of performance in the cockroach. *Journal of Personality and Social Psychology, 13,* 83–92.

Zander, A. (1982). *Making groups effective.* San Francisco: Jossey-Bass.

Zaremba, A. (1988). Working with the organizational grapevine. *Personnel Journal, 67*(6), 38–42.

Zdep, S. M., & Weaver, H. B. (1967). The graphoanalytic approach to selecting life insurance salesman. *Journal of Applied Psychology, 51,* 295–299.

Zemke, R. (1993). Rethinking the rush to team-up. *Training, 30*(11), 55–61.

Zuboff, S. (1982). New worlds of computer-mediated work. *Harvard Business Review, 60*(5), 142–152.

Zweigenhaft, R. L. (1976). Personal space in the faculty office: Desk placement and the student-faculty interaction. *Journal of Applied Psychology, 61,* 529–532.

# NAME INDEX

**553**

Lacho, K. J., 259
Laing, M., 411
LaMarre, S. E., 491
Lamm, H., 390
Lance, L. E., 262
Landau, K., 94, 96, 97
Landon, T. E., 233
Landy, F. J., 27, 83, 178, 260
Langdale, J. A., 179
Langer, E. J., 445
Langer, S., 304
Lapsley, D. K., 28
Larson, J. R., 291
Lasater, T. M., 362
Lasden, M., 492
Lasek, M., 208
LaShells, M. B., 301
Lassiter, G. D., 418
Latane, B., 382, 384, 388
Latham, D. R., 346
Latham, G. A., 304, 323, 326
Latham, G. P., 141, 181, 182, 276, 286, 466, 468
Latham, V. M., 348
Laumeyer, J., 291
Lawler, E. E., 283, 328, 446, 449, 456
Lawshe, C. H., 136, 137
Lazer, R. I., 260, 261
Leana, C. R., 296
Lease, J. E., 430
Ledford, G. E., 328
Ledvinka, J., 102
Lee, J. A., 121
Lehtela, K., 495
Lengnick-Hall, M. L., 46
Lentz, E., 374
Leppanen, A., 504
Lester, D., 492
Levine, E. L., 72, 88, 90, 103–104
Levine, M., 297
Levin-Epstein, M. D., 58
Levy, P. E., 262, 459
Lewecki, R. J., 363
Lichtenfels, P. A., 181
Lied, T. L., 458
Lierman, B., 316, 317
Lin, L., 496
Lin, T. R., 146, 182
Lindgren, H. C., 449
Linkous, R. A., 386
Liou, K. T., 468
Litterer, J. A., 391
Little, E. A., 494
Littlepage, G. E., 381
Livnech, N., 276
Locke, E. A., 449, 466, 468
Lockowandt, O., 244
Loewen, L. J., 496
Lofquist, L. H., 473

Loher, B. T., 326
London, M., 261
Long, G., 377
Long, W. S., 339
Lopez, F. E., 99, 100
Lopez, F. M., 99, 100
LoPresto, R. L., 191
Lord, R. G., 288, 289, 338, 400, 454
Lorge, I., 389
Lounsbury, J. W., 125
Love, K. G., 83, 179
Lowe, R. H., 8
Lozada-Larsen, S. R., 126
Lucas, J. A., 59

Maas, 184
Maasen, A., 487
Mabe, P. A., 261
Machungwa, P. D., 83
Mackie, D. M., 392
Maddux, J. E., 361
Mager, R. F., 306
Magjuka, R. J., 326
Magner, N. R., 391
Mahlin, S. J., 484
Mahoney, C. A., 386
Maier, N. R. F., 291, 389
Main, D. S., 90
Major, B., 418
Malandro, L. A., 417
Malaviya, P., 487
Manaugh, T. S., 212
Manligas, C. L., 182
Mann, F. C., 487, 492
Mann, K. O., 106
Mann, R. B., 173, 320
Manners, G. E., 381
Manson, T., 314
Manstead, A. S., 386
Manz, C. C., 349
Markham, S. E., 463, 491, 514
Markowich, M. M., 514
Marks, A., 390
Marriot, R., 487
Martin, 504
Martin, C. L., 179, 277, 288, 289
Martin, J. E., 182, 183, 184
Martinez, M. N., 67, 505
Maslow, A. H., 441
Mason, N. A., 158, 161, 502
Massengill, D., 151
Massey, M., 313
Matarazzo, J. D., 212
Matthes, K., 492
Mathews, K. E., 495
Matthews, M., 313
Maurer, S. D., 176, 182
Mawhinney, T. C., 465
Mayfield, E. C., 177, 181

Mayo, E., 373
McAlarnis, C., 2
McClelland, C. L., 444
McClelland, D. C., 340, 449
McCormick, E. J., 78, 86, 89, 91
McDaniel, M. A., 144, 176
McDaniel, Q. P., 170, 233
McElroy, J. C., 506, 507
McEvoy, G. M., 261
McGee, G. W., 352
McGehee, W., 308
McGowan, S. L., 90
McGregor, D., 290, 344
McIlvane, T., 510, 512
McIntosh, B., 291
McIntyre, R. M., 286
McKee, C., 317–318
McLemore, S. D., 130
McLoughlin, O., 487, 492
McShane, T., 121, 183, 511
Mecham, R. C., 89, 91
Meehan, B. T., 204
Meehl, P. E., 176, 177
Meers, A., 487
Mehrabian, A., 212
Melamed, S., 494
Mellor, E. F., 112
Mendel, R. M., 6
Mendleson, J. L., 323
Mento, A. J., 242, 466, 467
Menyhert, A., 218
Mershon, D. H., 496
Mesch, D. J., 517
Meyer, H. H., 261, 262
Meyer, J. P., 439, 440
Michaels, J. W., 386
Michals, J., 211, 212, 215, 217
Midkiff, K., 489
Mihal, W. L., 309
Mijares, T. C., 233
Miles, J. A., 388
Milkovich, G. T., 76
Miller, D., 187, 507
Miller, G. W., 492
Miller, J., 508
Miller, J. G., 422
Miller, R. K., 206
Miller, R. L., 93
Miller, S., 312
Miller, T. A., 162
Miller, T. I., 491
Milliman, R. E., 497
Millsap, R. E., 261
Miner, J. B., 313
Mischkind, L. A., 448
Mishra, A., 296
Mishra, J., 412
Mitcham, D. E., 191
Mitchell, J. V., 130
Mitchell, K., 291

Mitchell, T. R., 29, 350, 458
Mitchell, T. T., 291
Mitchell, V. F., 446
Mitra, A., 512
Modica, A. J., 397, 398
Moede, W., 387
Mohiuddin, S., 79
Molloy, J. T., 180
Montebello, H. R., 331
Moore, A. K., 90
Moore, H., 508
Moores, J., 480–481
Moreno, K. E., 121
Morrow, P. C., 506, 507
Morse, C. S., 208
Mosel, J. N., 206, 211
Moss, S. E., 339
Mossholder, K. W., 448
Motowidlo, S. J., 184, 288, 289
Mott, P. E., 487, 492
Mougdill, P., 446
Moulton, D. A., 64, 67
Mount, M. K., 76, 277, 290
Mouton, J. S., 344, 395
Moynahan, B., 67
Muchinsky, P. M., 191, 204, 206, 439, 440
Muczyk, J. P., 315
Mulder, M., 348
Mullen, B., 377
Mullins, W. C., 30, 83, 89
Mumford, M. D., 260
Munson, J. M., 325
Munsterberg, H., 4
Murphy, K. R., 228, 262, 277, 278, 285, 288, 289
Murray, 222
Mussio, S., 151
Myers, J. H., 206

Nadler, P., 321
Nagao, D. H., 179
Nail, P. R., 381, 468
Nanry, C., 292
Nanus, R., 360
Nash, A. N., 206, 207, 209, 217, 315
Nathan, B., 288, 289
Naughton, T. J., 76, 374
Naylor, J. C., 327
Nebeker, D. M., 458
Neufeldt, D., 378
Neuner, J., 410
Newman, R. L., 497
Newstrom, J. W., 315, 318
Nicholls, J. R., 352
Nichols, R. G., 424, 425
Nicholson, N., 487
Niebuhr, R. E., 64
Niemeyer, E. S., 315
Niemi, P., 495

Schmitt, N., 83, 237, 242, 244, 245
Schmitt, S. D., 6, 7
Schneider, J. R., 242
Schneier, C. E., 304
Schoenfeldt, L. F., 102, 238
Schramm, W., 313
Schriesheim, C. A., 346, 350
Schriesheim, J. F., 350
Schroeder, D., 29
Schulz, R., 445
Schuster, J. R., 460, 461, 464
Schwab, D. P., 174, 181, 278, 301, 473
Schwartz, B., 386
Schweitzer, S. C., 381
Sciarrino, J. A., 241
Scionti, C., 83
Scott, D., 491
Scott, K. D., 463, 514
Scott, W. D., 4
Sears, D. D., 418
Sears, D. O., 27
Seaton, F. W., 231, 241
Segal, J. A., 295
Segal, N. L., 453
Sego, D. J., 325
Seibert, P. S., 310
Seitz, D. D., 397, 398
Semmer, N., 487, 489
Serlin, R. C., 28
Sessa, V. T., 379
Seta, J. J., 385
Severance, L. J., 361
Shaffer, D. R., 207
Shaffer, G. S., 239
Shaffer, M. A., 515
Shapira, Z., 301
Shaw, I. M., 377
Shaw, J. B., 468
Shaw, M. E., 377
Sheets, P., 384
Shelton, S., 333
Shephard, H., 395
Shepperd, J. A., 388
Shetzer, L., 176
Shikiar, R., 209
Shirom, A., 301
Shneiderman, B., 374, 505
Sieber, J. E., 27
Siegfried, W. D., 6
Sieling, M. S., 111, 112
Silva, J. M., 59
Silverman, S. B., 244
Simonton, D. K., 340
Sims, H. P., 349
Sims, R. R., 305, 311
Sistrunk, F., 90, 103–104
Skinner, B. F., 328

Skinner, S. J., 22
Slade, L. A., 27
Sleezer, C. M., 304
Sloane, L. T., 375
Slocum, J. W., 468
Smart, R., 374
Smith, A. L., 486
Smith, B. N., 76
Smith, C., 489, 490
Smith, D. E., 286, 420
Smith, E. R., 392
Smith, J. E., 90
Smith, L., 488, 489
Smith, M. J., 502
Smith, M. L., 296
Smith, P. C., 96, 264, 301, 473, 474
Smith, P. L., 168
Smith, R. E., 12
Smith, T. J., 481
Smither, J. W., 238, 261, 285, 288
Smither, R., 449
Smits, S. J., 168
Smothers, R., 42
Snell, A. F., 239
Sniderman, M. S., 492
Snyder, A., 193
Snyman, J., 227, 228
Sommer, R., 385
Sommers, 400
Sonnemann, U., 244
Sorra, J. S., 325
South, J. C., 453
Sparks, C. P., 238
Spelten, E., 489
Speroff, B., 377
Spitzer, D., 331
Spivey, W. A., 172
Spock, G., 199
Springbett, B. M., 179
Srinivas, S., 288, 289
St. Clair, S., 170
Stackman, R., 176
Stackpole, C., 506
Stadelmaier, M. F., 378, 379
Stafford, E. M., 92, 93, 94
Stagner, R., 400
Stahl, M. J., 341, 449, 458
Stammerjohn, L. W., 502
Stanley, J. C., 331
Stathatos, P., 59
Staw, B. M., 27, 453
Steadham, S. V., 310
Stearns, G. K., 259
Steel, R. P., 467
Steers, R. M., 461
Steil, L. K., 428
Steinbrenner, G., 419
Steiner, I. D., 381
Stevens, L. A., 424, 425

Stevens, S., 199
Stewart, R., 168
Stoffey, R. W., 238
Stogdill, R. M., 338
Stokes, G. S., 239
Stone, D. L., 291
Stone, J. L., 418
Storer, T. S., 313
Stout, S. K., 468
Stradling, S. G., 386
Stramler, C. S., 191
Strauss, G., 322
Streit, T., 315
Strickland, W. J., 242
Stringfield, P., 261, 262
Stroebe, W., 390
Strube, M. J., 346
Stutzman, T., 83, 88
Stweart, D. W., 346
Suedfeld, P., 349, 496
Sulsky, L. M., 283, 286
Summer, C. E., 374
Sundstrom, E., 494, 496, 505, 506
Surrette, M. A., 49, 90, 468, 469, 517
Suttle, J. L., 446
Sutton, H. W., 412
Svec, C. M., 386
Swaroff, P. G., 172, 174
Sweetland, R. C., 129, 130
Swink, D. F., 318
Switzer, F., 6
Sylvia, R. D., 468
Sympson, J. R., 121

Tait, M., 453
Tanford, S., 384
Tannen, D., 416, 417
Tasto, D. L., 487
Taylor, H. C., 131, 134–135
Taylor, L. R., 90
Taylor, M. S., 174, 327
Taylor, R. R., 464
Taylor, S. E., 418
Taylor, S. M., 174
Teachout, M. S., 262
Tedeschi, J. T., 363
Teichner, W. H., 493
Telenson, P. A., 237
Tepper, B. J., 346
Terborg, J. R., 466
Terpstra, D. E., 235
Terris, W., 227
Tesser, A., 406
Tetrault, L. A., 346
Tett, R. P., 223, 439, 440
Thayer, P. W., 2, 308
Thomas, K. W., 391
Thomas, S. L., 400
Thombs, D. L., 386

Thompson, D. E., 103, 277
Thompson, K., 491
Thompson, T. A., 103
Thornburg, L., 481, 508
Thorne, A., 375
Thornton, G. C., 126, 242, 245
Tighe, E. M., 448
Tippins, N., 184
Titus, L. J., 385
Todd, R., 417
Tolman, C. W., 385
Tomarelli, M., 207
Tonowski, R. F., 510
Torsvall, L., 487
Toth, C., 194
Totterdell, P., 489
Town, J. P., 494, 496, 505
Trenn, K., 509, 510
Trent, J. T., 486
Trinkaus, J. W., 502
Triplett, N., 384
Trommsdorff, G., 390
Trumbo, D., 177
Tschirgia, H. D., 178
Tubbs, M. E., 465, 467
Tucker, J., 412
Turner, J. T., 510, 512
Twomey, D. P., 52
Tysinger, A., 433
Tziner, A., 276

Uhrbrock, R. S., 497
Ulrich, E., 487
Ulrich, L., 177

Valacich, J. S., 381, 382, 406
Vallance, T. R., 97, 310
Van Leeuwen, M., 381
Van Rybroek, G. J., 206
Van Zelt, R. H., 377
Vander Velden, L., 378
VanMarter, J., 182, 184
Vasey, J., 83
Vasilopoulos, N. L., 261
Vaughan, 184
Vecchio, R. P., 351, 352
Verhaagen, P., 487, 489
Veglahn, P. A., 243
Veres, J. G., 83, 305, 311
Verespes, M. A., 486
Verhage, J., 348
Vernon, H. M., 493
Vest, M. J., 463
Vettori, F. L., 315
Vidmar, N., 381
Villar, P., 52
Villere, M. R., 259
Viswesvaren, C., 227, 245

# SUBJECT INDEX

California Psychological Inventory, 222

*Canedy* v. *Bordman*, 49

Career Ability Placement Survey (CAPS), 224, 229, 230

Career Assessment Inventory, 452

Career Orientation Placement and Evaluation Survey (COPES), 452

Carpal-tunnel syndrome (CTS), 503

Case law, 42

Case studies, 315–316

*Caston* v. *Trigon Engineering*, 47

Cause-and-effect relationships, 17

*Chance* v. *Board of Examiners*, 72

Child care, 490–492
  on-site facility, 491
  organizations with, 490
  referral service, 492

Circadian rhythm, 487

*City of Richmond* v. *Croson*, 57

Civil Rights Acts, 6, 44, 45, 46, 52

Clinical versus statistical prediction, 176–177

Closed desk arrangement, 506, 507

Cluster grapevine, 412

Coaching, 322–323

Coaction, 384

Coefficient alpha formula, 122

Cognitive ability, 224–227, 429

Cognitive psychology, 6

Cognitive theories, 454–460
  consistency, 458–459
  equity, 454–456
  expectancy, 456–458

Color discrimination, 45

Communication
  downward, 408–411
  group, 383–384, 393
  horizontal, 411–413
  information in, 421–424
  interpersonal, 413–430
  nonverbal, 418–421
  persuasion by, 360–361
  serial, 406
  upward, 406–408
  verification, 423
  written, 431–433

Communication channel, 416–417

Communication overload, 421–424

Company manual, 409–411

Compensable job factors, 105–106

Compensation
  absolute amounts, 106, 109
  direct, 110
  indirect, 110–111
  performance appraisal and, 256–258
  relative amounts, 106

Competition for resources, 392

Complaint box, 407

Compressed work weeks, 480–481

Compromise, in conflict, 397

Computer-Assisted Instructed (CAI), 314

Computers
  to administer tests, 220
  fear of, 504–505
  hazards, 502–504
  keyboards, 503–504
  monitors, 502–503
  in programmed instruction, 314
  in recruitment, 169–170

Conciliation, in conflict, 397

Concurrent-validity design, 123

Conditional privilege, 207

Confidentiality, 60, 207

Conjunctive task, 381

Consequences, in learning, 328–329

Consideration, in leadership theory, 343–344

Consistency theory, 458–459

Construct validity, 125

Content validity, 122–123

Contrast effect, 178

Cooperative problem solving, 398

*Copeland* v. *Philadelphia Police Department*, 60

COPS Interest Inventory, 452

Counseling, 517

Cover letters, 188–191

Criterion, 235

Criterion groups, 236

Criterion validity, 123–124

Critical Incident Technique (CIT), 95–99, 310

Critical incidents, 310, 316

Critical-incident logs, 280, 282

Customer ratings, 261

Dale-Chall Index, 433

Dead-enders, 412

Debriefing, 28

Decision making, 444–445, 513

Decision making model, 354–358

Derivation sample, 237

*Detroit Police Officers Association* v. *Coleman Young*, 59

Devil's advocate, 389

*Diaz* v. *Pan American Airways*, 45, 49

Dictionary of Occupational Titles (DOT), 76

Differential Aptitude Test (DAT), 224

Differential validity, 144–145

Difficult people, types of, 396

*DiPompo* v. *West Point*, 47

Direct mail recruiting, 169, 170

Disability discrimination, 46–47

Discipline, for absenteeism, 514

Discipline problems, past, 205

Discrepancy theories, 449–453

Discrimination
  BFOQs and, 47, 49–50
  complaints, 39, 40–41

history of, 55–56

settlements, 42

Discrimination issues:
  age, 46
  color, 45
  disability, 46–47
  gender, 45
  national origin, 45
  pregnancy, 44, 47
  race, 44–45
  religion, 45–46
  veteran status, 47

Disjunctive task, 381

Dissertation, 9

Doctoral programs, 8–10, 34–35

Downward communication, 408–411

Drug testing, 60–63, 242–243
  confidentiality of results, 60
  federal guidelines, 61–63
  random, 60
  stages, 242–243

Earnings-at-risk (EAR) plan, 461

Edwards Personal Preference Schedule, 222

Effective temperature, 498

Ego needs, 443

Eleventh Mental Measurements Yearbook (MMY), 128, 129–130

E-mail, 409

Emphatic listening, 426

Employee Assistance Program (EAP), 517

Employee comparisons, 273–276
  forced-distribution method, 275
  paired comparisons, 274
  rank order, 273–274

Employee handbook, 410

Employee Performance Record, 281

Employee Polygraph Protection Act, 227

Employee referrals, 168–169, 172–174, 175

Employee screening, 510

Employee selection
  assessment centers, 239–242
  I/O developments in, 6
  handwriting analysis, 243–244
  interview, 176–187
  job analysis in, 73, 157
  linear criteria, 145–149
  nonlinear criteria, 149–151
  recruitment, 157–176
  references, 204–219
  rejection letters, 246–250
  top-down selection, 145–147
  weighted application blanks, 234–239

Employee selection techniques. *See* Tests

Employee violence. *See* Workplace violence

Training methods *(continued)*
  informal on-the-job, 321–324
  pass-through programs, 323
  performance appraisal, 323–324
  programmed instruction, 313–315
  seminars, 311–313
Training program evaluation:
  application of training, 333
  bottom-line measures, 333
  content validity, 332
  employee learning, 332–333
  employee reactions, 332
  posttest, 330
  pretest, 330
  research designs, 330–331
Training systems
  conducting the program, 324–326
  evaluation, 329–333
  needs analysis, 304–310
  program development, 310–324
  research designs, 330–333
Transformational leadership, 360
*Triblo* v. *Quality Clinical Laboratories,* 60
Trustworthiness, as leader trait, 361–362
Two-factor theory, 447–448

Union steward, 408
Upward communication, 406–408
Utility formula, 138–141

Validity generalization (VG), 124–125
Vertical dyad linkage (VDL), 350–351

Veteran's preference rights, 53
Video, 240–241, 313, 314
Vietnam-Era Veterans Readjustment Act, 44, 47
Virtual reality, 317
Vocational counseling, 224
Vocational interest and values tests, 452
Vocational Rehabilitation Act, 44, 46
Voice mail, 409
Voice stress analyzer, 227
Volunteerism, 321
Vroom-Yetton model, 354–358

Wage trend line, 107
*Walker* v. *Secretary of the Treasury,* 45
Weighted application blank (WAB), 234–239
  composite score, 236–237
  criticisms of, 238–239
  development, 235–238
  file approach, 235
  questionnaire approach, 235
  rare-response scoring, 237
  sample size, 237
  vertical percentage method, 236
Well pay, 513
Weschler Adult Intelligence Scale (WAIS), 219–220
Winning at all costs strategy, 395
Withdrawal, in group conflict, 395
Wonderlic Personnel Test, 219–220, 225, 226
Work environment, 492–504

computers, 502–505
in job analysis, 93–94
in job description, 78
music, 496–497
noise, 492–497
temperature, 497–501
Work Environment Preference Schedule, 452
Work samples, 241
Work schedules, 480–492
  child care and, 490–492
  compressed work week, 480–481
  flextime, 481–483
  homework, 485–486
  job sharing, 484–485
  moonlighting and, 492
  peak-time pay, 484
  shift work, 486–490
Work Values Inventory, 452
Worker Adjustment and Retraining Notification Act (WARN), 296
Worker mobility, 73
Workload, 500
Workplace violence, 508–512
  employee screening, 510
  management awareness, 510–512
  security measures, 509
Works-Preference Inventory, 448
Writing skills, 431–433
  improving, 431
  in manual writing, 410
  readability, 431–433